THEATRICAL DESIGNERS

THEATRICAL DESIGNERS

An International Biographical Dictionary

Edited by THOMAS J. MIKOTOWICZ

GREENWOOD PRESS
New York • Westport, Connecticut • London

Library of Congress Cataloging-in-Publication Data

Mikotowicz, Thomas J.
    Theatrical designers : an international biographical dictionary /
edited by Thomas J. Mikotowicz.
      p.   cm.
    Includes bibliographical references and index.
    ISBN 0–313–26270–5 (alk. paper)
    1. Set designers—Biography—Dictionaries. I. Title.
PN2096.A1AM54   1992   91–28086
792′.025′03—dc20

British Library Cataloguing in Publication Data is available.

Library of Congress Catalog Card Number: 91–28086
ISBN: 0–313–26270–5

First published in 1992

Greenwood Press, 88 Post Road West, Westport, CT 06881
An imprint of Greenwood Publishing Group, Inc.

Printed in the United States of America

The paper used in this book complies with the
Permanent Paper Standard issued by the National
Information Standards Organization (Z39.48–1984).

10 9 8 7 6 5 4 3 2 1

Contents

Preface   vii

Acknowledgments   ix

A History of Theatrical Design   xi

The Dictionary   1

APPENDIX A: Chronological List of Designers   269

APPENDIX B: Designers Listed by Country of Birth   277

APPENDIX C: Periodicals and Theatre Collections   287

Selected Bibliography   289

Index   297

About the Editor and Contributors   363

Preface

Although it is possible to find information on performers, directors, and writers in the theatre, obtaining information on designers has always proved a challenge to even the most rigorous of researchers. Unfortunately, it seems that design has not always been valued as a significant contribution to the creation of a production. As a result, those who document and critically analyze productions often omit information on the design process. The designers themselves, often keep poor records of their work. Nevertheless, design is as important as the other elements to the success of a production and should be valued as such. Thus, it is important to document design contributions and to be able to find biographical and analytical information regarding the careers of designers who have been instrumental in the growth and development of theatrical design, as well as those who may possibly make significant contributions in the future.

Therefore, this work seeks to provide for the reader or researcher a single reference source dedicated to theatrical designers. It includes approximately 270 set, costume, and lighting designers of drama, opera, dance, and film productions, as well as theatre architects and theoreticians. The selection represents a cross-section of designers, including both historical and contemporary figures. It includes primarily western designers because finding information in a timely manner on eastern designers proved to be almost impossible. The historical and contemporary figures included here were chosen based on their significance, the availability of research material, and, pragmatically, because the essay could be written within the time constraints of the project, among other more subjective reasons. There are additional designers who, arguably, should be in this book and, hopefully, will be included in further editions.

Entries vary in length, and again, the significance of a designer's contribution, the availability of material, and the amount of space for the most part were the determining factors. Generally, the longer, more detailed essays are on major contemporary designers who have amassed a large body of work and have contributed to the development of design in some manner.

Each entry includes an opening statement containing basic information on the name or pseudonym, the type of design, and the dates and places of birth and death as available. To facilitate cross-referencing, an asterisk will immediately follow the name of any designer who is featured in the dictionary. Some entries provide listings of shows, with the theatres, cities, and year of production when known. Please note that these lists do not include every production, but every attempt was made to document the designer's important contributions. Every entry, however, includes an essay that describes the growth of the designer's career, notable productions, style of design, and any specific contributions that the figure made to the development of design. Where applicable, an award section follows the essay, noting the most significant awards pertinent to design. The major entries end with a ''Further Reading'' section, which lists sources pertaining to the specific designer. Entries that do not include references can be additionally researched through the use of the Selected Bibliography. Additional material to aid in research includes two appendixes listing designers chronologically and by country of birth, a third appendix listing relevant periodicals and theatre collections, and a subject index.

Acknowledgments

I am greatly indebted to the United States Institute for Theatre Technology (USITT) and its members for their support. My appreciation also goes to the librarians at the New York Public Library, Yale, and Harvard theatre collections for their assistance in compiling information. Specifically, I should like to thank Arnold Aronson for his advice and inspiration in the creation and production of this book. Next, I should like to acknowledge the contributing writers for their hard work and dedication in compiling the entries. (Their names are appended to the entries, and brief biographical blurbs appear at the back of the book.) Also, I am thankful for the support of the Department of Theatre/Dance, and the College of Arts and Humanities at the University of Maine, which provided financial support for research. For the preparation of the manuscript, I should like to thank Kurt Lancaster, who spent many hours word processing and doing further research on the entries. Without the cooperation of my preschool daughter, Beth, I am certain that this book would not have been possible. Finally, I should like to thank Greenwood Press and my editor, Marilyn Browstein, for support and advice during the creation of this book.

A History of
Theatrical Design

From ancient rituals in open circles in the woods to present-day theatre complexes in the major cities of the world, performance spaces have served their communities and have been a reflection, as well as a celebration, of culture. It is difficult to separate the evolution of theatre building design from that of stage scenery because the theatre structure itself has served at various times as a background for performances. Thus, the architecture of the building, including the permanent stage structure, was the scenery in the early facilities of classical antiquity and continues to be in many modern productions. There have been many types of stage forms (the predominant ones include proscenium, thrust, and arena) in buildings ranging from intimate spaces to immense auditoriums that include both outdoor and indoor facilities.

Together with performance space, theatrical design has served in various ways to make the theatre event possible. Scenic design has usually consisted of set, lighting, and costume design, although new technologies are forcing the inclusion of sound, video, and film design in today's theatre. Throughout the ages design has been either generic, with stock elements used for a number of productions, or production-specific, with the individual elements tailored to a single show. The styles of design have varied from the illusionistic to the nonillusionistic and from the representational to the presentational, depending upon the technical capabilities and the aesthetics of the period.

Following is a brief history of the major trends and significant figures of the western tradition that have impacted upon the development of the theatre structure and scenic design. This history is broken down into eight sections: Ancient Ritual; Greek and Roman; Medieval; Renaissance, Elizabethan, and Seventeenth Century; Eighteenth Century; Nineteenth Century; Twentieth Century; and Contemporary.

ANCIENT RITUAL

Although very little is known about ancient ceremonies, many scholars agree that theatre grew out of religious ritual. One might imagine that the early humans cleared out the bush to create an area for a fire, gathered the rest of the community, and created a presentation. Basing many of their beliefs on contemporary, nonindustrialized societies, scholars postulate that these religious rituals perhaps included storytelling, dancing, and singing and that they served a variety of functions, including honoring ancestors and the gods, insuring favorable harvest, and teaching and passing along traditions from generation to generation.

Perhaps donning animal skins and specially decorated cloths, these primitive performers perhaps carried weapons, used drums and horns, and wore head-dresses and masks—all scenographic elements used to enhance the efficacy of performance. The mask, like all scenographic elements, not only is decorative but has significant symbolic powers. In the rituals, the wearer of the mask could heighten the reaction to his or her own appearance or perhaps assume a completely different identity. The mask could mystically transform a person into a god, a spirit, or even an animal. It could be a conventionalization or a symbol of some being or state of mind when priest-actors took on magical powers, ostensibly becoming possessed by otherworldly beings. All of this magic emanated from something that was fashioned from natural materials such as wood, cloth, animal hides, feathers, seashells, and metals.

As construction increased around the village, temples were built to serve as the central staging ground for religious ritual, although many outdoor spectacles continued to be produced. As the rituals grew in size, so did their scenographic demands. One of the most significant and massive ancient religious rituals took place in Egypt during the time of the pharaohs. It was called the Abydos Passion play and was described in an ancient document that has been estimated to be more than two thousand years old. The play was a retelling of the legend of King Osiris, who was dismembered by his enemies and was resurrected from the dead by his wife and son. In the ritual procession enactment of the legend, the part of the king was played by I-kher-nef-ert, who described the enactment: the sacred boat, the three-mile round-trip procession, and the actual killing of hundreds of slaves.

In the East, religious rituals, such as Hindu dance dramas used in temple ceremonies in India, eventually grew into festivals and other secular enter-tainments, which to this day have survived in such forms as Kathakali, Kabuki, and Noh plays. The scenography of these forms is highly decorative in costume and makeup, employs masks, and uses conventionalized scenery to represent real objects. Similarly, in the western tradition, specifically ancient Greece, the religious rituals became agricultural festivals featuring play competitions that honored the god Dionysus, and these eventually evolved into our present-day theatre.

GREEK AND ROMAN

In the age of the Greeks, in the latter half of the sixth century B.C., theatrical practice became more sophisticated. Out of their urbanized and socially and politically astute society developed the aesthetics of live theatrical performance. During the great period—the fourth and fifth centuries B.C.—such great poets as Aeschylus, Sophocles, and Euripides presented their works at playwriting festivals. Later, during the second and third centuries B.C., the comic poets Aristophanes and Menander produced plays. The first of these festivals was called the City Dionysia and was held in the spring of each year near Athens. As these classic plays emerged, the physical performance space became more formalized to serve their presentation.

The Theatre of Dionysus at Athens was first created out of a dancing circle that was placed at the foot of a hillside to worship the god of fertility, Dionysus. Sitting on the hillside, the audience surrounded the circle on three sides. Within the circle was an altar for sacrifices, and on its rear diameter was a scene building called the *skene*. Beyond this was a temple to Dionysus. In 499 B.C., the wooden benches that had been used for hillside seating collapsed and were replaced by a stone structure. This new performance space, outdoors on the hillside of the Acropolis, is believed to have seated from fifteen to twenty thousand spectators. Important city officials and wealthy citizens obtained the center seats close to the circle, and most people attended, some with government-subsidized tickets. After visiting the sites of existing ruins, most scholars agree that the outdoor amphitheatres were acoustically superb. Notably, three significant sections of the classical theatre building were formalized during this era: the auditorium, the orchestra, and the scene building.

The *skene* was a multipurpose building used for costume changes, entrances, and exits, as well as for a backdrop for the action. It probably started out as a temporary wooden structure with one front door, and it evolved into a more elaborate, roofed structure with several doors. Eventually, the roof functioned as a raised stage. This building could easily serve as the temple or palace scene within the tragic play and provided many opportunities for various entrances. The raised stage was useful for the appearance of the deities. By the fourth century B.C., the *skene* grew to be longer than the diameter of the dancing circle. Through the evidence of existing foundations, scholars know that two wings were built projecting forward and that eventually a *proskenion*, a temporary colonnade, was built between the two wings. This one-story structure in front of what became a two-story *skene* was the beginning of a prominent, neutral, architectural background for the drama.

There is much debate among scholars about the scenography used in Greek productions. Some argue that the Greeks used illusionistic or painted scenery to define a locale in a specific play. Some of this conjecture is based on the fact that in the *Poetics* Aristotle states that Sophocles invented *skenographia*. Some scholars believe, however, that this term may be interpreted in any number of ways and may not necessarily mean scene painting. Roman writer, architect, and engineer Vitruvius*, who wrote in the first century (four centuries after Sophocles presented his plays) about the Greek theatre, mentions painted scenery first created by Agatharchus. But the description implies that it was a permanent, decorative drawing on a backdrop, not necessarily an attempt at creating a realistic scene for a specific play.

There is evidence of other scenographic elements used by the Greeks. Vitruvius writes about *periaktoi*, three-sided units that were painted with a scene on each side. With only one side visible to the audience at a time, they could be revolved to reveal a different scene. Also, it is believed that by the fourth century B.C., there were painted panels that were mounted between the supporting columns of the *proskenion* called *pinakes*. These would serve as different backdrops for scenes, as well as sound baffles that would resonate the actors' voices for better projection.

Generally, though, most scholars agree that the architectural structure of the theatre served as the predominant visual backdrop to the action of a play, that the language of the text described the supposed locale to the audience, and that there is negligible evidence of illusionistic scenery in the Greek theatre. Further, the audience accepted the theatrical conventions in use at that time. Locations on and around the playing areas of the stage, together with the use of scenic machines, were familiar devices. These devices defined the locale of the play's action in the mind of the spectator.

The Greeks did use at least two major scene-shifting devices to assist in changing the locale from one scene to another: the *mechane* and the *ekkyklema*. The first machine was a crane for levitating a performer to simulate a god or for any number of effects. The term *deus ex machina* refers to the god-producing machine and became, through a parody by Aristophanes, the term commonly used today for a contrived ending. The *ekkyklema* was a revolving or movable platform that was used, perhaps, to show an interior scene. There is evidence that the Greeks used many different types of scene-shifting machines. The Roman writer Pollux, who lived in the second century A.D., refers in his Greek dictionary *Onamastikon* to several scenic effect machines in use in the Greek theatre.

Lighting for the Greek theatre was provided by the natural elements. The festival plays consisted of three tragedies and one satyr play. They would begin at dawn and continue until dusk, using the daily cycle of the sun, moon, and stars. The action of the plays would be written to coordinate roughly with the time of day. This cycle of light was coordinated with the religious aspects of the drama since ancient times. Even in Egypt, the theatricalized religious ceremonies incorporated this cycle of natural lighting into the action. In addition, it is reasonable to assume that torches, lanterns, candles, and other paraphernalia were used to illuminate and create dramatic effects onstage, particularly when the sun went down.

As with the stage decor, costume for the actor was conventionalized, and no attempt at historical accuracy seems to have been made. Tragic Greek plays were first presented by one actor and a chorus. Later, three actors and a chorus presented the dialogue. Since the actor or actors had to portray many roles in the play, their costumes defined the character that they assumed at the moment. Essentially, a tragic costume consisted of a mask with a tall headdress or high forehead called an *onkos*, a long robe called a *chiton*, and raised boots called *cothurni*. Specifically, the mask was the most vital distinguishing feature upon which a tragic actor depended. Its expression physicalized the psychological state of the character. Made of natural materials such as wood and cloth, the masks featured wide mouths that prompted some scholars to speculate upon the megaphonic qualities inherent in such a design. Also, the *onkos*, together with the *cothurni*, added to the height of the actor. The *chiton* had long sleeves, and extended down to the ankle, and some had elaborate decoration and images painted on them. The *chiton* approximated everyday dress, with the exception of the long sleeves. Over the *chiton* were thrown various colored cloaks, which would create slight delineations among, as well as progressions within, characters. It is also reasonable to assume that small accoutrements such as hats, crowns, scarves, and small props were used to define character further. This typical tragic costume was in use in Aeschylus's time; however, there were variations of it depending upon the character being played.

In comedy, such as in the plays of Aristophanes and Menander, costumes were ludicrously exaggerated. The comic actor wore a mask, as did his tragic counterpart, yet it generally did not have the *onkos*. Wigs and beards were added to the masks to designate age and character. Either a *chiton*, with ridiculous padding in front and behind, or a flesh-colored or striped tight was also worn. Often, a predominant feature of the comic actor was a phallus, made of padding. In Old Comedy, such as in Aristophanes's *The Wasps*, *The Birds*, and *The Frogs*, the chorus portrayed animals or insects by wearing skins and masks. As the New Comedy, popularized by Menander, came into being, there was a greater emphasis on naturalism. The characters were members of families and their servants, and the chorus was dressed as humans, appearing on the stage in ordinary street clothing.

The Hellenistic Greek theatre evolved into the Roman theatre over the course of a few centuries. After the second century B.C., the Romans gained power, and the Greek influence was slowly phased out. Existing theatres were remodeled, and new theatres were built to the new standards. The remodeled theatres contained architectural influences from both kinds of theatres, and they are referred to as Graeco-Roman theatres. The new Roman theatres took the disparate elements of the Greek amphitheatre—the auditorium, the orchestra, and the scene building—and unified them into a single structure.

The Romans are considered, by most scholars, to be late in their development of permanent playhouses. Whether it was the expense of a new building or the objections of a political faction is not known. The comedies of Terence and Plautus were performed during the time the Greek New Comedy was staged and were first presented on temporary wooden platform stages that were constructed for various festivals. These platform stages were backed by a simple changing house with three doorways that provided opportunities for the performers to enter and exit.

In 55 B.C., however, the first permanent theatre structure was erected in Rome. This theatre was unlike the Greek structures in that it was not built on a hill but was constructed as a free-standing structure that towered three stories tall. Within its architecture were included the auditorium, the orchestra, and the scene building of the Greek theatre, all in a single, unroofed building. Ruins of the Roman theatres can be viewed at present in Aspendus, Orange, and Pompeii.

Generally, the stage of the Roman structure was approximately three to five feet high, one hundred and twenty feet wide, and twenty feet deep. It increasingly accommodated more of the acting until eventually it was all located on the stage, which was partially protected by an awning. Trapdoors in the stage and steps led down to the orchestra, which was semi-circular in shape and was partially covered with an awning to protect the prime center seats from the elements. The orchestra typically seated tens of thousands of spectators.

The stage was backed on three sides by an architecturally elaborate *scaenae frons*, a three-story rear wall. Decorated with columns and pediments that formed small alcoves where statues were displayed, this wall had three openings for entrances in the center section and one on either side wing. The particular archways signified passage to or from specific locations: the center opening designated the royal palace; the two adjacent side openings led to various rooms in the palace; the stage-right archway led to the immediate neighboring countryside; and the stage-left opening presumably would direct a character to a distant countryside. Additionally, there were dressing rooms and corridors for crossing behind the *scaenae frons*.

There was no illusionistic scenery, as we know it today, in the Roman theatre. Audiences accepted the architecturally elaborate, yet neutral, *scaenae frons* as the backing for the various locations in the action of plays. As in the Greek theatre, scene changes occurred predominantly through the words of the playwright and in the conventions of the physical space. It is debatable, however, whether the Romans actually had any illusionistic scene painting or not. Vitruvius described the use of the painted, three-sided *periaktoi*, which were placed behind the openings in the *scaenae frons*. When a character would enter and the scene would change, these would revolve and display a different painted scene. Vitruvius also wrote that there were three types of scenery: tragic, comic, and satyric. Generally, the tragic scene included palatial scenography such as columns, statues, and other royal architectural features, while the comic scene consisted of a depiction of a private dwelling of the ordinary citizen. The satyric scene consisted of such landscape elements as mountains, trees, and rocks. Most scholars agree that the description of the three types of scenes applies to the drawings on the *periaktoi*, which were very small compared to the rest of the stage picture.

Vitruvius's writings also reveal that some Roman theatres had curtains that were in troughs on the edge of the stage and were pulled up to conceal the stage at the beginning and the end of the play. In some of the less elaborate theatrical structures, the use of two curtains became significant to the presentation of plays. The front curtain, called the *auleum*, was at first hidden in a trough in the front of the stage and pulled upward to conceal or reveal the onstage events. Later, after the second century A.D., it was mounted from above the front of the stage. There was also a back curtain, called the *siparium*, probably derived from the temporary wooden theatres, and it was used to conceal entrances and exits as well as costume changes. Almost nothing is known about the type of scene painting that may have appeared on these curtains.

The Romans, in contrast to their appreciation for the subtleties of theatre, grew to love the excitement of spectacle. The tragedies of Seneca, for example, featured horrific scenes of excessive violence, in which characters simulated ripping their own and others' flesh to the delight of the crowd. For this effect, animal entrails were probably used. While their drama dwindled into mediocrity, other events grew in popularity. At performance spaces such as the Colosseum and in the natural settings of lakes and mountains, major sea battles, called *naumachia*, were staged. For example, Julius Caesar is said to have staged a *naumachia* between the Tyrians and Egyptians on a lake with more than six thousand participants, many of whom were actually injured in the passion of the event. Conflagrations, animal fights, dances, gladiatorial contests, and water ballets also took place on a grand scale in various locations. There were many elaborate machines that created bold effects for the audience. Possibly, some of the machinery that made this spectacle possible in the amphitheatres was brought into the traditional theatre.

Costumes for the Roman theatre were almost entirely based on the Greek costumes. Tragic costume featured the same long robes and high boots, while comic costume displayed the shorter tunic. Wigs and beards were employed, and eventually masks were used. Some masks attempted to replicate natural features in their design, while others had highly exaggerated characteristics. Symbolic color was often used in costuming. In general, young men sported purple robes, old men wore white, and courtesans wore yellow.

MEDIEVAL

After the fall of the Roman Empire in the fifth century A.D., generally caused by the takeover of the Christian church, the theatrical tradition was passed along to the popular entertainers—mimes, jugglers, musicians, and possibly professional actors. These performers moved from one location to another and set up informal performance spaces. Some performers used the existing conditions on the street or town square to ply their craft, while others set up temporary wooden stages adorned with a simple backdrop. Almost nothing specific is known about these itinerant performances. By the tenth century A.D., however, the church adopted theatre as a means of heightening the effect of the religious ceremony, and the medieval theatre emerged.

The theatricalized rituals, called "miracle plays," were presented inside the church. They were, at first, presented on the major feast days of the church calendar and were enactments of biblical stories involving the lives of the saints. As part of the service, these plays were acted out in front of simple scenic structures that were rectangular booths sumptuously decorated with embroidered tapestries of religious emblems. These scenic buildings were called mansions and were too small to contain all of the acting. For most of the scene, the actors used a general acting area in front of the mansion called the *platea*. The mansions served many functions, such as providing a backing for the performers, providing entrances and exits, and housing props. They could be located anywhere in the church, and the action would move from one to the other. Normally, mansions were aligned on either side of the church, with heaven at the altar's end and hell at the opposite end. At first, the mansions were few and simple, but as time progressed, they increased in number as well as in size and grew more elaborate. As the mansions became large, disrupting the church services, and as the drama became more secular in its themes, the presentation was moved outside to the steps of the church. Similar to the structure of the classical theatre, the facade of the church served as an architectural background for the drama.

As the drama outside the church grew ever more secular, it moved farther away from the building and into the town. Using simple platforms with a curtain backdrop or an elaborate platform stage upon which several mansions were constructed, theatrical producers became increasingly inventive. In Germany, the mansions towered to three stories in height, and one platform stage is said to have held up to twenty-four mansions. One example of these fixed stages with multiple scenes on it is *The Valenciennes Passion Play* (1547). On stage right was the mansion representing "Paradise," on stage left was the one symbolizing "Hell," usually called the "Hellmouth," and in the center were such locations as "Herod's House" and "the Temple."

The scenography of the medieval theatre combined realistic elements with conventional symbols to designate locale and character. By convention, it did not disturb the sensibilities of the audience to see actors use the entire stage for each scene. The location was clear to the audience as long as they knew from which mansion the performer entered. This concept is called "simultaneous scene," in which all mansions are in view during the entire play. Special effects and machines were in use during this period. It is believed that the "Hellmouth" in *The Valenciennes Passion Play* belched real flames. Much as in Greek theatre, many effects relied on "flying in" characters from the heavens. For example, Christ would rise to heaven on a platform disguised as a cloud on the "Heaven" mansion. Trapdoors revealed and concealed devils, animals, and other characters. Disappearance effects were plentifully employed, and lighting was reflected off shiny surfaces to create a halo effect. Generally, however, there were no lighting instruments, with the exception of candles and torches, to illuminate the scene.

Day and night were sometimes designated with a backdrop painted with either the sun or the moon.

In England, individual mansions were placed upon, not a stationary platform, but a movable pageant wagon. Thus, the guilds, who produced plays in cycles, could present the different scenes of a play in sequence to a stationary audience by rolling wagons in and out of view. The spectators would watch a scene on one wagon, and, after it left, the next wagon would move into view with a new scene. Both the fixed and movable stages were in use in England and throughout Europe.

Costuming helped delineate male and female characters because all parts were played by men. Before elaborate costuming for these dramas came into being, most characters wore their everyday street clothing. Sometimes they would wear clothing appropriate to a character, but without regard to historical accuracy. In addition, emblematic costuming helped to define character. For example, the saints were associated with various birds, animals, or symbolic objects, so the performers playing them would wear these objects or a design of them. God, the angels, the devils, the saints, and mankind were all depicted with ornate, identifying emblems. In a more obvious manner, angels wore robes to which wings were attached. As the drama moved outdoors and the guilds took increasing pride in their presentations, costuming became extremely rich and elaborate. Wigs and beards, facial paint, and props all added to the effect.

Interludes, tournaments, mummer's plays, disguisings, and street pageants were other forms of performance during the Middle Ages. Interludes and tournaments were usually presented for royalty in the courtyard, an indoor banquet hall, or even the royal tennis court for the presentation of their spectacles. Scenery for the interludes was minimal and employed existing castle architecture and possibly some props. For the tournaments involving knights and soldiers, much of the scenography was emblematic, as in the religious plays. Mansions, arranged around the courtyard, represented such elements as the countryside, castles, and ships. Mummer's plays and disguisings were court entertainments sometimes associated with banquets and other special ceremonies and relied heavily on costume and props. Scenic elements for these mimicked the religious scenography in that several wheeled mansions were used that would enter the banquet hall in sequence. The street pageant, as well, reflected the emblematic approach to scenography of the Middle Ages. The performance space extended through the streets of a town with processioners, dressed in rich clothing and carrying elaborate banners, escorting visiting dignitaries or celebrating various civic events. A dignitary would be met on the edge of town and escorted to a civic building and would stop at the church and other prearranged locations along the way.

Toward the end of the medieval period, there were various stages in use. Simple, temporary structures were built by strolling popular entertainers, as in the commedia del l'arte, and other more complex platforms with solid rear facades with archways were constructed and placed in public areas by other groups.

These latter types of stages, situated in the town square, with the surrounding balconies of buildings for seating, most probably heralded the onset of the Elizabethan theatre.

RENAISSANCE, ELIZABETHAN, AND SEVENTEENTH CENTURY

The Italian Renaissance revived interest in the classics and thus created a link between the design of the theatres of antiquity and the modern theatre structure. In the academies during the latter part of the fifteenth century and throughout the sixteenth century, there was an attempt to stage the classic plays. In fact, some academies were formed solely for that purpose. Revivals of Greek and Roman classics were produced in academies in such cities as Rome, Florence, and Ferrara.

Possibly because not much was known about actual Greek and Roman stages until Virtruvius's *De Architectura* was first translated and published in 1484, the revivals of such classic texts as those by Terence and Plautus were staged on a simple platform with medieval mansionlike structures. This stage is usually referred to by scholars as the "Terence stage." On a raised stage approximately five feet in height, several curtained booths in various arrangements represented different locales, or individual houses of the characters. These combined booths, however, were more monolithic than the freestanding mansions of the medieval theatre.

Research of the classical plays, translations of Aristotle's *Poetics*, Horace's *Art of Poetry*, and Vitruvius's *De Architectura*, combined with contemporary treatises and commentaries, helped to create the basic precepts of the neoclassical ideal to which the theatres were built. The primary one was verisimilitude through unity of staging. Such Aristotelian concepts as the unity of time, place, and action strongly affected design during this period. No longer was simultaneous scene desirable; locales had to represent more closely those in real life. To do this, Italian painters developed the rules for perspective to illustrate life more truthfully. Although research shows that designers had for years been using perspective in theatrical performances, the first definitive record of such an occurrence was in 1508 when *Cassaria* by Ariosto was produced at Ferrara. The scenic art for this production was executed by Pellegrino da Udine and depicted a perspective landscape with houses, gardens, buildings, and churches.

Basing his work on Vitruvius's *De Architectura*, Sebastiano Serlio* synthesized the classical ideas put forth in the book and combined them with contemporary Renaissance ideals. As a result, he published the second volume of his own work, called *Architettura*, in 1545, in which he set out to suggest approaches to design and theatre architecture. Since there were no permanent Renaissance theatres in existence when Serlio wrote his book—most plays took place within the large rooms of palaces and academies—Serlio's design for a classical stage was intended to be temporary and was constructed for each production.

Although many believe that Vitruvius's descriptions (without accompanying illustrations) refer to drawings on *periaktoi*, Serlio's drawings were meant to be realized as full stage representations. Serlio took Vitruvius's description of the tragic, comic, and satyric scenes and rendered drawings of them. These three scenes were intended to meet the needs of all plays. They were all constructed on the same floor plan, which included four wing flats on each side of the stage, with a backdrop at the rear. The first three flats per side were angled and had many three-dimensional architectural details and openings. The first flats possibly extended to the auditorium walls and had an overhanging valance, which masked the upper regions above the stage. The scenery was meant to be permanently installed within a hall for a particular play.

Serlio's drawings intended that the scenery be constructed out of wood and canvas and be painted in one-point perspective. The set consisted of a painted backcloth that had a diminishing view on it, with side wing flats descending down a raked stage that continued the sight lines of the perspective toward the audience. The downstage side flats were L-shaped to convey further the impression of three-dimensionality. While simulating a realistic view of a street or landscape, the one-point perspective was most effective from one center vantage point in the auditorium. This seat was usually reserved for the royal viewer. Unfortunately, the perspective from the side seats was not as effective. Also, the actors who wandered upstage too far destroyed the effect because their height became obvious against the diminishing size of the painted buildings. Thus, acting was done on the forestage area in front of the scenery, not within it. The raked upstage portion, out of necessity, was basically reserved for the scenery.

Lighting developed during the Renaissance as well. For indoor entertainments, large chandeliers were hung over the apron of the stage and provided most of the illumination. As scenic lighting developed, however, it became more specific. Serlio engineered many schemes for aiming, focusing, and changing the character of light, which was provided mainly by candles and oil lamps. For example, he suggested such things as the use of colored light by shining light through bottles filled with colored liquid and amplifying the light by putting a highly reflective bowl behind them. Leone Di Ebreo Sommi*, another scenic designer, developed basic modern principles of lighting—illumination, focus, and mood. He, as well as other Renaissance designers, suggested the use of footlights, sidelights, and overhead strip lights to illuminate the stage. To focus on the stage, he suggested that the auditorium be dimmed. Finally, to create an appropriate mood and atmosphere, he stated that lighting for comedies should be at full intensity, while that for tragedies, when not used to illuminate the perspective, should be lower in intensity.

From about the latter half of the fifteenth century up to the middle of the sixteenth century, plays were performed with *intermezzi*, allegorical interludes that depended upon much spectacle. These *intermezzi* were intended to compliment certain royalty or dignitaries, who would actually take part in them. As a result, they were very elaborately done, incorporating the most complex scenery and machines to impress the royalty. There would be four *intermezzi* during the breaks between the five acts of a play. At first, the various *intermezzi* for a play were neither associated nor linked with the play. Later, they became thematically unified with the play. During *intermezzi*, the Serlian scenery remained stationary, and simple, additional, movable scenery was brought onstage by hand or on wagons. As time progressed, the scenery became more elaborate, and there was an increased interest in changeable scenery, both for the *intermezzi* and for the acts of a play. By the seventeenth century, the *intermezzi* eventually became absorbed into opera.

The permanent theatre building was introduced a bit later in this period because most plays were produced in palaces, academies, and elsewhere and, for the most part, only on special occasions. The Teatro Olimpico at Vicenza, founded in 1555 and opened in 1584, was a Renaissance model of a Roman theatre—a stage with a permanent architectural background, yet with a semi-elliptical rather than semicircular auditorium and orchestra. Designed by Andrea Palladio*, this theatre structure was an indoor theatre built in the classical mode that had an elaborate *scaenae frons*, featuring one large center archway flanked by two lesser ones. Each of two side wings contained a doorway, as in the Roman theatres. One year after Palladio's death, another stage architect, Vincenzo Scamozzi,* significantly altered the theatre by adding perspective vistas behind each of the five archways of the rear facade. In this manner, members of the audience could see down at least one aisle; thus the effect was created for everyone that the stage was a courtyard and each vista was a street running into it. These vistas were permanent and were built in relief and had a tremendous effect on the art of scene design throughout Europe at the time.

Shortly after working at Vicenza, Scamozzi had an opportunity to design a theatre that was in concept less a Roman stage than one dreamed about by Serlio. Moving closer to the concept of a modern theatre, Scamozzi designed the theatre in Duke Sabbioneta's palace in 1590, which had a widened central arch with two side exits. Unlike the theatre at Vicenza, which had five archways with different perspective scenes visible through them, this theatre had one continuous, perspective backdrop visible through its central, wide archway and its two smaller, side exit archways. It also incorporated side flats and the Serlian raked stage.

The theatre built at that time that most closely resembles the modern theatre, however, is the Farnese Theatre at Parma, built in 1618–1619 and designed by Giovanni Battista Aleotti*. Going further than Scamozzi at Sabbioneta, he combined the three arches into one wide proscenium arch. Similar in some ways to the Roman theatre structures, it deviates in design, though, through its proscenium arch with curtain. The development of the proscenium has prompted some scholars to suggest that it had its roots in the central arch of the Roman stage, others link it to the arches used in processions, while others cite the effect of easel painting and framing on the aesthetics of viewing. There were practical reasons for the proscenium as well, including concealing the ever-increasing stage machinery in use at this time. Nevertheless, the proscenium arch, while clearly separating audience and stage, did provide ample opportunity for the use of changeable perspective scenery.

Tapping the wealth of information concerning ancient Roman stage machinery, derived primarily from reading Vitruvius and Pollux as well as others, the Renaissance architects soon began experimentation with *periaktoi* and sliding panels. The first use of *periaktoi* was by Aristotile da San Gallo at Castro. Others experimented with these classical machines, such as Vignola, a painter who published *Two Rules of Perspective Practice*. With the publication of *Practica di fabricar Scene e Machine ne' Teatri* by Nicola Sabbatini* in 1638, the machinery to accomplish scene changes for *intermezzi* (allegorical entertainments between acts of Italian plays) and opera was created. Three such devices in the book for changing scenery are (1) *periaktoi* mounted on a central axle that has a rope wound around it for revolving; (2) duplicate side wing flats, one behind the other so that by removing the front one the rear one would be revealed; and (3) new wings or canvas to pull over the wings already visible. Since Serlio's time, the architectural bas-relief on the wing flats was replaced by painted details that made these types of changes possible. Many different types of effect machinery, such as ignitable *periaktoi*, collapsing buildings, rolling seas of painted cloth on rollers, disappearing characters through trapdoors and the flies, are only a few of the many devices suggested by Sabbatini.

There was much emphasis on concealing the machines that allowed performers to descend from the clouds and rise up into them again. By using clouds as tormentors, the machines were concealed. Sabbatini also suggests that a disturbance, such as trumpets blowing at the rear of the auditorium, occur to distract the audience from perceiving fully how the scene change was accomplished. Sabbatini's suggested diversion possibly indicates much about the lack of smoothness with which most changes occurred.

It was not until 1606 that changeable scenery had additional impetus when Aleotti designed a perspective set consisting of flat wings rather than the conventional, side, angled wings at Ferrara. Using techniques garnered from Guido Ubaldus's *Six Books of Perspective*, primarily for painters, Aleotti was the first to apply these to theatre. Up to this time, the single-point perspective had been painted by attaching a cord to the vanishing point on the back wall and stretching it to the stage side of the angled flats in order to trace the lines of the various buildings. The front side of the angled flats, parallel to the audience, merely required the straight lines of a surface flat to the picture plane. With only flat wings, the problem that Aleotti solved was that all receding lines had to be drawn on the flat walls. Overcoming this obstacle led to the use of entirely flat wings by the mid-seventeenth century and, thus, speedier ways of changing scenery by merely sliding the side wings on and off, in front of, and behind each other.

Other techniques for scene shifting involved sliding the side flats offstage in a groove cut in the floor. Thus, the next flat or scene would be revealed. The back shutter drop was sometimes created out of two large sliding flats that met in the center, and at other times it was a roll drop. Usually, up until the mid-sixteenth century, scenes depicted exterior settings with upper straight borders or billowed canvas painted to represent skies. When interior scenes came into being, the flats were painted to represent the architectural details of the given room, including the ceiling.

Such architects, designers, and machinists as Bernardo Buontalenti* and Giulio and Alfonso Parigi* were concerned with the mechanisms for scene changing and special effects. They created elaborate machinery for effects and beautiful scenery for plays performed for the De Médicis in Florence. Giacomo Torelli* is credited for the invention of the chariot and pole system of scene changing, which he developed while designing at the Teatro Novissimo in Venice in 1641. Simply stated, the movable flat wings were attached to poles that passed through the stage floor to a lower level and were mounted on chariots, or wheeled wagons. These chariots were attached to pulleys and winches and created such a magical effect in scene changing that most of Europe adopted the method, which lasted through the latter half of the nineteenth century.

Scenographic techniques spread from Italy to other parts of Europe. In England, however, there were two distinct theatrical styles coexisting during the latter half of the fifteenth century and the first half of the sixteenth century.

Influenced by the shape of performance space of medieval presentation, the freestanding, unroofed, English public theatres derived their form from bear-baiting pits and the innyard. Shakespeare's Globe Theatre and the Swan are prime examples of typical Elizabethan theatres. There were at least nine public theatres that were built from 1576 through 1642. Rising three stories, they varied in shape from circular to square to polygonal. The stage protruded outward and was elevated above a central courtyardlike area used for standing viewing, much like the trestle stages that were placed in innyards during the medieval period. Surrounding this area were three-tiered galleries for seating, some of which contained private boxes for important citizens. Again, this seating arrangement is similar to the surrounding balconies of innyards where patrons used to sit to watch a play below. At the rear of the playing area was a "tiring house," a backstage area that had up to three doors, used for entrances and exits. Over the stage was a roof supported by two columns. There may have been a second-story balcony, or gallery, over the stage area used for various scenes, such as in *Romeo and Juliet*. The audience sometimes sat onstage, either at the front of the stage or, possibly, in the balcony upstage.

In the Elizabethan public theatre, minimum scenery was used. Simple pieces may have been used to delineate a particular locale: a tree, a bed, a throne. As in the Greek theatre, dialogue revealed to the willing audience where a scene was transpiring. According to available evidence, theatres used stock pieces. Lighting was by daylight, by lanterns, and by torches, as required by the action of some plays.

As in Italy, there were indoor, private theatres that started out in converted halls during this time. Although called private, they were open to the public. Everyone was seated, but fewer people could be accommodated. These theatres charged more for admission. The Blackfriars opened in 1576 but was rebuilt in 1596 by James Burbage. The indoor, private theatres were similar to the outdoor, public theatres. The long, rectangular auditorium had one- to three-story galleries, some with boxes, along each of three walls. The center floor of the room had seats and benches. The raised stage was on one end of the room and extended out toward the audience. In the back were doorways for entrances and a backstage and second-floor gallery area. Chandeliers provided the general illumination of the hall and the stage. Costumes for the plays were contemporary Elizabethan dress, unless the character was a special historical figure or being. Fairies, ghosts, well-known royalty, and various nationalities were given conventionalized treatment, but no attempt at historical accuracy was made.

If the Italian ideal in scene design did not manifest itself in the public and private theatres, it certainly did in the court theatres of James I and Charles I. Inigo Jones* was England's most important scene designer to evolve out of this period. Jones studied in Italy several times and with Giulio Parigi,* Andrea Palladio,* Sebastiano Serlio,* and Vincenzo Scamozzi,* among others. As the court architect, he is singularly responsible for the Italianate staging introduced into England. He designed the court masques, England's counterpart to the Italian *intermezzi*, containing stunning perspective illusion, breathtaking costumes, and magnificent machinery and having no equal in Britain. Jones designed masques written by Ben Jonson, who finally complained to the king that too much emphasis was put on spectacle and too little on the text. Although Jones's early masques, such as Jonson's *The Masque of Blackness* in 1605, introduced perspective scenery to England, his designs for *Salmacida Spolia* in 1640 displayed elaborate, changeable scenery of four sets of wings and shutters that operated in grooves. Jones was subsequently fired by the Puritans in 1642 when they closed the theatres.

In 1660 when the monarchy was restored in England, neoclassicism and Italian scenery dominated scenic design. The Elizabethan-style theatres all but vanished. Plays were performed on converted tennis courts, at inns, and at private residences until permanent theatres were built.

During Spain's Golden Age, 1500–1700, plays were presented much as they were in England's public and private theatres. Religious plays, *auto sacramentales*, were presented in town squares during the feast of Corpus Christi on wagons called *carros*. At first there was one wagon, then two, until four wagons and a permanent, fixed stage were combined. Two wagons were placed behind the fixed stage for backing, and each of the other two was set adjacent to each end, forming a U-shaped theatre. The performances featured two to four plays, combined with farcical interludes. In addition, there were local parades that featured giant puppets and dances in a carnival spirit. Eventually, the church objected to the mixture of the farces and to dances being mixed with religious drama.

The Spanish public theatres, called *corrales*, were located in the major cities and were extensions of the courtyard theatres. In 1579 the Corral de la Cruz and in 1583 the Corral de la Principe both opened in Madrid. There were *corrales* subsequently built in other major cities. Although these theatres did not share a uniform design, they all had common traits and even resembled the Elizabethan public theatre. Most were square or rectangular, but one was oval. The stage was roofed and elevated with a rear, permanent facade. It had a front extension that was sometimes semicircular and two pillars at the rear to divide the stage for three entranceways. Like the "pit," there was the "patio" for standing spectators. Later, benches were provided in this area. There were three-tiered, side galleries with boxes for spectators and a rear gallery that usually contained a tavern on the ground floor. Directly above the tavern was a gallery for women, and above that, one for dignitaries. Because these theatres were converted from actual town squares surrounded with houses, much of their design incorporated connecting buildings in which seating space was rented by spectators. In the seventeenth century, the theatres were roofed. Scenery was minimal, and the staging was similar to that in the Elizabethan theatre in that action was played in front of the facade, a curtain, or a small scenic unit. Mansions were also placed onstage for various scenes but were soon replaced with painted flats having doors and windows.

The Italian influence on scene design and theatre buildings continued to spread throughout Europe during this period. In England, the Dorset Garden and the Drury Lane theatres, two typical facilities of the period, opened in 1671 and 1674, respectively, and were both designed by Christopher Wren. These seventeenth-century theatres had auditoriums containing three-story galleries that surrounded a central pit, or orchestra seating area. There were boxes on the first level, boxes and benches on the second, and benches on the third. The pit now had benches and was raked to assist the audience in seeing the stage, which was different from the Continental style in that there were a proscenium arch and an apron that thrust forward from it. In addition, there were two doors with balconies above that opened onto each side of the thrust stage and from which most characters entered.

Acting during this period took place on the front of the stage with the rear area reserved for the picture frame and scenery. The scenic area had grooves for changing scenes during plays. The chariot and pole system was possibly adopted only for opera productions. Trapdoors and machinery were used for special effects. These theatres continued to grow in size to accommodate the middle-class audiences through the eighteenth century. Ancillary space, such as dressing rooms, costume and prop storage, and a set construction area, was added to the facilities.

The Italian ideal was transmitted to Spain through the court of Philip IV (reigned 1621–1665). Designer Cosme Lotti was brought from Florence in 1626 and designed at the Buen Retiro, the palace hall used for plays, built in 1633. Lotti designed a permanent theatre in the Buen Retiro in 1640 called the Coliseo, which was sometimes open to the public. Although in some ways, particularly in the audience seating, the Coliseo resembled the *corrales*, it differed in that it had a proscenium arch. Lotti designed for this indoor stage, as well as for the outdoor extravaganzas, such as Calderón's *Love the Best Enchantment* (1635). For this entertainment, Lotti constructed a new stage that floated on a lake in which a shipwreck and a chariot pulled by dolphins were simulated.

Two events mark the beginnings of the Italian ideal in France. First, Serlio was published in the country in 1545, and second, *La Calandria*, with Italianate perspective scenery, was produced in 1548 for the wedding of Henry II and Catherine de Médici. By 1610, the year when Henry IV died, Italian designers were regularly being imported into France to produce in the Court theatres where the *ballet du cour*, an entertainment much like the English masques and Italian *intermezzi*, was performed. They brought with them the unified settings of the Italian theatre. In 1617 for *The Deliverance of Renaud*, the side wings and back shutter approach was introduced into the Court theatre.

In the public theatre, however, the progress toward Renaissance ideals was slow. Designer Laurent Mahelot* worked and published *Le Memoire de Mahelot, Laurent, et des Autre Décorateurs*, a record of his and others' productions from 1633 through 1678. Mahelot may have been the designer of these shows, but some scholars suggest that he was only the machinist. Settings for productions done at the Hôtel de Bourgogne Theatre, a converted, long, rectangular hall and one of Paris's permanent public theatres at the time, were primarily medieval in concept, employing simultaneous scene. Usually, there were five mansions onstage to represent the locales called for in the play—two on each side and one in the rear. These represented such locales as houses, palaces, seacoasts, temples, and forests. Sometimes, mansions would be altered with a curtain or drop to get an additional scene. Machines were employed such as boats, deus ex machina flying rigs, as well as elaborate effects, props, and costumes. Mahelot's work contained medieval as well as Renaissance ideals. For example, some of his drops were painted in perspective, and there were side mansions that recalled Serlio's angled side flats. Details in some of the productions were repeated throughout one simultaneous scene, thus unifying the entire structure to some degree.

The Théâtre du Marais, Paris's other public theatre, was created from a renovated tennis court in 1634 and rebuilt after a fire in 1644. The long, rectangular shape of the building—115 feet long, 38 feet wide, and 52 feet high—was ideally suited for the spectacle. The fifteen-hundred seat auditorium had a pit for standing viewing, and the side walls were divided into three galleries (the first two were divided into boxes). The rear wall of the auditorium had first-level boxes with an amphitheatre seating section above it. The proscenium stage was 6 feet above the parterre and was raked. It featured a *théâtre supériere*, which was a raised second stage from which heavenly scenes could possibly have been played.

Following Cardinal Richelieu's rise to power under Louis XIII, he tried to make France a cultural haven in Europe by encouraging artists who accepted the neoclassical ideal. In addition, he was responsible for having the architect Lemercier construct the first Italianate theatre in France. The Palais-Cardinal (later the Palais-Royal), which opened in 1641, had a permanent proscenium arch and a stage that was designed to accommodate wing flats.

Chief Minister Cardinal Mazarin, Richelieu's successor, brought the opera and, with it, designer Torelli to France. Torelli redesigned the Petit-Bourbon Theatre and the Palais-Royal Theatre into Italianate theatres and installed his chariot and pole system of scene changing in both of them. Molière eventually produced his comedies and housed his companies at both of these theatres, and used unified, interior drawing room settings constructed of wings and shutters. In 1645, Torelli established the Italian ideal in France with a successful production of the opera *La Finta Pazzi*. Torelli's acumen as designer-architect-machinist led to his creation of the sets and machines for Corneille's *Androméde*, the first machine play and the one that inspired a whole series of machine plays. The play was constructed like a conventional drama, only with pantomimic, musical interludes that highlighted Torelli's elaborate machinery. In 1659, Mazarin also brought Gaspare Vigarani,* who tore down the Petit-Bourbon Theatre and built Europe's largest theatre, the Salle des Machines in its place, in the Tuileries, adjacent to the Louvre. The Salle des Machines opened in 1662 with the opera *Hercules in Love*, in which the entire royal family and its attendants were elevated into the clouds. Suffering from poor acoustics and its relatively large size, the Salle des Machines saw little use after its first few years.

Hunger for opera increased in Paris toward the end of the seventeenth century. Vigarani died in 1663 and passed his post to his son Carlo, whose work was seen at the newly constructed theatre at Versailles and at the Paris Opera. At Versailles for Louis XIV, Carlo designed *The Pleasures of the Enchanted Island*, a combination play, procession, tournament, and ballet that lasted for three days. French opera design continued until the end of the century with the father and son, Jean Louis Bérain.*

During the sixteenth and seventeenth centuries, the Italian and French commedia dell'arte improvisational groups were a prevalent force in the shaping of the theatre and design. Performing on simple platform stages with a backcloth or on a typical Renaissance public stage, the commedia players, carrying on the Roman tradition of improvisational farce, brought to the theatre many stock characters adorned with identifiable costumes and individual masks, for example, Harlequin, Pulcinella, Il Doctore, Il Capitano, and Scapino.

The force of Italian scene design was felt through most of Europe by the end of the seventeenth century. The single-point perspective scene of symmetrically arranged buildings, streets, and trees, appearing on sets of wing, shutter, and border flats within a proscenium arch, dominated scenography during this period. Changeable scenery with spectacular effects created by elaborate machinery continued to dominate European design. Italian designers continued to be exported as commodities. Josef Furttenbach* took Serlio's ideas back to Germany, and later such designers as Ludovico Ottavio Burnacini* worked in Vienna at

the Austrian Court. Italian scenery, however, through infusion of energy from
the opera, continued to develop and change in style. The elaborate, intricate
baroque and rococo styles began to replace the symmetrical, orderly, and eco-
nomically detailed Renaissance scenery.

EIGHTEENTH CENTURY

Probably the most influential force in scene design throughout the seventeenth
and eighteenth centuries in Europe was the Bibiena family.* Because of their
mastery, they were in demand in most major European cities. Although there
were many of them, almost spanning two centuries of design, the four most
significant Bibienas were Ferdinando (1657–1743), Francesco (1659–1739), Giuseppe (1696–1757), and Carlo (1728–1787). Through their work, several significant developments occurred to improve the art of scenic design.

First of all, the size and splendor of the spectacle increased. Ferdinando can
be credited with several significant innovations. At Bologna in 1703, he altered
the single-point perspective by using "angled perspective" (*scena per angolo*),
that is, two or more vanishing points, or vistas, placed very low off to the side
of a central building or scenic unit. He thus created unusual size, scale, and
complexity in the stage picture. No longer were entire buildings visible on the
downstage flats. Bibiena painted only the lower section of architecture and thus
created the effect that the buildings were vast and continued out of sight, above
the upper borders of the scenery. Filippo Juvara* (1676–1736) independently
adopted the angled perspective while working in Naples about 1706. He also
experimented with changeable backgrounds in front of a fixed foreground. Juvara
placed flats or scenic units anywhere on the stage, not just to the sides. This
new scale and perspective, although possibly too elaborate, were more true to
real life. Performers could stand next to the scenery without the ridiculous effect
of being as tall as the building. The complexity of the stage picture possibly
detracted from the performer, but it also created a fantasy world for the spectators.

The Bibienas were not the only family of scene designers to win favor with
the European theatregoers. The Burnacinis,* another prominent dynasty, were
led by Giovanni (?–1656) and his son Ludovico Ottavio in Venice. The Mauro
family,* starting with Gaspare (1657–1719), worked in Italy, Austria, and Germany. The Quaglio family,* led by Giulio (1601–1658), dominated Germany.
The Galliari family,* including Bernardino (1707–1794) and Fabrizio (1709–
1790), worked during the seventeenth century and into the eighteenth and spread
new Italian methods throughout Italy and Germany.

During this period, scene design continued to use the wing, shutter, and border
system, with the addition of roll drops and front curtains. Scene changes, however, still took place in front of the audience. Because the neoclassic approach
emphasized the universality of the setting, stock or generic scenery was supplied
with some newly built theatres. Theatres had ready-made garden scenes, streets,
and interiors that were used many times for a multitude of different productions.

As the taste for ever-increasing spectacle took over, there grew a demand for fresh scenery for each play. Scenery was specifically designed to depict the locales called out in the text. Painters were employed in increasing numbers and at very high prices to execute these stage settings. Subsequently, theatres began hiring their own in-house scenic artists, and Continental designers such as Giovanni Nicolò Servandoni* were imported to England. Another prominent import was Philip DeLoutherbourg,* who was hired by actor-manager David Garrick to work at the Drury Lane. From 1771 to 1781, he designed more than thirty major productions that featured reproductions of actual locations onstage.

DeLoutherbourg was a total artist who coordinated and controlled all of the visual elements on the stage. Unlike sets for another production that were usually painted by several people, DeLoutherbourg's sets were entirely painted by him. His designs were influenced by the antiquarian movement, which was characterized by a renewed interest in history and local color. Exact locations, sometimes featuring ancient and classical ruins, were researched, sketched, and rendered for the stage. When DeLoutherbourg resigned from the Drury Lane, he opened a miniature theatre. Called the Eidophusikon, the theatre had a small stage that was six by eight feet in dimension. On it, he re-created specific locales and simulated actual weather conditions through painting, lighting, and sound. He experimented with various placements of scenic flats and units—such as using ground rows—remounted lighting instruments in unusual places, and employed semitransparent fabrics to create atmospheric moods.

Eighteenth-century theatre buildings sported elaborate proscenium arches with small thrust stages that had single side doors. The auditoriums were oval shaped, with seating for the masses. There were three levels of galleries, some of which had boxes with expensive seating, as well as an orchestra area that accommodated patrons on benches. The stage was raked, and the performers continued to play on the apron rather than in the setting.

At the beginning of the century, lighting was generalized, with chandeliers providing illumination for the actors on the front of the stage and the auditorium as well. Later, lighting became more advanced. New techniques and instruments were developed to help the scenery depict a specific locale. By mid-century, lights were hung on ladders behind the side flat wings to illuminate the scenery. "Scene blinds" were shutters that would block the light and were in use at the time as well. Footlights that receded into the floor were also in use. Lamps with reflectors, as well as candles, were common in theatres. Colored, semitransparent fabrics were used to color and filter the light. Garrick, in England, removed all visible fixtures from audience view and increased their intensity by employing more lights. The Argand lamp was introduced in 1785 and greatly improved the quality of light. Using a cylindrical wick, with a glass chimney that could be tinted, the Argand lamp provided greater control and intensity and superseded candles as the common light source.

Costuming during the eighteenth century remained dominated by contemporary dress, with conventionalized clothing for special characters. Garrick, after 1750, tried to present plays in Elizabethan dress, but the costumes may not have been totally historically accurate. Often, only the stars of a particular play, such as Garrick, Kemble, and Macklin in their Shakespearean roles, wore costumes that might be considered accurate. The rest of the cast was dressed in stock costumes that were used over and over again. Not until the nineteenth century was historical accuracy in costume a priority.

NINETEENTH CENTURY

Beginning in the late eighteenth century and continuing into the nineteenth century, there was an increased interest in historical accuracy, as well as an appetite for exotic landscapes and faraway places. Although the formal settings of the earlier period were still somewhat popular, highly accurate, locale-specific, architectural detail came into vogue and led to the historical romanticism of the early nineteenth century. Thus, the baroque and rococo settings of the seventeenth and eighteenth centuries were supplanted by either more subdued, simple, formal, neoclassic settings or exotic, romantic settings illustrating specific locations.

The theatre building during the nineteenth century underwent serious alterations. Because of the growing middle-class audience, theatres had become vast centers for entertainment. For example, the Drury Lane, which was built in 1794 and had a proscenium that was more than forty feet wide and more than ninety feet deep, was reconstructed after it burned down in 1809 as the Theatre Royal with a seating capacity of more than thirty-two hundred people. The Covent Garden, rebuilt after a fire in 1808, had a capacity of more than twenty-eight hundred. Acoustic problems abounded, together with insufficiently planned sight lines. Acting style must have been affected as performers attempted to project to the vast audience. In 1843, the Haymarket altered its stage and auditorium so that these problems could be addressed. The architects reduced the apron and removed the side proscenium doors. Thus, because the performance moved upstage, the proscenium arch became the separation line for performer and audience. The curtain could now fall between the two and create hitherto unknown effects.

To accommodate the increasing size of nineteenth-century theatres, spectacles and extravaganzas were presented to entertain the huge audiences. There were equestrian shows at Astley's Playhouse, where a circus ring was placed in the orchestra, and there were aquatic performances at Sadler's Wells, where a water tank was installed in the stage. Burlesques and extravaganzas were written incorporating these spectacular devices. Mme. Vestris, manager of the Olympic Theatre from 1831 to 1838, employed J. R. Planché* as playwright and designer. In addition to the horse races, sea battles, and other effects, the emphasis on spectacle included an antiquarian interest in historically accurate settings and costumes.

William Capon,* a major designer in the nineteenth century, was an early advocate for historically accurate costumes and scenery. In 1823, John Phillip

Kemble's production of *King John*, featuring Planché's historically researched costumes and scenery, was a huge success. Planché had to convince the actors that the audience would not laugh at them. Other actor-managers, such as William Charles MacReady and Charles Kean, followed suit and enjoyed success with scenery by such designers as Planché, Thomas Grieve, and William Telbin. This tradition was passed down a line of Shakespeare interpreters such as Henry Irving and Max Beerbohm Tree, who used such designers as Henry Hawes Craven* and William Roxby Beverley*. During the nineteenth century, this tendency reached its zenith.

A predominantly painterly approach to historical romanticism was dominant throughout Europe. Landscape painters, archaeologists, antiquarians, and scenic artists were regularly enlisted to work on a production. MacReady, for example, hired scenic painters such as Charles Marshall (1806–1880) and Clarkson Stanfield.* Detailed settings and spectacular effects were audience-pleasing elements of nineteenth-century production. Local color, ancient ruins, and exotic, historical locations made a formula for success. The larger houses could be filled if producers were sensitive to these requirements. It was not until about mid-century, however, that historical accuracy in production was consistent in that all scenes of a play were done by the same artist or that all characters in the same play were dressed in historical costume and not just the star.

In France, Louis-Jacques Daguerre (1787–1851), later the inventor of the photograph called the daguerreotype, refined the new invention, the panorama, and employed it in the theatre. Audiences had seen panoramas in buildings suited for that purpose. In the theatre, painted scenes on long canvas were rolled past the audience's view as background. For example, in some shows, riders on horses on treadmills would be viewed against the moving panorama. In England, Clarkson Stanfield introduced the moving diorama in a production of *Henry V* to portray the voyage by sea.

Another major development occurred in France. Pierre-Luc-Charles Ciceri* (1782–1868), Parisian designer of opera and ballet, opened the first scenic studio. He employed specialists in different fields to accomplish the various scenic effects. Since, the use of scenic studios rather than a specific theatre's scene shop has been a viable alternative. Ciceri designed at the then new Paris Opéra, where gas lighting and a water system for effects had been installed. Gas lighting allowed greater flexibility in control, although the illumination of the stage was still general. An operator could control the direction and illumination of the stage from one position, as he could not do with candles and oil. The carbon arc and limelight were experimented with in the mid-century and did not come into full use until the end of the century.

Methods for scene shifting evolved throughout the nineteenth century. With Henry Irving at the Lyceum in 1881, the grooves in the stage floor were abandoned for freestanding three-dimensional set units that could be moved or permanently placed for a production anywhere on the stage. The front curtain was used to mask many changes, while midstage drops were used for backing for downstage scenes while they masked upstage scene shifts. Elevators were utilized in major theatres to raise and lower scenery into position. New stage machinery made the chariot and pole system obsolete, and trapdoors in the stage floor were used extensively for regular dramas as well as for the emerging melodramas. In *The Corsican Brothers*, the Corsican trap was developed. Figures could appear and disappear while moving through space, but the audience could not see the trap because of a rolltop desk apparatus on the slot.

One of the most interesting aspects of scene design during the nineteenth century was the development of the box set. The box set was usually an interior surrounded by three canvas-on-wood frame walls painted to look like an actual room. The "fourth wall" was imaginary and faced the audience. Up to this time, most interiors were accomplished with the chariot and pole system of flats. Thus, the space between the back wall and the downstage flats, or proscenium, could not be closed off without impeding a sliding wing flat. It is possible that some designers experimented with actual box sets previous to the nineteenth century, but most scholars agree that they came into popular use during the 1830s throughout Europe. Mme. Vestris at the Olympic Theatre is credited with their introduction and consistent use in England at this time.

Early in the century, box sets had their details painted on them. Doors, windows, chairs, pots and pans on shelves, and the like were painted on the canvas. Later in the century, as the improved electric lighting and the realistic movement made this obviously artificial technique outmoded, actual furniture, props, and entrances were incorporated into the box set.

The realistic movement had its initial impetus with writer Émile Zola, who was a leading proponent of naturalism. Zola and his followers cried for a "slice of life" and obliteration of the barrier between art and life. Director André Antoine, at the Théâtre Libre in Paris in 1887, put the theories into practice and demanded that the sets for his dramas depict real life truthfully. Thus, actual food was used onstage, and authentic furniture was placed within the room as it would have been in everyday life. Antoine would then decide which side (the "fourth wall") would face the audience. In fact, Antoine would not let his actors concede to theatricality; they would sit with their backs to the audience if necessary. His approach emphasized the importance of environment to each play that he presented. Therefore, Antoine's approach to every play's environment was unique, and any type of stock setting was unacceptable. Ultimately, however, Antoine recognized that audiences were too enamored of the realistic scenic effects and did not necessarily concentrate on the play itself.

A theorist who laid the groundwork for the modernist era was the nineteenth-century, romantic opera composer Richard Wagner. An iconoclast whose writings still influence certain theorists, Wagner rebelled against the tendencies toward realism and also the type of theatre buildings of his era. In his writings he defined a concept called *Gesamkunstwerk*, a master artwork that called for a unified approach to production directorially and scenographically. Art should be distanced from real life. It should lift the audience up into another realm, an idealized drama "dipped into the magic fountain of music." Up to this time there had been little consistency in production style.

Wagner's dictatorial approach to his operas came through the concept of music, which exerts greater control over performers than is possible in regular drama. Further, he wanted to create a classless theatre, one in which music-drama would flourish. Together with the architect Gottfried Semper, he proceeded with plans that were later revised by several other architects. The building at Bayreuth was begun in 1872 and finished in 1876. The seating no longer indicated the social strata of the audience; the box, pit, and gallery arrangement gave way to a fan-shaped auditorium of thirty sloped rows of seats with side aisles and exits. There was no center aisle. In the rear of the auditorium was a single large, box seating area with a gallery above it. The auditorium accommodated 1,745 people, who all paid the same price of admission. Another innovation was that the auditorium was darkened during performance to heighten the illusion on the stage and thus take the audience into the fantasy world of the theatre.

Wagner believed in creating total illusion and meticulous historical accuracy. He saw the stage as an ideal world and the auditorium as the real world. Separating the stage from the auditorium was the orchestra pit, a "mystic chasm," most of which extended underneath the apron of the stage. To separate the audience further from the production were a double proscenium and a series of steam vents that would mask scene changes. The stage floor was raked and still employed the chariot and pole system of scene shifting.

Wagner's opera productions were rooted in the nineteenth century, but his writings inspired future theatricians for years to come. The Italianate-style theatre had dominated from the seventeenth century, but after Wagner's experiment at Bayreuth, theatre buildings slowly evolved. The wing and drop system was replaced by new machinery and scenery. Boxes, galleries, and center aisles were either reduced or eliminated altogether in new theatre buildings.

Other figures in addition to Wagner profoundly influenced the development of modern scene design. The French symbolists, toward the end of the nineteenth century, rejected realism as a way to get at the truth. Paul Fort spurned the efforts of the Théâtre Libre and espoused theories that led the way for the modern period. He founded the Théâtre d'Art in 1890, which became the Théâtre de l'Oevre in 1892, with Aurélian-Marie Lugné-Poe as its head. Such famous artists as Édouard Vuillard, Maurice Denis, Pierre Bonnard, and Toulouse-Lautrec were associated with Fort's new theatre. With the philosophy "the word creates the decor," Lugné-Poe and the symbolists created plays in an anti-realistic, highly stylized manner. Abstract paintings of lines and color on a backdrop; no furniture; gauze curtains in front of the actors; draping costumes; dim, general, overhead lighting; and chanting were some of the elements of a symbolist production. Out of this production approach came certain precepts that led into the modern era of scenic practice. For example, Lugné-Poe called for a unification of style between the actor and the scenery. Scenery should be simple yet evocative and should not be literal, descriptive, or illusionistically painted.

TWENTIETH CENTURY

Realism in design continued to flourish throughout the latter half of the nine-teenth and into the twentieth centuries. Producer Konstantin Stanislavsky at the Moscow Art Theatre experimented with realism, after being attracted to the Saxe Meiningen Troup's productions that played in Moscow in 1885. George II, Duke of Saxe Meiningen, revolutionized his productions by demanding consistent costuming and using real fabrics such as expensive embroidery and chain mail, together with settings that attempted to be authentic. When painted elements were called for, they were blended with the three-dimensional pieces. Most importantly, the Meiningen Troup had productions that were artistically unified, an effect that up to this time was not in the mainstream. In this manner, with his designer, V. A. Simov, Stanislavsky created realistic settings for such plays as Chekov's *The Seagull* (1896) and *The Cherry Orchard* (1904), as well as for Gorky's *The Lower Depths* (1902). Realism appealed to Stanislavsky and led him to research actual locations for his productions, as he did for Gorky's *The Lower Depths*, which takes place in a flophouse.

In America, in the beginning of the twentieth century, realism was passed on through the productions of Dion Boucicault to producer-director David Belasco.* Through his stage decorators, Belasco re-created an actual restaurant on the stage for *The Governor's Lady* (1912). It was stocked with food that was actually eaten for every performance. Belasco experimented heavily with lighting, spend-ing weeks on lighting rehearsals alone as he tried to create authentic-looking effects.

The aesthetics of the modern theatre, however, were solidified through the writings of European design theorists Adolphe Appia* and Edward Gordon Craig,* who both rejected the realistic approach. They called for a new theatre without the artificiality of pictorial realism, one in which productions were unified by a single artist so that the theatre might once again attain the greatness and sense of communion of the theatre of the Greeks.

Heavily influenced by the theories of Wagner as well as the symbolists, Appia published his ideas in several essays that were later published as books, *The Staging of Wagner's Musical Dramas* (1895), *Music and the Stage Setting* (1899), and *The Work of Living Art* (1921), all of which called for a reform of theatrical design practice. To Appia the disparity between the moving, three-dimensional actor and the obviously painted, two-dimensional scenery and flat floor was unacceptable for artistic unification. Also, Appia believed in a ''living light,'' which would shift and change along with the moods of the play and thus be unified with it. He suggested the use of three-dimensional platforms, steps, and ramps that would enhance the actor's movements and at the same time embody the rhythms of the production. After meeting choreographer Jaques-Dalcroze, who invented eurythmics, Appia was convinced that performance space was to be defined through the rhythms within the text. Although Appia actually designed several operas, he is mostly known as a theorist of modern stage design.

Craig was the son of Edward W. Godwin, a nineteenth-century scenic artist, and legendary English actress Ellen Terry. Beginning his career as an actor, Craig soon gravitated toward scenic design and theory. His manifestos against the typical and, to him, artificial nineteenth-century scenic practices were published in book form as *The Art of the Theatre* (1905) and *On the Art of the Theatre* (1911) and in the journal *The Mask* (1908 irregularly through 1929). Essentially, Craig followed in the footsteps of Wagner and Appia and called for directorial unification of productions in acting, directing, and designing. Craig, like Appia, saw a disparity when three-dimensional actors appeared against obviously painted backgrounds. He proposed using simplified, three-dimensional units that were abstract and could suggest a series of steps, walls, corridors, and doorways for settings. These units, through their avoidance of realism, could create a mood more synthesized with the text itself.

To this end, Craig developed a series of scenic screens meant to revolutionize scene design. His screens were used by Yeats at the Abbey Theatre and by Stanislavsky for *Hamlet* (1911) at the Moscow Art Theatre. They were meant to be an ever-changeable machine that could be used for every scene in a different configuration. Consisting mostly of very high walls made of natural fibers and other raw materials, they also incorporated movable step units so that their permutations could be endless. Unfortunately, as applied in the Moscow Art Theatre's *Hamlet*, they were huge and top-heavy. In fact, Stanislavsky writes in his biography, *My Life in Art* (1924), that they toppled over one hour before curtain and had to be fixed. Ultimately, they were not very successful on a wide scale. The theory behind the screens together with Craig's other ideas, however, did influence a whole generation of American designers.

Craig, like Appia, designed more than he actually produced and published his proposed designs with his theories. His writings have been criticized by his contemporaries and by later theorists for being more propagandist than theoretical and for being somewhat derivative of Appia's works. His designs, as well, have been criticized for being impractical to build in theatres because of their improbable scale. Nevertheless, Craig's impact on modern design has been incalculable.

Modern stage design was also ushered in by late nineteenth-century technological developments. The Industrial Revolution manifested itself in the theatre as well as in industry. As the nineteenth-century wing and drop settings on the chariot and pole system were declining in use, there was a need to find quick and easy ways to shift scenery. The German Karl Lautenschläger* introduced the revolving stage in 1896 in the Residenz Theatre in Munich. Later, in 1914, another German, Adolf Linnebach,* combined the sliding platforms developed by Fritz Brandt in Berlin with the elevator stage, flying apparatus, and small wagons at the Dresden State Theatre.

Electric lighting, as well, was evolving with lamps that were capable of producing one thousand watts each. Color media, lighting supports, and instruments were the subjects of much experiment. Mariano Fortuny (1871–1949) developed an elaborate lighting system in the early part of the century that incorporated colored silk, strong lamps, and reflectors and was capable of the most subtle shifts of color and intensity.

With improvements in lighting came the development of the cyclorama, made either of plaster or cloth. The cyclorama rendered the painted backcloth all but obsolete. The cyclorama used in Germany at this time, developed by Fortuny, was called a *kuppelhorizont* or ''sky dome.'' It was a curved, plaster surface on which all manner of lighting effects could be projected. The curved surface actually increased the square footage of the cyclorama and improved the vertical sight lines. The new cycloramas created moody, infinite voids when properly lit and were ideal, indefinite backgrounds appropriate for the new, three-dimensional scenery.

Reactions against realism were prevalent in Russia and Germany in the early part of the century through the work of a number of experimentalists who have had a profound effect on design. The most notable divergences include Russian constructivism through the directors Vsevolod Meyerhold (1874–1940), Nikolai Evreinov (1879–1953), and Aleksandr Tairov (1885–1950) and their designers, Isaac Rabinovitch,* Ignati Nivinski,* and Aleksandra Exter.* Constructivism in design was typified by such elements as an architectural, nonrepresentational acting machine with kinetic elements. Many of Meyerhold's productions employed a series of ramps, platforms, slides, steps, wheels, and swings that were more functional than ornamental. In Germany, Max Reinhardt, the famous director, with his designers Ernst Stern,* Oskar Strnad,* and Karl Walser, best embodied Craig's super-director theory. He too used semipermanent settings for some of his productions and built the mammoth theatre, the Grosses Schauspielhaus, from an old circus building. After the devastation of World War I, the expressionist movement manifested itself in scene design. In painting it emerged as the antithesis of impressionism in France. In Germany, it is best exemplified through the work of director Leopold Jessner with designer Emil Pirchan at the Berlin State Theatre. They imaginatively employed flights of steps, platforms, and light to symbolize the subjective world of the play. Finally, the Bauhaus theatre emerged through the impetus of Walter Gropius,* who attempted to shape the everyday world into art. Function and design were integrated into the whole, and the traditional barriers between art and craft were overcome. Gropius worked with Oskar Schlemmer,* who directed the stage workshop, and who conducted experiments to adapt the human form to theatrical space through the use of three-dimensional costumes. For director Erwin Piscator, Gropius developed unrealized plans for his ''total theatre,'' in which he incorporated a proscenium, a thrust, and an arena stage all in one building. In architecture, as well as design, the Bauhaus movement was a source of inspiration for later experimentalists, as well as for contemporary theatre architects.

The theories of playwright-director Berthold Brecht, however, had an immeasurable effect on scenography in the twentieth century. Working together with his scene designers Caspar Neher* and Teo Otto,* Brecht used production techniques that were developed in the Epic theatre by director Erwin Piscator. Piscator, a political reformist, was one of the first to use filmed projections and cartoons, as in his production of *The Good Soldier Schweik* (1927). Brecht formulated his theory of *verfremdungseffekt* or "alienation" effect. Brecht believed that the audience should not confuse the staging for real life. By separating the audience from the action, Brecht believed that he could induce critical evaluation from them. With designers Neher and Otto, he emphasized a theatrical approach to the staging of such productions as *Mother Courage and Her Children* (1937) and *The Caucasian Chalk Circle* (1944). He accomplished this approach scenographically through such techniques as projecting titles for scenes and not concealing the lighting instruments or the scene changes.

Later, in the 1940s, visionary Czechoslovakian designer Josef Svoboda* carried on in the tradition of Appia, Craig, and Brecht and extended the theories. Svoboda coined the term *scenographer*, which he feels is more inclusive of all the techniques available to a designer than the term *scene designer*, which implies a more "pictorial" or "painterly" approach. Using the modern theories of stagecraft, Svoboda has experimented with the latest technology. This contemporary approach to thinking about design has had an immeasurable effect upon current design practice and theory.

In America, the theories of Appia and Craig were carried through by such practitioners as Samuel Hume,* who studied with George Pierce Baker at Yale. Hume was also a student of Craig at his school in Florence when the teacher was developing his system of screens. After becoming impressed with the new theories of design, Hume mounted an exhibition in America of Continental stagecraft renderings that toured Cambridge, Chicago, Cleveland, Detroit, and New York during 1914 and 1915. Becoming the director of the Detroit Arts and Crafts Theatre, he developed a permanent, adaptable set made out of flats, pylons, and step units that could be made into any number of arrangements for a series of plays. Unfortunately, this style of setting was not used on a wide scale, but the theories of the "New Stagecraft," as Kenneth MacGowan called this style, emphasized simplification, suggestion, and synthesis and represented the basic design philosophy winning acceptance in America at that time.

At the Detroit theatre, Hume's friend Sheldon Cheney started *Theatre Arts Magazine*, which further promulgated the new European theories of design. Such major American designers as Robert Edmond Jones* and Lee Simonson* had also traveled to Europe to study the new theories of design. Jones, considered one of this century's greatest designers, applied these theories to all manner of plays, including those by O'Neill. Simonson, who was principal designer of the Theatre Guild during the 1920s and 1930s, on the other hand, criticized Craig in his book *The Stage Is Set* and leaned toward a more simplified, realistic approach. The Continental style was further developed in this country by Norman Bel Geddes,* whom many consider a visionary in the manner of Appia. Bel Geddes developed an unproduced design for Dante's *The Divine Comedy* that was composed of a series of steps, platforms, and mountainous units that soared in scale and incorporated dynamic, unusually angled lighting effects.

These theories were passed down to another generation of American designers who have just finished, or are still, working in the theatre today—Jo Mielziner,* Donald Oenslager,* Howard Bay,* and Ming Cho Lee.* In America, these designers and others experimented with variations on realism, such as simplified realism, poetic realism, and a theatricalized realism. Using Appia's theory of organic unity, the modern designers created settings that were an extension of the playwright's ideas or themes as derived from the text. These designers passed the traditions on to a third generation of designers who are working in New York and regional theatres today. This group includes Robin Wagner,* John Lee Beatty,* John Conklin,* and Marjorie Bradley Kellogg.* Current scenic design by these artists seems to employ most of the major ideas of the earlier part of this century and ranges from the realistic to the poetic in interpretation and from the illusionary to Brechtian theatricality.

Although realistic scenery was, and would continue to be, central to the popular theatre, the romantic, painterly scenery of the nineteenth century continued to develop and was practiced by such designers as Léon Bakst* for producer Diaghilev at the Ballets Russes, as well as by many other designers, including painters Pablo Picasso,* Alexandre Benois,* and Eugene Berman.* Bakst, heavily influenced by Oriental and folk arts, created many ornate and strikingly colorful backdrops for the ballet, and such artists as Picasso crossed disciplines to create sets and costumes for the dance, as did Marc Chagall,* Salvador Dalí,* and Pavel Tchelitchew.* A strong sculptural tradition also arose in dance design that was typified by the use of three-dimensional abstract units. Isamu Noguchi's* sculptures for Martha Graham's dances are perfect examples of this trend. Both the painterly and the sculptural approaches to dance design allowed plenty of bare floor space on which the dancers could move.

As the century progressed, techniques of dance design were integrated into other forms of performance. Such designers as Oliver Messel,* Cecil Beaton,* Oliver Smith,* Rouben Ter-Arutunian,* Boris Aronson,* and Jo Mielziner* plied their craft in both dance and dramatic theatre. As a result, a cross-fertilization occurred. Particularly in America, designers such as Smith, Aronson, Mielziner, and others integrated dance design techniques into plays and into the American musical. Perhaps as a result of director George Abbott, who called for such innovations as "traveler" curtain scenes to cover backstage scene shifts and quick and seamless transitions from scene to scene, musical design developed as an integral part of a production. Such shows as *On the Town* (1944), *Guys and Dolls* (1950), *West Side Story* (1957), and *Pacific Overtures* (1976) were designed so that the settings were moved in choreographic patterns and thus became part of the dance numbers. Modern musicals employ the same techniques but rely more on technology. Such Broadway musicals as *Dreamgirls* (1981), *Cats* (1981), *Les Misérables* (1987), *Into the Woods* (1988), and *Starlight Express*

(1989) use heavy machinery, complex, computerized, memory lighting consoles, projections, film, video, space-age fabrics, and other technologies. Perhaps designers John Napier,* Tony Walton,* and Robin Wagner are as much Renaissance machinists as they are contemporary scenographers. Thus, today's musical design is an amalgam of all past and current genres and technologies.

CONTEMPORARY

State-of-the-art theatrical design is in what some scholars refer to as the postmodern era. The seeds of this new trend in production were influenced by the early avant-gardists, as well as the experimental theatre groups of the 1960s and Performance Art of the 1970s. Performing in out-of-the-way theatres and transformed spaces, many of the groups now perform their works in major theatres with traditional proscenium setups. The aesthetics of design have evolved, however, and the productions are quite different from what they were throughout most of the twentieth century.

Reacting against the authoritarianism and capitalism of the popular theatre, while at the same time embracing the theories of Brecht, Artaud, Meyerhold, and others, the experimental theatre groups of the 1960s transformed non-theatrical structures such as old garages, stores, and warehouses into performance spaces. In addition, they produced theatre on the streets, in subways, in office buildings, and in other public places and transformed found space into performance space.

Eschewing the production techniques of the popular theatre, such groups as the Living Theatre, the Performance Group, the Open Theatre, Jerzy Grotowski's Polish Lab Theatre, Ariane Mnouchkine at the Théâtre du Soleil in Paris, and Luca Ronconi in Italy all used nontraditional performance arrangements of audience and performer. One major example of this unconventional use of space was in *Dionysus in '69* (1969) by director Richard Schechner, who worked with designer Jerry Rojo* to create an "environmental" setting. Rojo employed a series of platforms, steps, and ramps to transform the Performing Garage. Audiences sat in, on, and around the platforms and shared the same space as the performance. Director Joseph Chaikin's Open Theatre, which produced in this time period, was another example of environmental theatre. Many times designs were developed collaboratively by members of the group, and at other times a designer was appointed.

These groups questioned all of the previously held assumptions regarding production and directly influenced many of the experimental groups that produced in the 1970s and 1980s, such as Mabou Mines, Richard Foreman's* Ontological-Hysteric Theatre, the Performing Garage, and Robert Wilson's* Byrd Hoffman School of Byrds. Also, during the 1970s, Performance Art, a multimedia admixture, grew as a movement and in practice questioned the basic assumptions of performance and design.

The productions of these latter groups, whether their original works or their restaging of the classics, redefined design in fundamental ways through the use of technology. In the case of Mabou Mines, they did not credit any one designer for many of their shows but preferred a collaborative approach to the scenography. Similar to the experiments of Svoboda, as well as earlier designers, Mabou Mines employs a multimedia approach, with performers sometimes playing against the images of videotaped actors, rather than live ones. Their recent production of *Lear* (1990), an adaptation of Shakespeare's *King Lear*, was set in the Deep South during the 1950s. The design included facades of southern farmhouses, miniature cars to carry the performers around the stage, and performers dressed in 1950s, American clothing with facial microphones obviously taped to their faces. This multichannel production presented Shakespeare's historical text and ideas together with an Americanized locale and 1950s-costumed archetypes.

Other experimentalists, who performed in their own loft spaces that were transformed into theatres, are now performing in major proscenium houses. For example, avant-garde director-designer Richard Foreman has produced his plays at major regional theatres, and artist Robert Wilson, who produced performances in his Manhattan loft, had his opera *Einstein on the Beach* (1976) produced at the Metropolitan Opera House in New York and at the Next Wave Festival at the Brooklyn Academy of Music. This major work employed kinetic, imagistic designs on a mammoth scale and used projections. Wilson has applied his "moving painting" approach to classic plays as well.

Other major examples of contemporary approaches to classic opera can be seen in the works of director Peter Sellars. Together with such designers as George Tsypin and Adrianne Lobel, Sellars contemporized the action of the three Mozart/Da Ponte operas (*Le Nozze di Figaro*, *Don Giovanni*, and *Cosi fan tutte*, 1989), Wagner's *Tannhauser* (1985), as well as plays by Brecht, Sophocles, and Shakespeare. In these productions, no single point of view reigns, the past and present coexist simultaneously, and a multiplicity of meanings can be wrought out of a single moment of the production. Technology is an integral part of these productions. In the case of *Le Nozze di Figaro*, viewers heard the eighteenth-century text being sung while George Tsypin's visual elements were set in the twentieth-century luxury apartment building Trump Tower in Manhattan. Unlike the classic approach, which stresses an "organic" unity of time, place, and action, the style of postmodern design seems eclectic, drawing from all time periods simultaneously, and is not held to strict historical reproduction.

It seems likely that design will continue to evolve in this manner in the near future and shed many of the previously held assumptions of the first part of the twentieth century. Perhaps theatre architecture, as well, will be affected. No longer will facilities be built based only upon presenting a realistic setting with masking and sight lines, nor only on presenting a theatricalized setting. Facilities will have to provide for the increasing use of technology, such as film, video, computerized lighting control, and new stage machinery. As a result, the past theories of design will be combined with new technologies of the future, a combination that will thus further transform the possibilities of theatrical design.

THEATRICAL
DESIGNERS

A

Acquart, André. Set designer (b. 1922, France). In 1951, Acquart came to Paris after leaving Algiers, where he was educated at the Ecole Nationale des Beaux Arts. Within ten years, he had established himself as a first-rate designer by working with some of France's well-known directors. With director Roger Blin, he designed Genet's *The Blacks* (1959) and *The Screens* (1966). His designs were spare, abstract constructions, using stark platforms, steps, and flat screens that were mobile. He designed Brecht's *The Resistible Rise of Arturo Ui* (1960), codirected by Jean Vilar and Georges Wilson, and *Troilus and Cressida* (1964), directed by Roger Planchon. This latter play's design consisted of an adaptable arrangement of flat screens that were reconfigured throughout the performance. Although he has primarily worked in France, Acquart has also designed in Germany.

Thomas J. Mikotowicz

Adrian, Gilbert (Adrian Dolph Greenburg). Costume designer (b. October 12, 1903, Naugatuck, CT; d. September 3, 1959, Los Angeles, CA). Theatrical productions include *Music Box Revue of 1921*; *Scandals* (women's costumes, with Ada B. Fields)—1921; *Nifties of 1923* (with Cora MacGeachy); *Fashions of 1924*—1924 *Slightly Scandalous*, *In Bed We Cry* (Ilka Chase's gowns)—1944; *Obsession* (gowns)—1946; *Camelot* (with Tony Duquette*)—1960.

In addition, Adrian was chief costume designer at Metro-Goldwyn-Mayer in Hollywood from 1928 to 1941, where he designed the costumes for over 150 films, including *Grand Hotel* (1932), *Dinner at Eight* (1933), *The Great Ziegfeld* (1936), *Camille* (1937), *Marie Antoinette* (1938), *The Women* (1939), *The Wizard of Oz* (1939), and *The Philadelphia Story* (1940).

Adrian, known throughout most of his designing career simply as Adrian, attended the Parsons School of Fine and Applied Arts, where he studied theatre design. He received his first theatrical experience when Robert Kallock, a designer for the House of Lucile and a frequent lecturer at Parsons, recommended him as a designer at the Gloucester Playhouse in Massachusetts. Later, transferring to the Paris branch of Parsons, Adrian met Hassard Short and Irving Berlin at the Bal du Grand Prix, where Berlin asked him to return to New York and design the costumes for his *Music Box Revue of 1921*. Subsequently, Adrian designed the costumes for a number of musical revues on Broadway during the 1920s, most notably for George White. In 1925, Natacha Rambova, Rudolph Valentino's wife, secured Adrian to design Valentino's costumes for *The Hooded Falcon*, which was in production at Paramount's Astoria studios in Queens. Upon completion of the picture, Adrian moved to Hollywood. Eventually, he became the resident costume designer at Metro-Goldwyn-Mayer (MGM) and created gowns for the studio's top female stars, including Greta Garbo, Norma Shearer, Joan Crawford, Jean Harlow, Jeanette MacDonald, and Myrna Loy. Adrian's approach to costume design is perhaps best illustrated through the lavish period clothes he designed for such films as *Romeo and Juliet* (1936) and *Marie Antoinette* (1938). For MGM's film biography of the French queen, Adrian designed over four thousand individual costumes and scoured the museums and antique shops of France to buy authentic jewelry and material to be used in the picture. His most significant productions for the theatre include his work for Irving Berlin and George White in the 1920s and *Camelot* in 1960. Unfortunately, Adrian died before *Camelot* went into production, and his friend Tony Duquette* accepted the responsibility for completing Adrian's sumptuous costume designs.

Awards: Both Adrian and Duquette received Tony Awards for *Camelot* (1960); Adrian's was awarded posthumously.

Further Reading: Chierichetti, David. *Hollywood Costume Design*. New York: Harmony Books, 1976; Lavine, W. Robert. *In a Glamorous Fashion*. New York: Charles Scribner's Sons, 1980; Lee, Sarah Tomerlin, ed. *American Fashion: The Life and Times of Adrian, Mainbocher, McCardell, Norell, Trigere*. New York: Quadrangle Books, 1975; Leese, Elizabeth. *Costume Design in the Movies*. Bembridge, Isle of Wight: BCW, 1976; McConathy, Dale, and Diana Vreeland, *Hollywood Costume*. New York: Harry N. Abrams, 1976.

Howard Gutner

Alberti, Leon Battista. Theatre architect and theorist (b. 1404, Genoa, Italy; d. 1472). Having studied architecture in Padua under G. Barzizza, in 1428 Alberti entered the service of Cardinal Nicolo Albergati. Four years later he received an appointment to the Court of Eugenio IV, and by 1434 he was working for the papal Courts in Bologna and in Florence. A decade later Alberti came to Rome, and by 1452 he designed a theatre for Pope Nicholas V. Noted as the designer of both the Temple Malatestiano di Rimini and the Palazzo Rucellai, he was most important as a theorist. Alberti authored ten books on architecture as well as *De re aedificatoria*, a treatise on ancient classical theatre construction, and *De pictura*, the first treatise on practical directions for creating perspective drawings. These works represented the height of humanism in Italy and had a great influence on Serlio.* *Philodoxes*, a comedy in the classical tradition formerly attributed to Lapido, was apparently Alberti's single attempt at playwriting.

Andrea J. Nouryeh

Aldredge, Theoni V. (Theoni Athanasios Vachlioti). Costume designer (b. August 22, 1932, Salonika, Greece). Theatrical productions (all shows are in New York City unless otherwise specified) include *The Distaff Side* (Chicago)—1950; *The Importance of Being Earnest* (Chicago)—1953; *The Immoralist* (Chicago)—1956; *Much Ado About Nothing, A View from the Bridge, Lysistrata, The Guardsman* (all in Chicago)—1957; *Heloise, The Golden Six*—1958; *Sweet Bird of Youth* (costumes for Geraldine Page), *The Nervous Set, The Saintliness of Margery Kempe, Chic, The Geranium Hat, Flowering Cherry, Silent Night, Lonely Night*—1959; *A Distant Bell, The Best Man, Measure for Measure, Hedda Gabler, Rosemary, The Alligators, A Girl of the Night* (film; Warner Brothers)—1960; *Mary, Mary, Under Milkwood, Smiling the Boy Fell Dead, First Love, Ghosts, A Short Happy Life, Much Ado About Nothing, A Midsummer Night's Dream, The Devil's Advocate*—1961; *The Umbrella, Rosmersholm, I Can Get It for You Wholesale, MacBeth, King Lear, The Tempest, The Merchant of Venice, Mr. President, Tchin-Tchin, Who's Afraid of Virginia Woolf?*—1962; *Strange Interlude* (costumes for Geraldine Page), *The Blue Boy in Black, Memo, The Time of the Barracudas, Antony and Cleopatra, As You Like It, The Winter's Tale, The Trojan Women*—1963; *But for Whom Charlie?, Anyone Can Whistle, The Three Sisters, Hamlet, The Knack, Othello, Electra, Any Wednesday, Luv, P.S. I Love You* (costumes for Geraldine Page)—1964; *Coriolanus, Troilus and Cressida, Minor Miracle, The Porcelain Year, Skyscraper, The Playroom, Cactus Flower*—1965; *UTBU, First One Asleep, Whistle, Happily Never After, A Time for Singing, Serjeant Musgrave's Dance, All's Well That Ends Well, Measure for Measure, Richard III, A Delicate Balance*—1966; *You Know I Can't Hear You When the Water's Running, That Summer . . . That Fall, Illya Darling, Little Murders, The Comedy of Errors, Hamlet, Hair, King John, Titus Andronicus, Daphne in Cottage D, The Trial of Lee Harvey Oswald, You're a Big Boy Now* (film; Seven Arts), *No Way to Treat a Lady* (film; Paramount)—1967; *Before You Go, I Never Sang for My Father, Portrait of a Queen, Weekend, The Only Game in Town, The Memorandum, King Lear, Ballad for a Firing Squad, Huui, Huui, Henry IV: Parts 1 and 2, Hamlet, Romeo and Juliet, Don Rodrigo, Uptight* (film; Paramount)—1968; *Zelda, Billy, The Gingham Dog, Cities in Bezique, Invitation to a Beheading, Peer Gynt, Electra, Twelfth Night, Last Summer* (film; Paramount)—1969; *The Wars of the Roses, Parts 1 and 2, Richard III, The Happiness Cage, Trelawny of the 'Wells', Colette, The Works of Samuel Beckett* (costumes for Jack MacGowran)—1970; *Subject to Fits, Blood, Underground, The Basic Training of Pavlo Hummel, Timon of Athens, Two Gentlemen of Verona, The Tale of Cymbeline, The Incomparable Max, Sticks and Bones, The Wedding of Iphigenia, Iphigenia in Concert, Promise at Dawn* (film; Avco-Embassy), *I Never Sang for My Father* (film; Columbia)—

1971; *The Sign in Sidney Brustein's Window, Voices, That Championship Season, Older People, The Hunter, The Corner, Hamlet, Ti-Jean and His Brothers, Much Ado About Nothing, The Wedding Band, Children*—1972; *A Village Romeo and Juliet, The Three Sisters, No Hard Feelings, The Orphan, Nash at Noon, As You Like It, King Lear, In the Boom Boom Room, The Au Pair Man, Two Gentlemen of Verona* (London)—1973; *Find Your Way Home, The Killdeer, The Dance of Death, Music! Music!, An American Millionaire, In Praise of Love, Mert and Phil, Kid Champion, That Championship Season* (London), *The Great Gatsby* (film; Paramount), *Three Days of the Condor* (film; Paramount)—1974; *A Doll's House, Little Black Sheep, A Chorus Line, Trelawny of the 'Wells', Souvenir* (Los Angeles), *Harry and Walter Go to New York* (film; United Artists)—1975; *Rich and Famous, Mrs. Warren's Profession, The Belle of Amherst, The Baker's Wife, The Threepenny Opera, The Eccentricities of a Nightingale*—1976; *Marco Polo Sings a Solo, Annie, The Dream* (Philadelphia), *Semi-Tough* (film; United Artists)—1977; *Ballroom, The Cheap Detective* (film; Columbia)—1978; *The Grand Tour, Break a Leg, The Madwoman of Central Park West, Eyes of Laura Mars* (film; Columbia), *Network* (film; United Artists), *The Champ* (film; United Artists), *The Rose* (film; 20th Century Fox)—1979; *Onward, Victoria, Barnum, Middle Age Crazy* (film; 20th Century Fox)—1980; *Dreamgirls, Woman of the Year*—1981; *Hamlet, Ghosts, A Little Family Business, 42nd Street*—1982; *Buried Inside Extra, Merlin, Private Lives, The Corn Is Green, La Cage aux Folles, Annie* (film; Paramount)—1984; *Chess* (London)—1985; *Blithe Spirit, Dreamgirls* (revival), *Richard III, Henry IV, Part 1, Teddy and Alice*—1987; *Chess, Much Ado About Nothing* (Public Theatre), *La Cage aux Folles, Chorus Line*—1988; *Gypsy* (revival)—1989.

Aldredge has designed the costumes for more than one hundred Broadway and off-Broadway shows, as well as a number of films and operas. Aldredge began her career in the early 1950s at the Goodman Theater in Chicago, where she studied stage design. She created the costumes for the Goodman Theater production of *The Distaff Side* (1950), as well as for many local productions at Chicago's Studebaker Theater. In the late 1950s, Aldredge moved to New York when Goodman Theater alumnus Geraldine Page asked her to design her wardrobe for Tennessee Williams's *Sweet Bird of Youth* (1959). But it was not until the early 1960s and the beginning of her long association with Joseph Papp's Public Theatre in New York that Aldredge defined her approach toward the function of costume design on the stage. Working with a small production team, Aldredge came to regard costume as one aspect of a collaborative process, successful only if it served the producer's vision, the viewpoint of the director, and the comfort of the actor. In addition, she predicated a style based on fulfilling and heightening a sense of reality on the stage. Aldredge has referred to designing costumes as "designing real clothing that develops out of character. Good design is design you're not aware of."

Throughout a prolific and varied career that has included such Broadway hits as *Cactus Flower* (1965) and *Who's Afraid of Virginia Woolf?* (1962), as well as such ground-breaking off-Broadway productions as *The Basic Training of Pavlo Hummel* (1971) and *Colette* (1970), Aldredge's approach is perhaps best illustrated in the series of blockbuster musicals she designed in the late 1970s and early 1980s. Assessing the personalities of dancers at rehearsals of *A Chorus Line* (1975), she also took hundreds of snapshots of their rehearsal togs and later adapted what they had on for the costumes of the dancers in the play. Working without benefit of a literal set in *Dreamgirls* (1981), Aldredge studied photos from scores of fashion magazines of the 1960s and designed costumes that subtly suggested the passage of time over the ten-year period covered in the show. For *La Cage aux Folles* (1983), she created costumes that went beyond surface glitter and a surfeit of bugle beads. The gowns worn by the men in the musical displayed an elegance in both cut and line. Always working to enhance rather than take over the concept of a production, Aldredge continues to improve her craft after four decades of masterful work.

Awards: Aldredge has won three Tony Awards for "Best Costume Design" for *Annie* (1977), *Barnum* (1980), and *La Cage aux Folles* (1983). Her film work has earned her an Academy Award for "Best Achievement in Costume Design" and a British Society of Films and Television Award for *The Great Gatsby* (1974).

Further Reading: "Costumes and the Budget." *Theatre Crafts* November/December 1969; Lavine, W. Robert. *In a Glamorous Fashion*. New York: Charles Scribner's Sons, 1980; Leese, Elizabeth. *Costume Design in the Movies*. Bembridge, Isle of Wight: BCW, 1976; Russell, Douglas A. *Stage Costume Design: Theory, Technique, and Style*. New York: Prentice-Hall, 1985; "Theatres Top Twofer." *People* June 29, 1981.

Howard Gutner

Aleotti, Giovanni Battista. Theatrical architect, machinist, and scene designer (b. 1546, Italy; d. 1636). Aleotti made significant contributions to the development of scenography and the physical theatre. In 1606, working for the Court of the Estensi, he built the Teatro Intripidi in Ferrara, and in 1618, under the patronage of Raniccio I, he designed and constructed the Teatro Farnese in Parma, the first theatre with a permanent proscenium arch. This latter theatre has a U-shaped auditorium, seats approximately forty-five hundred spectators, and is still in existence today. Aleotti can also be credited with designing the settings and machines for the spectacle *La Difesa della*, which was to inaugurate the Teatro Farnese in 1618, but the building was not opened and remained closed until 1628. With its single proscenium arch opening, this baroque structure is the precursor of the modern theatre building. Up to this time existing theatres had several openings in their *scaenae frons*. This single opening together with a curtain created the first "picture-frame stage." In addition, Aleotti is credited with the development of sliding flat wings, which made it possible not only to display one continuous perspective scene behind this proscenium arch but, through mechanics, to change scenes entirely. In this invention, Aleotti overcame the inherent problems of painting perspective on side flats parallel to a backdrop. This system replaced the fixed, angled wing flats developed by Serlio* and was later carried further by the invention of the chariot and pole system of scene changing developed by Torelli.* Aleotti's contributions facilitated and encouraged more scene changing in the productions that followed.

Thomas J. Mikotowicz

Allio, René. Set and costume designer (b. 1924, Marseille, France). Allio, an influential scenographer, helped to redesign several theatres since the 1960s and has designed significant productions, mostly in his native France. His early work was with French director Roger Planchon, with whom he developed a number of his theories on design. Heavily influenced by the theories and conventions of Brecht's productions, as well as by those used in film, Allio used turntables to stage the action quickly and from multiple angles, particularly in Planchon's productions. Also, he used suggestive scenery rather than full stage sets and utilized scenic devices of his own invention that made his stage settings more architectural than painterly. Further, in trying to reconcile Brecht's "distancing" effect, Allio believes that the details of the set should support theatrical illusion; the props should be real for the audience, but the set as a whole should be a commentary on the play and therefore less realistic and more "presentational." This approach could be seen in his design for *Dead Souls*, in which there was an obviously painted cyclorama with small cloth drops, with real props and furniture in front of it to set the locale. For Planchon's production of *Tartuffe*, Allio explained that his design was a visual parallel of Tartuffe's uncovering. The set was a three-sided box with panels that moved so that the room appeared to get larger. The walls were covered with paintings chosen for their erotico-religious themes. Allio has also worked outside of France, including Britain's National Theatre, where he designed *The Recruiting Officer* (1963). His other productions include *Cymbeline* (1962); *Henry IV Part 1* (1965); *George Dandin* and *The Three Musketeers* (1968); and *The Beaux' Stratagem* (1970).

Ken Kloth

Anisfeld, Boris. Designer and artist (b. 1879, Russia; d. 1973). Educated at the Petrograd Academy of Fine Arts, Anisfeld began his career as one of a group of artists who revived painted scenery in Russia just before World War I. These painters shunned extensive use of constructed scenery in an attempt to create a realistic but decorative environment and employed painted, perspective settings with sweeping lines and rich colors derived from Russian art. In addition to designing sets and costumes for *Pavillon d'Armide*, *Sadko*, and *Cleopatra* (or *Egyptian Night*), he designed and wrote scenarios for both *Petrouchka* and *Scheherazade* and coauthored *Le Coq d'Or* with A. Bielski. Emigrating to the United States in 1918, Anisfeld was engaged by the Metropolitan Opera in New York City from 1918 to 1925 to design costumes and scenery for operas and ballets, including *La Rénè Fiomet*, *The Blue Bird*, *Le Roi de Labore*, *Mephistopheles*, and *The Snow Maiden*. He then moved to Chicago, where he designed the costumes and scenery for the world premiere of the opera *Love for Three Oranges*, presented by the Chicago Opera Company in 1921. Some of Anisfeld's other designs include sets and costumes for *Petrouchka* (1924), *The Idiot* (1925), and *Le Coq d'Or* (1927). Additionally, he designed for such theatres as *Théâtre de la Chauve-Souris* in Paris, the Ballets Russes de Monte Carlo, the Vienna State Opera, and the Paris Opera.

Jonet Buchanan

Appen, Karl von. Set designer (b. 1900, East Germany). Appen began his career working for the Frankfurt Kunstlertheater from 1921 to 1923 and has since worked for several prestigious theatres. He became designer at the Dresden National Theatre after World War II and went on to design for the Berliner Ensemble during the 1950s. Here he developed his epic style, which featured a few realistic set pieces against backcloths painted in an anti-illusory style. His skill in design resulted in a long relationship with the group and helped produce such significant works as Brecht's *Caucasian Chalk Circle* (1954), which won him first place in the International Theatre Festival in Paris. He continued to design into the 1970s, creating sets for such productions as Gozzi's *Turnadot*, directed by Kupla.

Thomas J. Mikotowicz

Appia, Adolphe. Designer and theorist (b. 1862, Geneva, Switzerland; d. February 29, 1928, Nyon, Switzerland). Theatrical productions include *Carmen* (designed Act II only), *Manfred*—1903; *Orpheus and Eurydice* (designed descent into hell segment only), *Echo and Narcissus*—1912; *Orfeo et Eurydice, Tidings Brought to Mary*—1913; *Echo and Narcissus*—1920; *Tristan und Isolde*—1923; *Das Rheingold*—1924; *Die Walküre, Prometheus*—1925.

Appia, along with Edward Gordon Craig* (1872–1966), had a profound influence on the development of modern scenography, despite the fact that he produced relatively few of his own designs during his lifetime. He first encountered music and theatre during his student days at the College de Vevey in Switzerland. In 1881 he saw his first opera, Gonoud's *Faust*, and the following year he saw Wagner's last Bayreuth production, which disappointed him tremendously, particularly in the area of stagecraft and design. In 1883, he again saw *Faust*, this time in a production staged by Otto Devrient (1838–1894), and was impressed with the simplicity and eloquence of the design. Like Craig, Appia rejected flat painted scenery as an inappropriate environment for the three-dimensional actor and, as well, turned away from the detailed realism employed in the production of most modern dramas. With an awareness of the theatrical possibilities of the newly invented electric light, Appia called for the use of light as a unifying visual counterpart to music that harmonized all of the diverse production elements. Appia found that the visual elements of operatic performances contributed virtually nothing to articulating the environment and mood of the piece in the manner that the music seemed to be able to accomplish so effectively. During the 1890s, Appia was attracted to the symbolists and began experimenting with designs and a scenario for Wagner's Ring cycle. In 1895, he wrote and published his first book, *La Mise en scene du drame wagnerien*, and continued from that time to publish occasional essays on the subjects of design and theatrical art. Appia's simple and evocative scenes were greatly influenced by Appia's encounter with Émile Jaques-Dalcroze (1865–1960), whose system of eurythmics suggested a performance style compatible with Appia's designs. In 1909, Appia collaborated with Dalcroze on a scenario and designs based on Aeschylus's *Prometheus Bound*, and the following year he helped Dalcroze establish the Hellerau Institute, where they began staging an annual summer festival in 1912. In 1914 he met Craig, with whom he began a long correspondence, although they never worked together. Appia was invited to contribute designs for *Tristan und Isolde* for La Scala in 1923, but critics were still slow to accept Appia's innovations. The following year Appia began work on the Ring cycle at Basel, but the critical storm generated over Appia's designs led to abandonment of plans to mount the entire cycle after performances of *Das Rheingold* and *Die Walküre*. He continued to design many projects for *King Lear*, *Macbeth*, *Lohengrin*, and *Faust*, among others, and the legacy of his designs, as well as his collected essays on theatrical art, insures that his influence will continue to inspire theatre artists in the future.

Further Reading: Books by Appia: *Music and the Art of the Theatre*, trans. Robert W. Corrigan and Mary Douglas Dirks. Miami: University of Miami Press, 1962; *The Work of Living Art & Man Is the Measure of All Things*, trans. H. D. Albright and Barnard Hewitt. Miami: University of Miami Press, 1960.

Books about Appia: *Adolphe Appia, 1862–1928. Actor-Space-Light*. Exhibition catalog produced by Pro Helvetia-Arts Council of Switzerland. Designed by Denis Bablet and Marie-Louise Bablet. London: John Caulder, 1982; Beacham, Richard C. *Adolphe Appia. Theatre Artist*. Cambridge: Cambridge University Press, 1987; Volbach, Walther R. *Adolphe Appia: Prophet of the Modern Theatre: A Profile*. Middletown, CT: Wesleyan University Press, 1968.

James Fisher

Armbruster, Mathias. Set designer and scenic artist (b. February 24, 1839, Wurttenburg, Germany; d. 1920). As a youngster, Armbruster studied portrait painting and spent one year of specialized study in Paris. He arrived in the United States in 1859 and settled in Cincinnati, where he became employed as an art glass painter and theatrical designer. Unfortunately, his career was interrupted by the Civil War. After it was over, he resettled in Columbus, Ohio, and founded the Armbruster Scenic Studio.

The studio paralleled the advent and decline of touring theatre in America to become a major scenic studio of the late nineteenth and early twentieth centuries. In 1896, the studio embarked upon its first commercial venture with a series of custom scenic drops for Al Field's minstrel show. "Leg" and "drop" scenery painted with aniline dyes in a romantic style was characteristic of the Armbruster approach for these shows, which were in business until 1923. The studio's first major contract was for Lewis Morrison's *Faust* (1884), which toured through the Midwest, on the East Coast, and eventually to New York City. A mixture of real and painted elements and the use of scrim transformations within realistic settings illustrated the studio's ability to employ current theatrical techniques. The show gave the Armbruster Studio its first important national recognition.

The Armbruster Studio's most productive period came between 1896 and 1908 when it supported traveling, classical repertories and spectacular melodrama. The touring companies of Alexander Salvini, Sarah Bernhardt, Madame Modjeska, and James O'Neill all contracted scenery by the studio. Salvini's contract for *Othello*, *Romeo and Juliet*, and *The Three Guardsmen* in 1896 began the studio's involvement in classical repertory. Subsequent productions in this area were MacLean and Tyler's *King John* and *Coriolanus* in 1901 and seventeen Shakespearean productions, as well as settings for such classics as *Richelieu*, *Mary Stuart*, *School for Scandal*, and *Virginius* between 1898 and 1907. Influenced by the historically accurate Shakespearean productions of Englishmen Henry Irving and Max Beerbohm Tree, Armbruster became fully allied with the antiquarian movement at the turn of the century. This firsthand knowledge of the international scenic styles of the day was applied to spectacular melodrama as well. The success of Elmer Vance's melodramatic production *The Limited Mail* (1890) was largely due to Armbruster's spectacular scenery. With the decline of touring theatre after 1908 came the decline and the eventual demise of the studio.

Further Reading: Joyce, Robert S. *The Armbruster Studio*. Ohio State University Theatre Collection Bulletin 12 (1965).

Brian R. Jones

Armstrong, Will Steven. Set, lighting, and costume designer (b. March 26, 1930, New Orleans, LA; d. August 12, 1969, NM). Theatrical productions include *Time of the Cuckoo*—1955; *Chaparral, Ivanov, The Family Reunion, The Power and the Glory*—1958; *The Beaux' Stratagem, Season of Choice, The Merry Wives of Windsor, All's Well That Ends Well, The Great God Brown, Lysistrata, The Andersonville Trial*—1959; *Peer Gynt, Caligula, Henry IV, Part 1 and 2, A Midsummer Night's Dream*—1960; *Carnival!, A Cook for Mr. General, Kwamina, Subways Are for Sleeping*—1961; *I Can Get It for You Wholesale, Tchin-Tchin*—1962; *The Passion of Jonathan Wade, Dear Me, the Sky Is Falling, Memo, King Lear, Comedy of Errors, One Flew Over the Cuckoo's Nest, Nobody Loves an Albatross, The Rehearsal, Semi-Detached*—1963; *The Passion of Josef D., Much Ado About Nothing, Richard III, The Three Sisters, Hamlet, My Kinsman, Major Molineux, Benito Cereno, Ready When You Are, C.B.!, I Had a Ball, The Old Glory, A Girl Could Get Lucky, Boris Godunov*—1964; *The Three Sisters, The Flaming Angel, The Wayward Stork, The Mad Woman of Chaillot, The Rivals, The Trojan Women, Katerina Ismailova, Coriolanus, Romeo and Juliet, King Lear*—1965; *3 Bags Full!, Pousse-Cafe, Twelfth Night, Julius Caesar*—1966; *The Deer Park, People Is the Thing That the World Is Fullest Of, Imaginary Invalid, A Touch of the Poet, Still Life, Fumed Oak, Ways and Means, Something Different*—1967; *Love's Labour's Lost, Forty Carats*—1968; *Zelda, The Front Page*—1969.

Armstrong began his professional career designing the sets, lights, and costumes for *Time of the Cuckoo* at the Williamstown Theatre in 1955. In addition to assisting other designers such as Donald Oenslager,* Jo Mielziner,* and Boris Aronson,* early in his career Armstrong designed numerous off-Broadway productions, including *Chaparral* and *Ivanov*, the latter earning him an Obie Award. He also designed many plays for the Phoenix Theatre, including *Peer Gynt*, *The Power and the Glory*, and *Henry IV, Part 1 and 2*. Armstrong made his Broadway debut in 1959 when he designed scenery, costumes, and lights for *The Andersonville Trial*. He continued to design for Broadway and created the scenic design for such shows as *Subways Are for Sleeping*, *I Can Get It for You Wholesale*, *Carnival!*, and *Forty Carats*. He was, however, also known for his work with groups like the Phoenix Theatre, the Williamstown Theatre Festival, and the New York City Opera, where his designs included *Boris Godunov* and *The Passion of Jonathan Wade*. In 1959, Armstrong began designing productions for the American Shakespeare Festival in Stratford, Connecticut, and in 1964 he created a permanent thrust stage for the group. His scenery adorned many Shakespearean productions, including *Much Ado About Nothing* and *Richard III*. Armstrong often designed costumes and lights as well as scenery, because he believed that all of the design elements must work together in creative interaction. His exploration of open staging by breaking the barrier of the proscenium arch was a common trait long before it was popularized in this country by other designers. Not necessarily drawn toward the decorative, Armstrong held a firm belief that the visual elements of a production should serve the play, rather than the designer's ego.

Awards: In addition to his Obie Award for *Ivanov* (1958), Armstrong also won a Tony Award for *Carnival!* (1961).

Further Reading: "Design Discipline." *Theatre Crafts* March/April 1967; "Designing a Mobile Theatre." *Theatre Crafts* September/October 1967; Oenslager, Donald. "Obituary." *Theatre Design & Technology* December 1969.

Ken Kloth

Aronson, Boris. Set designer, painter, and sculptor (b. October 15, 1900 [official date, but he may have been born a year or two earlier], Kiev, Russia; d. November 16, 1980, New York City). Aronson assisted Aleksandra Exter* in 1919 on *Romeo and Juliet* (Kamerny Theater, Moscow). He designed sets and costumes for the following: *Day and Night* (Unser Theatre, Bronx)—1924; *Final Balance* (Unser Theatre, Bronx), *Bronx Express* (Schildkraut Theatre, Bronx)—1925. Unless otherwise noted, the following productions opened in New York City: *String of Pearls* (Yiddish Art Theatre, Second Avenue)—1925; *Tenth Commandment* (Yiddish Art Theatre)—1926; *Menschen Stoib* (Yiddish Art Theatre), *Tragedy of Nothing* (Irving Place Theatre), *Yoshke Musikant* (Yiddish Art Theatre), *Red, Yellow, and Black*, *2x2 = 5* (Civic Repertory Theatre)—1927; *Lag Boimer*—1928; *The Golem* (unproduced), *Stempenyu, the Fiddler*, *Jew Süss*, *Angels on Earth* (latter three for Yiddish Art Theatre)—1929; *Roaming Stars* (Yiddish Art Theatre), *Jim Cooperkop* (Yiddish Worker's Art Theatre)—1930;

Walk a Little Faster (St. James Theatre)—1932; *Small Miracle* (John Golden Theatre), *Ladies' Money* (Ethel Barrymore Theatre)—1934; *Battleship Gertie* (Lyceum Theatre), *Three Men on a Horse* (The Playhouse), *Awake and Sing* (Belasco Theatre), Radio City Music Hall, sets for the 1935 season, *The Body Beautiful* (Plymouth Theatre), *Weep for the Virgins* (46th St. Theatre), *Paradise Lost* (Longacre Theatre)—1935; *Western Waters* (Hudson Theatre)—1937; *The Merchant of Yonkers* (Virginia Theatre)—1938; *The Time of Your Life* (Shubert Theatre), *The Gentle People* (Belasco Theatre), *Ladies and Gentlemen* (Martin Beck Theatre)—1939; *The Great American Goof* (ballet: set and costumes at the Center Theatre), *The Unconquered* (Biltmore Theatre), *Heavenly Express* (National Theatre), *Cabin in the Sky* (Martin Beck Theatre)—1940; *The Night Before Christmas* (Morosco Theatre), *Clash by Night* (Belasco Theatre)—1941; *Cafe Crown* (Cort Theatre), *The Snow Maiden* (Metropolitan Opera House), *R.U.R.* (Ethel Barrymore Theatre), *The Russian People* (Guild Theatre)—1942; *The Family* (Windsor Theatre), *The Red Poppy* (Music Hall Theatre), *What's Up* (National Theatre), *South Pacific* (Cort Theatre), *Miss Underground* (unproduced)—1943; *Pictures at an Exhibition* (International Theatre), *Sadie Thompson* (Alvin Theatre)—1944; *The Stranger* (The Playhouse), *The Desert Song* (Philharmonic Auditorium, Los Angeles), *The Assassin* (National Theatre)—1945; *Truckline Cafe* (Belasco Theatre), *The Gypsy Lady* (Century Theatre; and as *The Fortune Teller* in Los Angeles), *Sweet Bye and Bye* (Shubert Theatre)—1946; *The Big People* (Lyric Theatre), *The Changeling* (unproduced)—1947; *The Golden Door* (unproduced), *Sundown Beach* (Actor's Studio), *Skipper Next to God* (Maxine Elliott's Theatre), *The Survivors* (The Playhouse), *Love Life* (46th Street Theatre)—1948; *Detective Story* (Hudson Theatre)—1949; *The Bird Cage* (Coronet Theatre), *Season in the Sun* (Cort Theatre), *The Country Girl* (Lyceum Theatre)—1950; *The Rose Tattoo* (Martin Beck Theatre), *Barefoot in Athens* (Martin Beck Theatre), *I Am a Camera* (Empire Theatre), *Love Among the Ruins* (unproduced), *Ballade* (New York City Center), *I've Got Sixpence* (Ethel Barrymore Theatre)—1951; *The Crucible* (Martin Beck Theatre), *My Three Angels* (Morosco Theatre), *The Frogs of Spring* (Broadhurst Theatre)—1953; *Mademoiselle Colombe* (Longacre Theatre)—1954; *The Master Builder* (Phoenix Theatre), *Bus Stop* (Music Box Theatre), *Once Upon a Tailor* (Cort Theatre), *A View from the Bridge / A Memory of Two Mondays* (Coronet Theatre), *The Diary of Anne Frank* (Cort Theatre), *Dancing in the Chequered Shade* (McCarter Theatre, Princeton, New Jersey)—1955; *Girls of Summer* (Longacre Theatre)—1956; *Small War on Murray Hill* (Ethel Barrymore Theatre), *A Hole in the Head* (Plymouth Theatre), *Orpheus Descending* (Martin Beck Theatre), *The Rope Dancers* (Cort Theatre)—1957; *This is Goggle* (McCarter Theatre, Princeton, New Jersey), *The Firstborn* (Coronet theatre), *The Cold Wind and the Warm* (Morosco Theatre), *J.B.* (ANTA Theatre)—1958; *Coriolanus* (Shakespeare Memorial Theatre, Stratford-on-Avon, England), *The Flowering Cherry* (Lyceum Theatre), *A Loss of Roses* (Eugene O'Neill Theatre)—1959; *Semi-Detached* (Martin

Beck Theatre), *Do Re Mi* (St. James Theatre), *The Queen and the Rebels* (unproduced)—1960; *The Garden of Sweets* (ANTA Theatre)—1961; *A Gift of Time* (Ethel Barrymore Theatre), *Judith* (Her Majesty's Theatre, London)—1962; *Andorra* (Biltmore Theatre)—1963; *Fiddler on the Roof* (Imperial Theatre), *Incident at Vichy* (ANTA Theatre)—1964; *L'Histoire du Soldat* (Grand Ballroom, Waldorf-Astoria Hotel)—1965; *Cabaret*—1966; *Mourning Becomes Electra* (Metropolitan Opera House)—1967; *The Price* (Morosco Theatre), *Zorba* (Imperial Theatre)—1968; *Company* (Alvin Theatre), *Fidelio* (Metropolitan Opera House)—1970; *Follies* (Winter Garden Theatre)—1971; *The Creation of the World and Other Business* (also designed projections; Shubert Theatre), *The Great God Brown* (Lyceum Theatre)—1972; *A Little Night Music* (Shubert Theatre)—1973; *The Tzaddik* (ballet at the Newman Theatre Shakespeare Festival)—1974; *Dreyfus in Rehearsal* (Ethel Barrymore Theatre)—1975; *Pacific Overtures* (Winter Garden Theatre), *The Nutcracker* (ballet at the Kennedy Center in Washington, D.C.)—1976; *The Nutcracker* (CBS television production)—1977.

Aronson was regarded as one of the leading set designers of this century, and his prolific career lasted more than fifty-five years and included more than one hundred Broadway productions. He received his early training in Russia while studying art and stage design under Aleksandra Exter,* Tairov's principal designer and advocate of radical stage design. From early exposure to constructivist art, as well as to the theories of theatrical revolutionaries such as Meyerhold, Aronson developed concepts of stage design that refuted realistic/naturalistic scenery. Essentially, he came to believe that the set should allow for varied movement, that each scene should contain the mood and the feeling of the whole play, and that through organic fusion of color and form, the set should be beautiful. Most importantly, he realized that the set was complete only when the actor moved through it.

Coming to America in 1923 after a brief stay in Berlin, where he wrote two books, Aronson found work designing sets and costumes for the experimental Yiddish Theatre in the Bronx. His first work in America was *Day and Night* in 1924. His aversion to naturalism in design, which he believed to be slavish duplication of external details, was evident in his subjective and whimsical set for *The Tenth Commandment* (1926), for which he constructed the inside of a human skull to represent hell. For Eva LaGalliene's Civic Theatre, he designed *2x2 = 5* (1926). This type of creative work was soon recognized by major theatre critics and theorists and led Aronson to open his first major gallery showing of scene design models in New York City. Kenneth MacGowan, principal critic for the *New York Times* and coproducer of the gallery showing, was an early advocate of Aronson's futuristic work. Subsequently, the designer broke into the mainstream theatre and began designing for Broadway and Radio City Music Hall. On Broadway, his first design was the musical *Walk a Little Faster* (1932), featuring drop curtains that opened like an iris lens, unzipped from top to bottom, and concealed performers' upper bodies so that only their dancing feet were shown. Later, his set for *Do Re Mi* (1960) featured a curtain of juke boxes that were reminiscent of a stained-glass window in a cathedral.

Aronson was adept at creating settings that were derived either from research or from his imagination. For Harold Clurman's Group Theatre, he was called upon to design the naturalistic, bleak environments of the depression era. Yet even in the ostensibly realistic settings for Odet's *Awake and Sing* and *Paradise Lost* (both produced in 1935), Aronson evoked moods by creating simple impressionistic dwellings. Other shows, such as MacLeish's *J.B.* (1958) with its comic circus atmosphere, visually delighted the audience while stretching its imagination through the show's whimsical lines and forms.

The use of technology figured prominently throughout his career. In both *Battleship Gertie* (1935) and *The Great American Goof* (1940), Aronson used projected scenery. Using differently colored slides projected on abstract set units, he could change the appearance and thus the mood of a set. The Museum of Modern Art sponsored a showing in 1947 of Aronson's "Projected Scenery" and called it "Painting with Light."

In the latter half of his career, the designer developed a collaboration with director Harold Prince and used all of his previous experience to create some of the best-known designs of the twentieth century. His early Yiddish Art Theatre experience was put to use on *Fiddler on the Roof* (1964), and his Berlin days were expressed in his settings for *Cabaret* (1966). His work with Prince evidenced his pure versatility and organic use of technology in settings such as for *Zorba* (1968), with its house that revolved to reveal the occupant's bedroom, and for *Company* (1970), with its starkly vertical, plexiglass, and steel buildings with working elevators. In *Follies* (1971), he created the insides of a bare, semiderelict theatre, which transformed itself into a vision of glorious theatricality. His designs, for example, for *A Little Night Music* (1973), featured white birch trees painted on silk attached to plexiglass wing flats that moved in and out to create a striking forest perspective. His final creation for Prince was just as beautiful and technological as ever. *Pacific Overtures* (1976) featured a Japanese print style on screens and Commodore Perry's daunting sailing ship, which moved onto the stage like some massive creature.

Aronson's work in opera and ballet, specifically Baryshnikov's *The Nutcracker* (1976) and the Metropolitan Opera productions of *Mourning Becomes Electra* (1967) and *Fidelio* (1970), adds distinction to an already eclectic career. Along with the design of two synagogues, the writing of two books, and an active career as a sculptor and painter, Aronson's designs place him in a prominent position in twentieth-century scene design.

Awards: Aronson won Tony Awards for *The Country Girl* (1950), *Season in the Sun* (1950), and *The Rose Tattoo* (1951), as well as for *Cabaret* (1966), *Zorba* (1968), *Company* (1970), *Follies* (1971), and *Pacific Overtures* (1976). In addition, he earned the Joseph P. Maharam Foundation Award for his stage designs for *Fiddler on the Roof* (1965), *Cabaret* (1967), *Company* (1970), *Follies* (1971), and *Pacific Overtures* (1976). He also earned the Creative Arts Award, Brandeis University, 1969.

Further Reading: By Aronson: *Marc Chagall*. Berlin: Petropolis, 1923; *Contemporary Jewish Graphic Art*. Berlin, 1924.

About Aronson: George, Waldemar. *Boris Aronson et l'art du théâtre*. Paris: Croniques du Jour, 1928; Rich, Frank, with Lisa Aronson. *The Theatre Art of Boris Aronson*. New York: Alfred A. Knopf, 1987.

Thomas J. Mikotowicz

Arrocha Fernandez, Eduardo. Set and costume designer (b. May 17, 1934, Guanabacoa, Cuba). Arrocha was educated in the National School of Belles Artes "San Alejandro" and then at the Uffizi Gallery in Florence. Returning to Cuba, he primarily designed costumes for national ballet and modern dance companies. His most important stage designs have been *The Italian Straw Hat* (1961) and *The Threepenny Opera* (1967). His noted designs for dance include *Canto Campesino* for the Conjunto Nacional de Danza Moderna (1962) and *Giselle* for the Ballet National de Cuba (1964).

Andrea J. Nouryeh

Asakura, Setsu. Set designer and painter (b. ?, Japan). Director of both the Japan Art, Stage, and Television Association and the Japanese Center of the International Organization of Scenographers and Theatre Technicians, Asakura began her career as a painter. Among her earliest design efforts for the theatre were *Hakamadare wa dokoda* (1964) and *Vietnam Diskurs* by Peter Weiss (1964). Since the 1970s, she has worked primarily with the director Yukio Ninagawa. Their collaborative efforts include *Romeo and Juliet*, *King Lear*, *Macbeth*, *Oedipus Rex*, *Double Suicide*, and *Nigorie*. Characteristic of these productions are the use of vibrant colors and the grand scale of their sets, best exemplified by the staircase that filled the stage in *Romeo and Juliet* and the immense Buddhist temple that filled the stage in *Macbeth*. In 1984, she served as chief art director for the opera *Le Coq d'Or*, directed by Ennosuke Ichikawa and presented at the Theatre de Chatelet in Paris. Equally successful as a film designer, Asakura has received two Japanese Academy Awards.

Andrea J. Nouryeh

Ayrton, Michael. Set designer, artist, novelist, and theatrical producer (b. February 21, 1921, London, England; d. November 17, 1975, London, England). Ayrton, like Edward Burra,* was a classically trained artist who applied his crafts to theatre design. Trained as a painter and sculptor in London, Paris, and Italy, he soon became versatile in many of the arts. During his career, he wrote novels, illustrated books, produced films and television shows, and designed operas and ballets. His classically inspired designs for productions include *Macbeth* (1942) at the Opera House in Manchester; *The Spider's Banquet* (1944) and *Joan of Arc* (1947) at Sadler's Wells; and *The Fairy Queen* (1946) at Covent Garden.

Elbin L. Cleveland

B

Bakst, Léon (Lev Rozenberg). Set and costume designer, and artist (b. May 10, 1866, Grodno, Russia; d. December 28, 1924, Paris, France). Bakst began his career as a painter and graphics designer, and after becoming well known in Russian art circles, he emigrated to Paris in 1909. With Alexandre Benois,* he co-founded "The World of Art" group and exhibited his paintings. Like his companion Benois, Bakst soon found himself working with Sergey Diaghilev and the Ballets Russes, as well as for other troupes in Paris and London. His style of design for costumes and settings can be best described as ornate and colorful, taking their inspiration from the classical art and folk decorations of ancient Greece, Rome, Egypt, and the Orient. Such productions as *Cléopâtre* (1909), *Scheherazade* (1910), *Narcisse* (1911), *Le Dieu Bleu* (1912), *L'Après Midi d'un Faun* (1912), *La Légende de Joseph* (1914), *Les Femmes de bonne humeur* (1917), *The Sleeping Princess* (1921, revival), and *Broadway to Paris* (1911) are exemplary of his work, with their free-flowing lines, dynamic composition, and use of bold primary color. Of all the designers for the Ballets Russes, Bakst is considered to be one of the most significant because, through his designs, he attempted to capture the spirit of the dance.

Thomas J. Mikotowicz

Ballard, Lucinda. Costume and set designer (b. 1908, New Orleans, LA). Theatrical productions (all are in New York City, unless otherwise noted) include *As You Like It* (Ritz Theatre)—1937; *Great Lady* (Majestic Theatre)—1938; *American Jubilee* (New York World's Fair), *The Three Sisters* (Longacre Theatre), *Mornings at Seven* (Longacre Theatre)—1939; *Les Sylphide, Giselle, Peter and the Wolf, Swan Lake, Quintet, Higher and Higher* (all at the American Ballet Theatre)—1940; *Copacabana* (revue)—1941; *Solitaire* (Plymouth Theatre)—1942; *Moon Vine, Beggar on Horseback* (American Ballet Theatre), *My Dear Public* (47th Street Theatre), *Listen, Professor!* (Forrest Theatre)—1943;

Stove Pipe Hat (American Ballet Theatre), *Sing Out, Sweet Land!* (International Theatre), *I Remember Mama* (Music Box Theatre)—1944; *The Glass Menagerie* (Playhouse Theatre), *A Place of Our Own* (Royale Theatre), *Memphis Bound* (Broadway Theatre)—1945; *Show Boat* (revival; Ziegfeld Theatre), *One Shoe Off* (Nixon Theatre, Pittsburgh), *Annie Get Your Gun* (Imperial Theatre), *Happy Birthday* (Broadhurst Theatre), *Another Part of the Forest* (Fulton Theatre)—1946; *Street Scene* (Adelphi Theatre), *John Loves Mary* (Booth Theatre), *The Chocolate Soldier* (Century Theatre), *Allegro* (Majestic Theatre), *A Streetcar Named Desire* (Ethel Barrymore Theatre), *Show Boat*—1947; *Alice-Sit-By-the-Fire* (Playhouse Theatre, Greenwich, Connecticut), *The Glass Menagerie* (London), *Love Life* (48th Street Theatre), *Make Way for Lucia* (Cort Theatre), *Portrait of Jenny* (film)—1948; *The Rat Race* (Ethel Barrymore Theatre)—1949; *The Fourposter* (Ethel Barrymore Theatre), *A Streetcar Named Desire* (film)—1951; *Mrs. McThing* (Martin Beck Theatre)—1952; *My Three Angels* (Morosco Theatre), *Carnival in Flanders* (New Century Theatre)—1953; *The Wisteria Tree* (City Center), *Silk Stockings* (Imperial Theatre), *Cat on a Hot Tin Roof* (Morosco Theatre)—1955; *A Clearing in the Woods* (Belasco Theatre), *Orpheus Descending* (Martin Beck Theatre), *Dark at the Top of the Stairs* (Music Box Theatre)—1957; *Handful of Fire* (Martin Beck Theatre), *The Girls in 509* (Belasco Theatre), *J.B.* (ANTA Theatre)—1958; *The Sound of Music* (Lunt-Fontanne Theatre), *A Loss of Roses* (Eugene O'Neill Theatre)—1959; *Invitation to a March* (Music Box Theatre)—1960; *The Gay Life* (Shubert Theatre), *The Sound of Music* (London)—1961; *Romulus* (Music Box Theatre), *Lord Pengo* (Royale Theatre), *Tiger, Tiger, Burning Bright* (Booth Theatre)—1962.

Ballard was a leading designer in the theatre for more than fifty years. Her credits include designing a number of Broadway shows, as well as circuses, ice shows, the "American Jubilee" pageant at the 1940 New York World's Fair, and several films. She was appointed technical director when the American Ballet Theatre was formed in 1940 and designed both the scenery and costumes for a number of its productions. Throughout the early 1940s, Ballard designed both scenery and costumes for most of the productions she worked on but decided to concentrate solely on costumes after *I Remember Mama* in 1944. A year later, her decision became firm when she began a successful professional association with Tennessee Williams, and subsequently she created costumes for *The Glass Menagerie* (1945), as well as *A Streetcar Named Desire* (1947), *Cat on a Hot Tin Roof* (1955), and *Orpheus Descending* (1957).

Ballard credits director Elia Kazan, with whom she worked in *Sing Out, Sweet Land!* in 1944, with "teaching me how to work with actors, and how to think in terms of what the characters are like. Before that, I thought of costumes as paintings walking around." Yet, together with intensive research into period detail, Ballard's technique makes expert use of her background in painting, and she uses color to reveal both atmosphere and mood. For example, to create a sense of brilliant sunlight on the Mississippi levee in the 1947 revival of *Show Boat*, Ballard used more than forty shades of yellows and soft lime greens for both the props and the costumes. The ''tackiness'' Ballard wanted to emphasize in the World's Fair scene of the musical was achieved through the use of blazing reds contrasted with bright turquoise. Ballard also used large pieces of costume jewelry to accentuate the vivid color of the costumes worn by the female characters in the scene. Further, Ballard's ability to project mood and delineate character through the use of color helped to illuminate several of Tennessee Williams's plays, such as *A Streetcar Named Desire* (1947). It was Ballard's decision to make Blanche DuBois a ''pale ash blonde,'' and she persuaded Marlon Brando to dye his hair black for the play and dressed him in tight blue jeans and colorful T-shirts to accentuate the sharp contrast between Stanley Kowalski and the pale, fragile Blanche. All of Ballard's designs are a testament to her ability to delineate character through the use of costumes.

Awards: Ballard's costume designs have earned her two Tony Awards, the first in 1947 for her work in six productions: *Happy Birthday, Another Part of the Forest, Street Scene, John Loves Mary, The Chocolate Soldier*, and *A Streetcar Named Desire*. She won her second Tony for *The Gay Life* in 1961. Her designs have also earned her two Donaldson Awards, the New York Drama Critics' Award, and an Academy Award nomination for *A Streetcar Named Desire* (play, 1947; film, 1951).

Further Reading: Dietz, Howard. *Dancing in the Dark*. New York: Quadrangle Books, 1974; ''*Gay Life*: Costumes by Ballard.'' *Theatre Arts* November 1961; ''Glad Rags for a *Gay Life*.'' *Life* January 19, 1962; ''Lucinda Ballard.'' *New Yorker* November 29, 1947.

Howard Gutner

Bauchant, André. Painter and set and costume designer (b. 1873, France; d. 1958). Bauchant's earliest paintings were completed after he turned forty years old. These French primitive canvases on biblical, mythological, and classical subjects were exhibited in 1921, 1925, and 1927 at the Salon d'Autommne in Paris. At the 1927 exhibition Diaghilev became familiar with the muted blues, grays, browns, and greens of Bauchant's paintings. In January 1928, the painter was commissioned to design scenery and costumes for his only design effort, *Apollon Musagetes*. Bauchant painted still lifes and other canvases in Monte Carlo rather than fulfilling his commission for the Ballets Russes. Thus, the designs were never forthcoming. Rather, two 1928 variations on his 1925 canvas, *Apollon Apparaissant aux Bergers*, became the basis for the scene design. The act curtain, dominated by a huge vase of flowers, was based on another of Bauchant's canvases. Both designs were executed by the scene painter Schervashidze.

Andrea J. Nouryeh

Bay, Howard. Set and lighting designer, and teacher (b. May 3, 1912, Centralia, WA; d. November 21, 1986, New York City). Theatrical productions include *There's a Moon Tonight*—1933; *Chalk Dust, Battle Hymn*—1936; *Marching Song, Power, Native Ground, One Third of a Nation*—1937; *Sunup to Sundown, Merry Wives of Windsor*—1938; *The Little Foxes, Life and Death of an American,*

In a Jewish Grocery, Fifth Column, Pete Roleum and His Cousins (film)—1939; *Pagliacci, Gianni Schicchi, Suor Angelica, Abduction from the Seraglio, Morning Star, The Corn Is Green*—1940; *The Beggar's Opera, The Man with Blonde Hair, Brooklyn, U.S.A.*—1941; *Johnny 2X4, The Moon Is Down, The Strings, My Lord, Are False, Uncle Harry, The Eve of St. Mark, Count Me In, The Great Big Doorstep*—1942; *Something for the Boys, The Patriots, The Corn Is Green, The Merry Widow, A New Life, One Touch of Venus, Carmen Jones, Listen, Professor!*—1943; *Storm Operation, Chicken Every Sunday, Follow the Girls, The Searching Wind, Ten Little Indians, Catherine Was Great, Franklin Street, It's Up to You, Glad to See You, Men to the Sea, The Visitor, Violet*—1944; *Up in Central Park, Marinka, Devils Galore, Deep Are the Roots, Spring in Brazil, Polonaise*—1945; *The Would-Be Gentleman, Show Boat, Woman Bites Dog*—1946; *The Exile* (film)—1947; *Up in Central Park* (film)—1948; *The Big Knife, Montserrat, As the Girls Go, Magdalena*—1949; *Come Back, Little Sheba*—1950; *The Autumn Garden, Flahooley, Hilda Crane, Two on the Aisle, The Grand Tour*—1951; *Jollyanna, Les Noces, The Shrike, The Children's Hour, Mike Todd's Peepshow, A Certain Joy, Mid-Summer, Fred Waring Show* (television, through 1954), *Somerset Maugham Theatre* (television, through 1954)—1952; *Show Boat, Sandhog*—1954; *The Desperate Hours, Top Man, Finian's Rainbow, Red Roses for Me, Go Man Go!* (film)—1955; *Peer Gynt* (television), *Carmen Jones, A Very Special Baby, Build with One Hand, A Certain Joy, Night of the Auk*—1956; *Tevya and His Daughters, Look Back in Anger, The Music Man*—1957; *Interlock, Regina*—1958; *Desert Incident, The Fighting Cock, Carmen*—1959; *Cut of the Axe, The Cool World, Toys in the Attic, Show Boat, The Wall*—1960; *The Music Man, Show Boat, Pal Joey, Milk and Honey*—1961; *Isle of Children*—1962; *My Mother, My Father and Me, Bicycle Ride to Nevada*—1963; *Never Live over a Pretzel Factory, Natalya Petrovna*—1964; *Man of La Mancha, Capriccio, Mr. Broadway* (television)—1965; *Chu-Chem, A Midsummer Night's Dream* (film)—1966; *The Little Foxes*—1967; *Man of La Mancha*—1968; *Fire!*—1969; *Cry for Us All*—1970; *Knickerbocker Holiday*—1971; *Halloween*—1972; *The Pueblo Incident* (television)—1973; *Odyssey* (later retitled *Home Sweet Homer*)—1975; *Poor Murderer, The Utter Glory of Morrissey Hall*—1977; *Volpone, Oedipus*—1979; *The Little Foxes*—1982.

Like many designers of his generation, Bay started designing for the WPA Federal Theatre with such shows as *Marching Song, Battle Hymn, One Third of a Nation*, and *The Living Newspaper*. He moved quickly to Broadway and gained a reputation for realistic interiors, featured in such shows as *The Little Foxes, The Corn Is Green*, and *Brooklyn U.S.A.* His designs were known for their attention to detail, as well as their completeness through the suggestion of the set's continuing offstage. Adapting to the different needs of each show he designed, Bay did not believe that a designer should have one certain style. Certainly this varied approach is apparent in the diverse designs that he created throughout his entire career. Nevertheless, in the 1940s and 1950s, Bay became known as one of the designers to contact for musical comedies. This reputation led to his involvement with such popular shows as *Up in Central Park, One Touch of Venus, The Music Man*, and *Man of La Mancha*. Bay, however, displayed his virtuosity by concurrently designing such plays as the futuristic *Night of the Auk*, which had settings that were built out of metal and acrylic and were inspired by the designer's visit to a computer "gadget" convention. He believed strongly that scenery is imbued with its full meaning only when the performers are within it. This approach can be seen in his set for *Man of La Mancha*, the rendering of which is used on the cover of Gothic Color Company's *Scenic Artist Handbook*.

Bay found time throughout his career to write extensively about design in his own inimitable style. His book *Stage Design* is a highly readable account of his approach to design, rather than a text on the subject. He also lectured and was guest designer at Purdue, Yale, and Ohio universities. In 1965, Bay became a full professor at Brandeis. Subsequently, as chair of the Theatre Department, he built a professional theatre training program.

Awards: His design for *Up in Central Park* (1942) won the Drama Critics' and Donaldson Awards. In 1943, he again won the Donaldson Award for *Carmen Jones*. He won Tony Awards for *Toys in the Attic* (1960) and *Man of La Mancha* (1966), the latter of which also won the Drama Critics' Award.

Further Reading: By Howard Bay: *Stage Design*. New York: Drama Book Specialists, 1974.

About Bay: "A Howard Bay Design Potpourri." *Theatre Design & Technology* December 1969; "Designers on Designing: A Profile of Howard Bay." *Theatre Crafts* February 1983; "Scenic Design for Musical Comedy." *Theatre Arts Magazine* April 1959; Burdick, Elizabeth B., Peggy C. Hansen, and Brenda Zanger, eds. *Contemporary Stage Design—U.S.A.* Middletown, CT: Wesleyan University Press, 1974; Cocuzza, Ginnine, and Barbara Cohen-Stratyner, eds. *Performing Arts Resources: Volume 8.* New York: Theatre Library Association, 1983; Larson (see Bibliography); Pecktal (see Bibliography).

Ken Kloth

Baylis, Nadine. Designer (b. June 15, 1940, London, England). Receiving her training at the Central School of Art and Design, Baylis ventured into a theatrical design career that has focused primarily on dance. She is, perhaps, best known for the designs that she has rendered for choreographer Glenn Tetley and others at the Ballet Rambert, including such ballets as *Embrace Tiger and Return to Mountain* (1968), *Field Figures* (1970), *Rag Dances* (1971), *That Is the Snow* (1971), *There Was a Time* (1973), *Gemini* (1973), *Ancient Voices of Children* (1975), and *The Tempest* (1979). For the latter work, Baylis used large, billowing cloth sails that were altered through the use of projections, all against a sea made of nylon sheeting. She has also designed for a number of other dance companies, including the London Contemporary Dance Theatre, for which she designed *Phantasmagoria* (1987). In addition, she has designed theatrical productions in London, the United States, and elsewhere. Baylis's approach to design includes close collaboration with the director, or choreographer, and adding her own perspective to the work.

Thomas J. Mikotowicz

Beaton, Sir Cecil Walter Hardy. Set and costume designer, painter, photographer, and writer (b. January 14, 1904, London, England; d. January 18, 1980). Beaton's reputation as a professional photographer was established through his work during World War II for the Ministry of Information, his portraits of royalty, and his images of celebrities. His theatrical career began soon after he photographed Edith Sitwell, a celebrated personality who introduced him into the theatrical world. Beaton's style is decidedly neoromantic, illustrated in his stage work, which includes costumes for the musical *My Fair Lady* (1956) and the play *Lady Windmere's Fan* (1946). He also created stunning set designs for film with *Gigi* (1958) and *My Fair Lady* (1964), for which he won Oscars, and *On a Clear Day You Can See Forever* (1970), which he codesigned with Arnold Scarsi. Beaton is well known in ballet circles for his designs for Frederick Ashton's *Les Sirenes* (1946), *Swan Lake* (1952), and *Marguerite et Armand* (1963). In addition, he has written several books, among them *The Book of Beauty; Persona Non Grata*; his diary, *The Wandering Years*; and *Memoirs of the Forties*. As a painter, he has exhibited his creations in famous galleries worldwide. His celebrity and creative production in all of these areas led to his being knighted by Queen Elizabeth in 1972.

Thomas J. Mikotowicz

Beatty, John Lee. Set designer (b. 1948, Palo Alto, CA). Beatty's career began in 1969 with nine shows for College Light Opera in Falmouth, New Hampshire, followed by eight shows for the Weston Playhouse in Vermont in 1970. In 1972 and 1973, he designed six shows each season for Middletown, Virginia's Wayside Theatre. The following shows are for set design only and are in New York City, unless otherwise noted: *Marouf* (scenery and costumes, Manhattan Theatre Club)—1973; *The Amorous Flea* (scenery and costumes, Queens Playhouse), *Some People, Some Other People, and What They Finally Do* (Stage 73), *Room Service* (Queens Playhouse), *Come Back, Little Sheba* (Queens Playhouse), *An Evening with Cole Porter* (scenery and costumes, Manhattan Theatre Club), *The Wager* (Manhattan Theatre Club), *The Diary of a Scoundrel* (Gene Frankel Workshop), *Two Offenbach Operettas* (Theatre at Noon), *Battle of Angels* (Circle Repertory Company)—1974; *The Mound Builders* (Circle Repertory Company), *Down by the River Where Waterlilies Are Disfigured Every Day* (Circle Repertory Company), *Philadelphia, Here I Come!* (Queensboro Community College), *The Caucasian Chalk Circle* (Queensboro Community College), *Harry Outside* (Circle Repertory Company), *Not to Worry* (Circle Repertory Company), *Arms and the Man* (the Acting Company, Saratoga Springs, New York), *The Mound Builders* (art director for PBS television), *Golden Boy* (Manhattan Theatre Club), *The Elephant in the House* (Circle Repertory Company), *Jumpers* (Seattle Repertory

Theatre, Washington), *Long Day's Journey into Night* (Indiana Repertory Theatre, Indianapolis)—1975; *Knock, Knock* (Circle Repertory Company and Biltmore Theatre), *The Tot Family* (Arena Stage, Washington, D.C.), *La Perichole*
(scenery and costumes, San Francisco Opera), *The Contrast* (Cincinnati Playhouse in the Park, Ohio), *Serenading Louie* (Circle Repertory Company), *Rebel
Women* (New York Shakespeare Festival), *Mrs. Murray's Farm* (Circle Rep-
ertory Company), *Duck Variations* and *Rosemary* (The Acting Company), *The
Farm* (Circle Repertory Company), *The Innocents* (Morosco), *The Bed Before
Yesterday* (Wilmington Playhouse, Delaware), *A Tribute to Lily Lamont* (Circle
Repertory Company), *Ashes* (Manhattan Theatre Club)—1976; *A Month in the
Country* (Circle Repertory Company, Ohio), *Ashes* (New York Shakespeare
Festival), *Heartbreak House* (Circle Repertory Company, Ohio), *Irma La Douce*
(Los Angeles Civic Light Opera), *Hit the Deck* (Goodspeed Opera House, East
Haddam, Connecticut), *Sherlock Holmes* (Williamstown Theatre Festival, Mas-
sachusetts), *Tobacco Road* (Academy Festival Theatre, Lake Forest, Illinois),
Red-Bluegrass Western Flyer Show (Goodspeed Opera House, East Haddam,
Connecticut), *Old Times* (Academy Festival Theatre, Lake Forest, Illinois), *A
Life in the Theatre* (Theatre de Lys), *Out of Our Father's House* (Theatre of
Riverside Church), *Ulysses in Traction* (Circle Repertory Company), *The Water
Engine* (New York Shakespeare Festival)—1977; *The Middle Ages* (Hartford
Theatre, Stamford, Connecticut), *A Streetcar Named Desire* (Arena Stage, Wash-
ington, D.C.), *Lulu* (Circle Repertory Company), *The Water Engine* (Plymouth
Theatre), *The House of Bernarda Alba* (Circle Repertory Company, Ohio),
Catsplay (Manhattan Theatre Club and Promenade Theatre), *Tip Toes* (Good-
speed Opera House, Connecticut), *Duck Variations* (The Acting Company), *The
Fifth of July* (Circle Repertory Company), *Ain't Misbehavin'* (Longacre), *Out
of Our Father's House* (White House in Washington, D.C., and for WNET
television), *Catsplay* (Promenade), *Whoopee!* (Goodspeed Opera House, Connecticut), *After the Season* (Academy Festival Theatre, Illinois), *No Time for
Comedy* (scenery and costumes, McCarter Theatre, Princeton, New Jersey), *The
Rear Column* (Manhattan Theatre Club), *She Loves Me* (Goodspeed Opera
House, Connecticut), *Serenading Louie* (Academy Festival Theatre, Illinois)—
1978; *Broadway* (The Acting Company), *Storeyville* (Ford's Theatre, Washington, D.C.), *Whoopee!* (ANTA Theatre), *Merton of the Movies* (Milwaukee Repertory Theatre), *Tip Toes* (Brooklyn Academy of Music), *The Faith Healer*
(Longacre), *The Woods* (New York Shakespeare Festival), *Talley's Folly* (Circle
Repertory Company and Mark Taper Forum, Los Angeles, California), *Poet and
the Rent* (Circle Repertory Company), *The Curse of an Aching Heart* (St. Nicholas Theatre, Chicago), *Lone Canoe* (Goodman Theatre, Chicago), *The Five
O'Clock Girl* (Goodspeed Opera House, Connecticut), *The Rose Tattoo* (Berk-
shire Theatre Festival, Lenox, Massachusetts), *It's a Long Way to Boston* (Good-
speed Opera House, Connecticut), *Dark Pony* and *Reunion* (Circle Repertory
Company), *Jail Diary of Albie Sachs* (Manhattan Theatre Club), *Something
Wonderful* (Westchester Regional Theatre, New York)—1979; *Talley's Folly*

(Brooks Atkinson, New York; Goodman Theatre, Chicago), *Johnny on a Spot* (Brooklyn Academy of Music), *Biography* (Manhattan Theatre Club), *The Happy Time* (Goodspeed Opera House, Connecticut), *Hide and Seek* (Belasco), *Cyrano de Bergerac* (Goodman Theatre, Chicago), *Reverberation Fire Curtain* (Opera Lab of the University of Texas, Austin), *Little Johnny Jones* (Goodspeed Opera House, Connecticut), *The Lady and the Clarinet* (Mark Taper Forum, Los Angeles, California), *Holiday* (Center Theatre Group, Los Angeles, California), *The Diviners* (Circle Repertory Company), *The Fifth of July* (New Appollo), *Crimes of the Heart* (Manhattan Theatre Club)—1980; *The Five O'Clock Girl* (Helen Hayes), *Close of a Play* (Manhattan Theatre Club), *The Wild Duck* (Brooklyn Academy of Music), *Jitters* (Walnut Street Theatre, Philadelphia, Pennsylvania), *The Curse of Kulyenchikov* (later known as *Fools*; Eugene O'Neill Theatre), *Kaufman at Large* (Perry Street Theatre), *Is There Life After High School?* (Hartford Stage Company, Connecticut), *A Tale Told* (Circle Repertory Company, New York; Mark Taper Forum, Los Angeles, California), *The Diviners* (codesigned with David Potts, Saratoga Performing Arts Center, New York), *Foxfire* (Guthrie Theatre, Minneapolis, Minnesota), *Crimes of the Heart* (John Golden), *Medusa* (The First All Children's Theatre), *Monday After the Miracle* (Actor's Studio), *Duet for One* (Royale)—1981; *The Curse of an Aching Heart* (Little Theatre), *Livin' Dolls* (Manhattan Theatre Club), *Is There Life After High School?* (Ethel Barrymore), *Young Playwright's Festival* (Circle Repertory Company), *Monday After the Miracle* (Spoleto Festival, Charleston, South Carolina; Kennedy Center, Washington, D.C.; Eugene O'Neill Theatre), *Angels Fall* (Coconut Grove Playhouse, Miami, Florida; Saratoga Performing Arts Center, New York State; Circle Repertory Company), *The Holdup* (Saratoga Performing Arts Center, New York State), *Alice in Wonderland* (Virginia Theatre)—1982; *Cat on a Hot Tin Roof* (Mark Taper Forum, Los Angeles, California), *Passion* (Longacre), *Alice in Wonderland* (PBS television), *What I Did Last Summer* (Circle Repertory Company), *The Middle Ages* (St. Peter's Church), *Crimes of the Heart* (Ahmanson Theatre, Los Angeles, California), *The Seagull* (Saratoga Performing Arts Center, New York State, and Circle Repertory Company), *Baby* (Ethel Barrymore)—1981; *Park Your Car in Harvard Yard* (Manhattan Theatre Club), *Other Places* (Manhattan Theatre Club), *The Abduction of Figaro* (Minnesota Opera, Minneapolis), *The Miss Firecracker Contest* (Manhattan Theatre Club)—1984; *The Octette Bridge Club* (Music Box), *After the Fall* (Playhouse 91), *Angelo's Wedding* (Circle Repertory Company), *In Celebration* (Manhattan Theatre Club), *Hamlet* (Folger, Washington, D.C.; Long Wharf Theatre, New Haven, Connecticut), *Talley and Son* (Circle Repertory Company), *Tomorrow's Monday* (Circle Repertory Company), *It's Only a Play* (Manhattan Theatre Club), *Loot* (Manhattan Theatre Club), *Principia Scriptoriae* (Manhattan Theatre Club), *Picnic* (Ahmanson Theatre in Los Angeles), *Ain't Misbehavin'* (Buffalo Studio Arena; Syracuse Stage in New York State), *The Beastly Beatitudes of Balthazar*—1985; *The Nerd* (Helen Hayes), *The Hands of Its Enemy* (Manhattan Theatre Club), *Loot* and *Entertaining Mr. Sloane* (Taper

Too, Los Angeles, California, and Virginia Stage Company), *Loot* (Music Box), *Penn & Teller* (Westside Arts Theatre)—1986; *Bloody Poetry* (Manhattan Theatre Club), *The Lucky Spot* (Manhattan Theatre Club), *Burn This* (Plymouth), *Penn & Teller* (Ritz), *The Road to Mecca* (Lamb's Little Theatre)—1987; *Only You* (Circle Repertory Company), *Borderlines* (Circle Repertory Company), *V & V Only* (Circle Repertory Company), *Woman in Mind* (Manhattan Theatre Club), *Ain't Misbehavin'* (Ambassador Theatre)—1988; *Brilliant Traces, Florida Crackers* (two for the Circle Repertory Company), *What the Butler Saw, Aristocrats, Eleemosynary* (three for Manhattan Theatre Club), *The Rover* (Goodman Theatre, Chicago, Illinois), *Rebel Armies Deep into Chad* (Long Wharf Theatre, New Haven, Connecticut), *Men Should Weep* (Studio Arena Theatre, Buffalo, New York), *Look Homeward Angel* (Syracuse Stage Company, New York)—1989.

Beatty was among the first graduating class under the tutelage of Ming Cho Lee* at the Yale School of Drama, where he graduated with a master of fine arts degree in 1973. After working at regional theatres such as the Weston Theatre in Vermont and the Wayside Theatre in Virginia, Beatty moved to New York and became an assistant to designer Douglas Schmidt. Soon, however, he was designing on his own such productions as *Marouf* (1973) and *Ashes* (1976) at the Manhattan Theatre Club, *Diary of a Scoundrel* (1974) at the Gene Frankel Theatre Workshop, *The Amorous Flea* (1974) at the Queens Playhouse, and *The Battle of Angels* (1974) at the Circle Repertory Company. After working with Marshall Mason at the Queens Playhouse, he was hired to design at the Circle Repertory for the 1974–1975 season. By 1976, at the age of thirty-two, Beatty had established himself on Broadway with Jules Feiffer's *Knock Knock*, which began at the Circle Repertory Company. In fact, this company was an important connection for Beatty because it afforded an opportunity to design shows that eventually went to Broadway, including such major productions as *The Fifth of July* (1980), *Talley's Folly* (1980), and *Burn This* (1987). Similarly, his set at the Manhattan Theatre Club for *Crimes of the Heart* (1981) was adapted and moved to the John Golden Theatre on Broadway. Through his close association with directors Marshall Mason at the Circle Repertory Company and Lynne Meadow at the Manhattan Theatre Club, Beatty established connections with playwrights Lanford Wilson, David Mamet, and Beth Henley, to name only three. Many of their premiere productions were designed by Beatty, including Mamet's *A Life in the Theatre* (1977), *The Water Engine* (1978), and two short plays, *Dark Pony* and *Reunion* (1979). During the 1980s, Beatty designed such Broadway shows as *Monday After the Miracle* (1982) by William Gibson, the intimate musical *Baby* (1983), Athol Fugard's *The Road to Mecca* (1987), and *Woman in Mind* (1988) by Alan Ayckbourn. Over the course of working on a multitude of productions, Beatty has developed versatility, as he has designed works that have accommodated the different demands of plays, designs ranging from poetically realistic scenery to simple and stark presentational settings. In addition, he has designed for television, including *Out of Our Father's House* (1978) for WNET and Eva LeGallienne's revival of *Alice in Wonderland* (1983).

Awards: Beatty won a Tony Award for *Talley's Folly* (1980) and was nominated for *The Fifth of July* (1980).

Further Reading: Aronson (see Bibliography); Jenner, C. Lee. "From Neo-Realism . . ." *Theatre Crafts* October 1978: 43; Morrow, Lee Alan, and Frank Pike. *Creating Theatre*. New York: Vintage Books, 1986; Pollock, Steve. "Baby." *Theatre Crafts* 1985: 23; Sommers, Michael. "Designers at Work." *Theatre Crafts* May 1987: 37.

Brian R. Jones

Beazley, Samuel. Architect and playwright (b. 1786, England; d. 1851). Beazley was the author of innumerable short farces and comedies and several translations of opera libretti, but he is more appropriately remembered as the designer of a number of London's major theatre edifices. Critics have regarded his architectural designs as bland but serviceable structures. His designs include the Lyceum Theatre; St. James's Theatre; the facade of the Adelphi Theatre facing the Strand; the colonnade of the Drury Lane Theatre; and the twenty-five hundred-seat City of London Theatre, which opened in 1837.

James Fisher

Bel Geddes, Norman. Set and lighting designer, industrial designer, and producer (b. April 21, 1893, Adrian, MI; d. 1958). Theatrical productions include *Nju, Papa*—1916; *Shanwis*—1918; *La Nave, Boudoir, Chicago*—1919; *Divine Comedy, Ermine*—1920; *The Truth About Blayds, The Divine Comedy Project* (unproduced)—1921; *The Rivals*—1922; *Will Shakespeare, Fleet of Clay* (film), *The School for Scandal, The Miracle*—1923; *Arabesque* (produced), *The Follies of 1925*—1925; *The Sorrows of Satan* (film), *Devil in the Cheese*—1926; *Damn the Tears, Spread Eagle, Julius Caesar, Creoles, 5 O'Clock Girl, John*—1927; *The Patriot*—1928; *Fifty Million Frenchmen*—1929; *Lysistrata* (designed and produced)—1930; *Hamlet* (designed and produced)—1931; *Horizons* (produced), *Flying Colors*—1932; *Dead End* (produced)—1935; *Iron Men* (designed and produced)—1936; *The Eternal Road, Siege* (designed and produced)—1937; *The Eternal Road*—1939; *It Happens on Ice*—1940; *Sons and Soldiers*—1943; *The Seven Lively Arts*—1945.

Although Bel Geddes became a successful magazine and poster artist in Detroit by the time he was twenty-one, his strong interest in theatre led him to accept an assignment in Los Angeles with a fledgling company. While there, he designed his first shows, *Nju* and *Papa*, both in 1916. After the company folded, he returned to New York to establish a career and eventually met designer Robert Edmond Jones,* who gave him his first professional assignment designing summer stock in Milwaukee in 1918. Returning to New York that autumn, Bel Geddes designed his first Broadway show, *The Importance of Being Earnest*, followed by a number of other works that included ballets and operas. For these shows, Bel Geddes installed new lighting setups in the auditoriums that included the removal of footlights and the installation of balcony rail and auditorium positions for lighting the forestage with individually controlled lights.

After his Broadway success with *Ermine* (1920), Bel Geddes executed designs for a visionary project that was never produced, Dante's *The Divine Comedy* (1921). A scale model with lighting was created that was exhibited in Europe and photographed for *Theatre Arts Magazine*. The set for this production was a series of platforms, steps, and architectural units that towered more than five stories and led directly over the orchestra pit into the auditorium. The publicity that his design generated helped to earn Bel Geddes international attention.

Bel Geddes became an advocate for a style of scene design that depended on a permanent architectural unit enhanced with dramatic stage lighting to create the appropriate moods. He employed these techniques on such productions as Max Reinhardt's *The Miracle* (1924), for which Bel Geddes spent months in a Viennese castle developing the design with the German director. For this production, the designer transformed the Century Theatre into a massive medieval cathedral and used church pews for seating, gothic columns, stained-glass windows, and other accoutrements. As a director-designer, Bel Geddes applied his energies to Eva Le Gallienne's not very successful production of *Jeanne D'Arc* (1925) in Paris. For this production, Bel Geddes eliminated scenic ornamentation and focused wholly on three-dimensional forms of platforms and steps. At the other end of the spectrum were his more commercial Broadway productions, such as *Dead End* (1935) and *Iron Men* (1936), which were naturalistically detailed, creating a realistic New York City street and a half-constructed, steel-girded building at a construction site, respectively. Again serving as director and designer, Bel Geddes produced a tribute to the Jewish people called *The Eternal Road*, a huge production for which he redesigned the interior of the old Manhattan Opera House and installed a multilevel unit set. Although he worked on *The Seven Lively Arts* in 1945, many consider *The Eternal Road* to be Bel Geddes's final major theatrical achievement.

His other activities include founding an industrial design firm in 1926 comprised of designers, architects, and engineers that was intended to modernize industrial products and make them more artistically pleasing. Bel Geddes was also an architectural consultant for the Chicago World's Fair Exposition, which was to open in 1933, and designed a number of facilities, including theatres and restaurants, that were visionary in their conception. Unfortunately, none was ever built because of the depression. Later, General Motors hired him to design its Futurama exhibit at the 1937 New York World's Fair. After his final Broadway show in 1945, Bel Geddes spent the remainder of his career devoted to industrial design.

Further Reading: By Bel Geddes: *A Project for a Theatrical Presentation of The Divine Comedy of Dante Alighieri*. New York: Theatre Art, Inc., 1924; *Horizons*. Boston: Little, Brown, and Company, 1932; "The Theatre of the Future." *Miracle in an Evening: An Autobiography*, Ed. William Kelley. New York: Doubleday and Company, Inc., 1960. *A Project for The Divine Comedy*. New York, 1924.

About Bel Geddes: Bliven, Bruce. "Norman Bel Geddes: His Art and Ideas." *Theatre*

Arts Magazine 3 (July 1919): 179–90; Bogusch, George. "An American in Paris: Norman Bel Geddes Produces 'Jeanne D'Arc.' " *Theatre Design & Technology* 18 (October 1969): 4–11.

Thomas J. Mikotowicz

Belasco, David. Producer, director, designer, stage manager, and playwright (b. July 1853, San Francisco, CA; d. May 1931, New York City). In the area of design, Belasco is best known for his pioneering work in the area of lighting. Experimenting throughout his life with such qualities of light as color, intensity, distribution, and movement, he created a powerful, expressive medium, capable of engaging an audience's imagination and providing the artistic link between the actor and the stage setting.

As early as 1879, with his production of *The Passion Play* at the Grand Opera House in San Francisco, Belasco eliminated the use of footlights and replaced them with locomotive, bull's-eye headlights positioned at the upper front of house position. These headlights produced parallel beams capable of washing the stage at an angle different from that of the footlights. Belasco also eliminated footlighting for his productions of *The Darling of the Gods* (1902) and *The Return of Peter Grimm* (1911). In 1914, he decided to remove the footlights from the Belasco Theater. These early experiments with lighting instruments anticipated modern stage lighting and the practices of Reinhardt and Granville-Barker by twenty-five years. For *The Darling of the Gods* (1902), for example, Belasco created the effect of a Japanese purgatory, "The River of the Souls," by illuminating actors from behind a translucent backdrop. The bodies of the dead were seen as shadowy silhouettes that appeared to be floating.

Belasco also created innovative lighting systems and staging practices, dating from the time that he leased the Republic Theatre (eventually renamed the Belasco) in 1902. He collaborated with his chief electrician, Louis Hartmann, and the manufacturers, John H. and Anton Kliegl, in designing and experimenting with the most sophisticated lighting control and instrumentation in the country. The second Belasco Theatre, formerly the Stuyvesant Theatre, was the only theatre in the country that maintained an electrical laboratory where equipment was designed and manufactured. Here, Belasco experimented with the effects of color.

Belasco also collaborated with scenic artists and costume designers and embarked on detailed historical research for every production. Always maintaining that the theatre must be realistically accurate, he insisted on authentic, three-dimensional objects on the stage, instead of painted or simulated ones. To insure that the characters and their environment were properly matched, he and his staff constructed intricately scaled models for each production. Often, Belasco would send representatives across continents to purchase authentic materials. For *Du Barry* (1901), actual French drapery, furniture, and costume fabric were purchased. Likewise, costumes and furniture were imported from Japan for his production of *The Darling of the Gods* (1902). For the 1909 production of *The*

Easiest Way, Belasco purchased the contents of an entire bedroom located in an actors' boardinghouse and had the room completely rebuilt onstage. Responsible for more than 150 productions throughout his career, Belasco is now viewed as the main promulgator of realism/naturalism on the American stage.

Further Reading: By Belasco: *A History of the American Theatre: 1700–1950*. New York: Samuel French, 1951; *The Theatre Through Its Stage Door*. New York: Benjamin Blom, 1969.

    About Belasco: Lise-Lone, Marker. *David Belasco: Naturalism in the American Theatre*. Princeton: Princeton University Press, 1975; Winter, William. *The Life of David Belasco*. New York: Moffat, Yard and Company, 1918.

                                                                 Penny L. Remsen

Benois, Alexandre Nikolayevich. Set and costume designer, artist, and art critic (b. 1870, St. Petersburg, Russia; d. 1960). Theatrical productions include *The Queen of Spades* (Marinsky Theatre)—1890 and 1940; *The Story of Tzar Saltan* (Solodovn-Kikov Theatre, Moscow)—1900; *Le Pavillon d'Armide, Giselle, Petrouchka* (all with the Ballets Russes)—1911; *Le Malade Imaginaire* (Moscow Art Theatre)—1913; *Le Rossignol* (Paris Opera and London's Drury Lane)—1914; *Julius Caesar* (Pushkin Theatre)—1922; *Le Médecine Malgré Lui, Philemon et Baucis* (both for Diaghilev)—1923; *Les Noces de Psyche, Bolero, La Valse, La Baiser de la Fee, Princess Cygne* (Théâtre National de l'Opera, Paris)—1928; *Les Deux Tisserands* (Theatre Marique, Paris)—1940; *The Nutcracker* (London and Milan)—1957.

    Born into a prominent St. Petersburg family, Benois was schooled in art and culture at an early age. In the late 1880s at the Mai Academy, he met future fellow designers Bakst,* Golovine,* and Korovine.* With Benois as their leader, they developed a commitment to renewing the importance and focus of all of the arts in Russian society. Subsequently, he was also introduced to impresario Sergey Diaghilev, who, in collaboration with Benois, formed the "World of Art" group and published an art review magazine. Together, with Diaghilev as producer and Benois as art director, they formed an independent ballet company, employing Russian painters to design scenery and costumes for the productions. Each ballet was a synthesis created by the correct combination of composer, choreographer, and designer. Many famous performer-choreographers, such as Nijinsky, Pavlova, and Fokine, and famous composers, such as Debussy and Mussorgsky, were teamed with designers Bakst, Benois, and Golovine. With Diaghilev's Ballets Russes, Benois designed such productions as *Le Pavillon d'Armide* (1909) and *Petrouchka* (1911), and he traveled to Paris with the group to showcase Russian achievements. Parisians were stunned by the beauty, sweeping lines, and rich colors of the productions, which dared to go against the current trends toward naturalism in stage design. Benois also designed many significant play productions, including Moliere's *Le Malade Imaginaire* (1913), at the Moscow Art Theatre and *Julius Caesar* (1922) at the Pushkin Theatre. After 1927, Benois permanently left Russia and moved to Paris, where he designed several ballets for Ida Rubenstein, among them *Les Noces de Psyche* and *Bolero* (both

in 1928). For the rest of his career, he designed many classic ballets and operas at such major places as La Scala and Covent Garden and with the Ballets Russes de Monte Carlo in the United States.
Further Reading: Oenslager (see Bibliography).

                                                                    Thomas J. Mikotowicz

Bérain, Jean. Designer, theatrical architect, and engraver (b. 1637, Bar le Duc, France; d. 1711, possibly in Paris, France). Appointed official designer to Louis XIV in 1674, Bérain created elaborate costumes and decorations for special events taking place in the Court. These events, primarily presented at the palace at Versailles, included baptisms, marriages, and deaths, as well as the spectacular Court entertainments usually associated with the period. Ballets and operas were produced in the great halls of the palace, while outdoor festivities, in collaboration with such great playwrights as Molière, Racine, and Lully, were usually produced in the gardens. Bérain's designs for the Court masques were based on the iconography of the society. For example, Louis XIV was portrayed as the sun king, a lion, or some other majestic being. The designer's best-known work was *Le Triomphe de l'Amour* (1681), a combination of masques and aftermasques. In 1680, he replaced Vigarani* at the Académie Royale de Musique, now known as the Paris Opera, and designed many operas and ballets that featured his heavily ornamented sets and elaborate stage machinery. There, he collaborated with Lully and reaffirmed the classical French style of Louis XIV over the Italianate style dominating France up to that time. In addition to his design work, Bérain upheld a large atelier of students, among whom was his son, Jean (1678–1726). The younger Bérain eventually took over his father's position at the Paris Opera and designed such productions as *Les Muses* (1703), *Iphégénie en Tauride* (1704), and *Alcine* (1705).

                                                                    Thomas J. Mikotowicz

Bérard, Christian-Jacques. Set and costume designer, painter, and fashion designer (b. August 20, 1902, Paris, France; d. February 12, 1949, Paris, France). Theatre and ballet productions include *Les Elves*—1924; *La Nuit, La Voix Humaine*—1930; *Cotillon, Mozartiana*—1932; *La Machine Infernale*—1934; *La Reine Margot*—1935; *Symphonie Fantastique, L'Ecole des Femmes*—1936; *L'Illusion Comique*—1937; *Cyrano de Bergerac, Le Corsaire*, Massine's *Seventh Symphony*—1938; *Les Monstres Sacrés*—1940; *Renaud et Armide, Voulez-Vous Jouer Avec Moi?, Sodom et Gomorrhe*—1943; *Les Fourains, Les Folle de Chaillot*—1945; *La Belle et la Bête, L'Aigle à Deux Têtes*—1946; *Don Juan, Amphitryon*—1947; *Clock Symphony*—1948; *Les Fourberies de Scapin*—1949.

Similar to neoromantic artists Eugene Berman* and Pavel Tchelitchew,* Bérard merged his painting career with design for the theatre. At twenty-two, Bérard designed the ballet *Les Elves* (1924) for Michel Fokine. This subsequently led to collaborations with such famous choreographers as George Balanchine, for whom he created sets for *Cotillon* (1932) and *Mozartiana* (1933); Leonide Massine, for whom he devised settings for *Symphonie Fantastique* (1936); and Roland

Petit, for whom he designed *Les Forains* (1945). Along with Petit and Boris Kochno, Bérard established and served as codirector of the Ballet des Champs-Elysëes and designed many of its productions. His play designs were also featured at the Comedie Française and included boldy stylized shows such as Jean Cocteau's *The Infernal Machine* (1934) and Louis Jouvet's production of Jean Giradoux's *Madwoman of Chaillot* (1945). His *School for Wives* (1934) featured huge swinging doors that moved the audience from a Louis XIV interior to the outdoor garden. Other activities in design were equally successful for Bérard. He designed three films, but his most famous design was for Cocteau's *Beauty and the Beast* (1946). As a graphic artist, Bérard was well known for his portraits, posters, advertisement designs, and Steuben glass creations. In addition, his clothing sketches, submitted to such magazines as *Vogue* and *Harper's Bazaar*, were said to have inspired fashion designer Christian Dior to create the "New Look" in the mid-forties. An arresting personality, Bérard was a short, unkempt man with an uncombed beard whose personal appearance contradicted the beauty of his stage designs. Even his untimely death at forty-six, while at a final dress rehearsal, seemed to reflect the very theatrical quality of his life.

Thomas J. Mikotowicz

Berman, Eugene. Set and costume designer, and artist (b. 1899, St. Petersburg, Russia; d. 1972, Rome, Italy). Berman was born to a wealthy Russian family and studied painting and architecture until 1917, when he and his brother, Leonid, moved to Paris. There they developed a neoromantic style of painting that went against the prevailing modern, abstract art of the day. During this period, he spent much time visiting Italy, sketching its ruins, and studying the art of the Renaissance artists. Only when he moved to New York in 1935 did Berman become involved in theatrical design. Starting out as a designer of music festivals, Berman was soon commissioned by the Ballets Russes de Monte Carlo and Colonel de Basil's ballet company to design such works as *Icare* (1938), *Devil's Holiday* (1939), *Symphonie Italienne* (1939), and choreographer George Balanchine's *Concerto Barocco* (1941). Berman continued his work in ballet design in Europe and the United States and occasionally took dramatic assignments. After the group evolved into Ballet Theatre, Berman designed choreographer Anthony Tudor's *Romeo and Juliet* (1943) and *Giselle* (1944). For the dramatic stage, Berman's designs were few. He designed *Twelfth Night* (1938) for Louis Jouvet, but it was never produced. His classical, antiquarian style was suited to the operas that he designed for the Metropolitan Opera, including *Rigoletto, The Barber of Seville*, and *Don Giovanni*. One of his famous opera designs remains Gian Carlo Menotti's *Amahl and the Night Visitors* (1952), filmed for NBC television. Berman designed his final work for the Stravinsky Festival produced by the New York City Ballet in 1972, after a long hiatus from theatrical designing.

Thomas J. Mikotowicz

Bernini, Giovanni Lorenzo. Scenic designer, stage machinist, architect, and artist (b. 1598, Italy; d. 1680). Bernini is most significantly remembered as a prolific designer of stage machinery and spectacular theatrical effects in the baroque style. Although no drawings survive, Richard Lascelles, a friend of English designer Inigo Jones,* had the opportunity to see a number of Bernini's machines in operation in a Roman theatre. In his 1670 book, *Italian Voyage*, Lascelles describes such effects as fires, houses crumbling into ruins, sudden appearances of buildings and forests, boats floating on water, and elaborate monsters and dragons. Bernini also contributed designs for some of the decor and scenery for a Roman theatre built by the Barberini family in 1634. Also known as a true master artist of the theatre, Bernini wrote comedies and adaptations, acted in them, painted the scenery, invented the special effects and stage machinery for them, and even designed the theatres in which they were produced. Only one of his comedic plays, discovered in the 1960s, named *La Fontana di Trevi*, survives. Among the spectacles he produced were *De Due Teatri* (1637) and *L'Inondazione del Tevere* (1638).

James Fisher

Bernstein, Aline. Set and costume designer, and author (b. December 22, 1881, New York City; d. September 7, 1955, New York City). Theatrical productions include *The Queen's Enemies*—1916; *The Fair*—1920; *The Madras House, A Fairy Tale*—1921; *The Green Ring, Salut au Monde*—1922; *The School for Scandal, Grand Street Follies* (annual through 1929), *The Little Clay Cart*—1924; *The Dybbuk, Caesar and Cleopatra, The Critic, Hamlet*—1925; *The Apothecary, The Romantic Young Lady, Ned McCobb's Daughter, The Dybbuk, The Lion Tamer*—1926; *Tone Pictures and the White Peacock, If, The Love Nest*—1927; *The First Stone, Maya, Improvisation in June, Hedda Gabler, The Would-Be Gentleman, L'Invitation au Voyage, The Cherry Orchard, If, Peter Pan, Caprice*—1928; *The Lady from Albuquerque, On the High Road, Katerina, The Sea Gull, Mademoiselle Bourrat, The Game of Love and Death, The Living Corpse*—1929; *The Women Have Their Way, The Open Door, A Sunday Morning, Romeo and Juliet, The Green Cockatoo, Grand Hotel, Alison's House*—1930; *Tomorrow and Tomorrow, Camille, Getting Married, He, Reunion in Vienna*—1931; *The Animal Kingdom, Lenin's Dowry, Clear All Wires, Liliom, The Late Christopher Bean, Dear Jane, The Firebird*—1932; *The Porcelain Palace, A Good Woman, Poor Thing, We the People, Thunder on the Left*—1933; *Mackerel Skies, A Hat, A Coat, A Glove, Judgment Day, Between Two Worlds, L'Aiglon, The Children's Hour*—1934; *She* (film), *The Last Days of Pompeii* (film), *Night in the House*—1935; *And Stars Remain, Days to Come*—1936; *Storm over Patsy, To Quito and Back*—1937; *American Landscape*—1938; *The Little Foxes*—1939; *The Male Animal*—1940; *The Willow and I*—1942; *Harriet, The Innocent Voyage, Feathers in a Gale*—1943; *The Searching Wind*—1944; *Clover Ring*—1945; *Spellbound Child*—1946; *The Eagle Has Two Heads*—1947; *Regina*—1949; *The Happy Time, Burning Bright, Let's Make an Opera, An Enemy of the People*—1950; *Mary Rose*—1951; *The World of Sholom Aleichem*—1953.

Bernstein, the first prominent woman to be admitted as a member of the United

Scenic Artists' Union, designed more than one hundred productions in her forty-year career. She was also the cofounder in 1937 of the Museum of Costume Art. Although she worked with both Robert Edmond Jones* and Lee Simonson,* her work was, perhaps, not as well known, yet it evidenced a thorough approach. She was an active practitioner of the "New Stagecraft" of Jones and Mordecai Gorelik,* firmly believed in the subordinate nature of design to the script, and held an artistic commitment to the principle of simplicity in her work. Her designs were often described as being absolutely or quietly "right."

Her career began at the Neighborhood Playhouse, where she started as a volunteer and later executed others' designs. Her first design was for *The Queen's Enemies* in 1916. She continued to design for that theatre until 1929, including memorable productions like *The Little Clay Cart, The Dybbuk*, and several editions of *Grand Street Follies*, in which she would often parody contemporary designs. In 1924, Bernstein executed costumes for Max Reinhardt and Norman Bel Geddes's* production of *The Miracle* and began a long association with the Theatre Guild. Working with Eva Le Gallienne's Civic Repertory Theatre, she designed *Hedda Gabler, The Would-Be Gentleman*, and *The Cherry Orchard*, among others. For Le Gallienne, she designed a neutral box set with openings that could be changed with accoutrements or simple decor to accommodate a large repertory of multiple set shows.

In the 1930s, Bernstein designed several productions for Elmer Rice, including *We the People*. She also worked on many productions for producer-director Herman Schumlin that included *Grand Hotel, The Children's Hour*, and *The Little Foxes*. In the latter part of her career, Bernstein's designs began to rely increasingly on realism. Her later designs, however, although appropriate, did not show the same creativity and imagination of her earlier work.

Awards: She won the Tony Award in 1950 for her costumes for *Regina*, the Marc Blitzstein opera based on *The Little Foxes*.

Further Reading: By Bernstein: *Masterpieces of Women's Costume of the 18th and 19th Centuries*. New York: Crown, 1959.

About Bernstein: "The Craftsman." *Theatre Arts Monthly* April 1945; "Designer Sets the Stage: Jo Mielziner and Aline Bernstein." *Theatre Arts Magazine* February 1937; Gassner, John. *Producing the Play*. New York: Dryden, 1941; Klein, Carole. *Aline*. New York: Harper and Row, 1979; "Scissors and Sense." *Theatre Arts Magazine* August 1925; "Women Who Are Stage Designers." *Independent Woman* May 1946.

Ken Kloth

Beuther, Friedrich Christian. Scene designer (b. 1777, Germany; d. 1856). From the beginning, Beuther was known as an influential innovator and superior master designer in perspective and architecture. He began his theatrical career as an actor but soon turned to design. As a pupil of Giorgio Fuentes in Frankfurt, he was trained in a strong neoclassical style. Later, at Goethe's urging, Beuther became the scenic designer at the Hoftheater in Weimar. There, he added his own scenographic style to Goethe's principles of excellence in artistic presentation and homogeneity of style in production. Beuther converted the neoclassic and neo-Gothic modes to his own style, freely adapting linear perspective, using a warm color palette, and experimenting with color and light scales. He was an acclaimed modernist in his efforts to establish an integrated totality in the art of the theatre and anticipated many of the ideas later developed and promulgated by Richard Wagner. His popular productions included Mozart's *Titus* (1815) and *The Magic Flute* (1817), as well as a multitude of other plays and operas. In 1818, one year following Goethe's departure, Beuther left the Hoftheater to accept a new six-year contract in Braunschweig. Subsequently, he worked as guest designer in other German cities for the last thirty years of his career.

Further Reading: Oenslager (see Bibliography).

Annie Milton

Beverley, William Roxby. Artist and scene designer (b. 1814, England; d. 1889). Considered one of the most distinguished and influential painters of nineteenth-century English theatre, Beverley began his career with his father's company at the Theatre Royal in Manchester. In 1843, he became the theatre's chief designer, creating backdrops that were still in use after twenty-five years. From 1847 to 1856, Beverley worked at the Lyceum Theatre under Madame Vestris. His greatest success came with his designs for Planché's *The Island of Jewels* (1849), which included scene transformations that were renowned for their exceptional use of *trompe l'oeil* scene painting as well as their mechanical versatility. It is believed that Beverley developed a new method of painting by going over the raw cloth while the distemper was still wet in order to create new atmospheric effects. It is also probable that he used some sort of painted gauzes for scrim effects in his transformation scenes. From 1854 to 1868, Beverley worked at Drury Lane as a scene painter, remaining there as the theatre's exclusive designer until 1885. While there, he designed many Shakespearean revivals, including *Henry IV, Part 1* and *Antony and Cleopatra* (both in 1873). He was obviously attracted to jeweled settings, as could be seen in his *The Doge of Venice* (1867) and *The Shaughraun* (1875). Elsewhere, he designed, among others, several of Charles Kean's historically accurate productions at the Princess's Theatre, including *King John* and *Macbeth* (1852), and an elaborate production of Milton's *Comus*. He was not content to use only paint, canvas, and gauzes but employed such effects as an actual hansom cab and horse on the stage. In addition, he is reputed to have invented wing ladders fitted with gaslights. Through his inventive use of painted illusion together with other devices, Beverley became known as one of the period's most enchanting, inventive, and successful practitioners of stage illusion.

Jonet Buchanan

Bibiena Family. Scenic artists and theatre architects (1625 through 1787). Spanning four generations, the Bibienas, a family of designers and theatre architects, contributed enormously to the visual splendor of the baroque stage. The founder of the Bibiena dynasty was the designer Giovanni Maria Galli (1625–1665), who added "da Bibiena" to his name to differentiate himself from a fellow apprentice also named Galli. His enthusiasm for art was passed on to his four young sons, who in turn gave it to further generations. Two of his sons, Ferdinando (1657–1743) and Francesco (1659–1739), became especially well known in the theatre. Both were trained in the studio of a Bolognese painter and later under Rivani, a stage engineer responsible for some of the machinery in Louis XIV's Court theatre at Versailles.

Ferdinando was employed early in his life by the duke of Parma, for whom he worked in the beautiful Teatro Farnese, possibly under Giacomo Torelli.* During his twenty-eight years of service under the patronage of the Farnese, Ferdinando designed numerous theatre sets in Parma, Bologna, Venice, Turin, Rome, Naples, Milan, Florence, and other Italian cities. Ferdinando's work at Bologna and Parma firmly established the family's reputation. During his time in Bologna, he introduced what was perhaps the Bibienas' single most significant innovation—the *scena per angola* (angle perspective), first seen on the stage in 1703. He described and illustrated in his *L'Architettura Civile Preparata Nello Geometria* (1711) how he could give an accurate elevation of a scene from a drawing of an irregular plan. This new diagonal perspective, in which se $'4shing points were placed off the center line of the stage, replaced the single, central perspective commonly used in the seventeenth century. Gone were the central vistas of previous designers, and in their place were elaborate architectural stage settings, buildings, walls, statues, and courtyards, which became characteristic of the Bibiena stage. In addition to the introduction of the *scena per angola*, the Bibienas changed the scale of stage settings. Their designs were exceptional for their magnificence, size, and the seemingly infinite space depicted through the corridors that opened at angles to the stage. By 1708, Ferdinando was famous enough to be summoned to Barcelona, where he staged the festivities for the marriage of the future emperor Charles VI. In 1711, Charles VI appointed him Court architect at Vienna to succeed Burnacini. Thereafter he was in demand wherever an interest in opera developed and designed in such major cities as Paris, Lisbon, London, Stockholm, Berlin, Dresden, and St. Petersburg. Francesco first worked in Vienna but spent most of his life in Italy, and he worked at first with his brother Ferdinando and then on the Continent and developed his own style. He designed the festivities for Phillip V's arrival in Spain and designed the Theatre at Nancy and the Teatro Filarmonic.

Of Ferdinando's four sons, his eldest, Allessandro (1687–c.1769), was an architect but concerned himself less with theatrical work than did his three brothers. Ferdinando's second son, Giuseppe (1696–1757), inherited his father's post as theatrical engineer in Vienna after the latter went home to Bologna. Among his designs was the opera house in Bayreuth, which he codesigned with Joseph St. Pierre and which was finished in 1748. The vast structure contained a stage three times longer than the smaller auditorium. Giuseppe is also credited as one of the first designers to use transparent scenery lit from behind as early as 1723. Ferdinando's third son, Antonio (1700–1774), spent over twenty years in Austria and almost thirty in Italy and built more theatres than any one man of his time, including the Teatro Communale in Bologna, which opened in 1763. The youngest son, Giovanni Maria (c.1704–1769), went to Prague and is believed to have built a theatre near Lisbon. Giuseppe's son, Carlo (1728–1778), was also a famous designer of stage settings, one of which is preserved in the old Royal Theatre at Drottingholm. He created with his father the three-dimensional, golden, rococo decorations at the Bayreuth Opera House in 1748 and worked during the years 1750 to 1756 for the old Dresden Opera House. Later, he designed scenes for most of the great opera houses of Europe, including Naples, Stockholm, London, and St. Petersburg.

Through their work, the entire Bibiena family disseminated the Italian style of scene design throughout northern Europe. In addition to quality, the Bibienas produced a vast quantity of work—approximately 80 percent of all eighteenth-century stage designs have been attributed to the family. It is difficult to make individual attributions for many of their works because the family shared the same artistic values and a common architectural style in sketching. Known for skill, patience, ornamentation, and craftsmanship, their baroque settings achieved marvels of proportion, beauty, and scenic splendor.

Jonet Buchanan

Björnson, Maria. Scene designer (b. 1949, England). Björnson studied for three years at London's Central School before beginning her free-lance design career. Her preference has been for designing opera in which large, bold, romantic, and expressive sets as well as elaborate costumes are the norm. For her the world of an opera is one of "distorted reality," a reality either heightened or diminished by the stage design. Her job is to create visual effects that will expose the psychological realm of the opera and thereby enhance its emotional impact. Her earliest work was for provincial theatres, particularly the Citizen's Theatre in Glasgow. Since that time she has designed such works as *Toussaint* (1977) and Wagner's *Ring Cycle* (1983) for the English National Opera Company; *The Makropoulos Case* (1978) for the Welsh National Opera; *Katya Kabanova* (1979) for the Scottish Opera; and *A Midsummer Night's Dream* (1981) for the Royal Shakespeare Company. Her most recent design efforts have been for Andrew Lloyd Webber's *Phantom of the Opera* (1986) and *Follies* (1987), as well as the opera *Donnerstage Aus Licht* (1987).

Andrea J. Nouryeh

Bloodgood, William. Set designer (b. June 8, 1951, Glen Cove, NY). Bloodgood received his B.A. in 1973 from Franklin and Marshall College and his M.F.A. from Pennsylvania State University in 1976. From graduate school he went directly to the Shakespeare Festival in Ashland, Oregon, where he is now a resident designer. His more interesting projects were designs for *Spokesong*, Arthur Kopit's *Wings*, and Brendan Behan's *The Hostage*, all of which he designed at Ashland, and Philip Barry's *Holiday* at the Old Globe Theatre. Bloodgood has received several *Dramalogue Magazine* Awards and Bay Area

Critics' Circle Awards. Though born and raised on the East Coast, he has decided to live and do most of his work on the West Coast. He has designed sets for Houston's Alley Theatre, the Arizona Theatre Company, the Seattle Children's Theatre, the Alaska Repertory Theatre, the San Jose Repertory Company, and *Holiday* for the Old Globe Theatre in San Diego.

Further Reading: "Designers at Work." *Theatre Crafts* May 1987: 44.

Annie Milton

Bonnat, Yves. Set designer and painter (b. February 20, 1912, Voiron, France). Theatrical productions include *Il était trois navires*—1943; *Le Cid, Horace, Le Ville de la Mare, Les Muets*—1944; *Amphytrion*—1946; *Passage du Malin*—1947; *Jeux, Thermidor*—1948; *La Guerre involontaire, Mon Mari et toi*—1949; *Jeanne d'Arc au bucher, Septuor*—1950; *La Damnée, Madame Sans-Gens, Mephisto-Valse* and *Nocturne, Siegfried, Terrain Vague*—1951; *Ruy Blas, L'Isola del tesoro, The Man, Treize à table*—1952; *Boris Godunov, Il ètait une gare, La Troisieme femme*—1953; *Sogno d'una notte di mezza estate, La Femme a barb, L'Arlesienne, Mireille, Julius Caesar*—1954; *Monsieur Baucaire*—1955; *Oedipe-Roi*—1962; *Jazz-out*—1966.

Having studied at the National École des Beaux Arts in Devambert, Bonnat was invited to exhibit his paintings in the Salon d'Automne, which began his illustrious career. Since, his paintings have been exhibited in Lyon, Bordeaux, Paris, Vienna, Brussels, and Toronto. A great deal of his design career has been for the dance. He has designed sets and costumes for choreographer Serge Lifar and others, as well as for the Ballets de Moscou, the Festival International de la Danse, and the International Festival of Dance in Aix les Rains. In addition he has taken responsibility for the lighting at these festivals. Theatrical designs have been executed for Jean Louis-Barrault and for various operatic productions in Paris. His work has also been seen in various revues, operettas, and vaudevilles produced since 1945. As well, Bonnat has written about design and ballet. His most important writings are the series of books about design and a book about ballet.

Further Reading: By Bonnat (with Rene Hainaux): for the International Theatre Institute. *Stage Design Throughout the World (Since 1935, Since 1950) Since 1960*. New York: Theatre Arts Books, 1973.

Andrea J. Nouryeh

Borovsky, David. Set designer (b. 1934, Russia). Borovsky collaborated with director Yuri Lyubimov of the Taganka Theatre in Moscow to produce these most significant works: *Hamlet* (1972), *The Dawns Are Quiet* (1972), *Comrade Believe*, Maxime Gorky's *Mother* (1978), and *Valentin and Valentina* (1978). His designs are usually simple, using authentic objects that can be reconfigured for the various demands of a play's action. In *Hamlet*, Borovsky created a unit set, which used a large, movable curtain that was as wide as the stage. In addition, the set could spin on its central axis with a performer onboard, and it was illuminated by forceful lighting effects. With Lyubimov's choreographed movement, it served as the background, properties, and participant in the action. In the World War II drama *The Dawns Are Quiet*, he used old wooden boards configured in an abstract manner that served as an army truck and were used variously to represent a forest, the barracks, and ultimately the coffins of the soldiers.

Thomas J. Mikotowicz

Boucher, François. Scenic and costume designer, and artist (b. September 1703, France; d. May 1770, Paris, France). Boucher, one of the leading eighteenth-century French painters, executed scenic and costume designs for the Académie Royale de Musique, the theatre of the Parisian fairs, and Mme. de Pompadour's Theatre des Petits Appartements at Versailles. He collaborated with master designer Servandoni* on several theatrical spectacles produced by the Paris Opera as early as 1739 and succeeded him as designer, serving there from 1742 to 1748. Boucher's designs featured backdrops depicting idyllic landscapes of exotic charm. For the opera *Issé*, for example, he created a rustic inn surrounded by a picturesque landscape that included a bridge, a river, and a luminous sky. Some of his other significant designs were for the operas *Persée* (1746) and *Atys* (1747). In 1743, Boucher began working with his friend Charles-Simon Favart, designing scenery and costumes for a number of productions at the theatre fair of Saint Laurent, including *L'Ambigu de la Folie ou Le Ballet des Dindons* (1743), *Les Vendanges de Tempé* (1745), and *Cythere Assiegee* (1748). With the theatre fairs and the Opéra-Comique the neoclassical ideal, so long an institution of the French theatre, opera, and ballet, was challenged. In 1752, Favart became the director of the Opéra-Comique and began to explore ways in which the emotions of ordinary, rustic characters and the simplicity of rural life could be revealed on the stage. Boucher, assisting his colleague, created designs that reflected these objectives: pastoral landscapes with cottages and mills and with rustic furniture, props, ladders, wheelbarrows, baskets, and farming implements. In 1754, Boucher collaborated with choreographer Jean-Georges Noverre on *Les Fêtes Chinoises* and *La Fontaine de Jouvence*, both produced by the Opéra-Comique and staged at the Foire Saint Laurent. He returned to the Paris Opera in 1764 to design the revival of Rameau's *Castor et Pollux*, and, in the next year, he designed the scenery for Lully's *Thésee*. The last production designed by Boucher was a revival of Laujon's ballet *Sylvie*, which opened in 1766.

Further Reading: Oenslager (see Bibliography).

Penny L. Remsen

Bragdon, Claude. Set and lighting designer, architect, and artist (b. 1866, United States; d. 1946). Bragdon trained as a graphic artist and architect at Cornell University. In 1919, Walter Hampden, an actor, hired him to design the set for a production of *Hamlet*, after which a longtime relationship evolved. As a champion of the "New Stagecraft," Bragdon designed a classically styled set for the show that incorporated movable, multipurpose units that could be rear-

ranged to create different locales. Archways, towers, and staircases were constructed out of flats, platforms, step units, and curtains, in this as well as in
many of his other Shakespearean productions. His designs for such shows as
Macbeth (1921), *The Merchant of Venice* (1925), and *King Henry V* (1928)
tended to be economical, having a simple style that was later imitated by other
designers. His production of *Cyrano de Bergerac* at the Hampden Theatre in
New York was simply conceived and included dramatic lighting effects as silhouettes of soldiers before a lighted cyclorama on a bare stage. For the most
part, Bragdon's approach to design went against the realism of stage settings in
productions of the day, much like Lee Simonson's* and Robert Edmond Jones's*
designs. His work includes such productions as *Ruy Blas* (1923), *The Immortal
Thief* (1926), *Caponsacchi* (1926), *An Enemy of the People* (1927), *Light of
Asia* (1928), *Richelieu* (1929), and *Achilles Has a Heel* (1935). Skilled at dramatic lighting effects, Bragdon was referred to as the "Master of Light" for his
work on the "Song and Light Festival" in New York's Central Park in the early
part of this century.

Kurt Lancaster

Buontalenti, Bernardo. Set designer, theatrical machinist, and architect (b.
1536, Italy; d. 1608). Buontalenti began his career in 1547 as assistant to de-
signer-architect Giorgio Vasari, who worked in the Medici Court. In 1574, he
became chief designer and architect of the Florentine Court and, in addition to
creating palaces and villas, had full supervision over the scenery, machinery,
props, and costumes of the Court entertainments, including plays, pageants, and
processions. Nicknamed *delle Girandole* (of the fireworks), Buontalenti was
known for his pyrotechnic displays, as well as his elaborate hydraulic machinery
developed for the *intermezzi* of court presentations. For the marriage between
Virginia de'Medici and Cesare d'Este (1585), he designed the Teatro degli Uffizi.
This theatre was outfitted with an elaborate system of scene-changing devices,
including revolving *periaktoi* and other machinery. In 1589, he supervised the
festivities surrounding the marriage of Ferdinand I and Catherine de'Medici that
included outdoor events and the presentation of six *intermezzi* of *La Pelligrina*
by Bargagli in the Uffizi on May 2 of that year. Buontalenti's extravagant designs
for the *intermezzi* ushered in the new European genre of opera, with their impressive effects achieved through the use of machines for scene changing and
detailed painting techniques. Renaissance spectators were in awe of the special
effects created by flying cloud machines, *periaktoi*, sliding wing and shutter
flats, trapdoors, and other machinery associated with that period. As Buontalenti
inherited knowledge from Vasari, the great tradition of Court designers was
passed to his pupil, Giulio Parigi,* who eventually passed it along to his son.

Thomas J. Mikotowicz

Burian, Emil Frantisek. Composer, actor, director, writer, and designer (b.
April 11, 1904, Pizen, Czechoslovakia; d. August 9, 1955). Burian graduated
from the Prague Conservatory in 1927 and started a career as a composer and

actor. In 1932, he formed the left-wing cultural organization Leva Fronta, served as deputy to the National Assembly, and founded his own weekly paper, *Kulturni politika*.

Although musical composition remained the foundation of his work, Burian founded his Theatre D34 in 1934, after Czech independence was gained. Working in a concert hall with a small stage that measured twenty by twelve feet and an auditorium that seated 383 people, Burian sought a creative partnership among writers, designers, performers, directors, and stage personnel. With principal designer Miroslav Kouril, Burian experimented with placing emphasis on lights and music. This resulted in three significant, multimedia productions: Wedekind's *Spring's Awakening* in 1936; Pushkin's *Eugene Onegin* in 1937; and Goethe's *The Sorrows of Young Werther* in 1938. Burian seldom staged texts written for the stage, preferring to make his own adaptations that included his own musical compositions, such as *War* (1935). In addition, he created scenic elements with film and slide projections chosen for their symbolic value and light. In 1935, he created "Theatergraph," a technique of overlapping projected images with the live performer, and thus laid the foundation for Josef Svoboda's *Laterna Magika*. Though Burian's performers related physically to the projections, the projections were subordinated to the dramatic action, so that all elements of the action were integrated, rather than juxtaposed. In 1941, Burian's theatre was closed, and he was confined to a concentration camp.

Further Reading: Gillar, Jaroslav. "Theatre of Work 1936—1938." *Interscena* 3 (1969): 33–41; Muller, Robert. "A Talk with E. F. Burian." *Theatre Newsletter* October 16, 1948: 5.

Annie Milton

Burnacini, Ludovico Ottavio. Designer and architect (b. 1636, Venice, Italy; d. 1707). Burnacini designed more than four hundred operas, festivals, and plays, plus plans for theatres. His father, Giovanni Burnacini, held the position of imperial chief engineer under Ferdinand III and achieved a reputation as a theatrical designer during the Renaissance. Ludovico inherited his father's title in 1657 and held it until his death in 1707, and he worked for Leopold, Ferdinand III's successor. At the imperial summer residence, Burnacini designed aquatic displays that, perhaps, became the precedent for the extravagant designs of the Bibienas* a generation later. He is most notably associated, however, with the "high" baroque style of operatic production as a result of such elaborate designs as *Il Fuoco Eterno*, performed in 1674 at Theater auf der Cortina. His settings for the opera included detailed painting techniques and many pryotechnic displays. The theatre itself was designed by Burnacini and included three functional staging areas—the forestage, the midstage shutter area, and the inner stage beyond. His production of Cesti's opera, *Il Pomo D'Oro*, in 1662 included twenty-one huge sets and was a phenomenal success. Burnacini's theatrical design style depended on such spectacular effects as fireworks, formal baroque composition, and distinctive perspective views, as well as fanciful elements such as nymphs and fairies.

Brian R. Jones

Burra, Edward John. Set designer and artist (b. March 29, 1905, South Kensington, England; d. October 26, 1976). Burra belonged to a group of artists who were occasionally called upon to design ballets and operas. Although trained at the Royal College of Art, Burra took his influences from many sources, including various cultures, the Dadaists, and other artists such as Dali, Grosz, and Beardsley. His avant-garde painting style was welcomed at Sadler's Wells in such productions as *Barabau* (1936) and *The Miracle in the Gorbals* (1944) and at Covent Garden in *Carmen* (1947), *Don Juan* (1948), and *Don Quixote* (1950).

Elbin L. Cleveland

Bury, John. Set and costume designer (b. January 27, 1925, Wales). Theatrical productions include *Enemy of the People*—1954; *The Quare Fellow*—1956; *A Taste of Honey*—1958; *Fings Ain't Wot They Used T'Be*—1959; *Measure for Measure, Oh, What a Lovely War!*—(London), *The Physicists, The War of the Roses, York Mystery Cycle*—1963; *The Blood Knot*—1964; *Moses and Aron, The Homecoming*, David Warner's *Hamlet*—1965; *Macbeth*—1967; *Landscape* and *Silence, A Delicate Balance*—1969; *Battle of the Shrivings*—1970; *Hedda Gabler* and *A Doll's House* (New York)—1971; *Old Times*—1971; *All Over*—1972; *Hamlet*—1975; *Tamburlaine the Great*—1976; *Strife*—1978; *Amadeus*—1979; *Betrayal*—1979.

Bury began his career with Joan Littlewood's Theatre Workshop in 1945 and, designing approximately fifty productions, continued to work there until 1962. From there he joined the Royal Shakespeare Company as assistant head of design and was promoted in 1964 to head designer. Bury's distinguished career and his association with renowned director Peter Hall led to his appointment in 1973 as head designer and associate director of the National Theatre of Great Britain, a position he held until 1985. In addition to these theatre affiliations, Bury contracted many individual productions throughout the world and worked with many famous directors and performers. With a style described as unfussy and modern, Bury went against the prevalent seminaturalistic style in the fifties. His use of highly textured, natural materials, such as wood and metal, was an attempt to impart a sensory experience of an object. The style worked particularly well with such productions as the BBC version of Shakespeare's *The War of the Roses* (1965), Peter Hall's operas *Tristan und Isolde* (1971) and *The Magic Flute*, and the plays *A Taste of Honey* (London; 1963), *Oh, What a Lovely War!* (1963), *Amadeus* (1979), and *Betrayal* (1980).

Awards: Cowinner Gold Medal for Scene Design in Prague, 1976.

Thomas J. Mikotowicz

C

Campen, Jacob Van. Architect (b. c.1595, Holland; d. 1657). Borrowing on the style of Palladio's* Teatro Olimpico, theatre architect Jacob Van Campen designed the Schouwburg, the first permanent theatre built in Amsterdam. The Schouwburg featured a *scena stabile* (permanent setting), bordered by a balcony on each side, no proscenium arch, a single ceiling over both the stage and the auditorium, and a central arch not unlike the open-air theatres designed by members of the Chamber of Rhetoric. The Schouwburg was rebuilt in 1665 by Jan Voss (1615–1667), who added an Italianate proscenium arch and an orchestra pit and painted canvas scenery, but it was destroyed by fire in 1772.

James Fisher

Capon, William. Scenic designer and theatrical architect (b. 1757, England; d. 1827). When the Drury Lane Theatre was rebuilt in 1794 after a fire, Capon emerged as the chief designer, working with director John Phillip Kemble. Kemble and Capon shared an intense fondness for medieval and Gothic architecture. From his earliest designs, Capon satiated the public's growing appetite for spectacle and became one of the first advocates in England for historically accurate settings for drama. An antiquarian, Capon researched local historical sights and sketched and noted the types of construction materials. Most importantly, he observed light and shadow to represent them accurately on stage. For Handel's *Oratorio* (1794), which was performed for the reopening of the theatre, he created a background for the musicians that was an impressive and faithful replica of a Gothic chapel, replete with illuminated, stained-glass windows. In this production, he eliminated the wing flats and created a boxlike set. Similarly, he designed an even larger and more impressive fourteenth-century chapel in seven planes that included a choir loft, nave, and side aisles for *De Montfort* (1800). He applied the same energy to Shakespeare as he did to current drama. For *Macbeth* (1794), he created six chamber wings in the Gothic style and later re-created the Tower of London for *Richard III* (1805). His designs for Kemble's melodramas were in the same manner. His library and great hall for *The Iron Chest* (1796) and castle for *Adelmorn, the Outlaw* (1801) were both Gothically rendered. After Kemble became director at Covent Garden in 1809, Capon joined him and, together with other famous scene painters such as Thomas Greenwood and Gaetano Marinari, to name only two, painted many scenes for Shakespearean revivals, as well as generic scenes of various streets and buildings. Becoming part of a theatre's stock scenery, Capon's creations continued to be used for different productions of the same show and, indeed, for different shows entirely throughout the nineteenth century.

Thomas J. Mikotowicz

Carzou, Jean. Designer, painter, and graphic artist (b. January 1, 1907, Paris, France). Carzou had no formal artistic training when he began illustrating for magazines in the 1930s. He experimented with abstraction and collages in his early works but did little scenic design until the 1950s, when he produced highly evocative and surreal designs for several operas and ballets. Among these are *Les Indes Galantes* (1952), *Le Loup* (1953), *Giselle* (1954), *Athalie* (1955), and *La Perichole* (1969). Without a doubt, however, he made his greatest mark as a painter and graphic artist with exhibits in many European capitals. His fantastic surrealist paintings depicted a highly mechanized world and presented a memorable exhibition in 1957 under the title *Apocalypses*.

James Fisher

Chagall, Marc. Artist and set designer and artist (b. July 1887, Vitebsk, Russia; d. March 1985, Vence, France). Although he will be best remembered as an artist, Chagall designed a significant number of theatrical works. He was first introduced to design early in his career by fellow artist and theatrical designer Léon Bakst.* In 1915, Chagall accomplished his first production design, *Happy to Die*, at the Prival Komediante Theatre in Petrograd. For the design, he enlarged his cubist painting, *The Drinker* (1912), into a scenic backdrop. The costumes and makeup for this show were also under the supervision of Chagall, who insisted that the performers paint their faces green and their hands blue. In this first theatrical design, the artist embraced a nonnaturalistic style and began to explore his own personal sense of mythology. In 1921, he finished designs for *Mazeltov, The Agents*, and *The Lie*, all for the Kamerney State Jewish Theatre. For these shows, Chagall involved himself not only with the scenic and costume design but with the overall style of the performance, including acting and movement. His later career included designs for ballet. His first dance work was in 1942 on the New York City Ballet production of *Aleko*, choreographed by Leonide Massine. Subsequently, he created scenery and costumes for *The Firebird*, performed first in 1945 with choreography by Adolf Bolm and again in 1949 with choreography by George Balanchine. After settling in Vence, Alpes-Maritimes, in 1950, Chagall continued to pursue his interest in ballet design and designed the settings and costumes for such works as *Daphnis et Chloe* (1959) for the Paris Opera. The artist's final design for the stage was the only one he ever executed for an opera. Following a discussion in 1964 with Gunther Rennert and Rudolf Bing, Chagall worked intensely for three years and created thirty-nine painted drops and nearly 121 costumes and masks for a production of Mozart's *The Magic Flute*. The production opened in 1967 at the Metropolitan Opera House and continued a successful run. Chagall's artistic vision was applied to the design of several theatre interiors, including the Kamerny State Jewish Theatre in Moscow in 1921; the Winter Gate Theatre in London in 1949; the Frankfurt Theatre in Germany in 1959; the Paris Opera in 1966; and the Metropolitan Opera House at Lincoln Center in New York in 1966. Chagall's theatrical designs have been featured in museums in several countries, including Germany, France, and the United States.

Further Reading: Lassaigne, Jacques. *Marc Chagall: The Ceiling of the Paris Opera—Sketches, Drawings, and Paintings*. New York: Frederick A. Praeger, 1966; Lassaigne, Jacques. *Marc Chagall: Drawings and Water Colors for the Ballet*. New York: Tudor, 1965.

Penny L. Remsen

Chiaruttini, Francesco. Set designer (b. 1748, Cividale (Undine), Italy; d. 1796). Chiaruttini was schooled in Venice and studied the works of the contemporary Venetian painters and old masters in the Accademia di Belle Arti, as well as sketches in the shops of scene painters, such as Fossati. His most important work was accomplished at the Teatro Argentina in Rome from 1786 to 1788. Chiaruttini composed elaborate architectural scenes in the style of paintings like those of Pietro Gonzaga* that were used as backdrops for opera, ballet, and theatre.

Further Reading: Oenslager (see Bibliography).

Annie Milton

Ciceri, Pierre-Luc-Charles. Set designer and painter (b. August 17, 1782, Saint-Cloud, France; d. August 22, 1868, Saint-Cheron, France). Ciceri was one of the most influential French designers of the early nineteenth century. After apprenticing with F. J. Belanger from 1802 until 1806, Ciceri earned a position as a staff painter at the Paris Opera. He continued developing his craft and became principal designer at the Opera around 1810 but worked at several of the local Paris theatres on occasion. In 1822, he opened the first scenic studio in Paris, where he employed specialists to create the details of architecture and landscape painting. His students at the studio painted such popular scenes of the day as classical, romantic ruins, accurately rendered historical locales, and local settings. These sets were designed and painted on wing and shutter settings in perspective, and they were integrated with the new gas lighting systems that were installed in theatres of the day. Ciceri's independent scenic studio replaced individual theatres' shops and maintained the practice of several designers working on one show. Among his most famous designs were *Don Sancho* (1825),

Guillaume Tell (1829), and the historically accurate *Hernani* (1830), which he designed for the Comédie Français. Ciceri's style, continued through the work of his students, dominated French design throughout the rest of the century.

Thomas J. Mikotowicz

Ciulei, Liviu. Director, designer, actor, and filmmaker (b. July 7, 1923, Bucharest, Romania). Theatrical productions include *The Rainmaker* (directed), *Mrs. Warren's Profession, Saint Joan, The Man with the Gun, The Dark Years*—1958; *An Ideal Husband, Hamlet*—1959; *The Lower Depths, Passacaglia, The Glass Menagerie, As You Like It, Children of the Sun, The Waves of the Danube* (film)—1960; *Costake et la Vie Interieure*—1962; *The Threepenny Opera*—1964; *The Time of Your Life* (directed), *Love and Intrigue, A Streetcar Named Desire* (directed), *Forest of the Hanged* (film)—1965; *Danton's Death, Carnival Scenes*—1966; *As You Like It, The Sea Gull, Julius Caesar, Macbeth*—1968; *Richard II* (directed)—1969; *Volpone* (directed), *Leonce and Lena* (directed)—1970; *Macbeth*–1973; *Leonce and Lena, The Cherry Orchard* (directed)—1974; *Galileo* (directed), *Elizabeth I* (directed)—1976; *The Lower Depths* (directed), *Spring's Awakening* (directed)—1977; *The Inspector General, Hamlet, The Tempest*—1978; *Eve of Retirement* (directed), *Eli: A Mystery Play* (directed), *As You Like It* (directed)—1981; *Requiem for a Nun* (directed), *Peer Gynt* (directed)—1982; *The Threepenny Opera* (directed)—1983; *Twelfth Night* (directed), *Three Sisters* (directed)—1984; *A Midsummer Night's Dream* (directed)—1985; *The Bacchae* (directed)—1987; *Platonov* (adapted and directed; American Repertory Theatre, Cambridge, Massachusetts)—1988.

Ciulei is an example of the rare theatre artist who directs as well as designs. In recent years, he has become better known for his direction, but his productions always have a very strong visual style. They are highly original, and audiences have strong reactions, both positive and negative, to his productions. Ciulei made his reputation as one of the leading directors and designers in Europe. He was the artistic director of the Bulandra Theatre in Bucharest for ten years before coming to the United States, where his direction of shows like *Hamlet* and Buchner's *Leonce and Lena* for Arena Stage in Washington, D.C. led to his appointment as artistic director of the Guthrie Theatre in Minneapolis. He served in that position from 1981 to 1985. Initially trained as an architect, Ciulei favors stark, formal decor that serves as a scenic apparatus rather than as a setting. His set for *Macbeth* (1968) was a huge box of polished sycamore and brass. Inspired by Da Vinci's war machines, it had huge structural elements that interlocked and rearranged to form new configurations. At the Guthrie, he created an immediate furor by redesigning the shape of the stage from its original hexagon to a larger square. He also directed and designed a controversial production of *The Tempest* in which the stage was surrounded by a moat of blood littered with the artifacts of western civilization. With designer Santo Loquasto, he set *Peer Gynt* in the Industrial Revolution with a constructivist set backed by a wall of mirrors. During Ciulei's five-year tenure at the Guthrie, the theatre won a special Tony

Award, and avant-garde directors like Peter Sellars were given a place to experiment.

Further Reading: "Ciulei's Way: What Is This Tradition Thing?" *Connoisseur Magazine* August 1984; Henry III, W. A. "Moonbeams and Menaces." *Time* August 26, 1985: 65; Lieberman, Susan. "Style on Stage: Liviu Ciulei Reshapes the Guthrie." *Theatre Crafts* August/September 1983; "New Man at the Guthrie." *Newsweek* June 29, 1981.

Ken Kloth

Clare, Joseph. Scene designer (b. 1846, England; d. June 3, 1917). Clare began his career as an apprentice to William Bronson and painted scenery at the Theatre Royal in Liverpool. Soon after, he moved to New York City at the age of twenty-five to design scenery for plays produced for Wallack's Theatre. There he designed many plays, including Lester Wallack's production of *The World* (1880). A newspaper critic much admired Clare's scenery and effects, which consisted of an explosion of dynamite on a ship at sea, followed by the bursting of flames; a raft floating on a boundless sea; and other such melodramatic creations. The critic described Clare's work as a masterpiece of the stage carpenter's and painter's art, while he condemned the script as "dramatic rot." His other productions, as well, featured his highly pictorial scenery, such as *Cleopatra* (1891), produced at the Fifth Avenue Theatre. Clare also worked at the Standard Theatre and for many other American producers.

Further Reading: Oenslager (see Bibliography).

Annie Milton

Clark, Peggy. Lighting, set, and costume designer and technical supervisor (b. September 30, 1915, Baltimore, MD). Theatrical productions (all are for lighting design and were produced in New York City, unless otherwise noted) include *The Girl from Wyoming* (costumes; American Music Hall)—1938; *Wuthering Heights* (technical supervisor; Longacre Theatre)—1939; *Gabrielle* (set and lighting; Maxine Elliott's Theatre)—1941; *Uncle Harry* (costumes; Broadhurst Theatre), *It's Up to You* (U.S. Dept. of Agriculture tour), *The Great Big Doorstep* (Morosco Theatre), *Stage Door* (codesigner; American Theatre Wing), *Lunchtime Follies*—1942; *Counterattack* (Windsor Theatre), *A Connecticut Yankee* (technical supervisor; Martin Beck Theatre), *The Innocent Voyage* (technical supervisor; Belasco Theatre)—1943; *Ramshackle Inn* (costumes; Royale Theatre), *Laffing Room Only* (technical supervisor; Winter Garden Theatre), *On the Town* (technical supervisor and stage manager; Adelphi Theatre)—1944; *Dark of the Moon* (costumes; 46th Street Theatre), *Devils Galore* (Royale Theatre), *Billion Dollar Baby* (technical supervisor; Alvin Theatre)—1945; *Twilight Bar* (Ford's Theatre, Baltimore, Maryland), *Beggar's Holiday* (Broadway Theatre), *Brigadoon* (lighting and technical supervisor; Ziegfeld Theatre)—1946; *High Button Shoes* (Century Theatre), *Medea* (National Theatre), *Bonanza Bound!* (Shubert Theatre, Philadelphia), *Topaze* (technical supervisor; Morosco Theatre)—1947; *Look Ma, I'm Dancin'* (technical supervisor; Adelphi Theatre);

That's the Ticket (Shubert Theatre, Philadelphia), *Love Life* (46th Street Theatre), *The Rape of Lucretia* (Ziegfeld Theatre)—1948; *Along Fifth Avenue* (Broadhurst Theatre), *Miss Liberty* (Imperial Theatre), *Touch and Go* (Broadhurst Theatre), *Gentlemen Prefer Blondes* (Ziegfeld Theatre)—1949; *All You Need Is One Good Break* (Mansfield Theatre), *Cry of the Peacock* (Mansfield Theatre), *Bless You All* (Mark Hellinger Theatre)—1950; *The High Ground* (setting, lighting, and costumes; 48th Street Theatre), *Paint Your Wagon* (Shubert Theatre)—1951; *Pal Joey* (Broadhurst Theatre), *Curtain Going Up* (Forrest Theatre, Philadelphia), *Of Thee I Sing* (Ziegfeld Theatre), *Song of Norway* (Philharmonic Auditorium, Los Angeles), *Jollyanna* (Curran Theatre, San Francisco), Agnes de Mille Dance Theatre tour—1952; *Maggie* (National Theatre), *Wonderful Town* (Winter Garden Theatre), *Carnival in Flanders* (technical supervisor; New Century Theatre), *The Trip to Bountiful* (Henry Miller's Theatre); *Kismet* (Ziegfeld Theatre), *In the Summer House* (Playhouse Theatre)—1953; *Bullfight* (Theatre de Lys), *The Threepenny Opera* (Theatre de Lys), *Brigadoon* (Philharmonic Auditorium, Los Angeles), *On Your Toes* (46th Street Theatre), *Peter Pan* (Winter Garden), *Carousel* (New York City Center)—1954; *Plain and Fancy* (Mark Hellinger Theatre), *Kiss Me, Kate* (Philharmonic Auditorium, Los Angeles), *Will Success Spoil Rock Hunter?* (Belasco Theatre), *No Time for Sergeants* (Alvin Theatre), *The Righteous Are Bold* (Holiday Theatre)—1955; *The Amazing Adele* (Shubert Theatre, Philadelphia), *Mr. Wonderful* (Broadway Theatre), *The Ziegfeld Follies* (Shubert Theatre), *New Faces of 1956* (Ethel Barrymore Theatre), *Rosalinda* (Philharmonic Auditorium, Los Angeles), *No Time for Sergeants* (national tour), *Auntie Mame* (Broadhurst Theatre and national tour), *Bells Are Ringing* (Shubert Theatre)—1956; *Brigadoon, The Merry Widow, South Pacific, Carousel, The Pajama Game* (all for the New York City Center), *Annie Get Your Gun, South Pacific* (both for Curran Theatre, San Francisco, and Philharmonic Auditorium, Los Angeles), *The Carefree Heart* (Cass Theatre, Detroit), *Nude with Violin* (Belasco Theatre), *Eugenia* (Ambassador Theatre)—1957; *Annie Get Your Gun, Wonderful Town, Oklahoma!* (all for the New York City Center), *Say, Darling* (ANTA Theatre), *Carousel, Susannah, Wonderful Town* (all three for the Brussels World Exposition, Belgium), *Flower Drum Song* (St. James Theatre), *Present Laughter* (Belasco Theatre)—1958; *Juno* (Winter Garden Theatre), *Oklahoma!* (California), *Billy Barnes Revue* (York Theatre), *Cheri* (Morosco Theatre), *Goodbye Charlie* (Lyceum Theatre)—1959; *A Distant Bell* (Eugene O'Neill Theatre), *Bye Bye Birdie* (Martin Beck Theatre), *The Unsinkable Molly Brown* (Winter Garden Theatre), *Under the Yum-Yum Tree* (Henry Miller's Theatre)—1960; *Showgirl* (Eugene O'Neill Theatre), *Mary, Mary* (Helen Hayes Theatre), *The Merry Widow* (Philharmonic Auditorium, Los Angeles), *Guys and Dolls* (Philharmonic Auditorium, Los Angeles), *Sail Away* (Broadhurst Theatre)—1961; *Paradise Island* (Marine Theatre, Jones Beach, Long Island), *Romulus* (Music Box Theatre), *The Song of Norway* (Philharmonic Theatre, Los Angeles), *Kismet* (Curran Theatre, San Francisco), *Eddie Fisher at the Winter Garden* (Winter Garden Theatre)—1962; *Brigadoon, Wonderful Town, Okla-*

homa!, Pal Joey, The King and I (all at the New York City Center), *Carousel*
(Curran Theatre, San Francisco), *Around the World in 80 Days* (Marine Theatre,
Jones Beach, Long Island), 1964 Chevrolet industrial show (Masonic Temple,
Detroit), *The Time of the Barracudas* (Geary Theatre, San Francisco), *The Girl
Who Came to Supper* (Broadway Theatre)—1963; *Kiss Me, Kate* (Philharmonic
Auditorium, Los Angeles), *Bajour* (Shubert Theatre), *Poor Richard* (Helen
Hayes Theatre), *Brigadoon* (New York City Center)—1964; *Guys and Dolls,
Kiss Me, Kate, South Pacific, Oklahoma!* (all for the New York City Center
Light Opera Company), *The Great Waltz* (Los Angeles Civic Light Opera As-
sociation, Music Center)—1965; *How to Succeed in Business Without Really
Trying, The Most Happy Fella, Where's Charley?*, and *Guys and Dolls* (all for
the New York City Center Light Opera Company), *The Best Laid Plans* (Brooks
Atkinson Theatre), *Mardi Gras!* (Marine Theatre, Jones Beach, Long Island),
The Student Prince (Los Angeles Civic Light Opera Association, Music Center),
The Rose Tattoo (New York City Center)—1966; *Finian's Rainbow, The Sound
of Music, Wonderful Town, Brigadoon* (all at the New York City Center Light
Opera Company), *Dumas and Son* (Los Angeles Civic Light Opera Association,
Music Center), *Arabian Nights* (Marine Theatre, Jones Beach, Long Island),
Showboat (Los Angeles Civic Light Opera Association, Music Center), *People
Is the Thing That the World Is Fullest Of* (consultant; Bil Baird Puppet Theatre)—
1967; *Darling of the Day* (George Abbott Theatre), *Rosalinda* (Los Angeles
Civic Light Opera Association, Music Center), *South Pacific* (Marine Theatre,
Jones Beach, Long Island)—1968; *Jimmy* (Winter Garden Theatre), *Last of the
Red Hot Lovers* (Eugene O'Neill Theatre), *My Fair Lady* and *1491* (Los Angeles
Civic Light Opera Association, Music Center)—1969; *The Sound of Music* (Ma-
rine Theatre, Jones Beach, Long Island), *Cavalcade of Musical Theatre* (Los
Angeles Civic Light Opera Association, Music Center)—1970; *How the Other
Half Loves* (Royal Theatre), *Candide* (Opera House, Kennedy Center, Wash-
ington, D.C.)—1971; *The King and I* (Marine Theatre, Jones Beach, Long
Island)—1972; *Carousel* (Marine Theatre, Jones Beach), *The Whistling Wizard
and The Sultan of Tuffet, Pinocchio*, and *Bandwagon* (three at the Bil Baird
Puppet Theatre)—1973; *Alice in Wonderland*—1974; *Winnie the Pooh* and *Davy
Jones's Locker* (both at the Bil Baird Puppet Theatre), *The Student Prince* and
The Merry Widow (Light Opera of Manhattan)—1976; *Mlle. Modiste, Grand
Duchess, Babes in Toyland*—1978; *Musical Chairs* (Rialto Theatre)—1980; *A
Night In Venice* (Light Opera of Manhattan)—1982; *The Desert Song* (Light
Opera of Manhattan)—1988.

Clark is best known for her successful Broadway lighting designs. After
graduating from Smith College in 1935, she enrolled in the M.F.A. program at
Yale and received her degree in 1938. Her first scenic design job was in 1938
at the Green Mansions Summer Theatre in Warrentown, New York, and her
first Broadway show was *The Girl from Wyoming* as costume designer in the
same year. During World War II, she was involved with shows presented by
the American Theatre Wing, as well as the Department of Agriculture.

In 1944 Clark's career was advanced by meeting producer-designer Oliver Smith, who hired her to stage manage the musical *On the Town*. After the enormous success of this show, Clark and Smith embarked on a collaboration that would last for more than twenty years, beginning with *Beggar's Holiday* (1946). During this production Clark met her future husband, Lloyd R. Kelley, who was chief electrician on the show and with whom she formed a working partnership. With Smith, she designed lighting for approximately forty-three Broadway productions, including such shows as *Brigadoon* (1947), *High Button Shoes* (1947), *Gentlemen Prefer Blondes* (1949), *Miss Liberty* (1949), *The Unsinkable Molly Brown* (1960), *Mary, Mary* (1961), and *Last of the Red Hot Lovers* (1969). Her talents afforded her opportunities to work at other venues such as off-Broadway's Theatre de Lys as the lighting designer for Brecht's *The Threepenny Opera* in 1954 and at the New York City Center Theatre on such revivals as *The Sound of Music* (1967), *Oklahoma!* (1965), and *South Pacific* (1965). In addition, she has designed lighting for dance, including DeMille's *Fall River Legend* (1948) at American Ballet Theatre, and has technically supervised operas, including *Martha* (1960) at the Metropolitan Opera. Clark has an extensive number of lighting design credits for operas and musicals produced with the Manhattan Light Opera and the Los Angeles Civic Light Opera. In 1972, as a result of her husband's death, she reduced her work load but maintained her career by designing lighting on a less frequent basis.

Clark has not been content to limit herself to only theatre design activities and as a result engaged in many ancillary responsibilities. In 1968, for example, she was named the president of the United Scenic Artists, Local 829, the first woman to hold that post in the union. In addition, she has found it important to disseminate her ideas of design and has taught at the Polakov Studio and Forum of Stage Design and as a guest lecturer at the Yale School of Drama.

Further Reading: Chinoy, Helen, and Linda Walsh Jenkins. *Women in the American Theatre*. New York: Crown, 1981. Clark contributed a career reminiscence called "If Not an Actress, What . . . ?"

Thomas J. Mikotowicz

Clavé, Antoni. Set designer and painter (b. 1913, Barcelona, Spain). Theatrical productions include *Los Caprichos*—1946; *Carmen*—1949; *Ballabile, Feuerwerk*—1950; *The House of Bernarda Alba, Revanche*—1951; *Le Nozze di Figaro, Amor de Don Perlimplin con Belisa en su Jardin*—1952; *Deuil en 24 Heures*—1953; *Susanna and the Barber*—1956. In addition, he has designed two dance movies: *Revanche*—1951; *Carmen*—1980.

Born in Spain, Clavé came to Paris in 1939 as a refugee from the Spanish civil war. He became a student of Boris Kochno and was influenced by the works of Bonnard and Roualt. In 1946, Clavé produced his first decor for the Ballets des Champs-Elysées in London. This was *Los Caprichos*, which signaled the designer's preference for the stark use of red, white, and black. In his designs for *Carmen*, produced three years later, he added ladders, wooden chairs, shutters, staircases, scaffoldings, ropes, and draperies placed around the stage in a haphazard manner. In this way he wanted both to aid the action and utilize the three-dimensionality of the performance space. He repeatedly used these same elements to suggest circus tents, a Mediterranean seaport, and street scenes in the designs executed for choreographers Roland Petit and Ruth Page during the first decade of his career.

Further Reading: Hering, Doris. "Ballets de Paris." *Dance Magazine* November 1949: 10+.

Andrea J. Nouryeh

Colt, Alvin. Costume and set designer (b. July 5, 1916, Louisville, KY). Theatrical productions (all as costume designer, and produced in New York City, unless otherwise specified) include *Charade, Pastorale* (sets and costumes; both for American Ballet Caravan)—1940; *Saratoga* (ballet; Metropolitan Opera House), *Slavonika* (ballet; 44th Street Theatre)—1941; *On the Town* (Adelphi Theatre), *Waltz Academy* (ballet; Boston Opera House, Massachusetts)—1944; *On Stage!* (ballet; sets and costumes; Boston Opera House, Massachusetts), *Graziana* (ballet; sets and costumes; Metropolitan Opera House)—1945; *Around the World in Eighty Days* (Adelphi Theatre)—1946; *Barefoot Boy with Cheek* (Martin Beck Theatre), *Music in My Heart* (sets and costumes; Adelphi Theatre)—1947; *Clutterbuck* (Biltmore Theatre)—1949; *Guys and Dolls* (sets and costumes; 46th Street Theatre)—1950; *The Miraculous Mandarin* (sets and costumes; City Center Theatre), *Top Banana* (Winter Garden Theatre)—1951; *Kaleidoscope* (ballet; New York City Ballet, City Center Theatre)—1952; *The Frogs of Spring* (Broadhurst Theatre)—1953; *The Golden Apple* (Alvin Theatre), *Fanny* (Majestic Theatre), *Coriolanus* (Phoenix Repertory Theatre), *Top Banana* (film; United Artists)—1954; *Guys and Dolls, Finian's Rainbow* (both at City Center Theatre), *The Lark* (Longacre Theatre), *Pipe Dream* (Shubert Theatre), *The Doctor's Dilemma, The Master Builder, Phoenix '55, The Carefree Tree, Six Characters in Search of an Author* (all for the Phoenix Repertory Theatre)—1955; *Kiss Me, Kate* (City Center Theatre), *The Sleeping Prince* (Coronet Theatre), *L'il Abner* (St. James Theatre), *Miss Julie, The Stronger, A Month in the Country, The Littlest Revue, The Diary of a Scoundrel* (all for the Phoenix Repertory Theatre)—1956; *Copper and Brass* (Martin Beck Theatre), *Rumple* (Alvin Theatre), *Livin' the Life, Mary Stuart* (both for the Phoenix Repertory Theatre), *Maiden Voyage* (Forrest Theatre, Philadelphia, Pennsylvania)—1957; *Blue Denim* (Playhouse Theatre), *Say, Darling* (ANTA Theatre), *Hamlet* (American Shakespeare Festival, Stratford, Connecticut)—1958; *First Impressions* (Alvin Theatre), *Destry Rides Again* (Imperial Theatre), *L'il Abner* (film; Paramount)—1959; *Greenwillow, Wildcat* (both for the Alvin Theatre), *Christine* (46th Street Theatre)—1960; *13 Daughters* (54th Street Theatre)—1961; *The Beauty Part* (Music Box Theatre), *The Aspern Papers* (Playhouse Theatre), *The Turn of the Screw* (New York City Opera, City Center Theatre)—1962; *Here's Love* (Shubert Theatre), *The Infernal Machine, Abe Lincoln in Illinois* (both for the Phoenix Repertory Theatre)—1963; *Something More!* (Eugene O'Neill Theatre), *The Yeoman of the Guard* (City Center Theatre), *Wonderworld* (New York City World's Fair), *Ring 'Round the Moon, The Crucible* (both for the National Repertory Theatre, Belasco Theatre)—1964; *Anna Karenina* (Goodman Memorial Theatre, Chicago, Illinois)—1965; *Henry, Sweet Henry* (Palace Theatre), *The Paisley Convertible* (Henry Miller's Theatre), *The Imaginary Invalid, A Touch of the Poet, Tonight at Eight-Thirty* (all for the National Repertory Theatre, ANTA Theatre), *The Comedy of Errors* (with Jane Greenwood*; Ford's Theatre, Washington, D.C.)—1967; *The Goodbye People* (Ethel Barrymore Theatre), *John Brown's Body, She Stoops to Conquer* (both at Ford's Theatre, Washington, D.C.)—1968; *Stiletto* (film; Avco-Embassy)—1969; *The Ballad of Johnny Pot* (Theatre Four)—1971; *Sugar* (Majestic Theatre)—1972; *Lorelei* (Palace Theatre)—1974; *The Roast* (Winter Garden Theatre)—1980; *Broadway Follies* (Nederlander Theatre)—1981; *Night of 100 Stars* (Radio City Music Hall)—1982; *Parade of Stars Playing the Palace* (Palace Theatre)—1983; *Night of 100 Stars II* (Radio City Music Hall)—1985; *Night of 100 Stars III* (Radio City Music Hall)—1990.

Colt received his early theatre training at the Yale School of Drama, where he studied with Professor George Pierce Baker, and received a degree in theatre arts in 1937 as the youngest member of his graduating class. Following graduation, Colt went to Elitch Gardens in Denver, Colorado, where he assisted director Norris Houghton with the sets and costumes for a number of productions, including Michael Kidd's ballet *On Stage!* He received his first solo credits in 1940 when he designed both sets and costumes for the ballets *Charade* and *Pastorale* for the American Ballet Caravan. Four years later, he designed the costumes for *On the Town*, his first Broadway production. Throughout the 1940s, 1950s, and 1960s Colt remained one of Broadway's top costume designers and provided the designs for such productions as *Guys and Dolls* (1950), *The Golden Apple* (1954), *L'il Abner* (1956), and *Wildcat* (1960), as well as designing many productions at the Phoenix Repertory Theatre. In addition, he continued to design for both opera and ballet and provided costume designs for the New York City Ballet and the New York City Opera. In the 1970s and 1980s Colt slowed the pace somewhat but continued to remain active, providing costumes for the three Actors Equity "Night of 100 Stars" benefits, as well as awards programs such as the Emmy and Tony awards shows. In 1989, some of his musical costume designs were revived as part of *Jerome Robbins' Broadway*.

Colt feels that color is the most important element to consider onstage. But Colt's designing jobs do not end with the rough color sketches he makes of each costume on paper. Once the design is approved, he personally supervises the purchase of materials and the cutting and fitting of each garment. As a designer, however, Colt is probably best known for closing the gap between the everyday clothes people wear and the costumes they see onstage. For *Here's Love* (1963), Meredith Wilson's musical based on the film *Miracle on 34th Street*, Colt assayed a realistic approach for many of the costumes. He made sketches of certain scenes, then accompanied buyers from Macy's on their rounds of Seventh Avenue and the men's and children's wear markets to find clothes that fitted his specifications. Selections were made from manufacturers' regular lines, and many of the clothes that were selected for the stage were later made available at Macy's after the show opened. "People are very knowledgeable about clothes today," Colt has said. "You can't fool them with a lot of fur sequins on stage." Colt keeps up with offstage fashion design through his connection with the Neiman-Marcus department store. He is designer of special events for the Dallas store, under whose aegis he has attended couture fashion showings in Paris and wholesale collections in New York.

   Awards: Colt received the Tony Award for Best Costume Design in 1956 for his designs for *Pipe Dream, The Lark*, and *Phoenix '55*.

   Further Reading: "The Designing Mr. Colt." *Dance Magazine* November 1945.

                                                                                                                 Howard Gutner

Conklin, John. Designer (b. 1937, Farmington, CT). Theatrical productions include *The Lady's Not for Burning* (sets and costumes; Yale Dramatic Association, New Haven, Connecticut)—1956; *The Crucible, A View from the Bridge* (both for the Yale Dramatic Association, New Haven, Connecticut)—1957; *Cyrano de Bergerac, The Skin of Our Teeth, Danton's Death* (all for the Yale Dramatic Association, New Haven, Connecticut), *Time Remembered* (Williamstown Theatre Festival, Massachusetts)—1958; *The Brothers Karamazov, Charley's Aunt* (both at the Williamstown Theatre Festival, Massachusetts), *The Inspector General, Grand Tour* (both for the Yale Dramatic Association, New Haven, Connecticut), *Volpone* (Yale School of Drama, New Haven, Connecticut)—1959; *The Way of the World* (with Richard Casler; Institute for Advanced Studies in the Theatre Arts, New York), *Camino Real* (Yale Dramatic Association, New Haven, Connecticut)—1960; *Becket, The Sap of Life, Toys in the Attic, Once in a Lifetime* (sets and costumes), *The Five-Finger Exercise, Othello* (all for the Williamstown Theatre Festival), *Thieves' Carnival, Booth Is Back in Town* (both for the Yale Dramatic Association, New Haven, Connecticut), *The Decameron* (East 74th Street Theatre)—1961; *Peer Gynt* (Yale School of Drama, New Haven, Connecticut), *Mr. Booth, The Birthday Party, The Cherry Orchard* (all at the Williamstown Theatre Festival, Massachusetts), *Tambourines to Glory* (sets and costumes; The Little Theatre)—1963; *Othello* (sets and costumes; Hartford Stage Company, Connecticut), *The Rivals, As You Desire Me, The Birds* (all for the McCarter Theatre Company)—1964; *Uncle Vanya, She Stoops to Conquer, Waiting for Godot, The Tempest* (all for the Hartford Stage Company, Connecticut), *The Night Chanter* (Hunter College, New York), *Le Nozze di Figaro*—1965; *The Play of Daniel, The Play of Herod* (both for the New York Pro Musica, New York), *The Importance of Being Earnest, Twelfth Night, The Balcony* (all for the Hartford Stage Company, Connecticut), *Ondine, Marat/Sade, Annie Get Your Gun* (all at the Williamstown Theatre Festival, Massachusetts), *Dialogues of the Carmelites* (New York State Theatre), *The*

Beggar's Opera (Yale School of Drama, New Haven, Connecticut), *U.S.A.* (Theatre of the Living Arts, Philadelphia, Pennsylvania)—1966; *Enrico IV, The Servant of Two Masters, The Fantasticks, Who's Afraid of Virginia Woolf?, Skinflint Out West, A View from the Bridge* (all for the Hartford Theatre Company, Connecticut), *Beclch* (Theatre of the Living Arts, Philadelphia, Pennsylvania), *The Old Maid, Thief, The Medium* (Western Opera Theatre, San Francisco, California), *Saint Joan, Peer Gynt* (both at the Williamstown Theatre Festival), *The Playboy of the Western World* (Long Wharf Theatre, New Haven, Connecticut), *The Rivals* (Seattle Repertory Theatre, Washington)—1967; *Bagatelles* (Pennsylvania Ballet, Philadelphia), *Antigone, The Firebugs, The Threepenny Opera* (all for the Hartford Stage Company, Connecticut), *Galileo, Iphigenia in Aulis, Camino Real* (all at the Williamstown Theatre Festival, Massachusetts), *Six Characters in Search of an Author, Marat/Sade, The Threepenny Opera* (all at the Arena Stage, Washington, D.C.), *Salome* (Baltimore Civic Light Opera, Maryland), *The Duchess of Malfi* (Long Wharf Theatre, New Haven, Connecticut)—1968; *Cosi fan tutte* (Santa Fe Opera, New Mexico), *The Threepenny Opera* (sets and costumes; Williamstown Theatre Festival, Massachusetts)—1969; *Macbeth* (McCarter Theatre Company), *The Skin of Our Teeth, A Place Without Doors* (both at the Long Wharf Theatre, New Haven, Connecticut)—1970; *Mother Courage, Cyrano de Bergerac* (both at the Williamstown Theatre Festival, Massachusetts), *Scratch* (St. James Theatre, New York), *Beatrix Cenci* (Opera Society of Washington, D.C.), *What the Butler Saw* (Arena Stage, Washington, D.C.), *Hamlet* (Long Wharf Theatre, New Haven, Connecticut), *The Marriage of Figaro* (sets and costumes; Minnesota Opera, St. Paul), *Overture, The Grand Tour, O.W.* (both for the Royal Ballet, London)—1971; *Once in a Lifetime, The Resistible Rise of Arturo Ui, Mary Stuart* (all at the Williamstown Theatre Festival, Massachusetts), *The Hostage, Twelfth Night* (both at the Arena Stage, Washington, D.C.), *The Nutcracker, Swan Lake* (both for the Pennsylvania Ballet, Philadelphia), *Agamemnon* (McCarter Theatre Company), *The Misanthrope, Loot* (both for the Hartford Stage Company, Connecticut), *Orfeo* (sets and costumes; San Francisco Opera, California), *What Price Glory?* (Long Wharf Theatre, New Haven, Connecticut), *The Barber of Seville* (sets and costumes; Minnesota Opera)—1972; *The Master Builder, The Resistible Rise of Arturo Ui* (both at the Long Wharf Theatre, New Haven, Connecticut), *Nobody's Earnest, The Good Woman of Setzuan, Saint Joan* (all at the Williamstown Theatre Festival, Massachusetts), *Beatrix Cenci* (New York City Opera), *Indians* (Temple University, Philadelphia, Pennsylvania), *The Au Pair Man* (New York Shakespeare Festival, Vivian Beaumont Theatre), *Cosi fan tutte* (John F. Kennedy Center, Washington, D.C.), *Other Voices, Other Rooms* (Studio Arena Theatre, Buffalo, New York), *Ubu Roi* (Hartford Stage Company, Connecticut), *The Marriage of Figaro* (sets and costumes; Houston Grand Opera, Texas), *The Barber of Seville* (Opera Society of Washington, D.C.)—1973; *Lorelei* (The Palace Theatre), *Cat on a Hot Tin Roof, Romeo and Juliet, Twelfth Night* (all at the American Shakespeare Festival), *Pericles* (Delacorte Theatre), *Richard*

III (Vivan Beaumont Theatre), *Juno and the Paycock* (Mark Taper Forum, Los Angeles, California), *The Threepenny Opera* (Williamstown Theatre Festival, Massachusetts)—1974; *Room Service* (Hartford Stage Company, Connecticut), *Savages* (Williamstown Theatre Festival, Massachusetts), *A Death in Venice* (San Francisco Opera, California), *The Winter's Tale, Our Town* (both at the American Shakespeare Festival), *Kismet* (sets and costumes; Wolf Trap Theatre, Virginia), *The Scarecrow* (Kennedy Center, Eisenhower Theatre, Washington, D.C.), *The Leaf People* (Booth Theatre, New York)—1975; *Merton of the Movies* (Ahmanson Theatre), *Rex* (sets and costumes; Lunt-Fontanne Theatre, New York), *Cat on a Hot Tin Roof, Rosencrantz and Guildenstern Are Dead* (Guthrie Theatre, Minneapolis, Minnesota), *The Rose Tattoo* (Long Wharf Theatre, New Haven, Connecticut), *A History of the American Film* (Mark Taper Forum, Los Angeles, California), *As You Like It* (American Shakespeare Festival), *A Midsummer Night's Dream* (opera; sets and costumes; Wolf Trap Theatre, Virginia), *Waltz of the Toreadors* (Hartford Stage Company)—1976; *A Moon for the Misbegotten* (Guthrie Theatre, Minneapolis, Minnesota), *Un ballo in maschera* (sets and costumes; San Francisco Opera, California), *Fedora* (Santa Fe Opera, New Mexico), *Angel City* (Mark Taper Forum, Los Angeles, California), *Chez Nous* (Manhattan Theatre Club, New York), *Romeo and Juliet* (costumes; Circle in the Square, New York), *Julius Caesar* (costumes; American Conservatory Theatre, San Francisco, California), *The Recruiting Officer* (sets and costumes; Long Wharf Theatre, New Haven, Connecticut), *Bully!* (sets and costumes; 46th Street Theatre, New York), *All the Way Home* (Hartford Stage Company, Connecticut)—1977; *Rain* (Hartford Stage Company, Connecticut), *A Month in the Country* (Williamstown Theatre Festival, Massachusetts), *Eugene Onegin, The Duchess of Malfi* (both for the Santa Fe Opera, New Mexico), *Julius Caesar* (opera; sets and costumes; San Francisco Opera, California), *La Traviata* (Minnesota Opera), *The Turk in Italy* (sets and costumes; New York City Opera)—1978; *Medea, Miss Havisham's Fire* (both for the New York City Opera), *Galileo* (Hartford Stage Company, Connecticut), *Lulu* (Santa Fe Opera, New Mexico), *Cyrano de Bergerac, Journey's End* (both for the Long Wharf Theatre, New Haven, Connecticut), *Romeo and Juliet* (California Shakespeare Festival, Visalia), *The Resistible Rise of Arturo Ui, Camino Real* (both at the Williamstown Theatre Festival, Massachusetts), *Werther* (sets and costumes; Houston Opera, Texas), *The Merry Widow* (Central City Opera, Denver, Colorado), *A Lovely Sunday for Creve Coeur* (Hudson Guild Theatre, New York), *La Traviata* (St. Louis Opera, Missouri)—1979; *Ardèle* (Hartford Stage Company, Connecticut), *Chekhov in Yalta, Twelfth Night* (both for the Mark Taper Forum, Los Angeles, California), *Romeo and Juliet* (sets and costumes; Hartford Ballet, Connecticut), *The Bacchae* (sets and costumes; Circle in the Square, New York), *The Magic Flute* (sets and costumes; St. Louis Opera, Missouri), *Hamlet, A Midsummer Night's Dream* (sets and costumes; both at the California Shakespeare Festival), *The Philadelphia Story* (Vivian Beaumont Theatre, New York), *Don Pasquale* (San Francisco Opera, California)—1980; *Cymbeline, Kean, Antony and Cleo-*

patra (sets and costumes; all for the Hartford Stage Company, Connecticut), *Don Quichotte* (Netherlands Opera, Amsterdam), *Daphne* (Santa Fe Opera, New Mexico)—1981; *Colette* (Fifth Avenue Theatre, Seattle, Washington), *The Greeks* (set and costumes), *The Portage to San Cristobal of A.H.* (Hartford Stage Company, Connecticut)—1982; *Die Walküre, Das Rheingold* (both for the San Francisco Opera, California), *Pollichino* (sets and costumes; Cabrillo Festival, Aptos, California), *Arabella* (Santa Fe Opera, New Mexico), *Terra Nova* (Portland Stage Company, Maine), *La Grande-Duchesse de Gérolstein* (New York City Opera)—1983; *The Three Sisters* (Hartford Stage Company, Connecticut), *Awake and Sing!* (Circle in the Square, New York), *Siegfried* (San Francisco Opera, California), *Cosi fan tutte, Marriage of Figaro* (Netherlands Opera, Amsterdam), *We Come to the River* (Santa Fe Opera, New Mexico), *Battle of Legnano* (Pittsburgh Opera, Pennsylvania)—1984; *The Misanthrope, Pride and Prejudice*—1985; *Alcestis, The Tooth of Crime*—1986; *Sweet Table at the Richelieu, Infidelities*—1987; *A Streetcar Named Desire*—1988; *City of Angels*—1989; *Macbeth*—1990.

Conklin is among the most prolific American designers; his Broadway credits begin with *Tambourines to Glory* in 1963 and include the recent *City of Angels* (1989). He has designed classics and new works extensively for regional and repertory theatres, including a longtime association with the Williamstown Theatre Festival and the Hartford Stage Company. He has also designed for major opera and ballet companies, such as American Opera Society, Santa Fe Opera, Washington Opera Society, and Houston Grand Opera. He has served as a Visiting Professor of Design at Temple University.

Conklin respects past theatrical traditions; thus he seems to prefer large, romantic operatic works that allow him broad conceptual range, rather than naturalistic contemporary works. Such productions as his *Macbeth* (1990), as well as *The Misanthrope* (1985) and *Alcestis* (1986), evidence this preference. Further, he seems drawn to past plays and operas that remain, in some part, relevant to contemporary values and situations. In designing a work, Conklin seeks the aspects that resonate most completely with the present. His style ranges from his heavily detailed naturalism of *The Three Sisters* (1984) to his minimalistic and highly eclectic style for *The Tooth of Crime* (1986). Conklin emphasizes that a scenic design must move an audience emotionally, and he attempts to illuminate the psychological and social state of a play as well.

Further Reading: Aronson (see Bibliography).

James Fisher

Cook, Ansel. Scenic painter (b. ?, United States; d. ?). Cook was one of the scenic studio painters who worked extensively during the latter nineteenth and early twentieth centuries in America. His scenery appeared at the Castle Square Theatre in Boston, as well as at many other theatres in the United States. From 1897 to 1902, Cook was ''scenic artist'' of the Castle Square Stock Company and then worked at Chicago's Sosman and Landis Studio. Remembered as a ''fine drapery painter'' by Arthur Oberbec, elder scenic artist at the Peter Wolf Studio in Dallas, Texas, Cook used an effuse scenic style reminiscent of neoclassical European palace settings. His style anticipated that used in America's ornate movie palaces and was possibly an influence on such designers as Claude Bragdon.*

Further Reading: Oenslager (see Bibliography).

Annie Milton

Coutaud, Lucien. Set designer, painter, and illustrator (b. December 13, 1904, Meynes, France). Theatrical productions include *The Birds*—1928 and 1929; *La Vie en Rose*—1931; *Venus et Adonis*—1932; *Plutus, As You Like It*—1938; *800 Metres*—1941; *Le Soulier de Satin*—1943; *Le Poete*—1945; *Jeux de Printemps*—1948; *Elizabeth d'Angleterre*—1949; *Les Éléments*—1950; *Medea*—1953; *Le Seigneur de San Gor*—1954; *Jeanne d'Arc, Protee*—1955.

Internationally known painter, book illustrator, and creator of tapestries, Coutaud began his studies at the École des Beaux-Arts at Nimes in 1920. Four years later in Paris, he studied in various academies and at the École des Arts Decoratifs and came under the influence of such painters as Di Chirico, Ernst, and Klee. His first design was *The Birds*, directed by Charles Dullin in 1928. From 1930 until 1936, he developed a style quite similar to surrealism, but he never became a part of that movement. During this period he did only two pieces for the theatre: *La Vie en Rose* and *Venus et Adonis* for Michel St. Denis. After 1936, Coutaud entered a new phase where intense color and fragmented forms dominated his designs. This style typified his work for Dullin in *Plutus*, and for Jacques Copeau in *As You Like It*. Over the course of his stage design career, he has continued to collaborate with such directors as Copeau, Dullin, and Jean-Louis Barrault and has designed for choreographers Roland Petit and Serge Lifar.

Andrea J. Nouryeh

Craig, Edward Gordon. Designer, director, actor, and theorist (b. January 16, 1872, Stevenage, England; d. July 29, 1966, Vence, France). Craig served as director, scene designer, and costume designer for the following, unless otherwise indicated: *No Trifling With Love* (also acted)—1893; *Dido and Aeneas*—1900; *The Masque of Love*—1900; *Acis and Galatea*—1902; *Bethlehem*—1902; *For Sword and Song* (designed sets and costumes for a few scenes only), *The Vikings, Much Ado About Nothing*—1903; *Venice Preserved* (designed a few scenes only)—1904; *Rosmersholm* (designed only sets)—1906; *Hamlet* (codirected with Konstantin Stanislavsky and designed sets and costumes)—1912; *The Pretenders*—1926; *Macbeth* (contributed some set and costume designs only)—1928.

Without question, Craig was one of the most influential and controversial theatrical figures of the twentieth century. Illegitimate son of legendary English actress Ellen Terry and architect and scene designer Edward William Godwin, he began his career in 1889 as an actor in the company of his mother and actor-manager Henry Irving at London's Lyceum Theatre. Soon after, Craig himself dabbled in producing, beginning in 1893 with a production of Alfred de Musset's *No Trifling With Love* at the Uxbridge Town Hall. Under the management of Ben Greet, he played Hamlet in 1897, but shortly thereafter he terminated his acting career and began to develop a budding interest in designing, directing, and woodcutting. With the financial support of his mother, he published *The Page* in 1898, an eclectic journal of the arts. While still publishing this journal, for which he contributed most of the articles and artwork, often under pseudonyms, he was invited to direct and design a series of small operatic productions for the Purcell Opera Society. These productions, *Dido and Aeneas, The Masque of Love*, and *Acis and Galatea*, were staged with mostly amateur casts and on a limited budget. Craig's simple and evocative abstract designs, employing fabrics and pioneering lighting techniques, caught the attention of a number of critics and theatrical artists. His nonrealistic concepts, coupled with an emphasis on movement and music, seemed a revelation to Max Beerbohm, William Butler Yeats, and others who also yearned for a break with both the traditions of nineteenth-century production values and the naturalistic dramas of the contemporary theatre.

After terminating publication of *The Page* in 1901, Craig hoped to secure his own London theatre, in which he could experiment with his new ideas. But the English theatre was slow to accept change, and Craig's eccentric behavior and exorbitant demands for time and financial support kept him from the mainstream English theatres. In 1902, again on a limited budget and with an amateur cast, he designed and staged *Bethlehem* by Laurence Housman. Again, the critical response was enthusiastic, but no offers for his talents were forthcoming. The following year he convinced his mother to back him financially in a season at London's Imperial Theatre, where she would star in leading roles and he would design and direct. They opened with *The Vikings*, an early play by Henrik Ibsen based on tenth-century Scandinavian mythology. Mixed reviews with Terry's miscasting in the role of a fierce Viking woman, however, forced the play to close after three weeks. They rushed into a second production, Shakespeare's *Much Ado About Nothing*. Craig's simplified and fanciful settings, anticipating the similarly pared-down Shakespearean productions of Harley Granville Barker ten years later, were again well received. Poor ticket sales, however, forced Terry to terminate the Imperial Theatre season and perform in the provinces to recoup her losses. Craig, angry and frustrated by the Imperial failures, exiled himself from England, rarely to return.

In 1904, he met Isadora Duncan, whose free and seemingly spontaneous dancing style helped to solidify many of Craig's ideas about movement and its significance. While touring through Europe with Duncan as her sometime manager and lover, Craig completed and published his highly controversial manifesto *The Art of the Theatre* (1905; an expanded version was issued in 1911 as *On the Art of the Theatre*). In it, Craig called for a rejection of the literary and realistic theatre in favor of an ''art theatre'' to be created by a ''master artist of the theatre,'' an extraordinary individual who would be the dominant force in the production of the play and an expert actor, director, and designer. But his most controversial theory was expounded in his essay "The Actor and the Ueber-marionette," in which he seemed to be calling for the elimination of the living actor in favor of a life-sized puppet under the control of the "master artist." Craig later clarified this theory and suggested that the actor must become a highly controlled, well-trained artist minus the ego.

The diverse reactions to *The Art of the Theatre* and exhibitions of Craig's highly characteristic designs generated many offers of employment, but except for contributing some designs for a production of *Venice Preserved* for Otto Brahm in 1905 and an Italian production of Ibsen's *Rosmersholm* in 1906, starring Eleonora Duse, Craig rejected most offers or made demands that were too outrageous to be met. As a result, opportunities to work with famous German director Max Reinhardt, playwright George Bernard Shaw, and actor-manager Herbert Beerbohm Tree, among many others, vanished. Craig then turned his attention to launching a new journal called *The Mask*, which first appeared in 1908. It continued despite occasional financial setbacks until 1929. Eventually, Craig settled in Florence, where, through *The Mask* and an impressive series of books, articles, and another periodical, *The Marionnette* (1918–1919), he continued to promote his theories and designs.

In 1910, he contributed a few designs to an Abbey Theatre production of Yeats's *The Hour Glass* and gave the playwright a set of his patented scenic screens that he himself used in collaboration with Stanislavsky on a well-known production of *Hamlet* at the Moscow Art Theatre in 1912. The Moscow *Hamlet* was one of the few productions that made use of Craig's most representative designs: huge monolithic structures altered by changing lights. He published some of these designs in his 1913 book *Towards a New Theatre*, influencing many American designers such as Robert Edmond Jones* and Donald Oensla-ger.* Others, however, rejected Craig's theories and designs. Lee Simonson,* for example, condemned them as impractical in his book *The Stage Is Set* (1932).

After the Moscow *Hamlet*, Craig contributed designs to only two other productions, Ibsen's *The Pretenders* in Copenhagen in 1926 and *Macbeth* in New York in 1928. In 1957, his autobiography, covering his life to 1907, was published. He spent the last years of his life in Vence, France, where he was visited by many important artists and critics, including Peter Brook and Kenneth Tynan. Craig's influence on the modern theatre is incalculable, and despite the relatively few realizations of his designs in production during his life, his many publications continue to inspire theatre artists throughout the world.

Awards: Craig received several honors late in his career, including the Order of the Knights of Danneborg for his services to the Danish theatre in 1926; membership in the French Syndicat des metteurs en scene in 1946; Companion of Honour presented by Queen Elizabeth II for his services to the theatre in 1956; and an honorary membership in the United Scenic Artists in New York in 1961.

Further Reading: Books by Craig: *The Art of the Theatre*. Edinburgh: T. N. Foulis, 1905 (enlarged and reprinted as *On the Art of the Theatre*. London: Heinemann, 1911); *Ellen Terry and Her Secret Self*. London: Sampson, Low, Marston, 1931; *Gordon Craig*.

The Story of His Life. New York: Alfred A. Knopf, 1968; *Henry Irving*. London: J. M. Dent, 1930; *Index to the Story of My Days*. London: Hulton Press, 1957. *Nothing or the Bookplate*. London: Chatto and Windus, 1924; *Scene*. London: Humphrey Milford Oxford University Press, 1923; *Some Words*. London: J. M. Dent, 1924; *The Theatre Advancing*. Boston: Little, Brown, 1919; *Towards a New Theatre*. London: J. M. Dent, 1913; *Woodcuts and a Production. 1926*. London: Humphrey Milford Oxford University Press, 1930.

Books about Craig: Bablet, Denis. *Edward Gordon Craig*. Paris: L'Arche, 1962; Innes, Christopher. *Edward Gordon Craig*. Cambridge: Cambridge University Press, 1983; Leeper, Janet. *Edward Gordon Craig: Designs for the Theatre*. Harmondsworth: Penguin Books, 1948; Marker, Frederick J., and Lise-Lone Marker. *Edward Gordon Craig and "The Pretenders."* Carbondale: Southern Illinois University Press, 1981; Rose, Enid. *Gordon Craig and the Theatre*. London: Sampson Low, Marston, 1931; Senelick, Laurence. *Gordon Craig's Moscow "Hamlet."* Westport, CT: Greenwood Press, 1982.

A good source for information about articles by and about Craig, as well as exhibition catalogs, illustrated books, and the like, is Fletcher, Ifan Kyrle, and Arnold Rood. *Edward Gordon Craig. A Bibliography*. Society for Theatre Research, 1967 (covers Craig materials published through 1966).

James Fisher

Craven, Henry Hawes. Scene designer and painter (b. March 29, 1837, Leeds, England; d. July 27, 1910, London, England). Theatrical productions include *The Lighthouse*—1857; *Play*—1868; *School*—1869; *The Bells*—1871; *Hamlet*—1878; *The Merchant of Venice*—1879; *Two Roses, The Cup*—1881; *Romeo and Juliet*—1882; *The Mikado*—1885; *Faust*—1886; *Macbeth*—1888; *King Lear, Henry VIII*—1892; *Becket, Utopia Limited*—1893; *King Arthur*—1895; *Hamlet*—1897; *King John*—1899; *A Midsummer Night's Dream*—1900; *Twelfth Night, Coriolanus, The Only Way*—1901; *Ulysses, Three Little Maids, As You Like It*—1902; *The Merchant of Venice*—1905; *Cinderella, The Bondman*—1906.

Craven began his professional career in 1853 as scenic apprentice to John Gray at the Britannia Theatre in Hoxton and then at the Olympic Theatre. His first assignment came in 1857, when Gray's illness prevented him from completing a production of *The Lighthouse*. During his long career, Craven worked at many theatres, including Covent Garden and Drury Lane and the Theatre Royal in Dublin from 1862 to 1864. Most critics agree that his best work was with Sir Henry Irving at the Lyceum Theatre, where he assumed control in 1878 and remained the primary designer until the theatre was closed in 1902. While there, he worked with other designers such as William Telbin and Walter Hann and created romantic settings such as for *The Merchant of Venice* (1879), *Faust* (1886), and *Macbeth* (1888). Craven was a careful researcher and antiquarian who re-created ancient ruins and locales onstage for enthralled audiences. For example, to obtain authentic details he traveled to Nuremburg in 1885 to research *Faust*. He was capable of rapid work also, as exemplified by his creation in less than two months of elaborate sets for Irving's *Merchant of Venice*, featuring palaces and street scenes. Craven was an excellent painter, and his backdrop for Herbert Beerbohm Tree's *Twelfth Night* was highly praised, as was his *A Midsummer Night's Dream*, which included a blanket of real grass, blossoming bushes, and rabbits. In 1902, Craven used the vacated painting room at the Lyceum to open his own scenic studio and spent the remainder of his career there.

Elbin L. Cleveland

Creuz, Serge. Set designer and teacher (b. May 4, 1924, Molenbeck, Belgium). Creuz was educated at the Académie des Beaux-Arts and École National Supérieure d'Architecture et des Arts Décoratifs in Brussels and worked with designer Christian Bérard.* He has designed more than fifty operatic and theatrical productions since 1950. His most important designs include *Juliette ou la Cle des Songes* (1951); *La Boheme* (1960); *The Visit of the Old Lady* (1961); *The Caucasian Chalk Circle* (1962); and *The Threepenny Opera* (1969). As well as designing for the stage, Creuz has served as a teacher at the École Supérieure d'Art Dramatique in Strasbourg.

Andrea J. Nouryeh

Crow, Laura. Costume designer, teacher, and clothing designer (b. 1945, Hanover, NH). Theatrical productions (all were in New York City unless otherwise specified) include *Electra* (Greenwich Theatre, London)—1971; *Warp* (Ambassador Theatre; with Cookie Gluck), *Hot l Baltimore* (Center Stage, Baltimore, Maryland)—1973; *Sweet Bird of Youth* (Kennedy Center, Washington, D.C.)—1975; *The Farm, Misalliance* (both at the Circle Repertory Theatre)—1976; *Feed Lot, Ulysses in Traction, Brontosaurus* (all at the Circle Repertory Theatre), *Angel City* (McCarter Theatre, Princeton, New Jersey)—1977; *Fifth of July, Glorious Morning, In the Recovery Lounge* (all at the Circle Repertory Theatre), *A Streetcar Named Desire* (Arena Stage, Washington, D.C.), *The Water Engine and Mr. Happiness* (Plymouth Theatre), *The Blood Knot, Of Mice and Men* (both at the Pittsburgh Public Theatre, Pennsylvania)—1978; *Winter Signs, Mary Stuart, Hamlet* (all at the Circle Repertory Theatre), *Uncle Vanya* (Spreckles Theatre, San Diego, California)—1979; *Fifth of July* (Apollo Theatre), *The Taming of the Shrew, An Enemy of the People, Born Yesterday, The Dance of Death, Tintypes* (all at the Seattle Repertory Theatre, Washington)—1980; *A Tale Told* (Mark Taper Forum, Los Angeles, California), *Savages, Awake and Sing* (both at the Seattle Repertory Theatre, Washington), *The Great Grandson of Jedediah Kohler, Richard II* (both at the Entermedia Theatre)—1982; *Full Hookup* (Circle Repertory Theatre)—1983; *Levitation, Love's Labor's Lost* (both at the Circle Repertory Theatre)—1984; *Who's Afraid of Virginia Woolf?, Talley and Son* (both at the Circle Repertory Theatre), *Girl Crazy, The Real Thing* (both at the Seattle Repertory Theatre, Washington)—1985; *Orchards* (Lucille Lortel Theatre), *End Game, The Merry Wives of Windsor* (both at the Seattle Repertory Theatre, Washington)—1986; *Burn This* (Plymouth Theatre)—1987; *Road Show* (Circle Repertory Theatre)—1988; *Brilliant Traces* (Circle Repertory

Company), *Edith Stein* (GeVa, Rochester, New York), *Hedda Gabler* (Pittsburgh Public Theatre)—1989.

Crow received her B.F.A. at Boston University in 1967 and began her career as a teacher of design and construction techniques while still a master's candidate at the University of Wisconsin in 1968. Continuing her education in England, she studied at the Corthauld Institute of Art in London and, later, the London College of Fashion. Her first professional costumes were designed for a production of *Electra* at the Greenwich Theatre in London in 1971. In 1973, she returned to New York, where she created the costumes for *Warp* on Broadway with fellow costumer, Cookie Gluck. Throughout the 1970s, Crow continued to work on Broadway, and she became the resident costume designer at the Circle Repertory Theatre in New York. At Circle Rep, she designed the costumes for many plays, including the first productions of Lanford Wilson's *Fifth of July* (1980) and *Burn This* (1987). Later, she designed both Broadway productions of these plays. In addition, Crow also designed the first production of Wilson's *Hot l Baltimore* in 1973 and several plays at both the Arena Stage and the Kennedy Center in Washington, D.C. She also worked as a clothing and fabric designer for Wells, Rich, and Greene in New York and ATEX/USA in Asheville, North Carolina. In 1980, Crow became resident costume designer with the Seattle Repertory Theatre. There she employed her techniques of fastidious research and close attention to detail to productions ranging from Shakespeare's *The Taming of the Shrew* to Ibsen's *An Enemy of the People*, together with musicals such as Gershwin's *Girl Crazy*. In 1987, Crow returned to teaching and conducted classes in costume design at both Brandeis University and the University of Massachusetts.

Awards: Crow received the 1973 Drama Desk Award for "Best Costume Design" for *Warp* and the Joseph Jefferson Award in 1976 for *Misalliance*. In 1980, she won the Obie Award for her costume designs for *Mary Stuart* at the Circle Repertory Theatre.

Further Reading: Covey, Liz, and Rosemary Ingham. *The Costume Designer's Handbook*. Englewood Cliffs, NJ: Prentice Hall, 1983; Whiting, Frank M. *An Introduction to the Theater*. New York: Random House, 1980. Both books feature photographs of Crow's work.

Howard Gutner

Czettel, Ladislas. Costume and fashion designer and teacher (b. 1904, Hungary; d. 1949). Czettel studied at the Academy of Art in Munich and then went to Paris, where he studied with Léon Bakst.* In Paris, he became a successful dress designer with the larger couture houses. This success continued in Vienna, where he created evening gowns for the aristocracy and important prima donnas in the Vienna State Opera. Before emigrating to the United States in 1939, he created over 250,000 costumes for the Vienna State Opera, where he was guest designer from 1925 to 1935 and chief designer from 1935 to 1937; the Salzburg Festival; the Max Reinhardt Theater, where he was chief costume designer from 1932 to 1937; and the Folies Bergères. Perhaps the most important of these productions were Czettel's designs for Reinhardt's *Maria Stuart* (1933). From

1935 to 1938, he served as professor of costume design for the Max Reinhardt Seminary. Besides teaching and designing for the state opera company, Czettel created costumes for the Munich Carnivals from 1922 to 1933, the Great Exhibition in the Viennese Burg (1936), various operettas and revues in Vienna and Munich, and operatic festivals in Rome, Berlin, and Versailles. Known for his expert designs of sumptuous gowns, Czettel was awarded an honorary degree of doctor of arts from the Berlin State Art Academy. During this time he created the fashions worn in the German films *Der Einbrecher, Czibi*, and *Maria Baskirtscheff* and the British films *Gangway* and *Pygmalion* (1938).

After arriving in the United States in 1939, Czettel received an appointment as professor of costume and fashion history and taught ''Fashion Designing for Stage and Screen'' at the New School of Social Research. During his two-year tenure there, an exhibition of his designs was shown at the Museum of Modern Art, as well as at the New School, and his works received a national touring exhibition by the American Federation of Arts. Czettel was also engaged as one of the costume designers for the Metropolitan Opera House, where he rendered designs for *Falstaff, Der Rosenkavalier*, and *Tannhauser* (all in 1939); *Le Nozze di Figaro* (1940); and *The Masked Ball, Daughter of the Regiment, Manon*, and *Aida* (1941). Generally, the artist created only a selection of costumes for these operas: costumes worn by the prima donnas. After establishing himself, however, as a designer of formal evening wear for Henri Bendel and Jay Thorpe in the early 1940s, he was commissioned to design the costumes for *Rosalinda* (1943), *Helen Goes to Troy* (1944), and *La Vie Parisienne* (1945).

Czettel's costumes were shimmery, revealing creations made specifically with the text of the play or opera in mind, as well as the wearer's figure. They were cut in one piece with a minimum of seams and often had a low, deep-plunging back. This tendency to create for a specific woman made Czettel's couturier talents in great demand, and his ideas inspired entire lines of ''ready-to-wear'' evening gowns. In addition, just before his death in 1949, Czettel taught his fabric-cutting techniques at the Art School Laboratory Seminar of the Brooklyn Museum.

Andrea J. Nouryeh

D

Dahlstrom, Robert Andrew. Set and lighting designer (b. 1938, Billings, MT). Dahlstrom, theatrical designer and educator, has scenery and lighting design credits in theatre, opera, and dance. He received his M.F.A. degree from the University of Illinois and taught theatrical design at Northern Illinois University from 1967 until 1971. He moved to Seattle to join the theatre faculty at the University of Washington and subsequently became head of design for the School of Drama. Throughout his teaching career, Dahlstrom has maintained an active career in the professional theatre. He has had lengthy associations with the Seattle Repertory Theatre, Intiman Theatre Company, and the Seattle Opera Association. His first scenic design for the Seattle Repertory Theatre was *The Skin of Our Teeth* (1974). Since then, he has designed more than twenty-five productions for its repertory, including *Waltz of the Toreadors* (1975), *Private Lives* (1976), *Royal Family* (1977), *A Penny for a Song* (1978), *Catsplay* (1979), *Spokesong* (1980), *Another Part of the Forest* (1981), *Romeo and Juliet* (1982), *The Adventures of Huckleberry Finn* (1983), *Master Harold and the Boys* (1984), *The Mandrake* (1985), and *Danger Memory!* (1987). Dahlstrom has also designed shows for the American Conservatory Theatre in San Francisco that included *Man and Superman* (1976) and *Knock, Knock* (1977). At A Contemporary Theatre in Seattle, he designed such shows as *Educating Rita* (1983) and *Top Girls* (1984). Also, his work has been featured in productions at the Long Wharf Theatre in New Haven and Oregon Contemporary Theatre in Portland, among others. For the Seattle Opera, Dahlstrom has created designs for such significant productions as *The Ballad of Baby Doe* (1984), *Manon* (1985), and *Cosi Fan Tutte* (1986).

Awards: Dahlstrom received the Bay Area Critics' Award for design of *Knock, Knock* in 1977.

Further Reading: "Designers at Work." *Theatre Crafts* May 1987: 41.

Penny L. Remsen

Dalí, Salvador. Artist, set designer, and writer (b. May 1904, Figueras, Spain; d. January 1989, Figueras, Spain). Dalí brought his world of surrealism, prevalent in his painting, to theatrical design. His stage imagery was dislocated and irrational, yet juxtaposed with real objects, and was almost photographic in its accuracy. Dalí's designs virtually dominated the style of the productions in which they appeared. In 1927, at twenty-three, he designed the setting and costumes for *Mariana Pineda*. It was the first opportunity for him to work with friend and playwright García Lorca. They collaborated only once again, in 1944 for the ballet *Le Café de Chinitas*, choreographed by Argentinita. In 1929, Dalí's collaboration with Luis Bunuel resulted in the benchmark surrealist film *Un Chien Andalou*. During the following decade, Dalí suggested to choreographer Leonide Massine of the Ballets Russes de Monte Carlo that he create a ballet based on the hallucinations of Ludwig II of Bavaria. The development of that concept culminated in the ballet *Bachanale*, choreographed by Massine. Imbued with Dalí's surrealist images, the ballet was first performed in Monte Carlo in 1939 and subsequently moved to the New York City Metropolitan Opera House. Beginning in 1940, Dalí established residency in the United States and remained there throughout World War II. During this period, Dalí designed numerous ballets, including *Labyrinth*, written by Dalí and performed at the Metropolitan Opera with choreography by Massine; *Sentimental Colloquy*, produced by Ballet International with choreography by André Eglevsky; and *Mad Tristan*, produced by Ballet International with choreography by Massine. The latter two ballets were revised in 1948 and performed by the Grand Ballet du Marquis de Cuevas. After making his permanent home in Port Lligat, Spain, in 1945, Dalí was commissioned to design the dream sequence scenery for two films: Alfred Hitchcock's *Spellbound* and Vincente Minnelli's *Father of the Bride*. In addition, Dalí executed several drawings over a period of two years (1946 to 1947) for Walt Disney. These drawings were to have been used for a six-minute animated sequence that incorporated both real objects and animated characters. Unfortunately, the project never materialized. In 1948, Dalí collaborated with Luchino Visconti on Shakespeare's *As You Like It*, and, in 1949, he designed his first opera, *Salome*, with Peter Brook. Dalí ended his theatrical design career in 1961 with two ballets, *La Dama Spagnola e il Cavaliere Romano* and *Le Ballet de Galla*, with choreography by Maurice Béjart for the Teatro La Fenice in Venice. Like his other paintings, Dalí's theatrical renderings were exhibited throughout the world.

Penny L. Remsen

Damiani, Luciano. Scene designer (b. July 14, 1923, Bologna, Italy). Damiani began his design career at the Central University Theatre in Bologna, and he later worked for La Soffita and the Teatro Comunale. By 1954, he had begun working regularly for director Georgio Strehler at the Piccolo Teatro in Milan, where he succeeded designer Giovanni Ratto. During this period, he also obtained free-lance design work for the Teatro La Fenice in Venice, where he created sets for *Macbeth* (1955), and the Piccolo Scala in Milan, where he designed *The Secret Marriage* (1955). Throughout his career, Damiani has been able to obtain design assignments in many different European countries. Damiani's style is Brechtian, matching Strehler's directing style. His designs are nonrealistic, using strong textures in relief, dark, somber colors, and projections and frequently incorporating scene changes in view of the audience. These qualities can be seen in his designs for *Coriolanus* (1957), *The Good Woman of Setzuan* (1958), and *Baruffe Chiozzotte* (1965).

Elbin L. Cleveland

Davenport, Millia. Costume designer (b. 1895 Cambridge, MA; d. 1990). After attending Barnard College and the School of Fine and Applied Arts in New York, Davenport began designing sets and costumes for the Wits and Fingers Studio in Manhattan in 1918. Working with designers Yetta Kiviette and John N. Booth, Jr., she designed the costumes for her first Broadway play, *Helen of Troy*, in 1923. During the next thirty years, Davenport created the costumes for many Broadway shows, including the first productions of *Desire Under the Elms* (1924), *Love for Love* (1925), *East Lynne* (1926), *Falstaff* (1928), *Shoemaker's Holiday* (1938), and *Heartbreak House* (1938). In her work, she was rarely hindered by the limitations of available fabrics. For example, in 1940 Davenport designed the costumes for Maxwell Anderson's biblical play *Journey to Jerusalem* and commissioned craftsman Gilbert Blackman Rose to weave several natural fabrics together to create the material for the costumes. She also specified that the costumes should contain an off-white color so they would not distract the viewer from the simplicity of Jo Mielziner's* nonrepresentational sets. In 1946, Davenport was reunited with Maxwell Anderson when she designed the costumes for his play *Truckline Cafe*. Produced by the Group Theatre, the play examines the emotional dislocation caused by World War II and takes place at a busy truck stop between Los Angeles and San Francisco. Davenport's costumes, which included jeans and dresses that had been "distressed" and looked obviously worn, caught the essence of everyday life among the lower middle class after the war. Her other activities included publishing a two-volume reference work on costume in 1949, *The Book of Costume*, which is now out of print. This work was not only a history of fashion through the ages but also an examination of how climate, architecture, and the demands of current style affect the way people dress.

Howard Gutner

Davidson, Jeannie. Costume designer (b. March 21, 1938, San Francisco, CA). Davidson has designed costumes for over 120 shows in twenty-four years at the Ashland, Oregon, Shakespeare Festival, including every play in the Shakespeare canon except *Pericles*, as well as a variety of classic plays. She has also worked with the Denver Theatre Company, the American Conservatory Theatre in San Francisco, the Berkeley Repertory Theatre, the Children's Theatre Company in

Minneapolis, the Stanford Repertory Theatre, and the Colorado Shakespeare Festival, among others. Her efforts and talent have earned her the Los Angeles Drama Logue Award for *King Lear*, *'Tis a Pity She's a Whore*, *Romeo and Juliet*, and *She Stoops to Conquer* and many Drama Critics' Circle Awards. Her designs show a particular interest in painting and fabric modification.

Annie Milton

Daydé, Bernard. Set and costume designer, artist, and illustrator (b. February 3, 1921, Paris, France; d. 1986). Theatrical productions include *Coriolanus*, *Maria*—1945; *La Martyre de St. Sebastien*—1952; *Fantasio, La Guerre de Troie n'aura pas lieu*—1954; *Les Mouches*—1956; *Une Saison en Enfer*—1969; *L'Ecole des Femmes*—1970. Ballet productions include *Danses sur des poésie*, *Romeo and Juliet*—1944; *Sérénité, Sonata Pathétique*—1945; *La Belle au bois dormant, L'Oiseau Bleu, Les Sylphides*—1947; *Don Juan*—1948; *La Sylphide*—1953; *La Nuit est une Sorciere*—1954–1955; *Arcane, La Dryade, Études*—1955; *Ballets Africain, Ballets Haitians, Les Ballets de Pakistan*—1956; *Prometheus*—1956 and 1963; *Concerto, Les Liens*—1957; *Pulcinella, Señor de Manara, Swan Lake*—1959; *L'Étranger*—1960; *Carmen, Marines*—1961; *Symphonie Concertante*—1962; *The Three Musketeers*—1966; *Bacchus et Ariadne*—1967; *Amériques, Homage to Varèse, Hyperprism, Intergrales, Ionisation, Jeux, Octandre, Offandes, Orpheus and Eurydice, Le poème électronigue*—1973; *Densité 21.5*—1974; *Gaspard de la Nuit*—1976; *Deuil*—1977; *Salome, Sylvia*—1979. Opera productions include *Bacchus and Ariadne*—1967; *Malheurs d'Orphee*—1963; *The Miraculous Mandarin*—1967; *Orpheus in the Underworld*—1957; *La Victoire de L'Amour*—1962; *Werther, Opera d'aran*—1962; *Mariana pineda*—1969–1970; *Coeur revelateur*—1971; *Protocolo*—1972.

During his lifetime, Daydé designed over three hundred plays, ballets, and operas. His ballet designs were executed for such choreographers as Serge Lifar, Ruth Page, Béjart, and George Balanchine, and he designed for opera companies throughout France, Germany, Belgium, Denmark, Italy, Holland, Spain, Switzerland, England, and the United States. In addition to his posts as the resident designer and as director general for art and technical services for the Theatre National de l'Opera in Paris, Daydé designed ballet and opera productions for television, including the production of *Orphée aux enfers* for Hamburg film-TV. He was noted for using exposed stage machinery—bridges, metallic pipes—along with ramps as part of his stage settings. For example, in *Homage to Varèse* the percussion players sat up on a bridge that hung just below the proscenium arch. To this bridge were added screens and banners. The effect was described as reminiscent of a city skyline. Daydé's designs, paintings, and sculptures were first exhibited at the National Museum in Lisbon in 1949. Since then his works have been shown in galleries throughout Paris, and his designs for opera and ballet have appeared in scene designers' national and international exhibitions. One of his final works was illustrating the program for the 1984 Festival International de Danse in Paris.

Awards: Prix de la Critique Paris, 1957; Golden Star for Best Design, International Ballet Festival of Paris, 1963 and 1967; Prix Italia, Best Television Ballet in Europe, 1964; Chevalier de la Légion d'Honneur, 1975.

Further Reading: Percival, John, and Marie-Frencouse Christout. "Homage to Varèse." *Dance and Dancers* August 1973: 24–27; Percival, John. "Salome." *Dance and Dancers* January 1979; Stephant, Anne. "Bernard Dayde." *Danse* May 1979.

Andrea J. Nouryeh

Delfau, André. Set designer (b. 1914, Paris, France). Delfau studied at the École des Beaux Arts and began a career as a painter and illustrator before his first commission to design a ballet for Diaghilev. He began his theatrical design career in 1947, when he executed sets and costumes for *Sérénade* and *Apollon Musageté*, choreographed by George Balanchine at the Paris Opera Ballet. Continuing their collaboration with the Marquis de Cuevas's ballet company in 1950, Delfau and Balanchine combined efforts to create a splendidly atmospheric balletic version of Bellini's *La Sonnambula* and, subsequently, striking productions of Tchaikovsky's *Tragédie á Vérone* and Schiffman's *Annabel Lee*. In 1955, while working at the Royal Opera Ballet of Denmark, they created *Night Shadow*. Since 1961, Delfau has created scenery for Ruth Page's Chicago Opera Ballet, including such balletic works as *Die Fledermaus*, *Pygmalion*, and *Romeo and Juliet*. Occasionally, Delfau designed plays, such as *Les Serments Indiscrets* (1956) for the Comédie Française and others for the Opéra Comique. His work ranged from the pictorial to the abstract, depending on the needs of the script.

Further Reading: Oenslager (see Bibliography).

Annie Milton

DeLoutherbourg, Philip. Scene designer, stage machinist, and painter (b. October 31, 1740, Fulda, Germany; d. March 11, 1812, Chiswick, England). Theatrical productions include *The Chances*, *Alfred*, *A Christmas Tale* (all at the Drury Lane Theatre)—1773; *Sethona*, *The Maid of the Oaks* (both at the Drury Lane)—1774; *Queen Mab*, *The Sultan*, *The Runaway*, *Selim and Azor* (all at the Drury Lane Theatre)—1775; *The Camp* (Drury Lane)—1778; *The Wonders of Derbyshire*, *The Winter's Tale* (all at the Drury Lane)—1779; *The Fair Circassian*, *Almoran and Hamlet* (both at Drury Lane)—1780; *The Critic* (Drury Lane), *The Carnival of Venice* (Drury Lane), *Robinson Crusoe* (Drury Lane), "Eidophusikon" (Leicester Square)—1781; *Orpheus and Eurydice* (Kings Theatre), *Omai*—1785; "Eidophusikon" (The Strand)—1786 and 1787.

Although pressed by his mother to enter the ministry, DeLoutherbourg decided to become a painter instead. He first trained with his artist father, a miniaturist, and then took further training in painting in Germany and France under Italian artists. His romantically realistic paintings were well received in Paris and had many showings in galleries. He was so successful, in fact, that in 1767 DeLoutherbourg was elected to the French Royal Academy before he had reached the prescribed age. In England, he was admitted to the Royal

Academy of Art in 1772 and over the years exhibited more than 150 paintings there.

After returning to England to live, in 1771 he was hired as scene designer by David Garrick at the Drury Lane, largely as a result of his visionary approach to scenery of the day. As he had promised Garrick in a letter before he was hired, DeLoutherbourg completely reformed the standard scenery, machinery, costumes, and lighting of that time. DeLoutherbourg made use of colored or tinted glass in front of the lanterns, transparent gauzes, silks, and new mechanical scene-shifting devices, like roller drums and miniature models moving across stage, to create such effects as ship battles, thunderstorms, conflagrations, or a breathtaking dawn. His biggest innovation, however, was that he broke up the formal lines of the architectural perspective of Italianate scenery (back drop and wing and the groove system) and introduced the use of multiple pieces on the stage to create a more realistic stage picture. In *Alfred* (1773), his first play, and in *Queen Mab* (1775), DeLoutherbourg used small models of ships and barges, respectively, to depict a naval review and a regatta. For Garrick, he applied his inventiveness to such pantomimes as *Sethona* (1774), which employed an Egyptian setting, and *The Runaway* (1775).

With William Brinsley Sheridan, Garrick's successor at the Drury Lane, he designed ten new plays and five pantomimes. His designs for plays included *The Camp* (1778), *The Winter's Tale* (1779), and *The Critic* (1781), and his designs for pantomimes included *The Wonders of Derbyshire* (1779), which he depicted in twelve scenes, authentically re-created from original sketches of the country. One feature of this latter work was that his lighting of scenes dramatically illustrated different times of day. He left Drury Lane in 1781, after Sheridan reduced his salary by half.

He continued to design after leaving Drury Lane and created a model theatre in 1781 called the "Eidophusikon," a small, model proscenium theatre that was constructed and presented in various rooms in 1781, 1786, and 1787. On a stage six feet wide and eight feet deep, DeLoutherbourg created atmospheric and scenic effects for spectators to watch. It is highly probable that he was familiar with Servandoni's* earlier "silent play" in Paris and decided to create his own. DeLoutherbourg created natural lighting effects by removing the footlights and casting the main light from the top and sides of the stage. He made use of the recently invented Argand lamp and rigged up rolling cylinders in the back of the stage to create waves and moving sky effects, such as clouds and wind. Through his work in the model theatre, DeLoutherbourg's artistry made possible the changing of atmospheric effects within one scene rather than in a series of scenes.

As a designer, DeLoutherbourg emphasized careful planning. His work influenced the antiquarians, who carried the idea of researching and reproducing actual locations on stage to the limit, and called for a new respect for scene painters, who for the first time were listed in the program.

Further Reading: Nicoll, Allardyce. *The Development of the Theatre.* New York: Harcourt, Brace, 1927; Rosenfeld, Sybil. *A Short History of Scene Design in Great Britain.* Totowa, NJ: Rowman and Littlefield, 1973.

Elbin L. Cleveland

Derain, André. Set designer, painter, illustrator, and sculptor (b. June 10, 1880, Chaton, France; d. September 11, 1954, Chambourcy, France). Derain had already established himself as an important painter in the Fauvist style when Sergey Diaghilev enlisted him in 1919 to design scenery and costumes for the Ballets Russes. Just as he was successful in early modern art, Derain prospered in theatrical design. His first production, Léonide Massine's *La Boutique Fantasque* (1919), won him recognition as a first-rate theatrical designer and led to his collaboration with George Balanchine on *Jack-in-the-Box* (1926) and *Les Songes* (1933). Derain's painterly style interpreted reality into highly imaginative and decorative terms that insured a long career in ballet design. Some of his later works with Massine were *Mam'zelle Angot* (1947), *Les Femmes de bonne humeur* (1949), and *La Valse* (1950).

Thomas J. Mikotowicz

Dmitriev, Vladimir Vladimerovich. Set designer (b. 1900, Russia; d. 1948). Dmitriev, a student of Kuzma Petrov-Vodkin, was a noted Russian scene designer whose evocative settings were seen in productions at the Moscow Art Theatre, the Vakhtangov Theatre, and many others. After attending Vsevelod Meyerhold's classes in Petrograd, he designed the famous director's production of Émile Verhaeren's revolutionary tragedy *The Dawn* (1920), in striking settings influenced by the cubist and futurist schools. Unfortunately, several years later, Meyerhold turned down Dmitriev's designs for a production of *The Government Inspector*. Dmitriev's career was highlighted by his designs for Sergei Radlov's staging of Ernst Toller's expressionistic play *Eugene the Unlucky* (1923) and Maksim Gorky's last two plays, *Yegor Bulychov and Others* (1932) and *Dostigayev and Others* (1933). In the later part of his career, he created scenery for *The Last Sacrifice* (1944) and *Our Daily Bread* (1947).

James Fisher

Dobuzhinsky, Mstislav. Set and costume designer (b. 1875, Russia; d. 1957). Dobuzhinsky was a prolific designer who worked in Russia before and after the Revolution. The influences of his upbringing in a small village are seen in the folk art that he incorporated into his designs. After studying in Munich and Saint Petersburg, Dobuzhinsky painted for the World of Art group. His work was much admired by Stanislavsky, for whom he designed from 1909 to 1919. One of his most famous productions was Turgenev's *A Month in the Country* (1909) for the Moscow Art Theatre. In 1911, he designed sets and costumes for Diaghilev, and subsequently he participated in early experimental productions with Meyerhold, Komisarjevsky, and Granovsky. In Meyerhold's production of *Pe-*

trouchka (1908), Dobuzhinsky used a very painterly approach to create a highly decorative, rather than realistic, setting. His work could also be seen at the Gorky Theatre in Leningrad. His designs are in the constructivist style, although not as extreme as that of other designers. In 1921, Dobuzhinsky moved throughout Europe and designed productions across the Continent. At sixty-four, he emigrated to New York to retire but was soon designing productions in the American theatre until he was eighty-two.

Further Reading: Oenslager (see Bibliography).

Ken Kloth

Dorsey, Kent. Set and lighting designer (b. 1952, Los Angeles, CA). Scenic and lighting designer Dorsey received his M.F.A. in design from Temple University in 1979. In that same year, he joined the Old Globe Theatre in San Diego as the company's resident designer. For the past decade, in collaboration with directors Craig Noel and Jack O'Brien, he created the sets and lighting for such productions as *Orpheus Descending, Tartuffe,* and *On the Verge.* Becoming an unaffiliated free-lance designer in the latter half of the 1980s, Dorsey continued to design for the Old Globe in such productions as *Another Antigone, Talley's Folly, The Cocktail Hour,* and *Coriolanus.* Dorsey's additional training came as assistant to Gilbert Helmsley on the productions of *Nabucco* (1981), *King Lear* (1981), and *Sugar Babies* (1981). Over the years, Dorsey has collaborated with several other theatre companies in designing both scenery and lighting. In 1981, he collaborated on productions at the Arizona Theatre Company, including sets for *Glengarry Glen Ross, My Fair Lady,* and *The Rainmaker,* as well as lighting for *Fool for Love, What the Butler Saw,* and *Misalliance.* In 1983 and 1984, the Denver Center Theatre Company season featured Dorsey's designs for *The Front Page, Romeo and Juliet, The Tempest, Arms and the Man,* and *Spokesong.* He has also been commissioned to design scenery and lighting for several other California theatre companies, including the San Diego Opera, La Jolla Playhouse, and the Berkeley Repertory Theatre. Dorsey's interest in Hispanic theatre has resulted in his extensive work with local San Diego companies, including Jorge Huerta's Teatro Meta and Luis Valdez's Teatro Campesino. In September 1988, Dorsey's lighting design for *Suds, the Sixties Rocking Soap Opera* opened a new Broadway theatre called the Criterion.

Awards: Dorsey's designs have earned him several awards, including the Drama Logue Award for lighting design for *The Importance of Being Earnest, Of Mice and Men, Othello, Rashomon, Henry IV, Part One,* and *Wings.* He also earned the Drama Logue Award for scenic design for *The Tooth of Crime, Talley's Folly, Clap Your Hands,* and *Two Gentlemen of Verona,* all at the Globe Theatre. In addition, he was the recipient of the Bay Area Critics' Circle Award for scene design for *The Tooth of Crime* and for lighting for *The Tooth of Crime* and *Diary of a Scoundrel,* both at the Berkeley Repertory Theatre. His lighting design for *Othello* and *Night of the Iguana,* both at the Old Globe Theatre, earned him the San Diego Critics' Circle Award.

Further Reading: "Designers at Work." *Theatre Crafts* May 1987: 38.
Penny L. Remsen

Duquette, Tony. Costume and set designer (b. June 11, 1918, Los Angeles, CA). Theatrical productions include *Yolanda and the Thief* (film)—1945; *Ziegfeld Follies* (film)—1946; *Lovely to Look At* (film)—1952; *Kismet* (film)—1955; *Beauty and the Beast, Danses Concertantes*—1959; *Lady of Shalot, Caprice, Sinfonia, Danse Brilliant, Camelot, Can-Can* (film; sets for the ballet sequence)—1960; *Jederman*—1961; *Kismet, Jest of Cards, The Four Horsemen of the Apocalypse* (film)—1962; *The Magic Flute*—1963.

Duquette has created costumes for many plays, films, operas, and ballets, most of which have been produced almost exclusively on the West Coast. In the 1940s and 1950s, he worked closely with the Arthur Freed production unit at Metro-Goldwyn-Mayer (MGM) and created sets, costumes, and other properties for a number of classic musicals, including *Yolanda and the Thief* (1945), *Ziegfeld Follies* (1946), and *Kismet* (1955). For the theatre, his work is exemplified by the highly detailed, romantic sets that he created for such productions as *Jedermann* (1961) at the Salzburg Festival in Austria and the Los Angeles Light Opera Company production of *Kismet* (1962). When Gilbert Adrian,* the original costume designer for *Camelot* (1960), died during production, Duquette interceded and finished the show and won Tony Awards for both himself and Adrian.

Howard Gutner

E

Eckart, William. Costume and set designer, producer, and teacher (b. October 21, 1920, New Iberia, LA) and **Eckart, Jean** (née Jean Levy). Costume and set designer, producer, and teacher (b. August 18, 1921, Glencoe, IL). Theatrical productions (all in New York City unless otherwise specified) include *Glad Tidings* (Lyceum Theatre), *To Dorothy, a Son* (John Golden Theatre)—1951; *Gertie* (Plymouth Theatre)—1952; *Maya, The Scarecrow, The School for Scandal, The Little Clay Cart* (Theatre de Lys), *Dead Pigeon* (Vanderbilt Theatre), *Oh, Men! Oh, Women!* (Henry Miller's Theatre)—1953; *The Golden Apple* (Phoenix Repertory Theatre, Arizona), *Wedding Breakfast* (46th Street Theatre), *Portrait of a Lady* (ANTA Theatre)—1954; *Damn Yankees* (46th Street Theatre), *Reuben, Reuben* (Shubert Theatre, Boston)—1955; *Mister Johnson* (Martin Beck Theatre), *L'il Abner* (St. James Theatre)—1956; *Damn Yankees* (London), *Livin' the Life* (Phoenix Repertory Theatre), *Copper and Brass* (Martin Beck Theatre)—1957; *The Body Beautiful* (Broadway Theatre)—1958; *Once upon a Mattress* (coproducer; Phoenix Repertory Theatre, Arizona), *Fiorello!* (Broadhurst Theatre)—1959; *Viva Madison Avenue!* (Longacre Theatre), *Once upon a Mattress* (London)—1960; *The Happiest Girl in the World* (Martin Beck Theatre), *Let It Ride* (Eugene O'Neill Theatre), *Take Her, She's Mine* (Biltmore Theatre)—1961; *Oh Dad, Poor Dad, Mama's Hung You in the Closet and I'm Feelin' So Sad* (Phoenix Repertory Theatre), *Never Too Late* (Playhouse Theatre)—1962; *She Loves Me* (Eugene O'Neill Theatre), *Never Too Late* (London), *Here's Love* (Shubert Theatre)—1963; *Too Much Johnson* (Phoenix Repertory Theatre), *Anyone Can Whistle* (Majestic Theater), *She Loves Me* (London), *All About Elsie* (for the New York World's Fair), *Fade Out—Fade In* (Mark Hellinger Theatre)—1964; *A Sign of Affection* (Shubert Theatre, New Haven, Connecticut), *Flora, the Red Menace* (Alvin Theatre), *The Zulu and the Zayda* (Cort Theatre), *Oh Dad, Poor Dad, Mama's Hung You in the Closet and I'm Feelin' So Sad*

(London)—1965; *Mame* (Winter Garden Theater), *Where's Charley?* (tour), *Agatha Sue, I Love You* (Henry Miller's Theatre)—1966; *A Midsummer Night's Dream* (American Shakespeare Festival, Stratford, Connecticut), *Hallelujah, Baby!* (Martin Beck Theatre)—1967; *The Education of HYMAN KAPLAN* (Alvin Theatre), *Maggie Flynn* (ANTA Theatre), *A Mother's Kisses* (Shubert Theatre, New Haven, Connecticut)—1968; *The Fig Leaves Are Falling* (Broadhurst Theatre), *A Way of Life* (ANTA Theatre), *Mame* (London), *The Night They Raided Minsky's* (film, United Artists)—1969; *Norman, Is That You?* (Lyceum Theatre), *Sensations* (Theatre Four)—1970; *Of Mice and Men* (Phoenix Repertory Theatre, Arizona)—1971; *The Dining Room* (Plaza Theatre, Dallas, Texas)—1984.

Jean and William Eckart met at Tulane University and later attended Yale Drama School together, where they majored in stage and costume design. Although they are no longer married and working together, the credit line "scenery and costumes by the Eckarts" has graced the programs of many Broadway shows, including *Damn Yankees* (1957), *Fiorello!* (1959), *Flora, the Red Menace* (1965), *Mame* (1966), and *Hallelujah, Baby!* (1967). In addition, the Eckarts have created sets and costumes for opera, motion pictures, and a number of productions at the 1964–1965 World's Fair and were among the first designers to work in television in 1949.

Whether designing sets or costumes, the Eckarts inevitably try to find what they refer to as the "essence of a play—the feeling you get from reading the script, or talking with the director or author to determine their point of view." Discovering the essence of a particular scene may be as simple as studying an apple tree in upstate New York to design an orchard setting for *The Golden Apple* (1954), or it may be as difficult as designing the locker room set for the musical *Damn Yankees*. The Eckarts finally decided to design what they felt was the "essence" of any locker room, and the set was composed of nothing but stools and banks of lockers.

Always trying to refine a design idea, the Eckarts discarded a number of realistic sketches for the musical *Fiorello!* (1959); they decided that the focus of the show was not the city of New York, but rather the bubbly, enthusiastic personality of the title character, Fiorello LaGuardia. They decided to use crayons for the sketches so that their drawings would exhibit a childlike vigor and directness. *Fiorello!* was a landmark production for the Eckarts in another respect: to shift quickly from one full set to another, they evolved a mechanical device made of two adjoining turntables shaped like doughnuts. This determined the general shape and size of the sets, which had to be fairly shallow and set in a wide, inverted V-shape.

In 1971, the Eckarts left the New York theatre when William Eckart accepted a position as head of theatre design studies at Southern Methodist University in Dallas, Texas. Currently, he supervises the training of graduate and advanced undergraduate design students and plans the design/production curriculum of the theatre department. Jean Eckart changed careers entirely when she moved with her husband to Dallas and is now a social worker in a mental health clinic near the city. Still, she finds little difference between the two fields: "Psychology and theater design all relate around the notion of problem solving. You design for what the actors and directors need, based on what the play calls for, and what fits into the theater."

Awards: The Eckarts won the Donaldson Award in 1954 for their scenic design for *The Golden Apple.*

Further Reading: "Scenic Design and Lighting." *Theatre Arts* July 1960; "William and Jean Eckart." *Dramatics* November/December 1977; Owen (see Bibliography).

                                                                 Howard Gutner

Edwards, Ben. Set, costume, and lighting designer (b. 1916, Union Springs, AL). Theatrical productions include *Mrs. Moonlight, Pursuit of Happiness, Smiling Through, Beyond the Hills, The Silver Cord* (all at the Barten Theatre, Abingdon, Virginia)—1935; *Another Sun* (National Theatre)—1940; *Medea* (National Theatre)—1947; *Sundown Beach* (Belasco Theatre)—1948; *Diamond Lil* (with William DeForest; Coronet Theatre), *The Taming of the Shrew* (set and costumes), *Julius Caesar* (set and costumes; Woodstock Playhouse)—1949; *The Bird Cage* (costumes; Coronet Theatre), *Legend of Sarah* (costumes; Fulton Theatre), *Captain Brassbound's Conversion, Black Chiffon* (both for New York City Center)—1950; *The Royal Family, King Richard II, The Taming of the Shrew* (all for New York City Center)—1951; *Desire Under the Elms* (costumes; ANTA), *Sunday Breakfast* (set and costumes; Coronet Theatre), *The Time of the Cuckoo* (Empire Theatre), "The Ed Wynn Show" (NBC television)—1952; *The Remarkable Mr. Pennypacker* (set, lighting, and costumes; Coronet Theatre)—1953; *Lullaby* (Lyceum), *Sing Me No Lullaby* (Phoenix Theatre), *The Traveling Lady* (Playhouse Theatre), *Anastasia* (set and costumes; Lyceum Theatre)—1954; *Tonight in Samarkand* (set and lighting; Morosco Theatre), *The Honeys* (Longacre Theatre), the Armstrong Circle Theatre (CBS television)—1955; *Someone Waiting* (lighting; John Golden Theatre), *The Ponder Heart* (set and lighting; Music Box)—1956; *The Waltz of the Toreadors* (set, costume, and lighting; Coronet Theatre); *The Dark at the Top of the Stairs* (Music Box)—1957; *Jane Eyre* (set and lighting; Belasco Theatre), *A Touch of the Poet* (set, costumes, and lighting; Helen Hayes Theatre), *The Disenchanted* (Coronet Theatre)—1958; *God and Kate Murphy* (set and lighting; 54th Street Theatre), *Heartbreak House* (set and lighting; Billy Rose Theatre), *Ages of Man* (lighting; 46th Street Theatre)—1959; *Face of a Hero* (set and lighting; Eugene O'Neill Theatre)—1960; *Midgie Purvis* (Martin Beck Theatre), *Big Fish, Little Fish* (also produced with Lewis Allen; ANTA), *Purlie Victorious* (Cort Theatre), *A Shot in the Dark* (Booth Theatre)—1961; *The Aspern Papers* (Playhouse Theatre)—1962; *Harold* (also coproduced; Cort Theatre), *The Ballad of the Sad Cafe* (also coproduced; Martin Beck Theatre)—1962; *Hamlet* (Lunt-Fontanne Theatre)—1964; *The Family* (with George Jenkins), *The Royal Hunt of the Sun*—1965; *Nathan Weinstein, Mystic, Connecticut, Where's Daddy?, How's The World Treating You?*—1966; *What Do You Really Know About Your Husband?, More Stately Mansions, The Freaking Out of Stephanie Blake*—1967; *The Mother*

Lover—1969; *Purlie*—1972; *Look Away, Finishing Touches, The Prodigal Daughter* (Washington, D.C.), *A Moon for the Misbegotten*—1973; *Figures in the Sand, A Moon for the Misbegotten* (Los Angeles)—1974; *Long Day's Journey into Night, A Matter of Gravity, A Texas Trilogy* (New York and Washington, D.C.)—1976; *Anna Christie, A Very Private Life* (Buffalo, New York), *An Almost Perfect Person, A Touch of the Poet*—1977; *The West Side Waltz* (Spreckles Theatre, San Diego)—1980; *To Grandmother's House We Go* (Biltmore Theatre), *The West Side Waltz* (Ethel Barrymore Theatre)–1981; *Medea* (Cort Theatre)—1982; *Death of a Salesman*—1984; *The Iceman Cometh* (Lunt-Fontanne Theatre)—1985; *Lilian* (Ethel Barrymore Theatre)—1986; *Opera Comique* (Kennedy Center, Washington, D.C.), *The Chosen* (Second Avenue Theatre), *Long Day's Journey into Night* (Yale Repertory Theatre)—1987. In addition he worked on the following films: *Lovers and Other Strangers, Class of '44, Last of the Red Hot Lovers*.

Edwards received his first professional job at the Barter Theatre in Abingdon, Virginia, in 1936, where he designed such shows as *Mrs. Moonlight* and *Beyond the Hills*. After moving to New York, he improved his craft by working for Mordecai Gorelik* and Jo Mielziner.* One of his first Broadway shows was *Medea* (1947), produced at the National Theatre. Edwards's classical design received much notice and included an asymmetrical view of Medea's house, with wide steps, rising columns, and a set of massive front doors. Since then, he has spent more than forty years designing shows on Broadway ranging from *Julius Caesar* (1949) to *Long Day's Journey into Night* (1976), as well as working in regional theatres. Edwards's style includes the use of detail that brings out a special atmosphere—for example, his inclusion of a sagging door frame in the set for *The West Side Waltz* (1981) or a water-stained venetian courtyard wall in the production of *The Time of the Cuckoo* (1952) at the Empire Theatre. By using an approach to capture the essential, Edwards brought out an "impression of realism."

Awards: Edwards received the New York Critics' Circle Award for *Heartbreak House* in 1960.

Further Reading: Sommers, Michael. "Ben Edwards: The Gentleman from Alabama." *Theatre Crafts* August/September 1989: 48.

Kurt Lancaster

Eigsti, Karl. Set, lighting, and costume designer (b. 1938, Goshen, IN). Theatrical productions (the following are for set design and took place in New York City, unless otherwise specified) include *Billy Budd, Heartbreak House, Long Day's Journey into Night* (all at Arena Stage, Washington, D.C.), *The Critic, They* (sets and lighting for both, Theatre of the Living Arts, Philadelphia, Pennsylvania)—1965; *Thumby* (Long Wharf Theatre, New Haven, Connecticut), *The Three Sisters, Mr. Welk and Jersey Jim, The Lesson, The Collection* (Arena Stage, Washington, D.C.)—1966; *Marat/Sade* (Studio Arena Theatre, Buffalo, New York), *Fisher* (directed only, La Mama E.T.C.), *Inner-City Macbeth* (directed only, Cherry County Playhouse, Traverse City, Minnesota), *The Dumb-*

waiter, The Private Ear, The Miracle Worker (ATOL, Kentucky)—1967; *Ba-nanas* (Repertory Theatre of Lincoln Center, Forum Theatre) *Serjeant Mus-grave's Dance* (sets and costumes; Guthrie Theater, Minneapolis, Minnesota)—1968; *Henry V, Hamlet* (American Shakespeare Festival, Stratford, Connecticut), *Mourning Becomes Electra* (sets and costumes; Guthrie Theater), *Henry V* (ANTA Theatre)—1969; *Inquest* (Music Box Theatre), *Boesman and Lena* (Circle in the Square), *Othello* (American Shakespeare Festival), *Othello* (ANTA Theatre)—1970; *The House of Blue Leaves* (Truck and Warehouse Theatre), *Buying Out* (Studio Arena, Buffalo, New York), *The Passion of Antigona Perez* (Puerto Rico Traveling Theatre), Industrial show setting for Armstrong Cork Company, TV commercials—1971; *Grease* (lighting; Eden Theatre), *Sitting, The Saving Grace* (both at the Studio Arena, Buffalo, New York)—1972; *The Karl Marx Play* and *Baba Goya* (American Place Theatre), *Nourish the Beast* (retitled version of *Baba Goya*; Cherry Lane Playhouse)—1973; *The Resistible Rise of Arturo Ui, Horatio, Death of a Salesman, Who's Afraid of Virginia Woolf?, The Front Page* (Arena Stage, Washington, D.C.), *Yentl the Yeshiva Boy* (Chelsea Theater Center)—1974; *The Secret Place* (La Mama E.T.C.), *Wings* (Eastside Playhouse), *The Last Meeting of the Knights of the White Magnolia, The Dybbuk, Long Day's Journey into Night, Once in a Lifetime* (Arena Stage, Washington, D.C.), *Yentl* (Eugene O'Neill Theatre), *Sweet Bird of Youth* (Academy Festival Theatre, Lake Forest, Illinois; Kennedy Center, Washington, D.C.; Harkness Theatre)—1975; *Dandelion Wine, Saint Joan, Saturday, Sunday, Monday* (Arena Stage, Washington, D.C.), *Monty Python, Live!* (City Center), *The House of Blue Leaves* (Westport Country Playhouse, Connecticut), *When You Comin' Back Red Ryder?* (Cincinnati Playhouse in the Park, Ohio)—1976; *Catsplay* (Arena Stage, Washington, D.C.), *Guerramore, Diary of One Who Vanished, Aventures et Nouvelles Aventures* (Brooklyn Academy of Music), *On the Lock In* (New York Shakespeare Festival, Public Theater), *Sizwe Bansi Is Dead* (Pittsburgh Public Theatre, Pennsylvania; Studio Arena, Buffalo, New York), *JoAnne!* (Theatre of Riverside Church), *The Imaginary Invalid* (Cincinnati Playhouse in the Park, Ohio), *Daddy* (New Federal Theatre), *Cold Storage* (sets and costumes; Lyceum Theatre)—1977; *Slow Dance on the Killing Ground, Medal of Honor Rag* (Pittsburgh Public Theatre, Pennsylvania), *The National Health, Duck Hunting* (Arena Stage, Washington, D.C.), *Once in a Lifetime* (Circle in the Square), *Albee Directs Albee, Eubie!* (Ambassador Theatre), *Annie Get Your Gun* (Jones Beach Marine Theatre), *The Diary of Anne Frank* (Theatre Four)—1978; *Room Service, The Buddy System, Twelfth Night* (Cincinnati Playhouse in the Park, Ohio), *Curse of the Starving Class, You Can't Take It with You* (Arena Stage, Washington, D.C.), *Knockout* (Helen Hayes Theatre), *Murder at the Howard Johnson's* (John Golden Theatre), "Industrial" for Avon, *A Hundred Percent Alive* (Westwood Playhouse, Los Angeles, California), *Losing Time* (Manhattan Theatre Club)—1979; *The Caretaker* (Long Wharf Theatre, New Haven, Connecticut), *After the Fall, One Mo' Time* (Arena Stage, Washington, D.C.), *Julius Caesar* (Milwaukee Repertory Company, Wisconsin), *The*

Downstairs Boys, *The Baker's Wife* (Cincinnati Playhouse in the Park, Ohio), *The Guests of the Nation* (PBS television), *The Woolgatherer* (Circle Repertory Company), *Frimbo* (Grand Central Terminal, Tracks 39–42), *The American Clock* (Biltmore Theatre)—1980; *Disability: A Comedy*, *The Child*, *Cold Storage*, *Pantomime* (Arena Stage, Washington, D.C.), *Bodies* (Long Wharf Theatre, New Haven, Connecticut), *Julius Caesar* (Milwaukee Repertory Theatre, Wisconsin), *The Red Snake* (New York Shakespeare Festival, Public Theater), *Joseph and the Amazing Technicolor Dreamcoat* (Entermedia Theatre), *Our Town* (Guthrie Theatre, Minneapolis, Minnesota), *Shady Hill Kidnapping* (''American Playhouse,'' PBS television)—1981; *A Delicate Balance* (Arena Stage, Washington, D.C.), *Joseph and the Amazing Technicolor Dreamcoat* (Royale Theatre), *Macbeth* (Cincinnati Playhouse in the Park, Ohio), *The World of Sholom Aleichem* (Rialto Theatre), ''Industrial'' for IBM, *Richard II*, *The Great Grandson of Jedediah Kohler* (Circle Repertory Company; Entermedia Theatre), *The File on Jill Hatch* (PBS/BBC television), *May I Have This Dance?* (Tel Aviv, Israel), *Almost an Eagle* (Longacre Theatre)—1982; *Screenplay* (Arena Stage, Washington, D.C.), *Free and Clear* (Long Wharf Theatre, New Haven, Connecticut), *Amen Corner* (Nederlander Theatre), *Solomon Northrup's Odyssey* (PBS television), ''Industrial'' for IBM—1983; *Julius Caesar* (Cincinnati Playhouse in the Park, Ohio), *Accidental Death of an Anarchist* (Belasco Theatre), ''Industrial'' for IBM, ''Industrial'' for Equitable Life Assurance, *Winston Churchill Speaks* (David Susskind Productions, television), *Alone Together* (Music Box), *Translations* (Alaska Repertory Theatre in Fairbanks), *Terra Nova* (Huntington Theatre Company, Boston, Massachusetts)—1984; *The Beautiful Lady* (Mark Taper Forum, Los Angeles, California), *And a Nightingale Sang* (Cincinnati Playhouse in the Park, Ohio), *Saint Joan* (Huntington Theatre Company, Boston, Massachusetts), *Down River* (Musical Theatre Works)—1985; *Orphans* (sets and costumes; Pittsburgh Public Theatre, Pennsylvania), *Tartuffe* (Los Angeles Theatre Center, California), *Jumpers* (Huntington Theatre Company, Boston, Massachusetts)—1986; *Julius Caesar* (Philadelphia Drama Guild, Pennsylvania)—1988; *Les Blancs* (Huntington Theatre Company, Boston, Massachusetts)—1989.

Eigsti's training as a designer began in an eclectic fashion. He acted a bit in high school, and though he discovered art during a year-long trip to Europe with his parents, he entered Indiana University as a playwriting student. His first design experience was gained through designing the productions that he directed at the White Cloud Playhouse in Michigan in 1959. After studying at the Bristol Old Vic and the University of Bristol, where he earned a master's degree, he returned to the United States and found employment with the Arena Stage in Washington, D.C., as the supervisor of Robin Wagner's* sets. Before long, he was given the opportunity to design three productions that launched his design career, *Billy Budd*, *Heartbreak House*, and *Long Day's Journey into Night*, all produced in 1965. This experience led to work at other theatres, as well as assisting Ming Cho Lee* at the New York Shakespeare Festival.

After a brief hiatus as a directing student at New York University and as a director in several regional theatres, he returned to the design field at the Guthrie Theatre in 1968. His design for John Arden's production of *Serjeant Musgrave's Dance* that year was significant to his design career and typifies his affinity for placing images on stage that are linked to the heart of the play. In his design, he placed on stage a twelve-foot-diameter wheel, suggesting momentum and symbolizing the Industrial Revolution.

Returning to New York, he became head of the New Plays Program for Jules Irving at Lincoln Center and combined directing and designing. Subsequently, he took time off from designing to attend the School of Visual Arts in New York. He reestablished his career with the productions of *Boesman and Lena* (1970) and *The House of Blue Leaves* (1971). Since, his career has grown to include not only significant regional theatre productions at such institutions as Arena Stage in Washington, D.C., and Cincinnati's Playhouse in the Park, but several Broadway shows, as well. Some of his significant productions include the Broadway and off-Broadway productions of *Cold Storage* (1977), *The Woolgatherer* (1980), *Joseph and the Amazing Technicolor Dreamcoat* (1981), and *Amen Corner* (1983). Although Eigsti adapts his style to the demands of a particular show, he is generally recognized as a designer who can create evocative, realistic settings as well as emblematic scenery. His realistic interiors contain only enough elements to create a semblance of realism, and his non-representative designs may incorporate large symbolic elements that are tied to the themes of the play.

Eigsti's activities also include the art direction of four films for PBS, as well as teaching. His nineteen years of teaching theatre and design at New York University and his subsequent revitalization of the master's program at Brandeis University, after Howard Bay's departure, have given Eigsti the opportunity to influence countless students who will eventually work in the American theatre.

Awards: Eigsti earned a Tony nomination and a Joseph Maharam Foundation Award for *Knockout* in 1979.

Further Reading: Aronson (see Bibliography); Dolan, Jill. "Brandeis University: Enormous Changes." *Theatre Crafts* November 1985: 27; Larne, Michele. "Designers at Work." *Theatre Crafts* May 1987: 30.

Brian R. Jones

Elder, Eldon. Set and lighting designer, consultant, and educator (b. 1924, Atchison, KS). Theatrical productions include sets and lighting for *Shoemaker's Prodigious Wife, The Stronger, The Father, The Lower Depths*—1949; sets and lighting for *Angel in the Pawnshop, The Life of the Party, Within a Glass Bell, The Long Days, My Fiddle's Got Three Strings, Erdgeist, Measure for Measure, The Beggar's Opera*—1950; sets and lighting for *The Long Days* (New York), *Dream Girl, Idiot's Delight, Giants in the Earth, Candida, Love Revisited, Island Fling, Kin Hubbard, Legend of Lovers*—1951; *Venus Observed* (supervising designer), sets and lighting for *Hook 'n Ladder, Time Out for Ginger, The Grey-Eyed People*—1952; *Up in Central Park, Bloomer Girl,*

Cyrano de Bergerac, Rio Rita, Blossom Time, Rip Van Winkle, No, No, Nanette, One Touch of Venus, Carmen, Bitter Sweet, Kiss Me, Kate, Take a Giant Step—1953; sets and lighting for *The Girl in Pink Tights, Call Me Madam, Song of Norway, The New Moon, Roberta, The Mikado, Gentlemen Prefer Blondes, The Three Musketeers, Panama Hattie, Where's Charley?, The Red Mill, Oklahoma!, One Eye Closed*—1954; sets and lighting for *All in One* (including *Trouble in Tahiti* and *27 Wagons Full of Cotton*), *Phoenix '55, The Merry Widow, Brigadoon, Wonderful Town, The Young and the Beautiful, Heavenly Twins*—1955; *Fallen Angels, The Dybbuk*—1956; *Shinbone Alley, Billy Budd*—1957; *The Private Affairs of the Grand Duchess, The Merry Wives of Windsor, Othello, Twelfth Night, Lulu* (costumes and lighting)—1958; designed *Oedipus, Romeo and Juliet, Romanoff and Juliet, Saint Joan, H.M.S. Pinafore, Julius Caesar* (settings and costumes)—1959; *Suor Angelica, Prima Donna, Tiger at the Gates, A Night in Venice, Henry V* (settings and costumes), *The Taming of the Shrew, Measure for Measure, Drums Under the Window* (sets, lighting, and costumes)—1960; *The Caucasian Chalk Circle, Esther, Der Rosenkavalier* (sets and costumes), *The Ballad of Baby Doe, Much Ado About Nothing, A Midsummer Night's Dream, Richard II*—1961; *Three Sisters, Rehearsal Call, Richard II, Henry IV, Part 1, The Affair* (sets and lighting), *The Fun Couple* (and associate producer)—1962; *Morning Sun* (sets and lighting)—1963; *Hanging Judge, Rugantino* (supervising designer), *I Knock at the Door, Pictures in the Hallway, The Child Buyer* (sets and lighting)—1964; *The Golden Trumpet Ball, Madame Mouse* (sets and lighting), *The World of Ray Bradbury, Mating Dance*—1965; *The Oresteia, The Birds* (sets and costumes), *A Whitman Portrait* (sets and lighting), *The Entertainer* (costumes and lighting)—1966; *Of Love Remembered, Amazing Grace*—1967; *Mozart and Salieri, The Megilla of Itzik Manger* (lighting)—1968; *An Evening with Fannie Kemble, An Evening with Agee, Spiro Who?*—1969; *The Drexler Plays* (including *The Investigation* and *Hot Buttered Rolls*), *Will Rogers' USA, A Cry of Players, My Heart's in the Highlands*—1970; *Trial of the Catonville Nine, Helen Hayes: Portrait of an Actress* (film), *The Beaux' Stratagem* (sets and costumes), *Le Nozze Di Figaro*—1971; *An Unpleasant Evening with H. L. Mencken, Fidelio, Pygmalion, Cherry* (sets and costumes)—1972; *A Family and a Fortune, The Sea Gull, Pantagleize*—1973; *Twigs, Hamlet*—1974; *A Doll's House, Blasts and Bravos: An Unpleasant Evening With H. L. Mencken, Pictures in the Hallway, Cyrano de Bergerac*—1975; *The Madwoman of Chaillot, The Signalman's Apprentice, Music Is*—1976; *She Stoops to Conquer, Harry Outside, The Rivals*—1977; *Love Letters on Blue Paper, The End of the Beginning, Give My Regards to Broadway, National Health, Exit the King, Every Good Boy Deserves Favour*—1978; *The Master Builder*—1979.

Elder began his long career in design after graduating from the Yale School of Drama, where he earned an M.F.A. degree. He has designed the settings as well as the lighting for many Broadway, off-Broadway, regional, and educational theatres. On Broadway, he designed *Legend of Lovers* (1951), *Take a Giant*

Step (1953), *Shinbone Alley* (1957), and *The Affair* (1962). Off-Broadway, Elder is responsible for the set and lighting designs for such productions as *Morning Sun* (1963), *The Child Buyer* (1964), and *A Whitman Portrait* (1966). At the New York Shakespeare Festival, he designed many productions, including *Othello* (1958) and *Julius Caesar* (1959), both of which established his involvement with the group. His designs have been featured in the London productions of *A Whitman Portrait* (1966), *Hot Buttered Rolls* (1970), and *The Investigation* (1970). In addition, he has worked at such regional theatre and opera companies as the Seattle Repertory Theatre, the American Shakespeare Festival in Connecticut, the Ypsilanti Greek Festival in Michigan, the St. Louis Municipal Opera, and the Santa Fe Opera. His style is full of clear and simple forms that have the proper amount of decoration and detail. For example, his scenic design for the 1964 production of *The Child Buyer*, directed by Richard Altman, included a New England Senate hearing room with eighteen-foot-high pilasters, surmounted by busts of colonial leaders. Their strong vertical lines led the eye up to the ceiling decorated with the American flag and a Federalist portico that decorated the proscenium arch. Similarly, his sets for *Amazing Grace* and *A Whitman Portrait*, both in 1967, his costume designs for the Santa Fe Opera's production of *The Ballad of Baby Doe* in 1961, and his scenery for the 1972 production of *Fidelio* all rely on his strong use of line, verticality, and exact detail.

Theatre architecture and consulting were among the many activities in which Elder engaged. His credits in this area include the Wollman Memorial Rink Theatre and the Delacorte Theatre for the New York Shakespeare Festival, the American Shakespeare Festival's new stage in Stratford, and the stage for the Ypsilanti Greek Theatre, among others. With his expertise in theatre construction, in 1979, in association with the Off-Off Broadway Alliance (OOBA), Elder published *Will It Make a Theatre: A Guide to Finding, Renovating, Financing, Bringing up to Code, the Non-traditional Performance Space.*

Elder served as professor of stage design at Brooklyn College from 1956 to 1975 and influenced scores of students. In addition, his renderings have been shown at the International Exhibition of Stage Design in 1964, at the Kunstgewerbemuseum of Zurich, Switzerland, in 1966, and at the Third Prague Quadrennial as a part of "Contemporary Stage Design—U.S.A." in 1976.

Awards: Elder received the Ford Foundation Grant for Theatre Design, 1960; the Guggenheim Foundation Grant for Study of Classical Theatre in Greece, Italy, and Turkey in 1963. In addition, he was part of the Cultural Exchange Tour of the USSR and Poland for the United States Department of State in 1965 and a United States' delegate to the International Theatre Institute Congress in Budapest in 1969.

Further Reading: By Elder: *Designs for the Theatre.* New York: Drama Book Specialists, 1978; "The New International Designer." *Contemporary Stage Design—U.S.A.,* Exhibition Catalog. Middletown, CT: Wesleyan University Press, 1974; "An Open-Air Festival Theatre." *The Ideal Theatre: Eight Concepts.* Exhibition Catalog, New York Public Library at Lincoln Center, 1962; "Preparing the Professional Designer." *Theatre*

Crafts May 1969; "The Soviet Scene." *Opera News* 1966; *Will It Make a Theatre.* New York: Off-Off Broadway Alliance, 1979.

Brian R. Jones

Elson, Charles. Designer and teacher (b. 1909, Chicago, IL). Theatrical productions include *The Ticket of Leave Man* (Chase Barn Playhouse, Whitefield, New Hampshire)—1935; *The House of Connelly* (Mayan Theatre, Los Angeles, California)—1937; *As You Like It* (President Theatre)—1945; *Cordelia* (Shubert Theatre, New Haven, Connecticut), *The Temporary Mrs. Smith* (lighting and design assistant; The Playhouse), *Loco* (lighting and design assistant; Biltmore Theatre), *Hidden Horizon* (Plymouth Theatre), *Present Laughter* (lighting and design assistant; Plymouth Theatre), *Park Avenue* (Shubert Theatre), *The Fatal Weakness* (Royale Theatre), *Years Ago* (design assistant; Mansfield Theatre), *Land's End* (Playhouse Theatre), *Abduction from the Seraglio* (design assistant; Metropolitan Opera House), *Lovely Me* (lighting and design assistant; Adelphi Theatre)—1946; *Washington Square* (Shubert Theatre, New Haven, Connecticut), *A Dangerous Woman* (Erie Theatre, Schenectady, New York), *The Greatest of These* (lighting and design assistant; Shubert Theatre, Detroit, Michigan), *The Eagle Has Two Heads* (assistant; Plymouth Theatre), *Virginia Sampler* (New York City Center), *Portrait in Black* (lighting and design assistant; Booth Theatre), *Fidelio* (Central City Opera, Colorado), *Martha* (Central City Opera, Colorado), *The First Mrs. Fraser* (Shubert Theatre), *Duet for Two Hands* (Booth Theatre)—1947; *Power Without Glory* (Booth Theatre), *Kathleen* (Biltmore Theatre), *The Cup of Trembling* (Music Box Theatre), *Private Lives* (Plymouth Theatre), *Present Laughter* (Walnut Street Theatre, Philadelphia, Pennsylvania)—1948; *Albert Herring* (Tanglewood, Massachusetts), *Regina* (lighting; 46th Street Theatre)—1949; Katherine Dunham Ballet (Broadway Theatre), *The Lady's Not for Burning* (also technical director; Royale Theatre), *Out of This World* (also technical director; New Century Theatre), *An Enemy of the People* (lighting; Broadhurst Theatre), *The Flying Dutchman* (Metropolitan Opera House)—1950; *The Rose Tattoo* (Martin Beck Theatre), *Kiss Me, Kate* (also technical director; Coliseum Theatre, London), *Music in the Air* (lighting and technical director; Ziegfeld Theatre), *Nina* (Royale Theatre), *Borscht Capades* (Royale Theatre), *La Plume de Ma Tante, Lysistrata*—1951; *Collector's Item* (lighting; Booth Theatre), *The Deep Blue Sea* (Morosco Theatre), *La Clemenza di Tito, Lohengrin* (Metropolitan Opera House)—1952; *The Little Hut* (lighting; Coronet), *Don Giovanni* (Metropolitan Opera House)—1953; *His and Hers* (48th Street Theatre), *Norma* (Metropolitan Opera House), *A Star Is Born* (film, assistant art director), *Quadrille* (setting supervisor; Coronet Theatre)—1954; *The Champagne Complex* (Cort Theatre)—1955; *The Lovers* (Martin Beck Theatre)—1956; *Compulsion* (Ambassador Theatre)—1957; *Blue Denim* (Playhouse Theatre), *Maria Golovin* (Martin Beck Theatre), *La Plume de Ma Tante* (Royale Theatre), *Madame Butterfly* (Metropolitan Opera House)—1958; *First Impressions* (Alvin

Theatre)—1959, *Wildcat* (Alvin Theatre)—1960; *Troilus and Cressida* (lighting)—1961; *Henry IV*, *Richard II*, *Shakespeare Revisited* (all for the American Shakespeare Festival, Stratford, Connecticut), *Program for Two Players* (lighting; Fisher Theatre, Detroit, Michigan), *The Perfect Setup* (Cort Theatre)— 1962; *Photo Finish* (Brooks Atkinson Theatre)—1963; *Dialogues of the Carmelites* (City Center Opera, New York State Theatre)—1968.

Elson's career began in the 1930s with his design for *The Ticket of Leave Man* in 1934, at the Chase Barn Playhouse in Whitefield, New Hampshire. In 1937, he moved to Los Angeles and designed *The House of Connelly* at the Mayan Theatre, and, relocating to Maine, he designed forty-four productions at the Ogunquit Playhouse from 1939 to 1945. His first New York production was *As You Like It* in 1945, produced off-Broadway at the President Theatre. During the same year, like many of his contemporaries, he became an assistant to Donald Oenslager.* Together, they worked on such shows as *Pygmalion* (1945) at the Ethel Barrymore Theatre and *Born Yesterday* (1946) at the Lyceum Theatre. Elson's style was predominantly realistic, but with a strong classical, compositional style. This can be seen, for example, in *Private Lives* (1948), a revival that opened at the Plymouth Theatre and had sets that created formal, realistic scenes of the French hotel's classic terrace and of Amanda's sumptuous flat. Not limited to plays, Elson's designs have included such operas as *Fidelio* and *Martha* for the Central City Opera in Colorado in 1947, as well as works designed at the Metropolitan Opera House in New York, including *Lohengrin* (1953) and *Don Giovanni* (1953). His other activities included working on the film *A Star Is Born* (1954) and teaching scene design at the University of Oklahoma, the University of Iowa, and Hunter College in New York.

Kurt Lancaster

Erté (Romain de Tirtoff). Artist and theatrical designer (b. 1882, St. Petersburg, Russia; d. 1990). Theatrical productions (all were produced in Paris, unless otherwise noted) include *Le Minaret*–1913; *Aphrodite*, *Le Tango*, *La Revue de Saint Cyr*—1914; *Theatre Ba-Ta-Clan Revue*–1916; *La Planète Fémina*–1917; *Theatre Ba-Ta-Clan Revue*–1918; *Folies Bergère*, *La Marche à L'étoile*—1919; *Thais*, *Mauna Vanna*, *Aphrodite*, *Fedora*, *Tosca*, *Manon*, *La Bohème*, *Zaza*, *Louise*, *I Pagliacci*, *Faust*, *Marta L'Amour dei Trere* (Chicago), *Restless Sex* (film; United States, Cosmopolitan Films)—1920; *Folies Bergère*, *Theatre Alcazar Revue*, *Winter Garden Theater Revue* (New York)—1921; *Theatre des Ambassadeurs Revue*, *Theatre Alcazar Revue* (Marseilles), *George White's Scandals* (New York), *Winter Garden Theatre Revue* (New York), *Music Box Theatre Revue* (New York), *Fémina*—1922; *Folies Bergère*, *La Traviata* (costumes for Maria Kuznetov), *Ziegfeld Follies* (New York), *Music Box Theater Revue*— 1923; *Le Secret du Sphinx*, *Folies Bergère*, *Fémina*, *Winter Garden Theater Revue* (New York), *George White's Scandals* (New York), *Palladium Revue* (London)—1924; *George White's Scandals* (New York), *The Mystic* (film; MGM), *A Little Bit of Broadway* (film; MGM), *Time the Comedian* (film; MGM),

La Bohème (costumes for Renée Adorée; film, MGM); *Ben-Hur* (costumes for Carmel Byers; film, MGM)—1925; *Folies Bergère, George White's Scandals* (New York)—1926; *L'Amore de Tre Re, The Tales of Hoffman, Manhattan Mary* (New York)—1927; *Lindberg, Tosca, Manon, George White's Scandals* (New York)—1928; *Folies Bergère, La Princesse Lointaine, George White's Scandals* (New York)—1929; *Folies Bergère, Pelléas et Mélisande* (costumes for Ganna Walska)—1931; *Faust, Don Pasquale* (Rome)—1932; *Bal Tabarin, Les Travaux de Hercule, Au Temps des Merveilleuses*—1934; *Cécile Sorel, Les Joies du Capitol, Alhambra and Tabarin Theater Revues, French Casino* (New York)—1935; *Au Soleil du Mexique, Tabarin Theater Revue*—1936; *Plaisir de France, It's in the Bag* (London)—1937; *Le Chant du Tzigane, Les Heures sont Belles, Fleet's Lit Up* (London), *London Symphony* (London), *Scala Theater Revue* (Berlin)—1938; *Un Vrai Paradis, George White's Revue* (San Francisco), *Black Velvet* (London)—1939; *Phi-phi, Mes Amours*—1940; *Toi-C'est moi, Trois Jeunes Villes Nues, Lido Theater Revue, Dans Notre Miroir*—1941; *Les Cent Vierges, Coup de Roulis Revue*—1942; *Une Femme Par Jour, Belamour, Lido and Tabarin Theatre Revues*—1943; *Don Pasquale, Lido Theatre Revue*—1944; *The Barber of Seville, Lido and Tabarin Theater Revues*—1945; *On Cherche un Roi, Lido and Tabarin Theatre Revues, Il Matrimonio Segreto* (Rome), *Piccadilly Hayride* (London), *The Night and the Laughter* (London)—1946; *Les Mamelles de Tirésias, Tabarin Theater Revue*—1947; *Ma Mère l'Oye, Sueños de Viena* (Barcelona), *Bal Tabarin Revue* (Blackpool, England)—1948; *Puss in Boots* (London), *Bal Tabarin Revue* (Blackpool, England)—1949; *Palladium Theater Revue* (London), *La Nouvelle Eve Cabaret Revue*—1950; *La Traviata, Parfums, La Leç d'Amour dans un Parc, Histoires d'Eve, Fancy Free* (London), *Happy-Go-Lucky* (Blackpool, England)—1951; *Così fan Tutte, Les Filles d'Eve, Pelléas at Mélisande* (Naples, Padmavate (Naples)), *You Bet Your Life* (London), *Maske in Blau* (film; West Germany)—1952; *La Nouvelle Eve, Caccia al Tesoro* (Rome), *Die geschiedene Frau* (film; West Germany)—1953; *Mother Goose, Joker's Wild* (both in London)—1954; *Champagne-Cocktail, La Nouvelle Eve, Gonzague* (Cannes), *Companes de Viena* (Barcelona), *La Plume de Ma Tante* (London)—1955; *La Poule Noire, La Quincaillère de Chicago, Extravagances, Victoria Palace Theater Revue* (London), *Blackpool Theatre Revue* (Blackpool, England)—1956; *Capriccio, Pommes à l'Anglaise, La Nouvelle Eve, Blackpool Opera House Revue* (Blackpool, England)—1957; *Don Cézar de Bazan, Drap d'Or, Folies-Pigalle, La Nouvelle Eve, La Plume de Ma Tante* (New York)—1958; *Don Pasquale, Casino du Liban, Drap D'Or, Folies-Pigalle, Crown Jewels* (London), *Blackpool Opera House Revue* (Blackpool, England)—1959; *Phèdre, Piege pour un Homme Seul, Le Coiffeur-Miracle, Edition Speciale* (both ballet films of Louis Cuny), *Casino du Liban Revue* (Beirut), *Young in Heart* (London)—1960; *Moulin Rouge Revue, Castor et Pollux* (Lyons), *Olé* (Berlin)—1961; *Twist Appeal, La Java, La Chasse aux Folles*—1962; *Latin Quarter Revue* (New York)—1963; *The Eunuch, Wonderworld* (New York), *Latin Quarter Revue* (New York)—1964; *Flying Colors* (Montreal)—1967; *Zizi Jeanmaire*

Show—1970; *Zizi Je T'Aime*, *Ragtime Ballet*—1972; *Scheherazade*—1975; *Der Rosenkavalier*—1980; *Anatol* (Los Angeles)—1985.

In 1912 at the age of twenty, Romain de Tirtoff moved to Paris and arrived during Sergey Diaghilev's triumphant Ballets Russes tour. Tirtoff—adopting the pseudonym Erté from his initials, R. T., when he began to work as a fashion designer—became a sketch artist for the legendary Parisian couturier Paul Poiret. Through him, Erté had the opportunity to design costumes for several theatrical productions, including *Le Minaret* (1913) and *Aphrodite* (1914). Influenced by the lavish, Oriental-inspired costumes of the Ballets Russes and the designers Léon Bakst* and Ernst Stern,* Erté soon developed his own technique. Later, he united the stylized, minute attention to detail characteristic of the Oriental approach with the bold outlines and geometrical forms of the art deco style. This combination created a visual approach that was essentially modern, at the same time exhibiting a romantic escapism that bordered on the fantastic.

After he left Poiret in 1915, Erté became well known as an artist, and his designs were frequently featured in *Harper's Bazaar*, one of the most influential American fashion magazines. As a result, he was offered an opportunity to design for the French music hall Ba-ta-Clan by one of the pioneers of French revue, Madame Rasmini. Throughout the 1920s, he also designed sets and costumes for the American equivalents of these revues, the Broadway spectacles of Florenz Ziegfeld and George White. He also created sets and costumes for the vaudeville shows that appeared at the Winter Garden and Music Box theatres in New York. In 1925, Erté worked for a year in Hollywood at MGM and designed costumes for a number of films.

Following the gradual demise of the lavish revue after the economic collapse of 1929, Erté continued to design for small revues in Europe, as well as the legitimate theatre, opera, and ballet. He designed the sets and costumes for several productions at the Opèra and Opèra Comique in Paris. His later work adapted elements from both South American and Mexican art, while it maintained a studied devotion to detail.

Erté's designs were exhibited in London, Paris, Milan, and New York in 1966. After the New York exhibition, the entire collection, which consisted of designs for *Harper's Bazaar*, fashion houses, and Broadway, was purchased by the Metropolitan Museum of Art.

Further Reading: Barthes, Roland. *Erté*, trans. William Waver. Parma, Italy: Franco, Maria Ricci, 1972; *Erté Fashions*. New York: St. Martin's Press, 1972; "The Follies, Scandals, and Delights of Erté." *Horizon* Summer 1975; Spencer, Charles. *Erté*. New York: Clarkson Potter, 1970; Tirtoff, Romain de. *Things I Remember*. New York: Quadrangle Books, 1975.

Howard Gutner

Exter, Aleksandra. Designer and artist (b. January 6, 1882, Bielostock, Russia; d. March 17, 1949, Paris, France). Theatrical productions include *Famira Kifared*—1916; *Salome, Etudes de Bach* (costumes only)—1917; *Petrouchka*—1918; *Romeo and Juliet, Entremeses* (by Cervantes, a project for the Moscow

Art Theatre), *The Death of Tarelkin*, *The Modern Khlestakov*, *La Dama Duenda*—1921; *Aelita* (film), *Turandot*—1924; *Caucasia* (ballet)—1926; *La Donna Sullo Scudo*, *Le Cirque*—1927; *Night of Venice*—1928. Exter also designed theatre curtains (her most famous were for Tairov's Kamerny Theatre), numerous dance recitals, and many unproduced projects for stage and film.

Exter studied at the School of Fine Arts in Kiev and at the Academie de la Grande Chaumiére, where she met many of the greatest artists of her era, including Picasso, Apollinaire, and Braque. She began shuttling back and forth between Moscow and Paris, exhibiting with artists in her own country, and starting a studio school in Kiev in 1916. From the Revolution to the mid-1920s, she became increasingly interested in scene design and created the settings for many theatrical productions in Russia. Many of Exter's most important designs, featuring her cubist style, were done in collaboration with director Aleksandr Tairov at Moscow's Kamerny Theatre. In 1917, she designed settings and costumes for one of his greatest productions, *Salome*, with Alice Koonen, the noted Russian actress (and Tairov's wife), in the leading role. This production was a highly representative example of Exter's style, featuring bright colors and sharp lines in the costumes combined with a setting of rectangular steps, cylindrical columns, and many levels. In her experiments with cubism and her three-dimensional, ''constructed'' settings, she worked toward a harmonious relationship between the actor and the stage setting that suggested the theories of Appia* and Craig.* After the Soviet authorities ceased to support experimental works in the arts, Exter moved permanently to France and taught for a time in Leger's Academie de l'Art Moderne as well as in her own studio. She taught designers Pavel Tchelitchew* and Boris Aronson* and influenced several other important designers. Exter continued to work on theatre, film, and dance productions throughout Europe, and she also illustrated books and designed furniture, china, fabric, and lights, but she rarely exhibited as an artist after the mid–1930s. She died in obscurity in her last home in Fontenay-les-Roses, but in recent years there has been a significant revival of interest in her work.

Further Reading: Bowlt, John E. ''Aleksandra Exter.'' *Art News* April 1974; Lozowich, Louis. ''Alexandra Exter's Marionettes.'' *Theatre Arts Monthly* 12 (1928): 515–18; Nakov, Andrei B. *Alexandra Exter*. Paris: Galerie Jean Chauvelin, 1972; Oenslager (see Bibliography); Oliver, M. *The Russian Theatre*. New York: Brentano's, 1922; Yakov, A. T. *Alexandra Exter*. Berlin: ''Sarja'' Edition, 1922.

James Fisher

F

Fabris, Jacopo. Set designer, painter, and theatrical architect (b. 1689, Venice, Italy; d. 1761). After working as a painter in Italy in his youthful years, in 1719 Fabris went to Germany and became employed by the Margrave of Baden-Durlach as a Court designer. In 1724, he was assigned a position as designer at the Hamburg Opera House, where he produced the settings for twenty-five operas in six years. Subsequently, he married, and it is believed that he lived and worked in England for a period of ten years. As Court designer for Frederick the Great in Berlin in 1740, Fabris collaborated with the architect Knobelsdorff on a temporary palace theatre and then on the permanent royal opera house. In 1742, the new theatre was inaugurated with a production of *Cleopatra and Caesar*. After seven years of opera design, Fabris moved to Denmark, where he was installed as the Court designer for Christian VI. In Denmark, Fabris worked alongside architect Nicolas Eigtved on the construction of two theatres, the royal Charlottenborg Castle Theatre and the Kongens Nytorv Theatre, where he subsequently designed settings for plays. In addition to his practical design work, Fabris taught the principles of architecture and design and wrote a five-volume manuscript. Volume 4 is called *Instruction in der Theatralischen Architectur und Mechanique* and was reprinted in 1930. It is a firsthand description of eighteenth-century theatrical practice and design.

Further Reading: Oenslager (see Bibliography).

Thomas J. Mikotowicz

Farrah, Abdelkader. Designer (b. 1926, Algeria). A native Algerian who trained himself as a painter, Farrah worked with Michel Saint-Denis in France and England. Farrah employs strong architectural concepts in his stage designs that are noted for their bold use of color. In addition, he worked as a free-lance designer, mostly on the English stage for the Royal Shakespeare Company. Some of his major theatrical productions include *The Tempest* (1963), *Doctor*

Faustus (1968), *Richard III* (1970), *The Balcony* (1972), *Henry V* (1975), *Coriolanus* (1977), *As You Like It* (1980), and *Poppy* (1982).

James Fisher

Feder, Abraham. Lighting designer and theatre consultant (b. June 27, 1909, Milwaukee, WI). Theatrical productions include *Trick for Trick*—1932; *One Sunday Afternoon*—1933; *Four Saints in Three Acts, Calling All Stars, Gentlewoman*—1934; *The Hook-Up, Ghosts*—1935; *Conjur' Man Dies, Macbeth, New Faces of 1936, Horse Eats Hat, Walk Together Chillun, Triple-A Ploughed Under, Turpentine, Injunction Granted, Hedda Gabler*—1936; *The Tragical Historie of Doctor Faustus, Native Ground, Without Warning, I'd Rather Be Right*—1937; *Diff'rent, Pygmalion, Captain Jinks of the Horse Marines, Coriolanus, Prologue to Glory, Big Blow, Here Come the Clowns, The Cradle Will Rock, Androcles and the Lion, 13 of a Nation, The Father*—1938; *Sing for Your Supper, Speak of the Devil!*—1939; *A Passenger to Bali, Hold on to Your Hats, Johnny Belinda*—1940; *Giselle, Great American Goof, Peter and the Wolf, Angel Street*—1941; *Autumn Hill, The Skin of Our Teeth, Magic, Hello Out There, The Walking Gentleman*—1942; *Winged Victory*—1943; *Tower Beyond Tragedy, Out of This World*—1950; *Mary Rose, Sleep of Prisoners*—1951; *Three Wishes for Jamie, Dear Barbarians, The Sonja Henie Ice Revue*—1952; *A Pin to See the Peepshow*—1953; *The Immoralist, The Boy Friend, What Every Woman Knows, The Flowering Peach*—1954; *The Wisteria Tree, Inherit the Wind, Seventh Heaven, Skin of Our Teeth, The Young and the Beautiful*—1955; *My Fair Lady*—1956; *A Clearing in the Woods, Visit to a Small Planet, Orpheus Descending, Time Remembered*—1957; *Goldilocks, At the Grand, The Cold Wind and the Warm*—1958; *Come Play with Me, Can-Can, A Loss of Roses*—1959; *Greenwillow, Camelot*—1960; *Tiger, Tiger, Burning Bright*—1962; *Once for the Asking*—1963; *My Fair Lady, Blues for Mr. Charlie, The Three Sisters*—1964; *On a Clear Day You Can See Forever*—1965; *The Country Girl, Elizabeth the Queen, Carousel*—1966; *Beyond Desire, Salute to the American Musical Theatre* (the White House, Washington, D.C.)—1967; *The King and I, Carnival!, My Fair Lady*—1968; *Scratch*—1971; *Goodtime Charley, Doctor Jazz*—1975; *Carmelina*—1979; *Night of the Iguana*—1985.

Feder is a pioneer lighting designer and was the first independent lighting designer in both the theatrical and architectural worlds. After graduating from Carnegie Tech in 1929, he designed the lighting for his first Broadway production, *Trick for Trick* (1932). Starting when modern lighting was in its infancy, Feder has continued to be an innovator as well as a designer throughout his entire career and has created lighting for more than 125 Broadway productions. From 1935 to 1941, Feder oversaw the lighting for all WPA Theatre projects, including Orson Wells's production of *Dr. Faustus* (1935) and *The Living Newspaper* (1941). In 1940, he was the production coordinator and lighting designer for the first tour of the American Ballet Theatre and designed twenty-one ballets. Throughout the next two decades, Feder was responsible for many landmark

New York productions, including *The Cradle Will Rock* (1938), *Angel Street* (1941), *The Skin of Our Teeth* (1942), *My Fair Lady* (1956), and *Camelot* (1960). He worked with many of the major set designers on Broadway, including Oliver Smith,* and created more than mere illumination for the high demands of production. Feder used his engineering background to invent new lighting instruments, if needed, to serve the design of his shows. Two of his patents include the reflector bulb, which he codeveloped with Clarence Birdseye, and the sealed beam reflector lamp. Through his company, Lighting by Feder, he has consulted and designed many projects both theatrical and architectural. His architectural lighting includes Rockefeller Center, Central Park, Kennedy International Airport, the United Nations building, and the Pan-Am building. He has served as consultant and lighting designer for the New York World's Fair, Expo '67 in Montreal, the San Francisco Civic Center, and the Minskoff Theatre and designed the lighting for all of the theatres in the Kennedy Center, Washington, D.C.

Further Reading: By Feder: "Light as an Architectural Material." *Progressive Architecture* September 1958: 124–31; "Lighting, Awareness, and Discipline." *Lighting Dimensions* April 1978: 38; "Theatre Form Through Light." *American Institute of Architects' Journal* October 1960.

About Feder: Gassner, John, ed. *Producing the Play.* New York: Dryden Press, 1958; Pollack, Steve. "Lighting by Feder." *Lighting Dimensions* May/June 1986: 40–43.

Ken Kloth

Fedorovich, Sophie. Scene designer (b. December 15, 1893, Minsk, Russia; d. January 24, 1953, London, England). Fedorovich began her study of painting at age sixteen in Kraków, Poland. In 1921, she moved to London, where she eventually began designing ballets. One of her earlier designs was for *A Tragedy of Fashion* (1926), executed for the Ballet Rambert, a company with which she continued a long relationship. She especially enjoyed working with Frederick Ashton and designed many ballets for him and other choreographers at Sadler's Wells, including *The Scorpions of Ysitt* (1932), *Le Baiser de la Fee* (1935), and *Orpheus* (1953). Her scenic work was open and clean, frequently spartan, with economic use of line. The relative simplicity of her backgrounds made them especially successful for ballet. This tendency was helpful in the early days at Sadler's Wells when there was little budget for scenery. She believed ballet was the art of suggestion, not statement, and she retained this same style later at Covent Garden even though the budget and space were both larger. Her work there included *La Traviata* (1948), *Tosca* (1950), and *Madame Butterfly* (1950). Many of her designs employed drapes and swags of fabric. Her final design, *Orpheus,* for the Royal Opera House at Sadler's Wells, had to be completed by others after her untimely death due to gas poisoning caused by a malfunctioning thermostat in her home.

Elbin L. Cleveland

Ffolkes, David. Set, costume, and lighting designer (b. October 12, 1912, Hagley, Worcestershire, England). Theatrical productions (all were in London, unless otherwise specified) include *The Writing on the Wall* (sets), *Howell of*

Gurent (sets)—1934; *Trial in Camera* (sets)—1935; *Sunshine Sisters* (sets)—
1936; *King Richard II* (sets and costumes), *Young Mr. Disraeli* (sets and costumes)—1937; *Hamlet* (sets and costumes)—1938; *Henry IV, Part 1* (St. James
Theatre, New York), *Hamlet* (sets and costumes; St. James Theatre, New
York)—1939; *King Richard II* (costumes; St. James Theatre, New York)—1943;
Henry VIII (costumes; International Theatre, New York), *The Thracian Horses*
(sets), *The Day After Tomorrow* (sets), *What Every Woman Knows* (costumes;
International Theatre, New York)—1946; *Brigadoon* (costumes; Ziegfeld The-
atre, New York), *Man and Superman* (sets and costumes; Alvin Theatre, New
York)—1947; *Sleepy Hollow* (costumes; St. James Theatre, New York), *Where's
Charley?* (sets and costumes; St. James Theatre, New York)—1948; *Along Fifth
Avenue* (costumes; Broadhurst Theatre, New York), *The Browning Version* (cos-
tumes; Coronet Theatre), *A Harlequinade* (costumes)—1949; *Where's Charley?*
(sets and costumes; Broadway Theatre, New York), *Springtime for Henry* (costumes; John Golden Theatre, New York); *Flahooley* (costumes; Broadhurst Theatre, New York), *Seventeen* (sets and costumes; Broadhurst Theatre, New
York)—1951; *Montserrat* (sets and costumes), *Where's Charley?* (film)—1952;
Men of Distinction (sets and costumes; 48th Street Theatre, New York)—1953;
Scotch Symphony (costumes; New York City Ballet)—1954; *Alexander the Great*
(film)—1956; *Island in the Sun* (film)—1957; *Journey to the Center of the Earth*
(film)—1959; *Heavens Above!* (film)—1963; *The Long Ships* (film)—1964.

Working first for the Cambridge Theater Company as a paint mixer, Ffolkes
was soon promoted and designed the sets for their production of *The Writing on
the Wall*, which was presented in London in 1934. Later, he toured with the
company throughout the English countryside with the comedy *Howell of Gurent*
(1934), only to return to London, where he designed the sets for *Trial in Camera*
(1935) and Ivor Novello's *Sunshine Sisters* (1936). In 1936, John Gielgud introduced Ffolkes to Lillian Baylis at the Old Vic, where he later became chief
designer. Through his association with Maurice Evans and director Margaret
Webster at the Old Vic, Ffolkes achieved his first great successes in London
and designed the sets and costumes for *Hamlet* (1938) and *King Richard II*
(1943), both of which starred Evans and later opened to unanimous raves in
New York. Ffolkes continued his association with the Old Vic both in London
and in New York with the productions *What Every Woman Knows* (1946), *Henry
VIII* (1946), and the successful revival of George Bernard Shaw's *Man and
Superman* (1947). That same year, in league with set designer Oliver Smith,*
Ffolkes designed the costumes for his first musical, *Brigadoon*, as well as the
sets for his first ballet, *Highland Fling*, for the New York Ballet Society. In
1949, he again collaborated with Smith on the musical revue *Along Fifth Avenue*.
In the 1950s and early 1960s, Ffolkes began to design both sets and costumes
in Hollywood for such films as *Alexander the Great* (1956) and *Journey to the
Center of the Earth* (1959). Also in the 1950s, Ffolkes was a member of the
Division of Theater Arts at Boston University. Today he lives in retirement in
California.

Ffolkes's technique in set construction and costume design is perhaps best illustrated through his Shakespearean productions for the Old Vic. His credo for designing looks deceptively simple on the surface: comfortable, colorful costumes and uncluttered, easily shifted sets. A great deal of planning and careful consideration, however, goes into the construction of a unit set like the one Ffolkes designed for the 1939 New York production of *Hamlet*. His sets readily convertible from a castle parapet or throne room to a scenic view of a Danish plain or a row of tombstones for the graveyard scene, the critic from the *New York Herald Tribune* likened Ffolkes's drawings of the sets to a blueprint representing a "cross-section of the Maginot Line. . . . They are so expertly constructed that not so much as a mechanical tremor upsets the proceedings from curtain to curtain." Indeed, the settings, in the form of mobile units, advanced and receded as the action of play demanded. The actual scenic equipment was so extensive that a mere six inches intervened between some of the flying sets, all of which had a slight arc so that, when hauled upward, they would permit the interjection of a set that traveled horizontally. Ffolkes succeeded brilliantly at combining architectural knowledge with theatrical imagination. As a result, the platforms, uprights, and colonnades had such flexibility that they could be used for a variety of different scenes.

Ffolkes's costumes combined imagination with intense research into the dress of historical periods. Yet authenticity could sometimes be sacrificed for stage effect. When an infuriated Scotsman wrote Ffolkes that three patterns used in *Brigadoon* were not real Scotch plaids, Ffolkes defended his decision by replying that he had picked colors that would look good onstage. Ffolkes was consistent in his belief that truly functional design served both the production onstage as well as the audience.

Awards: Ffolkes's work has earned him a Tony Award for *Henry VIII* (1946), as well as two Donaldson Awards for *Brigadoon* and *Man and Superman* (1947).

Further Reading: "David Ffolkes." *Cue* October 9, 1948; "The English Designer in America." *Theatre Arts Monthly* October 1938; "Hamlet." *Life* November 28, 1938; Leese, Elizabeth. *Costume Design in the Movies*. Bembridge, Isle of Wight: BCW, 1976.

Howard Gutner

Fingerhut, Arden. Lighting designer (b. September 16, 1945, Minneapolis, MN). The majority of designs in Fingerhut's portfolio have been created for productions in the nonprofit theatre. After receiving a bachelor's degree from New York University in 1967 and a master's degree at Columbia in 1972, she began her career in lighting with the Open Theatre. While there, she worked for approximately five years with Joe Chaikin and Robert Ackerman on such successful productions as *Bent* and *Extremities*. Her lighting designs include the New York productions of *Da* (1978), *Plenty*, and *Driving Miss Daisy* (1987). In the past couple of years, Fingerhut worked on such projects as a collaboration with director Tadashi Suzuki on *A Tale of Lear* (1987) and *Julius Caesar* (1988) for the New York Shakespeare Festival. As an instructor, she has taught at New

York University for twelve years and currently serves as chair of the Theatre Department at Williams College. Fingerhut has also continued a fifteen-year relationship with the New York Shakespeare Festival as lighting designer.

Awards: Among her awards are the Village Voice Award for the lighting design for *The Diviners* (1981); an Obie Award in 1982 for "Sustained Excellence in Lighting Design"; and several Maharam Citations.

Further Reading: "Designers at Work." *Theatre Crafts* May 1987: 35; Flatow, Sheryl. "Lighting on Her Own Terms." *Theatre Crafts* October 1990: 47.

Annie Milton

Firth, Tazeena. Costume and scene designer (b. 1935, Southampton, England). Theatrical productions include *A Resounding Tinkle* (Theatre Royal, Windsor, London), *Two Gentlemen of Verona* (Royal Shakespeare Company, London)— 1969; *The Knot Garden* (Royal Opera, London)—1970; *Occupations, The Merchant of Venice, Enemies, The Man of Mode* (Royal Shakespeare Company, London)—1971; *The Lower Depths, The Island of the Mighty* (Royal Shakespeare Company, London), *La Cenerentola* (Royal Opera, Oslo, Norway)—1972; *Richard II, Love's Labor's Lost* (both at the Royal Shakespeare Company, London)— 1973; *Summerfolk* (Royal Shakespeare Company, London), *Pericles* (Comedie Française, Paris), *Next of Kin* (National Theatre, London)—1974; *The Merry Wives of Windsor* (Royal Shakespeare Company, London), *Peter Grimes* (Royal Opera, London), *The Marrying of Ann Leete* (Royal Shakespeare Company, London), *The Bassarids* (Opera, Frankfurt, Germany), *John Gabriel Borkman* (National Theatre, London)—1975; *The Zykovs* (Royal Shakespeare Company, London), *Woyzeck* (Berlin, Germany), *Troilus and Cressida, Force of Habit* (both at the National Theatre, London)—1976; *Tales from the Vienna Woods, Bedroom Farce* (National Theatre, London), *Falstaff* (Berlin, Germany)—1977; *Cunning Little Vixen* (Gothenburg, Germany), *A Midsummer Night's Dream* (Sydney, Australia), *Evita* (London)—1978; *Peter Grimes* (Opera, Gothenburg, Germany), *Evita* (Broadway Theatre, New York), *The Rake's Progress* (Royal Opera, London)—1979; *Lulu* (Royal Opera, London)—1981; *La Ronde* (Royal Shakespeare Company, London), *A Doll's Life* (Mark Hellinger Theatre, New York), *Le Grand Macabre* (English National Opera, London)—1982; *Turandot* (Vienna State Opera, Austria)—1983; *Tannhauser* (Royal Opera, London), *Tramway Road* (Lyric Theatre, London)—1984; *Samson* (Royal Opera, London)—1985; *Old Times* (Theatre Royal, Haymarket, London)—1986.

Educated in London, Firth first designed for the theatre for a *A Resounding Tinkle* at the Theatre Royal in Windsor. Two years later in 1971, Firth joined forces with designer Timothy O'Brien, and the two have been working as a team ever since. Together, they share the set and costume design responsibilities and variously trade different tasks, depending on the demands of the show.

O'Brien, former head of design at ABC television from 1955 to 1966, designed for the London stage throughout the late 1950s and early 1960s. In 1966, he became an associate artist for the Royal Shakespeare Company. With Firth, he designed a number of productions in the early 1970s, including *All's Well That*

Ends Well, Romeo and Juliet, The Latent Heterosexual, and *Measure for Measure.* Several of these plays, including *Summerfolk* and *Love's Labour's Lost,* toured the United States in the mid-1970s. In 1974, Firth and O'Brien began designing for the National Theatre in London and throughout the mid- and late 1970s, for the Royal Opera House, the Comedie Française, and the Berlin Opera.

Firth and O'Brien's technique—form follows function through simple efficiency—is perhaps best illustrated through their prodigious work on Harold Prince's *Evita,* both in London and New York. In 1977, Prince asked the designers to create a setting that would enable him to visualize a show. Using for inspiration the two long-playing records that composer Andrew Lloyd Webber had already published, Firth and O'Brien created an elaborate stage machine. It consisted of a projection screen with two parallel side walls that ran on a track, a floor with a recessed pattern of lights, and a balcony. Murals on the side panels and balcony represented the Argentine people as spectators of the events on stage. Projections of photos and newsreels turned the set into a cinema, a nightclub, a stadium, a bedroom, and the streets of Argentina with a minimum of sets and props. This efficiency is mirrored in the costume design, in which Firth and O'Brien used color to help the audience focus on specific characters in the crowds of people on stage. Their functional approach to design has been applied to such productions as *Turandot* for the Vienna State Opera and *Old Times* at the Theatre Royal in London.

Awards: Tazeena Firth and Timothy O'Brien were joint winners (with Ralph Koltai and John Bury) of the individual Gold Medal for set design at the Prague Quadriennale in 1975.

Further Reading: "*Evita.*" *Theatre Crafts* May 1985; "*Evita*: Staging on a Grand Opera Scale." *Theatre Crafts* November/December 1979; Owen (see Bibliography).

Howard Gutner

Fisher, Jules. Lighting designer, producer, and consultant (b. November 12, 1937, Norristown, PA). Theatrical productions include *All the King's Men*— 1959; *Tobacco Road, Here Come the Clowns, Greenwich Village U.S.A., Marcus in the High Grass*—1960; *The Eccentricities of Davy Crockett, Riding Hood Revisited, Willie the Weeper, Donogoo, Cicero, The Tiger Ray, Go Show Me a Dragon, All in Love, Red Roses for Me*—1961; *Moon on a Rainbow Shawl, The Banker's Daughter, Creditors, Fly Blackbird, The Book of Job, The Golden Apple, This Side of Paradise, Nathan the Wise, Half-Past Wednesday, O Say Can You See!, Riverwind*—1962; *The Love Nest, Six Characters in Search of an Author, Best Foot Forward, The Dragon, Spoon River Anthology, Telemachus Clay, The Ginger Man, The Trojan Women*—1963; *Anyone Can Whistle, High Spirits, Wonder World, The White House, The Subject Was Roses, A Girl Could Get Lucky, Tragical Historie of Doctor Faustus, Gogo Loves You, The Sign in Sidney Brustein's Window, P.S. I Love You*—1964; *Do I Hear a Waltz?, Decline and Fall of the Entire World As Seen Through the Eyes of Cole Porter Revisited, Half a Sixpence, And Things That Go Bump in the Night, Square in the Eye, Leonard Bernstein's Theater Songs, Pickwick, The Devils, The White Devil, Ben*

Bagley's New Cole Porter Revue, *The Yearling*—1965; *Suburban Tragedy*, *Make Like a Dog*, *Princess Rebecca Birnbaum*, *Young Marrieds Play Monopoly*, *Serjeant Musgrave's Dance*, *Hooray!*, *It's a Glorious Day . . . and All That*, *The Kitchen*, *A Hand Is on the Gate*, *Eh?*, *The Threepenny Opera*, *Hail Scrawdyke!*— 1966; *Black Comedy/White Lies*, *You're a Good Man Charlie Brown*, *The Natural Look*, *You Know I Can't Hear You When the Water's Running*, *Illya Darling*, *Little Murders*, *South Pacific*, *The Unknown Soldier and His Wife*, *A Minor Adjustment*, *Scuba Duba*, *Trial of Lee Harvey Oswald*, *Iphigenia in Aulis*—1967; *Before You Go*, *Grand Music Hall of Israel*, *Here's Where I Belong*, *Kongi's Harvest*, *Hair*, *The Only Game in Town*, *A Moon for the Misbegotten*, *The Happy Hypocrite*, *The Cuban Thing*, *The Man in the Glass Booth*, *Love Match*— 1968; *But*, *Seriously . . .*, *The Watering Place*, *Someone's Comin' Hungry*, *Trumpets of the Lord*, *Promenade*, *Butterflies Are Free*—1969; *Sheep on the Runway*, *Gantry*, *Minnie's Boys*, *Jakey Fat Boy*, *Dear Janet Rosenberg*, *Dear Mr. Kooning*, *Inquest*, *The Engagement Baby*, *Steambath*, *Home*—1970; *Soon*, *Hamlet*, *No*, *No*, *Nanette*, *Jesus Christ Superstar*, *Lenny*—1971; *Fun City*, *Pippin*, *Lysistrata*, *Mourning Becomes Electra*, *The Trials of Oz*—1972; *Seesaw*, *Molly*, *Full Circle*, *The Iceman Cometh*, *Uncle Vanya*, *Rachael Lily Rosenbloom and Don't You Ever Forget It*, *Joseph and the Amazing Technicolor Dreamcoat*, *Pippin*—1973; *Ulysses in Nighttown*, *Liza*, *Billy*—1974; *Rolling Stones Tour of U.S.A.* (Production Supervisor), *Man on the Moon*, *Chicago*—1975; *Rockabye Hamlet*, *A Star Is Born* (film)—1976; *American Buffalo*, *Beatlemania*, *Hair*, *Golda*—1977; *Dancin'*—1978; *Beatlemania*—1979; *Can't Stop the Music* (film)—1980; *Rock 'N' Roll! The First 5,000 Years*—1982; *La Cage aux Folles*— 1983; *Song and Dance*—1985; *Big Deal*, *Rags*—1986; *Birds of Paradise* (Promenade), *King Richard II* and *King Henry IV, Part I* (both at the New York Shakespeare Festival)—1987; *Songs of My Father* (Minskoff Theatre), *Legs Diamond* (Mark Hellinger), *La Cage aux Folles* (Paper Mill Playhouse, Millburn, New Jersey)—1988; *Grand Hotel*—1990.

With more than 150 Broadway shows to his credit and his own consulting firm, Fisher has been one of the busiest designers on Broadway. As a student, Fisher worked as an assistant stage manager and carpenter in summer stock. Before graduating from Carnegie Tech with a B.F.A. in theatre technology, he had worked as assistant electrician at the Shubert in Philadelphia on three touring musicals. These shows led to his becoming lighting designer for three shows at the Circle in the City Theatre. Thus, by the time he received his college degree in 1960, he had already designed a number of shows in off-Broadway theatres. Unlike many of his contemporaries, Fisher never interned with a major designer to learn his craft but learned it from experience.

His first New York show, *All the King's Men* (1959), established his career. For the next several years, Fisher worked at various New York City and regional theatres and designed dozens of productions. Fisher's early credits range from the musicals *Anyone Can Whistle* and *High Spirits*, both in 1964, to the classic and avant-garde productions of *Spoon River Anthology* (1963), *The Threepenny Opera* (1966), and *Little Murders* (1967).

Fisher's philosophy of design is that there is very little that is impossible in theatre if the designer carefully analyzes the problems to be solved. He also firmly believes that the lighting designer needs to be in on the production process from the beginning. Thus, he was involved in the early development of the "rock" musicals *Hair* (1968), *Jesus Christ Superstar* (1971), and *Pippin* (1972). All of these productions displayed a sophisticated application of theatrical lighting. Not only was the lighting for these shows a masterly execution of technology and design, but it was cross-fertilized with techniques used for "rock" show lighting. Not coincidentally, Fisher subsequently became production supervisor for the Rolling Stones tour of the United States in 1975.

In his work with director Bob Fosse, Fisher has demonstrated how the lighting designer can enhance a production. In *Pippin* (1972), Fisher's lighting was an integral part of the show, often functioning as scenery such as the "light curtain" used for the opening number. For Fosse's production of *Dancin'*, Fisher's lighting created the entire environment for the dancers. Although Fisher can create spectacular effects, he believes that good lighting should not be seen by the audience and that it works within the framework of the entire production. Fisher has carried his talent over to musical shows that Fosse did not direct, such as *Ulysses in Nighttown* (1974), for which he won a Tony Award, and *La Cage aux Folles* (1983).

In addition to lighting design, Fisher coproduced such shows as *Lenny* (1971), *Dancin'* (1978), *Beatlemania* (1977, 1979), *Rock 'N' Roll! The First 5,000 Years* (1982), *The Rink* (1983), and *Big Deal* (1985). As a theatre building consultant, Fisher has worked on such major performance and entertainment spaces as the Brooklyn Academy of Music, Circle in the Square Theatre, New York's Palladium Night Club, the Denver Symphony Hall, and the Minneapolis Orchestra Hall.

Awards: Fisher's work has earned him five Tony Awards, for *Pippin* (1973), *Ulysses in Nighttown* (1974), *Beatlemania* (1977), *Dancin'* (1978), and *Grand Hotel* (1990). He also won the Drama Desk Award for *Frankenstein* (1980) and *Grand Hotel*.

Further Reading: "An Evening in Four Acts: The Palladium Lights Up at Night." *Theatre Crafts* October 1985; "From Lighting Designer to Producer: Jules Fisher Tells About a Varied New York Practice." *Theatre Crafts* November 1971; "Jules Fisher." *Lighting Dimensions* March 1978; "Jules Fisher & Associates: Profile." *Theatre Crafts* May 1983; "Jules Fisher Talks About: What Does a Lighting Designer Do?" *New York Theatre Review* August/September 1978; "Lighting the Unknown Soldier and His Wife." *Theatre Crafts* November/December 1967; "Shadows in the Light." *Theatre Crafts* January 1974.

Ken Kloth

Foreman, Richard. Director, playwright, and designer (b. June 10, 1937, New York, NY). Theatrical productions (in most cases, Foreman served as playwright, director, and designer) include *Angelface, Elephant-Steps*—1968; *Ida-Eyed, Red Magic in New York*—1969; *Total Recall: Sophia = (Wisdom) Part 2*—1970; *Dream Tantras for Western Massachusetts, HcOhTiEnLa; or Hotel China*—

1971; *Evidence, Dr. Selavy's Magic Theatre, Sophia = (Wisdom) Part 3: The Cliffs*—1972; *Particle Theory, Honor, Classical Therapy; or, A Week Under the Influence*—1973; *Pain(t), Vertical Mobility: Sophia = (Wisdom) Part 4, RA-D-IO (Wisdom); or Sophia = (Wisdom) Part 1*—1974; *Pandering to the Masses: A Misrepresentation, Hotel for Criminals, Rhoda in Potatoland, Thinking (One Kind)*—1975; *Livre de Splendeurs (Part 1), Lines of Vision*—1976; *Slight, Book of Splendors (Part II): Book of Levers: Action at a Distance*—1977; *Blvd. de Paris (I've Got the Shakes)*—1978; *Luogo + Bersaglio (Place + Target)*—1979; *Madame Adare*—1980; *Penguin Touquet*—1981; *Cafe Amerique*—1982; *Egyptology: My Head Was a Sledgehammer*—1983; *George Bataille's Bathrobe*—1984; *Miss Universal Happiness*—1985; *Africanis Instructus, The Cure*—1986; *What Did He See?*—1989. As a director and/or designer, Foreman has also staged *The Threepenny Opera*—1976; *Stages*—1978; *Don Juan*—1981; *Three Acts of Recognition*—1982; *Die Fledermaus*—1984; *My Life My Death, The Birth of the Poet*—1985; *Largo Desolato*—1986.

After completing his education at Brown University and the Yale University School of Drama, Foreman began his career as a writer for the New Dramatists and Actors Theatre (1962–1965). From 1967 to 1968, he was the associate director of Film-Maker's Cinematheque. In 1968, he founded the Ontological-Hysteric Theatre to produce his own work in New York. He has written, directed, and designed an impressive number of productions, as well as occasionally working on classic or contemporary dramas by other writers. He has suggested that his extraordinary plays are an attempt to depict the mind at work and to disrupt the audience's thought processes. He has featured untrained actors in his plays, many of which ignore the usual dramatic conventions of plot and character, and as designer he employs nonrealistic settings, sound, lighting, and props and avoids the use of traditional scenery.

Awards: Obie Awards: 1970, 1973, 1976, 1986 (for directing); numerous grants.

Further Reading: By Foreman: *Plays and Manifestos*, ed. Kate Davy. New York: New York University Press, 1976. About Foreman: Benmussa, Simone, and Erika Kralik, eds. *Le Theatre de Richard Foreman*. Paris: Gallimard, 1975; Davy, Kate. *Richard Foreman and the Ontological-Hysteric Theatre*. Ann Arbor, MI: UMI Research Press, 1981; Kirby, Michael. "Richard Foreman's Ontological-Hysteric Theatre." *Drama Review* June 1973.

James Fisher

Fossati, Domenico di Morcate. Scene designer and painter (b. 1743, Venice, Italy; d. 1784). Fossati spent most of his working career in Venice. As a fresco painter, he worked on the walls and ceilings of palaces and churches. As a scene designer, he created machines for outdoor shows and spectacles. At the age of eighteen, he painted the scenes for Gozzi's *The Love for Three Oranges* (1761). Subsequently, he designed the scenery for many operas and dramatic works for the theatres of Venice and worked principally in the Teatro San Samuele. Fossati designed and painted scenes also for the Teatro San Moise, Teatro San Benedetto, and Teatro San Cassiano. His designs for theatre frequently combined picturesque motifs with Far Eastern evocations of fantastic palaces, triumphal arches, and ruins. Talented students such as Francesco Chiaruttini and Lorenzo Saccheti came to his studio to study with him. His drawings are preserved in Australia, England, and the United States in public and private collections. Fossati's work outside the theatre included the design of a triumphal arch, a scenic palace for the Piazza San Marco, scenic ornaments for the state visit of Pope Pius VI, and golden gondolas for regattas staged on the Grand Canal.

Further Reading: Oenslager (see Bibliography).

Annie Milton

Francini, Tomaso. Set designer and stage machinist (b. 1576 (or 1571), Italy; d. 1648). Among the group of influential Italian theatre artists Francini brought Italian scenic invention to the French Court of King Louis XIII. The *Ballet d'Alcina* (1610) is noted as a significant production, which revived the *ballet de cour*, and is thought to have been designed by Francini. Presented in a private hall theatre, either in La Salle du Petit Bourbon or in La Grande Salle du Louvre, the whole scenic display was shown as a unit at one end of the hall through a series of Italianate wings and backdrops. Working with his brother, a noted architect, Francini was responsible for many of these ballets. The *Ballet du triomphe de Minerve* (1615) included a shallow stage with cut-out, painted curtains, and the *Ballet de la delivrance de Renaud* (1617) included angle wings, both techniques brought from Italy. At the back, Francini sometimes employed a turning device, familiar in French street shows since 1485, to change scenes. To introduce it, Francini made a scale model to demonstrate to the queen how the device worked. He employed scene change devices on such productions as *Grand Ballet de la Reine représentant le Soleil*, in which the four seasons were represented in each act of the play. Most of the Italian scenic innovations of the Renaissance brought to the French Court by designers like Francini would be eventually used in the public theatres.

Further Reading: Lawrenson, T. E. *The French Stage in the XVIIth Century.* Oxford, England: University of Manchester, 1957; Oenslager (see Bibliography).

Annie Milton

Fraser, Claude Lovat. Artist and scene designer (b. 1890, London, England; d. 1921). The effect that Fraser had on the development of scenic design in England was significant, considering his early death. During his brief career, he introduced revolutionary ideas of simplicity to the English stage. Fraser's only formal training came from a year at the Westminster School of Art, at the end of which he left, rented a small studio, and spent the next two years experimenting with color and period motifs. During this time, Fraser befriended Edward Gordon Craig,* who strongly influenced him and turned his thoughts to theatre design. Another of Fraser's friends, Nigel Playfair, convinced him to design the sets and costumes for *As You Like It* for the Festival at Stratford in April 1919. It was both a sensation and a scandal. Audiences were astounded and incensed, calling it a futuristic treatment of a classic. The set depicted the Court and the forest scenes only, with changes made through the addition or removal of minor elements. Evident was Fraser's strong use of colors, with simple blue and green backgrounds and orange and vermilion costumes. In June 1920, Fraser created his most famous design, *The Beggar's Opera*, at the Lyric Theatre in Hammersmith. Using a single unit set, with simple period details, he depicted the many scenes of the play through the use of various curtains. Some of his other famous productions include Madame Karsavinas's ballets, *Nursery Rhymes* and *Divertissment*, at the Coliseum in London in 1921; John Drinkwater's *Mary Stuart*; Lord Dunsany's *If* at the Ambassador Theatre; Gustav Holst's *Savitri* at the Lyric Theatre; *La Serva Padrona* (1919); and *King Henry IV*. Paintings from the eighteenth and nineteenth centuries were the source of Fraser's inspiration for his many gay, brightly colored, romantic sets and costumes. He will be known for this attention to period detail and his nonrealistic, simple approach.

Jonet Buchanan

Freyer, Achim. Set designer, artist, and teacher (b. 1934, Berlin, Germany). Opera and theatre designs include *Le Barbier de Seville*—1968; *The Good Woman of Setzuan*—1969; *Clavigo*—1971; *Lear*—1973; *Woyzeck*—1975; *Fidelio*—1976; *Das Kathchen von Heilbronn, Maulwerke*—1977; *Pelleas and Melisande*—1979; *Satyagraha*–1981; *Akhnaten*—1983.

Freyer is the leading German stage designer of the 1970s, one of Germany's most important contemporary painters, and professor of stage design at the Hochschule fur Kunst in West Berlin. He began his career in 1954 at the Berliner Ensemble and studied with Brecht and Karl von Appen.* When Brecht died in 1956, Freyer left the theatre to paint and absorbed the ideas of Rauschenberg, Oldenburg, Kienholz, Beuys, and Cage. When the East German government prohibited his works in 1965, however, Freyer returned to scenic designing. Characteristic of Freyer's style in this period were artificiality and nonillusionistic effects. His design for Benno Besson's production of *Good Woman of Setzuan*, for example, was noted for his use of pop imagery, large cut-out figures, plastic foil, and masks. In *Clavigo* (1971), he covered the entire stage with bold, flower-printed fabric and hung a huge black heart above the stage to create a contemporary correlative to rococo. Reaction to these designs was negative, and Freyer was deemed a designer of decadent productions. With his artistic freedom again threatened, Freyer emigrated to West Germany in 1972. For the next six years he worked primarily with Hans Heugebauer and Hans Leitzau in Germany and with Claus Peymann's ensemble in Stuttgart. The most acclaimed designs from this period are *Lear*, *Woyzeck*, and *Das Kathchen von Heilbronn*.

In the last decade, Freyer has concentrated more on designing and directing opera. The most notable of these are *Satyagraha* and *Akhnaten*, two operas by minimalist composer Philip Glass. These works epitomize Freyer's characteristic style: his use of contemporary, ordinary materials, easily recognizable to the audience, juxtaposed to, and in tension with, the historical subject matter; and his use of color and light, as well as three-dimensional constructions, to create spectacular, dreamlike, or surrealistic stage pictures that interpret rather than illustrate the essence of what lies beneath the story line.

Further Reading: Graue, Martin. "West German Scenography." *The Drama Review* Summer 1984: 77–101; Riddell, Richard. "Achim Freyer: Designer of Interpretive Imagery." *Theatre Crafts* October 1979: 18+; Riddell, Richard. "The German Raum." *The Drama Review* March 1980: 39–52; Rockwell, John. "This 'Satyagraha' Is Distinguished by Its German Designer." *New York Times*, 12 August 1984: 24.

Andrea J. Nouryeh

Fuller, Isaac. Designer and painter (b. 1606, England; d. July 1672, London, England). Scene painter Fuller studied with François Perrier in Paris about 1630. He was probably at Oxford in 1641 when Charles I held Court there and possibly worked in Paris between 1645 and 1650. He returned to Oxford in 1650 and worked there until the early 1660s. He is known to have painted an Elysium scene for the Drury Lane production of John Dryden's *Tyrannic Love* in 1669 for approximately £335. Unfortunately, the managers of the theatre refused to pay more than £40 on the grounds that Fuller had contracted to finish the design in a fortnight in a manner similar to that of other artists working for the Drury Lane. In addition, the management argued that Fuller had failed to equal their quality and they sued him for £500. Fortunately, Fuller was awarded full payment by the Court. At various times, he worked in both Oxford and London, where he painted churches and taverns. His mural entitled *Last Judgment* in the chapel of All Souls College at Oxford and mythological scenes in the Mitre Tavern in London have survived.

James Fisher

Funicello, Ralph. Set designer (b. September 9, 1947, Mamaroneck, NY). Before graduating from New York University's design program in 1970, where he studied with Wolfgang Roth and Ming Cho Lee,* Funicello began his career designing off-Broadway shows. His New York debut in design was with the New York Shakespeare Festival's productions of *A Wonderfull Yeare* and *The Figures of Chartres* in 1969. After graduation, he worked as an assistant designer and traveled to Germany with Roth, where he observed European methods and styles of design. Returning to New York, he continued to design at off-Broadway and at regional theatres until he moved to California in 1972. Immediately, Funicello established a relationship with the American Conservatory Theatre in San Francisco that has lasted till this day. His first work there was *House of Blue Leaves* (1972), followed by such significant productions as *The Taming of the Shrew* (1972), *Pillars of the Community* (1974), *Another Part of the Forest* (1981), and *Uncle Vanya* (1983). Working as a free-lance designer, Funicello has designed primarily on the West Coast, but he has extended his work into many of the major regional theatres in the United States. Some of his more notable productions include *The Visit* (1974) and *Peer Gynt* (1975), both at the Pacific Conservatory Theatre; *Travesties* (1976), *The Importance of Being Earnest* (1977), *Division Street* (1980), *The American Clock* (1984), and *Measure* *for Measure* (1985) at the Mark Taper Forum; *Dr. Faustus* (1976) and *She Stoops to Conquer* (1977) at the Guthrie Theatre; *The Caucasian Chalk Circle* (1980) and *Learned Ladies* (1980) at the Denver Center Theatre Company; *The Front Page* (1982) at the Seattle Repertory Company; *La Rondine* (1984) at the New York City Opera; *Division Street* (1981) on Broadway; *A Streetcar Named Desire* at the Stratford Festival in Ontario; and *Misalliance* (1987) and *Tartuffe* (1987) at the South Coast Repertory Company.

Further Reading: Aronson (see Bibliography).

Elbin L. Cleveland

Furttenbach, Josef. Scene designer, stage machinist, and theatrical architect (b. 1591, Leutkirch, Germany; d. 1667). Furttenbach's contribution to stage design is that he disseminated the Italian theories of scene design throughout Germany. Freely adapting the ideas in Serlio's* *Architettura*, Furttenbach published three works, *Civil Architecture* in 1628, *Recreational Architecture* in 1640, and *The Noble Mirror of Art* in 1663, in which he outlined theatre architecture, machinery, special effects, and design. These works are important because they provide an in-depth view of Italian and German stage design and architecture of the period, as well as serving as the only existing example of Renaissance lighting. In the books, he discusses experimentation with lamps and reflectors, positions, and even oil mixtures to create varied lighting effects such as sunrises, heaven, and hell. Throughout his career, Furttenbach applied the principles that he and Englishman Inigo Jones* learned from Giulio Parigi* in Florence. As city architect at Ulm, a position he acquired in 1631, he designed many public buildings, among which was the Theater am Benderhof, a theatre school that opened in 1641. Although he designed a small number of productions, Furttenbach's creations were known for their Italianate influences such as a central, one-point perspective, use of *periaktoi*, machines, and elaborate scene shifts that would be accomplished in full view of an amazed audience. These designs, however, were not as elaborate or large as the Italian ones that influenced him, nor were the actual sets as big as the ones described in his books.

Further Reading: Hewitt, Barnard, ed. (see Bibliography).

Thomas J. Mikotowicz

G

Galliari Family. Set designers and stage machinists (1707 through 1823). Similar to the Bibienas, the Galliaris were the last significant family of Italian scene designers to work in Europe. After their painter-decorator father died in 1722, the Galliari brothers—Bernardino (1707–1794), and Fabrizio (1709–1790) and Giovanni Antonio (1714–1783)—moved to Milan from their small village and apprenticed at the scenic studio of the Teatro Regio Ducale. They studied painting, architecture, and the use of perspective. After collaborating with their teachers, the brothers were hired in 1738 to design Charles III and Maria Amalia's wedding festival in Innsbruck. After this initial success, their reputation grew, leading to design assignments in opera and ballet at theatres throughout Italy. Bernardino and Fabrizio succeeded their teachers, Barbieri and Righini, at the Teatro Ducale and, in 1748, became the Court designers at the Teatro Regio in Turin, where they stayed for the remainder of their lives. Their two nephews Giovanni Antonio (1714–1794) and Giuseppe (n.d.) carried on the family tradition in design. Not much is known about Giuseppe, but Giovanni stayed in Milan and became the principal designer at the Teatro Regio, which burned down in 1776 and was replaced by La Scala. Giovanni's son Gaspare (1761–1823) succeeded his father at La Scala and worked there for the remainder of his career on opera designs, royal festivities, and other public events. The family's neoclassic approach to their highly architectural settings in multipoint perspective included classic columns, crisscrossing staircases, archways, and domes. Their designs also showed a fondness for the romantic in the depiction of ruins in a rustic setting.

Kurt Lancaster

Georgiadis, Nicholas. Set designer (b. 1925, Athens, Greece). Theatrical productions include *Danses Concertantes, Noctambules, House of Birds, Julius Caesar, Swan Lake*—1955; *The Journey, The Burrow, Winter's Eve*—1957;

Agon, Lysistrata—1958; *The Invitation*—1960; *La Reine Morte*—1961; *Daphnis and Chloe*—1962; *Las Hermanas*—1963; *Swan Lake*—1964; *House of Bernarda Alba, Romeo and Juliet*—1965; *Romeo and Juliet* (film), *Sleeping Beauty*— 1966; *Aida, Swan Lake*—1967; *Les Troyennes, Swan Lake*—1969; *Sleeping Beauty*—1970 and 1975; *Raymonda, Swan Lake* (television)—1972; *Intimate Letters, Mayerling* (video)—1978; *Manon*—1982; *Don Quixote*—1983; *Bach Suite, Washington Square, Romeo and Juliet* (television)—1984.

Upon graduating as a student of architecture at the Technical University in Athens, Georgiadis came to the United States to study at Columbia University. His first design project was for the Choreographers' Workshop in 1952. Soon after, he went to London and began studying painting at the Slade School, where he won first prize for stage design. While he was still a student, Georgiadis was commissioned by Dame Ninette de Valois to design the set for *Danses Concertantes* (1955). Since that time he has designed ballets for choreographers Kenneth Macmillan, John Cranko, and Rudolf Nureyev. His first opera design was for *Aida* (1967). He has subsequently executed designs for operas at the Royal Opera House and in Frankfurt, Germany. The companies of the Old Vic, the Royal Court Repertory, and the Oxford Playhouse have also employed Georgiadis to design their plays.

Although Georgiadis has worked in all visual media, he is known for his ability to distinguish between the design requirements of dance, opera, and theatre and to allow painting to enhance rather than overwhelm his design ideas. For this designer, set design must be descriptive regardless of how abstract the design. Bright color, line, shape, pattern, and texture are all employed to evoke a sense of period and locale. For the dance, Georgiadis likes to use a juxtaposition of static figures and moving dancers. His ballet settings avoid the two-dimensionality of a painted backdrop. Yet, he is careful to push his settings back and to create spaces in which the dancers have freedom of movement. As a result, Georgiadis has made a major impact on design for dance and continues to exercise an influence on other designers in his role as the head of the department of stage design at the Slade School in London.

Further Reading: "Agon." *Dance and Dancers* October 1958: 7+; Billington, Michael. "Nicholas Georgiadis Talking to Michael Billington." *Plays and Players* September 1966: 54; Bland, Alexander. "Recent Ballet Decor." *Ballet Annual* 12 (1958): 78–83.

Andrea J. Nouryeh

Gérard, Rolf. Set and costume designer, painter, and sculptor (b. 1910, Berlin, Germany). Theatrical productions include *Figaro* (Royal Opera House, Covent Garden, London), *Cosi Fan Tutte* (Edinburgh Festival, England)—1936; *That Lady* (set and costumes; Martin Beck Theatre), *Caesar and Cleopatra* (National Theatre)—1949; *Captain Carvallo* (Erlanger Theatre, Buffalo, New York), *Don Carlos* (The Metropolitan Opera Company)—1950; *Aida, Die Fledermaus* (both for the Metropolitan Opera Company)—1951; *An Evening with Beatrice Lillie* (Booth Theatre), *La Boheme, Carmen, Cosi Fan Tutte* (all for the Metropolitan

Opera Company)—1952; *The Love of Four Colonels* (set and costumes; Shubert Theatre), *The Strong Are Lonely* (Broadhurst Theatre), *Faust, Tannhauser* (both for the Metropolitan Opera Company)—1953; *Les Contes d'Hoffmann*—1955; *Le Perichole*—1956; *Eugene Onegin, La Traviata*—1957; *Cavalleria Rusticana, Pagliacci* (both for the Metropolitan Opera Company)—1958; *The Fighting Cock* (ANTA)—1959; *Irma La Douce* (Plymouth Theatre), *The Gypsy Baron*—1960; *Tovarich* (Broadway Theatre)—1963; *Die Fledermaus, Arabella, Der Rosenkavalier, Les Sylphides, Romeo and Juliet, Orpheus and Eurydice, La Traviata* at the Metropolitan Opera from 1949 to 1969.

After receiving an education in medicine and art in Germany and Switzerland, Gérard fled Nazi terrorism in 1936 and moved to England. Because he did not have a license to practice medicine in England, he depended upon his painting skills to earn a living and in a short time he was working in scene design. His first major work was on the Mozart operas *Figaro* and *Cosi Fan Tutte* at the Royal Opera House and the Edinburgh Festival, respectively. He designed many ballets and plays as well during this time. In 1949, Gérard designed his first Broadway productions, *That Lady* at the Martin Beck Theatre and *Caesar and Cleopatra* at the National Theatre. During the same year, he made contact with the general manager of the Metropolitan Opera Association, Rudolph Bing, who helped his career immensely. At the Met from 1949 to 1969, Gérard designed such operas as *Don Carlos* (1950), *Cosi Fan Tutte* (1952), and *Carmen* (1952). His design for *Cosi Fan Tutte* incorporated a unified, latticework frame that created a wing and border arrangement. This minimalistic design utilized strong vertical elements, including pillars, drapes, trees, and French doors, against a simplified backdrop. The design for *An Evening With Beatrice Lillie* (1952) for the Booth Theatre in 1952 included sketched scenery and a curtain profile of Lillie. Gérard's work for Broadway included the musical *Irma La Douce* (1960), as well as the play *Tovarich* (1963). He exhibited his designs for opera in a show titled *Twenty Years at the Met* in New York City in 1969.

Kurt Lancaster

Gischia, Léon. Set designer and art historian (b. June 8, 1903, Dax, France). Theatrical productions include *Murder in the Cathedral*—1945 and 1952; *Richard II*—1947 and 1948; *Danton's Death*—1948; *Le Cid, Oedipus*—1949 (the latter also in 1951); *Pasiphae*—1949; *Henry IV, Enrico IV, La Profanateur*—1950; *The Prince of Homburg, La Calandria*—1951; *L'Avare*—1952; *Lorenzaccio*—1952 and 1953; *Don Juan, Le Médecine Malgré Lui, La Garde malade*—1953; *Ruy Blas*—1954; *Marie Tudor, La Ville, L'Etourdi, Le Triomphe de l'amour*—1955; *Les Femmes Savantes, Le Nozze di Figaro*—1956; *Le Faiseur*—1957.

Gischia, long associated with the productions directed by Simon Vilar for the Theatre National Populaire in Paris and at the festivals at Avignon, designed his first production, *Murder in the Cathedral*, for this director in 1945. In 1951, in the program notes for the Festival d'Avignon, he wrote that the terms *theatre* and *spectacle* were synonymous and that the visual presentation, for him, was the most important element in a theatrical production. Color and form in each design were not subservient to the plot but had to have an internal logic of their own. As well, costumes were not merely disguises for the performers, but details as essential as the gestures, the music, or the lighting for the *mise-en-scène*. To achieve a harmony of theatrical elements with the dramatic action, the scene designer and the director had to be equal partners in the creation of the spectacle. This type of collaboration characterized the many productions that he designed for Vilar over the years.

Andrea J. Nouryeh

Godwin, Edward William. Designer, architect, and archaeologist (b. 1833, England; d. October 6, 1886, London, England). Theatrical productions include *The Merchant of Venice* (adviser to the designers only)—1875; *Henry V* (adviser to the designer only)—1876; *Othello* (designed some costumes only)—1880; *The Cup* (designed some costumes and "the cup" only), *Juana, The Queen and the Cardinal*—1881; *The Cynic, Storm Beaten, The Merchant of Venice* (costumes only)—1882; *Claudian*—1883; *Romeo and Juliet*—1884; *As You Like It* (director and designer), *The Faithful Shepherdess, Junius*—1885; *Helena in Troas, The Cenci, Fair Rosamund, The Fool's Revenge*—1886.

Godwin's professional accomplishments have often been overshadowed by his seven-year liaison with legendary Victorian actress Ellen Terry (1847–1928). He fathered two children by Terry: Edith Craig (1867–1947), who later became an actress and noted director, and Edward Gordon Craig* (1872–1966), one of the greatest theatrical visionaries of the modern stage. Godwin had been interested in theatre from his childhood and began a career as a critic, reviewing many of the productions at the Theatre Royal, Bristol. During his years with Terry, Godwin worked as an architect and studied the history of theatre and stage architecture. In 1874, their relationship crumbled, although Godwin continued to advise her occasionally on theatrical matters until his premature death. His first important theatrical work was as adviser to the designers William Harford and George Gordon on an 1875 production of *The Merchant of Venice*, with Terry as Portia. The antiquarian production featured elaborate Italianate sets and costumes. Many of Godwin's later productions owed much to his archaeological interests, especially in his most important production, *Helena in Troas* by John Todhunter, for which he designed a painstakingly accurate classical theatre that was constructed inside the existing structure of Hengler's Circus.

Further Reading: Harbon, Dudley. *The Conscious Stone, The Life of Edward William Godwin.* New York: Benjamin Blom, 1971. Many biographical works on Craig or Terry contain considerable information on Godwin. Periodically, Craig reprinted many of Godwin's articles on theatre architecture and history in his esoteric journal, *The Mask.*

James Fisher

Golovine, Aleksandr. Set designer and artist (b. 1863, Moscow, Russia; d. 1930). Golovine's design career contains four distinct stylistic periods—naturalism, pictorialism, theatricalism, and social realism. His early years of naturalistic endeavor derived from his studies at the Moscow School of Painting, Sculpture, and Architecture, where he studied under the realistic masters of the day. In the late 1890s, Golovine found reward in applying his talents to the stage. His first productions, Koreshchenko's *The Ice House* and Rimsky-Korsakov's *The Maiden of Pskov* at the Bolshoi Theatre in Moscow, were in the realistic style of his training. In 1901, he moved to St. Petersburg and soon became the leading decorator for the Royal Stage and designed operas and plays in the Marinsky and Alexandrinsky Theatres. In St. Petersburg his association with the World of Art group brought about stylistic growth toward a pictorial style characterized by highly selective choices of elements genuine to character and period. For example, his design of Bizet's *Carmen* displayed a genuine Spain without the embellishments characteristic of the current operatic stage. Perhaps his greatest accomplishment of this pictorial period was his design for Diaghilev's Ballets Russes production of *L'Oiseau de Feu* in 1910. His wide recognition and maturity led to a long-lasting and mutually rewarding association with Vsevolod Meyerhold, which caused his turn to theatricalism in 1910. Each of Meyerhold and Golovine's productions, such as Lermontov's *The Masquerade* in 1917, attempted theatrically to re-create the atmosphere of the play rather than the realistic locale. In 1925, Golovine met Konstantin Stanislavsky, and their meeting became yet another turning point. The Moscow Art Theatre provided an arena and framework for Golovine's efforts in the state-directed style of social realism. Successful productions such as Beaumarchais's *The Marriage of Figaro* helped establish him as one of the outstanding masters of Soviet theatrical art.

Brian R. Jones

Gonzaga, Pietro Gottardo. Designer, architect, and artist (b. 1751, Italy; d. 1831). In his youth Gonzaga was fascinated with the work of Carlo Bibiena but was unable to fulfill his dream of studying with the master. Thus, he began his theatrical career in 1772 by working in the studio of the Galliari brothers.* Gonzaga admired the work of the Galliaris and favored the neoclassical style over the baroque, a preference followed by Russian designers of the early nineteenth century, many of whom were greatly influenced by Gonzaga's work. He became scene designer at La Scala in Milan in 1779 and for the next decade worked in a number of Italian theatres. In 1792, he went to Russia at the invitation of Prince Yusupov and became decor designer for the Imperial Theatres, including the Hermitage and the Bolshoi in St. Petersburg, the Petrovsky Theatre in Moscow, and others in Gatchina, Pavlovsk, and Peterhof. Most of his work in Russia was for operas or ballets. It is believed that he designed more than 320 productions in his career. He designed the scene for Ozerov's *Oedipus in Athens* in 1804, and in 1817, he was commissioned to design a theatre and a series of generic scenes for Prince Yusupov's country estate in Arkhangelskoye. Some of his more famous productions include the ballet *Amore e Psiché* and, with Fantaresi, *Il Giardino d'Agrigento*.

Further Reading: Oenslager (see Bibliography).

James Fisher

Gorelik, Mordecai. Set designer, playwright, director, and teacher (b. August 25, 1899, Minsk, Russia; d. March 7, 1990, Sarasota, FL). Theatrical productions include *King Hunger*—1924; *Processional*—1925; *The Last Love, Nirvana, The Moon Is a Gong*—1926; *Loud Speaker*—1927; *The Final Balance*—1928; *God, Man and Devil, Uncle Moses*—1928–1930; *Success Story*—1932; *Big Night, Little Ol' Boy, Men in White, All Good Americans*—1933; *They Shall Not Die, Sailors of Cattaro, Gentlewoman*—1934; *The Young Go First, Let Freedom Ring, The Mother*—1935; *Golden Boy*—1937; *Tortilla Flat, Casey Jones, Rocket to the Moon*—1938; *Thunder Rock, The Quiet City*—1939; *Night Music*—1940; *Walk into My Parlor*—1941; *Volpone, Days of Glory* (film), *Our Street* (film), *None but the Lonely Hearts* (film)—1944; *Dr. Knock*—1945; *All My Sons*—1947; *Desire Under the Elms, Danger, Men Working*—1952; *The Flowering Peach, St. Joan, L'Ennemi Publique No. 1* (film)—1954; *Hatful of Rain*—1955; *The Plough and the Stars*—1956; *Volpone, The Sin of Pat Muldoon*—1957; *Kantan*—1958; *A Distant Bell*—1960; *Hamlet, The Dybbuk*—1961; *House of Bernarda Alba*—1962; *Good Woman of Setzuan, The Firebugs*—1964; *Rainbow Terrace*—1966; *Divine Words*—1971.

After studying at the Pratt Institute of Fine Arts, Gorelik started as a scene painter in 1920 for the Neighborhood Playhouse and Provincetown Players. In the 1930s, Gorelik became the chief designer for the Group Theatre, where he applied the principles of the "New Stagecraft." Gorelik's approach to scene design was to find a metaphor for the set. For *Thunder Rock* (1939), his design was a simplified, yet realistic lighthouse, metaphorically described by him as a candle in the darkness. For *Golden Boy* (1937), all of the sets were in the shape of a boxing ring. Gorelik stated that the metaphor is implicit in the script, vivid in its evocative power, able to change and develop, and useful as well to the actors. He warned that the metaphor should not be too obvious. If it is too blatant, it is expressionism and crude poetry. For *All My Sons* (1947), Gorelik's metaphor was that the tree in the backyard was the son's grave. His metaphors for *The Flowering Peach* (1954), Clifford Odets's version of the Noah story, are wonderfully descriptive. The house of the first scene was a religious icon, and the hill, where the ark is built, was a church picnic.

Gorelik taught from the beginning of his career at such schools as the American Academy of Dramatic Arts, Biarritz American University in France, Brigham Young University, University of Southern California, and Southern Illinois University, where his archives are stored. His book *New Theatres for Old* is an important history of twentieth-century theatre. In addition, he has written and directed plays and authored more than one hundred articles concerning the theatre.

Further Reading: By Gorelik: "The Conquest of Stage Space." *Theatre Arts Monthly* March 1934; with Robert Edmund Jones, "Correspondence About 'New Theatres for Old.' " *Educational Theatre Journal* March 1968; "Epic Scene Design." *Theatre Arts*

Magazine October 1959; "In Search of a Metaphor." *Players Magazine* August/September 1969; "Metaphorically Speaking." *Theatre Arts Magazine* November 1954; *New Theatres for Old*. New York: Samuel French, 1955; Two essays on scene design in Larson, Orville K. *Scene Design for Stage and Screen*. Westport, CT: Greenwood, 1976.

Ken Kloth

Gray, Terence. Director, designer, and producer (b. September 14, 1895, Felikstowe, England; d. ?). Theatrical productions (all produced, directed, and/or designed by Gray at the Cambridge Festival Theatre) include *The Oresteia, The Man Who Ate the Popomack, King Lear's Wife, The Miracle of St. Anthony*— 1926; *Heraclius, The Pleasure Garden, The Glittering Gate, The Stronger, On Baile's Strand, Rout* (a ballet), *The Immortal Hour, The Workhouse Ward, The Rumour, Uncle Vanya, Love for Love, The Invisible Duke, Sweeney Todd the Barber, Androcles and the Lion, The Lost Silk Hat, The Adding Machine, Don Juan, The Player Queen, Dance Cameos, Red Nights of the Tcheka, The Insect Play, And in the Tomb Were Found . . . , Each in His Own Way, Miss Julie, Twelfth Night, Oedipus Tyrannus, Progress, Pompey the Great, Thirty Minutes in a Street, The Son of Learning, The Comedian, Absorbing Perdita, The Provok'd Wife, A Florentine Irony, The Dumb Man of Manchester*—1927; *Caesar and Cleopatra, Inheritors, The Carthaginian, From Morn to Midnight, Cheezo, Dr. Knock, Richard III, The Passion Flower, The Knight of the Burning Pestle, The Pretenders, The Devil's Disciple, The Riding to Lithend, A Royal Audience, The Last Hour, The Dreamy Kid, Emperor Jones, Madame Pepita, Adam and Creator, The Birds, Heartbreak House, The Man Who Ate the Popomack, The Show, The Subway, As You Like It, The Spook Sonata, The Hairy Ape, Marriage á la Mode*—1928; *Saint Joan, The Pleasure Garden, Prometheus, Dancing, The Witch, Romeo and Juliet, Hoppla!, The Carpenter of Rouen, Beggar on Horseback, Intoxication, The Playboy of the Western World, Twelve Thousand, Masses and Men, Les petits riens* (a ballet), *Periphery, The Shoemaker's Holiday, Salomé, Six Characters in Search of an Author, Marriage, Woman's Honor, The Mask and the Face, All for Love, Iphiginia in Tauris, Rosalind, The Dover Road, Deirdre of the Sorrows, Dandy Dick, The Rivals*—1929; *The Machine Wreckers, Measure for Measure, Box and Cox, Lady Audley's Secret, A Month in the Country, Lancelot of Denmark, Ballets, A Pair of Spectacles, A Valuable Rival, The Medium, Campbell of Kilmhor, C'est la guerre, Le Malade Imaginaire, Volpone, Naked, The Cherry Orchard, The Gentleman Dancing Master, The Kingdom of God, Rosmersholm, The Varsity Coach, The Unknown Warrior, Warren Hastings, Costanza, The Thought, Temptation, A Doll's House, Tobias and the Angel, The Merry Wives of Windsor*—1930; *Aladdin, The Oil Islands, Nichevo, Henry VIII, Wonderful Zoo, Hassan, Henry IV, The Insect Play, M. le Trouhadec, The Festival Revue, Julius Caesar, The Wild Duck, Judas, Lysistrata, Antigone, The Stronger, The Man with the Flower in His Mouth, Androcles and the Lion, 1066 and All That, From Morn to Midnight, Gustav Vasa, The Eunuch, Dr. Knock, The Alcestis, Salomé, The Sentimental Centaur, The Red Rover*—1931; *This World of Ours, Love for Love, Bastos the Bold, Marco*

Millions, Will You Play with Me?, Alison's House, In a Glass Darkly, The Knight of the Burning Pestle, Twice Nightly, The Witch, The Government Inspector, Troilus and Cressida, The Rose Without a Thorn, See Naples and Die, The Makropoulos Secret, The Servant of Two Masters, The Pride of the Regiment, Peer Gynt, One More River, Caesar and Cleopatra, The Three Sisters, Hotel Universe, The Merchant of Venice, The Eater of Dreams, London Docks, The Rope, Maya—1932; *Emperor Jones, The Dreamy Kid, The Lost Silk Hat, The Admirable Bashville, The Shewing Up of Blanco Posnet, The Man Who Ate the Popomack, Pericles, The Importance of Being Earnest, The Suppliants, The Circle of Chalk, The Dice of Death, Back to Methuselah, Pointe au Porc-épic, Happy and Glorious, Twelfth Night, The Birds, The Shoemaker's Holiday, Chantecler*—1933.

In 1926, Gray cofounded the Cambridge Festival Theatre and remained involved as director and designer until 1933. The more than one hundred experimental works produced there during Gray's tenure reflected the theories of such European theatre artists as Edward Gordon Craig,* Adolphe Appia,* Max Reinhardt, Aurelien Lugné-Poë, Jacques Copeau, Vsevolod Meyerhold, and others. Resisting the trend toward illusions of realism in the visual elements of the stage, Gray eliminated the proscenium and footlights and added a forestage connected to the auditorium by a staircase. Different levels on the stage offered a variety of staging options for a repertory of plays that ranged from Aeschylus's *Oresteia* to a variety of classics and modern European dramas. Perhaps his most significant innovation was his system of hollow boxes composed of cubes, columns, and steps in various sizes. Painted blue, gray, or terra cotta, these elements could be transformed by light and reconfiguration to suggest a variety of locations. They were very similar in concept to Craig's screen system. In fact, Gray also designed a luminous screen system of his own that, unlike Craig's system, could be used with three-dimensional elements. He used these multipurpose units to create all scenes in such productions as *The Oresteia* (1926) and *Romeo and Juliet* (1928). Gray's company included him as director and designer and Harold Ridge, a follower of Appia, as lighting designer. After 1930, Gray participated infrequently in productions at the theatre. Following his designs for the first English-language performance of Aeschylus's *The Suppliants* in 1933, Gray gave up the theatre.

Further Reading: By Gray: "The Festival Theatre in Cambridge." *Theatre Arts Monthly* September 1926: 585–86.

James Fisher

Greenwood, Jane. Costume designer and teacher (b. April 30, 1934, Liverpool, England). Theatrical productions (all took place in New York City, unless otherwise specified) include *Henry IV* (Oxford Repertory, Oxford, England), *The Hamlet of Stepney Green* (Lyric Theatre, London, England)—1958; *The Importance of Being Earnest* (Madison Avenue Playhouse), *The Ballad of the Sad Cafe* (Martin Beck Theatre)—1963; *Hamlet* (Lunt-Fontanne Theatre), *Half a*

Sixpence (Broadhurst Theatre), *A Race of Hairy Men* (Henry Miller's Theatre), *Tartuffe* (American Conservatory Theatre, Pittsburgh, Pennsylvania)—1965; *Nathan Weinstein, Mystic Connecticut* (Brooks Atkinson Theatre), *Where's Daddy?* (Billy Rose Theatre), *The Killing of Sister George* (Belasco Theatre), *How's the World Treating You?* (Music Box Theatre), *Murder in the Cathedral, Twelfth Night* (both at the American Shakespeare Festival, Stratford, Connecticut)—1966; *More Stately Mansions* (Broadhurst Theatre), *What Do You Really Know About Your Husband?* (pre-Broadway tryout), *The Comedy of Errors* (with Alvin Colt*), *She Stoops to Conquer* (both at Ford's Theatre, Washington, D.C.)—1967; *The Prime of Miss Jean Brodie* (Helen Hayes Theatre), *The Seven Descents of Myrtle* (Ethel Barrymore Theatre), *I'm Solomon* (Mark Hellinger Theatre)—1968; *The Wrong Way to Light a Bulb* (Booth Theatre), *The Penny Wars* (Royale Theatre), *Angela* (Music Box Theatre), *Crimes of Passion* (Astor Place Theatre), *Episode in the Life of an Author, The Orchestra* (both at Studio Arena, Buffalo, New York), *Much Ado About Nothing, Hamlet, The Three Sisters* (all at the American Shakespeare Festival, Stratford, Connecticut)—1969; *Hay Fever* (Helen Hayes Theatre), *Les Blancs* (Longacre Theatre), *Sheep on the Runway* (Helen Hayes Theatre), *Gandhi* (Playhouse Theatre), *Othello* (ANTA Theatre), *All's Well That Ends Well, The Devil's Disciple, Othello* (all for the American Shakespeare Festival, Stratford, Connecticut)—1970; *Seventy, Girls, Seventy* (Broadhurst Theatre), *The House of Blue Leaves* (Truck and Warehouse Theatre), *Wise Child* (Helen Hayes Theatre), *The Merry Wives of Windsor, The Tempest, Mourning Becomes Electra* (all for the American Shakespeare Festival, Stratford, Connecticut)—1971; *That's Entertainment* (Edison Theatre), *Julius Caesar, Antony and Cleopatra, Major Barbara* (all for the American Shakespeare Festival, Stratford, Connecticut)—1972; *A Moon for the Misbegotten* (Morosco Theatre), *Look Away* (Playhouse Theatre), *The Country Wife, Measure for Measure, Macbeth* (all for the American Shakespeare Festival, Stratford, Connecticut), *The Head Hunters, The Prodigal Daughter* (both for the Eisenhower Theatre, John F. Kennedy Center for the Performing Arts, Washington, D.C.), *Getting Married* (Hartford Stage Company, Connecticut), *Finishing Touches* (Ahmanson Theatre, Los Angeles, California)—1973; *Cat on a Hot Tin Roof* (ANTA Theatre), *Figures in the Sand* (Theatre at St. Clements), *Beyond the Horizon* (McCarter Theatre, Princeton, New Jersey), *Twelfth Night, Romeo and Juliet, Cat on a Hot Tin Roof* (all for the American Shakespeare Festival, Stratford, Connecticut)—1974; *Same Time, Next Year* (Brooks Atkinson Theatre), *Finn MacKool, the Grand Distraction* (Theatre de Lys), *King Lear, The Winter's Tale* (both for the American Shakespeare Festival, Stratford, Connecticut)—1975; *A Matter of Gravity* (Broadhurst Theatre), *Who's Afraid of Virginia Woolf?* (Music Box Theatre), *A Texas Trilogy* (Broadhurst Theatre), *California Suite* (Eugene O'Neill Theatre), *Long Day's Journey into Night* (Brooklyn Academy of Music)—1976; *Otherwise Engaged* (Plymouth Theatre), *Caesar and Cleopatra* (Palace Theatre), *Anna Christie* (Imperial Theatre), *Vieux Carre* (St. James Theatre), *The Night of the Tribades* (Helen Hayes Theatre), *An Almost Perfect Person* (Belasco

Theatre)—1977; *Cheaters* (Biltmore Theatre), *The Kingfisher* (Biltmore Theatre), *The Prince of Grand Street* (Forrest Theatre, Philadelphia, Pennsylvania)—1978; *Knockout* (Helen Hayes Theatre), *Romantic Comedy* (Ethel Barrymore Theatre), *Father's Day* (American Place Theatre), *Faith Healer* (Longacre Theatre), *Happy Days* (Newman Theatre at the Public Theatre), *The Umbrellas of Cherbourg* (Cabaret Theatre at the Public Theatre), *A Month in the Country* (Roundabout Stage One)—1979; *Judgement* (Theatre at St. Peter's Church), *Summer* (Hudson Guild Theatre), *The Sea Gull* (Newman Theatre at the Public Theatre), *Last Embrace* (film; United Artists), *Can't Stop the Music* (film; Associated Film Distributors)—1980; *The Supporting Cast* (Biltmore Theatre), *To Grandmother's House We Go* (Biltmore Theatre), *Duet for One* (Royale Theatre), *The West Side Waltz* (Ethel Barrymore Theatre), *Arthur* (film; Warner Brothers), *The Four Seasons* (film; Universal)—1981; *Plenty* (Plymouth Theatre)—1982; *Tartuffe* (American Place Theatre), *Heartbreak House* (Circle in the Square), *Tender Mercies* (film; EMI)—1983; *The Golden Age* (Jack Lawrence Theatre), *The Garden of Earthly Delights* (St. Clements Theatre), *Cinders* (New York Shakespeare Festival, LuEsther Theatre), *Alone Together* (Music Box Theatre), *Found a Peanut*, *La Boheme* (New York Shakespeare Festival, Anspacher Theatre)—1984; *A Map of the World* (Newman Theatre at the Public Theatre), *Wetherby* (film; MGM-United Artists)—1985; *The Iceman Cometh* (Lunt-Fontanne Theatre), *So Long on Lonely Street* (Jack Lawrence Theatre), *Lillian* (Ethel Barrymore Theatre), *The Perfect Party* (Astor Place Theatre), *Jacques and His Master* (Long Wharf Theatre, New Haven, Connecticut), *Sweet Liberty* (film; Universal)—1986; *The Knife* (Newman Theatre at the Public Theatre)—1987; *The O'Neill Plays* (Newman Theatre at the Public Theatre), *Long Day's Journey into Night* (Neil Simon Theatre), *Our Town* (Lyceum), *Jacknife* (film; United Artists)—1988; *What the Butler Saw* (City Center), *The Aristocrats*, *The Lisbo Traviata* (both at the Manhattan Theatre Club)—1989.

After studying theatre design at the Central School of Arts and Crafts in London, Greenwood became the resident designer of the Oxford Repertory Theatre in England for three seasons starting in 1958. Tanya Moiseiwitsch,* designer at the Stratford Shakespeare Festival in Ontario, brought her to Canada in 1960, where she worked as a draper. Scenery was so minimal and the audience was so close to this thrust stage that Greenwood soon realized the importance of fine fabrics and close attention to detail when designing for the productions. In 1962, Ray Diffen offered Greenwood a job in his New York costume shop, and a year later she designed the costumes for *The Ballad of the Sad Cafe*, her first Broadway production. Since the 1970s, Greenwood has remained one of Broadway's top costume designers and provided the designs for such productions as John Gielgud's *Hamlet* with Richard Burton, *More Stately Mansions*, *The House of Blue Leaves*, Jose Quintero's revival of Eugene O'Neill's *A Moon for the Misbegotten*, and *Plenty*. In addition, she has designed for the Metropolitan and San Francisco Opera, the Tyrone Guthrie Theater, and the Joffrey Ballet.

Greenwood's technique is perhaps best illustrated through her period costumes.

She is a firm believer in proper research into historical dress and states that it is better to do too much research than too little. Greenwood derives inspiration from paintings, textiles, even designs in china and pottery of the historical period she is researching. She continually returns to research periods that she has examined hundreds of times before, but she also attempts in her work to reinterpret past modes in terms that can be appreciated by a modern audience. For Joseph Papp's production of *La Boheme* in 1984, Greenwood studied the paintings of Toulouse-Lautrec and other French artists of the late nineteenth century and dressed the character of Musette in one scene in vivid green pantaloons. The colors recalled the cafe scenes of Lautrec, but the loosely cut pants also appealed to a modern audience that had made jumpsuits and harem pants fashionable in the 1980s. Studying American and primitive folk art of the mid-nineteenth century to research costume designs for *More Stately Mansions* (1967), Greenwood insisted on using natural, authentic fabrics of the period, even though they were more expensive to obtain.

In addition to her practical work as a costumer, Greenwood has taught at the Lester Polakov Design Studio and the Juilliard School of Drama. Today, as a professor of costume design at Yale University, Greenwood continues to inspire future designers with her appreciation of history, fashion, and style.

Awards: Greenwood received the Maharam Award for costume design for the 1965 production of *Tartuffe*. She was nominated for a Tony Award for "Best Costume Design" for *More Stately Mansions* (1967), *Hay Fever* and *Les Blancs* (1970), and *Heartbreak House* (1983).

Further Reading: "Jane Greenwood." *Theatre Crafts* March 1985; Smith, C. Ray, ed. *The Theatre Craft Book of Costumes.* Emanaus, PA: Rodale Press, 1973; "Three American Designers." *Theater* Fall/Winter 1981.

Howard Gutner

Grieve Family. Scene designers (1770 through 1882). The Grieve family held a prominent place in nineteenth-century English scene painting. There were three Grieves who were jointly responsible for most of the scenery at Covent Garden and Drury Lane during the early part of the century. John Henderson (1770–1845) had a long association with Covent Garden and designed scenery for spectacle plays and pantomimes under John Philip Kemble. In 1839, his elder son, Thomas (1799–1882), became principal scenic artist at Covent Garden under Madame Vestris's management, and later he held the same position at Drury Lane. Thomas was assisted by his son, Thomas Walford (1841—1882), who eventually became the leading painter for Charles Kean and was noted for his style and composition. John's younger son, William (1800–1844), was employed at Covent Garden in his youth but did his best work at Drury Lane. After the retirement of fellow scenic painter William Clarkson Stanfield,* William was considered the finest scenic artist of the day, known especially for his moonlit scenes.

In the extreme, the Grieve style was romantic, often portraying exotic locations under highly dramatic lighting conditions. Through exceptional use of color, perspective, highlight and shadow, cut scenes, transparencies, and gauzes, the Grieves produced scenes unequaled in design and execution. Although the Grieves were not especially known for their use of technical innovations, they are credited with introducing the diorama on the stage with *Harlequin and Cinderella* in 1820. In short, dioramas created moving backgrounds by rolling painted canvas from one backstage drum across stage to another. The Grieves' dioramas for the annual Covent Garden pantomimes were flights of fancy, with numerous exotic countries portrayed on them. Together, the members of this family of designers provided scenery for more than seven hundred productions, including such staged novels as *Rob Roy* (1818); *Kenilworth* (ballet, 1832); *A Vision of the Bard*; Byron's *Manfred*; and the world premiere of Weber's *Oberon* in 1826.

Jonet Buchanan

Gropius, Walter. Theatre architect and artist (b. 1883, Germany; d. 1969). In an effort to infuse everyday life with art, in 1920 Gropius founded the Staatliches Bauhaus in Weimar, Germany, a school of fine arts and arts and crafts. This school was dedicated to functional architecture, industrial design, painting, and sculpture, as well as theatre. Collaborating with Oskar Schlemmer,* who was in charge of the theatre workshop, and avant-gardist director Erwin Piscator, in 1926 Gropius conceived of a new type of theatre structure, one he would call the Total Theatre. Through its design, this facility intended to change the performer-spectator relationship. Integrated within the structure's design were three types of stages—the thrust, the arena, and the proscenium. The building was shaped like an ellipse, with a two thousand-seat arena and a proscenium stage. In front of the proscenium was a circular apron that thrust into the arena and could be rotated into the center of the auditorium to create a theatre-in-the-round. The ceiling was dome-shaped to accommodate projections. In addition, twelve pillars supported the ceiling and provided additional projection surfaces with screens that could be mounted between them. To surround the spectators further with the presentation, a translucent cyclorama was hung at the rear of the proscenium stage. Unfortunately, the Total Theatre was never built because the Nazis came to power and disbanded the controversial Bauhaus organization. Its influence, however, can be seen in many current theatre facilities.

Further Reading: By Gropius: Intro. and ed. *The Theatre of the Bauhaus: Schlemmer, O., L. Mohol Nagy, and F. Molnar*, trans. Arthur S. Wensinger. Middletown, CT: Wesleyan University Press, 1961.

Thomas J. Mikotowicz

H

Hammond, Aubrey. Artist and theatrical designer (b. 1893, England; d. 1940). Hammond's atmospheric sets and handsome costumes were seen in a variety of theatres, including the Haymarket, Wyndhams, and the Vaudeville in London, as well as such regional ones as the New Liverpool Repertory and Stratford Shakespeare Festival. As the scenic supervisor in 1932 at Stratford, Hammond used various mechanical scenic devices for his productions, including a rolling stage in *Julius Caesar* and a movable cave in *The Tempest*. His productions included *The Rose and the Ring* (Wyndham's Theatre); *The Man with a Load of Mischief* (Theatre Royal, Haymarket, 1925); *The Pilgrim of Love; Now and Then* (Vaudeville Theatre); *Masses and Men* (1925); and *Wild Violets* (Drury Lane Theatre, 1932). In addition to his theatrical work, he designed revue settings for C. B. Cochran and André Charlot, as well as for numerous films.

Jonet Buchanan

Hay, Richard L. Set designer and theatre architect (b. May 28, 1929, Wichita, KS). Hay has been principal scenic designer for the Oregon Shakespearean Festival since 1969 and has been associate artistic director for design at the Denver Center Theatre Company since 1984. He received his bachelor's degree in architecture from Stanford University in 1952. This was followed by a master's degree in scenic design in 1955 and a Fulbright Study Grant at the University of Bristol in England. Hay then worked in New York and assisted Ming Cho Lee,* Motley,* Boris Aronson,* and Robert Randolph* between the years 1962 and 1965. Since then, he has worked primarily in regional repertory theatre. His work includes designs for productions at the Guthrie Theatre, the American Conservatory Theatre, the Missouri Repertory Theatre, the Berkeley Repertory Theatre, the Mark Taper Forum, the Old Globe Theatre in San Diego, and the Denver Center Theatre Company. In the course of his career in repertory theatre, he has designed over 225 productions, including the entire Shakespearean canon.

His favorite designs were for the productions *South Pacific* and *Emperor Jones*, produced at the Denver Center Theatre Company, and for *The Timon of Athens* and Ibsen's *Brand*, produced at the Oregon Shakespeare Festival.

In addition, Hay has designed theatre buildings and stages, taught scenic design, and exhibited his work. The three theatres that comprise the Oregon Shakespeare Festival complex—the Elizabethan Theatre, the Angus Bowmer Theatre, and the Black Swan Theatre—are his creations. At the Denver Center Theatre, he designed the Source Theatre and the Space Theatre. He created the Festival Stage at the Old Globe Theatre, as well as the one at the new Old Globe Theatre. He has also been involved with the designs for the Intiman Theatre in Seattle and for the Milwaukee Repertory Theatre. Hay served as instructor and associate professor of scene design at Stanford University, Palo Alto, California, for eleven years. Further, Hay was a participant at the British Council Theatre Planning Conference held in London in 1983, was a member of the United States' delegation to the Prague Quadrennial ''Exposition of Theatre Design and Scenography'' in 1983 and 1987, and exhibited at the Prague Quadrennial in 1987, among other places.

Further Reading: ''Designers at Work.'' *Theatre Crafts* May 1987: 40.

Annie Milton

Heeley, Desmond. Set and costume designer (b. June 1, 1931, Staffordshire, England). Beginning his career at the Birmingham Repertory Theatre, Heeley soon moved on to design at the Shakespeare Memorial Theatre (renamed the Royal Shakespeare). In 1955, he assisted director Peter Brook on *Titus Andronicus* and followed this success with innumerable others. From the start of his career, Heeley developed a characteristic style in costume design suited to period classic plays and operas and noted for its use of rich color and texture. Since, he has designed both costumes and settings for productions outside of England, many at the Shakespearean Theatre at Stratford, Ontario, and some at the Tyrone Guthrie Theatre in Minneapolis, and worked with director Michael Langham. He has also worked on Broadway, where he designed one of his more significant works, Tom Stoppard's *Rosencrantz and Guildenstern Are Dead* (1967), for which he won two Tony Awards. This success led to his being hired by Rudolf Bing to design *Norma* (1970) at the Metropolitan Opera House. In opera and ballet he has designed both costumes and settings for many productions at such important venues as La Scala, Glyndebourne, and the Royal Swedish Opera House.

Thomas J. Mikotowicz

Heinrich, Rudolf. Scenic designer, director, and teacher (b. February 10, 1925, Halle, Germany; d. December 1, 1975, London, England). Theatrical productions include *Hansel und Gretel*—1949; *The Cunning Little Vixen*—1956; *Otello, La Traviata, Tales of Hoffman*—1958; *A Midsummer Night's Dream*—1961;

Flying Dutchman, *The Magic Flute*, *Lulu*—1963; *Lohengrin*—1964; *Salome*— 1965; *Macbeth*—1967; *The Ring Cycle*—1973; *Don Carlos*—1975.

Receiving his education at the Kunsteschule in Halle, Germany, Heinrich became a disciple of artists Max Elton and Paul Pilowski. He then began an apprenticeship at the Leipzig Theater in 1948, where, as an assistant to director Walter Felsenstein, he designed his first opera, *Hansel and Gretel* (1949). Heinrich left the Leipzig Theater in 1950, and he began designing operas and plays in East Germany, many for his mentor Felsenstein. Between 1948 and 1963, he designed twelve operas for the Handel festivals in Halle, and from 1954 until he fled East Berlin in 1963, he headed the department of design at the Komishe Oper.

After escaping to the West, Heinrich began an international directing and designing career for the opera. His designs have been seen on the major operatic stages of the United States, Austria, Canada, Switzerland, and Italy. Characteristic of his style is the depiction of the social and historical context of the drama through abstract and suggestive settings. In 1973, at the National Theater of Mannheim, Heinrich's designs were exhibited. Subsequently, his influence on the future of German design was exerted in his years as professor of design at the Munich Academy of Fine Arts.

Awards: National Prize of GDR, Handel Festival 1955 and 1960.

Further Reading: Ericson, Raymond. "A Director with Designs." *New York Times* September 26, 1971; Loney, Glenn. "New Visions in Opera Design: Rudolph Heinrich in Retrospect." *Theatre Crafts* November/December 1976: 13 + ; Smith, Patrick J. "A Man Engaged." *Opera News* March 6, 1965: 14–15.

Andrea J. Nouryeh

Herbert, Jocelyn. Scene designer (b. February 2, 1917, London, England). Trained in her youth as an art student in France, Herbert returned to London to enroll in Saint-Denis's Theatre Studio. Not until she was forty, however, did she embark upon a theatrical career. After raising a family, Herbert joined the Royal Court Theatre as a staff scene painter in 1956. The following year, she designed the first of many productions there, Ionesco's *The Chairs*. She designed such original premiere productions as playwright Arnold Wesker's *Roots* (1959), *The Kitchen* (1959), and *Chicken Soup with Barley* (1960). Other significant productions at the Royal Court include *Krapp's Last Tape* (1958), *Serjeant Musgrave's Dance* (1959), and *Saint Joan of the Stockyards* (1964). She has also designed many Shakespearean productions for the Royal Shakespeare Company, and at the National Theatre her productions include *Mother Courage* (1965), *Galileo*, and *The Oresteia* (1981). Additionally, she has designed works at the Metropolitan Opera in New York, including *Lulu* (1977) and *The Rise and Fall of the City of Mahagonny* (1979). Herbert has served as art director on a number of major films, including *Isadora* (1968) and *The Hotel New Hampshire*

(1983). Much of her stage work shows a Brechtian influence and is typified by realistic details placed in open or highly simplified stage spaces.

Elbin L. Cleveland

Herrman, Karl-Ernst. Scenic designer (b.?, Germany). Herrman is best known for his work at the Schaubuhne am Helleschen Ufer. In 1970, director Peter Stein picked him to be the resident designer of his theatre. Since the auditorium of the building had no proscenium arch, Herrman, using such materials as earth, trees, and other visual quotations of nature, altered the shape of the auditorium for each new production. As part of this new approach to the theatrical space, he designed productions so that the audience would become a part of the stage. The most notable of these include *As You Like It*, *The Art of Comedy*, *Al Gran sole carico d'Amore*, and *Peer Gynt* (1972). Herrman's design solutions to the problem created by the lack of a stage in the original theatre were incorporated in the stage architecture of the new theatre building. His approach to scenic design is to create backgrounds for the action rather than self-sufficient settings. In his collaborations with Stein, such as *Trilogue des Wiedersehens* (1978), *Oresteia* (1980), *Kalldeway Farce* (1982), and *Cami* (1983), he has attempted to give each production a unified statement. In addition to designing for the theatre, Herrman has created a group of "raums"—total spatial compositions or settings that function as works of art independent of theatrical production. These were exhibited at the Theatre of Nations Festivals in Hamburg in 1980.

Andrea J. Nouryeh

Hersey, David. Lighting designer (b. November 30, 1939, Rochester, NY). Theatrical productions include *Evita* (Prince Edward Theatre); *Mayerling* (London's West End, Royal Ballet)—1978; *The King and I*, *The Sound of Music*, *Camelot*, *The Little Shop of Horrors*, *Evita*, *Merrily We Roll Along*, *Old Times*, *The Turn of the Screw* (English National Opera)—1979; *Peter Pan*, *Mother Courage*, *As You Like It*, *The Crucifer of Blood*—1980; *The Life and Adventures of Nicholas Nickleby*—1981; *Henry VI Part 1* (Royal Shakespeare Company), *Guys and Dolls* (National Theatre)—1982; *Cats*—1983; *Starlight Express* (Apollo Victoria), *Rough Crossing* (National Theatre)—1984; *Les Miserables* (Royal Shakespeare Company), *Albert Herring*, *Old Times* (Theatre Royal, Haymarket), *Starlight Express* (Apollo Victorio Theatre)—1985; *Porgy and Bess* (Glyndebourne), *The Life and Adventures of Nicholas Nickleby* (Broadhurst Theatre)—1986; *La Traviata* (Glyndebourne), *Starlight Express*—1987; *Bartholomew Fair* (National Theatre)—1988; *Carmen* (Earls Court), *Metropolis* (Piccadilly Theatre, London), *Miss Saigon*—1989.

From 1961 to 1967, Hersey worked primarily as a lighting designer, though he did act in a show in 1962 and was the stage manager for *Six Characters in Search of an Author* at the Martinique Theatre in New York. In 1968, he moved to England and joined Theatre Projects Limited. Soon after, he designed *She*

Stoops to Conquer at the Garrick Theatre in London (1969) and launched a design career that included lighting plots for such award-winning productions as *Evita* (1979), *The Crucifer of Blood* (1980), and *Cats* (1983), among work that includes opera and ballet. His lighting for the 1985 production of *Les Miserables* was described in *Time Magazine* as a haze that at times flashed with "otherworldly bursts of white glare." In *Starlight Express*, which opened in 1985 at the Apollo Victoria Theatre in London and went on to New York, Hersey devised computer-controlled, movable spotlights able to shine directly down on the technical control bridge. To create the effect of starlight projected on the back wall of a stage, he used eight thousand meters of fiber optics and different sheets of metal gauze with thousands of pea bulbs attached to it. His design work has been supplemented by his own firm. In 1975, Hersey founded David Hersey Associates, Limited, in London. Special lighting effects that he has developed include light curtains and gobos—a pattern template for light.

Awards: Hersey has won many awards for his lighting designs, including the Los Angeles Drama Critics' Circle Award for *Evita* (1979), the Drama-Logue Critics' Award for *The Crucifer of Blood* (1980), the Antoinette Perry Award for *Evita* (1979); the Maharam Foundation Design Award for *The Life and Adventures of Nicholas Nickleby* (1981); the Antoinette Perry Award and the Drama Desk Award for *Cats* (1983); and the Drama-Logue Critics' Award for *Old Times* (1985).

Kurt Lancaster

Hockney, David. Artist and set designer (b. July 9, 1937, Yorkshire, England). Trained at the Royal College of Art from 1959 to 1962, Hockney is better known as a painter and photographer than as a scene designer. His first foray into the theatrical world was with the Royal Court Theatre's production of *Ubu Roi* (1966). Hockney's sets and costumes revealed a strong use of assemblage and color. His forceful artistic vision has been applied to the sets and costumes for a number of opera and ballet productions, including *The Rake's Progress* (1974) and *The Magic Flute* (1978), both at the Glyndebourne Festival Opera House; *Parade* (1979), *Le Sacre du Printemps* (1980), and *Oedipus Rex* (1980), all at the Metropolitan Opera House in New York; *Varii Capricci* (1983) by the British Royal Ballet at the Metropolitan Opera in New York; and *Tristan und Isolde* (1987) at the Los Angeles Music Center Opera. Hockney's work, like his art, is typified by several prominent and recurring themes; strongly shaped human forms, animals, trees, fire, boxes, and especially water. Much of his design work is a mixture of abstract expressionist and pop images.

Further Reading: Friedman, Martin. *Hockney Paints the Stage.* New York: Abbeville Press, 1983.

Elbin L. Cleveland

Hould-Ward, Ann. Costume designer (b. 1951, Glasgow, MT). After pursuing studies at the Art Students League in New York, Hould-Ward designed the costumes for a number of productions at regional theatres across the United States, including *The Cherry Orchard* and *Don Juan* at the Denver Center Theater

Company, *Merrily We Roll Along* at the La Jolla Theater Company, and *Fiorello!* and *The Jokers* at the Goodspeed Opera House. In the 1970s, Hould-Ward worked as an assistant to costume designer Patricia Zipprodt,* with whom she worked on many shows prior to her own Broadway debut with *Sunday in the Park with George* (1984), which she codesigned with Zipprodt. In 1985, Hould-Ward designed the costumes for the musical *Harrigan 'n' Hart*, and in 1988 she was nominated for a Tony Award for her costumes on her second Sondheim musical, *Into the Woods*. The costumes were based on original concepts by Hould-Ward and Zipprodt.

Hould-Ward's technique takes into consideration both research and the colors and textures of the fabrics she uses to create her costumes. To design the costumes for the diverse number of fairy tales that interweave to create the musical *Into the Woods*, Hould-Ward studied the paintings of Breughel. Her original costume sketches included notes and reference art that helped to shape the characters as well as their costumes. For *Sunday in the Park with George*, the designers were faced with the task of re-creating the shimmering style of pointillism, not just arranging actors in historical costumes against a background. Using a method that involved painting and dyeing fabric a number of colors, then rubbing it to reveal the layered colors underneath, Zipprodt and Hould-Ward succeeded in creating a third "color" by the juxtaposition of two other colors—a method developed by Seurat himself and a major tenet of pointillism.

Awards: Hould-Ward won the 1984 Tony Award for Best Costume Design, as well as the Maharam Award, for *Sunday in the Park with George*, awards that she shared with Patricia Zipprodt. She was also nominated for a Tony in 1988 for *Into the Woods*.

Further Reading: "Beyond Happily Ever After." *New York Times Magazine: The New Season* August 30, 1987; "Recreating Seurat: 'Sunday in the Park with George.'" *Theatre Design and Technology* Winter 1985.

Howard Gutner

Howard, Pamela. Set and costume designer (b. January 5, 1939, Birmingham, England). Howard received her formative training in art at the Birmingham College of Arts and the Slade School of Fine Art, from which she graduated in 1959. Since 1960, she has designed major productions for many of the theatre companies in England, including *Blues, Whites and Reds* (1974) at the Birmingham Repertory Theatre; *War Music* (1977) at the Old Vic; *The Philanderer* (1978) at the National Theatre; *On the Rocks* (1982) at the Chichester Festival Theatre; *The Taming of the Shrew* (1985) at the Royal Shakespeare Theatre; and *Border Warfare* (1988) at the Old Museum of Transport in Glasgow. In addition, her work has been seen in the United States in such productions as *Gilles de Rais* (1981) at the CSC Repertory in New York and *Waiting for Godot* (1986) at the Power Center at the University of Michigan. She has been a lecturer at the Birmingham College of Art and the University of Michigan and is currently head of the department of theatre design at the Central School of Art and Design in England. In addition, she has designed exhibits for several galleries and has presented lectures at many colleges and conferences in England and abroad. Howard served on the Drama Advisory Panel for the Arts Council of Great Britain and the Advisory Committee for the International Theatre Institute, and she was named honorary secretary of the Society of British Theatre Design.

Elbin L. Cleveland

Hume, Samuel. Set designer, director, theorist, and teacher (b. June 14, 1885, Berkeley, CA; d. September 1, 1962, Berkeley, CA). Hume's early career in theatre coincides with the "Little Theatre" and the "New Stagecraft" movements of the early twentieth century. After attending the University of California, Hume went to Europe, where he studied theatre and met Edward Gordon Craig.* After attending Craig's workshop at the Arena Goldoni in Florence, Hume returned to the United States as a disciple of Craig and the New Stagecraft. He subsequently finished his senior year and his master's degree at Harvard, where he studied under Professor George Pierce Baker. As an enthusiast of the new European theories, Hume organized "The New Stagecraft Exhibition" in 1914, which featured his own work as well as that of Robert Edmond Jones,* and was shown in Cambridge, New York, Chicago, and Detroit. As a result of this exhibition, Hume was hired as the director of the Detroit Arts and Crafts Theatre, where he put many of his newfound theories into practice. Here he experimented and popularized the neo-Craigian permanent adaptable setting that emphasized simplification, suggestion, and synthesis. Constructed of three-dimensional pieces that could serve as such things as walls, fences, doorways, or buildings, this system of flats, platforms, and pylons could be used for many plays or many scenes within a play. In addition, by changing their position on stage and adding such accoutrements as pottery, curtains, and suggestive lighting, their appearance could suggest many moods and exotic locations in a very economical manner. In keeping with Craig's theory of the single unifying artist of the theatre, Hume both directed and designed such plays as *The Tents of the Arabs* (1916), *The Wonder Hat* (1916), *The Chinese Lantern* (1917), and *Helena's Husband* (1917), in Detroit.

Hume's influence in disseminating the European theories was evident in many of his other activities as well. As a proponent of the New Stagecraft and director of the Detroit Arts and Crafts Theatre, he found financial support and provided an office for Sheldon Cheney to found *Theatre Arts Magazine.* In 1929, he co-wrote with Walter Réne Fuerst *Twentieth-Century Stage Decoration*, which had an introduction by Adolphe Appia.* This treatise on the new theories of stagecraft railed against naturalistic scenery and became highly influential in American theatre design practice. Finally, Hume went on to become professor at the University of California and was in charge of its Greek theatre project, and eventually he founded the drama department. His second book, *Theatre and School*, continued to demonstrate his lifelong commitment to educational theatre.

Further Reading: By Hume: *Theatre and School*. New York: Samuel French, 1932; with Walter Réne Fuerst. *Twentieth-Century Stage Decoration*. New York: Benjamin Blom, 1967.

Thomas J. Mikotowicz

Hurry, Leslie. Set designer and artist (b. February 10, 1909, London, England; d. November 20, 1978). Scene designer and artist, Hurry was educated at the St. John's Wood Art School and the Royal Academy Schools. His atmospheric stage designs were seen more in opera and ballet than in the drama, although he designed many Shakespearean productions for England's Old Vic and the Shakespeare Memorial Theatre. Hurry's settings for tragedies were dark and somber, with occasional bright touches of red and gold. This approach created a sense of mystery and space that worked most effectively in operas and verse dramas and allowed his visual style to accentuate the poetic nature of the work. Some of his most significant productions include *Hamlet* (1944) at the Old Vic, *Turandot* (1947) at Covent Garden, *Medea* (1948), *Cymbeline* (1949), *King Lear* (1950), *Tamburlaine the Great* (1951) at the Old Vic, *The Ring of the Nibelung* (1956), *Cat on a Hot Tin Roof* (1958; London), *The Duchess of Malfi* (1960), and *Becket* (1961).

James Fisher

I

Ingegneri, Angelo. Set designer and stage machinist (b. c.1550, Italy; d. c.1613). Ingegneri wrote one of the most significant treatises on lighting, *Della poesia rappresentativa e del modo di rappresentare le favole sceniche* (Discourse on representational poetry and the manner of presenting stage plays), in 1598. His most important suggestions included concealing the lighting instruments, focusing light sharply on the actors' faces by using tinsel reflectors and valances to keep light off the audience, and darkening the auditorium. Unfortunately, this last idea was not well received since fashionable audiences of the day wished to be seen.

James Fisher

Irving, Laurence Henry Forester. Set designer and artist (b. April 11, 1897, London, England; d. 1983). Theatrical productions include *Vaudeville Vanities—* 1926; *The Five O'Clock Girl, Heat Wave—*1929; *The Mulberry Bush, Petticoat Influence, An Object of Virtue—*1930; *The Man Who Pays the Piper, The Circle, Lean Harvest, The Good Companions, Viktoria and Her Hussar, The Painted Veil, There's Always Juliet, The Nelson Touch—*1931; *Punchinello, Evensong, Never Come Back—*1932; *Becket—*1933; *Clive of India, The Laughing Woman, The Young King—*1934; *Murder in the Cathedral—1935; Bees on the Boat, Cranmer of Canterbury—*1936; *Zeal of Thy House, Yes and No, I Have Been Here Before, Ninety Sail, Thank You, Mr. Pepys!, People at Sea—*1937; *Mary Goes to See, Banana Ridge, The Sun Never Sets, Christ's Comet—*1938; *She Follows Me About—*1943; *Desert Rats, The First Gentleman—*1945; *Marriage à la Mode—*1946; *Hamlet—*1950; *Man and Superman—*1951; *The Happy Marriage, Sweet Peril—*1952; *Out of the Whirlwind, Pygmalion—*1953; *The Shadow of Doubt, The Wild Duck—*1955; *The Broken Jug, The Court Singer—*1958.

As the son of actor H. B. Irving (1875–1919) and grandson of the great Victorian actor-manager Sir Henry Irving (1838–1905), Laurence Irving was well prepared for a life in the theatre. Following a term in the Royal Naval Air Service during World War I, he studied art at the Byam Shaw School and the Royal Academy Schools. After a successful exhibit at the Fine Arts Society in 1924, Irving planned a career as an artist and illustrator. In 1928, however, after a few small jobs as a scenic designer, he was invited to contribute designs for John Masefield's play *The Coming of Christ*, staged at the Canterbury Cathedral. This led to many scene design projects, including work on a number of films, including Douglas Fairbanks's *The Man in the Iron Mask* and the Fairbanks-Mary Pickford early talkie version of Shakespeare's *The Taming of the Shrew* in 1929. Later film projects included *Diamond Cut Diamond* (1932), *Captain Blood* (1935), and *Pygmalion* (1938). Irving's most important stage designs were for a 1933 production of Tennyson's *Becket*, which had been one of his grandfather's greatest vehicles, and the first production of T. S. Eliot's *Murder in the Cathedral* (1935). He designed less frequently after 1950 but continued to work as an artist. In 1951, Irving published an important biography of his grandfather entitled *Henry Irving: The Actor and His World*.

James Fisher

Izenour, George C. Theatre architect and engineering consultant (b. July 24, 1912, New Brighton, PA). Design and engineering projects include Art Center at the University of South Florida, Dallas Theatre Center in Texas, Art Center at the University of Bahia in Brazil—1958; Leob Drama Center at Harvard University—1959; Phillips Andover Academy, Jewish Community Art Center at Hartford, Connecticut, Madison Performing Arts Hall in Wisconsin—1961; Little Carib Theatre at Port of Spain-Trinidad, Atlanta Arts Center in Georgia, Columbia Arts Center in South Carolina—1962; Goucher College Arts Center—1963; Gammage Auditorium at Arizona State University, Drama Center at Carnegie Institute of Technology, Drama Center at Wittenberg University, Art Center at the University of New Mexico, Art Center for the Fathers of the Confederation in Charlottetown in Prince Edward Island, Canada, Art Center at Macalester College in St. Paul, Minnesota, Jesse Jones Hall for the Performing Arts in Houston, Texas, restoration of the Chicago Auditorium in Illinois, Municipal Auditorium in Jackson, Mississippi, Art Center at Wheelock College in Boston, Massachusetts, Viterbo College Concert Hall/Theatre in LaCrosse, Wisconsin, Loretto Hilton Art Center at Webster College, Webster Groves, Missouri—1965; Erie Art Center in Pennsylvania, Milwaukee Performing Arts Center in Wisconsin, Theatre Center at Women's College of the University of North Carolina, Wichita Cultural Center in Kansas, Juilliard School at the Lincoln Center of the Performing Arts in New York, Orlando Music Hall in Florida, Performing Arts Hall in Roanoke, Virginia, Auditorium-Coliseum and Moise Hall at McGill University, Performing Arts Hall at the University of Virginia, Manitoba Arts Center at Winnipeg, Canada, Brandon Auditorium in Manitoba, Canada, Creative Arts Center at West Virginia University, Akron Performing Arts Hall at the University of Akron in Ohio, Krannert Center at the University of Illinois—1967; Kansas State University Concert Hall/Theatre in Manhattan, Kansas, Theatre of Performing Arts in Fort Wayne, Indiana, Performing Arts Hall-Civic Center in El Paso, Texas, Edwin Thomas Hall at Ohio University, Arts Center at Choate School in Wallingford, Connecticut, Arts Center at St. Catherine College in St. Paul, Minnesota, Sala Rios Reyna at Caracas in Venezuela, Arts Center and Long Street Theatre at the University of South Carolina, remodeling of Bushnell Memorial Hall in Hartford, Connecticut, Mabee Center at Oral Roberts University in Tulsa, Oklahoma, Speech Arts Building and multiple-use coliseum at Washington State University in Pullman, Washington, Festival Theatre in Caesarea, Israel.

Izenour is one of the leading theatre consultants in the country today, having influenced the design of scores of performing art centers and theatres. Since 1955, he has designed or consulted on more than one-hundred theatre projects all over the world. There is hardly a major city in this country that does not have an Izenour theatre or performing arts center. A leading proponent of flexible arrangement theatres, Izenour put his theories into practice on such facilities as the Loeb Drama Center at Harvard University and the drama school complex at Carnegie Institute of Technology. At the Edwin Thomas Performing Arts Hall at the University of Akron, Izenour changed the volume and acoustics of the auditorium by movable ceiling panels to block off part of the audience. He worked with Frank Lloyd Wright on several projects, including the Dallas Theatre Center.

Izenour founded the research lab in technical theatre at Yale in 1939 and was the professor of theatre design and technology from 1961 to 1977. He has more than eighteen patents in related fields, including ones for the electronic lighting console (1947), the synchronous winch system (1958), and the first steel-acoustical shell for the Minneapolis Symphony Orchestra (1962). His writings on theatre technology are extensive. His latest book, *Theatre Technology* (1988), deals with design and use of stage equipment and follows the same theories expounded in his earlier work, *Theatre Design* (1977). This first work is a detailed look at contemporary theatre architecture and engineering problems in multiuse performing arts centers. It also includes an excellent survey of the history of theatre architecture.

Further Reading: By Izenour: "Building for the Performing Arts." *Tulane Drama Review* Summer 1963; "The Consultant: Then and Now." *Theatre Design & Technology* Summer 1975; with Jo Mielziner* and Gilbert Helmsby, Jr. "On Training Technicians, Theatre Engineers, and Scenographers." *Theatre Design & Technology* Spring 1976; "The Origins, Evolution and Development of Theatre Design Since World War II in the United States." *Theatre Design & Technology* Summer 1978; "Revolution in Light: The Electronic Console Control." *Theatre Arts Magazine* October 1947; *Theatre Design.* New York: McGraw-Hill, 1977; *Theatre Technology.* New York: McGraw-Hill, 1988.

About Izenour: Silvermann, Maxwell. *Contemporary Theatre Architecture.* New York: New York Public Library, 1965.

Ken Kloth

J

Jacobs, Sally. Theatrical and film designer (b. 1932, London, England). Educated at St. Martin's School of Art and the Central School of Arts and Crafts in London, Jacobs began her career as a "film continuity" person. She designed her first theatrical production, *Five Plus One*, for the Edinburgh Festival in August 1961 and her first London production, *Twists, Arts*, in February 1962. She has also designed frequently for the Royal Shakespeare Company, including her famous design for Peter Brook's production of *A Midsummer Night's Dream* (1970). The design scheme placed the action in a white box in which players swung from trapezes, wore elements of clown costume, and used bits and pieces of circus juggling props. Her other significant productions include *Women Beware Women* (1962); *Marat/Sade* (London, 1964; New York, 1965); *Brecht: Sacred and Profane* (1973); Director Andrei Serban's *Turandot* (1984); and *Fidelio* (1986) at the Royal Opera House in London. In addition, she has lectured on theatre design at the California Institute of the Arts, Los Angeles, and has designed at various theatres in the United States and Europe.

Jonet Buchanan

Jenkins, George. Set and lighting designer (b. 1909, Baltimore, MD). Theatrical productions (all theatres were in New York, unless otherwise specified) include *Early to Bed* (Broadhurst Theatre)—1943; *Mexican Hayride* (Winter Garden Theatre), *Allah Be Praised, I Remember Mama* (Music Box Theatre)—1944; *Dark of the Moon* (46th Street Theatre), *Common Ground* (Fulton Theatre), *Memphis Bound, Are You with It?* (Century Theatre), *Strange Fruit* (Royale Theatre), *The French Touch*—1945; *Tonight at Eight-Thirty, Time for Elizabeth*—1948; *Lost in the Stars* (Music Box Theatre)—1949; *The Curious Savage, Bell, Book, and Candle* (Ethel Barrymore Theatre)—1950; *Three Wishes for Jamie* (Mark Hellinger Theatre)—1952; *Touchstone, Gently Does It* (Playhouse Theatre)—1953; *The Immoralist* (Royale Theatre), *The Bad Seed* (46th Street

Theatre)—1954; *Ankles Aweigh* (Mark Hellinger Theatre), *The Desk Set* (Broadhurst Theatre)—1955; *Too Late the Phalarope* (Belasco Theatre), *The Happiest Millionaire* (Lyceum Theatre)—1956; *The Merry Widow* (New York City Center), *Rumble* (Alvin Theatre)—1957; *Song of Norway* (Marine Theatre, Jones Beach, Long Island), *Two for the See-saw* (Booth Theatre)—1958; *Tall Story* (Belasco Theatre), *The Miracle Worker* (Playhouse Theatre)—1959; *One More River* (Ambassador Theatre), *Critic's Choice* (Ethel Barrymore Theatre), *Hit the Deck* (Marine Theatre, Jones Beach, Long Island)—1960; *Paradise Island* (Marine Theatre, Jones Beach, Long Island)—1961; *A Thousand Clowns* (Eugene O'Neill Theatre)—1962; *Jennie* (Majestic Theatre), *Around the World in Eighty Days* (Marine Theatre, Jones Beach, Long Island)—1963; *A Thousand Clowns* (Comedy Theatre, London), *Everybody Out, the Castle Is Sinking* (Colonial Theatre, Boston)—1964; *Catch Me If You Can* (Morosco Theatre), *Mardi Gras!* (Marine Theatre, Jones Beach, Long Island), *Generation* (Morosco Theatre), *The Royal Hunt of the Sun* (with Ben Edwards; ANTA)—1965; *Wait Until Dark* (Ethel Barrymore Theatre and Strand Theatre, London), *Student Prince* (San Francisco)—1966; *The Only Game in Town*—1968.

Although Jenkins trained as an interior and industrial designer, he soon turned to scene design and became an assistant to designer Jo Mielziner* from 1937 to 1941. His first New York production was in 1943, with *Early to Bed* at the Broadhurst Theatre. In 1944, he earned the Donaldson Award for his design of *I Remember Mama*. For the next two decades, his work continued to be highly visible on Broadway with such shows as *Dark of the Moon* (1945), *Bell, Book, and Candle* (1950), and *The Miracle Worker* (1959). As an example of his style, the set for *13 Daughters* (1961) consisted of architectural units depicting a realistic, two-story house with decorated porches and stairways. His realistic design for *Wait Until Dark* (1966) created a suspenseful effect by depicting a photographer's basement apartment that has been adapted for his blind wife, who is being held hostage by murderous smugglers.

Kurt Lancaster

Jensen, John. Set and costume designer (b. 1933, Weiser, ID). Jensen has maintained a prolific design career in both professional and educational theatre. After graduating from the University of Oregon in 1958, he moved to New York City with the hopes of becoming a professional dancer. Soon, however, his interest turned to art history and theatrical design, and he enrolled as a student at the Pratt Institute, the School of Visual Arts, the Art Students' League, and Lester Polakov's School of Stage Design. In 1964, he was hired at C. W. Post College as designer and technical director, and in 1966 he left there to assist designer Jo Mielziner.* Two years later, he was hired to work in the Guthrie Theatre prop shop and continued there for the next eight years. His first full design assignments were for sets and costumes for Ben Jonson's *The Alchemist* and sets for Anouilh's *Ardèle*, both in 1969. Other productions at the Guthrie include *The Tempest* (1970), *A Play by Aleksandr Solzhenitsyn* (1970), *Of Mice* *and Men* (1972), and *The Crucible* (1974). In 1972, Jensen, together with Desmond Heeley* and Robert Scales, designed the stage for the international tour of the Stratford Festival Theatre of Canada. He has also collaborated with a number of regional theatre companies throughout the United States and created designs for such productions as *The Lion in Winter* (1970) for the Actor's Theatre in Louisville; *The Whitehouse Murder Case* (1971) for the Milwaukee Repertory Theatre; *The Ruling Class* (1975) for the American Conservatory Theatre; *Mourning Becomes Electra* (1976) for the Goodman Theatre; *The Cherry Orchard* (1976) for the Center Stage; *Uncle Vanya* (1977) for the Pittsburgh Public Theatre; *The Sea Plays* (1978) for the Long Wharf Theatre; *Damn Yankees* (1979) for the Brooklyn Academy of Music; *Talley's Folly* (1982) for the Cincinnati Playhouse; *All My Sons* (1983) for the Philadelphia Drama Guild; and *Curse of the Starving Class* (1986) for the Portland Stage Company. Jensen was the principal scenic designer for the McCarter Theatre's 1979–1980 season and created scenery for *The Visions of Simone Machard* (1979) and *1959 Pink Thunderbird* (1980). Since 1975, he has taught design at Carnegie-Mellon University and is currently head of the design/technical program at Rutgers University.

Further Reading: "Designers at Work." *Theatre Crafts* May 1987: 32.

Penny L. Remsen

Jones, Inigo. Scene and costume designer, architect, and artist (b. July 15, 1573, Smithfield, England; d. June 21, 1652, London, England). Theatrical productions include *The Masque of Blackness*—1605; *Hymenaei*—1606; *Hue and Cry After Cupid*—1608; *The Masque of Queens*—1609; *Tethys' Festival, Prince Henry's Barriers*—1610; *Oberon, the Fairy Prince*—1611; *Lords' Masque, Inns of Court Masque*—1613; *Pleasure Reconciled to Virtue*—1618; *Palace of Augures*—1622; *Time Vindicated*—1623; *Neptune's Triumph*—1624; *The Fortune's Isles*—1625; *A French Pastoral*—1626; *Love's Triumph Through Callipolis, Chloridia*—1631; *Albion's Triumph, Tempe Restor'd*—1632; *The Shepherd's Paradise*—1633; *The Triumph of Peace*—1634; *The Temple of Love, Florimène*—1635; *The Triumphs of the Prince d'Amour*—1636; *Britannia Triumphans, Luminalia, The Passionate Lovers*—1638; *Salmacida Spolia, The Queen of Aragon*—1640.

Not much is known about Jones's early years, although it is believed that he may have apprenticed with a carpenter in St. Paul's Churchyard and worked as a painter. Jones's first theatrical work was in 1605, when he designed scenery for the student plays at Oxford; his first known production, *The Masque of Blackness*, was performed at Court. During his career, he was responsible for most of the significant Stuart masques produced at Court. From 1605 until 1631, Jones worked closely with playwright Ben Jonson in creating masques for the Court; however, they had a serious disagreement during preparations for *Chloridia* (1631) over whether the poetry or the spectacle was more important in the masques. Jonson left, and Jones never worked with him again.

Jones's designs for the masques and plays are important for several reasons.

He carried the Italian mode of scenery into England through the use of three-sided *periaktoi* to change scenery; the use of a decorative frame to mask the wings and fly area—a forerunner of the proscenium; the use of a curtain that opened to reveal the scene and was closed to indicate the end of the play; the employment of tinted water to color the light; and the use of several other mechanical, scene-shifting devices. Later he elaborated on Italian methods with multiple side wings and back shutters in the Serlian manner, particularly in *Florimène* (1635) and *Salmacida Spolia* (1640).

Early in his career, in 1610, Jones was appointed surveyor of works to the royal heir, Henry, Prince of Wales. After Prince Henry's death in 1612, Jones traveled again to Italy, where he stayed from 1613 to 1615 and was influenced by the theatrical works of Serlio,* Parigi,* and others. In 1615, Jones won the enviable position as surveyor of the king's works, which he held until 1642. During his career, Jones produced several significant architectural projects, including his work at Somerset House, St. Paul's Church in Covent Garden, and a number of theatres: the Cockpit-in-court, the Paved Court Theatre at Somerset, the Surgeon's Theatre, and the Masquing House at Whitehall in 1637. Jones's architectural designs brought to England the latest ideas of the Italian masters, primarily Palladio,* whose classically influenced formulas and philosophy he employed in proportioning and decorating his architecture.

Elbin L. Cleveland

Jones, Robert Edmond. Designer, producer, director, and theorist (b. December 12, 1887, Milton, NH; d. November 26, 1954, Milton, NH). Theatrical productions include *The Glittering Gate*—1914; *The Man Who Married a Dumb Wife, Interior, The Devil's Garden*—1915; *Caliban by the Yellow Sands, The Happy Ending, The Merry Death, Til Eulenspiegel, Good Gracious Annabelle*—1916; *A Successful Calamity, Three One-Act Plays for a Negro Theatre: The Rider of Dreams, Granny Maumee, Simon the Cyrenian* (also directed), *Caliban by the Yellow Sands* (produced only); *The Deluge, The Rescuing Angel*—1917; *The Wild Duck, Hedda Gabler, The Magical City, Fanny's First Play, Trilby, The Garden of Paradise, The Little Shepherd, An Ideal Husband, Hempfield, Redemption, Be Calm Camilla, The Gentile Wife*—1918; *Guibour, The Jest, The Will of Song*—1919; *The Birthday of Infanta, George Washington: The Man Who Made Us, The Tragedy of Richard III, Samson and Delilah*—1920; *Macbeth, Daddy's Gone A-Hunting, Swords, The Claw, Anna Christie, The Mountain Man, The Idle Inn*—1921; *The S.S. Tenacity, The Deluge, The Hairy Ape, Voltaire, Rose Bernd, Hamlet, Romeo and Juliet*—1922; *The Laughing Lady, Launzi, A Royal Fandango, The Show Booth*—1923; *The Spook Sonata* (also codirected with James Light), *The Living Mask, Fashion* (also codirected with James Light), *Welded* (also produced with Kenneth Macgowan and Eugene O'Neill), *George Dandin, The Ancient Mariner* (also codirected with James Light), *At the Gateway, The Emperor Jones, Hedda Gabler* (also directed), *All God's Chillun Got Wings, The Crime in the Whistler Room, The Saint* (also codirected with Richard Boleslavsky and Stark Young), *S. S. Glencairn, Desire Under the Elms* (also directed), *Patience* (also directed)—1924; *Beyond, The Triumph of the Egg, Diff'rent, Michel Auclair* (also director), *Love for Love* (also director), *Ruint, Trelawny of the 'Wells', Outside Looking In* (also coproduced with Kenneth Macgowan and Eugene O'Neill), *The Buccaneer, The Last Night of Don Juan* (also coproduced with Kenneth Macgowan and Eugene O'Neill), *The Pilgrimage, In a Garden, The Fountain* (also coproduced with Kenneth Macgowan and Eugene O'Neill)—1925; *The Great God Brown* (also directed), *Little Eyolf, The Jest, Skyscrapers, Bride of the Lamb* (also coproduced with Kenneth Macgowan and Eugene O'Neill), *Martine*—1926; *The House of Women, Paris Bound*—1927; *Faust, Salvation, Machinal, Mr. Moneypenny, These Days, Holiday*—1928; *Serena Blandish, Becky Sharp, See Naples and Die, Ladies Leave, Yolanda of Cyprus, The Channel Road, Week-End, Seven-Year Love, Cross Roads*—1929; *Children of Darkness, Rebound, The Green Pastures, Die Gluckliche Hand, Roadside, Le Prezione Ridicole*—1930; *Woyzeck, Oedipus Rex, Mourning Becomes Electra, The Lady with a Lamp, The Passing Present*—1931; *Night over Taos, Camille* (also directed and produced); *Lucrece*—1932; *Inaugural Program of the Radio City Music Hall, Pierrot Lunaire, Enchantment* (also directed); *Nine Pine Street, The Merry Widow* (also produced and directed); *Ah, Wilderness!, The Green Bay Tree, Mary of Scotland*—1933; *The Joyous Season, Othello* (also produced and directed), *Dark Victory, La Cucaracha* (film)—1934; *Becky Sharp* (film), *Central City Lights* (also produced and directed)—1935; *The Dancing Pirate* (film)—1936; *Othello* (also directed)—1937; *The Sea Gull, Ruy Blas* (also produced and directed), *Everywhere I Roam*—1938; *The Philadelphia Story, The Devil and Daniel Webster, Susanna Don't You Cry, Madam Will You Walk?, Kindred* (also directed)—1939; *Juno and the Paycock, Romeo and Juliet* (lights only), *Love for Love* (also directed), *Tonight at Eight-Thirty*—1940; *Orpheus, The Barber of Seville*—1941; *Without Love*—1942; *The Crucifixion of Christ, Othello*—1943; *Jackpot, Helen Goes to Troy, The Children's Christmas Story*—1944; *Lute Song, The Iceman Cometh*—1946; *A Moon for the Misbegotten*—1947; *Out of Dust*—1949; *The Enchanted, The Flying Dutchman*—1950; *The Green Pastures*—1951.

Jones, perhaps the most important American scene designer of the first half of the twentieth century, was an early proponent of the "New Stagecraft," best exemplified in the work of European theorists Adolphe Appia* and Edward Gordon Craig.* Born in New Hampshire and educated at Harvard University, Jones began his design work as early as 1911.

His first important design, for *The Man Who Married a Dumb Wife* (1915), began the revolution in American scene design against realistically detailed settings in favor of simpler, often abstract environments. Among his most memorable and important designs were many of the original productions of the plays of Eugene O'Neill, especially during the 1920s and 1930s, including *Anna Christie* (1921), *The Hairy Ape* (1922), *The Emperor Jones* (1924), *Desire Under the Elms* (1924), *Mourning Becomes Electra* (1931), and *Ah, Wilderness!* (1933).

Jones, along with O'Neill and Kenneth Macgowan, produced many of these works, as well as a diverse sampling of contemporary and classical plays. In the late 1940s, Jones designed the last two productions of O'Neill's plays staged during the playwright's lifetime: *The Iceman Cometh* (1946) and *A Moon for the Misbegotten* (1947). Jones's designs continually set a standard in American scene design; his designs for two Shakespearean productions, *Richard III* (1920) and *Hamlet* (1922), both starring John Barrymore, were critically acclaimed and the first innovative American productions of Shakespeare in the twentieth century. In addition, he designed several operas and two films.

Aside from his work as a designer and occasional producer, he also directed plays, including the original productions of O'Neill's *The Fountain* (1925) and *The Great God Brown* (1926). As a theorist, Jones was involved in two influential publications; in 1922 he collaborated with Macgowan on *Continental Stagecraft*, a study of the significance of developments in the modern European theatre, and in 1941 several of his essays for *Theatre Arts Monthly* were collected and published as *The Dramatic Imagination*.

Further Reading: By Jones: with Kenneth Macgowan. *Continental Stagecraft*. New York: Harcourt, Brace, 1922; *The Dramatic Imagination*. New York: Duell, Sloan, and Pearce, 1941. "The Artist's Approach to the Theatre," *Theatre Arts Monthly*, September 1928: 629–34; "The Gloves of Isadora," *Theatre Arts Monthly*, October 1948: 17–22; "Nijinsky and *Til Eulenspiegel*," *Dance Index*, April 1944: 44–54; "Notes on the Theatre," *Theatre Arts Monthly*, May 1923: 323–25; "The Robe of Light," *Theatre Arts Monthly*, August 1925: 493–99; *The Theatre of Robert Edmond Jones*. Ralph Pendleton, ed. Middletown, CT: Wesleyan University Press, 1958.

James Fisher

Juvara, Filippo. Architect and scene designer (b. 1676, Italy; d. 1736). Juvara studied architecture in Rome and subsequently took a job as an assistant designer at the San Barolomeo Opera House in Naples. Working there with Giuseppe Capelli, he became familiar with angled perspective scenery. In 1708, Juvara was asked by Cardinal Pietro Ottoboni to come to Rome to design a small baroque theatre to be installed in the Palazzo della Cancellaria. Working there until approximately 1714, Juvara designed many productions and, elaborating on the wing and shutter method of stage design, experimented with freestanding flats in various positions on the stage. Later in his career, he used a circular rear backdrop of a garden overlooking a city rather than the usual straight shutter flat and further experimented on established traditions of existing scenography. Concurrently, in 1713, he designed opera productions in the Teatro Capronica and the private theatre of the queen of Poland. In 1714, he became chief architect at the Savoy Court in Turin. Juvara's technique was known throughout Europe and passed down to his students and assistants. He was a master at perspective, elaborate architectural vistas, and ingenious theatrical effects and scenic tricks.

Further Reading: Oenslager (see Bibliography).

Thomas J. Mikotowicz

K

Kantor, Tadeusz. Director, designer, and artist (b. April 6, 1915, Wielopole, Poland; d. December 8, 1990, Warsaw, Poland). Forming the Independent Theatre in Poland during the Nazi occupation, Kantor staged *Balladyna* (1943) and *Return of Odysseus* (1944). He began his significant work at the Teatr Stary in Kraków in 1945, where for the following ten years he was responsible for the designs of most of the productions presented there. In 1955, he founded the Teatr Stary's experimental stage, Cricot II, in which he mounted performances of the surrealist plays of Stanislaw Ignancy Witkiewicz, in which improvisational acting techniques were prominently used. In the 1960s, Kantor staged his own "Happenings" in Poland. His most important productions of the era include *Cuttlefish* (1956), *In a Small Country House* (1961), *The Madman and the Nun* (1963), *Happening-Cricotage* (1965), *Water-hen* (1967), and *Lovelies and Dowdies* (1973). Kantor achieved international critical acclaim with his "Theatre of Death." His company toured Europe, America, and Australia with *Dead Class* (1975), most of which is performed in mime; it shows a classroom full of corpses doomed to repeat in death the mistakes they made in life. In Florence, he produced *Wielopole, Wielopole* (1980), a grotesque portrait mixing elements of childhood reminiscences, familial and religious mythology, and striking visual images of the carnage of World War I. Other recent productions include *Ou sont les neiges d'antan* (1978), *Where Are the Snows of Yesteryear?* (1982), and *Let the Artists Die* (1985). Kantor has also exhibited at numerous art galleries and participated in many theatrical festivals throughout Europe.

James Fisher

Kellogg, Marjorie Bradley. Designer (b. 1946, United States). Theatrical productions include *Sambo* (with Ming Cho Lee*; New York Shakespeare Festival, Public Theatre)—1969; *The Happiness Cage* (New York Shakespeare Festival, Public Theatre)—1970; *A Gun Play* (with Ralph Funicello; Cherry Lane Theatre,

New York), *The Black Terror* (New York Shakespeare Festival, Public Theatre)—1971; *A Swansong, The Lady's Not for Burning* (both for the Long Wharf Theatre, New Haven, Connecticut), *Death of a Salesman* (Center Stage, Baltimore, Maryland), *Old Times* (Goodman Theatre, Chicago, Illinois), *The Country Girl* (Williamstown Theatre Festival, Massachusetts)—1972; *Juno and the Paycock* (Long Wharf Theatre, New Haven, Connecticut), *Getting Married* (Hartford Stage Company, Connecticut), *Three Men on a Horse* (Arena Stage, Washington, D.C.), *Candida, Twelfth Night* (both at the PAF Playhouse, Huntington Station, New York), *The Country Girl* (Williamstown Theatre Festival, Massachusetts)—1973; *The Killdeer, Sweet Talk* (both for the New York Shakespeare Festival, Public Theatre), *Private Lives* (Williamstown Theatre Festival, Massachusetts), *A Touch of the Poet, The Hot l Baltimore* (both for the Hartford Stage Company, Connecticut), *Where's Charley?* (Circle in the Square, New York), *Studs Edsel* (Ensemble Studio Theatre), *La Cambiale di Matrimonio* (Opera Buffa of New York), *The Merry Wives of Windsor* (Augusta Repertory Theatre, Maine), *Bits and Pieces* (Manhattan Theatre Club, New York)—1974; *Pygmalion* (Long Wharf Theatre, New Haven, Connecticut), *Afternoon Tea, All Over* (both at the Hartford Stage Company, Connecticut), *The Beggar's Opera* (Williams College, Williamstown, Massachusetts), *Death of a Salesman, All God's Chillun Got Wings* (both at the Circle in the Square, New York), *Life Class, Sea Marks, The Sea* (all for the Manhattan Theatre Club, New York), *The Front* (film, assistant art director; Columbia Pictures), *The Poison Tree* (Ambassador Theatre, New York)—1975; *The Estate* (Hartford Stage Company, Connecticut), *Awake and Sing!, Major Barbara* (McCarter Theatre Company, Princeton, New Jersey), *The House of Mirth, Alphabetical Order* (both for the Long Wharf Theatre, New Haven, Connecticut), *Seven Keys to Baldpate, Twelfth Night* (both for the American Stage Festival, Milford, New Hampshire), *Children* (Manhattan Theatre Club), *The Show-Off* (Goodman Theatre, Chicago, Illinois), *Green Pond* (sets and costumes; Stage South, Columbia, South Carolina), *All Over* (Theatre in America, PBS television)—1976; *Sleuth* (Syracuse Stage, New York), *Saint Joan* (Long Wharf Theatre, New Haven, Connecticut), *Paul Bunyan* (Manhattan School of Music, New York), *Molly* (sets and costumes; Spoleto Festival, Charleston, South Carolina), *Green Pond* (Chelsea Theatre Center, New York), *Arms and the Man, A Flea in Her Ear* (both for the American Stage Festival, Milford, New Hampshire), *The Confirmation* (McCarter Theatre Company)—1977; *The Sea Gull* (Indiana Repertory Theatre, Indianapolis), *A Flea in Her Ear* (Hartford Stage Company, Connecticut), *The Trial of the Moke* (Great Performances, PBS television), *Spokesong* (Long Wharf Theatre, New Haven, Connecticut), *Da* (Hudson Guild Theatre, New York), *The Best Little Whorehouse in Texas* (Entermedia Theatre, New York), *Bonjour, La Bonjour* (Guthrie Theatre, Minneapolis, Minnesota), *Fathers and Sons* (New York Shakespeare Festival, Public Theatre), *Under This Sky* (film; Red Cloud Productions), *The Taming of the Shrew* (Milwaukee Repertory Theatre, Wisconsin)—1978; *Hedda Gabler* (Cincinnati Playhouse in the Park, Ohio), *Spokesong* (Circle in the Square, New York), *Summerfolk* (Long Wharf Theatre, New Haven, Connecticut), *Right of Way* (Guthrie Theatre, Minneapolis, Minnesota), *Wine Untouched* (Harold Clurman Theatre, New York), *Open Window* (film; Park Lane Productions)—1979; *Salt Lake City Skyline* (New York Shakespeare Festival, Public Theatre), *A Midsummer Night's Dream* (Denver Theatre Center, Colorado), *Mary Barnes*, *American Buffalo*, *Solomon's Child* (all for the Long Wharf Theatre, New Haven, Connecticut), *Second Avenue Rag*, *Bonjour, La Bonjour* (both for the Phoenix Theatre, New York), *After the Season* (Wilmington Playhouse, Delaware, and Colonial Theatre, Boston)—1980; *Children's Crusade* (the First All Children's Theatre, New York), *The Medal of Honor Rag* (American Playhouse, PBS television), *Showdown at the Adobe Motel* (Hartman Theatre, Stamford, Connecticut), *Plenty* (Goodman Theatre, Chicago, Illinois), *Kean* (Arena Stage, Washington, D.C.), *The Father*, *American Buffalo* (both for the Circle in the Square, New York), *Isn't It Romantic?*, *Kaufman at Large* (both for the Phoenix Theatre, New York), *Hedda Gabler* (Boston University, Massachusetts), *A Day in the Death of Joe Egg* (Long Wharf Theatre, New Haven, Connecticut)—1981; *Solomon's Child* (Little Theatre, New York), *Ethan Frome*, *Open Admissions* (both for the Long Wharf Theatre, New Haven, Connecticut), *The Woods* (The Second Stage, New York), *Corpse!* (American Stage Festival, Milford, New Hampshire), *Present Laughter* (Circle in the Square, New York), *Steaming* (Brooks Atkinson Theatre, New York), *Extremities* (Cheryl Crawford Theatre, New York)—1982; *Another Country* (Long Wharf Theatre, New Haven, Connecticut), *The Misanthrope*, *Heartbreak House* (both at the Circle in the Square, New York), *Moose Murders* (Eugene O'Neill Theatre, New York), *A Lesson from Aloes*, *A Mad World, My Masters* (both for the La Jolla Playhouse, California), *Wild Life* (Vandam Street Theatre, New York), *Under the Ilex* (The Repertory Theatre of St. Louis, Missouri), *Hot Lunch Apostles* (La Mama E.T.C., New York), *American Buffalo* (Booth Theatre, New York), *Extremities* (Los Angeles Public Theatre, California), *Lunching* (New Broadway Theatre, Chicago, Illinois), *Old Times* (Roundabout Theatre, New York), *A Private View* (New York Shakespeare Festival, Public Theatre)—1983; *The Value of Names* (Hartford Stage Company, Connecticut), *Cantorial* (Hartman Theatre, Stamford, Connecticut), *Requiem for a Heavyweight*, *The Bathers*, *Under the Ilex* (all for the Long Wharf Theatre, New Haven, Connecticut)—1984; *Arsenic and Old Lace*, *The Gilded Age*, *A Country Doctor*, *Distant Fires*—1986; *A Month of Sundays*, *Self Defense*, *Babbitt: A Marriage*, *Self Defense* (ATE), *Elmer Gantry* (Ford Theatre, Washington, D.C.), *Serenading Louie* (Hartford Stage Company, Connecticut), *Fighting Chance* (Long Wharf Theatre, New Haven, Connecticut)—1987; *Annula, An Autobiography* (TNT Playhouse), *Enrico IV* (Roundabout Theatre, New York)—1988.

Kellogg is one of a growing number of American women scene designers working regularly on and off-Broadway, as well as on regional stages. Greatly influenced by Ming Cho Lee,* for whom she worked as an assistant, Kellogg has also assisted Robin Wagner* and David Mitchell.* Although she has designed for a number of theatres and directors, she has had an especially productive collaboration with director Arvin Brown and the Long Wharf Theatre in particular. Although Kellogg's most effective designs have involved painstakingly detailed realistic settings, such as for David Mamet's *American Buffalo* (1980), she has worked on a variety of contemporary and classic works. For Vaclav Havel's *A Private View* (1983), as in many of her designs, Kellogg combined selective, realistic elements with abstract, conceptual elements and a masterful manipulation of space.

Further Reading: Aronson (see Bibliography).

James Fisher

Kerz, Leo. Set and lighting designer (b. November 1, 1912, Berlin, Germany; d. November 4, 1976, New York City). Theatrical productions include *Artzte im Kampf*—1932; *The Threepenny Opera, The Hairy Ape, Golden Boy, Gas*— 1937 to 1942; *The Private Life of the Master Race*—1945; *The World of Christopher Blake, Me and Molly, Antony and Cleopatra*—1947; *Bravo, All You Need Is One Good Break*—1949; *A Long Way from Home*—1950; *The Biggest Thief in Town, Edwina Black*—1951; *The Sign of Winter*—1952; *The Victim, The Sacred Flame, The Gypsies Wore High Hats*—1954; *Troilus and Cressida, Macbeth, Aida, Lohengrin, Der Rosenkavalier, Die Walküre*—1955; *The Magic Flute, Parsifal, Boris Godunov, Francesca da Rimini, Landara, Die Fledermaus*—1956; *Susannah, Orpheus in the Underworld, The Moon, The Tempest*— 1957; *Clerambard, Listen to the Mockingbird*—1958; *Rhinoceros*—1961; *The Deputy*—1963; *The Threepenny Opera*—1964; *Burn Me to Ashes, Riverside Drive*—1965; *Parsifal*—1966; *Dance of Death, Chemmy Circle*—1969; *The Ruling Class*—1970; *Cavalcade of Musical Theatre, Dance of Death, Two by Pinter, Andorra, School for Scandal*—1971; *Children of the Wind*—1973. Films include *Guilty Bystander, Mister Universe*—1952; *This Is Cinerama*—1953; *Teresa*—1954; *Never Love a Stranger, New York Confidential*—1958; *The Goddess, Middle of the Night*—1959; *Odds Against Tomorrow*—1960.

While attending school in Berlin from 1929 to 1933, Kerz became a student of director Erwin Piscator and worked with Laszlo Moholy-Nagy and Traugott Müller.* As a young man, he was assistant to designer Caspar Neher* on the original 1928 production of Bertolt Brecht's *The Threepenny Opera*. He designed his first studio productions in 1932 at the Theater am Schiffbauerdamm and was awarded the Goethe Prize for stage design. During this period, Kerz absorbed Piscator's design ideas that architectural structure, projected images, and light should replace painted scenery. Subsequently, Kerz's own style became defined by its three-dimensionality, its sparse architectural units, and its attempt to unify the play's action, locale, and theme in the setting.

With the rise of Hitler to power in 1933, Kerz left Germany to embark on a long and successful career. Eventually, he migrated to Johannesburg and founded the Pioneer Theatre, an interracial company for which he designed and staged American plays and an English version of *The Threepenny Opera*. By 1941, he emigrated to the United States, where he remained for the rest of his life. His first work in New York was assisting such designers as Jo Mielziner* and Stewart Chaney and teaching design, lighting, and makeup at the New School for Social Research, where Piscator was director of the Dramatic Workshop. By 1947, he designed *Antony and Cleopatra* for Katherine Cornell and Guthrie McClintic. With the success of this production, Kerz went on to design plays for the Broadway stage while serving as staff designer and art director for the film division of CBS. From 1955 through 1960, Kerz designed operas for the San Francisco Opera Company, The Metropolitan Opera, and the New York City Opera. In 1961, Kerz secured the American rights for Ionesco's *Rhinoceros* and produced and designed the show. For his efforts he was awarded the Outer Critics Circle Award for the most creative overall contribution to the season. One year later, Piscator invited Kerz to the Freie Volksbuhne to design the world premiere of Rolf Hochhuth's controversial play *The Deputy*, which received international attention.

Over the course of the final decade of Kerz's life, he taught courses at Montana State University, Rutgers University at Lawrenceville, and the College of Fine Arts at Illinois State University. His sketches and models were exhibited at the Library and Museum of Performing Arts, Lincoln Center, in 1968. As art director for *Seeds of Discovery*, a feature film produced by NASA in 1969, he won a special award at the International Film and Television Festival. He also continued designing for the New York stage as well as for the Arena Stage in Washington, D.C., and Center Stage in Baltimore. Just before his death, Kerz was actively involved in designing sets for Sarah Caldwell's Boston Opera Company production of *The Triumph of Honor, or the Rake's Reform*, but the designs were never completed.

Further Reading: Larson, Orville K. "Leo Kerz's Designs for *Richard III.*" *Players Magazine* February 1959: 100–102; "Settings Designed by Leo Kerz" (a catalog of an exhibition at the Harvard Theatre Collection), 1987.

Andrea J. Nouryeh

Kiesler, Frederick. Set designer, architect, and artist (b. September 22, 1896, Vienna, Austria; d. December 27, 1965, New York City). Theatrical productions include *R.U.R.*—1922; *Methusalah, Emperor Jones, Francesca*—1923; *Mouchoir des Nuages, Gas II*—1924; *Jack and the Beanstalk*—1931; *Helen Retires, Ariadne in Naxos*—1934; *In the Pasha's Garden, Poisoned Kiss*—1935; *Joseph and His Brethren, Garrick, Maria Malibran*—1936; *Sleeping Beauty*—1937; *The Abduction from the Seraglio, The Marriage of Figaro*—1938; *L'Heure Espagnole, The Tales of Hoffman, Dido and Aeneas*—1939; *Cosi Fan Tutte, Le Donne Curiose, The Magic Flute*—1940; *Falstaff, Orpheus, The Barber of Seville, Don Pasquale*—1941; *Iphigenia in Tauris, Solomon and Balkis, The Mother*—1942; *The Old Maid and the Thief, Fashions of the Times*—1944; *No Exit, Der Freischutz, Riders to the Sea*—1946; *Oedipus Rex, Angelique, The Soldier's Tale, The Poor Sailor, Gianni Schicchi*—1948; *The Magic Flute*—

1949; *Ballet Ballads, Fidelio, The Beggar's Opera*—1950; *The Prisoner, Triple Sec, The Triumph of Saint Joan*—1951; *Canticle for Innocent Comedians, Falstaff, The Play of Robin and Marian*—1952; *Cosi Fan Tutte, Venus and Adonis, Britannia Triumphans, Facade*—1953; *Capriccio, The Tempest*—1954; *Idomeneo, The Tempest*—1955; *The Wife of Martin Guerre, Pantaloon, He Who Gets Slapped*—1956; *L'Enfant et les sortileges, The Child and the Apparitions, Gianni Schicchi*—1957; *Enrico IV, Bolivar*—1958; *Canticle for Innocent Comedians* (posthumously)—1969; *Shadows* (posthumously)—1977.

After studying art in Vienna, Kiesler began his auspicious theatre design career with a futuristic set for Capek's *R.U.R.* in Berlin (1922). The set featured a number of technical innovations, including the first use of motion pictures in place of backdrops, a device that simulated a television screen, and neon lights. His next design, for *Emperor Jones* (Berlin, 1923), demonstrated some of Kiesler's theories of kinetic stage space. In this production the set was in continuous motion, coordinated with the acting and lighting.

Kiesler emigrated to the United States in 1926 as the director of the International Theatre Exhibition in New York and officially became an American citizen in 1932. From 1933 to 1957, Kiesler served as the scenic director for the Juilliard School, where he produced the majority of his theatrical work, including *Ariadne in Naxos* (1934), *The Magic Flute* (1949), and *The Prisoner* (1951). He did at times, however, work in other theatres. For example, in 1935 he designed *In the Pasha's Garden* for the Metropolitan Opera. Kiesler's style was a combination of futurism, expressionism, and constructivism. His sets were inexpensive, with an uncluttered, simple use of line and with smooth and flat textures, employing a bold use of color.

Kiesler's 1924 design of the first modern theatre-in-the-round in Vienna was the start of a long career in architecture as both a practitioner and a visionary theorist. He served as the director of the Design Laboratory of the Columbia University School of Architecture from 1936 to 1942. In 1961, he was commissioned by the Ford Foundation to design the Universal Theatre, an urban theatre center. Although it was never realized, an aluminum model of it is on display at the Harvard Theatre Collection. This ellipsoidal theatre is designed without a single column or beam and so integrates the performers and the audience into one unified space. The space is enveloped in continuous shells of reinforced concrete. He included no fly space because Kiesler felt that designers would use projections and plastic scenery rather than old-fashioned drops. Stating that theatres cannot exist by themselves, Kiesler incorporated a thirty-story skyscraper into the complex, a precursor of the Marriott Marquee Theatre in New York City. As a result of his work, his ideas have influenced many theatre architects, including George Izenour,* who has claimed to have studied Kiesler's designs of multiuse theatres.

Further Reading: "Art in Orbit: Excerpts from Kiesler's Journals." *The Nation* May 11, 1964; Held, R. L. *Endless Innovations: Frederick Kiesler's Theory and Scenic Design.* Ann Arbor, MI: U.M.I. Research Press, 1982; *The Ideal Theatre: Eight Concepts.*

New York: American Federation of Arts, 1962; "Kiesler's Pursuit of an Idea." *Progressive Architecture* July 1961; "Notes on Improving Theatre Design." *Theatre Arts Magazine* September 1934.

Ken Kloth

Kim, Willa. Costume designer (b. 1937, Los Angeles, CA). Theatrical productions (all productions took place in New York City, unless otherwise specified) include *Red Eye of Love*—1961; *Fortuna, Birds of Sorrow* (ballet)—1962; *The Saving Grace, Have I Got a Girl for You!, Gamelan* (ballet; Leningrad, USSR)—1963; *Funnyhouse of a Negro, Dynamite Tonight, A Midsummer Night's Dream, The Old Glory, Helen*—1964; *The Day the Whores Came Out to Play Tennis, Sing to Me Through Open Windows, Song of Noah* (ballet; the Netherlands), *The Stage King* (ballet; Santa Fe, New Mexico)—1965; *Malcolm, The Office, Hail Scrawdyke!, Chu-Chem* (with Howard Bay*; Philadelphia, Pennsylvania)—1966; *Scuba Duba, The Ceremony of Innocence*—1967; *Papp, Promenade*—1969; *Operation Sidewinder, Sunday Dinner*—1970; *The Screens*—1971; *Sleep, Lysistrata*—1972; *Jumpers* (Washington, D.C.)—1974; *Goodtime Charley*—1975; *Dancin'*—1978; *Bosoms and Neglect*—1979; *Family Devotions, Sophisticated Ladies*—1981; *Lydie Breeze*—1982; *Song and Dance*—1985; *Long Day's Journey into Night, The Front Page*—1986; *Legs Diamond*—1987; *Legs Diamond* (Mark Hellinger Theatre)—1988; *Sophisticated Ladies* (Moscow)—1989.

Educated at the Chouinard Institute of Art in Los Angeles, Kim assisted designer Raoul Pène du Bois* for several years before designing the costumes for her first production, *Red Eye of Love*, which opened off-Broadway in 1961. Her introduction to dance came in 1962, when she designed costumes for choreographer Glen Tetley's ballet *Birds of Sorrow*. When critics raved about the costumes, Kim received offers from the Joffrey Ballet, the San Francisco Ballet, and American Ballet Theatre. Early on, Kim recognized that with dance, one is concerned with movement, but with theatre, one is focused on character. A desire to help the actor reveal character through costume design, combined with intense research for period accuracy, is the hallmark of Kim's technique. According to Kim, for all designers, more of an emphasis is being placed today on period accuracy than ever before. Preparation, she emphasizes, is endless. For *Sophisticated Ladies* (1981), Kim read every book she could find on Duke Ellington, including his son's books. She went to museums to research black history and listened over and again to the lyrics of Ellington's songs. Kim's costumes for the 1986 revival of *The Front Page* at Lincoln Center are an excellent example of just how she helps reveal character through costume design. The character of Sheriff Hartmann, for example, is a wimpish, well-to-do bureaucratic pawn, completely out of place among the seedy reporters of the pressroom. So in contrast to the reporters in their array of unmatched stripes and checks, argyles and polka dots, Kim designed an outfit for Hartmann that consisted of cream-colored trousers, a green and gold, brocade satin vest, and a forest green tweed jacket. The difference in attire was startling and helped to delineate the differences between the characters in the play. Kim's resourcefulness knows no bounds when it comes to searching out just the right costume. She scoured secondhand shops all along the eastern seaboard for months to find old clothes and accessories for some of the reporters in the play. After decades of hard work, Kim continues to apply her resourcefulness and passion for accuracy to productions on Broadway and throughout the country.

Awards: Kim won a Tony Award in 1981 for "Best Costume Design" for *Sophisticated Ladies*. In addition, she won an Obie Award for her costume designs for *The Old Glory* (1964); the Drama Desk Award for "Best Costume Design" in 1969 for *Promenade* and *Operation Sidewinder*; and the Joseph Maharam Foundation Award in 1971 for her designs for *The Screens*.

Howard Gutner

Klotz, Florence. Costume designer (b. 1928, New York City). Theatrical productions (all were in New York City, unless otherwise specified) include *A Call on Kuprin* (Broadhurst Theatre), *Take Her, She's Mine* (Biltmore Theatre)—1961; *Never Too Late* (Playhouse Theatre)—1962; *On an Open Roof* (Booth Theatre), *Nobody Loves an Albatross* (Lyceum Theatre)—1963; *Everybody Out, the Castle Is Sinking* (Colonial Theatre, Boston, Massachusetts), *One by One* (Belasco Theatre), *The Owl and the Pussycat* (ANTA Theatre)—1964; *The Mating Dance* (Eugene O'Neill Theatre)—1965; *The Best Laid Plans* (Brooks Atkinson Theatre), *This Winter's Hobby* (Shubert Theatre, New Haven, Connecticut), *It's a Bird . . . It's a Plane . . . It's Superman* (Alvin Theatre)—1966; *Golden Boy* (tour; costume coordinator)—1968; *Something for Everyone* (film; Paramount)—1969; *Norman, Is That You?* (Lyceum Theatre), *Paris Is Out* (Brooks Atkinson Theatre)—1970; *Follies* (Winter Garden Theatre)—1971; *A Little Night Music* (Shubert Theatre), *Sondheim: A Musical Tribute* (Shubert Theatre)—1973; *Dreyfus in Rehearsal* (Ethel Barrymore Theatre)—1974; *Pacific Overtures* (Winter Garden Theatre), *Legend* (Ethel Barrymore Theatre)—1976; *Side by Side by Sondheim* (Music Box Theatre), *A Little Night Music* (film; New World Picture)—1977; *On the Twentieth Century* (St. James Theatre), *Broadway, Broadway* (tour)—1978; *Harold and Maude* (Martin Beck Theatre), *Goodbye, Fidel* (New Ambassador Theatre)—1980; *The Little Foxes* (revival; Martin Beck Theatre)—1981; *A Doll's Life* (Mark Hellinger Theatre)—1982; *Peg* (Lunt-Fontanne Theatre)—1983; *Jerry's Girls* (St. James Theatre)—1984; *Grind* (Mark Hellinger Theatre), *I'm Old-Fashioned* (New York City Ballet)—1985; *Rags* (Mark Hellinger Theatre)—1986; *Roza* (Mark Taper Forum, Los Angeles)—1987; *City of Angels* (Virginia Theatre)—1989.

Educated at the Parsons School of Design, Klotz began her career at Brooks Costume Company in New York, where she both painted and aged material. Here she met Irene Sharaff,* who took her on as an apprentice for *The King and I* in 1951. Klotz was also an apprentice on the musicals *Carousel, Oklahoma!*, and *The Sound of Music*. After assisting Lucinda Ballard* on *The Gay Life* in 1961, Klotz received her first solo credit as a costume designer for the

Broadway show *A Call on Kuprin* in May of that same year. Since then, Klotz has designed costumes for a number of Broadway shows, as well as the New York City Ballet and the Lyric Opera in Chicago. In 1969, she received her first credit as a costume designer for motion pictures with *Something for Everyone*.

With a series of musical shows for Stephen Sondheim in the 1970s, however, Klotz established herself as a major creative force on Broadway, as she designed the costumes for *Follies* (1971), *A Little Night Music* (1973), *Sondheim: A Musical Tribute* (1973), *Pacific Overtures* (1976), and *Side by Side by Sondheim* (1977). For *Follies* Klotz used a technique that combined exhaustive research of the original Ziegfeld Follies and study of Watteau and other baroque painters before designing the costumes for the show's "Loveland" sequence. For *Pacific Overtures*, which was set in nineteenth-century Japan, Klotz traveled to Kyoto to observe Japanese fabric weaving and brought back books related to the period covered in the musical. With each costume, Klotz tried to create for the audience an immediate sense of the character's role in the production. For example, the Peter Pan collar worn by actress Dorothy Collins for her first appearance in *Follies* indicated the reserved attitude of the character before she even spoke. In *A Little Night Music*, the countess makes her initial appearance in a towering felt hat that gives her a distinctive, regal bearing and also makes her taller than anyone else on stage. Through such skillful application of her craft, Klotz continues to be one of the most popular designers in the New York theatre.

Awards: Klotz has won four Tony Awards: *Follies* (1971), *A Little Night Music* (1973), *Pacific Overtures* (1976), and *Grind* (1985). In addition, she has won three Drama Desk Awards and two Los Angeles Drama Critics' Awards. In 1975, she was named "Best Theater Designer" in the United States by Fashion Awards.

Further Reading: "Follies." *London Theatre Record* April 24/May 7, 1985; "A Little Night Music." *Take One* March 1978; "No Fooling Around with *Follies*." *Theatre Crafts* May/June 1971.

Howard Gutner

Kochergin, Edward Stepanovich. Set designer (b. 1937, Russia). Regarded as one of the Soviet Union's most important designers, Kochergin received his initial training under the Soviet artists Bruni and Akimov. In 1963, Kochergin became head of design of the Leningrad Theatre of Drama and Comedy, where he designed many productions. Later, in 1966, he became designer of the Kommissarjevskaya Dramatic Theatre. His work here led to his taking a position as chief artist of the Gorky Theatre in Leningrad. For the Gorky Theatre he designed *Hamlet* (1972), *Boris Godunov* (1973), *The Story of a Horse* (1976), and Nicholai Gogol's *Notes of a Madman* (1978), as well as *Energetic People*, *Valentin and Valentina*, *Last Summer in Shulimsk*, *Moliere*, and *Summerfolk*. Since then he has worked with important directors at major theatres throughout Russia. Kochergin developed a style that compares to Grotowski's "poor theatre" productions. Usually, he designs sparse, textured settings integral to the action of the play. For *Monologue About Marriage*, he provided a bentwood chair, kitchen table, one flower, and two potted plants on a bare stage. Many of his settings consist of metaphorical, nonrepresentational objects. At Leningrad's Maly Dramatic Theatre, he designed the setting for *The House*, which consisted of only five wooden horses, the kind used to adorn Russian farmhouses. His work with director Lyubimov at the Taganka on *The Inspector's Recounting* showed an equal amount of imagination. His set was made up of a huge backcloth of felt, representing an overcoat currently being fabricated. Performers entered and exited through slits in the felt as well as from above on movable platforms.

                                                                                            Thomas J. Mikotowicz

Kokkos, Yannis. Set designer (b. 1944, Greece). Arriving in Paris in 1963, this Greek-born designer has contributed the settings for many of the major productions produced in France. Among his productions are *Hamlet* (1983), *Ubu Roi* (1986), *Hernani* (1985), and *Electra* (1986). In 1987, he won the Gold Medal in Scenic Design at the Prague Quadrennial.

                                                                                            Thomas J. Mikotowicz

Koltai, Ralph. Set designer (b. 1924, Germany). Although born in Germany, Koltai is considered a British designer. He is known for his contemporary and sometimes experimental approach to scenic design and employs modern-day materials and techniques to such classic productions as *Doctor Faustus* (1964), *Back to Methuselah* (1968), and *Brand* (1978). He has worked for such major institutions as the National Theatre and the Royal Shakespeare Company and, at the latter, designed *Baal* (1979) and *Troilus and Cressida* (1985). Much of his work has been in opera, in which he employs the same contemporary approach. His significant productions in this area include the *Taverner* (1972) and Wagner's *The Ring* (1970–1973). For his designs, Koltai employs such materials as plastic tubing, metals, and mirrors, as well as projections, to give the sets a contemporary look and function. In his designs for *Les Soldat* (1983), directed by Ken Russell at the Opéra de Lyon, Koltai created four acting areas on various levels that contained flat vertical surfaces, on which female body parts and other images were projected. His recent designs for the musical *Metropolis* (1989) at the Piccadilly Theatre in London created the same cold, dark, industrial feeling present in Fritz Lang's 1926 film.

    Further Reading: Goodwin (see Bibliography); Rosenfeld (see Bibliography).

                                                                                            Thomas J. Mikotowicz

Komisarjevsky, Theodore. Designer and director (b. May 23, 1882, Venice, Italy; d. April 17, 1954, United States). Theatrical productions include *Black Masks, The Master Builder*—1907–1909; *Nota Kopek and Suddenly a Rouble*—1910; *The Bourgeois Gentleman*—1911; *Faust*—1912; *The Idiot*—1913; *Dmitry Donskoi*—1914; *The Golden Cockerel*—1917; *Lohengrin, Boris Godunov*—1918; *Prince Igor*—1919; *The Government Inspector*—1920; *The Race with a Shadow, The Love Thief, Uncle Vanya*—1921; *Six Characters in Search of an Author, At the Gates of the Kingdom*—1922; *The Bright Island, Ivanov*—1925; *Uncle Vanya, The Three Sisters, The Snow Man, Katerina, The Government*

Inspector, Hearts and Diamonds, The Cherry Orchard, Liliom—1926; *The Four-teenth of July, King Lear, Naked, The Pretenders, Paul I, Mr. Prohack*—1927; *The Man with Red Hair, The Brass Paperweight*—1928; *The Three Sisters, Red Sunday*—1929; *Man with Portfolio*—1930; *The Queen of Spades, Take Two from One, Musical Chairs, Robin Hood*—1931; *Musical Chairs, The Heart Line, Le Cocu Magnifique, Hatter's Castle, The Merchant of Venice, Fraulein Elsa*—1932; *Macbeth, The Merchant of Venice, Escape Me Never*—1933; *Magnolia Street, The Maitlands*—1934; *The Merry Wives of Windsor, Mesmer, Further Outlook*—1935; *King Lear, The Sea Gull, Antony and Cleopatra, The Boy David*—1936; *King Lear*—1937; *The Comedy of Errors*—1938; *The Taming of the Shrew, The Comedy of Errors*—1939; *Russian Bank*—1940; *Crime and Punishment*—1947; *Cymbeline*—1950.

Komisarjevsky was born to Russian parents in Venice but spent most of his active career as a director and designer working in English and American theatres. He began his work in Russia on the pre-Revolutionary stage in 1907, sometimes in collaboration with his sister, Vera Komisarjevsky (1864–1910), staging plays and operas with powerful symbolist and futurist designs, and sometimes in collaboration with director Nikolai Evreinov. Between the years 1910 and 1918, Komisarjevsky ran a studio theatre in Moscow and staged plays by playwrights Andreyev, Kuzmin, and Sologub. As a prolific director and designer, he was associated with the Free School of Scenic Art (1910–1919), the Gay Theatre (1910–1911), the Moscow Nezlobin Dramatic Theatre (1910–1913), the Maly and Bolshoi theatres in Moscow (1913–1914), the Moscow Opera House (1914–1919), the Vera Komisarjevsky Memorial Theatre (1914–1918), and the Bolshoi Ballet and Opera (1918–1919). After moving to England in 1919, he was able to find only occasional work as a scene designer. After an extraordinarily suc-cessful season at the Barnes Theatre in Hammersmith, however, he was offered a variety of major assignments. Subsequently, he married actress Peggy Ashcroft, who performed leading roles in a number of his productions, ranging from Shakespeare to the Russian classics. His most acclaimed productions were several Shakespearean plays, including *Macbeth* (1933), *The Merry Wives of Windsor* (1935), *King Lear* (1936), *The Comedy of Errors* (1938), and *The Taming of the Shrew* (1939), all staged at the Shakespeare Memorial Theatre. During the 1930s, Komisarjevsky also produced several plays; his last was J. M. Barrie's *The Boy David* (1936). In addition, he authored several books, including *The Theatre and a Changing Civilization* (London: John Lane the Bodley Head Limited, 1935).

Further Reading: Oenslager (see Bibliography).

James Fisher

Kook, Edward Frankel. Designer of stage lighting equipment (b. 1903, New York, NY; d. September 29, 1990, New York, NY). Educated as an accountant, Kook used his business skills to form Century Lighting, Inc., in 1929 in part-nership with Saul Joseph and Irving Levy. Century Lighting developed state-of-the-art lighting equipment and effects for theatres throughout the country. Among their most important early innovations were the successful development and manufacture of the profile spot lighting instrument called "Leko," a name compounded from "Levy" and "Kook." In 1946, he founded Portovox, a company that manufactured permanent and portable wireless microphones and sound equipment. With his wife, Hilda H. Silverson, Kook formed the Arts of the Theatre Foundation in 1947 to provide grants and fellowships to playwriting students and to support of other educational theatre projects. Kook has assisted numerous important young artists at the beginning of their careers, most notably scene designer Ming Cho Lee.* In addition to his management of Century Lighting, he taught lighting at Columbia University and the Yale Drama School, served on the board of the Phoenix Theatre from 1957 to 1963, and worked as a lighting consultant in partnership with designer Jo Mielziner.* In collaboration with Joel M. Schenker, he produced *Love Me, Love My Children* at the Mercer-O'Casey Theatre in 1971.

Awards: He received a special Tony Award in 1952 for contributing to and encouraging the development of stage lighting and electronics; a Ford Foundation Grant; a Kelcey Allen Award in 1962; and a USITT Founders Award in 1974.

Further Reading: By Kook: *Image in Light for the Living Theatre*. New York: Ford Foundation, 1963.

James Fisher

Korovine, Konstantin Alexeevich. Designer (b. December 23, 1861, Moscow, Russia; d. September 11, 1939, Paris, France). Theatrical productions include *Snegurochka*—1885; *The Little Hump-backed Horse*—1902; *Sadko*—1906; *The Tale of the Invisible City of Kitezh and the Maid Fevronia*—1907; *Prince Igor*—1909; *Les Orientales*—1910; *Snegurochka*—1911; *The Tale of the Tsar Saltan*—1913; *La Belle au Bois Dormant*—1915; *Snegurochka*—1929.

In 1874, Korovine enrolled in the Moscow Institute of Painting, Sculpture, and Architecture and studied under Vasilii Polenov and Alexei Savrasov. Korovine later became a member of the Abramtsevo artist's colony, under the patronage of Savva Mamontov, who later encouraged Korovine as a scenic designer and employed him to design settings for a number of operas during the 1890s. In his career, he designed as many as 130 operas, ballets, and plays. His work as a painter and a scene designer was greatly influenced by the impressionist movement. In 1900, Korovine became resident designer for the Bolshoi in Moscow. He also taught at the Moscow Institute of Painting, Sculpture, and Architecture before emigrating to Paris in 1923, where, unfortunately, he found little of the success he had achieved in his homeland.

Further Reading: Bowlt, John E. *Russian Stage Design. Scenic Innovation, 1900–1930*. Jackson, MS: Mississippi Museum of Art, 1982; Kogan, D. *K. Korovine*. Moscow: Iskusstvo, 1964; Kusubova, T. "A Note on Konstantin Korovine (1861–1939)." *Tri-Quarterly* 1973: 558–69; Oenslager (see Bibliography); Vlasova, R. *Konstantin Korovine*. Leningrad: Khudozhnik RSFSR, 1969.

James Fisher

L

Landesman, Heidi. Set designer and producer (b. 1951, United States). Theatrical productions include *Holeville*—1979; *Table Settings, The Marriage Dance*—1980: *How It All Began, Twelve Dreams, Penguin Touquet, A Midsummer Night's Dream*—1981; *Maybe I'm Doing It All Wrong, Pastorale*—1982; *'Night, Mother, Painting Churches, The Lady and the Clarinet, Romeo and Juliet, American Passion* (scenic consultant)—1983; *Big River*—1985; *Hunting Cockroaches* (Manhattan Theatre Club), *Into the Woods* (produced only; Martin Beck Theatre)—1987; *Romeo and Juliet*—1988; *Approaching Zanzibar* (Second Stage), *Dutch Landscape* (Mark Taper Forum, Los Angeles, California)—1989.

Since graduating from Yale, Landesman has won critical acclaim for her designs and has worked extensively in regional theatres and for Joseph Papp's New York Shakespeare Festival. Her designs are compelling in their frightening banality, as was the home setting for *'Night, Mother* (1983), her first Broadway production. For *A Midsummer Night's Dream* (1981), she transformed the Delacorte Theatre into a magic glade of real grass, trees, and flowers. Her design for *Big River* (1985), which she also co-produced on Broadway, was a warm impression of the Mississippi River in rough-hewn wood and sepia. For her efforts, Landesman was the first woman singly to win a Tony Award for set design.

Awards: In 1983, she won the Obie Award for *A Midsummer Night's Dream* and *Painting Churches*. Her set for *Big River* (1985) won the Tony Award, Drama Desk Award, and the Joseph Maharam Foundation Award.

Further Reading: "Sets and the Working Girl." *Vogue Magazine* September 1985; "Women in Design: A Discussion." *Theatre Design & Technology* Summer 1985.

Ken Kloth

Larionov, Michel. Scene designer and painter (b. May 22, 1881, Tiraspot, Bessarabia; d. May 10, 1964, Foteny-aux-Rosse, France). Theatrical productions include *Soleil de Minuit*—1915; *Histoires Naturelles, Kikimora*—1916; *Contes*

Russes—1917; *Chout*—1921; *Renard*—1922 and 1929; *Karaguez*—1924; *Sur le Borysthene*—1932; *Port Said*—1935; *Donna Serpente, Jour de Fete au Village, Le Bureau des Idees*—1936 to 1938.

After studying from 1898 to 1904 at the Moscow Institute of Painting, Sculpture, and Architecture, Larionov met fellow designer Nathalie Goncharova, who became his lifelong companion. In 1906, the two artists joined Diaghilev in Paris to exhibit in the Russian section of the Salon d'Automne. After serving one year in the Russian army, Larionov returned to Paris to design his first major ballet for Diaghilev, *Soleil de Minuit* (1915). With this ballet Larionov illustrated in practice the ideals of cubism, futurism, and rayonism that he had been associated with as a painter. The essential element of his style was a return to a primitivism inspired by Russian folklore and folk art. Popular arts, particularly farce and the buffoonery of the fairground clowns, were the prime arenas from which Larionov took his subject matter for the ballets. The colors and shapes found in toys, painted trays, woodcuts, embroidery, and icons made by Russian craftsmen were brought to life in his designs. To this decoration, he added flat figures, inverted perspective, geometric, cubist constructions, and clear, "vulgar" color lit by white light.

Larionov did not just design ballets for Diaghilev—he helped to create them. Because of his thorough knowledge of the theatre, Larionov was given the job of training choreographer Leonide Massine. From this collaboration were created *Soleil de Minuit*, *Kikimora*, and *Contes Russes*. When Larionov again returned to work for Diaghilev in 1921, he was made artistic director of the company. He designed and conceived *Chout*, his cubist ballet, which was translated into movement by a young dancer in the company named Slavinsky. Perhaps his most important designs from this period were for Nijinska's ballet *Renard*, based on a Russian folktale.

Larionov continued to design for the Ballets Russes after Diaghilev's death. Some of his last designs were executed for choreographers Serge Lifar, De Basil, Adolf Bolm, and Gsovsky. For the next fifteen years he and Goncharova lived in poverty and obscurity until Richard Buckle's 1954 Diaghilev exhibition in Edinburgh. He died in France ten years later.

Further Reading: By Larionov: with Nathalie Goncharova. *L'art theatral decorative modern.* Paris: Le Cible, 1919. About Larionov: "Diaghilev and His First Collaborators." *Ballet* September 1949: 9–15; Hastings, Baird. "The Contribution of Michel Larionov to Ballet Design." *Dance Magazine* 23:11 November 1949: 12 + .

Andrea J. Nouryeh

Larkin, Peter. Set designer (b. August 25, 1926, Boston, MA). Theatrical productions (all are in New York unless otherwise specified) include *The Wild Duck*—1951; *First Lady, Dial "M" for Murder, A Streetcar Named Desire* (Canada, ballet)—1952; *The Teahouse of the August Moon*—1953; *Ondine, Peter Pan*—1954; *Inherit the Wind, No Time for Sergeants*—1955; *Shangri-La, New Faces of 1956, Protective Custody*—1956; *Good as Gold, Compulsion, Miss Isobel*—1957; *Blue Denim, Goldilocks* (Lunt-Fontanne Theatre), *The*

Shadow of a Gunman—1958; *First Impressions, Only in America*—1959; *Greenwillow, Laurette*—1960; *Giants, Sons of Giants, We Take the Town, Nowhere to Go But Up*—1962; *Marathon '33, The Seagull, The Crucible, Ring 'Round the Moon*—1963; *Rich Little Rich Girl, Liliom, She Stoops to Conquer*—1964; *The Porcelain Year*—1965; *The Great Indoors, Happily Never After, Anna Christie* (Los Angeles), *Hail Scrawdyke!*—1966; *Scuba Duba*—1967; *Les Blancs, Sheep on the Runway*—1970; *Twigs, WC*—1971; *Wise Child* (Helen Hayes Theatre)—1972; *Let Me Hear You Smile*—1973; *Thieves' Carnival*—1974; *Cracks*—1976; *Ladies at the Alamo*—1977; *Dancin'*—1978; *G. R. Point, Break a Leg*—1979.

After a brief career in New York as an illustrator and cartoonist, Larkin enrolled at the Yale Drama School in 1946. While there, he was influenced by such luminaries as Orin Parker, Donald Oenslager,* and guest lecturer Robert Edmond Jones.* After two years at Yale he decided to leave school and begin a career in design. He worked first at the Artillery Lane Playhouse in St. Augustine, Florida, and continued with several summer theatres over a span of three years. When George Schaefer, artistic director for the New York City Center, interviewed Larkin in 1951, he immediately contracted the designer to create the sets for *The Wild Duck*, and Larkin's career became established.

During the 1950s, Larkin was successful on Broadway with designs for such productions as *Dial "M" for Murder* (1952) and *The Teahouse of the August Moon* (1953). Larkin's style revealed a penchant for simplicity that has led to his work being called skeletal and constructivist. This style is evident in his designs for *Inherit the Wind* (1955) and *Goldilocks* (1958), in which large structural elements were placed against large expanses of sky. His designs for *No Time for Sergeants* (1955) were well received and became part of the show when the latrine lids flipped open at "attention" when the inspection officer entered. His subtle use of forced perspective in the architectural elements for *A Streetcar Named Desire* (1952), for example, showed Larkin's ability to simplify the complex.

For Larkin, scenic simplification is part of the intricate puzzle of using theatrical conventions creatively. For example, in 1966, for the Eugene O'Neill Theatre Center's New Playwright's Conference, he developed a series of simple scenic modules to overcome the expanding scenic needs of the conference. These modules were capable of serving for the sets for several shows. Further, his creative use of stage mechanics in *Goldilocks* (1958), his use of concentric turntables for *Protective Custody* (1956), and his ingenious scene shifts in full view of the audience for *Peter Pan* (1954) created a scenic magic unique to his designs. He has since applied his design talents at the Stratford Shakespeare Festival in Connecticut and at the New York City Center Ballet.

Further Reading: Weaver, Arden Walter. "A Look at the Stage Designs of Peter Larkin Through a System of Critical Analysis." Ph.D. diss., University of Michigan, 1982.

Brian R. Jones

Laurencin, Marie. Ballet designer and painter (b. 1886, France; d. 1956). Laurencin studied art at the Academie Hubert in Paris and subsequently became Apollinaire's lover. He classified her as a "scientific cubist," one who painted "new structures out of elements borrowed not from the reality of sight, but from insight." When she was commissioned to design the set, costumes, and act-curtain for the Ballets Russes production of *Les Biches* (1924), starring Nijinsky, she relied on the pastel colors and simple organic lines that characterized her paintings. The set, a living room suggested by a window, balcony rail, and lavender curtains painted on a backdrop and a large sofa upholstered in lavender, was complemented by the designer's reliance on pink, black, and beige for the women's costumes, and blue, bluish gray, and white for the men's. Laurencin designed several productions for Roland Petit as well as other choreographers after the war. Her most famous designs include *Le Déjeuner sur l'Herbe*, *Paul et Virginie*, and *L'eventail de Jeanne*.

                                                                                      Andrea J. Nouryeh

Lautenschläger, Karl. Set designer, technical director, and inventor (b. 1843, Germany; d. 1906). Lautenschläger is best known for introducing the revolving stage in 1896 at the Residenz Theater in Munich. Although this type of stage is believed to have been first invented in Japan, its introduction into German theatres led to its wide acceptance into western theatres after 1900. This device helped solve the problem of changing the heavy, three-dimensional scenery and was supplanting the wing and drop method in the last quarter of the nineteenth century. The revolving stage accommodated several different settings that could be shifted into the audience's view by simply revolving the turntable, thus allowing for quick scene changes. In addition, if changes to a scene had to be made during the course of a show, scenes could easily be prepared backstage, while another was onstage, and rotated into view. Lautenschläger also designed what was called the *Shakespearebühne*. For a production of *King Lear* in 1889 at the Hoftheater in Munich, Lautenschläger created a multipurpose stage consisting of three different sections: an architecturally decorated facade within the pros-cenium, an inner stage with scenery, and a semicircular forestage in front of the proscenium arch. In 1900, he also redesigned the stage for the Oberammergau Passion Play. Lautenschläger incorporated electricity, electric motors, and other stage machinery into productions that allowed for changes in the aesthetic and technical approaches to scene design of the day.

                                                                                      Kurt Lancaster

Lee, Eugene. Set and lighting designer (b. March 9, 1939, Beloit, WI). Theatre productions (all are designed by Lee and were in New York City, unless otherwise noted) include *Endgame* (Theatre of the Living Arts, Philadelphia)—1965; *Poor Bitos* (Theatre of the Living Arts, Philadelphia), *Fitz and Biscuit* (Circle in the Square), *A Dream of Love*, *Beclch* (costumes), *Endgame* (all three for the Theatre of the Living Arts, Philadelphia)—1966; *The Threepenny Opera*, *The Imaginary Invalid*, *H.M.S. Pinafore* (all for Studio Arena, Buffalo, New York), *The Three-penny Opera*, *The Importance of Being Earnest* (both for the Trinity Square Repertory Company, Providence, Rhode Island)—1967; *Enrico IV*, *A Delicate*

Balance (both for Studio Arena, Buffalo); *Years of the Locust, An Enemy of the People, Phaedra* (all for Trinity Square Repertory Company, Providence, Rhode Island)—1968; *Macbeth, The Homecoming, Billy Budd, Exiles, The Old Glory, House of Breathe, Black/White, Wilson in the Promised Land* (all for Trinity Square Repertory Company, Providence, Rhode Island), *World War 2 1/2* (Martinique Theatre), *Slave Ship* (Brooklyn Academy of Music, New York), *The Recruiting Officer* (Theatre of the Living Arts, Philadelphia), *Harry Noon and Night* (Franne Lee designed costumes; Theatre of the Living Arts, Philadelphia)—1969; *The Skin of Our Teeth, Lovecraft's Follies* (both for the Trinity Square Repertory Company, Providence, Rhode Island), *A Line of Least Existence* (with Franne; Theatre of the Living Arts, Philadelphia), *Alice in Wonderland, Saved* (Franne designed costumes; The Extension), *Mother Courage* (Franne designed costumes; Studio Arena, Buffalo), *You Can't Take It with You* (Trinity Square Repertory Company, Providence, Rhode Island), *Son of Man and the Family, The Taming of the Shrew* (both at the Rhode Island School of Design Theatre)—1970; *The Good and Bad Times of Cady Francis McCullum and Friends* (Franne designed costumes), *Troilus and Cressida, Down by the River Where Waterlilies Are Disfigured Every Day* (all three at the Trinity Square Repertory Company, Providence, Rhode Island), *The Threepenny Opera* (Rhode Island School of Design Theatre), *Orghast* (Shiraz Festival, Iran)—1971; *Dude* (with Franne and Roger Morgan; Broadway Theatre), *Old Times* (Trinity Square Repertory Company, Providence, Rhode Island)—1972; *The Royal Hunt of the Sun* (Trinity Square Repertory Company, Providence, Rhode Island), *Feasting with Panthers* (Trinity Square Repertory Company, Providence, Rhode Island and PBS television), *Candide* (with Franne; Chelsea Theatre Center, Brooklyn Academy of Music and Broadway Theatre), *Brother to Dragons, Ghost Dance, Aimee* (all for Trinity Square Repertory Company, Providence, Rhode Island), *The Tooth of Crime* (with Franne; Performing Garage)—1973; *A Man for All Seasons* (Trinity Square Repertory Company, Providence, Rhode Island), *Well Hung* (Trinity Square Repertory Company, Providence, Rhode Island), *Gabrielle* (Franne designed costumes; Studio Arena, Buffalo), *Love for Love* (with Franne)—1974; *Peer Gynt, Tom Jones, Seven Keys to Baldpate, The Skin of Our Teeth* (Franne designed costumes; Mark Hellinger Theatre), *Cathedral of Ice, Two Gentlemen of Verona* (both for the Trinity Square Repertory Company, Providence, Rhode Island), *Brother to Dragons* (PBS television)—1975; *Dream on Monkey Mountain* (Center Stage, Baltimore), *Bastard Son, Eustace Chisholm and the Works, Of Mice and Men* (all three for the Trinity Square Repertory Company, Providence, Rhode Island), *Life Among the Lowly* (PBS television)—1976; *King Lear* (Trinity Square Repertory Company, Providence, Rhode Island), *Some of My Best Friends* (Longacre Theatre), *Ethan Frome, Rosmersholm, Seduced* (all three for the Trinity Square Repertory Company, Providence, Rhode Island)—1977; *Uncle Tom's Cabin: A History* (lights only; Trinity Square Repertory Company, Providence, Rhode Island), *La Fanciulla del West* (Lyric Opera, Chicago)—1978; *Sweeney Todd* (Uris Theatre in New York City and

London), *Gilda Radner Live from New York* (Winter Garden Theatre), *The Scarlet Letter* (PBS television)—1979; *Kaspar* (International Center for Theatre Research, Paris); *It's Me, Sylvia* (Playhouse Theatre), *Willie Stark* (Kennedy Center Opera House), *Inherit the Wind* (Trinity Square Repertory Company, Providence, Rhode Island), *Simon and Garfunkel Concert* (Central Park), *Faust* (Opera Company of Boston), *Of Mice and Men, Buried Child* (both toured for the Trinity Square Repertory Company, Providence, Rhode Island), *Steve Martin Special* (NBC television), *Merrily We Roll Along* (Alvin Theatre), *House of Mirth* (PBS television)—1981; *Little Prince and the Aviator* (Alvin Theatre), *The Hothouse* (Trinity Square Repertory Company, Providence, Rhode Island, and Playhouse Theatre), *Agnes of God* (Music Box), *Simon and Garfunkel* (Tokyo), *Hammett* (Zoetrope Studios Films), *The Web* (Trinity Square Repertory Company, Providence, Rhode Island), *Bone Songs* (Cubiculo Theatre), *Easy Money* (Orion Films)—1982; *The Tempest, Letter from Prison: In the Belly of the Beast* (both for the Trinity Square Repertory Company, Providence, Rhode Island), *Newsweek 50th Anniversary* (New York State Theatre), *Galileo, The Wild Duck* (both for the Trinity Square Repertory Company, Providence, Rhode Island), *Ballad of Soapy Smith* (Seattle Repertory Company, Washington, and the Public Theatre), *Billy Bishop Goes to War* (Bradford Theatre, Boston), *Randy Newman Live at the Odeon* (Showtime television)—1983; *The New Show* (NBC television), *The Wild Duck* (Dallas Theatre Center, Texas), *Jonestown Express* (Trinity Square Repertory Company, Providence, Rhode Island), *Tom Jones, Seven Keys to Baldpate, Galileo, Fool for Love, Misalliance* (all for the Dallas Theatre Center)—1984; *Tom Jones* (Dallas Theatre Center), *The Normal Heart* (Public Theatre, New York), *Streetheat* (with Franne; Studio 54), *The Dark and Mr. Stone* (with Franne; La Mama Experimental Theatre Club)—1985; *The Widow Clair*—1986; *Sweeney Todd* (Franne designed costumes; New York City Opera), *The Little Rascals* (with Franne; Goodspeed Opera House, East Haddam, Connecticut)—1987.

After attending the Yale School of Drama, Lee started designing at the Theatre of the Living Arts in Philadelphia in 1966. There he met his former wife and collaborator, Franne Newman Lee (b. December 30, 1941). Together, they worked on many of director André Gregory's productions. In 1967 Lee found a position as resident designer with the Trinity Square Repertory Company, Providence, Rhode Island, under the direction of Adrian Hall. He stayed at Trinity for a number of years, designed many productions, and continues to work there occasionally. His work there eventually led him to the New York theatre, where he and Franne became responsible for many designs throughout the 1970s and 1980s.

Lee is mostly known for his environmental settings that tend to convert the entire theatre building, rather than just the stage area, into the performance space, such as in *Slave Ship* (1969) and in André Gregory's *Alice in Wonderland* (1970). Director Peter Brook noticed Lee's work in *Slave Ship* and invited the designer to collaborate on *Orghast* (1971) at the Shiraz Festival near Persepolis,

Iran. With Franne, Lee designed director Harold Prince's very successful production of *Candide* at the Brooklyn Academy of Music in 1973 that transformed the proscenium stage and auditorium into the playing area. Platforms at different levels were situated throughout the building. Audience members sat on benches and stools, with one group in the center surrounded by a walkway, while others watched from the outside of the walkways. Lee's other work with Prince includes *Sweeney Todd* (1979), for which he designed a massive setting using an actual, re-created metal warehouse that towered several stories high and had machinery to elevate the performers.

Both Franne and Eugene designed for the television show *Saturday Night Live* from 1975 to 1980 and other special shows, including television movies and rock concerts. Though Franne was credited for being the costume designer, many times her efforts crossed over into set design. During the eighties, Lee remarried and designed shows on his own, but he continues to collaborate with Franne on many productions.

Awards: Both Eugene and Franne won the Tony, the Maharam Foundation, and the Drama Desk awards for *Candide* (1973). Lee also won a Tony Award for *Sweeney Todd* (1974).

Further Reading: Aronson (see Bibliography).

Kurt Lancaster

Lee, Ming Cho. Set designer (b. October 3, 1930, Shanghai, China). Theatrical productions (all were in New York City, unless otherwise noted) include *Guys and Dolls* (Grist Mill Playhouse, Andover, New Jersey)—1955; *The Infernal Machine* (Phoenix Theatre), *Missa Brevis* (Juilliard Opera Theatre), *The Crucible* (Martinique Theatre), *Triad* (Theatre Marquee)—1958; *Three Short Dances* (Connecticut College), *The Turk in Italy* (Peabody Arts Theatre, Baltimore, Maryland)—1959; *The Old Maid and the Thief*, *The Fall of the City*, *La Bohème* (three for the Peabody Arts Theatre), *Kata Kabanova*, *Peter Ibbetson* (both for the Empire State Music Festival, Bear Mountain, New York)—1960; *Amahl and the Night Visitors*, *Three by Offenbach*, *Don Giovanni* (three for the Peabody Arts Theatre, Baltimore, Maryland), *The Pearl Fishers* (Empire State Music Festival), *Tristan und Isolde* (Baltimore Civic Opera), *Werther* (Peabody Arts Theatre, Baltimore, Maryland), *The Merchant of Venice*, *The Tempest*, *King Lear*, *Macbeth* (four for the New York Shakespeare Festival, Delacorte Theatre), *A Look at Lightning* (Martha Graham Dance Company), *The Moon Besieged* (Lyceum Theatre), *Hamlet* (Peabody Arts Theatre, Baltimore, Maryland), *Madame Butterfly* (Opera Company of Boston)—1962; *Antony and Cleopatra*, *As You Like It*, *The Winter's Tale*, *Twelfth Night* (four for the New York Shakespeare Festival), *Mother Courage and Her Children* (Martin Beck Theatre), *Conversations in the Dark*, *Walk in Darkness* (Greenwich Mews Theatre), *Sea Shadow* (Joffrey Ballet), *Sideshow*—1963; *Hamlet*, *Othello*, *Electra*, *A Midsummer Night's Dream* (four for the New York Shakespeare Festival), *Il Tabarro*, *Gianni Schicchi*, *Kata Kabanova* (four for the Juilliard Opera Theatre)—1964; *Love's Labour's Lost*, *Coriolanus*, *Troilus and Cressida*, *The Taming of the Shrew*,

Henry V (five for the New York Shakespeare Festival), *Ariadne* (Alvin Ailey
Dance Company), *The Witch of Endor* (Martha Graham Dance Company), *Ma-
dame Butterfly* (Metropolitan Opera House), *Fidelio, The Magic Flute* (two for
the Juilliard Opera Theatre)—1965; *All's Well That Ends Well, Measure for
Measure, Richard III* (three for the New York Shakespeare Festival), *Slapstick
Tragedy* (Longacre Theatre), *A Time for Singing* (Broadway Theatre), *Olympics,
Night Wings* (two for the Joffrey Ballet), *Don Rodrigo* (New York City Opera),
Julius Caesar, The Marriage of Figaro (Metropolitan Opera House), *The Trial
of Lucullus* (Juilliard Opera Theatre)—1966; *The Comedy of Errors, Titus An-
dronicus, Hair* (three for the New York Shakespeare Festival), *Little Murders*
(Broadhurst Theatre), *The Crucible* (Arena Stage, Washington, D.C.), *Elegy*
(Joffrey Ballet), *The Rape of Lucretia* (Juilliard Opera Theatre), *Bomarzo* (Opera
Society of Washington, D.C.), *Le Coq d'Or, Boris Godunov* (Associated Opera
Companies of America)—1967; *Henry IV, Parts 1 and 2, Romeo and Juliet,
Ergo* (three for the New York Shakespeare Festival), *Here's Where I Belong*
(Billy Rose Theatre), *The Tenth Man, Room Service, The Iceman Cometh* (three
for the Arena Stage, Washington, D.C.), *King Lear* (Repertory Theatre of Lin-
coln Center), *A Light Fantastic* (Joffrey Ballet), *The Lady of the House of Sleep*
(Martha Graham Dance Company), *Secret Places* (Joffrey Ballet), *Bomarzo,
L'Ormindo* (Juilliard Opera Theatre), *Faust*—1968; *Peer Gynt, Cities in Bezique,
Invitation to a Beheading, Electra, Sambo* (codesigned with Marjorie Kellogg),
(five for the New York Shakespeare Festival), *Billy* (Billy Rose Theatre), *La
Strada* (Lunt-Fontanne Theatre), *Animus, The Poppet* (two for Joffrey Ballet),
Julius Caesar (Hamburg State Opera, Germany), *The Barber of Seville* (Amer-
ican Opera Center), *Help! Help! The Globolinks* (New York City Center)—1969;
*The Wars of the Roses (Henry VI, Parts I, II, and III), Jack MacGowran in the
Works of Samuel Beckett* (two for the New York Shakespeare Festival), *Gandhi*
(Playhouse Theatre), *The Night Thoreau Spent in Jail* (Arena Stage, Washington,
D.C.), *Roberto Devereux, The Rake's Progress* (Juilliard Opera Theatre), *Il
Giuramento* (American Opera Center), *Othello* (unproduced)—1970; *Timon of
Athens, Two Gentlemen of Verona* (two for the New York Shakespeare Festival),
Lolita, My Love (Shubert Theatre, Philadelphia), *Remote Asylum* (Ahmanson
Theatre, Los Angeles), *Ariodante* (Kennedy Center, Washington, D.C.), *Su-
sannah, Two Gentlemen of Verona* (St. James Theatre)—1971; *Hamlet, Much
Ado About Nothing, Older People, Wedding Band* (four for the New York
Shakespeare Festival), *Volpone, Henry IV* (Mark Taper Forum, Los Angeles),
Much Ado About Nothing (Winter Garden Theatre), *Our Town* (Arena Stage,
Washington, D.C.), *Maria Stuarda, Tales of Hoffman, La Bohème* (American
Opera Center), *Lucia di Lammermoor, Bomarzo* (two for Teatro Colon, Buenos
Aires)—1972; *Inherit the Wind* (Arena Stage, Washington, D.C.), *Lear* (Yale
Repertory Theatre, New Haven, Connecticut), *Don Juan* (San Francisco Ballet,
California), *Myth of a Voyage* (Martha Graham Dance Company), *Four Saints
in Three Acts, Syllabaire Pour Phedre, Dido and Aeneas* (three for the Metro-
politan Opera at the Forum), *Anna Bolena, St. Matthews Passion, La Favorita*

(San Francisco Opera), *Le Coq d'Or* (Dallas Civic Center)—1973; *The Seagull* (New York Shakespeare Festival), *Whispers of Darkness* (National Ballet of Canada), *Boris Godunov* (Metropolitan Opera House), *Idomeneo* (Kennedy Center, Washington, D.C.)—1974; *All God's Children Got Wings* (Circle in the Square), *The Glass Menagerie* (Circle in the Square), *Julius Caesar, The Ascent of Mt. Fuji* (two for the Arena Stage, Washington, D.C.), *In Quest of the Sun* (Royal Winnepeg Ballet, Canada), *The Leaves Are Fading* (American Ballet Theatre), *Idomeneo*—1975; *For Colored Girls Who Have Considered Suicide/ When the Rainbow Is Enuf* (New York Shakespeare Festival), *Waiting for Godot* (Arena Stage, Washington, D.C.), *I Puritani, Lohengrin* (two for the Metropolitan Opera House), *Bilby's Doll* (Houston Grand Opera, Texas)—1976; *Caesar and Cleopatra* (Palace Theatre), *Romeo and Juliet* (Circle in the Square), *The Shadow Box* (Morosco Theatre), *For Colored Girls . . .* (Mark Taper Forum, Los Angeles, California)—1977; *Mother Courage* (The Acting Company), *Angel* (Minskoff Theatre), *The Grand Tour* (Palace Theatre), *King Lear* (The Acting Company), *Hamlet* (Arena Stage), *Twelfth Night* (American Shakespeare Festival, Stratford, Connecticut), *The Tiller in the Fields* (American Ballet Theatre), *Madame Butterfly* (Lyrica Opera of Chicago, Illinois), designed the Astor Court Garden and Chinese Wing of the Metropolitan Museum of Art—1978; *Don Juan* (Arena Stage, Washington, D.C.), *The Tempest* (Mark Taper Forum, Los Angeles, California), *The Glass Menagerie* (Guthrie Theatre, Minneapolis, Minnesota), *Saint Joan* (Seattle Repertory Theatre), *The Tempest* (American Shakespeare Festival)—1979; *Plenty* (Arena Stage, Washington, D.C.), *Boris Godunov, Attila* (two for the Lyric Opera of Chicago, Illinois)—1980; *Oedipus* (Brooklyn Academy of Music), *Attila, La Donna del Lago* (Houston Grand Opera, Texas), *Madame Butterfly* (Chilean Opera Society)—1981; *K2* (Brooks Atkinson Theatre), *Mary Stuart, Alceste, Montezuma* (American Opera Center)—1982; *K2* (Brooks Atkinson Theatre), *Death of a Salesman* (Stratford Festival), *Desire Under the Elms* (Indiana Repertory Theatre, Indianapolis), *I Capuleti e I Montecchi* (American Opera Center), *The Glass Menagerie* (Eugene O'Neill Theatre), *Turandot* (Opera Company of Boston, Massachusetts)—1983; *The Cuban Swimmer, Dog Lady* (both for Intar Theatre)—1984; *Execution of Justice* (Guthrie Theatre, Minneapolis, Minnesota)—1986; *Camille* (Long Wharf Theatre, New Haven, Connecticut)—1987.

Currently cochairperson of the Yale Drama School's design program, Lee has designed the stage settings for many productions both on and off-Broadway, as well as in regional and educational theatres. After entering the United States as an adolescent and studying at Occidental College in Los Angeles and UCLA, Lee soon made his way to New York. He entered the world of professional design in the mid–1950s as an assistant to Jo Mielziner,* with whom he worked for five years. During this period, he also worked with George Jenkins,* Rouben Ter-Arutunian,* and Boris Aronson.* By the end of the 1950s, he was designing off-Broadway, establishing himself there with his set design for Jean Cocteau's *The Infernal Machine* (1958) at the Phoenix Theatre.

Lee's sense of design was established in his early career years. His style leaned toward the nonliteral approach, leading some of his critics eventually to accuse him of being "too Brechtian." Basically a traditionalist, Lee emphasized simplicity and sparseness, and attempted to eliminate unnecessary details from the scenography and thus to integrate the setting organically within the framework of the entire production. In conference with the director, Lee's work pattern was to move from the general to the specific as he decided on a basic concept, chose materials, and eventually rendered the design. Essentially, his basic approach to design has remained intact throughout the years.

Soon after his initial successes, Lee became principal designer for Joe Papp's New York Shakespeare Festival and served in this position from 1962 until 1973. His productions with this organization include *King Lear* (1962), *Electra* (1964), *Peer Gynt* (1969), *The Wars of the Roses* (*Henry VI Parts I, II and III*) (1970), *Two Gentlemen of Verona* (1973), and *Much Ado About Nothing* (1976). For many of these productions, Lee overcame a limited budget by designing sets that were spare and that sometimes employed multipurpose unit settings. Further, his ingenious settings triumphed over budget restraints when one of his basic unit structures would be used for three separate summer shows and consequently saved the expense of separate scenery.

His designs for the Broadway stage were sometimes no less austere. The design for Brecht's *Mother Courage* (initially in 1963, then with the Acting Company in 1978) consisted of a stark environment inhabited only by Mother Courage's battered wagon. Other significant productions continued this style, such as Tennessee Williams's *Slapstick Tragedy* (1963), *Billy* (1969), *Colored Girls* (1976), and *The Shadow Box* (1977). This latter production incorporated a multipurpose unit setting. In contrast, Lee's later Broadway work, such as *K2* (1983), relied more on an elaborate, realistic environment. For this play, he transformed the stage into a section of a magnificent, snowy mountainside, where two climbers are trapped.

Lee continued to work in many regional theatres and act as designer or design adviser. One of his proud achievements was his production of *The Glass Menagerie*, which was presented at the Guthrie Theater in Minneapolis, with a design quite unlike Jo Mielziner's original. Although it was realistic in design, Lee states that he tried to unify it organically by making "connections between the verbal and the visual." He also designed *Our Town* and *Inherit the Wind*, both of which he executed for the Washington Arena Stage and took on tour to the Soviet Union in 1972. Later, he created the sets for *Camille*, presented at the Long Wharf Theatre in 1987.

His work is also well represented in the worlds of opera and dance, both in New York and regionally. Perhaps his best known are sets for *Madame Butterfly* (1965), *Boris Godunov* (1975), *I Puritani* (1977), and *Lohengrin* (1978), all produced for the Metropolitan Opera. He has designed extensively for such prominent choreographers and dance companies as Alvin Ailey, José Limon, and the Joffrey Ballet. For Martha Graham's dance company, his efforts include

The Witch of Endor (1965), for which he designed a sparse set consisting of only two thrones and a metal configuration, and *Myth of a Voyage* (1973).

An energetic designer, Lee also consulted on the design of the two theatres within the Public Theater complex, as well as on several regional performance spaces, and maintained a full teaching schedule at Yale's Drama School, where he serves as co-chair of the design program and adviser to the Yale Repertory Company. As a teacher, Lee trains his students and apprentices as he was taught by Mielziner and others. In this way, Lee's influence on design will be evident through future generations of designers.

Further Reading: By Lee: "Designing Opera." In Burdick, Hansen, and Zanger (see Bibliography).

About Lee: Aronson (see Bibliography); Oenslager (see Bibliography); "Three Stage Designers." *Theatre* Fall/Winter 1981–1982.

Thomas J. Mikotowicz

Linnebach, Adolf. Set and lighting designer, architect, and inventor (b. 1876, Germany). Linnebach was the resident designer and technical director at the Dresden Schauspielhaus in the early part of this century and introduced all manner of hydraulic stage machinery and lighting innovations. Linnebach's elevator stage was divided into three sections, each of which could be raised and lowered to its original level. He installed the hydraulic stage in Dresden in 1914 and other various types of it at the Operhaus in Hamburg in 1926 and the Schauspielhaus at Chemnitz in 1925. In addition, he experimented with revolving stages and projection equipment. He is perhaps best known for the Linnebach projector (or lantern), a simple box containing a light source and aperture that is meant to shine through large painted slides. For his play designs, Linnebach's style was typically formal, yet his sets were simple in composition, such as for *Gyges und sein Ring*, produced at the Hoftheater in Dresden.

Thomas J. Mikotowicz

Lissim, Simon. Set and costume designer, and decorative artist (b. 1900, Kiev, Russia; d. 1981). Lissim, well-known international scenic designer, trained as a painter in Russia and began his theatrical career as an assistant stage designer at the Kiev Repertory Theatre. Influenced by his contemporaries Léon Bakst,* Serge Soudekine,* and others, Lissim developed a decorative, painterly style. After the Russian Revolution, he emigrated to Paris, where he designed a significant number of productions, including *L'Autre Messie* (1923) and *La Farce des Encore* (1924). His most outstanding production, however, was in 1925 when his designs for *Hamlet* at Lugné-Poe's Theatre de l'Oeuvre won him recognition as a scenic designer. For his efforts, he was awarded a silver medal in the Paris Decorative Arts Exposition. Characteristically, this stage design blends into the decorative arts, and he saw little distinction between them. At a time when the preeminence of the playwright was assumed, his designs were equally assertive as the script. His approach to design was to frame the action through use of appropriate mood and atmosphere. His imaginative designs went beyond the text to create dreamlike worlds, such as those for the 1931 Paris production of *A Love for Three Oranges*. He moved to the United States in 1937 and continued to design and teach at City University in New York. His later designs include *L'Annonce Faite A Marie* (1942), *La Barbe Bleue* (1947), and *The Infinite* (1952). His attitude toward theatrical design as a decorative art is evident in his many unrealized project designs. In 1973, he reworked his designs from the 1924 production of *The Legend of Tsar Saltan*, produced in Barcelona, into fanciful creations without regard to production limitations. The result was a series of decorative renderings reminiscent of Bakst, but with the sophistication of the French impressionists.

Further Reading: By Lissim: "Designing for the Theatre." *Dreams in the Theatre: Designs of Simon Lissim*. New York: New York Public Library, 1975.

About Lissim: Freedley, George. *Simon Lissim*. New York: J. Hendrickson, 1949; Leon, M. Paul. *Simon Lissim*. Paris: Editions du Cygne, 1933; Paolucci, Ann, ed. "Simon Lissim's Stage Designs for Hamlet." *Shakespeare Encomium*. City College Papers I. New York: City College, 1964; Wood, Thor. "The Embodiment of Dreams." *Dreams in the Theatre: Designs of Simon Lissim*. New York: New York Public Library, 1975; Young, Mahonri Sharp. "The Man from Kiev." *Dreams in the Theatre: Designs of Simon Lissim*. New York: New York Public Library, 1975.

Brian R. Jones

Loquasto, Santo. Set and costume designer for theatre and film (b. 1944, Wilkes-Barre, PA). Theatrical productions include *Cat on a Hot Tin Roof*—1965; *The Subject Was Roses*—1966; *Luv, The Little Foxes, Little Malcolm and His Struggle Against the Eunuchs*—1967; *The Hostage, Tiny Alice, Black Comedy/White Lies, Camino Real, Wait Until Dark, Galileo, How To Succeed in Business Without Really Trying, The Rose Tattoo*—1968; *The Waltz Invention, The Homecoming, The Bacchae, Ring 'Round the Moon, Tartuffe, The Cherry Orchard, The Unseen Hand, Forensic and the Navigators, A Delicate Balance, Narrow Road to the Deep North, The Farce of Scapin*—1969; *A Day in the Death of Joe Egg, Misalliance, The Trial of A. Lincoln, Anything Goes, Rosencrantz and Guildenstern Are Dead, The Price, Yale Repertory Season of Story Theatre, The Skin of Our Teeth, The Revenger's Tragedy*—1970; *Ring 'Round the Moon, A Gun Play, Long Day's Journey into Night, The Seven Deadly Sins, Wipe-Out Games, The Sign in Sidney Brustein's Window, The Birthday Party, Plaza Suite, Mother Courage and Her Children, Hedda Gabler, Pantagleize, The House of Blue Leaves, Uptight, Sticks and Bones, The Barber of Seville*—1971; *That Championship Season, Old Times, Henry V, The Resistible Rise of Arturo Ui, Uncle Vanya, A Streetcar Named Desire, Sticks and Bones, The Secret Affairs of Mildred Wild, The Rake's Progress, Sunset, A Public Prosecutor Is Sick of It All*—1972; *The Orphan, The Siamese Connection, You Can't Take It with You, As You Like It, King Lear, La Dafne, In the Boom Boom Room, The Tempest, What the Wine Sellers Buy*—1973; *The Dance of Death, Macbeth, Pericles, The Merry Wives of Windsor, Ah, Wilderness!, Mert and Phil, Richard III, A Midsummer Night's Dream*—1974; *A Doll's House, The Cherry Orchard,*

Hamlet, The Comedy of Errors, Kennedy's Children, Rusalka, Murder Among Friends, Sue's Leg, The Double Cross, Ocean's Motion, Awake and Sing!, Measure for Measure—1975; *Legend, The Glass Menagerie, Other Dances, Push Comes to Shove, Heartbreak House, Give and Take, Once More Frank, Country Dances, Happily Ever After, After All, Washington Square*—1976; *The Cherry Orchard, American Buffalo, Agamemnon, The Lower Depths, The Italian Straw Hat, Golda, Miss Margarida's Way, Landscape of the Body, The Caucasian Chalk Circle, Mud Cacklin' Hen*—1977; *Don Quixote, The Mighty Gents, The Play's the Thing, Curse of the Starving Class, Heptagon, Stop the World, I Want to Get Off, King of Hearts, Sarava, Simon*—1978; *The Four Seasons, Baker's Dozen, The Goodbye People, Daddy Goodness, Sylvia, Pas de Deux, Old World, Bent*—1979; *Stardust Memories* (film), *Chapters and Verses, Celebration, Le Corsaire Pas de Deux, The Fan* (film), *The Member of the Wedding, Emigres, The Suicide, Twyla Tharp and Dancers on Broadway, Dances of Albion, Raymonda*—1980; *A Midsummer Night's Dream, So Fien* (film), *The Floating Light Bulb, A Midsummer Night's Sex Comedy* (film), *Concerto, Jardin Animé, Bournonville Pas de Trois, La Fille Mal Gardee Pas de Deux, Flower Festival Pas de Deux, Twyla Tharp and Dancers on Broadway, The Catherine Wheel, Crossing Niagara*—1981; *The Wake of Jamey Foster, Gershwin Concerto, As You Like It, Gardenia, A Harlequinade, Inconsequentials, The Catherine Wheel* (television), *The Three Sisters*—1982; *Follow the Feet, Theme and Variations, Peer Gynt, America Kicks Up Its Heels, Once Upon a Time, The Glass Menagerie, Richard III, Booth Is Back in Town, Orgasmo Adulto Escapes from the Zoo* (scenic consultant), *Uncle Vanya, The Photographer, Fait Accompli, Zelig* (film)—1983; *Cinderella, Falling in Love* (film), *Desperately Seeking Susan* (film)—1984; *California Dog Fight, Virginia, In Trousers, Singing' in the Rain*—1985; *Radio Days* (film), *Sweet Sue*—1987; *Cafe Crown*—1989; *Grand Hotel, Alice* (film)—1990.

After graduating from Yale, Loquasto designed for such repertory companies as the Hartford Stage and the Long Wharf Theatre. His New York debut came in 1970 with an evening of one-acts, *The Unseen Hand* and *Forensic and the Navigators*. Within the following two years, he established his career with the award-winning settings for two shows that opened at the New York Shakespeare Festival, then were transferred to Broadway, *Sticks and Bones* and *That Championship Season*. Although both plays are set in living rooms, Loquasto created unique settings for each. In the same week in 1977, Loquasto again had two vastly different styles on view when *The Cherry Orchard* opened at the Vivian Beaumont, with a setting that was an evocative, surrealistic, white landscape with minimal furniture carefully placed, and *American Buffalo* opened on Broadway, with a stage heaped with the realistic clutter of a secondhand shop. More recently, his style has expanded into the experimental with such nonrealistic and unified works as *The Photographer*, directed by postmodernist director JoAnne Akalaitis in 1983 at the Brooklyn Academy of Music.

Loquasto continues to design for many of the major regional theatres and modern dance companies, although for dance, he mostly designs costumes. He has worked with Baryshnikov, Glen Tetley, Jerome Robbins, and Twyla Tharp, to name only a few. In recent years Loquasto has been production designer for films, including several with Woody Allen. In 1985, he came back to Broadway with *Singin' in the Rain*, complete with an actual rainstorm re-created onstage, many mobile units to accomplish the change of scenes, and a much more subtle and romantic color scheme than usual. Overall, Loquasto's designs have been compared to the work of Ming Cho Lee* and Boris Aronson.* His actual settings can be monumental structures, immense cubes, heavily textural, or they can be constructed out of interesting components such as pipe, wood, or other found materials. At the other extreme, they can be highly realistic, filled with the clutter of everyday life.

Awards: Sticks and Bones (1971) and *That Championship Season* (1972) earned Loquasto the New York Drama Desk and the New York Drama Critics' Circle awards. In 1977, his work for *The Cherry Orchard* received a Tony Award for costumes and the Drama Desk Award, *American Buffalo* earned him the Drama Desk and the Maharam Foundation Awards, and his costume designs for *Agamemnon* received a Maharam Award. Recently, he won a Tony Award for set design for *Cafe Crown* (1989) and a Tony and a Drama Desk Award for his costume designs for *Grand Hotel* (1990).

Further Reading: "Contemporary American Designers: Santo Loquasto." *Theatre Design & Technology* Fall 1981; "Designers at Work." *Theatre Crafts* May 1987: 33; "Santo's Championship Season: Interview with Designer Santo Loquasto." *Theatre Crafts* October 1973; Aronson (see Bibliography).

Ken Kloth

Luzzati, Emanuele. Designer, painter, and illustrator (b. June 3, 1921, Genoa, Italy). Prolific Italian artist and designer, Luzzati studied at the School of Fine Arts in Lausanne and, after some work as a potter and illustrator, began his theatrical work at the Teatro Nuovo in Milan in 1947. Although he has mostly designed for opera, he has also had considerable experience in theatre, film, and television while continuing his work as a painter and illustrator. He has designed settings and costumes for virtually every major opera and every major opera company in the world, including the Vienna Staatsoper, Munich Staatsoper, La Scala, Aldeburgh, and Glyndebourne. Among his better-known productions are *Diavolessa* (1952), *Per un Don Chisciotte* (1961), *Vassiliev* (1967), and *Maria Stuarda* (1974).

Awards: Prize S Genesio for best scenography, Italy, 1962; Academy Award nomination for *Gazza ladra*, 1966; Academy Award nomination for *Pulcinella*, 1974.

James Fisher

M

Mahelot, Laurent. Designer, director and machinist (b.?, France; d.?). Mahelot was a seventeenth-century French scene designer and director for the Comédiens du Roi at the Hôtel de Bourgogne and is remembered more for his *Memoire* than for any specific designs of his own. In this volume, Mahelot described the plays in the repertoire of the company in the 1630s and the scenography used in the productions. The scenic approach shown in the book reveals the influence of Italian Renaissance perspective as well as the ''simultaneous scene'' method derived from medieval drama. The ''simultaneous scene'' method consisted of a multitude of set units depicting various locales surrounded by a central acting area. This method precedes the eventual single set format that was to become typical for French classical drama. *Memoire* continued to be compiled by other theatricians and was published in 1920, thus providing the contemporary scholar with a rather extensive view of seventeenth-century French scenic methods.

James Fisher

Martin, Jean-Baptiste. Designer and artist (b. 1659, Paris, France; d. 1735). Influenced by the style of Bérain,* Martin designed settings and costumes for ballets at the opera in Paris. Among the ballets he designed were *Le Provencale*, *Psyche*, and the *Ballet des Elements*. Martin's son, Jean-Baptiste Martin (the Younger, 1700–1741), was a noted painter.

James Fisher

Matisse, Henri-Émile-Benoît. Artist and ballet designer (b. December 1869, Le Cateau-Chambresis, France; d. November 1954, Nice, France). Matisse was fifty years old when he first became involved in theatrical design through the influence of Sergey Diaghilev of the Ballets Russes. Although his involvement in this area was short-lived, like many of his contemporaries he designed several ballets and thus cross-fertilized the worlds of art and theatre. Diaghilev first commissioned Matisse to design sets and costumes for *Le Chant du Rossignol*, produced in 1919 with choreography by Léonide Massine. The designs that eventually graced the stage for the ballet were Oriental in style and featured a geometrical cut-out technique to create an expressive environment. This cut-out technique, essentially decorative, created a strong background in which the dancers appeared as living sculptures. During the 1927–1928 theatrical season, Matisse worked on several drawings for *Scheherazade* for the Ballets Russes de Monte Carlo, but the production never materialized. Another noteworthy ballet production of Matisse's design was *L'Etrange Farandole*, originally performed as *Rouge et Noir* in 1937. The design employed his earlier cut-out technique, which eventually developed into his later artistic style. The designs for this work exhibited Matisse's appreciation for spatial relationships among the dancers and the sets and the forceful use of color and abstract shapes. His theatrical designs have been exhibited in Paris in 1939, London in 1954, and New York in 1963 and 1965.

Further Reading: Schneider, Pierre. *Matisse.* New York: Rizzoli International, 1984; Williams, Peter. *Masterpieces of Ballet Design.* London: Phaidon Press, 1981.

Penny L. Remsen

Mauro Family. Designers and theatrical architects (c.1650 through 1820). The Mauros are typical of the large families who developed and maintained business specialties in the arts, agriculture, and banking in Europe during the eighteenth century. As designers, the family worked together and collaborated with others on many theatrical and architectural production projects. Because they frequently signed their work "Mauro Cousins" or "Mauro Brothers" and because several family members had the same first name, it is sometimes difficult to distinguish one individual's work from another's. Although the family was centered in Venice, Italy, they worked in Germany and in other countries as well. The opera and play designs of the Mauro family span a century and a half and date roughly from the end of the seventeenth century until 1820 and thus reflect the change from full baroque style through rococo and into neoclassicism.

The dynasty begins with Francesco (c.1650–1692), who was the father of Gaspare, Pietro, and Domenico I. In 1662, he assisted Francesco Santurnini as an engineer in Munich and also worked for Francesco Santi in a similar venture. Gaspare (before 1657–1719), however, was the real founder of the dynasty. He collaborated with Santurnini for a presentation of *Le Fortune di Rodope e di Damira* (1657) and *Teseo* at the theatres of St. Appollonaire and St. Cassiano in Venice. Between 1659 and 1679, he collaborated several times with the painter Mazzarini. In 1679 he became the permanent chief engineer for the Theatre of San Giovanni Crisostomo. He worked with his brothers Pietro on *Artaxerse* (1669) and *Servio Tullio* (1685) and with Domenico I on theatre and celebration projects in Venice, Turin, and Parma, including a mock naval battle, *La Gloria d'Amore* (1690), which included floating scenery, ships, and monsters. Pietro (before 1662–1697) is one of the least known. Together with helping his brothers on productions, he was the architect for the Teatro Novissimo of Fabriano in 1692, and he decorated the renovated Teatro del Sole in Pesaro in 1695. Domenico I (before 1669–1707) collaborated as engineer with Fumiani and Mazzarini on the production of *Coriolanus* (1669) at the ducal palace in Piacenza. He also worked with his relatives in Munich, Venice, Turin, and Parma at various theatres or events, including *Il Favore degli Dei* (1690). Some of the scenes he created incorporated new perspective based on intersecting diagonals.

Domenico I had four sons who continued the family tradition. Gerolamo I (before 1692–1719), whose work is most obscure, assisted his father and his uncles, Pietro and Gaspare. Romualdo (before 1699–1756) worked on several family projects, and between 1718 and 1722, he worked at the Teatro San Giovanni and San Samuele and continued at the latter from 1744 to 1756. His production designs include *Lamano* (1719), *Temistocle* (1744), and *Le Nozze di Paride* (1756). The third son, Alessandro (before 1709–1748), worked throughout Italy and western Europe. With Romualdo, he oversaw construction of the opera house in Dresden from 1717 to 1719. The facility had a typical horseshoe shape, a huge stage that measured twenty-three meters wide and forty-three meters deep, and an auditorium with two-thousand seats. He is credited with the designs for *Semiramide* (with cousin Giuseppe, 1714), *Arminio* (1722), and *Berenice* (1734). He also worked with Romualdo on rebuilding the Teatro San Samuele into a horseshoe configuration after it was destroyed by fire. About the fourth brother, Antonio I (before 1692–1733), very little is known about his work. He collaborated with his brother Gerolamo and his cousin Antonio II on the two operas *Scipio Africano* (1692) and *Argenide* (1733).

Gaspare had two sons who carried on the family design tradition. The first was Antonio II (before 1709–1736), and it is believed that he designed *La Partenope* (1709), *Agrippo* (1722), *Rosilena e Oronta* (1728), and *Elisa Regina de Tiro* (1726). It is not possible, however, to know which Antonio (I or II) should be credited with designs signed "A.M." But it is certain that one of the cousins worked in Ferraro (1709), Padua (1721), and Pesaro (1735). The other son, Giuseppe (before 1699–1722), apparently had greater technical than artistic strengths. He collaborated with his cousin Romualdo on the scenery for *l'Amfione* (1699) in Milan. He also worked with other relatives at the Teatro San Giovanni Crisostomo from 1714 to 1722, including such productions as *Semiramide* (with Alessandro, 1714), *Leucippe e Teonoe* (with Antonio I, 1719), and *Guilio Flavio Crispo* (with Romualdo, 1722).

The third generation of Mauros descended from Alessandro. Domenico II (before 1725–1766) worked independently from 1733 to 1755 and, after 1758, worked mostly in collaboration with others as one of the "Mauro Cousins." In 1761, he repainted the interior of Teatro San Samuele. His productions include *L'Ambizione depressa* (1733) and *Statira* (1751), both at the Teatro San Angelo, as well as *Antigono* (1761) and *Cresco* (1770), both at the Teatro San Benedetto. The second son is Gerolamo II (before 1725–1766), who worked with his cousin Gerolamo III at the Teatro San Moise. As a result, it is not possible to distinguish between them before the death of Gerolamo II in 1766, because they worked in the same theatre and collaborated with each other. But it is believed that Gerolamo I worked on such productions as *Arcifanfano Re Dei Matti* (1749) and *Il Tamerlano* (1765).

Romualdo's sons include Gerolamo III (before 1750–1788), who began work with his father in 1754 and worked with his cousin Domenico II until 1780. He worked at several theatres, including San Giacomo in Corfu, San Salvatore, San Moise, San Giovanni Crisostomo, and San Benedetto. His production designs include *Il Mondo della Luna* (with Gerolamo II, 1750), *L'Amor in Ballo* (with Gerolamo II, 1765), *Rinaldo* (1775), *Il Trionfo d'Arianna* (1781), and *L'Arbore di Diana* (with Sacchetti, 1788).

The fourth generation Mauros include Antonio III (before 1774–1807), who was the son of Domenico II. By the 1780s, he was working at the Teatro San Benedetto and remained there until 1798. In 1795, he directed the building of the Teatro Dei Nobili. His designs for interiors were done in the newest neoclassical style and moved away from the older rococo forms. His productions include *Narbale* (with Domenico II, 1774), *Osmane* (1784), *La Morte di Semiramide* (1791), *La Bella Lauretta* (1795), and *Eroe* (1798). In addition, the fourth generation included two sons of unknown lineage, Alessandro (before 1782–?) and Gaetano (before 1806–1820). Alessandro was more of a manager than a painter, and there are no confirmed examples of any design work. Gaetano worked in theatres in Venice, Milan, and Padua as a scene painter. His design works include *Amore Vince l'inganno* and *La Sorpresa* (1806), *Romilda e Constanza* (1817), and *Zenobia* (1820).

Further Reading: Baur-Heinhold, Margarete. *Baroque Theatre*, trans. Mary Whittal. London: Thames and Hudson, 1967; *Enciclopedia della Spettacolo*, Vol. 7. Rome G. C. Sansoni, 1960; Nicoll, Allardyce. *A History of Early Eighteenth-Century Drama.* Cambridge: Cambridge University Press, 1929; Weil, Mark S. *Baroque Theatre and Stage Design.* St. Louis: Washington University Press, 1983.

Elbin L. Cleveland

Mayrhauser, Jennifer von. Costume designer (b. 1948, Ithaca, NY). Mayrhauser has been credited with numerous costume designs for Broadway, off-Broadway, regional theatre, television, and film productions. Following her graduation from Northwestern University with a degree in theatre in 1971, Mayrhauser settled in New York and began working in the Crafts Department at the New York Shakespeare Festival, where she built costume armor. Also in 1971, she assisted costume designer Carrie Robbins on the production of *The Beggar's Opera.*

In 1973, she was introduced to Marshall Mason, the artistic director of the Circle Repertory Theatre Company, a meeting that led to her being hired as a full-time designer. She worked there until 1977, designing costumes for more than twenty productions, many of which she collaborated on with set designer John Lee Beatty* and lighting designer Dennis Parichy. Her credits there include

The Prodigal (1973), *The Persians* (1974), *The Mound Builders* (1975), *Down by the River Where Waterlilies Are Disfigured Every Day* (1975), *Dancing for the Kaiser* (1975), *Serenading Louie* (1976), and *Exiles* (1977). Over the years, she has continued to design for the Circle Repertory Theatre such productions as *The Diviners* (1980), *Angels Fall* (1982), *What I Did Last Summer* (1983), *The Early Girl* (1986), *El Salvador* (1987), *Borderlines* (1988), and *Keeping an Eye on Louie* (1988). Some of these productions moved to Broadway, such as *Knock, Knock* (1976) and *Talley's Folly* (1980). Increasingly, her work was featured on Broadway in such productions as *Beyond Therapy* (1982), *Hay Fever* (1986), *The Musical Comedy Murders of 1940* (1987), and *Night of the Iguana* (1988). Her solid approach to costume design worked well for the many off-Broadway theatres for which she worked. Those productions include *Catsplay* (1978), *The Miss Firecracker Contest* (1984), and *The Lucky Spot* (1987). She has also been busy in such regional theatres as the Guthrie Theatre in Minneapolis, the Folger Theatre in Washington, D.C., the La Jolla Playhouse in California, and the McCarter Theatre in Princeton, New Jersey. Her virtuosity afforded opportunities in costume design for television and film. For PBS, she designed *The Mound Builders* (1975) for the "Theatre in America" series, as well as specials for the major networks including *Kennedy's Children* (CBS Cable, 1981), *The Electric Grandmother* (NBC, 1981), and *Kingdom Chums* (ABC Entertainment, 1986). Her feature film credits include *Mystic Pizza* for the Samuel Goldwyn Company, *Eugene O'Neill: Journey Towards Genius* (1988) for the Lumiere Production Company, and *Lean On Me* (1988) for Warner Brothers.

Awards: She received a nomination for the San Diego Critics' Award for "Outstanding Costume Design" for her work on *Hedda Gabler* in 1987 at the La Jolla Playhouse.

Further Reading: "Designers at Work." *Theatre Crafts* May 1987: 38; "Jennifer von Mayrhauser: Costumes in Character." *Theatre Crafts* April 1983.

Penny L. Remsen

Messel, Oliver. Set and costume designer, and artist (b. January 13, 1904, Cuckfield, England; d. July 13, 1978, Bridgeton, Barbados). Designing costumes and sets for C. B. Cochran's annual *Revues* from 1926 through 1931, Messel developed his colorful style and set his career as a theatrical designer in motion. Since, he designed many well-known productions such as *The Infernal Machine* (1940), *The Lady's Not for Burning* (1949), *Ring 'Round the Moon* (1950), *Roshomon* (1959), and costumes for *Gigi* (1972). Messel's traditional style for the ballet, a style using perspective backdrops painted in a classical manner, is evident in such works as *Francesca da Rimini* (1937), Frederick Ashton and Ninette Valois's *Sleeping Beauty* (1946), and Ashton's *Homage to the Queen* (1953). He also applied his talents in design to such films as *Caesar and Cleopatra* and *Suddenly Last Summer*, as well as to a painting career and architectural consulting. In addition, Messel authored several texts on scene design; his most significant work was *Stage Designs and Costumes* (London, 1934).

Thomas J. Mikotowicz

Mielziner, Jo. Set and lighting designer, theatre architect, and consultant (b. March 19, 1901, Paris, France; d. March 15, 1976, New York). Theatrical productions (all were in New York City and include both sets and lighting, unless otherwise noted) include *Nerves* (Comedy Theatre), *That Awful Mrs. Eaton* (Morosco Theatre), *The Guardsman* (Garrick Theatre)—1924; *Mrs. Partridge Presents* (Belmont Theatre), *The Wild Duck* (48th Street Theatre), *First Flight* (Plymouth Theatre), *Caught* (39th Street Theatre), *The Call of Life* (Comedy Theatre), *The Enemy* (Times Square Theatre), *Lucky Sam McCarver* (Playhouse Theatre), *Unseen*—1925; *Little Eyolf* (Guild Theatre), *The Masque of Venice* (Mansfield Theatre), *Seed of the Brute* (Little Theatre), *Pygmalion* (Guild Theatre)—1926; *Saturday's Children* (Booth Theatre), *Right You Are If You Think You Are* (Guild Theatre), *Mariners* (Plymouth Theatre), *The Second Man* (Guild Theatre), *The Marquise* (Biltmore Theatre), *The Doctor's Dilemma* (Guild Theatre), *Fallen Angels* (48th Street Theatre)—1927; *Cock Robin* (48th Street Theatre), *Strange Interlude* (John Golden Theatre), *The Grey Fox* (Playhouse Theatre), *The Jealous Moon* (Majestic Theatre), *The Lady Lies* (Little Theatre), *A Most Immoral Lady* (Cort Theatre)—1928; *Street Scene* (Playhouse Theatre), *The Skyrocket* (Lyceum Theatre), *Judas* (Longacre Theatre), *Meet the Prince* (Lyceum Theatre), *Young Alexander* (Biltmore Theatre), *The First Little Show* (Music Box Theatre), *Karl and Anna* (Guild Theatre), *Jenny* (Booth Theatre), *First Mortgage* (Broadhurst Theatre), *Dread* (pre-Broadway, Washington, D.C., and Brooklyn, New York), *The Amorous Antic* (Masque Theatre), *Mrs. Cook's Tour* (pre-Broadway, Chicago, Illinois), *The Red General* (unproduced)—1929; *Uncle Vanya* (Cort Theatre), *Second Little Show* (Royale Theatre), *Mr. Gilhooley* (Broadhurst Theatre), *Solid South* (Lyceum Theatre), *Sweet and Low* (46th Street Theatre)—1930; *Anatol* (Lyceum Theatre), *The Barretts of Wimpole Street* (Empire Theatre), *The House Beautiful* (Apollo Theatre), *Crazy Quilt* (44th Street Theatre), *The Third Little Show* (Music Box Theatre), *I Love an Actress* (Times Square Theatre), *Brief Moment* (Belasco Theatre), *Of Thee I Sing* (Music Box Theatre)—1931; *Never No More* (Hudson Theatre), *Distant Drums* (Belasco Theatre), *Bloodstream* (Times Square Theatre), *Bridal Wise* (Cort Theatre), *Gay Divorce* (Ethel Barrymore Theatre), *Biography* (Guild Theatre)—1932; *Emperor Jones* (Metropolitan Opera House), *Champagne Sec* (Morosco Theatre), *A Divine Drudge* (Royale Theatre), *I Was Waiting for You* (Booth Theatre), *The Dark Tower* (Morosco Theatre), *The Lake* (Martin Beck Theatre)—1933; *By Your Leave* (Morosco Theatre), *Merrymount* (Metropolitan Opera House), *Dodsworth* (Shubert Theatre), *Yellow Jack* (Martin Beck Theatre), *The Pure in Heart* (Longacre Theatre), *Merrily We Roll Along* (Music Box Theatre), *Spring Song* (Morosco Theatre), *Bird of Our Fathers* (pre-Broadway, Philadelphia), *Romeo and Juliet* (Martin Beck Theatre), *Accent on Youth* (Plymouth Theatre), *Gather Ye*

Rosebuds—1934; *Deluxe* (Booth Theatre), *Panic* (Imperial Theatre), *Flowers of the Forest* (Martin Beck Theatre), *Kind Lady* (Longacre Theatre), *Winterset* (Martin Beck Theatre), *Jubilee* (Imperial Theatre), *Pride and Prejudice* (Music Box Theatre), *Hell Freezes Over* (Ritz Theatre), *Old Love*—1935; *A Room in Red and White* (46th Street Theatre), *Ethan Frome* (National Theatre), *Co-Respondent Unknown* (Ritz Theatre), *The Postman Always Rings Twice* (Lyceum Theatre), *Saint Joan* (Martin Beck Theatre), *On Your Toes* (Imperial Theatre), *St. Helena* (Lyceum Theatre), *Hamlet* (Empire Theatre), *Daughters of Atreus* (44th Street Theatre), *The Wingless Victory* (Empire Theatre), *The Women* (Ethel Barrymore Theatre)—1936; *High Tor* (Martin Beck Theatre), *The Star-Wagon* (Empire Theatre), *Susan and God* (Plymouth Theatre), *Antony and Cleopatra* (Mansfield Theatre), *Too Many Heroes* (Hudson Theatre), *Father Malachy's Miracle* (St. James Theatre), *Barchester Towers* (Martin Beck Theatre)—1937; *Yr. Obedient Husband* (Broadhurst Theatre), *On Borrowed Time* (Longacre Theatre), *Save Me a Waltz* (Martin Beck Theatre), *I Married an Angel* (Shubert Theatre), *Sing Out the News* (Music Box Theatre), *Abe Lincoln in Illinois* (Plymouth Theatre), *Knickerbocker Holiday* (Ethel Barrymore Theatre), *The Boys from Syracuse* (Alvin Theatre)—1938; *Mrs. O'Brien Entertains* (Lyceum Theatre), *Stars in Your Eyes* (Majestic Theatre), *No Time for Comedy* (Ethel Barrymore Theatre), *Too Many Girls* (Imperial Theatre), *Key Largo* (Ethel Barrymore Theatre), *Mornings at Seven* (Longacre Theatre), *Christmas Eve* (Henry Miller's Theatre), *The Merchant of Venice, Abe Lincoln in Illinois*—1939; *Two on an Island* (Broadhurst Theatre), *Higher and Higher* (Shubert Theatre), *Journey to Jerusalem* (National Theatre), *Pal Joey* (Ethel Barrymore Theatre), *Flight to the West* (Guild Theatre), *The Little Dog Laughed* (pre-Broadway)—1940; *Mr. and Mrs. North* (Belasco Theatre), *The Cream in the Well* (Booth Theatre), *The Talley Method* (Henry Miller's Theatre), *Watch on the Rhine* (Martin Beck Theatre), *The Wookey* (Plymouth Theatre), *Best Foot Forward* (Ethel Barrymore Theatre), *Candle in the Wind* (Shubert Theatre), *The Land Is Bright* (Music Box Theatre), *The Seventh Trumpet* (Mansfield Theatre)—1941; *Solitaire* (Plymouth Theatre), *Pillar of Fire* (Metropolitan Opera House), *By Jupiter* (Shubert Theatre)—1942; *Foolish Notion* (Martin Beck Theatre), *The Firebrand of Florance* (Alvin Theatre), *The Glass Menagerie* (Plymouth Theatre), *Carousel* (Majestic Theatre), *Hollywood Pinafore* (Alvin Theatre), *Carib Song* (Adelphi Theatre), *Beggars Are Coming to Town* (Coronet Theatre), *The Rugged Path* (Plymouth Theatre), *St. Lazare's Pharmacy* (pre-Broadway, Chicago), *Happy Time*—1945; *Jeb* (Martin Beck Theatre), *Annie Get Your Gun* (Imperial Theatre), *Happy Birthday* (Broadhurst Theatre), *Another Part of the Forest* (Fulton Theatre), *Windy City* (pre-Broadway, New Haven, Connecticut)—1946; *The Big Two* (Booth Theatre), *Street Scene* (Adelphi Theatre), *Finian's Rainbow* (46th Street Theatre), *The Chocolate Soldier* (Century Theatre), *Barefoot Boy with Cheek* (Martin Beck Theatre), *Command Decision* (Fulton Theatre), *Allegro* (Majestic Theatre), *A Streetcar Named Desire* (Ethel Barrymore Theatre)—1947; *Mister Roberts* (Alvin Theatre), *Shadow of the Wind* (Metropolitan Opera House Theatre), *The Legend of Sleepy Hollow* (St. James Theatre), *Summer and Smoke* (Music Box Theatre), *Anne of the Thousand Days* (Shubert Theatre)—1948; *Death of a Salesman* (Morosco Theatre), *South Pacific* (Majestic Theatre)—1949; *The Man* (Fulton Theatre), *Dance Me a Song* (Royale Theatre), *The Real McCoy* (Catholic University, Washington, D.C.), *The Innocents* (Playhouse Theatre), *The Wisteria Tree* (Martin Beck Theatre), *Mister Roberts*, *Burning Bright* (Broadhurst Theatre), *Guys and Dolls* (46th Street Theatre), *Desire Under the Elms*—1950; *The King and I* (St. James Theatre), *A Tree Grows in Brooklyn* (Alvin Theatre), *Top Banana* (Winter Garden Theatre), *Point of No Return* (Alvin Theatre), *A Month of Sundays* (pre-Broadway, closed Philadelphia), *Camino Real*—1951; *Flight into Egypt* (Music Box Theatre), *Wish You Were Here* (Imperial Theatre), *The Gambler* (Lyceum Theatre)—1952; *Picnic* (Music Box Theatre), *Can-Can* (Shubert Theatre), *Me and Juliet* (Majestic Theatre), *Tea and Sympathy* (Ethel Barrymore Theatre), *Kind Sir* (Alvin Theatre)—1953; *By the Beautiful Sea* (Majestic Theatre), *All Summer Long* (Coronet Theatre), *Fanny* (Majestic Theatre)—1954; *Silk Stockings* (Imperial Theatre), *Cat on a Hot Tin Roof* (Morosco Theatre), *Islands of Goats* (Fulton Theatre), *The Lark* (Longacre Theatre), *Pipe Dream* (Shubert Theatre), *The Oldsmobile Show*, *Picnic* (Film)—1955; *Middle of the Night* (assisted by John Harvey; ANTA Theatre), *The Most Happy Fella* (Imperial Theatre), *Happy Hunting* (Majestic Theatre)—1956; *Miss Lonelyhearts* (Music Box Theatre), *The Square Root of Wonderful* (National Theatre), *Look Homeward, Angel* (Ethel Barrymore Theatre), *Maiden Voyage* (pre-Broadway, closed Philadelphia)—1957; *Oh Captain!* (Alvin Theatre), *The Day the Money Stopped* (Belasco Theatre), *Handful of Fire* (Martin Beck Theatre), *The World of Suzie Wong* (Broadhurst Theatre), *The Gazebo* (Lyceum Theatre), *Whoop-Up!* (Shubert Theatre)—1958; *Rashomon* (Music Box Theatre), *Sweet Bird of Youth* (Martin Beck Theatre), *Gypsy* (Broadway Theatre), *The Gang's All Here* (Ambassador Theatre), *Silent Night, Lonely Night* (Morosco Theatre)—1959; *There Was a Little Girl* (Cort Theatre), *The Best Man* (Morosco Theatre), *Christine* (46th Street Theatre), *Period of Adjustment* (Helen Hayes Theatre), *Little Moon of Alban* (Longacre Theatre), *White Alice* (pre-Broadway)—1960; *The Devil's Advocate* (Billy Rose Theatre), *Everybody Loves Opal* (Longacre Theatre), *A Short Happy Life* (pre-Broadway)—1961; *All American* (Winter Garden Theatre), *Mr. President* (St. James Theatre)—1962; *The Milk Train Doesn't Stop Here Anymore* (Morosco Theatre)—1963; *After the Fall* (ANTA, Washington, D.C.), *But for Whom Charlie?* (ANTA, Washington Square), *After the Fall* (national tour, opened in Wilmington, Delaware), *The Owl and the Pussycat* (ANTA)—1964; *Danton's Death* (Vivian Beaumont Theatre), *The Playroom* (Brooks Atkinson Theatre), *Venus Is* (Billy Rose Theatre), *Don't Drink the Water* (Morosco Theatre), *My Sweet Charlie* (Longacre Theatre)—1966; *The Paisley Convertible* (Henry Miller's Theatre), *That Summer— That Fall* (Helen Hayes Theatre), *The Unemployed Saint* (Royal Poinciana Playhouse, Palm Beach, Florida), *Daphne in Cottage D* (Longacre Theatre), *Mata Hari* (pre-Broadway, Washington, D.C.)—1967; *The Prime of Miss Jean Brodie*

(Henry Miller's Theatre), *I Never Sang for My Father* (Longacre Theatre), *The Seven Descents of Myrtle* (Ethel Barrymore Theatre), *Slaughter on Tenth Avenue* (New York State Theatre, New York City Ballet), *Possibilities* (Players Theatre)—1968; *1776* (46th Street Theatre), *The Conjuror* (University of Michigan, Ann Arbor), *Galileo* (University of Illinois, Urbana)—1969; *Who Cares?* (New York State Theatre, New York City Ballet), *Child's Play* (Royale Theatre), *Georgy* (Winter Garden Theatre), *Look to the Lillies* (Lunt-Fontanne Theatre), *1776* (46th Street Theatre)—1970; *Father's Day* (John Golden Theatre), *PAMTGG* (New York State Theatre, New York City Ballet)—1971; *Caravaggio* (Playhouse in the Park, Cincinnati, Ohio), *Love Me, Love My Children* (scenery only, Mercer-O'Casey Theatre)—1971; *Children! Children!* (Ritz Theatre), *Voices* (Ethel Barrymore Theatre), *Sugar* (Majestic Theatre), *The Crucible* (revival, Vivian Beaumont Theatre)—1972; *Outcry* (Lyceum Theatre)—1973.

Mielziner, one of the most significant American designers of the twentieth century, was born in Paris to artistic parents. His father was a prominent easel painter, and his mother was a journalist and the Paris representative of *Vogue* magazine. In 1910, the family returned to live in New York. When Mielziner was fourteen, he saw Robert Edmond Jones's* design for *The Man Who Married a Dumb Wife* and was inspired to go into theatrical set design. After attending the Ethical Culture School in New York City, the Philadelphia Institute of Fine Arts, and the Arts Students League of New York City and apprenticing with designer Joseph Urban* in 1921, Mielziner traveled to Europe on scholarship and studied the latest trends in European scene design in Germany.

When he returned to the United States in 1923, it was not long before he acquired a design apprentice position at the Theatre Guild. Here he made lasting relationships with several members of the company that led to the design of many shows. One of his first was *The Guardsman* (1924), a big success starring the team of Lunt and Fontanne. Toward the end of the decade, Mielziner designed Elmer Rice's *Street Scene* (1929), and created an extremely realistic and very detailed set that depicted a New York street replete with tenements.

During the 1930s, Mielziner established himself as a major designer and dominated the Broadway stage for the next two decades. His career was helped along by his becoming chief designer for the Playwright's Company, founded by writers Elmer Rice, Maxwell Anderson, and Robert E. Sherwood. Mielziner's reputation grew as a result of his creating the settings for such significant American dramas as Anderson's *Winterset* (1935). His ethereal set of the Brooklyn Bridge and the New York skyline for this show was considered a masterpiece. Other significant American productions that Mielziner designed were Lillian Hellman's *Another Part of the Forest* (1946); Tennessee Williams's *The Glass Menagerie* (1945), *A Streetcar Named Desire* (1947), *Cat on a Hot Tin Roof* (1955), and *The Milk Train Doesn't Stop Here Anymore* (1963); and Arthur Miller's *Death of a Salesman* (1949) and *After the Fall* (1964), to name only a few. Although rooted in realism, his sets went beyond that into a "poetic realism," which depicted not only the locale for the play, but the inner moods and feelings of the characters. He accomplished this type of approach through the innovative use of materials such as transparent scrims, skeletal metal frameworks for houses, and projections. For the musical theatre, Mielziner also created a distinguished list of credits, including the dark and moody *Pal Joey* (1940), the bright and cheerful *South Pacific* (1949), and the stylistically exaggerated *Guys and Dolls* (1950).

In addition to sets, Mielziner designed costumes and created the lighting schemes for most of his productions. Early on, he struck up a companionship with Edward F. Kook, who was to become the president of Century Lighting, and together they developed more efficient lighting instruments. As well, Mielziner designed lighting for political events, television, and various festivals. He also advised on the building of several theatres, including the ANTA Theatre in Washington, D.C., the Vivian Beaumont and the Forum theatres at Lincoln Center in New York City, and the Loretto-Hilton Theatre in Missouri, as well as a number of university facilities. During his lifetime, Mielziner produced many renderings for his shows that have been exhibited worldwide and purchased for private collections. Many of them are considered to be masterpieces of art.

Awards: Mielziner earned five Tony Awards for best scene design for his contributions to the 1948–1949 season, "Best Scene Design" for *The Innocents* (1950) and *The King and I* (1951), as well as for "Best Set and Lighting Design" for *Child's Play* (1970); in addition, he was nominated for Tonys for *1776* (1969) and *Father's Day* (1971). He won five Donaldson Awards for scene design for *Dream Girl* (1946), *A Streetcar Named Desire* (1948), *Death of a Salesman* (1949), *The Innocents* (1950), *The King and I* (1951) and an individual one for distinguished contributions to the theatre (1952); nine *Variety* New York Drama Critics' Poll Awards for scene design for *Dream Girl*, *Another Part of the Forest* (1947), *A Streetcar Named Desire* (1948), *Death of a Salesman* (1949), *The Innocents*, *The King and I*, *Flight into Egypt* (1952), *Can-Can* (1953), and *The Most Happy Fella* (1956); a Drama Desk Award for *Child's Play*; two Joseph P. Maharam Foundation Awards for *1776* and *Child's Play*; and one Oscar for the color art direction of the film *Picnic* (1955).

Further Reading: By Mielziner: *Designing for the Theatre: A Memoir and a Portfolio.* New York: Atheneum, 1965; *The Shapes of Our Theatre.* New York: C. N. Potter (dist. by Crown), 1970.

About Mielziner: Larson. *Scene Design for Stage and Screen* (see Bibliography).

Thomas J. Mikotowicz

Militello, Anne E. Lighting designer (b. April 29, 1957, Buffalo, NY). Militello began her career lighting punk bands on the West Coast in the late 1970s. Eventually working her way to the Magic Theatre in Omaha, she met and worked with Sam Shepard and Michael McClure. Subsequently, Militello moved to New York in 1980, where she financed her early design career by working as an electrician in local lighting rental houses and lighting shows for rock clubs. During this time she designed many shows for LaMama E.T.C. and worked with playwrights and directors such as Tom Eyen, Tom O'Horgan, Elizabeth Swados, and John Vaccaro. Eventually, she began to work as a lighting designer in theatre on a full-time basis. Militello's credits include the New York premieres of the Broadway and off-Broadway productions of *Cuba and His Teddy Bear* (1986), starring Robert DeNiro and produced by Joseph Papp; *A Lie of the Mind* (1985), written and directed by Sam Shepard and starring Geraldine Page; eight new productions (1983–1988) written and directed by Maria Irene Fornes in various theatres in New York City; *Rapmaster Ronnie* (1984) by Elizabeth Swados and G. B. Trudeau; *La Puta Vida* (1987) at the Public Theatre; and *Three Ways Home* (1988), starring Malcolm-Jamal Warner. Her work with experimental theatre includes designs for Mabou Mines, Squat Theatre, Ping Chong, and the Fiji Co., Winston Tong and many shows at Theatre for the New City. Her regional theatre experience includes work at the Milwaukee Repertory Theatre, the Studio Arena Theatre in Buffalo, the McCarter Theatre in Princeton, and the Boston Shakespeare Company. She expands her work to include international tours with dance companies and electronic music artists, MTV videos, and interior lighting designs. In 1984, she received the Obie Award for "Sustained Excellence in Lighting Design."

Annie Milton

Miller, Craig. Lighting designer (b. 1950, Hugoton, KS). Miller is credited with the lighting designs for numerous Broadway and off-Broadway productions, as well as for many major regional theatres and opera and dance companies throughout the country. After graduating from Northwestern University in 1971 and teaching at a small college until 1975, he moved to New York, where he began designing lights for several small dance companies and assisted well-known professionals Thomas Skelton, Jules Fisher,* and others. His credits include productions with the Lars Lubovitch, the Laura Dean, and Alvin Ailey dance companies, as well as the Stuttgart and Royal Danish Ballet companies. Through the influence of Skelton, Miller was given the opportunity to design several operas at the Spoleto Festival USA in 1977. This work led to assignments at the Dallas Opera, Juilliard Opera, and the Manhattan School of Music, among many others. He designed the lighting for *Lulu* (1979) at the Santa Fe Opera and maintains a relationship with the organization. In addition, he has designed many plays in regional theatre, off-Broadway, and on Broadway. For the Guthrie Theatre in Minneapolis, he created the lighting for *Romeo and Juliet* in 1979, and, for the Goodspeed Opera House, he lit *One Touch of Venus* and *The Little Rascals* in 1987. Off-Broadway, Miller has created lighting schemes for *Trixie True, Teen Detective* (1980), *Company* (1981), *Gardenia* (1982), *Jeeves Takes Charge* (1983), and *Spookhouse* (1984). On Broadway, his credits include *On Golden Pond* at the New Apollo Theatre in 1979; *Barnum* at the St. James Theatre in 1980; *I Won't Dance* and *Five O'Clock Girl*, both at the Helen Hayes Theatre in 1980; *Brothers* at the Music Box Theatre in 1983; *Take Me Along* at the Martin Beck Theatre, *Doubles* at the Ritz Theatre, and *Wind in the Willows* at the Nederlander Theatre, all in 1985; *Safe Sex* at the Lyceum Theatre in 1987; and *Romance, Romance* at the Helen Hayes Theatre in 1988.

Awards: He was nominated for a Tony Award for his lighting for *Barnum* (1980) and won Maharam Awards for Samuel Beckett's *Company* (1981) and John Guare's *Gardenia* (1982).

Further Reading: "Designers at Work." *Theatre Crafts* May 1987: 40; "Onstage and off the Shelf." *Lighting Dimensions* November/December 1985; "Using Your Apple Computer to Handle Lighting Paperwork." *Theatre Crafts* March 1985.

Penny L. Remsen

Minks, Wilfried. Set designer and director (b. February 21, 1930, Binai, Czechoslovakia). Theatrical productions include *Don Carlos*—1959; *Die Vershworung des Fresco zu Genua, Maid of Orleans*—1960; *Die Kunst eine Widerbellerum zu zahmen*—1961; *La Cena del Rey Baltazar, The Hostage, Luther*—1962; *The Music Man*—1963; *Henry V, The Quare Fellow, L'Avare*—1964; *Romeo and Juliet, Hamlet, Die Unberaten, Fruhlings Erunchen*—1965; *Die Rauber, Antigone, Macbeth*—1966; *Measure for Measure, Soldaten, War of the Roses*—1967; *Schwyk in zwesten Weltkrieg, Peer Gynt*—1968; *La Bottega del Caffe, Torquato Tasso*—1969; *The Tempest*—1970; *The Revenger's Tragedy*—1972; *The Tempest*—1976.

Minks has become one of the most influential scenic designers in Germany since the 1970s. He began his training at the age of seventeen at the Arts and Crafts School in Leipzig. Later, he studied in Berlin at the Hochschule fur Bildende Kunste under the direction of Willi Schmidt. The most important start of his career, however, was in 1959, when he moved to the Stadttheater Ulm and began his collaborations with directors Hubner, Palizsch, and Zadek. Three years later, they all moved to the Bremen Stadttheater, which from 1967 to 1973 became the most radical theatre in Germany. Minks did all the designs for this theatre's productions. Designs for these directors as well as other directors like Fassbinder, Gruber, Neuenfels, Peymann, and Stein, who came to Bremen to work under Hubner's artistic direction, established Minks's reputation. The words "Bremen stil" were coined to characterize these productions.

One important watchword for the Bremen group was to take Artaud's motto, "No more masterpieces," seriously. As a result, design in these productions worked against the status quo, against the script as literature. Minks used projections and white light and borrowed imagery from the visual arts, particularly American pop art. No definitive style was established. Rather, each production designed by Minks was an experiment created by the tensions between a realistic "kernel" in the setting described by the playwright and the formal and abstract structures inherent in the play.

When Hubner lost financial support in Bremen in 1973, Minks began designing in Berlin, Bochen, and Stuttgart. Since that time, he has often served as his own director for these projects. This fact explains, to some degree, why his design career appears to have slowed down in recent years. His influence has been enormous. Many of Germany's younger designers are Minks's disciples. They are not only taking his classes in scene design at the Hochschule fur dildende

Kunste in Hamburg but also absorbing his design ideas as expressed on the German stage.

Further Reading: Canaris, Volker. "Peter Zadek and Hamlet." *The Drama Review* March 1980: 53–62; Riddell, Richard. "The German Raum." *The Drama Review* March 1980: 39–52; Riddell, Richard. "Wilfried Minks: The Influential West German Designer in Mid-Career." *Theatre Crafts* January/February 1978: 27 + .

Andrea J. Nouryeh

Mitchell, David. Set designer (b. May 12, 1932, Honesdale, PA). Theatrical productions include *Henry V, Medea*—1965; *Macbeth, Madama Butterfly*—1966; *Volpone, Falstaff, La Boheme, Naked Hamlet*—1967; *Aida, Take One Step, A Cry of Players*—1968; *Pelleas and Melisande, Mefistofele, The Increased Difficulty of Concentration*—1969; *Journeys, Grin and Bare It, Postcards, Colette, Steambath, Trelawny of the 'Wells'*—1970; *How the Other Half Loves, Fire in the Mindhouse, The Basic Training of Pavlo Hummel, Manon Lescaut, The Incomparable Max*—1971; *Aida, Lord Byron, The Cherry Orchard*—1972; *Il Trovatore, Macbeth, Cosi Fan Tutte, Barbary Shore*—1973; *Short Eyes, Boris Godunov, The Cherry Orchard, The Wager, In the Boom Boom Room, Enter a Free Man*—1974; *Little Black Sheep, The Ravel Festival, Shoe Shine Parlor, Trelawny of the 'Wells'*—1975; *Apple Pie, Mrs. Warren's Profession, The Steadfast Tin Soldier, Henry V*—1976; *Mondongo, I Love My Wife, Annie, The Gin Game, The Italian Straw Hat, A Photograph*—1977; *The Prince of Grand Street, Working, End of the War, Funny Face, The Steadfast Tin Soldier* (television), *Rich Kids* (film)—1978; *I Remember Mama, The Price, One Trick Pony* (film)—1979; *Barnum*—1980; *Bring Back Birdie, Can Can, The Tempest, My Dinner with Andre* (film), *Sizwe Bansi Is Dead* (television), *Gertrude Stein* (television)—1981; *The Magic Flute, The Bournonville Dances* (television), *Foxfire, Creation of the World*—1982; *Brighton Beach Memoirs, Private Lives, Dance a Little Closer* (musical based on *Idiot's Delight*), *La Cage aux Folles*—1983; *The Old Flag, The Cabal of Hypocrites*—1984; *Harrigan 'n' Hart, Biloxi Blues, The Odd Couple, The Boys of Winter*—1985; *Broadway Bound*—1986; *King Henry IV, Part 1*—1987; *The Big Love, Legs Diamond*—1988; *Young Rube*—1989.

Mitchell began his career as an assistant to Ming Cho Lee,* whose influence can be seen in his early designs for the Public Theatre, starting with *Henry V* (1965) and continuing with *Medea* (1965), *Macbeth* (1966), *Volpone* (1967), and *Hamlet* (1967). These designs tended to be frontal, with a clean sharpness of right angles and parallel lines. Mitchell has stated that he prefers to have the set self-contained within the stage space and dislikes sets that suggest a continuation off-stage or through the proscenium. Like Lee, he uses a type of Brechtian stagecraft and often combines very realistic elements and details with more stylized scenic techniques. This style can be seen in his settings for *Steambath* (1970), *Short Eyes* (1974), and *Foxfire* (1982), in which such realistic details as real steam and running water were placed in obviously theatricalized environments. He has continued to work with the New York Shakespeare Festival as well as other regional theatres, ballet, and opera companies throughout the world.

Mitchell earned his first major Broadway credits in 1977 with the three Broadway hits *The Gin Game, I Love My Wife*, and *Annie*. With the musical *Annie* and later, with the musical *La Cage aux Folles* (1983), Mitchell earned a reputation for kinetic scenery that had cinematic movement. In *Annie*, through the use of treadmills and cut-out automobiles, Mitchell developed a rhythm and pace through the scene changes that resembled a cinematic "pan shot." This was carried even further with *La Cage aux Folles*, in which the scenery again traveled from side to side. Through the overture and first two musical numbers of the show, the scenery simulated a long pan shot down the street: going into the club, onto the stage, through the wings, and into the apartment. These two production designs created a whole new "look" to musicals, while harkening back to the more elaborate style of previous decades.

Awards: Mitchell won the Drama Desk Award for *Short Eyes* in 1974. *Annie* earned Mitchell a Tony Award, the Outer Critics' Circle Award, and the Los Angeles Critics' Circle Award in 1977. In 1980, he won a Tony Award and the Joseph Maharam Award for *Barnum*.

Further Reading: Aronson (see Bibliography); "La Cage aux Folles: It Is What It Is, A Hit." *Theatre Crafts* November/December 1983; "Orphan Annie Goes from a Hard-Knock Life to Easy Street." *Theatre Crafts* November/December 1977; "Special Effects in Barnum." *Theatre Design & Technology* Spring 1981.

Ken Kloth

Moiseiwitsch, Tanya. Theatrical designer and architectural consultant (b. December 3, 1914, London, England). Theatrical productions include *The Faithful, Westminster, Alien Corn*—1934; *A Deuce o' Jacks, Bird's Nest, Blind Man's Bluff, Baintighearna An Ghorta, Boyd's Shop, Candida, Cartney and Kevney, Casadh ant Sugain, Church Street, Coggerers, Coriolanus, Damer's Gold, Deidre, The Dear Queen, Dervorgilla, End of the Beginning, Grand House in the City, The Great Adventure, Hassan, In the Train, Invincibles, Jailbird, Katie Roche, Killycreggs in Twilight, The Lost Leader, The Man in a Cloak, Moses' Rock, Neal Maquade, Noah, Parnell of Avondale, Passing Day, The Patriot, Pilgrims, Playboy of the Western World, Plough and the Stars, Quin's Secret, Saint in a Hurry, Silver Jubilee, Shadow and Substance, Shadowy Waters, Shrewing Up of Blanco Posnet, She Had to Do Something, A Spot in the Sun, Thomas Muskerry, Times Pocket, Village Wooing, Well of the Saints, Who Will Remember?, The Wild Goose, Wind from the West, Words on the Window Pane*—1935–1939; *Golden Cuckoo, High Temperature*—1940; *Androcles and the Lion, The Doctor's Dilemma, The Gentle People, George and Margaret, Goodness How Sad, Merchant of Venice, Romeo and Juliet, Rope*—1941–1944; *The Alchemist, Dr. Faustus, John Gabriel Borkman, Point Valaine, Uncle Vanya, The Critic*—1944–1945; *The Beaux' Stratagem, Twelfth Night, Cyrano de Bergerac, Time of Your Life*—1945–1946; *Bless the Bride, Peter Grimes*—1947; *Beggar's Opera, Lady of Rohesia, Cherry Orchard*—1948; *Henry VIII, Treasure Hunt,*

A Month in the Country—1949; *Captain Carvallo, Don Giovanni, Holly and the Ivy, Home at Seven*—1950; *Figure of Fun, The Passing Day, A Midsummer Night's Dream, Richard II, Henry IV, Part 1, Henry IV, Part 2, Henry V*—1951; *The Deep Blue Sea, Othello, Timon of Athens*—1952; *Henry VIII, Julius Caesar, Richard III, All's Well That Ends Well*—1953; *The Matchmaker, Measure for Measure, Oedipus Rex, The Taming of the Shrew*—1954; *A Life in the Sun, The Cherry Orchard, Julius Caesar, Merchant of Venice, Oedipus Rex*—1955; *Measure for Measure, Henry V, Merry Wives of Windsor*—1956; *Twelfth Night, Two Gentlemen of Verona*—1957; *The Bright One, Much Ado About Nothing, The Winter's Tale, Henry IV, Part 1, Two Gentlemen of Verona, The Broken Jug*—1958; *Merchant of Venice, All's Well That Ends Well*—1959; *Wrong Side of the Park, King John, Romeo and Juliet*—1960; *Ondine, Coriolanus, Love's Labour's Lost*—1961; *The Alchemist, Cyrano de Bergerac, Taming of the Shrew*—1962; *Hamlet, The Miser, The Three Sisters*—1963; *Saint Joan, Volpone*—1964; *The Way of the World, The Cherry Orchard*—1965; *As You Like It, The Skin of Our Teeth*—1966; *The House of Atreus, Antony and Cleopatra, Peter Grimes*—1967; *House of Atreus, Volpone*—1968; *Macook's Corner, Swift, Uncle Vanya, Caucasian Chalk Circle*—1969; *Cymbeline*—1970; *Barber of Seville, Shoemaker's Holiday*—1971; *A Man for All Seasons, The Persians*—1972; *The Government Inspector, Stirrings in Sheffield on a Saturday Night, The Misanthrope*—1973; *The Imaginary Invalid*—1974; *The Misanthrope, Phaedra Brittanica*—1975; *The Voyage of Edgar Allan Poe, Rigoletto, All's Well That Ends Well*—1977; *Oedipus Rex, Oedipus at Colonnus*—1978; *Double Dealer*—1979; *Red Roses for Me, La Traviata*—1980; *Kidnapped in London*—1981; *Mary Stuart*—1982; *King Lear* (television), *Tartuffe*—1983; *Tartuffe* (television), *The Clandestine Marriage*—1984; *The Government Inspector*—1985.

Moiseiwitsch is one of the most influential designers of the twentieth century, partly because of her innovation and development, with Tyrone Guthrie, of the open stage. Moiseiwitsch started her career at the Abbey Theatre in Dublin, where she designed more than fifty productions from 1935 to 1939. Soon after, she began a long association with the Old Vic, where she designed such legendary productions as *Uncle Vanya* and *The Critic* (both in 1944). Her production of *Henry VIII* (1949) was her first experimentation with a permanent unit set, using no front curtain. This production was directed by Tyrone Guthrie, with whom she formed a lasting partnership. In 1953 for Guthrie, Moiseiwitsch designed an open stage at the newly built Stratford Festival in Ontario and created settings for *Richard III* and *All's Well That Ends Well*. She has continued to design regularly for Stratford and has served as associate director since 1974. In 1963, Moiseiwitsch went to Minneapolis with Guthrie and was instrumental in the design of the open hexagonal stage at the Guthrie Theatre. She also created settings for the premiere season and was resident designer through 1967. Her production of *The House of Atreus* in 1967originated at the Guthrie and later toured the United States.

In addition, Moiseiwitsch has designed costumes, props, and settings for major companies around the world, including such institutions as the National Theatre of Great Britain, the Mark Taper Forum, the Piccolo Teatro in Milan, and the Habimah Theatre in Tel-Aviv. She has served as scenic designer on such operas as *La Traviata* and *Rigoletto* for the Metropolitan Opera. Moiseiwitsch's influence can be seen with the wide use of unit sets and acceptance of the open stage design, modeled after the Guthrie Theatre, at such facilities as the Festival Theatre in Chichester, the Vivian Beaumont Theatre, and many regional, college, and university theatres.

Awards: Her striking designs for *The House of Atreus* earned Moiseiwitsch the New York Drama Desk Award and the Los Angeles Critic's Circle Award.

Further Reading: By Moiseiwitsch: "Problems in Design." *Drama Survey* May 1963.

About Moiseiwitsch: Behl, Dennis. "Architect of the Open Stage: Tanya Moiseiwitsch's Alliance with Art and Craft." *Theatre Crafts* August/September 1986; "Genius in Stitches." *Plays and Players* April 1985.

Ken Kloth

Montresor, Beni. Designer, artist, and illustrator (b. March 31, 1926, Verona, Italy). With training from the Academia di Belle Arte in Venice, Montresor designed more than thirty films for Fellini, De Sica, and Rossellini from 1952 to 1959. He engaged in a wide variety of activities, including writing film scripts, ballets, and children's books, as well as theatrical design. His first opera design was Barber's *Vanessa* (1960), after which he came to New York and created the settings for Menotti's *The Last Savage* (1964) at the Metropolitan Opera House. Subsequent designs for this company included *La Gioconda*, *Esclaramonde*, and *La Cenerentola*. The New York City Opera maintains his designs for *The Magic Flute*, *Daughter of the Regiment*, *Turandot*, and *L'Amore de Tre Re*. In 1982 at the Guthrie Theatre in Minneapolis, he designed Andrei Serban's *The Marriage of Figaro*, which won the Kudos Award for best design. His work has been seen at the major opera houses and theatres all over the world. Ethereal and magical, his design style is characterized by the use of lighting to alter the rich colors and forms of his painted drops and scrims. His renderings and paintings have been exhibited in New York at the Knoedler Gallery and at the Library and Museum of Performing Arts.

Andrea J. Nouryeh

Moses, Thomas. Scenic artist (b. 1856, England; d. 1931). Although his father had planned for him to be a tanner in England, Moses left Liverpool as a young man and sailed to America, where he studied with various artists in Chicago, New York, and California. He was soon hired to paint scenery in Sosman & Landis Scenic Studio, one of the largest in the country. Staying with the firm from 1877 to 1929, he eventually became manager and vice president. As a designer, Moses is best known for scenery that included work for the shows of Buffalo Bill, Edwin Booth, and Sarah Bernhardt. Believing that the theatre should be filled with romance and happiness, Moses mostly painted exteriors. While he had a fine style that was initially distinctive, it became, however, repetitive and stereotyped. Thus, his peers thought that his ornamentation was easily recognizable. Moses left Sosman & Landis when it was sold and it became the Chicago Studio. For the rest of his career, Moses continued as a scenic artist, touring the country, "touching up" Masonic scenery.

Jonet Buchanan

Motley (Harris, Audrey Sophia, 1901–1966; Harris, Margaret F., 1904–   ; Montgomery, Elizabeth, 1904–   ). Scenic and costume designers (all were born in England). Theatrical productions include *Romeo and Juliet, Men About the House, Strange Orchestra, The Merchant of Venice*—1932; *Richard of Bordeaux, A Midsummer Night's Dream, Ball at the Savoy*—1933; *Hamlet, Spring 1600, Jack and Jill, The Haunted Ballroom*—1934; *Romeo and Juliet, Noah, The Old Ladies*—1935; *The Sea Gull, Dusty Ermine, Aucassin and Nicolette, Richard II, The Happy Hypocrite, Farewell Performance, Charles the King, The Witch of Edmonton*—1936; *Richard II, The School for Scandal, The Three Sisters, Henry V, He Was Born Gay, Great Romance, Macbeth*—1937; *The Three Sisters, The Merchant of Venice, Dear Octopus*—1938; *The Importance of Being Earnest, Rhonda Roundabout, Weep for Spring, Great Expectations*—1939; *Beggar's Opera*—1940; *The Doctor's Dilemma, The Cherry Orchard*—1941; *The Doctor's Dilemma, Watch on the Rhine, The Three Sisters*—1942; *Richard III, Lovers and Friends*—1943; *The Cherry Orchard, A Highland Fling, A Bell for Adano*—1944; *The Tempest, Hope for the Best, The Wind of Heaven, You Touched Me!, Carib Song, Skydrift, Pygmalion*—1945; *Antony and Cleopatra*—1946; *The Importance of Being Earnest*—1947; *Anne of the Thousand Days*—1948; *The Heiress, Antigone, Miss Liberty, South Pacific*—1949; *Happy as a Lark, The Innocents, Peter Pan, The Liar, Bartholomew Fair*—1950; *Hassan, Othello, Paint Your Wagon, The Grand Tour*—1951; *The Happy Time, Candida, To Be Continued, The Innocents, The River Line*—1952; *Midsummer, Paint Your Wagon, King John, Antony and Cleopatra, Can-Can*—1953; *Mademoiselle Colombe, The Immoralist, Charley's Aunt, I Capture the Castle, Wedding in Paris, Can-Can, Peter Pan*—1954; *The Honeys, The Merry Wives of Windsor, The Young and the Beautiful, Island of Goats*—1955; *A Likely Tale, The Mulberry Bush, The Crucible, Middle of the Night, The Most Happy Fella, Long Day's Journey into Night, Othello, Cards of Identity, The Sea Gull*—1956; *The Magic Flute, Eugene Onegin, As You Like It, Shinbone Alley, South Pacific, First Gentleman, Julius Caesar, The Merchant of Venice, Look Back in Anger, Requiem for a Nun, The Country Wife, Look Homeward, Angel*—1957; *A Majority of One, Love Me Little, Romeo and Juliet, Jane Eyre, Hamlet, Much Ado About Nothing, The Cold Wind and the Warm*—1958; *Requiem for a Nun, The Rivalry, The Magistrate, The Merry Wives of Windsor, The Aspern Papers, King Lear, Rosmersholm, Il Trovatore*—1959; *Ross, A Man for All Seasons, Waiting in the Wings, Simon Boccanegra, Caprice, Becket*—1960; *As You Like It, Macbeth, Troilus and Cressida*—1961; *We Take the Town, Richard II, Henry IV,*

Part I, Kwamina—1962; *Tovarich, 110 in the Shade, Mother Courage and Her Children*—1963; *Baker Street, Ben Franklin in Paris*—1964.

Montgomery and the Harris sisters, under the name Motley, designed a staggeringly diverse collection of costumes and a small number of settings, beginning in England in the early 1930s. While designing many West End productions during the 1930s, Motley formed an especially close alliance with John Gielgud for several of his finest Shakespearean productions of that era. After enjoying success on the English stage, they turned to America after 1941 and from that time on worked on both sides of the Atlantic. As their work with Gielgud suggests, the Motley trio were among the first designers to engage in a sophisticated collaboration with the director that included not only creating pictorial effects through harmony in color, line, shape, and texture, but contributing costumes and visual effects that served as a means of interpretation of the author's deeper intentions. Their costumes were featured in such classic plays as *Othello* (1956) and *King Lear* (1959) and such Broadway hits as *The Most Happy Fella* (1956), *A Man for All Seasons* (1960), and *Becket* (1960).

Awards: Motley won Tony Awards for *First Gentleman* (1957) and for *Becket* (1960).

Further Reading: By Motley: *Designing and Making Stage Costumes.* New York: Watson-Guptill, 1964.

James Fisher

Motta, Fabrizio Carini. Scene designer, theatrical architect, and stage machinist (b. 1627, Italy; d. 1699). After being educated as a painter, Motta served the Gonzago Court, located in Mantova, Italy, as the prefect of theatres and architect to Duke Ferdinando Carlo IV between the years 1671 and 1699. He was in charge of designing Court theatricals and events at the public playhouses, as well as theatre and municipal architecture. During his lifetime, he wrote two works on theatrical buildings and practice. The first, a published manuscript titled *Treatise on the Structures of Theatres & Scenes*, discusses the fundamental requirements for a functional theatre facility by teaching lessons in sight lines, vanishing points, and fire exits and shows several variations on theatre buildings. The writing offers a different view from that in the writings of Serlio,* Sabbatini,* and Josef Furttenbach* in that it treats the theatre auditorium apart from the stage. The second, an unpublished manuscript written in 1688 titled ''Construction of Theatres and Theatrical Machines,'' is one of the first comprehensive studies that combines text and illustrations of the seventeenth-century Italian stage house and its equipment.

Further Reading: By Motta: *The Theatrical Writings of Fabrizio Carini Motta, Translations of Trattato sopra la struttura de' Theatrie scene, 1676 and Costruzione de teatri e machine teatrali, 1688,* intro. Orville K. Larson, trans. C. Thomas Ault and Orville K. Larson. Carbondale and Edwardsville: Southern Illinois University Press, 1987.

Thomas J. Mikotowicz

Müller, Traugott. Set designer (b. 1895, Germany; d. 1944). Müller began his theatrical career working under the guidance of German director Erwin Piscator, known for his epic theatre productions in the early part of this century. For many of his shows, Müller devised a complex, multipurpose setting of ramps, steps, and levels on a revolving stage. Although his best designs were seen in contemporary and classic German dramas, he also created some effective settings for the plays of Shakespeare. Among his best-known productions are *Segel am Horizont* (1924), *Desire Under the Elms* (1925), *Die Räuber* (1926), *Rasputin* (1927), *Richard III* (1937), *Richard II* (1939), and *Turandot* (1941).

James Fisher

Musser, Tharon. Lighting designer (b. 1925, Roanoke, VA). Theatrical productions (all theatres listed are in New York, unless otherwise specified) include *Long Day's Journey into Night* (Helen Hayes Theatre)—1956; *Shinbone Alley* (Broadway Theatre), *Much Ado About Nothing* (American Shakespeare Festival), *Monique* (John Golden Theatre), *The Makropoulos Secret* (Phoenix Theatre)—1957; *The Chairs* (Phoenix Theatre), *The Lesson* (Phoenix Theatre), *The Infernal Machine* (Phoenix Theatre), *The Entertainer* (Royale Theatre), *The Firstborn* (Habimah Theatre, Tel Aviv, Israel), *A Midsummer Night's Dream* (American Shakespeare Festival, Stratford, Connecticut), *Murder in the Cathedral* (Carnegie Hall), *Shadow of a Gunman* (Bijou Theatre), *J. B.* (ANTA)—1958; *The Beaux' Stratagem* (Phoenix Theatre), *Once Upon a Mattress* (Phoenix Theatre), *Romeo and Juliet* (American Shakespeare Festival), *A Midsummer Night's Dream* (American Shakespeare Festival), *The Merry Wives of Windsor* (American Shakespeare Festival), *The Great God Brown* (Coronet Theatre), *Only in America* (Cort Theatre), *Five Finger Exercise* (Music Box Theatre)—1959; *Peer Gynt* (Phoenix Theatre), *The Long Dream* (Ambassador Theatre), *The Tumbler* (Helen Hayes Theatre), *Twelfth Night* (American Shakespeare Festival), *The Tempest* (American Shakespeare Festival), *Antony and Cleopatra* (American Shakespeare Festival)—1960; *The Glass Menagerie*, *The Skin of Our Teeth*, *The Miracle Worker* (all three for the American Repertory Company tour, Europe and South America), *As You Like It* (American Shakespeare Festival), *Macbeth* (American Shakespeare Festival), *The Turn of the Screw* (American Festival, Boston), *Anatol* (American Festival, Boston), *Elizabeth the Queen* (American Festival, Boston), *Advise and Consent* (Shubert Theatre, Cincinnati), *Mary Stuart* (Academy of Music, Northampton, Massachusetts, toured), *Elizabeth the Queen* (Academy of Music, Northampton, Massachusetts, toured), *Garden of Sweets* (ANTA)—1961; *Giants, Sons of Giants* (Alvin Theatre), *H.M.S. Pinafore*, *Androcles and the Lion* (both at the Arts Festival, Boston), *Calculated Risk* (Ambassador Theatre), *Nowhere To Go But Up* (Winter Garden)—1962; *Andorra* (Biltmore Theatre), *Mother Courage and Her Children* (Martin Beck Theatre), *King Lear* (American Shakespeare Festival), *The Comedy of Errors* (American Shakespeare Festival), *Henry V* (American Shakespeare Festival), *Here's Love* (Shubert Theatre), *Ring 'Round the Moon* (National Repertory Theatre tour), *The Sea Gull* (Belasco Theatre), *The Crucible* (Belasco Theatre), *Marathon '33* (ANTA)—1963; *Any Wednesday* (Music Box Theatre), *Much Ado About Nothing* (American Shakespeare Festival), *Richard III* (American Shakespeare

Festival), *Hamlet* (American Shakespeare Festival), *Hedda Gabler*, *Liliom*, *She Stoops To Conquer* (National Repertory Theatre tour for above three), *Golden Boy* (Majestic Theatre), *Alfie* (Morosco Theatre)—1964; *Kelly* (Broadhurst Theatre), *All in Good Time* (Royale Theatre), *Flora, the Red Menace* (Alvin Theatre), *Romeo and Juliet* (American Shakespeare Festival), *Coriolanus* (American Shakespeare Festival), *The Taming of the Shrew* (American Shakespeare Festival), *King Lear* (American Shakespeare Festival), *Mais Oui* (Casino du Leban, Beirut, Lebanon), *Minor Miracle* (Henry Miller's Theatre), *The Rivals*, *The Madwoman of Chaillot* (both for National Repertory Theatre tour, Greensboro, North Carolina), *The Trojan Women* (National Repertory Theatre tour, Columbus, Ohio)—1965; *Malcolm* (Shubert Theatre), *Great Indoors* (Eugene O'Neill Theatre), *The Lion in Winter* (Ambassador Theatre), *Mame* (Winter Garden), *Falstaff* (American Shakespeare Festival), *Murder in the Cathedral* (American Shakespeare Festival), *Twelfth Night* (American Shakespeare Festival), *Julius Caesar* (American Shakespeare Festival), *A Delicate Balance* (Martin Beck Theatre), *Tonight at Eight-Thirty*, *A Touch of the Poet* (both for the National Repertory Theatre tour, Greensboro, North Carolina), *The Imaginary Invalid* (National Repertory Theatre tour, Columbus, Ohio)—1966; *Hallelujah, Baby!* (Martin Beck Theatre), *A Touch of the Poet* (ANTA), *A Midsummer Night's Dream*, *Antigone*, *The Merchant of Venice* (all three for the American Shakespeare Festival), *The Birthday Party* (Booth Theatre), *After the Rain* (Golden Theatre), *John Brown's Body*, *The Comedy of Errors* (both for the National Repertory Theatre tour, Greensboro, North Carolina), *The Promise* (Henry Miller's Theatre), *Everything in the Garden* (Plymouth Theatre)—1967; *House of Flowers* (Theatre de Lys), *Catch My Soul* (Ahmanson Theatre, Los Angeles), *Man and the Universe* (Hemis Fair Exhibit, San Antonio, Texas), *Golden Boy* (Palladium, London), *As You Like It*, *Androcles and the Lion* (both at the American Shakespeare Festival), *The Lovers* (Vivian Beaumont Theatre), *Maggie Flynn* (ANTA)—1968; *Fig Leaves Are Falling* (Broadhurst Theatre), *Mame* (Drury Lane Theatre, London), *The Gingham Dog* (Golden Theatre), *Spofford* (Fisher Theatre, Detroit, Michigan), *Fedora* (Dallas Civic Opera, Texas)—1969; *Blood Red Roses* (John Golden Theatre), *Applause* (Palace Theatre), *The Boy Friend* (Ambassador Theatre), *Dream on Monkey Mountain*, *Rosebloom* (both at Center Theatre Group, Mark Taper Forum, Los Angeles), *The Merry Widow*, *Madame Butterfly*, *Il Tabarro*, *Carmina Burana* (all four at the Dallas Civic Opera, Texas)—1970; *Follies* (Winter Garden), *Trial of the Catonsville Nine* (Lyceum and for the Center Theatre Group, Los Angeles), *Major Barbara* (Center Theatre Group, Mark Taper Forum, Los Angeles), *On the Town* (Imperial Theatre), *Prisoner of Second Avenue* (Eugene O'Neill Theatre), *Fidelio* (Dallas Civic Opera)—1971; *Night Watch* (Morosco Theatre), *Old Times* (Center Theatre Group, Mark Taper Forum, Los Angeles), *Dream on Monkey Mountain* (Kammerspiele Theatre, Munich, Germany), *Applause* (Her Majesty's Theatre, London), *The Creation of the World and Other Matters* (Shubert Theatre), *Lucia di Lammermoor* (Dallas Civic Opera), *The Great God Brown* (Lyceum Theatre),

Don Juan (Lyceum Theatre), *The Sunshine Boys* (Broadhurst Theatre)—1972; *A Little Night Music* (Shubert Theatre), *The Orphan* (Public Theatre and the Anspacher Theatre), *Forget-Me-Not Lane* (Center Theatre Group, Los Angeles), *The Good Doctor* (Eugene O'Neill Theatre), *Andre Chenier* (Dallas Civic Opera)—1973; *Saint Joan* (Center Theatre Group, Ahmanson Theatre, Los Angeles), *Candide* (Broadway Theatre), *The Pearl Fishers* (Miami Opera Guild, Florida), *The Charlatan* (Center Theatre Group, Mark Taper Forum, Los Angeles)—1974; *A Little Night Music* (London), *The Wiz, A Chorus Line*—1975; *Pacific Overtures*—1976; *Romeo and Juliet* (London Ballet Festival)—1977; *Ballroom*—1978; *They're Playing Our Song* (London)—1979; *42nd Street*—1980; *Dreamgirls, Children of a Lesser God* (London)—1981; *Merlin* (Mark Hellinger Theatre), *Brighton Beach Memoirs* (Alvin Theatre), *Private Lives* (Lunt-Fontanne Theatre)—1983; *The Real Thing* (Plymouth Theatre), *Open Admissions* (The Music Box)—1984; *Biloxi Blues* (Ahmanson Theatre), *The Odd Couple, Jerry's Girls*—1985; *Broadway Bound* (Broadhurst Theatre)—1986; *A Month of Sundays, The Knife* (NYSF), *Teddy and Alice* (Minskoff Theatre)—1987; *Rumors, Ziegfeld* (London)—1988; *Welcome to the Club*—1989.

Musser began her lighting design career after attending the Yale School of Drama and designed for the José Limon Dance Company, as well as other companies in New York. This work led into designing plays in 1956, when she was hired by director José Quintero to design lights for the premiere of *Long Day's Journey into Night*. Following this early success, she formed relationships with several performing groups: the American Shakespeare Festival, for which she designed approximately twenty-nine productions between 1958 and 1967; the Phoenix Theatre, for which she designed six productions between 1957 and 1960; and the National Repertory Theatre, for which she lit sixteen productions between 1961 and 1968. Since, she has worked on more than one-hundred productions and provided the lighting for such Broadway shows as *J. B.* (1958), *Mame* (1966), *A Delicate Balance* (1966), and *Prisoner of Second Avenue* (1971). Her most famous recent achievements were, perhaps, her collaborations with set designer Robin Wagner,* costume designer Theoni Aldredge,* and the late director Michael Bennett on such musicals as *Ballroom* (1978), *Dreamgirls* (1981), and *A Chorus Line* (1975). For the latter, she introduced the computer-controlled memory board to Broadway. Musser's approach to lighting design emphasizes that the designer should have a point of view to the show, use only the necessary instruments, and collaborate with the other artists.

Awards: Musser won Tony Awards for her lighting of *Follies* (1971), *A Chorus Line* (1975), and *Dreamgirls* (1981).

Further Reading: "Designers at Work." *Theatre Crafts* May 1987: 95; Sommers, Michael. "Designers on Design: Tharon Musser, A Leading Light of the Great White Way." *Theatre Crafts* October 1989: 42 + .

Kurt Lancaster

N

Napier, John. Set designer (b. 1944, England). Napier trained as a sculptor at Hornsey College of Art and received his theatre training under designer Ralph Koltai at London's Central School. Subsequently, he applied this training to productions for many British companies, including the Royal Shakespeare Company. He is responsible for designing many of its significant productions, by both Shakespeare and contemporary authors. Notable ones include *Twelfth Night* (1978), *Equus* (1973), *Nicholas Nickleby* (1980), *Cats* (1981), and *Les Misérables* (1987). His designs for *Nicholas Nickleby*, *Cats*, and *Les Misérables* won Tony Awards for "Best Set Design." His significant play designs include *The Ruling Class* and Edward Bond's *Lear* at the Royal Court Theatre. His current style of design rejects pictorial realism and replaces it with scenic environments that rely heavily on technology and require rearrangement of auditorium and stage space. For example, his design for *Cats* was a sculpted arrangement of junkyard debris that extended throughout the auditorium and was transformed into magnificent permutations through rising platforms, lighting, and fog effects. His set design for *Starlight Express* (1989), also indicative of this style, was a series of mobile ramps, platforms, and bridges on which the performers roller-skated with breathtaking speed and timing. Recently, he designed the London and Broadway productions of *Miss Saigon* (1989, 1990), employing such technical spectacle as a flying helicopter and a giant statute of Ho Chi Min.

Thomas J. Mikotowicz

Neher, Caspar. Designer and librettist (b. April 11, 1897, Augsburg, Germany; d. June 30, 1962, Vienna, Austria). Theatrical productions include *Katchen von Heilbronn, In the Jungle of Cities*—1923; *Life of Edward II, In the Jungle, Katalaunische Schlacht*—1924; *Coriolanus, Chalk Circle, You Never Can Tell*—1925; *Lysistrata, Baal, Man Equals Man, Lulu, Hamlet*—1926; *The Little Mahagonny, Die Wupper, Palestrina*—1927; *Man Equals Man, Kalkutta 4 Mai,*

The Threepenny Opera, Carmen, Die Petroleuminseln, Von Teufel geholt, Danton's Death—1928; *Woyzeck, Giftgas uber Berlin, Pioniere in Ingolstadt, Moritat, Moschopoulos, Sganarelle, Happy End, Flieg roter Adler von Tirol, King John, What Price Glory?*—1929; *The Rise and Fall of the City of Mahagonny, The Front Page, Draw the Fires*—1930; *The Threepenny Opera* (film version with costumes by Neher), *Man Equals Man, From the House of the Dead, Macbeth*—1931; *Die Burgschaft, Un Ballo in Maschera, The Rise and Fall of the City of Mahagonny, Oliver Cromwell's Sendung*—1932; *Silver Lake, The Seven Deadly Sins, The Flying Dutchman, Schinderhannes*—1933; *Tannhauser, Land in der Dammerung*—1934; *Der Gunstling, Zauber-geige, Die Fledermaus*—1935; *Carmen, Datterich*—1936; *Macbeth, Coriolanus, Carmen, Struensee, Gregor und Heinrich*—1937; *The Tempest, Macbeth, Der Untergang Karthagos*—1938; *Die Burger von Calais, Othello, Twelfth Night*—1939; *King Lear, A Midsummer Night's Dream, Richard II, La Traviata*—1940; *Johanna Balk, Pfarr Pedr*—1941; *Carmina Burana*—1942; *Fidelio*—1945; *Mother Courage and Her Children, The Devil's General*—1946; *Fear and Misery of the Third Reich, Rigoletto, Peter Grimes, Orfeo, Danton's Death, Antigone*—1947; *Antigone, Parsifal, King Lear, Orpheus, Carmen, The Marriage of Figaro*—1948; *Faust, Parts I and II, The Threepenny Opera, The Magic Flute, Puntila, Un Ballo in Maschera*—1949; *The Mother, Puntila, Richard II, The Tutor, Don Giovanni*—1950; *The Mother, Freischutz, The Cocktail Party, Woyzeck, The Condemnation of Lucullus, Egmont, Puntila*—1951; *Woyzeck, La Forza del Destino, Urfaust, Lulu, Jedermann, Macbeth*—1952; *The Trial, Woyzeck, The Rose Tattoo*—1953; *The Good Person of Setzuan, The Dark Is Light Enough, The Lady's Not for Burning, Julius Caesar, The Power and the Glory, Eroffnung des indischen Zeitalters*—1955; *The Threepenny Opera, Danton's Death, Un Ballo in Maschera*—1956; *Galileo, Jeptha, Woyzeck, Leonce und Lena*—1957; *Macbeth, Woyzeck, Saint Joan of the Stockyards, Julietta*—1959.

Neher, probably the most prolific scene designer in Germany after World War I, is mostly remembered today for his evocative designs for several of the original productions of the plays of Bertolt Brecht. Their long relationship began in 1917, while Neher was recovering from injuries suffered during World War I. Their collaborations began with illustrations for early, unproduced versions of Brecht's *Baal* in 1919 and continued through numerous productions (and several versions of some of the plays) of *In the Jungle of Cities* (1923), *Life of Edward II* (1924), *Baal* (1926), *Man Equals Man* (1926), *The Threepenny Opera* (1928), *Happy End* (1929), *Mother Courage and Her Children* (1946), *Puntila* (1949), *The Mother* (1950), *The Good Woman of Setzuan* (1955), and G. W. Pabst's film version of *The Threepenny Opera* (1931). Neher's stark and primitive designs owe much to the influence of the cabaret and speakeasy environment of Berlin between the wars, and, aside from his work with Brecht, he designed productions for directors Max Reinhardt and Erwin Piscator and composor Kurt Weill. His work displayed an impressive diversity in an array of designs for international plays from both the classical and contemporary canon, and some of his finest creations were for operatic works, especially those by Mozart.

Further Reading: Cushing, Mary Watking. "Caspar Neher." *Opera News* February 1959: 13+; Melchinger, Siegfried. "Neher and Brecht." *The Drama Review* Winter 1968: 134–45; Willett, John. *Caspar Neher: Brecht's Designer.* London: Methuen, 1986.

James Fisher

Nelson, Richard. Lighting designer (b. 1938, Flushing, NY). Theatrical productions include *Hamlet of Stepney Green*—1958; *Lysistrata, Curtains Up!, The Drunkard, Mardi Gras!, Scaramouche, Dreams . . . , The Redemptor, What Did You Say "What" For?, Ezio, Paris, The Girls in 509, Separate Tables, Say, Darling, Speaking of Murder, Red Letter Day, The Tunnel of Love, Vincent, Guitar, Time of Vengeance, Marching Song*—1959; *The Geranium Hat, Oh, Kay!, The Idiot, Man and Superman, Emmanuel, Nat Turner*—1960; *Montserrat, Five Posts in the Marketplace, Hobo, The Pleasure of His Company, A Raisin in the Sun, The Biggest Thief in Town, See How They Run, The Interpreter, Two Queens of Love and Beauty, A Man Around the House, A Whiff of Melancholy, The Fantastics, The Beauty Part, Not While I'm Eating*—1961; *Mummers and Men, The Storm, Yankee Doodle Comes to London*—1962; *King Lear, The Firebugs, The Lady's Not For Burning*—1963; *La Voix Humaine, Death of a Salesman, Shadow of Heroes, A Midsummer Night's Dream, Twelfth Night, Man and Superman, Ah, Wilderness!*—1964; *The Conquest of Everest, The Sandbox, Passion, Poison and Putrefaction, The Rooming House, The Bald Soprano, Hamlet, Kiss Me, Kate, Bye Bye Birdie, Peer Gynt, The Importance of Being Earnest, Julius Caesar, Long Day's Journey into Night, Ah, Wilderness!, The Tinder Box*—1965; *The Cherry Orchard, Heartbreak House, Galileo, The Caucasian Chalk Circle, Beclch*—1966; *The Time of Your Life, U.S.A., Tartuffe, The Glass Menagerie, The Flies*—1967; *The Sea Gull, This Was Burlesque*—1968; *The King of Spain, George M!, The Student Prince, Mame, Uncle Vanya, Crimes of Passion, The Life and Times of Sigmund Freud, Deafman Glance*—1969; *Watercolor, Criss-Crossing, The Fisherman and His Wife, Macbeth*—1970; *All Over* (Martin Beck Theatre), *Six, Any Resemblance to Persons Living or Dead, Drat!*—1971; *The Sign in Sidney Brustein's Window* (Longacre Theatre), *The Real Inspector Hound, After Magritte, Anna K., The Mother of Us All*—1972; *All Over, The Tavern, Jacques Brel Is Alive and Living in Paris, That Championship Season, Three Men on a Horse*—1973; *A Family and a Fortune, The Seagull, The Skin of Our Teeth, The Magic Show* (Cort Theatre), *Hamlet, A Grave Undertaking*—1974; *Waltz of the Toreadors, A Doll's House, The Taking of Miss Janie, Finn Mackool, The Grand Distraction*—1975; *Zalmen, or the Madness of God* (Lyceum Theatre), *Every Night When the Sun Goes Down, So Long, 174th Street* (Harkness Theatre), *Showboat*—1976; *The Trip Back Down* (Longacre Theatre), *Lily* (Lincoln Center), *Finian's Rainbow, 3 Wilder Plays*—1977; *Much Ado About Nothing, Annie Get Your Gun, End of the War*—1978; *Heartbreak House, Murder at the Howard Johnson's* (John Golden Theatre), *The Price* (the Playhouse Theatre), *The Interview, King of Schnorrers* (The Playhouse Theatre), *Holeville*—1979; *The Lady from Dubuque*

(Morosco Theatre), *Changes, Censored Scenes from King Kong* (Princess Theatre), *Mornings at Seven* (Lyceum Theatre), *Onward, Victoria* (Martin Beck)—1980; *Beyond Therapy, Sarah in America, The Dance of Death, The Supporting Cast* (Biltmore Theatre), *Henry IV, Part One, Oh Brother!* (ANTA Theatre), *Another Part of the Forest, Two Gentlemen of Verona*—1981; *Beside the Seaside, Antigone, Savages, Solomon's Child* (Helen Hayes Theatre), *The Misunderstanding, Present Laughter* (Circle in the Square), *The Death of Von Richthofen as Witnessed from Earth, Sweet Prince, Knickerbocker Follies, The Price of Genius* (Lamb's Theatre), *A Little Family Business* (Martin Beck Theatre)—1982; *The Misanthrope* (Circle in the Square), *Good Sports, The Caine Mutiny Court Martial* (Circle in the Square), *Five, Six, Seven, Eight . . . Dance!* (Radio City Music Hall), *The Corn Is Green, A Mad World, My Masters, Romeo and Juliet, The Tap Dance Kid* (Broadhurst Theatre)—1983; *Serenading Louie, The Tap Dance Kid* (Minskoff Theatre), *Awake and Sing!* (Circle in the Square), *Sunday in the Park with George* (Booth Theatre), *Pump Boys and Dinettes, Danny and the Deep Blue Sea, Oliver, Oliver, Personals, Total Eclipse, Raggedy Ann*—1984; *Harrigan 'n' Hart* (Longacre Theatre), *Peccadillo, Arms and the Man* (Circle in the Square), *Measure for Measure, Oliver, Oliver, Personals*—1985; *Miami, Loot* (Music Box Theatre), *Precious Sons* (Longacre Theatre), *Long Day's Journey into Night* (Broadhurst Theatre), *The Boy's in Autumn* (Circle in the Square), *You Never Can Tell* (Circle in the Square), *Brownstone*—1986; *Hunting Cockroaches* (Manhattan Theatre Club), *Blithe Spirit* (Neil Simon Theatre), *Sleight of Hand* (Cort Theatre), *Beautiful Bodies, Into The Woods* (Martin Beck Theatre)—1987; *Juan Darien* (St. Clement's Church), *Mail* (Music Box Theatre), *Night of the Iguana* (Circle in the Square), *Cafe Crown*—1988.

Nelson's prolific career began almost immediately after his graduation in 1956 from the High School of Performing Arts in New York City. In 1958, he designed his first off-Broadway production, the musical *Hamlet of Stepney Green*. Since, he has designed scores of productions in that venue, including *The Real Inspector Hound* (1972), *Serenading Louie* (1984), and *Hunting Cockroaches* (1987).

In 1963, Nelson became the production manager and technical director for the Seattle Repertory Theatre, and his lighting design for *King Lear* "christened" the new theatre. He continued to work with the company until 1982 and designed many of their shows, as well as shows for other theatres on a free-lance basis. His productions include *Julius Caesar* (1965), *Waltz of the Toreadors* (1975), and *The Dance of Death* (1981). While in Washington, he and two associates founded the Port Townsend Festival Theatre in 1965. During the 1960s, he collaborated with experimental director André Gregory, first in Philadelphia at the Theatre of the Living Arts in 1966 and then in Los Angeles at the Inner-City Cultural Center in 1967. He and Gregory collaborated on *Beclch* (1966), *U.S.A.* (1967), and *The Flies* (1967).

His first Broadway production was *The Caucasian Chalk Circle* in 1966. Since then, his lighting designs have added to the success of many Broadway shows, including such famous productions as *The Sign in Sidney Brustein's Window*

(1972), *The Magic Show* (1974), *The Price* (1979), *Mornings at Seven* (1980), and *The Tap Dance Kid* (1983). His award-winning lighting for Stephen Sondheim's *Sunday in the Park with George* (1984) truly enhanced the Seurat-styled setting, painted in impressionistic dots, and his lighting scheme for Sondheim's *Into the Woods* (1987) created appropriately lit scenes to convey the storybook details and character of the script.

In addition, Nelson has created lighting plans for productions by many major dance companies. Among them are performance events by the Martha Graham Company, the Laura Dean Dancers, and the Alvin Ailey American Dance Company. His other activities include designing the lighting for many industrials and exhibits. In 1988, he accepted a position at the University of Michigan at Ann Arbor, where he currently serves as associate professor of theatre.

Awards: Nelson won the Drama Logue and the Drama Desk awards for lighting design for *Mornings at Seven* in 1980. In 1982, for the production of *The Death of Von Richthofen as Witnessed from Earth*, he was given the Drama Desk and Maharam awards for lighting design. Two years later, he received the Tony, Drama Desk, and Maharam awards in lighting design for *Sunday in the Park with George* (1984). In the same year, he received nominations for the Drama Critics' Circle Award in lighting for *Serenading Louie*, *The Tap Dance Kid*, and *Sunday in the Park with George*. In 1988, he was nominated for both the Tony and Drama Desk awards for his lighting for *Into the Woods*.

Further Reading: "Designers at Work." *Theatre Crafts* May 1987: 24; "*Sunday in the Park with George*: An Artist's Collaboration Brings Seurat to Broadway." *Theatre Crafts* August/September 1984; "Traveling History of Film." *Lighting Dimensions* July/August 1986.

Penny L. Remsen

Nikolais, Alwin. Choreographer and designer (b. 1912, Southington, CT). Known mostly for his nonrealistic and nonlinear dance choreography, Nikolais incorporates symbolic set designs into his dance pieces. From 1939 to 1942, he worked as the director of the Nikolais School of Dance in Hartford, Connecticut. He also taught intermittently at the University of Hartford from 1940 to 1948. During this time period, he assisted Hanya Holm in New York City, and in 1953, he formed the Nikolais Dance Theatre. In 1989, he and Murray Louis merged their respective companies into Nikolais and Louis Dance. In his works, some of which are still popular today, Nikolais incorporates abstract color, light, motion, and sound into what has been described as kaleidoscopic designs. In *Tensile Involvement* (1953), dancers in different positions on the stage manipulated elastic bands into geometric shapes that moved as a solid object. In *Crucible* (1985), a large mirror-table sat on the stage floor at such an angle that the dancers' bodies were hidden from audience view. As the musical score began with a metallic banging and thumping, the dancers' hands popped up from behind the table and created double images in the reflection that appeared as alienlike shapes. Nikolais works to create a visual effect and not emotional-psychological tensions. He has also been described as a master puppeteer. In *Intrados* (1989), two dancers are fitted into meter-length hoops attached to stilts that they manipulate by moving inside the rim, balancing on top, and swinging on the edges of the hoops, while lights cast shadows on each other. His creative use of scenography for dance and his unique talent for creating elaborate sound plots have influenced many other choreographers, as well as theatrical designers.

Kurt Lancaster

Nivinski, Ignati. Set designer and painter (b. ?, Russia, d. ?). Not much has been written about the designer Nivinski, but he was noted for his collaboration with Eugene Vakhtangov during the last year of the famous Russian director's life. His cubist and futurist painting styles lent themselves to the distorted perspective and angularity of both *Princess Turandot* and *Eric XIV* (both in 1922). The former's eastern motif was enhanced by Nivinski's yellow sun, silk banners, and sign indicating that the action was taking place in Peking. In the latter, angular streaks of lightning, bent columns, rusted gold ornaments, and numerous stairs and passageways created an expressionistic rendering of the interior world of the main character. His other designs for Vakhtangov included *Short Plays by Merimee* and *The Invisible Lady* (both in 1922).

Further Reading: Gorchakov, Nikolai. *Theater in Soviet Russia.* New York: Columbia University Press, 1957; Slonim, Marc. *Russian Theater: From the Empire to the Soviets.* New York: World, 1961.

Andrea J. Nouryeh

Noguchi, Isamu. Set designer and sculptor (b. 1904, Los Angeles, CA). Theatrical productions include Dance—*Frontier*—1935; *El Penetente*—1940; *Appalachian Spring, Herodiade, The Bells*—1944; *Dark Meadow, Cave of the Heart*—1946; *Errand into the Maze, Night Journey, The Seasons*—1947; *Diversion of Angels, Orpheus*—1948; *Judith*—1950; *Voyage*—1953; *Seraphic Dialogue*—1955; *Embattled Garden, Clytemnestra*—1958; *Acrobats of God, Alcestis*—1960; *Phaedra*—1962; *Circe*—1963; *Cortege of Eagles*—1966; Theatre—*King Lear*—1955.

Noguchi is perhaps best known for his work in dance, although he is responsible for many sculptural works of art. His first theatrical design assignment was to create masks for Yeats's *At the Hawk's Well* in 1926. In 1925, he embarked upon a lifelong collaboration with Martha Graham and designed his first theatrical set for her *Frontier* ten years later. That set became his point of departure for years of theatre work that treated dance spaces as volumes to be handled sculpturally. His simple use of hemp rope from the proscenium arch to a point on the floor, upper center stage, simultaneously penetrated the space and defined its ever-changing relationship to the dancer. His sculptural approach to space was evident throughout twenty designs that he did for Graham that included *Appalachian Spring* (1944) and *Seraphic Dialogue* (1958). Noguchi also designed for other choreographers. In 1960, he designed the dance *Alcestis*. His work with Merce Cunningham on *The Seasons* in 1947 and with Balanchine on *Orpheus* in 1946 are only two examples.

Brian R. Jones

O

O'Hearn, Robert. Designer (b. July 19, 1921, Elkhart, IN). Theatrical productions include *The Relapse*—1950; *Love's Labour's Lost, A Date with April, Kismet* (assistant designer)—1953; *Pajama Game* (assistant designer), *Festival, Othello, Henry IV, Part I, A Clerical Error* (film)—1955; *Child of Fortune, The Apple Cart, My Fair Lady* (assistant designer)—1956; *West Side Story* (assistant designer)—1958; *L'Elixir d'Amore*—1960; *As You Like It, Macbeth, Troilus and Cressida*—1961; *Die Meistersinger* (also costumes)—1962; *Aida* (also costumes)—1963; *Abraham and Cochrane, La Sylphide, Samson and Delilah*—1964; *Porgy and Bess, Kiss Me Kate, Pique Dame*—1965; *Die Frau Ohne Schattan*—1966; *Otello, Nutcracker Ballet*—1967; *La Traviata, Rosalinda*—1968; *Der Rosenkavalier, Tallis Fantasia*—1969; *Parsifal, Boris Godunov*—1970; *Bregenzer Festspiele, Porgy and Bess*—1971; *Falstaff, The Marriage of Figaro, Gianni Schicchi*—1972; *Barber of Seville, The Enchanted, The Mind with the Dirty Man*—1973; *A Midsummer Night's Dream, Coppelia, Carmen, The Pearl Fishers*—1974; *Don Pasquale, The Marriage of Figaro, Die Meistersinger*—1975; *The Girl of the Golden West, Boris Godunov, Der Rosenkavalier*—1976; *Don Quixote, Die Meistersinger*—1977; *Adriana Lecouvreur, La Boheme, Coppelia, Andrea Chenier, Der Rosenkavalier*—1978; *The Taming of the Shrew, Die Fledermaus*—1980; *Tosca, West Side Story*—1981; *Pique Dame, La Traviata*—1982; *Lucia di Lammermoor*—1984; *L'Italiana in Algeri, Porgy and Bess*—1985; *Aida, Don Giovanni*—1986.

After attending Indiana University, O'Hearn studied at the Art Student's League from 1945 to 1946. His first important works were the more than sixty productions he designed for the Brattle Theatre in Cambridge, Massachusetts, between 1948 and 1952. He designed both settings and costumes for his first Broadway production, *The Relapse*, in 1950. During the 1950s he continued to design regularly for Broadway, but he increasingly turned his attention to opera. He designed nine operas for the Central City Opera House between 1959 and

1963, as well as several productions for the American Shakespeare Festival between 1961 and 1964. O'Hearn has also designed many works for the Metropolitan Opera Association since 1966. His work since the early 1970s has been almost exclusively devoted to the opera stage, with occasional designs for ballets. He had an exhibition of his scene and costume designs at the Lincoln Center Library of Performing Arts in 1974 and currently teaches at the Studio and Forum of Stage Design in New York.

James Fisher

Oenslager, Donald. Scenic designer, theatre consultant, author, and teacher (b. March 7, 1902, Harrisburg, PA; d. June 21, 1975, Bedford, NY). Theatrical productions include *Sooner and Later, A Bit O'Love, Celeste, Morals*—1925; *The Fall of the House of Usher, Plots and Playwrights, The Patriarch*—1926; *Pinwheel, Machiavelli, Good News, Pueblo*—1927; *L'Histoire du Soldat, Anna, Brand, The New Moon*—1928; *Follow Thru, Stepping Out, Heads Up!, Fortnight*—1929; *The Searcher, Girl Crazy, Trade Winds, Overture*—1930; *You Said It, Rock Me, Julie, America's Sweetheart, The Winter's Tale, Free for All, Singin' the Blues, East Wind, The Emperor Jones*—1931; *Whistling in the Dark, Adam Had Two Sons, A Thousand Summers, The King's Coat*—1932; *Forsaking All Others, Uncle Tom's Cabin, Keeper of the Keys, Venice Preserved*—1933; *Jezebel, Salome, Sweet Bells Jangled, Lady from the Sea, Hide and Seek, Divided by Three, Dance with Your Gods, Tristan und Isolde, The Farmer Takes a Wife, Anything Goes, Gold Eagle Guy, Der Rosenkavalier, Christmas Oratorio*—1934; *Hollywood Holiday, Something Gay, The Ascending Dragon, Sweet Mystery of Life, First Lady, Tapestry in Gray, Land of the Living*—1935; *Russet Mantle, Timber House, Stage Door, Ten Million Ghosts, Sweet River: An Adaptation of Harriet Beecher Stowe's Uncle Tom's Cabin, Matrimony Pfd., Red, Hot and Blue!, Johnny Johnson, 200 Were Chosen, You Can't Take It with You*—1936; *Le Bourgeois Gentilhomme, Le Pauvre Matelot, Amelia Goes to the Ball, Miss Quis, I'd Rather Be Right, Robin Landing, Of Mice and Men, Edna His Wife, Otello, A Doll's House*—1937; *Amelia Goes to the Ball, I Am My Youth, Spring Thaw, The Circle, The Good, The Fabulous Invalid, A Woman's a Fool—To Be Clever, The Flying Ginzburgs*—1938; *The American Way, The Birds Stop Singing, Off to Buffalo, Candida, From Vienna, Skylark, The Man Who Came to Dinner, Margin for Error, I Know What I Like, Prometheus Bound, The Merchant*—1939; *Young Couple Wanted, My Dear Children, The White-Haired Boy, Beverly Hills, Out West It's Different, Retreat to Pleasure, The Old Foolishness, My Sister Eileen*—1940; *The Lady Who Came to Stay, The Doctor's Dilemma, Claudia, As You Like It, Mr. Big, Father's Day, Spring Again, Theatre, Pie in the Sky, Portrait of a Lady*—1941; *Rose Burke, Flowers of Virtue, Punch and Julia*—1942; *Pygmalion*—1945; *Born Yesterday, Three to Make Ready, On Whitman Avenue, The Abduction from the Seraglio, La Traviata, Loco, Present Laughter, The Fatal Weakness, The Temporary Mrs. Smith, Years Ago, Park Avenue, Land's End*—1946; *Washington Square, The Greatest of*

These, The Eagle Has Two Heads, Message for Margaret, Portrait in Black, Martha, Fidelio, How I Wonder, Eastward in Eden, Angel in the Wings—1947; *The Men We Marry, Tales of Hoffman, Cosi Fan Tutte, Town House, The Leading Lady, Life with Mother, Goodbye My Fancy*—1948;—Smile of the World, *At War with the Army, The Father, The Rat Race, The Velvet Glove*—1949; *The Liar, The Live Wire, Springboard to Nowhere*—1950; *Second Threshold, Peer Gynt, The Small Hours, The Beautiful Galatea, Amelia Goes to the Ball, The Constant Wife*—1951; *Paris '90, Candida, To Be Continued, La Boheme*—1952; *Comedy on the Bridge, Dido and Aeneas, Horses in Midstream, Carmen, Sabrina Fair, Escapade, Madam, Will You Walk, The Prescott Proposals*—1953; *Coriolanus, Dear Charles*—1954; *The Wooden Dish, A Roomful of Roses, Janus, A Quiet Place, Readings from the Bible by Judith Anderson*—1955; *The Ballad of Baby Doe, Major Barbara*—1956; *The Man in the Dog Suit, Four Winds, Mary Stuart, Nature's Way, A Shadow of My Enemy*—1957; *J. B., And Perhaps Happiness, The Girls in 509, The Pleasure of His Company, The Marriage Go Round*—1958; *A Majority of One, Orpheus and Eurydice, The Mikado, The Pink Jungle, The Highest Tree*—1959; *Dear Liar, Orfeo, The Prisoner*—1960; *A Far Country, A Call on Kuprin, Blood, Sweat and Stanley Poole, The Wings of the Dove, First Love*—1961; *Venus at Large, Il Ballo Delle Ingrate*—1962; *The Irregular Verb to Love, A Case of Libel*—1963; *Madama Butterfly, The Lady from Colorado, One by One*—1964; *Carmen, The Italian Lady from Algiers, Tosca*—1966; *Love in E Flat, Der Rosenkavalier, Antigone, The Merry Widow, Don Pasquale, The Masked Ball, Spofford*—1967; *Avanti! Don Carlos*—1968; *The Wrong Way to Light a Bulb*—1969; *Good News, Mikado*—1974.

Oenslager began his career by studying under George Pierce Baker at Harvard. After a year in Europe, he served as Robert Edmond Jones's* design assistant at the Provincetown Playhouse, where other artists such as Eugene O'Neill, Kenneth Macgowan, Lee Simonson,* and Jo Mielziner* also worked. Oenslager designed more than 250 Broadway shows, beginning with *A Bit O' Love* in 1925. Although his early designs for *Pinwheel* (1927) and *L'Histoire du Soldat* (1928) evidence the constructivist influence of Russian design, Oenslager did not work in any one particular style. He drew from many influences; for example, his designs for *Tristan und Isolde* (1934) and *Prometheus Bound* (1939) are reminiscent of Bel Geddes, while the style of Robert Edmond Jones and the "New Stagecraft" can be seen in his designs for *The Emperor Jones* (1931), *The Doctor's Dilemma* (1941), and *Major Barbara* (1956). Oenslager designed naturalistic scenery for such plays as *Of Mice and Men* (1937) but was probably best known for his splashy sets for musicals like *Girl Crazy* (1930), *I'd Rather Be Right* (1937), and *Anything Goes* (1934) and his stylish interiors for plays like *You Can't Take It with You* (1936), *The Leading Lady* (1948), *Life with Mother* (1948), and *Born Yesterday* (1946).

Oenslager was also involved with consulting and teaching. As a theatre consultant, he worked on many performing arts complexes, including Lincoln Center in New York, the Kennedy Center in Washington, D.C., and the Montreal

Cultural Center. In 1925, Oenslager helped found the Yale School of Drama and continued to teach there for the next forty-five years. He held a firm belief that a designer needs a strong background in the liberal arts and that designers must study the past. These beliefs are reflected in his books, *Scenery, Then and Now*, and *Stage Design: Four Centuries of Scenic Invention*. In both, he drew on his extensive archives to give both a history and a theoretical view of stage-craft. In addition, he was a mentor and inspiration to scores of talented designers, including Will Steven Armstrong,* John Conklin,* Eldon Elder,* Peter Larkin,* Santo Loquasto,* and Jean Rosenthal.*

Further Reading: By Oenslager: "Let There Be Light." *Theatre Arts Magazine* September 1947; "Let There Be Light." *Theatre Design & Technology* May 1971; Interview in Pecktal (see Bibliography); with Edward F. Kook. "Porto Theatre." *Theatre Crafts Magazine* May 1969; "Project for the Ring." *Theatre Arts Monthly* January 1927; Essays in Larson, Orville K. *Scene Design for Stage and Screen*. East Lansing, MI: Michigan University Press, 1961; *Scenery, Then and Now*. New York: Russell and Russell, 1966; *Stage Design: Four Centuries of Scenic Invention*. New York: Viking Press, 1975; *The Theatre of Donald Oenslager*. Middletown, CT: Wesleyan University Press, 1978.

Ken Kloth

Otto, Teo. Set designer (b. February 4, 1904, Remscheid, Germany; d. June 9, 1968, Frankfurt, Germany). With training from the Academy of Fine Arts in Kassel and from the theatre school at the Bauhaus, Otto's early design career began at the Proletkult Kassel in 1926, followed by positions at the Kroll Opera in Berlin in 1927 and at the Berlin State Theater, where he worked until 1931. He emigrated to Switzerland in 1933 and subsequently became involved with the Schauspielhaus in Zurich. Here he collaborated with Brecht on the first productions of *Mother Courage* (1941), and *Galileo* (1943), and *The Good Woman of Setzuan* (1943) and developed an epic style of design that would influence future designers. Emphasizing theatricalism, the exposing of the stage as part of the design, Otto's sets used realistic elements combined with painted, decorative screens, projections, and harsh or moody lighting to suggest the scene. While in Zurich, Otto designed many productions of plays by Durrenmatt and Max Frisch. Throughout the next two decades, his designs were installed in major opera houses and theatres in Europe. In New York in 1960, he designed productions of *Nabucco* and *Tristan und Isolde* for the Metropolitan Opera. While working as professor of stage design at the Academy of Fine Arts in Düsseldorf, a position he held until his death, he wrote two books on design theory: *Nie wieder* and *Meine Szene*.

Thomas J. Mikotowicz

P

Palladio, Andrea. Designer, stage machinist, and architect (b. 1518, Italy; d. 1580). Andrea di Pietro, better known as Andrea Palladio, was one of the most significant designers and architects of the Italian Renaissance theatre. His theories and style owe much to the influence of Vitruvius* (Marcus Vitruvius Pollio) and were published in Venice in 1570 under the title *Quattro libri dell' architettura*. English designer Inigo Jones* admired the Palladian style and translated the book, which had a considerable impact on architectural design in England and the rest of Europe. Palladio was a founding member of the Olympic Academy, for which he designed the Teatro Olimpico in the tradition of the Roman theatres of antiquity. Unfortunately, he did not live to see it completed, and the final work was carried out by his student, Vincenzo Scamozzi,* who altered the stage background and spurred on the development of stage scenery. The Teatro Olimpico, built into a preexisting hall, held thirteen ovoid tiers of seating surrounding a small orchestra, in front of which was a seventy-foot-long by eighteen-foot-deep stage. This was backed by a decorated facade with five openings, one at each side of the stage platform and three in the rear. Scamozzi opened the theatre with a production of *Oedipus Rex* in 1585 and added perspective street scenes made of lathe and plaster behind each of the openings to create a sense of a city. The vanishing point for each of these street scenes lined up perfectly with the center of the orchestra, and a drop curtain was added to reveal the action of the play.

James Fisher

Parigi, Alfonso. Scene designer, architect, and engineer (b. ?, Florence, Italy; d. 1656). Alfonso was the son of the famed architect, engineer, and scene designer Giulio Parigi* (1580–1635) and the grandson of Alfonso Parigi, who was an architect. Apparently Alfonso was the only one of Giulio's seven sons who followed in his father's profession. He received his training from his father, who had been a student of Buontalenti,* and succeeded him as designer for the Medici Court in 1628. He retained that position until his death in 1656, although in later years the Medici Court called upon other designers as well as Parigi. During his tenure with the Medicis, he produced designs for entertainments staged at Court weddings, celebrations, birthdays, and visits of other nobility; one of these designs was for *La Flora* (1628). Many of his entertainments included mock naval battles on the Arno River, for which special ships and artificial islands with castles were built and decorated. Alfonso's stage designs were as elaborate as those of his father, but it is clear from extant illustrations that they were less rigidly balanced symmetrically. Alfonso's use of foliage in exterior scenes was freer. Like his peers, he also used oil lamps and candelabra with reflectors to produce lighting effects by changing color and intensity. His architectural work includes the Church of San Giovanni and the facade of the Pitti Palace. It is possible that both Giulio and Alfonso were primary influences on Inigo Jones,* who visited Florence in the early 1600s.

                                                                                                    Elbin L. Cleveland

Parigi, Giulio. Set designer, theatrical architect, and stage machinist (b. 1580, Italy; d. 1635). Parigi succeeded Bernardo Buontalenti* in 1608 as architect of the Medici Court and carried on the scenic grandeur established by his teacher. Designing Court entertainments of magnificent detail and with elaborate scene-shifting machinery, Parigi designed such productions as *Il Guidizio di Parade* (1608), *Eros and Anteros* (1613), *The Liberation of Tyrrhenus* (1616), and *La Guerra d'Amore* (1616). These Court entertainments included naumachia, equestrian shows, and plays with *intermezzi*. Particularly striking are Parigi's existing sketches of *The Inferno*, with its large hellmouth replete with devil creatures lurking about. Parigi's work possibly influenced German architect Josef Furttenbach* and definitely influenced English designer Inigo Jones,* and these influences helped disseminate the Italian stage technology to other parts of Europe. In 1620, he was succeeded by his son Alfonso (d. 1656), who carried on the grand traditions of chief designer for the Medici Court.

                                                                                                    Thomas J. Mikotowicz

Pène du Bois, Raoul. Set and costume designer (b. 1913, New Orleans, LA; d. 1985). Coming from a family involved in art, Pène du Bois designed costumes for a production of *The Garrick Gaieties*, produced in the late 1920s, when he was only sixteen years old. Although he thought of himself as a painter, Pène du Bois earned a living designing various revues for the Shubert brothers and others. While in New York, he studied at the Grand Central Art School, where he developed an affinity for bold use of color. His designs graced the stages of the Ballets Russes du Monte Carlo and the New York City Ballet in such productions as *Ghost Town* (1939) and *Jeux* (1966). Pène du Bois also designed the sets and costumes for such spectacles as *Jumbo*, produced at the Hippodrome Theatre by Billy Rose. Throughout his work, which included Broadway plays, operas, ballets, ice shows, stage spectacles, and films, he tried to bring out some semblance of reality in the obviously spectacular scenes. In 1939, his black and white design for the set of *One for the Money* at the Booth Theatre in New York earned him the American School of Design Award. In this show there was an iridescent nightclub scene, in which most of the light shone upward from beneath the glass floor. Over the years, he was responsible for sets and costumes for many Broadway musicals such as *Bells Are Ringing* (1956) and *Plain and Fancy* (1955). In addition, he designed costumes for such musicals as *Music Man* (1957) and *Gypsy* (1959, 1975). His art direction for film includes *Kitty* (1945), *Bring on the Girls* (1945), and *Louisiana Purchase* (1941).

Awards: His work on Broadway earned Pène du Bois a Tony Award in 1952 for the sets and costumes for *Wonderful Town.* Also, in 1971, he received the Tony, Drama Desk, and Joseph Maharam awards for *No, No, Nanette.*

Further Reading: Pecktal (see Bibliography).

Kurt Lancaster

Peruzzi, Baldassare. Set designer, architect, and painter (b. 1481, Italy; d. 1537). Architect of the Farnese Palace and a painter of importance in his day, Peruzzi did his most famous theatrical design for *La Calandria* (1518) by Cardinal Bibiena, which was noted for its exceptional ornamentation, detail, and striking perspective views. It is credited with reviving the art of scenic representation in the drama. Peruzzi also designed settings for a performance given in honor of Giulio de'Medici's arrival in Rome. Peruzzi studied with Piero dal Borgo, who built up generalized rules for perspective drawing, and was also a student of Vitruvius. As he was the teacher of Sebastiano Serlio,* Peruzzi's theories and settings were probably the basis of Serlio's rules for designing tragic, comic, and pastoral stage scenery. Certainly, Serlio used many drawings and notes prepared by Peruzzi on the ten books of Vitruvius, and Serlio's emphasis on architecture and perspective is easily traced back to Peruzzi's designs.

Jonet Buchanan

Peters, Charles Rollo, III. Designer and actor (b. September 25, 1892, Paris, France; d. January 21, 1967). Theatrical productions (Peters appeared as an actor in all of these and designed those indicated) include *Salome*—1918; *The Bonds of Interest* (designer), *John Ferguson* (designer), *The Faithful*—1919; *Mixed Marriage*—1920; *The Varying Shore*—1921; *Romeo and Juliet* (designer), *Pelleas and Melisande*—1923; *Antony and Cleopatra* (designer), *The Depths*—1924; *The Depths, Stolen Fruit*—1925; *Trelawny of the 'Wells', Out of the Sea*—1927; *Diplomacy, The Age of Innocence*—1928; *The Rivals, Café*—1930; *The Streets of New York* (designer), *The Pillars of Society* (designer), *The Bride the Sun Shines On* (designer)—1931; *Peter Ibbetson*—1932; *Autumn Crocus, The Shining Hour, Home Chat*—1934; *The Taming of the Shrew, Within the Gates*—1935.

Born in Paris, Peters was raised in the United States before going to Europe to study art. Upon completing his studies, he returned to America and worked as a scene designer and actor with the Washington Square Players. Shortly thereafter, he became a founding member of the prestigious Theatre Guild, for which he designed several productions with an inventory of modest materials. Peters's sets were simple and suggestive in the manner of the "New Stagecraft" that was influencing scores of American designers. He designed the first Guild production, *The Bonds of Interest* (1919), and played the role of Leander. Immediately after, he designed and played the role of Andrew in *John Ferguson*, which was the second Guild production and its first critical and box office success. Later, he worked closely with actress Jane Cowl (1884–1950), designed several of her shows, and often played opposite her in such productions as *Romeo and Juliet* (1923).

James Fisher

Picasso, Pablo. Painter, sculptor, and set and costume designer (b. October 25, 1881, Málaga, Spain; d. April 8, 1973, Mougins, France). Possibly the world's most significant modernist artist, Picasso delved into the realm of theatre on occasion. A chief proponent of the cubist movement, he cross-fertilized painting and theatre and produced some of the most unique designs for ballet and drama while he was working primarily in France. Working with Diaghilev's Ballets Russes, Picasso created the set and costumes for *Parade* (1917), for which he created a nonrepresentational act curtain and matched the design to the two cubist costumes for the Managers. Other creations for the Ballets Russes include the designs for *Le Tricorne* (1919), *Pulcinella* (1920), *Cuadro Flamenco* (1921), and *Mecure* (1924). In the designs for the sets and costumes for all of these ballets, he was influenced by his art. This tendency also was foremost in his designs for Cocteau's drama *Antigone* (1922) and for Stravinsky's opera *Oedipus Rex* (1947). Throughout the 1950s and 1960s, Picasso continued to provide painted curtains for several ballets in Paris and simple scenery for plays, including Honneger's drama *Icare* (1962). In addition to his design activities, he authored two plays: *Desire Caught by the Tale* (1941) and *The Four Little Girls* (1965).

Thomas J. Mikotowicz

Pilbrow, Richard. Lighting designer, producer, and consultant (b. 1933, London, England). Pilbrow started a career in the theatre as a stage manager but soon became involved in lighting design when he was commissioned for *Arlecchino* in 1957 at the Lyric Hammersmith Theatre. Since, he has maintained a prolific career in England and the United States and designed the lighting for such productions as *Any Other Business* (1958), *Danton's Death* (1959), *Miss Julie* (1960), *Richard III* (1961), *Peer Gynt* (1962), *Baal* (1963), *She Loves Me* (1964), *Love for Love* (1965), *The Prime of Miss Jean Brodie* (1966), *Wise Child* (1967), *A Streetcar Named Desire* (1974), *Annie* (1978), *Windy City* (1982), and *Singin' in the Rain* (1983). In 1957, Pilbrow founded Theatre Projects, a consulting organization. Over the years, Theatre Projects introduced the latest concepts and technologies to theatres, including innovations in architecture, theatre technology, and management. These theatres include the Barbicon of the

Royal Shakespeare Company, Covent Garden, the Performing Arts Center in Calgary, Canada, and the Portland, Oregon, Performing Arts Center.

Always maintaining his design career, Pilbrow created lighting plans for Lord Lawrence Olivier's productions at the National Theatre, on some of which he collaborated with famous scenographer Josef Svoboda.* These were *The Storm* (1966) and *The Three Sisters* (1967). In New York, Pilbrow was the first British national to design an original Broadway musical. The show was *Zorba* (1968), directed by Harold Prince and designed by Boris Aronson* at the Imperial Theatre. His other New York credits include *Rosencrantz and Guildenstern Are Dead* (1967), *The Rothchilds* (1970), and *Shelter* (1973). His technological abilities were put to use on other productions when he was asked to design projections for *A Funny Thing Happened on the Way to the Forum* and *Golden Boy* on Broadway. As a result of his expertise, he was the first British lighting designer admitted to New York's United Scenic Artists' Union, Local 829. In 1970, using his technological knowledge acquired from years of designing, he authored the book *Stage Lighting*, which has become a standard text at a large number of colleges and universities.

As producer, Pilbrow collaborated in 1965 with the Berliner Ensemble to present *The Resistible Rise of Arturo Ui*, *Coriolanus*, *The Threepenny Opera*, and *The Days of the Commune*, all at the Old Vic. Since the 1970s, in partnership with Harold Prince, Pilbrow produced more than thirty West End productions, including *Fiddler on the Roof*, *Cabaret*, and *A Little Night Music*. He brought many popular and award-winning Broadway plays to London, such as *I'm Not Rappaport* in 1986. In film, he produced the feature *Swallows and Amazons* (1973) and, in television, the seventeen-part series "All You Need Is Love: The Story of Popular Music" for the BBC and PBS.

Awards: In 1982, Pilbrow received a lifetime achievement award from USITT for his many years of contributions to the art of lighting.

Further Reading: By Pilbrow: *Stage Lighting*, 2d ed. New York: Drama Book Specialists, 1979.

Penny L. Remsen

Pitkin, William. Set, lighting, and costume designer (b. 1925, Omaha, NE). After attending the Universidad Nacional de Mexico and the University of Texas and serving with the United States Air Force, Pitkin traveled to Paris to study design with Christian Bérard and to study at the Ecole Paul Colin. After returning to the United States, he became involved in theatre and designed the sets for his first show, *Thunder Rock* (1947), at the Maverick Theatre in Woodstock, New York. Subsequently, in 1949 he finished his schooling at Bard College in upstate New York, where he received his B.A. degree. Immediately following, he went to Italy in 1950 and designed *Born Yesterday* and *Napoleon* for the Theatre Guild in Rome. Since, he has designed for the New York stage, as well as regionally. His most significant work includes the design for *The Threepenny Opera* at the Theatre de Lys in 1954 and *The Impossible Years* at the Playhouse in 1965. Pitkin's designs have also been featured in Shakespearean productions such as *Othello* (1970) for the National Shakespeare Company and *The Taming of the Shrew* for the American Shakespeare Festival in Stamford, Connecticut. In ballet design, he has created designs for such works as *Coppelia* (1968) for American Ballet Theatre, *Romeo and Juliet* (1976) for the San Francisco Ballet, and *The Nutcracker* (1984) for the Lone Star Ballet. Other work included such operas as *Madame Butterfly* for the Washington Opera Society and *The Wizard of Oz* for the Children's Theatre and Nicolo Marionettes. In television, Pitkin's designs earned him an Emmy Award for costumes for the PBS production of *Romeo and Juliet* (1978). He also served as a lecturer in scene design at the University of Texas from 1978 to 1981.

Kurt Lancaster

Planché, James Robinson. Playwright, designer, and musician (b. 1795, England; d. 1880). Planché is best known as the author of over 150 plays and opera librettos, many of which were written for Madame Vestris at the Olympic Theatre and later influenced the works of Gilbert and Sullivan. Planché's first play, however, *The Vampire*, was produced in 1818 and was popular for its scenic innovation of the "vampire trap," which provided the means for quick entrances and exits of the supernatural antihero. As one of the first designers to do so, he applied his interests in historically accurate detail to all of the costumes for Charles Kemble's Covent Garden production of Shakespeare's *King John* (1823). Although the actors believed that the audience would not accept the attempt at historical re-creation, the production was lauded. The following year, he designed historically accurate costumes and scenery for Kemble's successful production of *Henry IV, Part I*. Planché continued advocating accuracy in design with such later productions as Webster's *Taming of the Shrew* (1844) and Charles Kean's archaeologically accurate *A Midsummer Night's Dream* (1856). His membership as a fellow in the Society of Antiquaries led to his involvement in the British Archaeological Association, and he was invited to join the College of Heralds. He wrote several publications on historical costuming to make production research easier: *Costumes of Shakespeare's King Henry IV, Parts 1 and 2* (1824); *The History of British Costume* (1834); and *A Cyclopedia of Costume or Dictionary of Dress* (1876–1879).

Thomas J. Mikotowicz

Poelzig, Hans. Theatrical architect (b. 1839, Germany; d. 1936). When director Max Reinhardt decided to convert the Zirkus Schumann into the Grosses Schauspielhaus in Berlin, he was persuaded to commission one of Germany's outstanding new architects, Hans Poelzig. The design that Poelzig created attempted to unify the auditorium and the stage while breaking away from the reliance on the proscenium arch. The theatre, which housed over three thousand spectators, was made of a U-shaped forestage, with banks of steps and a movable wall that separated it from a huge, domed cyclorama. The "cyc" was lit from the flies by banks of spotlights. Along the walls of the auditorium and in concentric circles inside the theatre's dome, Poelzig created a light-tipped, stalactite motif reminiscent of Moorish arches. Although Kenneth Macgowan felt the auditorium was misdesigned and horrible, Poelzig's theatre influenced other architects to create designs for theatrical spaces that were distinct departures from the traditional proscenium stage. In addition to designing the theatre, Poelzig did several large-scale scenic designs for opera. Among them were *Don Giovanni*, *Gilles und Jeanne*, and *King Lear*.

Andrea J. Nouryeh

Polidori, Gianni. Set designer, art director, and painter (b. November 7, 1923, Rome, Italy). During the 1940s, Polidori received training in design in three disciplines: painting, theatre, and film. He studied painting with the famous artists Renato Guttuso, Vittorio Grassi, and Corrado Cagli and studied stage design from 1945 to 1946 at the Accademia di Belle Arti, located in Rome. Immediately afterward, he enrolled in the Centro Sperimentale di Cinematografia, also in Rome, and completed the film design program in 1948. In 1959, Polidori extended his training by working in television.

Polidori's stage designs have spanned five decades and include drama, opera, and ballet, and he has variously functioned as set, lighting, and costume designer. His first professional design was for Buchner's *Woyzeck* (1946). This production was followed by *L'Uomo e il fucile* (1947) and Arthur Miller's *All My Sons* (Italy; 1947). In 1950, he married Misa D'Andrea, a costumer with whom he had worked on Ibsen's *The Master Builder* and *Enemy of the People* (Italy; both 1950). In fact, Polidori has designed many American and British plays that were produced in Italy. Among them are Arthur Miller's *Death of a Salesman* (1951), Eugene O'Neill's *The Iceman Cometh* (1965), John Osborne's *Look Back in Anger* (1957), Thornton Wilder's *Our Town* (1975), and Ben Hecht and Charles McArthur's *The Front Page* (1988). He has also designed works for contemporary Italian playwrights, including *Affabulazione* (1986) by Pier Paolo Pasolini, *Two Farces* (1988) by Dario Fo, and *Il Vizio Assurdo* (1974) by Diego Fabbri, the last produced at the Teatro Verdi in Padua. Adept at designing for the classical theatre, Polidori has applied his craft to such works as Moliere's *The Bourgeois Gentleman* (1953), Shakespeare's *Measure for Measure* (1957), and Goldsmith's *She Stoops to Conquer* (1981). Also, he has designed the ballets *Il Cappello a tre punte* and *Scarlattiana* (1954), both choreographed by T. Wallmann. In film, Polidori has designed for major international film directors.

Polidori established himself in the international film community by designing Luchino Visconti's* neorealistic film *Belissima* (1952) and sustained his career with designs for Alberto Lattuada's production of Gogol's *Il Cappotto* (1953) and Michelangelo Antonioni's *I vinti* (1953), *La Signora senza Camelie* (1953), and *Le Amiche* (1955). Polidori continued his designs for film into the 1960s with such works as *Il mondo di notte 2* (1960) and *Liola* (1963) and into the 1970s with *La proprieta' non e' piu' un furto* (1971) and Sergio Leone's "spaghetti western,'' *Il mio nome e' nessuno* (released in the United States as *My Name Is Nobody* and starring Henry Fonda, 1973).

Polidori's career includes other activities such as consulting, painting, and teaching. As a consultant, he has advised on the laboratory theatre at the Nazionale d'Arte Drammatica Art in Rome, the Carlo Felice Theatre in Genoa, and the Teatro Cavour in Imperia. As a painter, his paintings have been shown at major galleries, primarily in Italy. As a teacher, he has instructed students in scenography at the Centro Sperimentale di Cinematographia in Rome in 1967–1968 and has served as associate professor of scenography at the Universitá degli Studi in Bologna from 1971 to 1986. In 1983, he and Emmanuele Luzzati* founded the Polytechnico 'G. Byron' Scuola di Communicazione visiva e scenografia in Genoa.

Further Reading: Barsacq, Léon. *Décor de Film.* Paris, 1970; Hainaux (see Bibliography); Stein, Elliot, ed. *Caligari's Cabinet and Other Grand Illusions: A History of Film Design.* Boston: New York Graphic Society, 1970.

Thomas J. Mikotowicz

Ponnelle, Jean-Pierre. Designer and director (b. February 19, 1932, Paris, France). Considered by many to be one of the preeminent opera designers in the world, Ponnelle studied art under Fedinand Léger and first designed with a production of Henze's opera *Boulevarde Solitude* in 1952. For the next ten years, he continued opera design at major theatres in Europe and America. In 1962, Ponnelle combined designing with directing in his production of *Tristan und Isolde* in Düsseldorf. This led to many subsequent successful productions and a double career, similar to that of Franco Zefferelli.* Some memorable productions include *Barbiere di Siviglia* (1968) and *Le Nozze di Figaro* (1976), both of which he created in Salzburg; *Pelleas and Melisande* (1973), produced in Munich; and *La Cenerentola* (1969) and *Lear* (1981), both directed and designed in San Francisco.

Thomas J. Mikotowicz

Pons, Helene (née Weinncheff). Costume designer, dressmaker, and teacher (b. ?, Tiflis, Russia; d. 1990). Pons was responsible for both the design and execution of costumes for the Broadway stage for more than forty years. As a dressmaker, she has constructed the clothes for more than one thousand shows, including *Kiss Me Kate* (1954), *My Fair Lady* (1956), *Jamaica* (1957), and *Camelot* (1960), as well as fourteen Theater Guild productions, with stars such as Nazimova, Alfred Lunt, and Lynn Fontanne. As a designer in her own right, she has created costumes for such landmark productions as *Our Town* (1938), *A View from the Bridge* (1955), *The Diary of Anne Frank* (1955), and *The Skin of Our Teeth* (1955). In addition, Pons has created costumes for the Metropolitan Opera productions of *Faust*, *Carmen*, *Aida*, and *La Boheme*. Pons began making costumes in her New York apartment and eventually developed the business into one of the leading theatrical costume houses, the Pons Studio. Her studio also turned out masks, helmets, armor, jeweled ornaments, and stylized wigs for a multitude of productions. Never keeping a stock of standard costumes to rent out to small productions or college theatres, Pons insisted that everything be specially designed for a particular show or person. This personalized touch, along with a keen instinct for what will and will not work onstage, was the hallmark of Pons's technique. In the opening scene of *My Fair Lady*, which had costumes designed by Cecil Beaton,* Pons created "brocade" capes for a number of aristocratic characters by using white tufted bedspreads she had purchased at Macy's. Pons knew that, from a distance, the material, dyed and trimmed, would suggest the stuffiness of brocade much better than the original article. Similarly, Pons used dog collars to double as scabbards in *Camelot*. She left New York in the late 1960s to live in Italy, where she worked with oils and silk screen. Before her death, she was still creating costumes, had three shows in New York, and wrote a children's book.

Howard Gutner

Popova, Liubov Sergeevna. Set designer, painter, and textile designer (b. April 24, 1889, outskirts of Moscow, Russia; d. May 25, 1924, Moscow, Russia). Throughout the first decades of the twentieth century, Popova studied at the private studios of Konstantin Yuon and Stanislav Zhukovsky in Moscow and traveled to ancient cities in Russia, France, and Italy to study art and architecture. From 1914 to 1916, she used a nonobjective style for her paintings, and also her style began to take on a three-dimensional quality. Consequently, her works from 1916 to 1921 were dubbed either "architectonic" or "painterly" constructions. By the end of the Revolution, Popova had been made a professor at the Free State Arts Studios in 1918 and a member of the Institute of Artistic Culture in 1920. Her one theatre design effort during this period was in 1919: *The Tale of the Country Priest and His Dunderhead Servant* for the Theater of Marionettes in Moscow. After contributing to the "$5 \times 5 = 25$" exhibit in Moscow in 1921, Popova turned her artistic talents toward designing stage constructions and costumes as well as other utilitarian constructivist activities such as designing book covers, porcelain, and textiles. With the stage, Popova's artistic concerns for using real form and real space rather than relying upon the two-dimensionality of painting had their clearest expression. These famous stage designs were done for Meyerhold: *The Magnificent Cuckold* (1922), in which she created a construction made up of platforms, wheels, revolving doors, stairs, ladders, chutes, and geometric shapes; and *Earth on End* (1923), which was similarly designed.

Further Reading: Bowlt, John E. "From Surface to Space: The Art of Liubov Popova." *Structuralist* 1976: 80–88; Law, Alma. "Meyerhold's 'The Magnanimous Cuckhold.' " *The Drama Review* Spring 1982: 61–86.

Andrea J. Nouryeh

Pronaszko, Andrzej. Set and costume designer (b. 1888, Debreczyn, Poland; d. 1961). Theatrical productions include *The Winter's Tale*—1924; *Achilles, The Battleship Potemkin*—1925, *The Rose*—1926; *Forefather's Eve, Cry Aloud, China* (Tretiakov), *The Return of Odysseus, Samuel Zborowski*—1932; *The*

Undivine Comedy, The Bacchae, The Captives, Caesar and Cleopatra, Cleopatra, Die Rauber—1933, *The Man Who Was Thursday*—1934; *The Revisor*—1935; *The Battleship Potemkin, All God's Chillun' Got Wings*—1932 to 1936; *Peer Gynt, Father Marek*—1936; *Life Is a Dream*—1937; *Antigone*—1946; *The Anathema, Balladyna*—1945 to 1947; *Fuente Ovejuna*—1948; *Fantazy*—1954; *Kordian*—1957; *The Madwoman of Chaillot*—1958; *Beatrix Cenci*—1959.

Pronaszko studied painting at the Academy of Belles Arts in Kraków and began his design career at the Theatre of Lodz in 1918. In 1922, he began designing for the Theatre Slowacki of Kraków, where he introduced the principles of cubism to the staging of Polish romantic and neoromantic dramas. As he experimented with architectural planes and three-dimensional forms, Pronaszko changed the relationship of the audience to the action. This is best exemplified by his designs for the auditorium; in 1927, with the help of architect S. Syrkas, he designed two ring-shaped platforms, which encircled the audience, and in 1934, with engineer St. Bryla's help, he designed a mobile set for touring in which the audience revolved. From the mid-1920s to the mid-1930s, Pronaszko worked in Warsaw and did most of his designs in collaboration with director Leon Schiller.* The most important of these was *Forefather's Eve*, characterized by its geometric simplicity. Although cubism generally defined Pronaszko's aesthetic, he did design neorealistic settings for dramas with political or social subjects such as *The Battleship Potemkin* and *The Captives*. After the war until his death, he worked at theatres in Kraków and at the Teatr Polski in Warsaw, where he designed *The Madwoman of Chaillot* and *Beatrix Cenci*.

Further Reading: Strzelecki, Z. "Illustrations on the Cover." *Le Theatre en Pologne* 1964:2; Strzelecki, Z. "Polish Theatrical Plastic Arts." *PIW Edition.* Warsaw, 1963; Szydlowski, Roman. *The Theatre in Poland.* Warsaw: Interpress, 1972.

Andrea J. Nouryeh

Pyle, Russel. Set and lighting designer, and art director (b. 1941, El Centro, CA). Noted as a distinguished southern California designer, Pyle has worked primarily in Los Angeles and some in New York and has designed more than two hundred productions in the past two decades. After brief schooling as a graduate student in directing at California State University, he took an administrative job at a small college. During his eight-year employment and without any formal design training, Pyle began free-lancing as a set and lighting designer. His work was primarily with the Company Theatre, where he designed such shows as *Johnny Johnson* (1969), *Comings and Goings* (1969), *The Martyrdom of Peter Ohey* (1971), *The Empire Builders* (1971), *James Joyce Memorial Liquid Theatre* (1971), *The Plague* (1972), *Endgame* (1973), *The Hashish Club* (1973), *Mary Stuart* (1974), *Mirror to Mirror* (1977), and *Salt* (1979). During this time he established relationships with many other theatres, including Odyssey Theatre Ensemble, Los Angeles Actors' Theatre, Mark Taper Forum, Westwood Playhouse, Long Beach Civic Light Opera, Theatre Forty, and Teatro Campesino. At the Los Angeles Actors' Theatre, Pyle designed *Park Your Car in Harvard*

Yard (1982), for which he won a Drama Logue Award for design, and *The Last Tape and Testament of Richard Nixon* (later named *Secret Honor*, 1983). In 1985, when the Actors' Theatre moved into a new theatre complex, becoming the Los Angeles Theatre Center, Pyle was named the resident scenic and lighting designer. Some of his significant productions there were *Quartered Man* (1986), *A Rich Full Life* (1986), and *I Don't Have To Show You No Stinking Badges* (1986). Pyle's work has been briefly glimpsed in New York in revivals of *The Hashish Club* (1973) at the Bijou Theatre and *Secret Honor* (1983) at the Provincetown Playhouse. With Catalina Coast to Coast Productions, he designed the lighting for *Journey's End* (1982), *The Wrong Box* (1983), and *Billy Budd* (1984), all of which won awards for his design. He does not attempt to embrace a unique style for all of his shows. His approach, he says "is to be as innovative and true to the script as possible, while giving the actors the most exciting environment in which to work."

By 1976, he established his career and expanded his activities to include opera, dance, television, and film. For the Los Angeles Opera Theatre, he designed the lighting for *La Boheme* (1980), *Cosi Fan Tutte* (1981), *Madame Butterfly* (1981), *La Traviata* (1982), *Elixer of Love* (1983), and *Die Fledermaus* (1984). His dance credits include productions by the Gene Marinaccio Ballet Company, most notably *Into Light We Shall Return* and *Cantique de la Vie* (both in 1975) and the lighting for the Arlene Erb Dancers' production of *Cry* (1981). His television credits include art direction for several specials, including "Beach Music Awards," "The Christmas Party," and "Strip Tease." In addition, he has served as art director on the two feature films *Rainy Day Friends* and *Swap Meet*.

Awards: Pyle received the Los Angeles Drama Critics' CircleAward for *The Emergence* (1969), *The Hashish Club* (the Company Theater, 1973), *Journey's End* (Catalina Coast to Coast Productions, 1982), *Billy Budd* (Catalina Coast to Coast, 1984), and *I Don't Have To Show You No Stinking Badges* (Los Angeles Actors' Theatre, 1986). He has also received Drama Logue Awards for *Shooter's Bible* (1977), *Something's Rockin' in Denmark, Baal* (1981), *Equus, Park Your Car in Harvard Yard, Journey's End, A Doll's House* (1982), *The Last Tape and Testament of Richard Nixon, Through the Leaves, The Wrong Box* (1983), *Foolin' Around with Infinity* (1987).

Further Reading: "Designers at Work." *Theatre Crafts* May 1987: 27.

Penny L. Remsen

Q

Quaglio Family. Designers, stage machinists, and architects (1668 through 1942). Second only to the Bibienas, the Quaglio family was the most celebrated dynasty of scenographers in Italy. The family included several generations of scene designers in an unbroken line, beginning with Giulio Quaglio I (1668–1751), who was active at the middle of the seventeenth century, through Eugene Quaglio (1857–1942), who died in Berlin in 1942. Each member of the family passed his craft on to the next and influenced the development of scenic art from the baroque era to the latter half of the nineteenth century. The first Quaglio whose work is recorded in any detail was Giovanni Maria Quaglio I (1700?–1765?), who, beginning in 1754, designed settings for most of the operas of composer Christoph Willibald Gluck. His design for Gluck's *Le Cinesi* so impressed Emperor Franz I that he presented Giovanni Maria with a snuffbox filled with a hundred ducats. In 1762, Quaglio's innovative use of light, mechanical tricks, and autumnal colors was seen in Vienna's Burgtheater in Gluck's *Orfeo*. The sons of Giovanni Maria, Lorenzo (1730–1804) and Giuseppe (1747–1828), were born in Italy but spent their active careers working mainly at foreign Courts. Lorenzo became Court architect at Mannheim in the Court of Carl Theodore, and he assisted with the construction of the National Komodienhaus and renovated Alessandro Bibiena's* Schlosstheater. In 1778, Lorenzo became firmly established in Munich, where he had the opportunity to design many productions, most notably Wolfgang Amadeus Mozart's opera *Idomeneo*, presented during the Carnival of 1781. The Quaglio sons, grandsons, and great-grandsons dominated scenic design for many years, with many of them still working in Munich and Berlin at the end of the nineteenth century. Lorenzo's great-nephew, Simon (1795–1878), succeeded his brother, Domenic II (1787–1832), in restoring the Schloss Hohenschwangau for the king of Bavaria. He later became chief designer of Munich's Hoftheater, remained in that position for thirty-two years, and trained his son, Angelo II (1829–1890), to succeed him. Simon successfully combined his neoclassic sensibilities with a growing interest in romanticism, seen especially in his 1818 production of Mozart's *The Magic Flute*. Angelo II assisted his father for many years, and while working on productions of *Tannhauser* (1855) and *Lohengrin* (1858), he began a fruitful collaboration with composer Richard Wagner that culminated in the world premieres, between 1865 and 1870, of *Tristan und Isolde*, *Die Meistersinger*, *Das Rheingold*, and *Die Walküre*.

James Fisher

R

Rabinovitch, Isaac. Scene designer (b. February 27, 1894, Russia; d.?). Theatrical productions include *Four Plunderers*—1919; *The Inspector General*—1920; *Le Bourgeois Gentilhomme, Phillip II, Truth Is Good But Happiness Is Better*—1921; *Don Carlos, The Sorceress, The Death of Tarelkin*—1922; *Lysistrata*—1923; *Carmencita and the Soldier, Aelita* (film), *The Trial of Three Million* (film), *The Marriage, Prazdnik and Kasrilovka*—1924; *The Fruits of Education, The Love for Three Oranges, The Wastrels, Now*—1927; *The White Eagle* (film)—1928; *The Intervention*—1929; *Pervaja Konnaja*, decorations for the May Day celebrations—1930; *Till, Nit-Gedajget*—1931; *Evgeny Onegin*—1933; *The Storm*—1934; *The Sleeping Beauty*—1936; *Uriel Acosta*—1940; *The Great Cyril*—1957; *The Idiot, Hamlet*—1958.

Rabinovitch was a student with Pavel Tchelitchew* under the tutelage of Aleksandra Exter* in Kiev from 1918 to 1920. Together, they designed the scenery and costumes for the film *Aelita* in 1924. Directed by Protazanov and based on the Tolstoy novel, the film featured a futuristic model "Martian" city that was designed solely by Rabinovitch. Rabinovitch designed for a number of the more important Russian theatres in Moscow, Leningrad, and Minsk and for a time was the leading designer at the Moscow State Jewish Theatre. Later, he became famous for his work at the Vakhtangov, Maly, and Moscow art theatres. His work is perhaps best known to westerners through his design for *Lysistrata* (1923) at the Nemirovich-Danchenko Studio. His revolving set with its clean lines and graceful, curving colonnades was highly sculptural and multifunctional and avoided the use of two-dimensional painting. Rabinovitch placed more emphasis on lighting to achieve scenic effects than most other Russian scene designers. In addition, he often referred to himself as a "regisseur-designer" because he recognized that the set is not complete without the performer. According to scholar Norris Houghton, who interviewed him, Rabinovitch distinguished himself from Russian constructivists by claiming to use simplified architectural forms, rather than abstract construction, to express the meaning of the play.

Elbin L. Cleveland

Randolph, Robert. Set, lighting, and costume designer (b. March 9, 1926, Centerville, IA). Theatrical productions include *The Saint of Bleecker Street*— 1954; *The Desperate Hours*—1955; *Bye Bye Birdie*—1960; *How To Succeed in Business Without Really Trying*—1961; *Bravo Giovanni, Calculated Risk, Little Me*—1962; *Sophie*—1963; *Foxy, Any Wednesday, Funny Girl, Something More!*—1964; *Pleasures and Palaces, Minor Miracle, Christmas in Las Vegas, Skyscraper, Anya*—1965; *Sweet Charity, It's a Bird... It's a Plane... It's Superman, Walking Happy*—1966; *Sherry, Sweet Charity, Henry Sweet Henry, How to Be a Jewish Mother*—1967; *Golden Rainbow*—1968; *A Teaspoon Every Four Hours, Angela*—1969; *Applause*—1970; *Ari, 70 Girls 70*—1971; *Applause*—1972; *Gypsy, No Hard Feelings, Good Evening, The Enclave*—1973; *Words and Music: Sammy Cahn's Songbook, Gypsy, The King and I*—1974; *We Interrupt This Program, How To Succeed in Business Without Really Trying, Wonderful Town, The Norman Conquests*—1975; *Porgy and Bess, Hellzapoppin*—1976; *Annie Get Your Gun*—1977; *Spotlight*—1978; *A Partridge in a Pear Tree*—1980; *Little Johnny Jones, Seven Brides for Seven Brothers*—1982; *A Partridge in a Pear Tree, Little Johnny Jones, Seven Brides for Seven Brothers*— 1985; *Sweet Charity*—1986. Television productions include The Tony Awards Show from 1967 to 1984; "That's Life," "Liza with a Z," and "Night of 100 Stars"—1985.

Randolph is credited with more than fifty Broadway productions, most of them musicals. He would often design lights as well as sets and felt that the two were integral. After working as an industrial and architectural designer and teaching at the University of Iowa, Randolph debuted on Broadway with set and costume designs for *The Saint of Bleecker Street* in 1954. It was his sets for *Bye Bye Birdie* in 1960, though, that gained prominence and established his most recognizable style. Randolph's constructivist cubes for the telephone song in that show set a style that reappeared in such 1960s' musicals as *How to Succeed in Business Without Really Trying, Skyscraper,* and *It's a Bird... It's a Plane... It's Superman.* One of a number of designers to move away from the old look of painted drops for musicals, Randolph preferred three-dimensional units to give his sets a fresh, sleek, and modern look. His design for *Sweet Charity* (1966) moved totally away from static painted scenery. It used changing light that provided a fluidity that complemented director Bob Fosse's staging. With the musical *Applause* (1970), Randolph designed a unique way of showing the backstage of a theatre: the audience viewed the stage from the wings and saw battens and lights hanging in forced perspective. *Applause* also employed a scene-shifting technique that used thin "plates" on which furniture glided. It is now a common practice, but then it was unique when Randolph helped to develop it. In addition to his stage work, Randolph designed the Tony Awards Show from 1967 to 1984 and the television specials "That's Life," "Liza with a Z," and "Night of 100 Stars" (1985).

Further Reading: "Applause from the Wings: Interview with Set Designer Robert Randolph." *Theatre Crafts* May/June 1970; Interview in Pecktal (see Bibliography); "Sets and Lights for 'Sherry.'" *Theatre Crafts* March/April 1967.

Ken Kloth

Rennagel, Marilyn. Lighting designer (b. 1943, Los Angeles, CA). After graduating from UCLA in 1971 with an M.F.A. in theatre technology, Rennagel began a career as a lighting designer that has covered the worlds of drama, dance, opera, concert, television, and film. Early in her career she designed the lighting for more than one hundred rock concerts at such auditoriums as the Hollywood Paladium, the Santa Monica Civic Center, and the Los Angeles Forum. During this time, she formed her own company with a colleague called Sundance Lighting, which was oriented toward the rock concert market. By 1973, she became disillusioned with this type of design and found much repetition and gimmicry involved in it. She soon became the assistant lighting designer for the Mark Taper Forum and assisted Tharon Musser on many productions there, as well as on the Broadway shows *A Chorus Line*, *Same Time, Next Year*, *Pacific Overtures*, and *The Act*. As a result of these experiences, Rennagel has gone on to design the lighting for the Broadway productions *Faith Healer* (1979), *Peter Allen—Up in One* (1979), *Clothes for a Summer Hotel* (1980), *Woman of the Year* (1981), *Do Black Patent Leather Shoes Really Reflect Up?* (1981), and *Social Security* (1986). Rennagel parallels her artistic origins in rock with her move into opera. Her numerous credits include works at the Miami Opera, the Dallas Opera, the Opera Company of Philadelphia, and the Syracuse Opera. She has been staff lighting designer for the Michigan Opera since 1979 and for the Opera Pacific since 1986. In addition, she has taught master classes in lighting design at Southern Methodist University and UCLA.

Awards: Her efforts have earned her three Drama Logue Critics' Awards for lighting design, for *Metamorphosis* (1982), *Traveler in the Dark* (1985), and *West Side Story* (1987).

Further Reading: "Designers at Work." *Theatre Crafts* May 1987: 97; "Getting Your Show On the Road." *Theatre Crafts* August/September 1987; "Springtime in New York." *Lighting Dimensions* May/June 1985.

Penny L. Remsen

Ricketts, Charles. Designer and painter (b. 1866, Switzerland; d. October 7, 1931, London, England). Theatrical productions include *Astarte*, *Paris and Oenone*, *Aphrodite Against Artemis*, *Salome*—1906; *A Miracle*, *Persians*, *Don Juan in Hell*, *The Man of Destiny*, *Attila*, *Arms and the Man*—1907; *Lanval*, *A Florentine Tragedy*, *Electra*—1908; *King Lear*—1909; *The Dark Lady of the Sonnets*—1910; *Fanny's First Play*, *King Lear*, *One Act Plays* (by Gordon Bottomley)—1911; *Oedipus Rex*, *The Death of Tintagiles*—1912; *The King's Threshold*, *Philip the King*, *The Dynasts*—1914; *The Man Who Married a Dumb*

Wife, The Well of the Saints—1915; *Judith, Lithuania, A Door Must Be Open or Shut, The Admirable Crichton*—1916; *Annajanska, Twelfth Night, The Merchant of Venice, Two Gentlemen of Verona*—1918; *Judith, Nail, Salome*—1919; *Alcestis, Medea, Iphigenia in Tauris*—1920; *The Betrothal*—1921; *Saint Joan*—1924; *Henry VIII*—1925; *The Mikado, Macbeth*—1926; *The Coming of Christ*—1928; *The Gondoliers*—1929; *Sarah Siddons, the Greatest of the Kembles, Elizabeth of England*—1931.

Swiss-born English designer Ricketts was most devoted to his work as a painter but periodically turned to projects in scene design. Although some critics have found Ricketts's scene and costume designs, especially for his early productions, to be imitative of the works of Edward Gordon Craig* or Léon Bakst,* such later designs as *The Death of Tintagiles* (1912) and *The Judith Plays*, designed for Lillah McCarthy in 1916 and 1919, demonstrate greater originality. Some of his early works were realized in Ireland through his long friendship with William Butler Yeats. At the Abbey Theatre, Yeats had begun experimenting with nonrealistic visual schemes employing a set of his variable moving screens by Craig that were occasionally on the same bill with Ricketts's designs. The combined work of Craig and Ricketts was, unfortunately, seen only in Ireland, but in his writings Yeats later recalled the exceptional beauty of the works. Ricketts also designed several of the first productions of the plays of George Bernard Shaw, including *Saint Joan* (1924). Shaw greatly admired Ricketts's designs, and despite his distress with certain aspects of the original production, he felt that the acting of Sybil Thorndike, combined with Ricketts's designs, greatly elevated the production's quality.

Further Reading: Binnie, Eric. *The Theatrical Designs of Charles Ricketts*. Ann Arbor: UMI Research Press, 1985.

James Fisher

Robbins, Carrie. Costume designer (b. February 7, 1943, Baltimore, MD). Theatrical productions (all were in New York City, unless otherwise specified) include *Bells Are Ringing* (Schwab Auditorium, University Park, Pennsylvania)—1962; *Bye Bye Birdie* (Schwab Auditorium, University Park, Pennsylvania)—1963; *A Midsummer Night's Dream, Come Back, Little Sheba* (both at Schwab Auditorium, University Park, Pennsylvania)—1964; *The Hostage, The Merry Widow, Prometheus Bound* (all at Schwab Auditorium, University Park, Pennsylvania)—1965; *Tartuffe, The Mikado* (both at the Studio Arena Theatre, Buffalo, New York)—1966; *Pantagleize, The Lesson, Antigone* (all at the Studio Arena Theatre, Buffalo, New York)—1967; *The Barber of Seville, The Lion in Winter* (both at the Studio Arena Theatre, Buffalo, New York), *Tartuffe, The Flies, The Glass Menagerie, The Sea Gull* (all at the Mark Taper Forum, Los Angeles, California), *Leda Had a Little Swan* (Cort Theatre), *Trainer, Dean, Liepolt and Company* (American Place Theatre)—1968; *Inner Journey, The Year Boston Won the Pennant* (both at the Mark Taper Forum, Los Angeles, California), *The Millionairess, Julius Caesar* (both at the Tyrone Guthrie Theatre,

Minneapolis), *The Time of Your Life* (Vivian Beaumont Theatre)—1969; *Look to the Lilies* (Lunt-Fontanne Theatre), *The Good Woman of Setzuan* (Vivian Beaumont Theatre)—1970; *An Enemy of the People* (Vivian Beaumont Theatre)—1971; *Narrow Road to the Deep North*, *The Crucible* (both at the Vivian Beaumont Theatre), *The Beggar's Opera*, *Sunset* (both at the Chelsea Theatre Center), *The Hostage* (Good Shepherd-Faith Church), *Grease* (Royale Theatre), *The Secret Affairs of Mildred Wild* (Ambassador Theatre)—1972; *Grease* (national company), *The Plough and the Stars* (Vivian Beaumont Theatre), *Let Me Hear You Smile* (Biltmore Theatre), *the Rake's Progress* (Kennedy Center, Washington, D.C.), *Grease* (London), *Sisters of Mercy* (Theatre de Lys), *The Beggar's Opera* (Saratoga), *Molly* (Alvin Theatre), *The Iceman Cometh* (Circle in the Square)—1973; *Over Here!* (Shubert Theatre), *Yentl—the Yeshiva Boy* (Chelsea Theatre Center), *Joan of Lorraine* (Good Shepherd-Faith Church)—1974; *Polly* (Chelsea Theatre Center)—1975; *The Boss*, *Marco Polo* (both at Chelsea Theatre Center)—1976; *Happy End* (Martin Beck Theatre), *The Creditors*, *The Stronger* (both at the Public Theatre)—1977; *The Old Man and His Family*—1978; *The Sun Always Shines in the Cool* (with Tricia Blackburn; 78th Street Theatre Lab)—1979; *Sidewalkin'*, *Really Rosie* (Chelsea Theatre Center), *Fearless Frank* (Princess Theatre), *Arms and the Man* (Playwrights Horizons), *Mother Courage and Her Children* (Center Stage, Baltimore, Maryland)—1980; *Frankenstein* (Palace Theatre), *Macbeth* (Vivian Beaumont Theatre), *The First* (Martin Beck Theatre), *The Stitch in Time* (ANTA Theatre) *It Had To Be You* (John Golden Theatre), *El Bravo!* (Entermedia Theatre)—1981; *Agnes of God* (Music Box Theatre)—1982; *Raggedy Ann* (State Theatre, Albany, New York)—1984; *The Octette Bridge Club* (Music Box Theatre), *The Boys of Winter* (Biltmore Theatre)—1985; *Twelfth Night* (Alaska Repertory Theatre, Anchorage, Alaska)—1986; *Sweet Bird of Youth* (Ahmanson Theatre, Los Angeles)—1987.

Robbins holds a degree in art education and theatre arts from Pennsylvania State University, as well as an M.F.A. from the Yale Drama School. She began her work in the theatre while still an undergraduate, designing such Penn State productions as *Bells Are Ringing* and *Bye Bye Birdie*. After receiving her M.F.A., Robbins worked for the Studio Arena in Buffalo, New York, and the Inner-City Cultural Center in Los Angeles before designing costumes for her first Broadway show, *Leda Had a Little Swan*, in 1968. Since then, she has designed the costumes for several productions at New York's Chelsea Theater Group, as well as the Repertory Theater of Lincoln Center, Sarah Caldwell's Boston Opera, John Houseman's City Center Acting Company, and the Kennedy Center in Washington, D.C. In the early 1980s, Robbins became a visiting guest professor in advanced costume design at the University of Illinois in Champaign.

Robbins describes herself as a "stickler for details," and her technique combines intensive research with a concern for the director's visual understanding of the play and casting. For John Gay's production of *The Beggar's Opera* (1972) at New York's Chelsea Theater Group, Robbins was inspired by the warm, muddy colors in Hogarth's paintings of the period. After a long discussion with the director about the time period, they both reached the conclusion that there was little sanitation in Europe during the fifteenth century and that the women probably dragged their long skirts through the dirty streets. Additionally, Robbins bought grain and seeds in quantity and sewed them onto the lower portion of the costumes.

For the musical *Grease* (1972), Robbins used old *Life* magazines, as well as high school and college yearbooks from the 1950s as research tools. To re-create the depression era for the 1973 musical *Molly*, Robbins initially looked at old issues of *Vogue* and *Harper's Bazaar*. As the project evolved, however, she felt that the clothes should be more realistic and less fashion-oriented. Figuring that the characters in the play were too poor to afford the latest 1932 styles, the year in which the play was set, Robbins found inspiration in the 1931 Sears Roebuck catalog.

Throughout her work Robbins displays a vivid imagination, coupled with an innate common sense and a far-reaching knowledge of fashion history. Currently head of the costume department at New York University, she continues to pass this knowledge along to both students and peers.

Awards: Robbins was nominated for a Tony Award for Best Costume Design for *Grease* in 1972 and *Over Here!* in 1974. She received the Drama Desk Award as "most promising costume designer" for *Grease* and *The Beggar's Opera* in 1972, and the Drama Desk Award for *Over Here!* and *The Iceman Cometh* in 1974.

Further Reading: "Carrie Robbins." *Dramatics* September/October 1979; "Costumes by Carrie Robbins." *Theatre Crafts* January/February 1974; Owen (see Bibliography).

Howard Gutner

Rojo, Jerry. Set designer, director, teacher, and architectural consultant (b. 1935, Alton, IL). Theatrical productions include *Sourball, Dionysus in '69*— 1969; *Macbeth*—1970; *Commune*—1971; *The Tooth of Crime*—1972; *A Great Hoss Pistol, Endgame*—1973; *Mother Courage*—1974; *Ghosts*—1975; *Sleuth*— 1976; *When We Dead Awaken, In the Well of the House, A Christmas Carol*— 1977; *Three Sisters, Scapino*—1978; *The Balcony*—1979; *A Body of Bricks*— 1980; *Front Street, Norman, Is That You?*—1983; *Prometheus Project*—1985; *The Yellow House*—1986; *The Bell Witch Variations, Virgin Forest*—1987; *Dr. Faustus, Misanthrope, Dr. Charcot's Hysteria Shows*—1988. Architectural designs include Environmental Theatre, Sarah Lawrence College, 1970; Environmental Theatre, University of Connecticut, 1971; Portable Thrust Theatre, University of Connecticut, 1972; Environmental Theatre, Section 10, 1974; Fixed Unit Stage, StageWest, 1976; Thrust Stage, Clockwork Repertory Theatre, 1981; Fleet Colonial Faire-Providence 350, 1986; Performing Arts Facility, Eastern Connecticut State University, 1987.

Rojo received a master of fine arts degree from Tulane University in 1960 and began his career teaching theatrical design at the University of Omaha. After his departure from the University of Omaha in 1961, he joined the theatre faculty at the University of Connecticut, Storrs, where he taught and designed over sixty productions until his retirement in 1985.

He has been credited with several benchmark, environmental theatrical designs, many of which were produced in collaboration with Richard Schechner and the Performance Group. These designs included *Victims of Duty* (1967), *Dionysus in '69* (1969), *Macbeth* (1970), *Commune* (1971), *The Tooth of Crime* (1972), *Mother Courage* (1974), *The Balcony* (1979), and *Prometheus Project* (1985). In all of them Rojo sought to engender the audience's active participation and its total involvement with the space, time, and action of the play. The designs were notable for joining the playing area and the audience seating area into a unified, architectural whole. Rojo feels that one of his most successful environmental designs was for the 1973 production of *Endgame*. Collaborating with André Gregory, Rojo created "an environment vaguely reminiscent of a carnival midway," where the audience viewed the performers from six sides through cyclone fencing. This design earned a Drama Desk Award in 1973.

Rojo's architectural designs are similar to his theatrical designs in that they are "less decorative and more functional," and in all cases they emphasize "verticality" as an aesthetic objective. In these designs, Rojo has created fixed environments in which "space becomes the concept for the play," and costumes, lighting, and sound (not traditional scenic units) become the crucial design elements. He has also consulted on the architectural planning for the Museum of Contemporary Art, Chicago (1976), Cabaret Theatre at Westbeth, New York (1972), and the Department of Theatre at the University of Delaware (1972). In addition, his designs have been exhibited at Lincoln Center under the title "Contemporary Stage Design, USA"; at the Hudson River Museum under the title "Theatrical Evolution 1776–1976" in 1976; and at the Jorgensen Gallery as "Retrospect IV—Environmental Designs of Jerry Rojo" in 1978.

Awards: His efforts have earned him an Obie Award for his work on *Dionysus in '69* in 1969; an Obie Award nomination for his designs of *The Tooth of Crime* and *Endgame*, both in 1973; and the Drama Desk Award for *Endgame*.

Further Reading: McNamara, Brooks, Jerry Rojo, and Richard Schechner. *Theatres, Spaces, Environments*. New York: Drama Book Specialists, 1975.

Penny L. Remsen

Roller, Andreas Leonhard. Designer and stage machinist (b. 1805, Germany; d. 1891). Roller studied for a time in Vienna before working as scene designer and stage mechanic in theatres in England, France, and Austria. In 1834, he was appointed chief scene designer and machinist for the Imperial Theatres in St. Petersburg (after which time he was called Andrei Ivanovitch). His many innovations, used for productions of operas such as Gounod's *Faust*, included interesting experiments in lighting, such as shafts of light through windows and exterior light leaking through cracks into an interior scene; ingenious transformation scenes and tableaux; and overtly romantic designs. He also assisted on the restoration of the Tsarskoye Selo Hermitage, the Bolshoi Theatre, the Hermitage Theatre, and the Winter Palace.

James Fisher

Ronconi, Luca. Designer, director, and performer (b. 1933, Italy). Ronconi was trained at Rome's Accademia Nazionale d'Arte Drammatica and for several years appeared as an actor with Vittorio Gassman's company. His first important success as a director came in 1966 with his production of Thomas Middleton's *The Changeling* (1966). He also staged Shakespeare's *Measure for Measure* (1967), *Richard III* (1968), and Giordano Bruno's *Il Candelaio* (1968) for the Turin's Teatro Stabile. For a 1969 production of Ariosto's *Orlando Furioso*, Ronconi revived Italian folk spectacle in a production utilizing a freely structured space. In other shows, he attempted to combine environmental theatre techniques with a medieval street pageant. For example, for his production of *XX* (1971), Ronconi transformed the auditorium of the Odéon in Paris into a two-story structure, each story divided into ten rooms. At the beginning of the performance, approximately two dozen spectators were shut into each cubicle, and actors occasionally burst in to speak, while sounds and music were audible from other areas. Periodically a wall would be removed between cubicles, revealing some audience members to other audience members, and all of the walls were removed eventually. Similarly, he redefined performance space in *Oresteia* (1972), a six-hour production that was impressive in its visual imagery, as well as *The Barber of Seville* (1972) and *Utopia* (1975). Ronconi has continued to experiment with his novel uses of space and symbolic theatricality with such productions as Middleton's *A Game of Chess*, Ibsen's *Ghosts* (1982), and several other works at the Prato Theatre Workshop. His virtuosity has been applied to the opera, as well, with designs for *Faust*, *Siegfried*, and *Orpheus and Eurydice*.

James Fisher

Rose, Jürgen. Set designer (b. 1937, West Germany). Theatrical productions include *Romeo and Juliet*—1962; *Cosi fan Tutte, The Firebug, Poema Extaza*—1962 and 1972; *The Firebird, Electre*—1964; *Eugene Onegin*—1965; *Valse Nobles et Sentimentales*—1966; *Rosencrantz and Guildenstern Are Dead*—1967; *Cinderella, Les Paravents*—1968; *Uncle Vanya*—1970; *Die Mitschuldigen, The Nutcracker, Le Baiser de la Fee, Daphnis and Chloe, R.B.M.E.*—1972; *Traces*—1973; *Un Ballo in Maschera*—1975; *Swan Lake*—1976; *A Midsummer Night's Dream*—1977; *Kameliendame, The Sleeping Beauty*—1978; *Salome*—1979; *Woyzeck*—1983; *John Falstaff*—1984.

Throughout the past three decades, Rose has designed ballets for choreographer John Cranko and for the National Ballet of Canada. His designs for the theatre have been executed primarily for the German director Hans Lietzau, and his most successful opera collaborations have been with director Otto Schenk. One of his most impressive designs was for *Woyzeck* in Munich in 1983. The stage, littered with wooden chairs, was enclosed on three sides with walls pierced with doors. Above these walls was a second playing area used for intimate scenes. The stage floor itself contained a series of transparent rings that, when lit, gave off a glow that matched the light of the moon. So important were Rose's designs for the production that an album reproducing his color sketches for the opera was given with the program. Although Rose is primarily a designer for the opera stages of Germany, his work for the Vienna State Opera has led him to design *Un ballo in maschera* (1975) for Covent Garden and *Salome* (1979) for the Metropolitan Opera House.

Further Reading: Barzel, Ann. *Dance Magazine* November 1978: 57–62; Clarke, Mary, and Clement Crispe. *Design for Ballet*. New York: Hawthorne Books, 1978; Loney, Glenn. "Innovative Designs on European Stages: From Salzburg to Glasgow." *Performing Arts Journal* 1984: 97–112; Pepys, Tom. *Dance and Dancers* February 1977: 16–17.

Andrea J. Nouryeh

Rosenthal, Jean. Lighting designer (b. March 16, 1912, New York City; d. 1969). Theatrical productions (all were in New York City and are for lighting design, unless otherwise noted) include *Macbeth* (Lafayette Theatre), *Hamlet* (Imperial Theatre), *Horse Eats Hat* (Maxine Elliott's Theatre)—1936; *Julius Caesar* (Mercury Theatre), *The Cradle Will Rock* (Mercury Theatre)—1937; *Shoemaker's Holiday* (Mercury Theatre)—1938; *Native Son* (St. James Theatre)—1941; *The Telephone* and *The Medium* (Ethel Barrymore Theatre)—1947; *Joy to the World* (Plymouth Theatre), *Sundown Beach* (Belasco Theatre), *The Telephone* and *The Medium* (revival at New York City Center)—1948; *Caesar and Cleopatra*—1949; *The Consul* (Ethel Barrymore Theatre)—1950; *Woyzeck*—1952; *The Climate of Eden* (Martin Beck Theatre), *Blue Beard's Castle* (New York City Center)—1952; *La Cenerentola* and *The Trial* (both at New York City Center)—1953; *Ondine* (46th Street Theatre), *Falstaff*, *Showboat*, *Die Fledermaus* (all at New York City Center), *Quadrille* (Coronet Theatre) *The Saint of Bleeker Street* (Broadway Theatre), *House of Flowers* (Alvin Theatre), *The Time of Your Life* (New York City Center)—1954; *Julius Caesar* and *The Tempest* (both at the American Shakespeare Festival, Stratford, Connecticut)—1955; *The Great Sebastians* (Coronet Theatre), *King John, Measure for Measure*, and *The Taming of the Shrew* (all at the American Shakespeare Festival, Stratford, Connecticut)—1956; *The Taming of the Shrew, Measure for Measure, The Duchess of Malfi* (all at the American Shakespeare Festival, Stratford, Connecticut), *A Hole in the Head* (Plymouth Theatre), *The Beggar's Opera* (New York City Center), *Othello, The Merchant of Venice, Much Ado About Nothing* (all at the American Shakespeare Festival, Stratford, Connecticut), *West Side Story* (Winter Garden Theatre), *The Dark at the Top of the Stairs* (Music Box Theatre)—1957; *Winesburg, Ohio* (National Theatre), *Hamlet* and *The Winter's Tale* (both at the American Shakespeare Festival, Stratford, Connecticut), *Ballets: U.S.A.* (Alvin Theatre), *The Disenchanted* (Coronet Theatre), *Redhead* (46th Street Theatre), *Destry Rides Again* (Imperial Theatre)—1958; *Judy Garland* (Metropolitan Opera House), *All's Well*

That Ends Well (American Shakespeare Festival), *Take Me Along* (Shubert Theatre), *The Sound of Music* (Lunt-Fontanne Theatre), *Saratoga* (Winter Garden Theatre), *Juniper and the Pagans* (Colonial Theatre, Boston)—1959; *Caligula* (54th Street Theatre), *Dear Liar* (Billy Rose Theatre), *Henry IV, Part 1 and 2* (Phoenix Theatre), *A Taste of Honey* (Lyceum Theatre), *Becket* (St. James Theater)—1960; *The Conquering Hero* and *Ballets: U.S.A.* (American National Theatre and Academy), *The Gay Life* (Shubert Theatre), *Night of the Iguana* (Royale Theatre)—1961; *A Gift of Time* (Ethel Barrymore Theatre), *A Funny Thing Happened on the Way to the Forum, Lord Pengo* (Royale Theatre)—1962; *On an Open Roof* (Cort Theatre), *The Beast in Me* (Plymouth Theatre), *Jennie* (Majestic Theatre), *Barefoot in the Park* (Biltmore Theatre), *The Ballad of the Sad Cafe* (Martin Beck Theatre)—1963; *The Chinese Prime Minister* (Royale Theatre), *Hello, Dolly!* (St. James Theatre), *Fiddler on the Roof* (Imperial Theatre), *Luv* (Booth Theatre), *Poor Bitos* (Cort Theatre)—1964.

Rosenthal's training in theatre began in 1928 at the Neighborhood Playhouse and continued at the Yale School of Drama. In 1935 she joined the Federal Theatre Project (later the Mercury Theatre) and worked with directors Orson Welles and John Houseman. At this time the role of the lighting designer had not yet been formally established, and it was usually left to the stage manager to arrange the lighting. Rosenthal eagerly met the task and almost single-handedly invented the field of lighting design along the way. She took great pains and gained great fame for her lighting of such productions as *Macbeth* (1936), Marc Blitzstein's *The Cradle Will Rock* (1937), *Julius Caesar* (1937), and *Native Son* (1941). In 1938, she became Martha Graham's lighting and production supervisor, designing dance until her death in 1969. Her lighting designs for dance were equally impressive, elevating the craft of illuminating the stage to an art. She went on to design the lighting for hundreds of productions, including such significant Broadway plays and musicals as *West Side Story* (1957), *A Taste of Honey* (1960), *Night of the Iguana* (1961), and *Hello, Dolly!* (1964). Critics hailed her effects as magical, probably stemming from her ability to create moods and realistic atmospheres through the artistic use of color and intensity. She always attempted to unify the production through the lighting. Her other activities include consulting on the lighting of many theatres, municipal buildings, and public gathering places. Some of her theatre lighting installations include the Juilliard School of Music, Lincoln Center for the Performing Arts, the Tyrone Guthrie Theatre in Minneapolis, and the Memorial Pavilion and Center Theatre of the Los Angeles Music Center. With Lael Wertenbaker, she put her theories into a book titled *The Magic of Light* (1972), used for many years as a standard text for lighting students.

Further Reading: By Rosenthal: with Lael Wertenbaker. *The Magic of Light: The Craft and Career of Jean Rosenthal, Pioneer in Lighting for the Modern Stage*. Boston: Little, Brown, and Co., 1972.

Thomas J. Mikotowicz

Rosse, Herman. Set designer, artist, architect, and teacher (b. 1887, Denmark (some sources state Holland); d. 1965). Theatrical productions include *The Drama of the Nativity and the Murder of the Innocents*, *La Serva Padrona*— 1919; *Madame Chrysantheme*, *The Yellow Mask*—1920; *It's Getting Dark on Old Broadway* (Ziegfeld Follies) and *Casanova*—1923; *Mister Pitt*—1924; *Chauve Souris*, *Mandragola*—1925; *South Seas Island Fantasy*—1926; *The Dime Museum Revue*, *Parisian Nights*, *Hearts and Flowers*—1927; *Americana*— 1928; *The Bridal Veil*, *Hamlet*, *Macbeth*, *Romeo and Juliet*, *Julius Caesar*, *Othello*, *The Merchant of Venice*—1929; *Bow Bells*, *The Great Magoo*, *The Clowns in Clover* (Billy Rose Revue), *Rain or Shine*—1932; *Tyl Eulenspiegel*, *Elisabeth*—1935; *The Rivals*—1945; *Victoria Regina*—1946; *Banjo on My Knee*, *Song of Norway*, *The Merry Widow*—1949; *Baroque Ballet*, *May Time*—1950; *Up in Central Park*—1951; *Carousel*, *Kiss Me Kate*, *The Chocolate Soldier*— 1952; *High Button Shoes*, *Die Fledermaus*—1953; *Carmen*, *My Three Angels*, *Paint Your Wagon*—1954; *Guys and Dolls*, *Mother Was a Bachelor*—1955. Film productions include *The King of Jazz*—1929, *Frankenstein*—1930; *Murder in the Rue Morgue*, *Take a Chance*—1932; *The Emperor Jones*—1933; *Rubber*— 1936; *Ulysses in Nighttown*—1958.

Like his contemporaries Lee Simonson,* Robert Edmond Jones,* and Kenneth Macgowan, Herman Rosse brought the theories of Adolphe Appia* and Edward Gordon Craig* to the United States through his designs for more than two hundred theatrical productions and through his prolific writings. He has also been credited with variously promoting the rise of postimpressionism, expressionism, and dadaism in American theatrical design.

Initially, he came to the United States to supervise the design of Holland's building for the 1915 San Francisco Exposition. He did not return to Holland, however, but remained in the United States and designed such productions as *The Drama of the Nativity and the Murder of the Innocents* and *La Serva Padrona*. In 1919, Rosse was appointed head of the School of Design at the Art Institute of Chicago. His significance as a designer who experimented with new theories led to his becoming a regular contributor to *Theatre Arts Monthly* throughout the 1920s. To this activity he added designing productions for the Chicago Civic Shakespeare Society, the Little Opera of America, and the Chicago Grand Opera Company.

By 1929, Rosse had designed his first of a series of movies for Universal and Paramount Pictures, *The King of Jazz*, for which he won an Academy Award for "Best Art Direction." Before he returned to Holland to become professor of decorative art at the Technical University of Delft in the mid-1930s, Rosse had designed approximately eight films and had his renderings exhibited at the Arden Galleries. Further, he had designed the Nyack Amusement Park Theatre, illustrated a 1930 translation of the *Canterbury Tales*, and created the scenery for lavish shows for Florence Ziegfeld and Billy Rose in New York and for John Murray Anderson at the London Hippodrome. Rosse returned to the United

States in 1947 and became the resident designer for the Paper Mill Playhouse until 1960. His other later activities included the founding and managing of the American Designer's Gallery, the first artists' cooperative gallery in New York, as well as serving from 1955 until his death as the art director of *Chapter One*, the American National Theatre Association's newsletter.

Further Reading: By Rosse: *Designs and Impressions*. Chicago: Seymour, 1920; with Macgowan, Kenneth. *Masks and Demons*. New York: Harcourt Brace, 1925.

About Rosse: Cheney, Sheldon. "Herman Rosse's Stage Designs." *Theatre Arts Monthly* April 1921: 148–56; Dorr, Charles H. "The Stage Designs of Herman Rosse." *Theatre* February 1921: 162–63.

Andrea J. Nouryeh

Roth, Ann. Costume designer (b. 1932, United States). Unlike many designers who work in the theatre, Roth received her first professional experience in Hollywood, where she assisted Irene Sharaff* with such films as *Brigadoon* (1953), *A Star Is Born* (1954), and *The King and I* (1956). Before she came to New York in 1957, Roth was an assistant designer on the movies *Oklahoma!* (1955) and *Around the World in 80 Days* (1956). After assisting Miles White* on this last film, Roth received her first solo credit as a costume designer in 1958 for the production *Maybe Tuesday* at the Playhouse Theatre. Since the 1960s, Roth has designed the costumes for a number of Broadway shows, including Neil Simon's *The Odd Couple* (1965) and *The Star-Spangled Girl* (1966), *Tiny Alice* (1969), *Six Rms Riv Vu* (1972), *First Monday in October* (1978), *They're Playing Our Song* (1979), *Singin' in the Rain* (1983), and *Hurlyburly* (1985). In addition, she has created costumes for a number of productions at the American Conservatory Theater in San Francisco and the Kennedy Center in Washington, D.C. In the late 1960s, Roth returned to motion picture work as a solo designer and created the costumes for an extensive number of films, including *Midnight Cowboy* (1969), *The Owl and the Pussycat* (1970), *Klute* (1971), *The Day of the Locust* (1975), *Hair* (1979), *The World According to Garp* (1982), *Places in the Heart* (1984), *Silkwood* (1984), and *Sweet Dreams* (1985). Claiming that she is not a fashion-oriented costume designer, Roth maintains that she would not have been happy working on the Hollywood star vehicles of the 1930s and 1940s. She views helping the performer develop the character as her principal job. Roth's designs have continued to the present to delineate character both onstage and in motion pictures.

Howard Gutner

S

Sabbatini, Nicola. Set designer, stage machinist, and theorist (b. 1574, Italy; d. 1654). Sabbatini's treatise, *Practica di Fabricar Scene e Macchine ne' Teatri* (The practice of making scenes and machines) describes and illustrates the scenic practices of Italian theatres in the late sixteenth and early seventeenth centuries. Although Sabbatini did not invent the methods he describes, and many of the practices were outdated when his books were published, he attempted to show the progression from the three-dimensional scenery of Serlio* a century before to the use of the pole and chariot method invented by his apprentice, Giacomo Torelli.* Sabbatini's first book, published in 1637, describes the problems of theatre construction, audience arrangement, and scenery building and painting. It also devotes much discussion to various lighting methods. In the book, he suggested that candles or oil lamps were more effective if placed on the side of the stage, rather than over the audience or behind the upper borders, as was the common practice. He also described means of coloring light by using bottles filled with colored water in front of the light source and primitive dimming systems, using various shutters. The second book, published the next year, dealt with *intermezzi* and describes methods of changing scenery using "Serlian wings," *periaktoi*, and shutters. Sabbatini described numerous techniques to create special effects, including hell scenes and the use of traps, ships, and seas. His books also include elaborate drawings of cloud machines and methods of simulating rain, thunder, lightning, sunsets, and rainbows.

Further Reading: Hewitt, Barnard, ed. (see Bibliography).

Ken Kloth

Sacchetti, Lorenzo. Theatrical designer, architect, and artist (b. 1759, Padua, Italy; d. 1829). Sacchetti's artistic career began with royal commissions for frescoes and interior decorations in Padua and Venice. He received his first scenic training as an apprentice to Domenico Morcate di Fossati* in the Teatro

San Giovanni Crisostomo and subsequently spent ten years refurbishing and designing for the theatres of San Samuele and San Moisè. In 1794, the choreographer Salvatore Vigano arranged for Sacchetti's transfer to Vienna, where he became an assistant in the Hoftheater to the extremely talented Austrian stage designer, Josef Platzer. In 1818, Emperor Francis II appointed Sacchetti Court painter and designer of the Hoftheater. As architect, he also redecorated the Redoutensaal and other buildings in Brno. Sacchetti was known for his use of diagonal perspective in his designs, as well as his bold use of color in such productions as *Caius Marius* and Collin's *Coriolanus*, both in Vienna (1806). He also applied his design talents to Court festivities, palaces, and lithographs. In addition, he wrote a practical handbook on scene design, *Quanto Sia Facile l'Inventore Decorazioni Teatrali*, published in Prague in 1830. From 1817 until his death, Sacchetti resided chiefly in Prague, where he was appointed designer of the National Theatre.

Jonet Buchanan

Sagert, Horst. Painter and scene designer (b. 1934, Dramburg, Germany). Sagert, a major German artist and designer of theatre and films, was a student of artist Heinrich Kilger and began his career as a practicing graphic artist. From 1963 through 1972, Sagert created six theatre designs: *Red Roses for Me* and *Tartuffe* (both in 1963); *The Rise and Fall of Mahagonny* (1964); *Drakon* (1965); and *Oedipus Tyrannus* (1966). A further design that was very influential was *A Midsummer Night's Dream*, produced in West Germany in 1976. It was characterized by Sagert's unique hand-sewn and haphazard style, created by cutting up and sewing cloth pieces together to give the three-dimensional set pieces a special look and texture. At the Prague Quadrennial in 1979, his designs were exhibited for *King Bamba* (1978) and *Medea* (1979), the latter of which was awarded a gold medal for scenography. His film credits are extensive and include *Jolanda, the Daughter of the Coraro Nero* (1952); *Public Opinion* (1954); *Era de Venerdi 17* (1956); and *Extra concubale* (1965).

Further Reading: Fielding, Eric. "3 Award-Winning Exhibitions." *Theatre Design and Technology* Spring 1980: 22–25; Riddell, Richard. "East and West Germany." *Theatre Design and Technology* Spring 1980: 15–17.

Andrea J. Nouryeh

Sainthill, Loudon. Scenery and costume designer (b. 1919, Tasmania, Australia; d. 1969). When Colonel de Basil's Ballets Russes de Monte Carlo toured Australia in the late 1930s, Sainthill showed some of his paintings to Anton Dolin, a member of the ballet. Dolin was impressed enough with Sainthill's work to invite him back to London as an unofficial member of the company, but war intervened before Sainthill was able to design any productions. After the war, Sainthill designed the sets for Giraudoux's *Amphitryon '38* in Australia. In 1950, he returned to England, where Robert Helpmann, Tony Richardson, and Michael Benthall asked him to design *The Tempest* for the Stratford Memorial Theater. This production—and the subsequent acclaim it received—formally launched Sainthill's prolific career. Throughout the 1950s and 1960s, Sainthill designed sets and costumes for more than a dozen Shakespearean productions at Stratford, as well as a number of contemporary theatrical productions, including Wolf Mankowitz's *Expresso Bongo* (1959) in London, Tennessee Williams's *Orpheus Descending* (1957), and Rodgers and Hammerstein's musical version of *Cinderella* (1961). In the late 1950s, Sainthill began to design for motion pictures as well, with *Look Back in Anger* (1958) and *Day of the Triffids* (1963) among his credits. In whatever medium he was working, Sainthill was always concerned that his work be convincing, and he tried to take the audience into another "world." As a testament to his designs, just before his death in 1969, Sainthill won a Tony Award for "Best Costume Design" for his work on *The Canterbury Tales*.

Howard Gutner

Sanquirico, Alessandro. Set designer (b. 1777, Milan, Italy; d. 1849). Although he designed only at La Scala, Sanquirico has a prominent place in nineteenth-century scenic design. From 1806 to 1832, he designed hundreds of grand operas and ballets at La Scala. In about 1817, he was named chief designer at the theatre, and, in 1829, he supervised redecoration of the theatre in the style of Pompeiian architecture. Like his contemporaries, Sanquirico also afforded his services to the local aristocracy and designed palaces, courtyards, and public events such as coronations, weddings, and other royal occasions. As a pupil of Paolo Landriani and assistant to Giovanni Pedroni, he learned his art and thus carried on the traditions passed down from the Galliari family.* Sanquirico blended his neoclassic training with the newly embraced trends toward romanticism. Some of his most important designs include Rossini's *La Gazza Ladra* (1827), Pacini's *The Last Days of Pompeii* (1827), Bellini's *Norma* (1831), and Donizetti's *Lucretia Borgia* (1834). His style incorporated large architectural units, constructed and painted in perspective with much use of chiaroscuro to create dramatic effects of light and shadow. His designs were published in two collections; the first was between the years 1819 and 1824 (in a collection of several designers' work), and the second was in 1827 in a volume solely dedicated to Sanquirico's work. As a result, his technique set an example for subsequent designers of grand opera throughout the nineteenth century.

Thomas J. Mikotowicz

Scamozzi, Vincenzo. Stage designer and architect (b. 1552, Italy; d. 1616). Scamozzi is best known for his alteration of Andrea Palladio's* Renaissance model of a Roman theatre, the Teatro Olimpico at Vicenza, in 1585. The alteration consisted of installing permanent perspective vistas behind each of the five archways that led from the stage. In 1590, he completed an entire theatre on his own at Sabbioneta and helped bring about the transition from the Roman style to the Renaissance style proposed by Serlio.* This theatre had only one large central archway opening, behind which Scamozzi installed the Serlian raked stage, side flats, and rear backdrop painted in perspective. Most scholars agree that this design was an integral step in the growth of the modern proscenium theatre.

Thomas J. Mikotowicz

Schiller, Leon de Schildenfeld. Designer and director (b. 1887, Poland; d. 1954). Schiller was born in Kraków and spent his early twenties working as a cabaret singer and journalist in Paris and as a music student in Vienna. After World War I, Schiller worked for a time for the Polski Teatr in Warsaw and the Reduta Theatre in Osterwa before starting the Boguslawski Theater in 1924. At this theatre, he directed a number of European classics and contemporary plays, including Brecht's *The Threepenny Opera*, which, together with his well-known left-wing political interests, led to the closing of the theatre in 1930. He moved his base of operations to Lwów and staged works in a number of Polish cities until he was interned at Auschwitz until 1941. The Nazis had closed Polish theatres, so Schiller secretly produced early Polish liturgical dramas at a Warsaw convent. At the conclusion of the war he became director of the theatre in Lódz. Some of Schiller's significant productions are *The Undivine Comedy* (1926), *Forefather's Eve* (1934 and 1937), *The Tempest* and *La Celestina* (both in 1947), *The Lower Depths* (1949), and *Halka* (1953). While in Paris, Schiller had met Edward Gordon Craig,* who greatly influenced his ideas about theatre. In addition, his commitment to "total theatre," as well as his love for both realistic and romantic drama, was derived from his admiration for the works of Polish playwright Stanislaw Wyspianski and Russian actor-director Konstantin Stanislavsky. Thus, Schiller's productions strongly reflected his single vision and were both directed and designed by him. A collection of his theoretical writings on theatre, *Teatr Ogromny*, was published following Schiller's death. Schiller was perhaps the most important theatrical figure in Polish drama in the years between the two world wars.

James Fisher

Schlemmer, Oskar. Designer, sculptor, and painter (b. 1888, Germany; d. 1943). Schlemmer is best known for his extraordinary work with the Bauhaus theatre workshop. First joining the staff of the Bauhaus in 1921 as a sculptor, within two years he was in charge of its theatre workshop and led the troupe until 1929. The essential problem in stage design, as Schlemmer saw it, was to reconcile the three-dimensional body of the performer as it moved through the stage space. By mathematically analyzing the human form, he came up with geometrically shaped costumes and masks for such experimental works as *The Triadic Ballet* (1912 and 1922). The work was presented in three parts, with each section having its own set of abstract costumes that showed a transformation in the dancers from beginning to end. Schlemmer also created designs that were assemblages of images, much like an abstract painting. For example, in *The Figural Cabinet* (1922), described by the designer as "Half shooting gallery - half *metaphysicum abstractum*," a giant hand slowly lowers and says "Stop!", differently colored balls "walk" across the stage, and one of them becomes a pendulum. Schlemmer's experiments influenced scores of artists, designers, and dancers in post–World War II Germany, as well as throughout the rest of the world.

Further Reading: Gropius (see Bibliography).

Thomas J. Mikotowicz

Schneider-Siemssen, Gunther. Set, costume and lighting designer (b. June 7, 1926, Augsberg, Germany). Schneider-Siemssen, the resident designer at the Staatoper, Volksoper, and Burgtheater in Vienna and teacher at the International Sommerakad fur bildende Kunst in Salzburg, has had a long and prolific career. While beginning his studies of design with Ludwig Sievert, Emil Preetorius, and Rudolf Hartman in Munich, he became apprentice to designer Clemens Krauss at the Staatoper in Munich from 1941 to 1944. After the war, from 1947 until 1954, he designed for theatre and film in Munich, Berlin, and Salzburg. In 1952, he began his twenty-year association with the Salzburg Marionettes, for whom he created new puppet stages and designed several of their productions of opera. By 1954, he was given his first official appointment as chief of design at the Bremen State Theater. After collaborating with Herbert Von Karajan on his *Pelleas and Melisande* for the Vienna State Opera company in 1960, Schneider-Siemssen moved to Vienna permanently and became von Karajan's production adviser. By 1962, he received his appointments as the chief designer for the Staatoper, Burgtheater, and Volksoper in Vienna.

Since his Covent Garden debut as the designer for Peter Ustinov's production of Schoenberg's *Erwartung* in 1962, Schneider-Siemssen has developed an international design career. He has created the settings and costumes for over seventy-five operas at numerous summer and Easter opera festivals, as well as for the major opera companies of Germany, Austria, Switzerland, Italy, Holland, Argentina, Bulgaria, England, the Soviet Union, the United States, and Yugoslavia. From 1969 through 1972, his stage designs were exhibited in Vienna, New York, Berlin, and Salzburg. He even designed an opera for Austrian television, *Daphne*. His work has been noted for its use of painted gauze and complicated series of patterns with colors for the spotlights. In his recent designs for the *Ring Cycle* (1990) at the Metropolitan Opera House, he created spectacular illusions such as Rhine maidens swimming, rainbow bridges, and a luminescent Valhalla. He has used projection and a ring-shaped platform to create the symbolic settings for Wagner's operas. Perhaps most notable is the designer's ability to use these elements to transform the stage into visual metaphors for the emotional states of the characters that Wagner expressed in his music.

Further Reading: Loney, Glenn. "Scenery for Salzburg's Super Stage: Von Karajan's challenge met by Designers Teo Otto and Gunther Schneider-Siemssen." *Theatre Design and Technology* December 1971: 13 + .

Andrea J. Nouryeh

Sequi, Sandro. Set and lighting designer, director, producer, and author (b. November 10, 1935, Rome, Italy). An accomplished director, musician, and set and lighting designer, Sequi began his studies at the National Academy of

Dramatic Arts in Rome. His debut as a director and designer in theatre came at the Spoleto Festival in 1960. One year later, he directed and designed his first opera, Respighi's *Lucrezia*, performed at La Fenice in Venice. Since then, he has both staged and designed numerous productions for opera, theatre, and television. Serving as the director-designer of operas for major companies in Argentina, Belgium, France, Greece, Holland, Portugal, the United Kingdom, and the United States, as well as the companies in all the major Italian cities, Sequi has earned an international reputation. Although he has staged over forty operas from the repertory, among his most noted are Verdi's *Otello*, Mozart's *Don Giovanni*, Puccini's *Madame Butterfly*, and Wagner's *Lohengrin*. For Sequi a faithful visual interpretation of the music takes precedence over realism in a design. Although his work is often highly stylized, Sequi will use an artistic quality that is most appropriate for the particular opera.

Andrea J. Nouryeh

Serlio, Sebastiano. Scenic designer, painter, theatrical architect, and theorist (b. 1475, Bologna, Italy; d. 1554, Paris, France). Serlio learned the crafts of drawing and painting from his father and worked for the first forty years of his life decorating churches, public buildings, and private palaces. In 1525 at the age of fifty, Serlio moved to Rome to study with Baldassare Peruzzi.* While in Rome, he accepted a few architectural commissions to make a living, including designing a wooden theatre at Vicenza. In 1541, he went to Paris to help decorate the Fontainbleau palace. After François I died in 1547, Serlio fell out of favor of the Court and took minor assignments in Lyon, but he returned to Paris and hoped for a reappointment until he died.

In 1537 Serlio began the major work of his life and wrote a commentary on architecture that appeared in seven separate books. The final work of *Architettura* was published in 1551. Basing much of his thought on Vitruvius's *De Archi-tectura* as well as some on the influence of Peruzzi, Serlio in the second book focused on theatre architecture and stage scenery. Serlio's theatre plans influenced the growth of the proscenium theatre and of illusionistic scenery. His proposed theatre included a semicircular seating plan in a rectangular auditorium and a deeply raked stage. For scenery, Serlio called for three stock scenes to be used for various plays: the tragic, the comic, and the satyric. The first was a street scene containing classical buildings, the second contained buildings and houses of the middle and low classes, and the third used pastoral landscapes in its composition. Serlio's books created for the first time an accurate account of Renaissance stage practice and were translated into many languages. Thus, they had a profound influence on production through the eighteenth century and are still valuable to scholars today.

Further Reading: Hewitt (see Bibliography); Oenslager (see Bibliography).

Thomas J. Mikotowicz

Servandoni, Giovanni Nicolò. Scene designer, stage machinist, architect, and painter (b. May 2, 1695, Florence, Italy; d. January 19, 1766, Paris, France). Servandoni began his art training with Pannini and then studied architecture in

Rome with Rossi. In 1724, he traveled to Paris, where he collaborated on designs for the operas *Pyramis and Thisbe* (1726) and *Prosperpine* at the Académie Royale de Musique. By 1728, he was promoted to head painter at the academy, succeeding the Bérains,* where he continued to work until 1735. In addition, at this time he became closely associated with the French Court and designed a number of plays, festivals, weddings, and celebrations for them. He was elected to the Academy of Painting and Sculpture in 1731 and was sought after to design many architectural projects. From 1738 to 1742, he produced several exhibitions of spectacular lighting and scenery. At the Salle des Machines, he produced a son et lumière (a diorama combining sound, light, and motion) of St. Peter's Cathedral in Rome. In 1742, he collaborated with Giovanni Bibiena* at the Opera de Tejo and the Ajuda Theatre. During this time he designed more than sixty productions for the Paris Opera and created a new entertainment called the "silent play"—a succession of theatrical scenes with accompanying music but without actors. He continued to work throughout western Europe for various royal houses for the remainder of his life. In 1749, he moved to London, where he designed a grand festival with pyrotechnics in St. James Park and worked in Covent Garden. By 1754, he had returned to Paris, where he continued to design at least until 1758. In 1760, he was hired by the Hapsburg grand duke of Vienna to design a wedding, and, in 1763, he was contracted in Württemberg to design a series of opera scenes.

Elbin L. Cleveland

Sharaff, Irene. Costume and scenery designer (b. 1912, Boston, MA). Theatrical productions (all were in New York City, unless otherwise specified) include *Alice in Wonderland* (scenery and costumes; Civic Repertory Theatre)—1932; *As Thousands Cheer* (Music Box Theatre)—1933; *Life Begins at 8:40* (Winter Garden Theatre), *The Great Waltz* (Center Theatre)—1934; *Crime and Punishment* (Biltmore Theatre), *Parade* (Guild Theatre), *Jubilee* (Imperial Theatre), *Rosmersholm* (Shubert Theatre), *Union Pacific* (Ballets Russes)—1935; *Idiot's Delight* (Shubert Theatre), *On Your Toes* (Majestic Theatre), *White Horse Inn* (Center Theatre)—1936; *Virginia* (Center Theatre), *I'd Rather Be Right* (Alvin Theatre), *Jeu de Cartes* (American Ballet Theatre)—1937; *Boys from Syracuse* (Alvin Theatre)—1938; *The American Way* (Center Theatre), *Streets of Paris*, *Gay New Orleans* (both at the Hall of Music, New York World's Fair)—1939; *Boys and Girls Together* (Broadhurst Theatre), *All in Fun* (Majestic Theatre)—1940; *Lady in the Dark* (Alvin Theatre), *The Land Is Bright* (Music Box Theatre), *Sunny River* (St. James Theatre), *Banjo Eyes* (Hollywood Theatre)—1941; *By Jupiter* (Hollywood Theatre), *Star and Garter* (Music Box Theatre), *Count Me In* (Ethel Barrymore Theatre)—1942; *Madame Curie* (film, MGM)—1943; *Meet Me in St. Louis* (film, MGM), *Ziegfeld Follies* (film, MGM)—1945; *The Would-Be Gentleman* (Booth Theatre), *Hamlet* (City Center), *Facsimile* (American Ballet Theatre), *The Best Years of Our Lives* (film, Goldwyn)—1946; *The Secret Life of Walter Mitty* (film, Goldwyn)—1946; *The Bishop's Wife* (film, Goldwyn)—1947; *Bonanza Bound* (Shubert Theater, Philadelphia), *Magdalena* (Ziegfeld Theatre), *A Song Is Born* (film, Goldwyn), *Every Girl Should Be Married* (film, RKO)—1948; *Montserrat* (Fulton Theatre)—1949; *Dance Me a Song* (Royal Theatre), *Mike Todd's Peepshow* (Winter Garden Theatre), *Age of Anxiety*, *Design with Strings* (both at the American Ballet Theatre)—1950; *The King and I* (St. James Theatre), *A Tree Grows in Brooklyn* (Alvin Theatre), *An American in Paris* (film, MGM; costumes and scenery for ballet sequence), *Huckleberry Finn* (film, MGM)—1951; *Of Thee I Sing* (Ziegfeld Theatre), *Call Me Madam* (film, 20th Century Fox)—1952; *Me and Juliet* (Majestic Theatre), *Fanfare* (American Ballet Theatre), *The King and I* (London), *Brigadoon* (film, MGM)—1953; *By the Beautiful Sea* (Majestic Theatre), *On Your Toes* (46th Street Theatre), *A Star Is Born* (film, Warner Brothers; costumes and scenery for the "born in a Trunk" number)—1954; *Guys and Dolls* (film, Goldwyn)—1955; *Shangri-La* (Winter Garden Theatre), *Candide* (Martin Beck Theatre), *Happy Hunting* (Majestic Theatre), *The Concert* (American Ballet Theatre), *Rib of Eve* (American Ballet Theatre), *The King and I* (film, 20th Century Fox)—1956; *Small War on Murray Hill* (Ethel Barrymore Theatre), *West Side Story* (Winter Garden Theatre)—1957; *Flower Drum Song* (St. James Theatre), *Three x Three* (American Ballet Theatre)—1958; *Juno* (Shubert Theatre), *Porgy and Bess* (film, Goldwyn)—1959; *Do Re Mi* (St. James Theatre), *Can-Can* (film, 20th Century Fox)—1960; *West Side Story* (film, United Artists), *Flower Drum Song* (film, Universal Pictures)—1961; *Jenny* (Colonial Theatre, Boston), *The Girl Who Came to Supper* (Broadway Theatre), *Boys from Syracuse* (London), *Cleopatra* (film, 20th Century Fox; costumes for Elizabeth Taylor)—1963; *Funny Girl* (Winter Garden Theatre), *The King and I* (New York State Theatre)—1964; *Sweet Charity* (Palace Theatre), *The Sandpiper* (film, MGM)—1965; *Who's Afraid of Virginia Woolf?* (film, Warner Brothers)—1966; *Hallelujah, Baby!* (Martin Beck Theatre), *The Taming of the Shrew* (film, Columbia; costumes for Elizabeth Taylor)—1967; *Slaughter on Tenth Avenue* (American Ballet Theatre), *Funny Girl* (film; costumes for Barbra Streisand)—1968; *Hello, Dolly!* (film, 20th Century Fox), *Justine* (film, 20th Century Fox)—1969; *The Great White Hope* (film, 20th Century Fox)—1970; *PAMTGG, Printemps, The Concert* (New York City Ballet)—1971; *Interplay* (American Ballet Theatre), *Irene* (Minskoff Theatre; costumes for Debbie Reynolds)—1972; *Fanfare* (American Ballet Theatre), *The Other Side of Midnight* (film, 20th Century Fox)—1976; *The King and I* (Uris Theatre)—1970; *West Side Story* (Minskoff Theatre)—1980.

Sharaff, a major costume and scenery designer for both theatre and motion pictures for over fifty years, has worked with many accomplished theatrical producers, including George Abbott, the Shuberts, Sam Harris, and David Merrick, and was the first American to design for the Ballets Russes. She began her career in 1928 as an assistant to Aline Bernstein,* who succeeded Gladys Calthorp as Eva Le Gallienne's scenic designer at the Civic Repertory Theater in New York. In 1932, when Le Gallienne asked Sharaff to design the scenery and costumes for a new Civic production of *Alice in Wonderland*, her career as a major designer was formally launched. Soon after she began work on *Alice*, Sharaff realized that Le Gallienne wanted the scenery and costumes to look as if they had been drawn by Tenniel, so she copied the artist's cross-hatched technique and even added painted shadows to the costumes and scenery for a chiaroscuro effect. The settings were drawn on a huge scroll like a typewriter ribbon and were fed scene by scene from a spool on the left across the back of the stage to the right. All scene changes took place in front of the audience, and in the words of New York *World-Journal* critic John Anderson, "They keep the entire production moving without unnecessary delays, and are ingeniously scaled to suggest Alice's changes in height." The following year, Sharaff created her first period costumes when she designed the clothes for Irving Berlin's "Easter Parade" number in the musical revue *As Thousands Cheer*. Berlin wanted to re-create a scene from the old rotogravure section of the *New York Times* Sunday edition. Sharaff spent many hours in the library to research the styles of the 1880s and finally achieved the sepia tone effect she wanted through the use of color—a wide range of brown tones—and a variety of fabrics in different textures.

Research, authenticity, and the use of color to heighten and contrast are the hallmarks of Sharaff's technique. She has been quoted as saying that no one can be a designer without knowing history, and the first thing she works out in complete detail when she begins to design for a new production is the color scheme. For example, Sharaff spent months studying photographs and pictures of the royal family of Siam and used authentic Thai fabrics and brocades to create the brilliant reds, blues, and greens of the Siamese Court in *The King and I*. Sharaff's costumes for Gertrude Lawrence, as Anna, were designed in pale tones of gray and yellow and stood in stark contrast to the bright Oriental background. Realizing that exaggeration and fantasy had no place in the urban landscape of *West Side Story*, Sharaff simply used color to contrast the T-shirts worn by members of the two teenage gangs in the musical: bright purple, crimson, violet, and black for the Sharks, and muted indigos, musty yellows, and ochers for the Jets.

In 1942, when producer Arthur Freed asked Sharaff to design costumes for Metro-Goldwyn-Mayer (MGM) studios in Hollywood, she began a second career designing for motion pictures, which continued into the 1970s. In addition to designing costumes for such classic films as *Meet Me in St. Louis*, *The Best Years of Our Lives*, and *An American in Paris*, Sharaff is one of the few designers who has had the opportunity to design costumes for the film versions of many of her original Broadway successes, including *The King and I*, *West Side Story*, *Flower Drum Song*, and *Funny Girl*. On screen, her work will continue to inspire future designers for many years to come.

Awards: Sharaff's designs have earned her two Donaldson Awards (for *Alice in Wonderland*, 1932, and *The King and I*, 1951), as well as a Tony Award for *The King and I*. In addition, she has earned five Academy Awards for Best Achievement in Costume Design for *An American in Paris* (1951), *The King and I* (1956), *West Side Story* (1961), *Cleopatra* (1963), and *Who's Afraid of Virginia Woolf?* (1966).

Further Reading: By Sharaff: *Broadway to Hollywood: Costumes Designed by Irene Sharaff.* New York: Van Nostrand Reinhold, 1976.

About Sharaff: "Costume Designs for *All in Fun* and *Lady in the Dark.*" *Theatre Arts* January 1941; LaVine, W. Robert. *In a Glamorous Fashion.* New York: Charles Scribner's Sons, 1980; Leese, Elizabeth. *Costume Design in the Movies.* Bembridge, Isle of Wight: BCW, 1976; "Theater Costumes of Irene Sharaff." *Harper's Bazaar* April 1941.

Howard Gutner

Shelving, Paul. Set and costume designer (b. October 29, 1889, Staffordshire, England; d. June 5, 1968, Warwick, England). Shelving began his theatre career as assistant scenographer with the Moody-Manners Opera Company in 1905. He produced his first professional design, which included both scenery and costumes, for *Dame Julian's Window* in 1913. After military service in World War I, he returned in 1919 and began a lifelong relationship with the Birmingham Repertory Theatre. He was an excellent scene painter, praised for his fine use of color, but equally capable with highly stylized expressionistic shows, realistic works, and period reproductions. Much of his early recognition, however, came from his stylized work *Gas* and *The Immortal Hour* (1922), in which he used simple forms and large flat areas, much like Adolphe Appia.* Also, he designed many classic plays, including *Henry V*, which depicted a very symmetrical, monolithic castle entrance, and *Back to Methuselah* (1925), which used a bright color scheme and whimsically curving lines to depict a nonrepresentative forest. During his fifty-five-year career, he designed more than one hundred productions in Birmingham and London and some historical plays with the Malvern Festival Theatre. Many of the productions he designed for the Birmingham Repertory Theatre moved on to London's West End, including *The Immortal Hour* (1922) and *The Marvellous History of St. Bernard* (1926).

Further Reading: Trewin, V. C. *The Birmingham Repertory Theatre: 1913–1963.* London: Barrie and Rockliff, 1963.

Elbin L. Cleveland

Sheringham, George. Set designer (b. 1885, England; d. 1937). Sheringham, like his contemporaries Claude Lovat Fraser* and Aubrey Hammond,* was an artist who infused his settings with a strong sense of painting and design. But because he was influenced by Edward Gordon Craig,* his sets were never overly burdensome. They were often simple unit settings that could be altered through the use of curtains. His most significant productions include Sheridan's *The Duenna*, which he designed for director Nigel Playfair in 1924. The setting was a simple unit comprised of archways and doors on two levels, over which was mounted a crescent-shaped drop, elaborately painted in art nouveau style. The model is currently on display in the Victoria and Albert Museum in London. His other productions followed the same simple, yet decorative style: *Love in a Village* (1928); *The Lady of The Camellias*, produced at the Garrick Theatre in London; *Midsummer Madness*; and the *Swindburne Ballet* in London. Sheringham was also involved in remounting Gilbert and Sullivan's operas in 1928 and subsequently designed *Twelfth Night* (1932) and other productions at the Stratford-on-Avon Shakespeare Festival. Working with director Walter Bridges-Adams and alongside a group of designers that included Norman Wilkinson*and Theodore Komisarjevsky,* Sheringham had strong ideas about the role of design in the theatre. Among his many beliefs was that only one artist should design both sets and costumes, a practice not commonly followed in his time. In 1925, as a way of inciting interest in new design aesthetics, he published *Design in the Theatre*, a collection of design plates by Continental designers whose work was exceptional.

Further Reading: By Sheringham: with James Laver. *Design in the Theatre*. London, 1927.

Thomas J. Mikotowicz

Simonson, Lee. Set designer, director, author, and artist (b. June 26, 1888, New York City; d. 1967). Theatrical productions include *Love of Our Neighbor*, *The Miracle of St. Anthony*, *Overtones*—1915; *The Magical City*, *Pierre Patelin*, *The Red Cloak*—1916; *The Faithful*, *The Rise of Silas Lapham*, *Molière*—1919; *The Power of Darkness*, *The Cat Bird*, *Jane Clegg*, *Martinique*, *The Dance of Death*, *The Treasure*, *Heartbreak House*—1920; *Mr. Pim Passes By*, *Liliom*, *Don Juan*—1921; *He Who Gets Slapped*, *Back to Methuselah*, *From Morn to Midnight*, *R.U.R.*, *The World We Live In (The Insect Comedy)*, *The Lucky One*, *The Tidings Brought to Mary*—1922; *Peer Gynt*, *The Adding Machine*, *As You Like It*, *The Devil's Disciple*, *The Failures*, *Les Rates*—1923; *Sweet Little Evil*, *Fata Morgana*, *Man and the Masses*, *Bewitched*, *The Mongrel*, *Carnival!*—1924; *Arms and the Man*, *The Glass Slipper*—1925; *The Goat Song*, *Juarez and Maximillian*—1926; *The Road to Rome*—1927; *Marco Millions*, *Volpone*, *Faust*—1928; *Dynamo*, *Camel Through a Needle's Eye*, *Damn Your Humour*—1929; *Roar China*, *The Apple Cart*, *Hotel Universe*, *Elizabeth the Queen*—1930; *Miracle at Verdun*, *The Insect Play*, *As You Like It*, *Lean Harvest*, *Pas d'Acier*—1931; *Collision*, *The Good Earth*, *Red Planet*—1932; *American Dream*, *The Mask and the Face*, *The School for Husbands*—1933; *Days Without End*, *They Shall Not Die*, *Jigsaw*, *Rain from Heaven*, *A Sleeping Clergyman*—1934; *The Simpleton of the Unexpected Isle*, *Parade*—1935; *Call It a Day*, *End of Summer*, *Idiot's Delight*, *Prelude to Exile*—1936; *The Masque of Kings*, *Virginia*, *Amphytrion 38*, *Madame Bovary*, *Swan Lake*, *Voices of Spring*—1937; *Lorelei*, *Wine of Choice*—1938; *The Streets Are Guarded*—1944; *Foxhole in the Parlor*—1945; *Joan of Lorraine*—1946; *The Ring*—1947.

Simonson graduated from the Ethical Culture High School in 1905 and Harvard in 1908, where he was a member of Professor George Pierce Baker's contemporary playwriting class. Immediately afterward, he traveled to Paris and continued his studies of art and theatrical design at the Academie Julien, as well as at various studios. He returned to the United States in 1912, became involved with the Washington Square Players, and designed his first show in 1915.

In 1919, he and director Philip Moeller founded the Theatre Guild, a professional company dedicated to the production of noncommercial and classic plays. Simonson remained on the board of the theatre as artistic director and principal designer until his resignation in 1939. Among his designs were *The Faithful* (1919), *Back to Methuselah* (1922), and *Marco Millions* (1928).

Simonson, together with such American designers as Robert Edmond Jones* and Samuel Hume,* was a proponent of the "New Stagecraft" movement. Studying the new European theories of design by such theorists as Adolphe Appia* and Edward Gordon Craig,* Simonson developed a style of design that was simple and suggestive. Using simple masses and dramatic lighting effects, Simonson, who had recently traveled to Germany to view productions, created stunning effects for his productions, including *Liliom* (1921). For *Dynamo* (1929), another Theatre Guild production, Simonson re-created an electrical power plant on the stage that towered above the performers' heads but that contained only enough elements to create the environment—a simplified realism. Similarly, his designs for *Roar China* (1930) were equally effective. For this show, he created a battleship onstage and used only selected views of it.

Later, Simonson became involved in opera and designed such works as *The Ring* (1947) by Wagner at the Metropolitan Opera House and *Le Pas d'Acier* by Stravinsky. As a theorist, Simonson authored several books, among them *The Stage Is Set* (1932), a description of current design and a critique of Craig's theories; *Part of a Lifetime* (1943), an autobiography; and *The Art of Scene Design* (1950), a text on design for beginners.

Further Reading: Books by Simonson: *The Art of Scene Design*. New York, Harper and Brothers, 1950; *Part of a Lifetime*. New York: Duell, Sloan, and Pearce, 1943; *Settings and Costumes in the United States*, ed. with Theodore Komisarjevsky. London: The Studio, Limited, 1933; *The Stage Is Set*. New York: Theatre Arts Books, 1970 (seventh printing). In addition, he wrote many articles.

About Simonson: Larson, Orville K. *Scene Design in the American Theatre: From 1915 to 1960*. Fayetteville, AR: University of Arkansas Press, 1989; Larson, Orville K. "Settings and Costumes by Lee Simonson." *Theatre Design & Technology* February 1963.

Thomas J. Mikotowicz

Smith, Oliver. Set designer, theatrical producer, and teacher (b. February 13, 1918, Waupun, WI). Theatrical productions (all had sets designed by Smith and opened in New York City, unless otherwise noted) include *Saratoga* (ballet at Metropolitan Opera House)—1941; *Hello Out There*, *Coming Through the Rye*, *The End of the Beginning* (co-produced and designed sets for three plays for McCarter Theatre, Princeton, New Jersey), *Rodeo* (ballet at Metropolitan Opera House), *Rosalinda* (operetta at 44th Street Theatre)—1942; *The Wind Remains* (Museum of Modern Theatre)—1943; *Fancy Free* (ballet at Metropolitan Opera House), *The New Moon* (operetta at New York City Center), *Waltz Academy* (ballet at Metropolitan Opera House), *The Perfect Marriage* (Ethel Barrymore Theatre), *Sebastian* (ballet at Phoenix Theatre), *Rhapsody* (operetta at Century Theatre), *On the Town* (coproduced and designed sets, Adelphi Theatre)—1944;

Interplay (ballet at Metropolitan Opera House), *On Stage!* (ballet at Metropolitan Opera House), *Billion Dollar Baby* (coproduced and designed, Alvin Theatre)— 1945; *Twilight Bar* (pre-Broadway run), *The Medium* (opera at Columbia University), *Facsimile* (ballet at Broadway Theatre), *No Exit* (co-produced), *Beggar's Holiday* (Broadway Theatre)—1946; *Brigadoon* (Ziegfeld Theatre), *High Button Shoes* (Century Theatre), *Bonanza Bound!* (coproduced and designed, pre-Broadway run), *Topaze* (Morosco Theatre)—1947; *Look, Ma, I'm Dancin'!* (Adelphi Theatre), *Me and Molly* (coproduced and designed, Belasco Theatre), *Fall River Legend* (ballet at Metropolitan Opera House), *That's the Ticket* (Shubert Theatre)—1948; *Along Fifth Avenue* (Broadhurst Theatre), *Miss Liberty* (Imperial Theatre), *Gentlemen Prefer Blondes* (coproduced and designed, Ziegfeld Theatre)—1949; *Age of Anxiety*, *Nimbus* (two ballets at Center Theatre), *Bless You All* (coproduced and designed, Mark Hellinger Theatre)—1950; *Paint Your Wagon* (Shubert Theatre)—1951; *Pal Joey* (Ethel Barrymore Theatre)—1952; *The Band Wagon* (MGM film), *Carnival in Flanders* (New Century Theatre), *At Home with Ethel Waters* (48th Street Theatre), *In the Summer House* (coproduced and designed, Playhouse)—1953; *The Burning Glass* (Longacre Theatre), *The Tender Land* (opera at New York State Theatre), *Carousel* (New York City Center), *On Your Toes* (46th Street Theatre)—1954; *Oklahoma!* (A Sam Goldwyn Company film), *Guys and Dolls* (MGM film), *Will Success Spoil Rock Hunter?* (Belasco Theatre), *The Amazing Adele* (Shubert Theatre)—1955; *My Fair Lady* (Mark Hellinger Theatre), *Mr. Wonderful* (Broadway Theatre), *Rib of Eve* (ballet at Metropolitan Opera House), *Auntie Mame* (Broadhurst Theatre), *Candide* (Martin Beck Theatre)—1956; *A Clearing in the Woods* (coproduced and designed, Belasco Theatre), *Eugenia* (Ambassador Theatre), *A Visit to a Small Planet* (Booth Theatre), *La Traviata* (opera at Metropolitan Opera House), *The Saturday Night Kid* (coproduced and designed, pre-Broadway), *West Side Story* (Winter Garden Theatre), *The Carefree Heart* (Cass Theatre), *Jamaica* (Imperial Theatre), *Time Remembered* (Morosco Theatre), *Nude with Violin* (Belasco Theatre)—1957; *Present Laughter* (Belasco Theatre), *Winesburg, Ohio* (National Theatre), *Say, Darling* (ANTA Theatre), *Tristan* (ballet at Metropolitan Opera House), *Flower Drum Song* (St. James Theatre)—1958; *Porgy and Bess* (MGM film), *Juno* (coproduced and designed, Winter Garden Theatre), *Destry Rides Again* (Imperial Theatre), *Cheri* (Morosco Theatre), *Take Me Along* (Shubert Theatre), *The Sound of Music* (Lunt-Fontanne Theatre), *Five Finger Exercise* (Music Box Theatre), *Juniper and the Pagans* (pre-Broadway run), *Goodbye Charlie* (Lyceum Theatre)—1959; *A Taste of Honey* (Lyceum Theatre), *Becket* (St. James Theatre), *The Unsinkable Molly Brown* (Winter Garden Theatre), *Under the Yum-Yum Tree* (Henry Miller's Theatre), *Camelot* (Majestic Theatre)—1960; *Martha* (opera at Metropolitan Opera House), *Show Girl* (coproduced and designed, Eugene O'Neill Theatre), *Mary, Mary* (Helen Hayes Theatre), *Points on Jazz* (ballet at Broadway Theatre), *Sail Away* (Broadhurst Theatre), *The Gay Life* (Shubert Theatre), *The Harvest* (opera, Lyric Opera of Chicago), *Daughter of Silence* (Music Box Theatre), *The Night of the Iguana* (Royale Theatre)—1961; *Romulus* (Music

Box Theatre), *Eddie Fisher at the Winter Garden* (Winter Garden Theatre), *Come On Strong* (Morosco Theatre), *Lord Pengo* (Royale Theatre), *Tiger, Tiger Burning Bright* (coproduced and designed, Booth Theatre)—1962; *Natural Affection* (coproduced and designed, Booth Theatre), *Children from Their Games* (Morosco Theatre), *The Time of the Barracudas* (pre-Broadway run), *Barefoot in the Park* (Biltmore Theatre), *110 in the Shade* (Broadhurst Theatre), *The Girl Who Came to Supper* (Broadway Theatre)—1963; *The Chinese Prime Minister* (Royale Theatre), *Hello, Dolly!* (St. James Theatre), *Dylan* (Plymouth Theatre), *Beekman Place* (Morosco Theatre), *Ben Franklin in Paris* (Lunt-Fontanne Theatre), *I Was Dancing* (Lyceum Theatre), *Luv* (Booth Theatre), *Bajour* (Shubert Theatre), *Slow Dance on the Killing Ground* (Plymouth Theatre), *Poor Richard* (Helen Hayes Theatre), *The Great Waltz* (Drury Lane, London/San Francisco Civic Opera, California)—1964; *Kelly* (Broadhurst Theatre), *Baker Street* (Broadway Theatre), *The Odd Couple* (Plymouth Theatre), *The Four Marys* (ballet at New York State Theatre), *Les Noces* (ballet at Metropolitan Opera House), *Hot September* (pre-Broadway run), *A Very Rich Woman* (Belasco Theatre), *Don Giovanni* (Opera Company of Boston, Massachusetts), *On a Clear Day You Can See Forever* (Mark Hellinger Theatre), *The Cactus Flower* (Royale Theatre)—1965; *This Winter's Hobby* (pre-Broadway run), *The Best Laid Plans* (Brooks Atkinson Theatre), *Dido and Aeneas* (opera at Kansas City Music Hall, Kansas), *Show Boat* (New York State Theatre)—1966; *Breakfast at Tiffany's* (Majestic Theatre), *Moses and Aron* (opera at Boston's Back Bay Theatre, Massachusetts), *I Do! I Do!* (46th Street Theatre), *The Star-Spangled Girl* (Plymouth Theatre)—1966; *Dumas and Son* (Los Angeles Civic Light Opera, California), *Illya Darling* (Mark Hellinger Theatre), *Swan Lake*, *Harbinger* (two ballets at New York State Theatre), *Falstaff* (Washington, D.C., Opera), *Stephen D.* (coproduced at East 74th Street Theatre), *Song of the Grasshopper* (ANTA Theatre), *The Niggerlovers* (coproduced at Orpheum Theatre), *How Now, Dow Jones* (Lunt-Fontanne Theatre), *The Catherine Wheel* (ballet at New York City Center)—1967; *Darling of the Day* (George Abbott Theatre), *Plaza Suite* (Plymouth Theatre), *Weekend* (pre-Broadway run), *Carmen* (National Opera Company), *The Exercise* (coproduced and designed, John Golden Theatre), *Collision Course* (coproduced at Café Au Go Go), *Giselle* (ballet at Metropolitan Opera House)—1968; *1491* (San Francisco Civic Opera, California), *Dear World* (Mark Hellinger Theatre), *Adaptation/Next* (coproduced at Greenwich Mews Theatre), *But, Seriously . . .* (Henry Miller's Theatre), *Come Summer* (Lunt-Fontanne Theatre), *A Patriot for Me* (Imperial Theatre), *Indians* (coproduced and designed, Brooks Atkinson Theatre), *Jimmy* (Winter Garden Theatre), *Last of the Red Hot Lovers* (Eugene O'Neill Theatre)—1969; *Petrouchka* (ballet at New York State Theatre), *Bequest to the Nation* (Theatre Royal/Haymarket, London), *Alice in Wonderland* (coproduced at Extension Theatre), *Lovely Ladies, Kind Gentlemen* (Majestic Theatre)—1970; *Four on a Garden* (Broadhurst Theatre), *Prettybelle* (pre-Broadway run), *The Most Important Man* (opera at New York State Theatre)—1971; *The Time of Your Life* (Kennedy Center, Washington, D.C.), *Eccentrique* (ballet at New York City Center), *Lost* *in the Stars* (Imperial Theatre), *The Little Black Book* (Kennedy Center), *Mass* (Kennedy Center, Washington, D.C.), *Verdi's Requiem* (coproduced at St. Paul's Cathedral, London), *Doctor Selavy's Magic Theatre* (coproduced at Mercer/O'Casey Theatre), *The Mother of Us All* (coproduced and designed, opera at Guggenheim Museum)—1972; *Tricks* (Alvin Theatre), *The Women* (46th Street Theatre), *Gigi* (L.A. Civic Light Opera)—1973; *Endgame* (coproduced at Manhattan Project), *Present Laughter* (Kennedy Center, Washington, D.C.), *Perfect Pitch* (Kennedy Center, Washington, D.C.), *Sleeping Beauty* (ballet at New York State Theatre), *All Over Town* (Booth Theatre)—1974; *Don't Call Back* (Helen Hayes Theatre), *The Royal Family* (Helen Hayes Theatre)—1975; *The Heiress* (Kennedy Center, Washington, D.C.), *Kismet* (Los Angeles Civic Light Opera, California), *Texas Fourth* (ballet at New York State Theatre)—1976; *Do You Turn Somersaults?* (46th Street Theatre), *Gracious Living* (Kennedy Center, Washington, D.C.), *Naughty Marietta* (operetta at New York State Theatre), *First Monday in October* (Majestic Theatre)—1978; *Carmelina* (St. James Theatre), *Contredances* (ballet at Metropolitan Opera House), *Home and Beauty* (Kennedy Center, Washington, D.C.)—1979; *Clothes for a Summer Hotel* (Cort Theatre), *Lunch Hour* (Ethel Barrymore Theatre), *Mixed Couples* (Brooks Atkinson Theatre)—1980; *Talent for Murder* (Biltmore Theatre), *Wild Boy* (Kennedy Center), *The Nutcracker* (ballet in Milwaukee, Wisconsin)—1981; *The Nightingale* (First All Children's Theatre), *84, Charing Cross Road* (Nederlander Theatre)—1982; *Estuary* (ballet at Metropolitan Opera House)—1983; *Amnon V'Tamar* (ballet at Metropolitan Opera House), *The Golden Age* (Jack Lawrence Theatre), *Beloved Friend* (Hartman Theatre, Stamford, Connecticut), *Wind in the Willows* (pre-Broadway)—1984; *Night of the Iguana, Twelfth Night* (Repertory of St. Louis, Missouri)—1986; *Jerome Robbins' Broadway* (several of Smith's original designs for musicals were re-created by Robin Wagner*)—1988; *Fall River Legend*—1990.

Smith, one of the world's most accomplished designers, is credited with designing more than four hundred productions, including theatre, dance, opera, and four movie musicals. He and the late Lucia Chase served as codirectors of American Ballet Theatre (ABT) from 1945 to 1980. The company's management was turned over to Russian emigré and dancer Mikhail Barishnikov, who resigned in 1991, and Smith was asked to return as director. Smith also produced many successful Broadway plays. In addition, his efforts have been applied to the redesigning of the interiors of several theatres, including the National Theatre in Washington, D.C. Currently, he holds a post at New York University as "master teacher of scene design."

After attending the University of Pennsylvania as an architectural student who then switched to a degree in fine arts, Smith considered continuing his formal education in the theatre. He was sidetracked to New York City, however, where he intended to work a year before attending Yale. After a number of menial jobs, he began his career as a ballet designer in his early twenties. Smith created the decor for *Saratoga* (1941), his first major ballet, and then for *Rodeo* (1942) by Agnes De Mille and won praise from the critics. This was followed by the ballet *Fancy Free* in 1944 and solidified an alliance among him, choreographer Jerome Robbins, and composer Leonard Bernstein. Transforming this ballet into a musical, the trio mounted its first Broadway hit, *On the Town*, with Smith as both designer and coproducer. His future as a force on Broadway was launched, and he soon became codirector of the American Ballet Theatre as well. On Broadway, he provided the lavish designs for such forties musicals as *Gentlemen Prefer Blondes*, *High Button Shoes*, and *Brigadoon*. In the fifties, he proved his mastery of design with the shows *My Fair Lady*, *West Side Story*, and *The Sound of Music*, as well as many Broadway plays, operas, ballets, and such movie musicals as *The Bandwagon* and *Oklahoma!* His prolific career continued throughout the sixties and seventies with such successful shows as *Indians*, *Night of the Iguana*, and Neil Simon's *The Odd Couple*. Throughout the eighties and nineties, Smith has continued to design many revivals of his earlier hits as well as new theatre and dance productions.

Perhaps Smith's technique is best illustrated through his approach to designing for the musical and ballet; he states that the design is not a static thing in itself, but part of the choreography. For example, Lizzie Borden's eerie house in the ballet *Fall River Legend* is reassembled by the dancers into a gallows, a church, and various street scenes. In the musical *Hello, Dolly!* the locales moved gracefully from the feed store to the millinery shop and to the Harmonia Garden's Restaurant. Similarly, his sets for *West Side Story* moved with equal grace, seeming to reappear and dissolve as the story unfolded. Yet Smith adheres to one concept that runs throughout all of his work: the set should be simple, free from unessential details and fussiness. He continues to pass this knowledge on to new generations of designers through his teaching as well as through the continuing example of his work.

Awards: His efforts have earned him eight Tony Awards for *My Fair Lady* (1956), *West Side Story* (1957), *The Sound of Music* (1959), *Camelot* (1960), *Becket* (1960), *Hello, Dolly!* (1964), and *Baker Street* (1965) and one special Tony Award in 1965 for "Sustained Achievement." His work and design have also garnered for him four Donaldson Awards for *Brigadoon* (1947), *High Button Shoes* (1947), *Gentlemen Prefer Blondes* (1949), and *Pal Joey* (revival, 1952); four New York Drama Critics' Awards for *My Fair Lady*, *Candide* (1956), *Destry Rides Again* (1959), and *Camelot*; an Oscar nomination for the movie *Guys and Dolls* (1955); the Sam S. Shubert Award (1960) for distinguished contributions to the theatre; the Handel Medallion (1975) from the city of New York as an outstanding figure in the arts; and special awards at the Kennedy Center and the Waldorf Astoria Hotel for his work with American Ballet Theatre.

Further Reading: By Smith: "Ballet Design." *Dance News Annual* 1953: 93–102; "More Than Just Interior Decoration." *Theatre Arts Magazine* June 1958; essay on musical theatre design in Larsen, Orville K. *Scene Design for Stage and Screen*. East Lansing, MI: Michigan University Press, 1961; "Setting the Stage: 'A Taste of Honey.' " *Theatre Arts* February 1961.

About Smith: "Designers on Designing: A Profile of Oliver Smith." *Theatre Crafts Magazine* April 1982; interview in Pecktal, Lynn. *Designing and Painting for the Theatre*.

New York: Holt, Rinehart, and Winston, 1975; ''A Man for All Scenes.'' *Time* March 19, 1965.

Thomas J. Mikotowicz

Sommi, Leone Di Ebreo. Producer of Court entertainments and dramatist (b. 1525, Mantua, Italy; d. 1592). Patronized by Mantuan nobility, di Sommi was the producer of theatrical entertainments for the Court and became the official author for the Accademia degli Invaghiti, directed by Prince Cesare Gonzaga. He is best known for *I doni*, a historic pastoral; *The Comedy of a Marriage*, a Hebrew play; and *L'Hirifile*, an Italian play. An expert in the stage practice of his day, di Sommi wrote *Dialogues on Stage Affairs*, which has been translated and appears in the appendix of Allardyce Nicoll's *The Development of the Theatre* (see Bibliography). The dialogues are accounts of lighting, makeup artistry for indoor lighting, costuming, and histrionic techniques. Of particular interest is the information these dialogues provide on artificial light on the sixteenth-century Italian stage: how shading, atmosphere, and bright lights were achieved by using careful placement of lamps, mirror reflectors, and candles.

Andrea J. Nouryeh

Soudekine, Serge. Set designer and studio artist (b. 1882, Smolensk, Russia; d. 1946). Soudekine's development as a designer occurred when he was a student and studio artist at the Moscow Institute of Painting, Sculpture, and Architecture from 1897 to 1909. He was associated with such artists as Aleksandr Golovine* in Diaghilev's World of Art group. Unlike Golovine, Soudekine ended his career by designing highly decorative scenery rather than scenery of social realism. After his first highly symbolic design work for Maurice Maeterlinck's *Soeur Beatrice* in 1906, Soudekine went on to design scenery and costumes for a variety of theatre, dance, and especially opera productions. Throughout his career, he created new designs two or three times for many titles. The highlight of his career in Russia was with the design for Aleksandr Tairov's production of *The Marriage of Figaro* (1915) at the Chamber Theatre in Moscow. Although enthusiastically received by the public and critics, Tairov was not satisfied with the highly stylized, sumptuous red and gold scenery because it did not unite the production. Nevertheless, his flamboyant, highly decorative style remained Soudekine's strength and formed the approach to his other play and opera designs. His painterly design for Diaghilev's Paris production of *La Tragedie de Salome* in 1913 is remembered for its ability to evoke the malevolence and mysticism of its lead character. After the Revolution, Soudekine emigrated to Paris, and eventually to New York. His work for the New York Metropolitan Opera in the 1920s rivaled the sumptuousness of his work in Paris. His bold, vivid costumes and scenery for *Petrouchka* (1925), *Le Rossignol* (1926), and *Porgy and Bess* are exemplary of his ability to provide rich decoration for evocative music and dance. Up to his death Soudekine continued to design for American ballet companies and created the decor for such productions as *Reminicience* for American Ballet and *La Fille Mal Gardée* for Ballet Theatre.

Brian R. Jones

Stanfield, William Clarkson. Scene painter, designer, and artist (b. 1793, England; d. 1867). Stanfield was considered a preeminent scenic artist during the nineteenth century and was responsible for more than five hundred scenic drops. His work challenged that of the famous Grieve family.* After leaving the Merchant Navy in 1815, he began painting scenery at the Royalty Theatre in Wellclose Square. In 1831, he worked in the Theatre Royal, Edinburgh, and later returned to London to become the scenic director at the Coburg Theatre and eventually at the Drury Lane Theatre. While employed by William Charles Macready as one of the principal designers at Covent Garden, Stanfield used a scenic device that was relatively new to the London theatre—the diorama. For *Henry V* (1839), Stanfield used this device, which moved painted scenery across the stage to illustrate the sea voyage from Southhampton to Harfleur. The mechanical device, together with Stanfield's exceptional painting abilities, created extraordinary effects for the audience. In addition to his theatre designs, Stanfield was known for his sea and landscape paintings, many of which were exhibited at the Royal Academy with considerable success. He was elected a member of that prestigious group in 1835. In 1834, he left scene painting as a profession, although he did provide scenery for Macready's pantomimes in 1837 and 1842, as well as the backcloth for Charles Dickens's production of *The Frozen Deep* at Tavistock House. His final drop scene was painted for Benjamin Webster in 1858 at the New Adelphi Theatre.

Jonet Buchanan

Stern, Ernst. Set and costume designer, and artist (b. 1876, Bucharest, Romania; d. 1954). Theatrical productions include *Lysistrata, The Doctor's Dilemma, Twelfth Night, Turnadot, Sumurun* (all at the Deutsches and Kammerspiele theatres, Berlin)—1906 to 1911; *Othello, The Taming of the Shrew, The Comedy of Errors, Julius Caesar, A Midsummer Night's Dream, Macbeth, Romeo and Juliet, The Merchant of Venice, Much Ado About Nothing, King Lear, Hamlet, Cymbeline, King Henry IV, Parts 1 and 2, As You Like It, Faust, Don Carlos, Maria Stuart, Fiesco, Wallenstein, Le Bourgeois Gentilhomme, George Dandin, Oedipus Rex, The Oresteia, Amphytrion, La Belle Hélène, Orphée aux Enfers* (all produced at the Deutsches and Kammerspiele theatres, Berlin)—1911 to 1921; *Madame Pompadour*—1923; *Three Musketeers* and *Merry Widow*—dates unknown. Designed the following in London: *Sumurun*—1911; *The Miracle*—1912; *Bitter Sweet*—1929; *Evergreen*—1930; *White Horse Inn, The Song of the Drum*—1931; *Helen*—1932; *Follow the Sun*—1936; *The Merry Widow, King Lear, Twelfth Night, As You Like It*—1943; *The Lilac Domino*—1944; *The Merchant of Venice, Much Ado About Nothing*—1945; *Can-Can*—1946; *The Bird Seller*—1947.

Stern is considered one of a number of significant designers who worked in Germany before World War I. Through his work, specifically in collaboration with director Max Reinhardt, Stern advanced the artistic development of the German theatre past the realistic stage. Stern's consistent practice of the theories of Appia* and Craig* gave strength to the turn-of-the-century movement to unify scenery with the internal, rather than the external, requirements of a play. Stern is associated with nearly all of Reinhardt's great successes, such as *The Miracle* at London's Olympia Theatre in 1912, *Don Carlos* (1909), *Oedipus Rex* (1910), *Much Ado About Nothing* (1912), *George Dandin* (1912), and *Le Bourgeois Gentilhomme* (1918) at the Deutsches and Kammerspiele Theatres in Berlin. In addition, he designed such Reinhardt masterpieces as *Danton* (1920) and *Lysistrata* (1923) at the Grosses Schauspielhaus in Berlin. By the sculptural nature of his work, Stern influenced the direction of Reinhardt's productions. In fact, it may be that stylization of production remains associated with Reinhardt's name because of Stern's ability to inspire the eclectic director beyond his preference for naturalistic scenery.

In addition to his influence on Reinhardt, Stern served as an example for such "New Stagecraft" designers as Robert Edmond Jones,* who traveled to Europe and studied Continental design of the day. Stern's costumes for the Grosses Schauspielhaus's 1928 production of *The Merry Widow*, with its heavily lined style and bold washes of color and vibrant draftsmanship of the human figure, have a similar style to Jones's subsequent work. Stern is also remembered for his technical facility with the German invention of revolving stages, such as in *The Merchant of Venice* and *Othello*, produced at the Deutsches Theatre in Berlin sometime between the years 1911 to 1921. In addition to his work for Reinhardt, in 1921 Stern joined famous film director Ernst Lubitsch as art director for several films. Subsequently, he served as art director for films in London and Hollywood.

Further Reading: Books by Stern: *Ariadne auf Naxos; Skizzen fur die Kostume und Dekorationen*. Berlin: Furstner, 1921; *Buhnenbilder bei Max Reinhardt*. Berlin: Henschelverlag, 1955; *My Life, My Stage*. London: Gollancz, 1951; Stern and Heinz Herald. *Reinhardt und seine Buhne*. Berlin: Eysler, 1918.

Books about Stern: Carter, Huntley. *The Theatre of Max Reinhardt*. New York: Benjamin Blom, 1914; Macgowan, Kenneth, and R. E. Jones. *Continental Stagecraft*. New York: Benjamin Blom, 1922; Reinhardt, Gottfried. *The Genius*. New York: Alfred Knopf, 1979.

Brian R. Jones

Stettheimer, Florine. Painter, poet, and theatrical designer (b. 1871, Rochester, NY; d. May 12, 1944, New York, NY). Known primarily as a painter, Stettheimer was responsible for the design of one show. Born to a family of moderate wealth, Stettheimer and her two sisters devoted their lives to the arts. They traveled in Europe from 1906 to 1914 with their mother. After returning, they soon established a salon for the avant-garde. Although she may have been involved in designing for the theatre informally, her only known work was for

Gertrude Stein's opera *Four Saints in Three Acts* (1934). After a brief run in Hartford, Connecticut, the show opened at the 44th Street Theatre in New York City for a four-week run and then moved to Chicago and other cities. Stein's text, as well as the sets, was praised by the critics. Stettheimer's cellophane scenery and unique costumes made up of long robes, halos, and gloves were so unique that they seemed to baffle the audience as much as Stein's nonsensical dialogue.

Elbin L. Cleveland

Straiges, Anthony J. Set and costume designer (b. October 31, 1942, Pottsville, PA). Theatrical productions (all productions were in New York City, unless otherwise noted) include *La Boheme* (San Francisco Summer Opera Festival, California)—1969; *Exit the King, Oh Dad, Poor Dad, Ariadne auf Naxos, The Lower Depths* (costumes only), *How Music Came to Earth* (costumes only) (all at Brooklyn College)—1970 to 1972; *Women Beware Women, The Rise and Fall of the City of Mahagonny, Don Juan* (three for the Yale Repertory Theatre, New Haven, Connecticut), *Ring 'Round the Moon* (Williamstown Theatre, Massachusetts)—1973 to 1974; *Streamers* (Arena Stage, Washington, D.C.)—1977; *Timbuktu* (Mark Hellinger Theatre), *A History of the American Film* (ANTA Theatre), *Comedians* (Arena Stage, Washington, D.C.), *The Beggar's Opera* (Guthrie Theatre, Minneapolis, Minnesota)—1978; *Romeo and Juliet* (Guthrie Theatre, Minnesota)—1979; *An American Tragedy* (Arena Stage, Washington, D.C.)—1980; *The Great Magoo* (Hartford Stage, Connecticut)—1982; *Buried Child* (Arena Stage, Washington, D.C.), *Summer, On the Swing Shift* (two for the Manhattan Theatre Club), *Sunday in the Park with George* (Playwright's Horizons Theatre City)—1983; *Sunday in the Park with George* (Broadway Theatre), *Diamond* (Circle in the Square)—1984; *A Long Day's Journey into Night* (Broadway)—1986; *Into the Woods* (Martin Beck Theatre), *Rumors* (Broadhurst Theatre)—1988.

Straiges began his formal theatre design training at Brooklyn College with Eldon Elder* and then moved on to Yale to work with Ming Cho Lee.* From 1970 to 1972, at Brooklyn College, he designed sets for *Exit the King, Oh Dad, Poor Dad*, and *Ariadne auf Naxos* and costumes for *The Lower Depths* and *How Music Came to Earth*. At the Yale Repertory Theatre, his most striking design was for *The Rise and Fall of the City of Mahagonny* (1974). Since that time, he has designed scenery for more than eighty productions, produced in regional theatres and on Broadway. On Broadway, he designed sets for such productions as *Timbuktu* (1978), *A History of the American Film* (1978), *Sunday in the Park with George* (1984), and *Into the Woods* (1988). Many of his designs have received critical acclaim, and he has won a number of awards, including a Tony for *Sunday in the Park with George*. His striking design for this show re-created for the first act, in three dimensions, George Seurat's nineteenth-century impressionist painting "A Sunday Afternoon on the Island of La Grande Jatte." For the second act, Straiges employed a laser beam device and a modern setting to depict a contemporary art museum.

Awards: Straiges won several awards for his design for *Sunday in the Park with George* (1984): Drama Desk, Tony, Maharam Foundation, and Outer Critics' Circle awards.

Further Reading: Burdick, Elizabeth, Peggy C. Hanson, and Brenda Zanger, eds. *Contemporary Stage Design—U.S.A.* Middletown, CT: Wesleyan University Press, 1974.

Elbin L. Cleveland

Strnad, Oskar. Set designer and theatre architect (b. 1879, Vienna, Austria; d. 1935). Theatrical productions include *Jeremias, Kaiser in Messalina, Antony and Cleopatra*—1919; *Faust, Don Carlos, Wilhelm Tell*—1920; *Danton's Death, Brand*—1921; *Hamlet, Rausch, Die Namenlosen*—1922; *Danton's Death, La Dama Luende, Mr. Pim Passes By, Der Weisse Heiland*—1923; *Der Schweirige, The Merchant of Venice, Danton's Death, St. Joan, Das Apostelspiel*—1924, *Romeo and Juliet, L'Homme et les Tantimes, King Lear, Der Weisse Heiland*— 1925; *Julius Caesar, Spiel im Schloss, Ariadne auf Naxos, Turandot, Periferie*— 1926; *Oesterreichische Komodie, Das Lockende Phantom, Escape, Zu ebener Ende und erster Stock, King Lear, Periferie, A Midsummer Night's Dream, The Miracle, Ein besserer Herr, Der Diamant des Geisterkonigs, Jonny Spielt auf, The Merchant of Venice, Peer Gynt*—1927; *Leinen aus Ireland, Tristan und Isolde, Das gerhume Konig reich, Periferie, The Magic Flute, Die Rauber, Der Boxen Oktaton Konig reich*—1928; *Juarez and Maximillian, Die Verbrecher, Danton's Death, L'Ennemie, Speck, Don Juan*—1929; *Das Reich Gottes in Bohmen, Die Verschworien des Fiesko zu Genua, The Tales of Hoffman, Schwanda, Woyzeck, Olympia, Die Kraetur, The Ring Cycle, Das Leben des Orest*—1930; *The Tempest, Der Schweirige, Hoffman's erazhlungen, Timon of Athens, Oberon*—1931; *Oberon, Tannhauser, The Magic Flute, The Miracle, Der Kliene Niemans*—1932; *Das Salzburger grosse Welttheater, Much Ado About Nothing, Kaiser Franz Joseph van Oesterreich, Tristan und Isolde, The Magic Flute, The Young Baron Neuhaus*—1933; *Maria Stuart, Christiano zwischen Himmel und Holle, Die Reise einer Frau, Don Giovanni, Die Strasse der Verheissung*—1934; *Ariadne auf Naxos, Adrienne Ambrossat, Abduction from the Seraglio*—1935.

Strnad was primarily known for his designs done for German director Max Reinhardt during the 1920s and 1930s. His style was characterized by the extreme use of the stage's vertical space, which he filled with such scenic elements as huge columns, pillars, stairs, and platforms. For example, in his famous design for *Danton's Death*, an enormous guillotine on the stage floor extended upward all the way into the flies, and massive rectangular columns for *Hamlet*, produced at the Burgtheater in Vienna, disappeared into the upper reaches of the theatre. Not only did Strnad have a prolific career with designing Reinhardt's productions and with designing operas in Austria, but he was also a theorist. Interested in changing the audience's relationship to the stage action, Strnad invented the ''Ringbuhne'' in 1923. In this theatre, a sliding and revolving stage encircled the auditorium and was divided by pillars into three to five compartments. The primary problem with this design was that there was no easy access to exits in case of fire.

Andrea J. Nouryeh

Svoboda, Josef. Scenographer (b. May 10, 1920, Caslav, Czechoslovakia). Theatrical productions (all works opened in Prague, unless otherwise noted) include *Empedokles* and *The Bride* (both at the Smetana Museum)—1943; *The Fox Trap* (Municipal Chamber Theatre)—1944; *Manon Lescaut* (Municipal Theatre, Teplice), *Tales of Hoffman* (Grand Opera), *Andre and the Dragon* (Horacka Theatre, Jihlava), *The Bartered Bride* (Grand Opera of 5 May), *Insect Comedy* (National Theatre)—1946; *Aida* (Grand Opera of 5 May), *The Mayor of Stilmond* (Theatre of 5 May), *The Purge* (Satire Theatre)—1947; *The Little Foxes* (National Theatre), *El Amor Brujo*, *The Rogue's Ballad* (both at the Grand Opera of 5 May), *Marysa* (National Theatre)—1948; *The Czech Manager* (Smetana Theatre), *The Flaming Border*, *The Bride of Chod* (both at the Tyl Theatre)—1949; *The 11th Commandment* (State Film Theatre)—1950; *Der Freischutz* (Smetana Theatre)—1952; *The Robber* (Tyl Theatre)—1954; *A High Summer Sky* (Tyl Theatre)—1955; *Janosik* (State Opera, Dresden)—1956; *The Entertainer* (Tyl Theatre)—1957; *Rusalka* (Teatro La Fenice, Venice), *Polyekran*, *Laterna Magika* (both at the Brussels World Fair, Belgium)—1958; *The Flying Dutchman* (Smetana Theatre)—1959; *The Seagull* (Tyl Theatre)—1960; *Intoleranza* (Teatro La Venice, Venice), *The Story of a Right Man* (National Theatre)—1961; *Julietta* and *Romeo and Juliet* (both at the National Theatre)—1963; *La Sonnambula* (the National Ballet, Amsterdam), *The Whirlpool* (National Theatre)—1964; *Hamlet* (Belgian National Theatre, Brussels), *Atomtod* (Teatro La Scala, Milan), *The Makropoulos Affair* (National Theatre)—1965; *The Last Ones* (Tyl Theatre), *The Storm* (National Theatre, London)—1966; *The Three Sisters* (National Theatre, London), *Dalibor* (National Theatre), *One-Ended Rope* (Theatre Behind the Gate), *Tristan und Isolde* (Wiesbaden, West Germany)—1967; *Faust* (State Theatre, Wiesbaden, West Germany)—1968; *The Soldiers* (State Opera, Munich), *The Fiery Angel* (Municipal Theatre, Frankfurt), *Pelleas and Melisande* (Royal Opera House, Covent Garden, London)—1969; *The Clown* (Municipal Theatre, Düsseldorf), *Waiting for Godot* (State Theatre, Salzburg), *Mother Courage* (Tyl Theatre)—1970; *Romeo and Juliet* (National Theatre), *Idomeneo* (State Opera, Vienna), *Eugene Onegin* (Municipal Theatre, Frankfurt), *Simone Boccanegra* (Municipal Theatre)—1971; *Operetta* (Schiller Theatre, Berlin), *From the House of the Dead* (State Opera, Hamburg), *The Sea Gull* (Theatre Behind the Gate), *The School for Scandal* (National Theatre), *Nabucco* (Covent Garden, London), *Don Juan*, *Tyl Eulenspiegel*, *Le Sacre Du Printemps*, *The Rake's Progress* (all at the National Theatre), *Carmen* (Metropolitan Opera House, New York), *Boris Godunov* (State Opera, Hamburg), *The Effect of Gamma Rays on Man-in-the-Moon Marigolds* (National Theatre), *Poem of Fire* (La Scala, Milan), *L'Oiseau de Feu* (Royal Theatre, Copenhagen), *Die Dreigroschenoper* (Municipal Theatre, Zurich)—1972; *The Whirlpool* (National Theatre), *Kata Kabanová*

(Opera House, Zurich), *The Secret* (National Theatre), *The Jumpers* (Burg-theatre, Vienna), *Children of the Sun* (National Theatre), *Tannhäuser* (Royal Opera House, Covent Garden, London), *The Man from Elsewhere* and *Sleeping Beauty* (both at the National Theatre), *A Dream of Reason* (Moscow Art Theatre, Moscow)—1973; *I vespri siciliani* (Metropolitan Opera House, New York), *The Jumpers* (Kennedy Center, Washington, D.C.), *Phedré* (Slovene National The-atre, Ljubljana), *Coriolanus* (National Theatre), *Don Carlos* (Municipal Theatre, Cologne), *Prague Carnival* (Laterna Magika), *Snow on the Limba*, *The Devil's Wall* (both at National Theatre), *Tristan und Isolde* (Festival Theatre, Bayreuth), *Cyrano de Bergerac* (Festival Theatre, Prague), *Les Troyens* (Grand Theatre, Geneva), *Das Rheingold*, *Die Walküre* (both Royal Opera House, Covent Gar-den, London)—1974; *An Optimistic Tragedy* (National Theatre), *Das Rheingold* (Grand Theatre, Geneva), *The Snow Laughed As It Fell* (National Theatre Studio), *Symphonie Fantastique* (National Opera, Paris), *Kabale und Liege* (Aka-demie Theatre, Vienna), *War and Peace* (National Theatre), *Love in Carnival Colors* (Laterna Magika), *Bartolucci* (Théâtre Espace Pierre Cardin, Paris), *Fi-delio* (Opera House, Zurich), *Jenufa* (National Theatre), *Siegfried* (Covent Gar-den, London), *The Lost Fairy Tale* (Laterna Magika), *Mahagonny* (Grand Theatre, Geneva), *Simone Boccanegra* (Opera House, Zurich)—1975; *König Otakar* (Burgtheatre, Vienna), *Die Walküre* (Grand Theatre, Geneva), *Passion* (National Theatre), *Turnadot* (Teatro Reggio, Turin), *Fidelio* (National Theatre), *Siegfried* (Grand Theatre, Geneva), *Otello* (National Opera, Paris), *Queen of Spades* (National Arts Center, Ottawa), *Götterdämmerung* (Covent Garden, Lon-don), *The Tempest* (Berlin Tournament, Munich), *The Trial of Love* (National Theatre), *Die Soldaten* (Hamburg, West Germany)—1976; *Don Carlos* (Grand Theatre, Geneva), *The Magic Circus* (Laterna Magika), *The Last Vacation* (Na-tional Theatre), *Faust* (State Opera, Berlin), *Götterdämmerung* (Grand Theatre, Geneva), *Ariadne auf Naxos* (National Arts Center, Ottawa), *Ein Engel kommt nach Babylon* (Opera House, Zurich), *Closed Circuit* (Moscow Art Theatre, Moscow), *White Storks Above Brest* (National Theatre)—1977; *Die Frau ohne Schatten* (Grand Theatre, Geneva), *Macbeth* (National Theatre), *Il Trovatore* (Opera House, Zurich), *Il Campiello* (National Theatre), *Jenufa* (Juilliard School, New York), *Nabucco* and *Tristan und Isolde* (both at the Grand Theatre, Geneva), *The Bartered Bride* (Metropolitan Opera House, New York), *Die Meistersinger* (National Theatre), *From the House of the Dead* (Opera House, Zurich), *Fidelio* (Grand Theatre, Geneva)—1978; *La Traviata* (National Theatre), *The Makro-poulos Affair* (State Theatre, Hannover), *Our Militants* (National Theatre), *The Snow Queen (Laterna Magika), The Good Soldier Schweik* (Schiller Theatre, Berlin), *Gianni Schicchi* and *Suor Angelica* (National Arts Center, Banff, Can-ada), *Parisiana* (Municipal Theatre, Marseilles), *Don Carlos* (Opera House, Zurich)—1979; *The White Disease* (Tyl Theatre), *The Dream Play* (State Uni-versity, Albany, New York), *The Miraculous Mandarin* (La Scala, Milan), *Jenufa* (Grand Theatre, Geneva), *Rusalka* (State Threatre, Stuttgart), *Grief Over the Message from Ur*, *The Hero*, and *A Flawless Life* (all three at the National

Theatre), *Otello* (Grand Theatre, Geneva), *Time Out of Mind* (National Arts Center, Banff, Canada), *The Duchess of Wallenstein's Armies* (National Theatre)—1980; *Night Rehearsal* (Laterna Magika), *Josefs Legende* (La Scala, Milan), *Faust* (National Theatre), *Idomeneo* (National Arts Center, Ottawa), *Die Kluge* and *Duke Bluebeard's Castle* (both at the Smetana Theatre), *From the House of the Dead* (Deutsche Opera, Berlin), *The Tales of Hoffman* (Smetana Theatre), *The Oresteia* (Tyl Theatre)—1981; *The Road* (Smetana Theatre), *Queen of Spades* (Houston Grand Opera, Texas), *Hamlet* (National Theatre), *Dalibor* (Smetana Theatre)—1982; *Idomeneo* (Ottawa)—1983; *Partage de Midi* (Louvain)—1984; *Blue Angel* (New York City Opera)—1985.

Born in Czechoslovakia, Svoboda is regarded by many to be one of the most significant designers of the twentieth century. Trained as an architect, he began his career in the early 1940s by designing amateur productions. It was not until the end of the 1950s, when social realism became less dominant in his native country, that his career flourished. In 1958, working along with director Alfred Radok, he created *Polyekran* and *Laterna Magika*, two multimedia entertainments for the Brussels World Fair that incorporated live actors with previously filmed projections of the same performers. He has continued through the years to explore the limits of this technique and eventually formed a separate theatre that is an adjunct to the National Theatre in Prague and that he now heads. He has carried this fascination for projections into his stage work and has since become known for this emphasis on technology in his designs.

Svoboda prefers the term *scenographer* to the traditional one of *scene designer* because it implies the actual, three-dimensional use of space. Carrying on in the tradition of Appia* and Craig,* he believes that scenery should be a synthesis of the total theatrical work. Svoboda demands that the design bring the play to life by incorporating spatial relationships, movement, light, and sound, as well as using any type of material, equipment, or technique that will elucidate the production. Jarka Burian, American scholar and author of two books on Svoboda, states that the designer chooses a metaphoric rather than a realistic approach to integrate the design as an organic, dynamic, and kinetic part of the production. Rather than a static depiction of locale, limited to the traditional techniques of painting and arranging elements on the stage, Svoboda gives the design life and character of its own, capable of transformation throughout the course of the dramatic action. As a result of his method, Svoboda has created some of the most technologically advanced scenography of his time and stunning machines for performance. His work usually includes a flexible stage design that can be altered, scene to scene, through the use of lighting, projections on screens, scrims, or even mirrors, as well as motorized platforms that move in all directions, horizontally as well as vertically.

Some of his most significant productions have been *The Insect Comedy* (1946), *Hamlet* (1959), *The Seagull* (1960), *The Last Ones* (1966), and *Mother Courage* (1970). Svoboda's opera productions evidence Svoboda's ingenious use of technology, as well as his use of all manner of modern materials, such as plastics, hydraulics, and lasers. In *Tristan und Isolde*, performed in Wiesbaden in 1967, Svoboda created one of his best-known effects, the three-dimensional "pillar of light," with an aerosol mixture through which shone low-voltage luminaires. In Richard Wagner's *The Ring Cycle*, performed in London between the years 1974 and 1976, the central unit was a platform that raised, lowered, tilted, and transformed into stairs that leveled no matter at what pitch the platform was. In addition, its underside had a large mirror to reflect performers who were below stage level.

For more than thirty years, he was the principal designer at the Czech National Theatre, a position he obtained in 1948 and one that included management. Since 1969, he has been professor of architecture at the Prague Academy of Fine and Industrial Arts. In addition to his designs for more than five hundred productions for the theatre, ballet, and opera, he has taught his theories, exhibited his works, and lectured extensively on scenography and art.

Awards: Svoboda has earned the State Prize, Prague, 1954; the Industrial Design Award and two Gold Medals, World's Fair, Brussels, 1958; the Scenography Award, Bienal, São Paulo, 1961; the Merited Artist of CSSR, Prague, 1968; an Honorary Doctorate for the Royal College of Art, London, 1969; and the Sikkens Prize, Amsterdam, 1969.

Further Reading: Burian, Jarka. *The Scenography of Josef Svoboda*. Middletown, CT: Wesleyan University Press, 1971; Burian, Jarka. *Svoboda: Wagner—Josef Svoboda's Scenography for Richard Wagner's Operas*. Middletown, CT: Wesleyan University Press, 1983.

Thomas J. Mikotowicz

Szajna, Josef. Director, designer, and artist (b. 1922, Rzeszow, Poland). Szajna began his theatrical activities at Nowy Huta in the People's Theatre, where he designed such plays as *Princess Turnadot* and *Of Mice and Men* (both in 1956). He eventually became its artistic and managing director, as well as its head designer, retaining these responsibilities from 1963 to 1966 while availing himself to work on several productions throughout Poland. His best-known work at that time was for director Jerzy Grotowski's seminal revival of Wyspianski's *Akropolis* (1962). Szajna's nonrepresentational set consisted of a central playing area surrounded by the audience and inhabited by platforms, various ramps and steps, and stove pipes hung at odd angles. From 1966 to 1971, he worked variously at the Stary Theatre in Kraków, the Slaski Theatre in Katowice, the Wspolczesny Theatre in Szczecin, and the Polish Theatre in Warsaw. In 1971, Szajna became head director-designer for the Studio Theatre Gallery in Warsaw. He held this position until 1982 and directed many significant productions. A total theatre artist in the spirit of Edward Gordon Craig,* Szajna has functioned as playwright and dramaturge, working up scripts from sections of literary texts by such authors as Dante, Goethe, and Shakespeare. His graphic arts background, combined with his directing talents, resulted in productions that were highly visual and that employed kinetic scenography to create the dramatic action. His work in this realm includes the productions of *Faust* (1971), *Dante* (1974), *Cervantes* (1976), and *Macbeth* (1963) in England. During this period, he toured several of his novel productions, including *Death on a Pear Tree* (1978), throughout Europe and North America. Szajna, who became professor of scenography at the Warsaw Academy of Fine Arts, has taught, published, and exhibited his design works. In 1982, he retired and only occasionally directs and designs in Poland.

Thomas J. Mikotowicz

T

Tchelitchew, Pavel. Designer and painter (b. September 21, 1898, Moscow, Russia; d. July 31, 1957, Frascati, Italy). As a young man of twenty, Tchelitchew assisted Isaac Rabinovitch,* a famous Soviet designer, and created sets and costumes for a small music hall production. This early interest in design led to further training in abstract art and stage decor under Aleksandra Exter,* the famed artist-designer who also taught Boris Aronson.* But unlike Aronson, Tchelitchew renounced the cubist style, and subsequently moved to Berlin, where he designed the opera *Le Coq d'Or* and met Sergey Diaghilev. In Paris in 1923, he adopted a neoromantic style, influenced by artist-friends such as Christian Bérard* and the brothers Eugene* and Leonide Berman. During this period he developed his unique method of multiple perspectives, which gave his painting style a quality of surrealism. In 1934, he employed this technique on director Louis Jouvet's successful production *Ondine* in Paris and soon after moved to the United States and acquired citizenship. In the United States, his predominant designs were for the Ballets Russes de Monte Carlo, including sets for *Nobilissima Visione* (1938) and *Balustrade* (1940), both choreographed by George Balanchine. During the forties, Tchelitchew became disenchanted with the stage. When he was offered the design of Agnes De Mille's *Rodeo*, he instead recommended Oliver Smith,* who started his auspicious career with this ballet. Tchelitchew spent his later career painting and exhibiting at such venues as the Museum of Modern Art in 1942, as well as in Paris in 1956.

Thomas J. Mikotowicz

Telbin, William. Designer (b. 1813, England; d. 1873). Scenic artist and designer Telbin worked for several provincial theatres before he was engaged by actor William Charles Macready for an important production of Shakespeare's *King John* in 1842. The design was so well received that Macready hired Telbin to paint a panoramic drop, the first of several that he painted during his career.

He exhibited in a number of galleries, including the British Institution and the Royal Academy. In 1856, Telbin worked for actor-manager Charles Kean on a production of *The Winter's Tale*, and in 1861 he worked on designs for Charles Fechter's production of *Othello*. He periodically worked in the theatre with his two sons, William Lewis Telbin (1846–1931) and Henry Telbin (1840–1865). But after Henry was killed in a fall, Telbin withdrew from most work. Some of his other well-known productions are *King John* (1842), *The Tempest* (1857), *The Merchant of Venice* (1858), and *Hamlet* (1861).

James Fisher

Ter-Arutunian, Rouben. Set and costume designer (b. July 24, 1920, Tiflis, Soviet Georgia, Russia). Ter-Arutunian's costume and set designs have appeared in theatre, dance, opera, film, and television productions. As an adolescent, he studied the humanities at the universities of Berlin and Vienna and also classical painting at the Ecole des Beaux Arts. His first professional design assignment was for costumes for *The Bartered Bride* at the Dresden Opera House in 1943 and was followed by several other successful shows. Subsequently, he emigrated to America in 1951 and worked as a designer in television until his affiliation with the American Shakespeare Festival at Stratford, Connecticut, in 1956. Here he designed such significant productions as *King John* (1956), *Measure for Measure* (1956), and *Much Ado About Nothing* (1957). The following year he began designing on Broadway, beginning with George Abbott's *New Girl in Town* (1957) and followed with *Who Was That Lady I Saw You With?* (1958), for which he won the Outer Critics' Circle Award for ''Best Scenic Design.'' He was equally successful with *Redhead* (1959), for which he received a Tony Award for costumes. His other Broadway credits include *Advise and Consent* (1960), *Arturo Ui* (1963), *The Devils* (1965), *Ivanov* (1965), Tennessee Williams's *The Milk Train Doesn't Stop Here Anymore* (1964), *All Over* (1971), *Goodtime Charley* (1975), and *The Lady from Dubuque* (1980). In addition, he has designed for major ballet companies throughout the world, including the New York City Ballet productions of *Souvenirs* (1955), *The Seven Deadly Sins* (1958), a once legendary *Nutcracker* (1964), *Coppelia* (1974), and *Vienna Waltzes* (1975). His work for American Ballet Theater includes *Sargasso* (1966) and Glenn Tetley's *Ricercare* (1966), for which he designed scenery and costumes. Ter-Arutunian divides dance decor into four basic approaches: the ''classic,'' using a decor-less stage; the ''romantic,'' employing a representational stage picture; the ''sculptural,'' utilizing three-dimensional units; and the ''decorative,'' which is based on the easel-painting tradition. He has also designed settings for the Hamburg Opera, the San Francisco Opera, the Los Angeles Civic Light Opera, and the New York City Opera. His media work includes costume and set designs for the films *The Loved One* and *Such Good Friends* and the television productions of *Twelfth Night*, an Emmy award-winner for Hallmark's ''Hall of Fame.'' He also designed two other television productions: *The Magic Flute* and *Maria Golovin* (NBC). In all of his work, Ter-Arutunian stresses simplicity and clarity in regard to the arrangement of stage space and costuming the human body.

Further Reading: By Ter-Arutunian: "Decor for Dance" in Burdick, Hansen, and Zanger (see Bibliography).

Thomas J. Mikotowicz

Thompson, Woodman. Designer (b. c.1889, Pittsburgh, PA; d. 1955). Thompson taught costume and scene design at the Carnegie Institute of Technology in Pittsburgh from 1915 to 1921, where he had received his degree in commercial illustration. In 1921, he went to New York and became an assistant to Lee Simonson* for the Broadway production of *Back to Methuselah*. During the 1920s, he designed many of Winthrop Ames's revivals of Gilbert and Sullivan operettas, including *Iolanthe* (1926) and *Pirates of Penzance* (1926). His work in New York includes such significant productions as *Beggar on Horseback* (1924), *What Price Glory?* (1924), *The Desert Song* (1926), *The Barretts of Wimpole Street* (1931), *Romeo and Juliet* (1934), and *The Magnificent Yankee* (1946). In all, Thompson designed over seventy productions in his lifetime. His style was heavily influenced by the "New Stagecraft" precepts of simplicity, suggestion, and synthesis. In addition, Thompson taught scene design at Columbia University until the time of his death.

Kurt Lancaster

Throckmorton, Cleon. Set designer, theatre architect, producer, and playwright (b. October 8, 1897, Atlantic City, N.J.; d. 1965).

Theatrical productions include *The Hairy Ape* (with Robert Edmond Jones*)— 1922; *George Dandin* (with Robert Edmond Jones; Provincetown Playhouse), *S. S. Glencairn, All God's Chillun Got Wings* (both at the Provincetown Playhouse)—1924; *The Emperor Jones, The Dreamy Kid, The Blue Peter, Ruint, Rosmersholm, Outside Looking In, Weak Sisters, A Man's Man, Lovely Lady, Adam Solitaire, The Joker, The Devil to Pay, The Man Who Never Died, The Wisecrackers*—1925; *The Makropoulos Secret, East Lynne, Bride of the Lamb, Beyond Evil, Service for Two, Sandalwood, Beyond the Horizon, The Silver Cord, In Abraham's Bosom*—1926; *Earth, Menace, Rapid Transit, Wall Street, Triple Crossed, Burlesque, In Abraham's Bosom, The Triumphant Bachelor, Jacob Slovak, Porgy, The Good Hope, The Ivory Door, The Stairs, The King Can Do No Wrong, Paradise* (all for the American Grand Guignol Players)— 1927; *These Modern Women, Hot Pan, Rope, Napoleon, Killers, The Scarlet Fox, Porgy and Bess, On Call, Congai, The Good Hope*—1928; *Solitaire* (designed only the "Coney Island" effect), *Man's Estate, Mystery Square, Getting Even, Porgy, Fiesta, Top o' the Hill, Red Dust, Inspector Kennedy, The Unsophisticates*—1929; *Penny Arcade, The Old Rascal, Stepping Sisters, Change Your Luck* (also produced), *Torch Song, The Good Hope*—1930; *She Means Business, Doxtor X, Hobo, Gray Shadow, Lady Beyond the Moon, Six Characters in Search of an Author, Brass Ankle, A Regular Guy, Just To Remind You, Did*

I Say No?, The House of Connelly, Two Seconds, Hot Money, Louder, Please, A Widow in Green, Springtime for Henry, Sentinels, The Bride the Sun Shines On—1931; *Monkey, The Moon in the Yellow River, The Truth About Blayds, Another Language, Bulls, Bears and Asses, Back Fire, Page Pygmalion, The Other One, Criminal at Large, Rendezvous, The Dark Hours, Chrysalis, Take a Chance*—1933; *Alien Corn, Run, Little Chillun!, The Threepenny Opera, For Services Rendered, Give Us This Day, Eight Bells, Is Life Worth Living?, Birthright, Peace on Earth*—1933; *The Gods We Make, Sing and Whistle, The Lord Blesses the Bishop, Ode to Liberty*—1934; *Creeping Fire, Prisoners of War, Noah, I Want a Policeman!*—1935; *Searching for the Sun, Bitter Stream*—1936; *Curtain Call, Love in My Fashion*—1937; *Ghost for Sale*—1941; *Nathan the Wise*—1942.

Throckmorton designed the settings for more than 150 plays, including the original productions of Eugene O'Neill's *The Hairy Ape* (1922), *All God's Chillun Got Wings* (1924), *The Glencairn Cycle* (1924), and *The Emperor Jones* (1925). His expressionistic settings, particularly for the first two O'Neill plays, transformed what would have been ordinary locales into highly distorted, subjective views and helped to insure the success of the productions. Throckmorton was also the stage designer for a number of musicals, among them *The Three-penny Opera* (1933), *Greenwich Village Follies*, and *Porgy and Bess* (1929). An important designer in the "New Stagecraft" movement, Throckmorton was one of a group of Broadway designers, including Norman Bel Geddes,* Robert Edmond Jones,* Jo Mielziner,* Donald Oenslager,* and Lee Simonson,* who brought the new European design theories to Broadway. Through the use of a few simplified, suggestive, and symbolic elements, a dramatic stylized effect was achieved. Through simple line, color, and the suggestive use of light, he created such emotionally charged locales as the death house scene for *The Last Mile*. Throckmorton also designed and supervised the building and equipping of theatres, produced revivals of old melodramas of the "gaslight era," and wrote the plays *Bowery After Art, Shoestring Revue, South of Broadway, Stage Hand's Lament*, and *The Art Photographer*, as well as serving as producer or coproducer for eighteen Broadway plays.

Thomas J. Mikotowicz

Tilton, James. Set and lighting designer, and art director (b. 1937, Rochelle, IL). Theatrical productions (all productions were in New York City and include both set and lighting design, unless otherwise noted) include *Scapin, Impromptu de Versailles, The Lower Depths*—1964; *You Can't Take It with You*—1965; *Pantagleize*—1967; *The Cocktail Party, The Misanthrope, Ballad of a Firing Squad*—1968; *Oh! Calcutta!* (off-Broadway), *Hamlet, Cock-A-Doodle Dandy, Private Lives* (Nederlander)—1969; *The Criminals, Harvey* (Virginia)—1970; *The School for Wives* (Lyceum), *The Grass Harp* (Martin Beck)—1971; *Rainbow, Oh! Calcutta!* (scenery only, Eden)—1972; *The Seagull, The Inspector General, The Merchant of Venice* (Vivian Beaumont)—1973; *Malacon, Miracle*

Play—1974; *Knuckle, Macrunes Guevarra, Seascape* (Shubert)—1975; *The Cat and the Fiddle, Oh! Calcutta!* (revival, Edison)—1976; *Vieux Carre* (St. James)—1977; *Galileo*—1978; *Flying Blind* (scenery), *Later, Big and Little, Getting Out*—1979; *A Christmas Carol* (scenery only), *Twice Around the Park* (Court)—1982; *You Can't Take It with You* (Plymouth)—1984; *The Madwoman of Chaillot, Clarence, Vivat! Vivat, Regina!, The Loves of Anatol* (lighting only, Circle in the Square)—1985; *The Time of Your Life, Children of the Sun, The Circle*—1986.

Tilton's extensive career has included set and lighting designs for play and opera productions in regional, off-Broadway, and Broadway theatres, as well as television and film. Arriving in New York in 1963, Tilton established a collaboration with director-actor Ellis Rabb and the Association of Performing Artists Repertory Theatre (APA). With the APA company, Tilton designed such Broadway shows as *You Can't Take It with You* (1965), *Pantagleize* (1967), *The Cocktail Party* (1968), and *Hamlet* (1969). Tilton also designed for the Phoenix Theatre, the group that was the producing organization for APA. His work with them occurred between 1975 and 1979 and included such productions as *27 Wagons Full of Cotton, Ladyhouse Blues*, and *City Sugar*. Off-Broadway, Tilton designed *The Lower Depths* (1964), *The Madwoman of Chaillot* (1985), and *The Time of Your Life* (1986). His work in regional theatre began in 1963 when he became the resident designer for the Front Street Theatre in Memphis, after designing *My Fair Lady* for the group. Since, he has designed many productions at such regional theatres as the Syracuse Stage, the Hartman Theatre, the Buffalo Studio Arena, the Cleveland Playhouse, the Asolo Theatre, the Huntington-Hartford Theatre, and the American Conservatory Theatre. The diversity of Tilton's work is evident in his designs for the opera. He has designed *Evol Spelled Backward Is Love* (1962) in Germany, *The Disappointment* (1976) at the Library of Congress, and *The Maid of Milan* (1980) at the John Drew Theatre. His art direction includes the film *Dear, Dead Delilah* (1970) and several television specials, including his two designs for PBS's "Theatre in America" series: *Secret Service* (1977) and *Uncommon Women and Others* (1978). In addition, he has designed such Showtime cable television productions as *Conflict of Interest* (1980) and the award-winning *Purlie* (1982).

Awards: Tilton received a Tony Award nomination in lighting design for the 1975 production of *Seascape*. He also was nominated for a Drama Desk Award for the Phoenix Theatre's productions of *27 Wagons Full of Cotton* and *A Memory of Two Mondays*. In 1982, Tilton received an Ace Award for his art direction on *Purlie* for Showtime cable television.

Further Reading: "Designers at Work." *Theatre Crafts* May 1987: 31; Pecktal (see Bibliography); "Repertory Theatre: The Problems of a Complete Concept in Stage Design." *Theatre Crafts* March/April 1967.

Penny L. Remsen

Tipton, Jennifer. Lighting designer (b. 1937, Columbus, OH). Theatrical productions (all theatres listed are in New York City, unless otherwise specified) include *Richard II* (American Shakespeare Festival, HB Studios, New York),

Love's Labour's Lost (American Shakespeare Festival, HB Studios, New York)—1968; *Horseman Pass By* (Fortune Theatre), *Our Town* (ANTA Theatre)—1969; *Airs, Amnon V'Tamar, Bach Partita*—1972; *The Tempest, Macbeth, A Midsummer Night's Dream* (New York Shakespeare Festival, Newhouse Theatre), *The Killdeer* (Newman Theatre), *The Dybbuk, Dreyfus in Rehearsal* (Barrymore Theatre)—1974; *The Leaves Are Fading, Habeas Corpus* (Martin Beck Theatre), *Murder Among Friends* (Biltmore Theatre)—1975; *Rex* (Lunt-Fontanne Theatre), *For Colored Girls Who Consider Suicide When the Rainbow Is Enuf* (Booth Theatre), *The Nutcracker* (American Ballet Theatre)—1976; *The Landscape of the Body* (Newman Theatre), *The Cherry Orchard*—1977; *Museum* (Public Theatre), *Runaways* (Public Theatre and Plymouth Theatre), *All's Well That Ends Well, Taming of the Shrew* (Delacorte Theatre), *After the Season* (Academy Festival Theatre), *Agamemnon* (Beaumont Theatre and Delacorte Theatre), *Happy End* (Martin Beck Theatre), *A Month in the Country* (Williamstown Theatre Festival), *Don Quixote* (American Ballet Theatre), *The Goodbye People* (Westport Playhouse), *Funny Face* (Studio Arena, Buffalo, New York), *Drinks Before Dinner* (Public Theatre), *Alice in Wonderland, The Pirates of Penzance* (Public Theatre)—1978; *Two Part Inventions* (Goodman Theatre, Chicago), *Bosoms and Neglect* (Goodman Theatre, Chicago)—1979; *Lunch Hour, Billy Bishop Goes to War, The Seagull*—1980; *Sophisticated Ladies*—1981; *The Wake of Jamey Foster*—1982; *Uncle Vanya, Orgasmo Adulto Escapes from the Zoo*—1983; *Baby with the Bathwater, Hurlyburly, Whoopi Goldberg, Endgame, The Ballad of Soapy Smith*—1984; *Singin' in the Rain* (Gershwin Theatre)—1985; *Principia Scriptoriae* (Manhattan Theatre Club), *Hamlet* (Public/Newman Theatre), *The Juniper Tree* (ART, Cambridge, Massachusetts), *Little Eyolf* (Yale Repertory Theatre), *Under Statements* (Repertory Theatre of St. Louis), *The Return of Pinocchio* (47th Street Theatre), *A Walk in the Woods* (Yale Repertory Company, New Haven, Connecticut)—1986; *Uncle Vanya* (Classic Stage Company), *Paradise Lost* (Center Stage), *Leonce and Lena (and Lenz)* (Guthrie Theatre, Minneapolis)—1987; *Ah, Wilderness!, A Long Day's Journey into Night* (Yale Repertory Company, New Haven, Connecticut)—1988; *Jerome Robbins's Broadway, Waiting for Godot* (Lincoln Center Theatre Company)—1989; *The Screens* (Guthrie Theatre, Minneapolis)—1990.

Tipton started her career as a dance student at Cornell University, then later studied under and assisted Tom Skelton, a lighting designer at Connecticut College and in New York. In the mid-1960s, she began working for the Paul Taylor Dance Company and with Twyla Tharp's company, as well as other dance and ballet companies. She has also worked in the theatre and designed on and off-Broadway as well as in regional theatres. Her Broadway credits include *For Colored Girls Who Consider Suicide When the Rainbow is Enuf* (1976), *Lunch Hour* (1980), and *Singin' in the Rain* (1985). Off-Broadway, Tipton has designed for the Manhattan Theatre Club and the Public Theatre, as well as for experimental theatre directors Joanne Akalaitis, Robert Wilson, and Peter Sellars. Regionally, she has been active as well. For director Joanne Akalaitis, she lit

Leonce and Lena (and Lenz) in 1987 and *The Screens* in 1990, both at the Guthrie Theatre in Minneapolis. Her approach to her lighting designs emphasizes bringing out textures and sculptures in space. Sometimes she uses a predominantly white-based palette to accomplish this effect, particularly in her dance work. But she admits that her approach and thoughts about lighting change frequently. In addition, she has been a contributing editor for *American Theatre* magazine, a consultant for the Performing Arts Center at Cornell University, and an associate director at Goodman Theatre.

Awards: Tipton earned an Obie Award for her work done at the Public Theatre in 1979. She also received the Creative Arts Award Medal in Dance from Brandeis University in 1982. In 1987, she received a New York Dance and Performance Award for her design for *Circumstantial Evidence*. She earned two awards in 1989: the Commonwealth Award of Distinguished Service in Dramatic Arts and the Drama Desk Award for her work for *Jerome Robbins's Broadway*, *A Long Day's Journey into Night*, and *Waiting for Godot*.

Further Reading: Sommers, Michael. "Designers on Design: Jennifer Tipton, Architect of the Air." *Theatre Crafts* October 1990: 38 + .

Kurt Lancaster

Toms, Carl. Set designer (b. 1927, Kirkby-in-Ashfield, England). Theatrical productions (all were in London, unless otherwise specified) include *La Cener-entola* (Sadler's Wells)—1959; *The Barber of Seville* (Sadler's Wells), *A Mid-summer Night's Dream* (Aldeburgh)—1960; *Iphigenie en Tauride*—1961; *Ballet Imperial, Our Man in Havana*—1963; *The Tricks of Scapin, The Lesson* (both at the Edinburgh International Festival), *Die Frau ohne Schatten* (costumes only)—1967; *Love's Labour's Lost, Edward II* (both at the National Theatre)—1968; *Taming of the Shrew* (Young Vic Theatre), *Sleuth* (New York and London), *Vivat! Vivat, Regina!* (Chichester and London), *Cyrano de Bergerac* (National Theatre)—1970; *Peter Grimes* (San Francisco Opera), *I Puritani* (New York City Opera), *Fanfare for Europe*—1973; *Travesties, Sherlock Holmes*—1974; *Die Meistersinger* (New York City Opera), *The Winter's Tale*—1975; *Norma* (San Diego Opera Company), *La Traviata* (San Diego Opera), *Thais* (San Francisco Opera)—1976; *The Merry Widow* (San Diego Opera), *The Marriage of Figaro* and *The Voice of Ariadne* (both at the New York City Opera), *Man and Superman* (Malvern Festival and London), *Travesties* (National Theater), *A Long Day's Journey into Night* (Los Angeles), *Queen's Silver Jubilee Gala, The Merry Widow* (San Diego Opera)—1977; *The Devil's Disciple* (New York), *She Stoops to Conquer* (National Theater), *Betrayal* (National Theater), *Thais* (Metropolitan Opera, New York), *Hamlet* (San Diego Opera Company)—1978; *Stage Struck, For Services Rendered, The Guardsman* (National Theater)—1979; *Playbill, Night and Day* (National Theater), *The Provok'd Wife*—1980; *The Second Mrs. Tanqueray, On the Razzle* (both at the National Theatre), *Der Freischutz* (New York City Opera)—1981; *Windy City* (Victoria Palace), *The Real Thing* (Strand Theatre), *Swan Lake* (Festival Ballet), *Romeo and Juliet* (both at the San Diego Opera), *Macbeth* (Vienna State Opera)—1982; *The Winslow Boy* (Lyric Theatre), *The Hothouse* (Vienna Burgtheater), *Jeeves Takes Charge* (New York), *Hay*

Fever (Queen's Theatre), *A Patriot for Me*—1983; *The Aspern Papers*, *The Happiest Days of Your Life* (Royal Shakespeare Company), *The Italian Girl in Algiers* (costumes only; San Francisco Opera and Geneva), *Rough Crossing* (National Theatre)—1984; *Jumpers* (Aldwych Theatre, London), *The Dragon's Tail* (Apollo Theatre), *Faust* (Vienna State Opera)—1985; *Hapgood* (Ahmanson Theatre, Los Angeles, California)—1988.

Educated at the Mansfield College of Art, the Royal College of Art, and the Old Vic School, Toms first designed for the London Stage in 1957. He is credited with many sets for drama productions for the West End, the Edinburgh Festival, and the Chichester Festival and for many ballets for the Royal Opera House, Glyndebourne, and Sadler's Wells, among others. In 1965, he completed the redesigning of the Theatre Royal in Windsor and, in 1982, the Theatre Royal in Bath. He was initially head of design for the Young Vic at the National Theatre, and in 1970, he was made associate director. Always adapting his style to suit the textual material, for Tom Stoppard's *Rough Crossing*, Toms created a nautical environment onstage without actually depicting a realistic luxury liner. Similarly, his designs for the revival of Stoppard's *Jumpers* in 1985 used stylized sets to depict realistic locales. On the other hand, his work for Stoppard's farce *On the Razzle* (1981) employed very detailed, realistic units that tracked diagonally and concealed each other onstage. Other design work of Toms's has included the decoration of restaurants, hotels, houses, exhibitions, programs, and cards.

Awards: In 1969, Toms earned Obie, Tony, and Drama Desk awards for *Sherlock Holmes* (London and New York). For *A Patriot for Me* produced in Los Angeles in 1983, Toms received the Hollywood Drama Logue Critics' Award. He also won the SWET Designer of the Year Award for the 1980 production of *The Provok'd Wife*.

Jonet Buchanan

Torelli, Giacomo. Scenic designer, stage machinist, and architect (b. 1608, Italy; d. 1678). Torelli learned his craft in Italy and was influenced by architect Aleotti,* who designed the Teatro Farnese in 1628, and he also learned as an apprentice in the Teatro del Sole in Pesaro, where the designer-machinist Sabbatini* worked. By 1640, Torelli designed the new Teatro Novissimo in Venice and several of its productions. Here Torelli improved on stage machinery, lighting, and scene-changing methods used by such designers as Sabbatini.

Torelli's most significant invention was the chariot and pole system of scene shifting. In this system, sixteen wing flats (eight sets) were connected to their own small carriages in the basement with poles that extended through slots in the stage floor. The "chariots" were able to roll in unison in their own tracks because they were all connected to a single counterweighted drum that was controlled by a single stagehand. The upper borders of scenery were similarly counterweighted and moved with precision. The overall effect of this capability was impressive as the entire stage picture instantly transformed from one scene to another. Several operas, such as *La Finta Pazzi* (1641), *Bellerofonte* (1642), and *Venere Gelosa* (1643), featured his clever machinery, which caused his contemporaries to nickname him "the great magician." The chariot and pole system was eventually adopted by many theatres and used well into the eighteenth century.

In 1645, Torelli left for Paris at the request of the duke of Parma, who was asked by Queen Anne of France to supply a stage designer. Torelli arrived and soon transformed Molière's Petit-Bourbon Theatre into an Italianate house, replete with all of his newly developed machinery. He soon re-created his work for the opera *La Finta Pazzi* but, to the delight of the French, reset the action in France, with scenes of the Seine River. This production, as well as many other Italian operas, brought the "Italian ideal" in staging to France. Torelli's magnificent work continued with sets for Corneille's machine play, *Andromeda* (1650), as well as many subsequent productions of opera and ballet.

In 1659, a jealous competitor, Gaspare Vigarani,* was brought to France to design a theatre for the king, an event that signaled Torelli's lessening influence in the Court. In 1661, Torelli offended the king with his elaborate design for Molière's *Les Fâcheux* and returned to Italy to design at his new Teatro della Fortuno and to live peacefully until his death. Meanwhile, the jealous Vigarani had Torelli's machinery removed from the Petit-Bourbon Theatre, ostensibly to use it in the Salle des Machines in the palace in 1666, but he burned it instead. Torelli's drawings, however, were preserved and, many years after his death, appeared in Diderot's *Encyclopedia* (1772) under "Machines du Thèâtre."

Further Reading: Oenslager (see Bibliography).

Thomas J. Mikotowicz

Troester, Frantisek. Scenographer (b. December 20, 1904, Vrbicany, Czechoslovakia; d. 1968). Theatrical productions include *Periferie, Egor Balycev, The Winter's Tale, Tartuffe*—1934; *King Svatopluk, Fuente Ovejuna, Public Enemy, Julius Caesar*—1935; *Lady Precious Stream, Revizor*—1936; *Table Ronde, A Charmed Life*—1937; *Romeo and Juliet*—1938; *l diavoletto di Zvikov*—1944; *La Malade imaginaire, Macbeth, Theseus*—1946; *A Midsummer Night's Dream, Gore ot ouma*—1947; *Carmen, I Brandembergahesi in Bohemia, Boris Godunov*—1948; *Enspigl, Merry Wives of Windsor*—1949; *The Marriage of Figaro*—1950; *Daughter of the Regiment*—1951; *Nascosta sulle scale, L'avventura della volpe furba*—1952; *The Three Musketeers*—1953; *Dalibor*—1955; *L'Affair Makropoulos*—1956; *Aida, Don Juan, The Eccentric*—1957; *Beg Bajazid, Die Meistersinger, The Atonement of Tantalus, Cunning Little Vixen*—1958; *Mirandolina, Woyzeck*—1959.

Troester, known as the "father" of postwar scene design in Czechoslovakia, trained as a painter and an architect in Prague. As an urban architect in Algeria in the 1920s, he designed ramps and podiums to accommodate the Algerian terrain. When he turned his attention to designing sets for the theatre, he brought this architectonic propensity to the stage. In addition to relying on ramps, platforms, turntables, and sculptural set pieces to alter the stage space, Troester added lighting and film projections to his kinetic designs. What he created on the stage, primarily in collaboration with director Jiri Frejka, were expressionistic designs that they called "hyperbolic realism." At the end of World War II, Troester cofounded the Akademie Muzickyck lemeni and headed its design division until his death in 1968. By the early 1950s, his theatrical designs were out of favor with the government because they were not in the style of social realism; however, he continued to teach and design operas. As a result of his prolific approach, by 1957 his career had a rebirth, and his nonrealistic, kinetic stage designs were again seen on the stages of Prague. In 1959, he received international recognition for his designs when he won first prize for scenography at the São Paolo Bienniale. Over the course of his lifetime, Troester designed more than 350 productions.

Further Reading: By Troester: "Measured by Today." *Divadio* December 1964: 62; "Remarks about the Setting." *Zivot* (1937): 3–4.

About Troester: Burian, Jarka. "Czechoslovakian Stage Design and Scenography, 1914–1938, A Survey." *Theatre Design and Technology* Summer 1975.

Andrea J. Nouryeh

U

Urban, Joseph. Set designer (b. 1872, Vienna, Austria; d. 1933). Theatrical productions include *Pelleas and Melisande, Hansel and Gretel, Tristan und Isolde, Tales of Hoffman, Faust, Mona Vanna*—1912; *Don Giovanni, Love of Three Kings, Jewels of the Madonna, Louise, Djamileh, Die Meistersinger*—1913; *Ziegfeld Follies, Macbeth, The Garden of Paradise, Twelfth Night, Here Comes Tootsie, Behold My Wife*—1915; *Caliban of the Yellow Sands, Ziegfeld Follies, Nju, Merry Wives of Windsor, The Country Girl*—1916; *Ziegfeld Follies, St. Elizabeth, Faust, Women and Song, The Riviera Girl*—1917; *Ziegfeld Follies*—1918; *Parsifal, Tristan und Isolde, A Young Man's Fancy, Prince Charming, Ziegfeld Follies, Rose of China*—1919; *Ziegfeld Follies, Sally, Don Carlos*—1920; *Cosi Fan Tutte, Ernani, Ziegfeld Follies*—1921; *Ziegfeld Follies*—1922; *Ziegfeld Follies, Fedora*—1923; *Carmen, Falstaff, Le Vestale, Ziegfeld Follies*—1924; *Ziegfeld Follies, Pelléas and Mélisande*—1925; *Fidelio, La Vide Breve, Ziegfeld Follies*—1926; *La Rondine, Hansel and Gretel, Ziegfeld Follies, Rio Rita, Show Boat*—1927; *The Three Musketeers, Die Aegyptische Helena*—1928; *Don Giovanni*—1929; *Flying High, Boccaccio*—1930; *Electra, Ziegfeld Follies*—1931; *Il Signor Bruschind*—1932.

After working in Europe in the 1890s designing palaces, pavilions, and a bridge, Urban found employment as a designer for the Burgtheater in Vienna in 1904. Here he established himself as an opera designer, eventually taking assignments all over Europe. Urban came to the United States and worked for the Boston Opera Company in 1911 and designed such shows as *Die Meistersinger, Don Giovanni, Faust, Pelléas et Mélisande,* and *Tristan und Isolde.* Urban stimulated the "New Stagecraft" movement that was occurring in America at that time by using some of its techniques of simplicity and suggestion in these operas. For example, in *Tristan und Isolde* (1912), he placed a couch, surrounded by dimly lit yellow curtains, in the middle of a bare stage to represent a ship at sea. American designers such as Robert Edmond Jones* and Lee Simonson* were influenced by these Continental theories of design. Urban, however, remained a decorative artist, rather than an actual practitioner of this new movement, which called for a more internal approach to design.

For the Broadway stage, Urban designed such shows as *The Garden of Paradise* (1915), in which he included two elaborately painted backdrops depicting a city street at night with skyscrapers and streetlights and a rustic house with trees and stars. As Urban's work could be very elaborate in terms of painting and detail, he was discovered by producer Florenz Ziegfeld to design the *Ziegfeld Follies*. In a scene from a design for one of the shows, Urban included such effects as a backdrop of elephants spouting water from their trunks.

After the Boston Opera closed, Urban moved permanently to New York. There, he designed Shakespearean settings for James K. Hackett, operas at the Metropolitan Opera House, and, subsequently, sets for film companies. Besides his stage designs, he decorated apartments, charity balls, cocktail lounges, restaurants, and store windows. His architecture skills included designing the Ziegfeld Theatre.

Urban is credited for introducing to the United States the Continental method of painting flat scenes on the floor, rather than the usual method of hanging a scene against a wall. He also introduced the concept of spattering or sponging differently colored paint speckles on the surface of a scene painting, which caused different sections of the surface to appear or disappear under differently colored lights. It was called "pointellage" by the critics and was borrowed from the French impressionists. Further, he utilized platforms and portals in his designs, such as for *Tales of Hoffman* (1912) and for his New York Shakespeare productions. The portal, a decorative framing device, served to unify the design of the individual sets for a show. With the production of *Women and Song* (1917), he developed a new background color, which later became known as Urban blue.

Further Reading: Larson, *Scene Design in the American Theatre from 1915 to 1960* (see Bibliography).

Kurt Lancaster

V

Vanbrugh, Sir John. Architect and playwright (b. January 1664, London, England; d. March 26, 1726, London, England). Playwright John Vanbrugh had little, if any, formal training as an architect when he indulged his interest in that area by designing Castle Howard, Blenheim Palace, and the Queen's Theatre. The latter was finished in 1705 on the site of the present Her Majesty's Theatre and was commissioned for Thomas Betterton's company. He is remembered mostly for his playwriting, and his most produced work, *The Relapse* (1696), was a popular favorite in the late seventeenth century and later in the 1770s with Richard Brinsley Sheridan's sanitized version, *A Trip to Scarborough*.

Further Reading: Barman, C. *Sir John Vanbrugh*. London: 1924; Whistler, L. *Sir John Vanbrugh, Architect and Dramatist, 1664–1726*. London: 1938.

James Fisher

Vesnin, Aleksandr. Architect and theatrical designer (b. May 16, 1883, Yu-ravets, Volga Province, Russia; d. November 7, 1959, Moscow). Vesnin began his studies as an architect at the Moscow Practical Academy and at the Institute of Civil Engineers in St. Petersburg. From 1912 through 1914 he worked in Vladimir Tatlin's studio with artist-designers Liubov Sergeevna Popova* and others. After the Revolution, Vesnin created decorations for agitprop theatre in the streets and squares of Moscow. In 1919 he began his formal theatrical design career for the Maly Theater with *The Inspector General* and *Oliver Cromwell*. His successful partnership with director Aleksandr Tairov commenced one year later with *L'Annonce faite a Marie*. Their collaborations culminated with the cubist *Phedre* (1921) and with Vesnin's constructivist theatre work, *The Man Who Was Thursday* (1923). Among his various activities during this period were his membership in the Institute of Artistic Culture, his contribution to the "5 x 5 = 25" exhibition in Moscow, and his work in the Moscow Children's Theatre. By 1923, he became associated with the Left Front of the Arts and a supporter of the constructivist movement. At the same time, he began to work with his brothers on the architectural projects for which he has primarily been known: the Lenin Library and the Palace of Soviets in Moscow. The cofounded the Association of Contemporary Architects and continued to create buildings such as the house communes for Stalingrad until 1933, when Leonid Vesnin died and constructivism was officially censured.

Andrea J. Nouryeh

Vigarani, Gaspare. Set designer, stage machinist, and theatrical architect (b. 1586, Italy; d. 1663). Known in Italy as a successful machinist and builder of theatres, Vigarani was summoned to Paris in 1659 by Cardinal Mazarin, chief minister to King Louis XIV. Vigarani was assigned to supervise the design for the performances that were to be held as part of the royal wedding. As a further extension of his duties, he was instructed to design a new theatre because the Petit-Bourbon was to be torn down to enlarge the Louvre. Modeled on his Teatro Modena in Italy, built in 1654, the Salle des Machines was Vigarani's triumph as Europe's largest theatre and was located in the Tuileries Palace. With a seating capacity of more than seven thousand people, the theatre opened in 1662 with a performance of the opera *Hercules in Love*, featuring Vigarani's elaborate stage machinery, which actually levitated the royal family. Because Vigarani became extremely jealous of his rival Giacomo Torelli,* he destroyed the latter's stage machinery, which was installed in the Petit-Bourbon Theatre, instead of transferring it to the new theatre as had been planned. When Vigarani died in 1663, he was succeeded by his son Carlo (1663–1713), who, as a designer for the Court, worked principally at the Palace of Versailles. Carlo's best-known work was the *Pleasures of the Enchanted Island* (1664), a three-day spectacle.

Further Reading: Oenslager (see Bibliography).

Thomas J. Mikotowicz

Visconti, Luchino. Film and theatre director and designer (b. November 2, 1906, Milan, Italy; d. March 17, 1976, Rome, Italy). Theatrical productions include *Parenti terribles, Antigone*—1945; *Le Nozze di Figaro, The Glass Menagerie*—1946; *Eurydice*—1947; *As You Like It* (produced under the title *Rosalinda*)—1948; *Death of a Salesman*—1951; *Three Sisters*—1952; *La vestale*—1954; *Uncle Vanya, La Traviata*—1955; *Mario e il mago*—1956; *Maratondi danza*—1957; *A View from the Bridge, Don Carlos, Macbeth, The Impresario from Smyrna*—1958; *Figli d'Arte, Duca d'Alba*—1959; *'Tis a Pity She's a Whore, Salome*—1961; *Il diavolo in giardino, La Traviata*—1963; *Manon Lescaut*—1972; *Old Times*—1973. Also, Visconti is known for his work on many films.

Known in the United States primarily for his film direction, Visconti was a theatre director-designer in his native Italy. He was educated at private schools in Milan and Como before working as a scene designer and actor in 1928 for productions directed by G. A. Traversi. In 1936, Coco Chanel introduced Visconti to Jean Renoir, and for several years Visconti worked in various capacities on the great director's films. During this same period, however, he continued to work in theatre. While with the Teatro Eliseo in Rome, he was energetic in encouraging production of works by contemporary European and American dramatists. As a director and designer, Visconti created unique productions of plays by Shakespeare and Beaumarchais, as well as Chekhov, Anouilh, Tennessee Williams, and Arthur Miller. During his later career, he returned to film work, although he occasionally worked in theatre, as when he staged Harold Pinter's *Old Times* (1973) in Rome, which was his last production. Visconti also directed many operas, but his greatest fame rests on his work as a film director.

Further Reading: Baldelli, P. *Luchino Visconti*. Milan: 1973; Estéve, M., ed. *Luchino Visconti*. Paris: 1963; Guillaume, Y. *Luchino Visconti*. Paris: 1966; Smith, G. N. *Luchino Visconti*. London: 1967.

James Fisher

Vitruvius (Marcus Vitruvius Pollio). Designer and architect (b. 84 B.C., Italy; d. 14 B.C.). Roman architect Vitruvius was the author of a ten-volume treatise, *De Architectura*, of which volume five offers a detailed, diagrammatic study of classical theatre construction and stage machinery. The work was found in 1414 and published with illustrations in 1511, from which time it had considerable influence on Italian Renaissance artists and scene designers and served as an especially useful model for designers Palladio* and Scamozzi* in the building of the Teatro Olimpico in 1585 in Vicenza.

James Fisher

W

Wagner, Robin. Set designer (b. August 31, 1933, San Francisco, CA). Theatrical productions include *Don Pasquale, Amahl and the Night Visitors, Zanetto, Contemporary Dancers Company*—1953; *Tea and Sympathy, Mr. Roberts*—1954; *The Immoralist, Dark of the Moon*—1955; *Waiting for Godot*—1957; *The Miser, The Ticklish Acrobat, Waiting for Godot, Filling Station, The Guardsman*—1958; *And the Wind Blows, The Plaster Bambino*—1959; *The Prodigal, Between Two Thieves, Borak*—1960; *A Worm in Horseradish*—1961; *Entertain a Ghost, The Days and Nights of Beebee Fenstermaker, The Playboy of the Western World, Come Blow Your Horn, West Side Story*—1962; *Major Barbara, Cages, In White America, The Burning*—1963; *The White Rose and the Red, Dark of the Moon, Galileo*—1964; *A View from the Bridge, An Evening's Frost, He Who Gets Slapped, Lonesome Train and Hard Travelin', Saint Joan, The Skin of Our Teeth*—1965; *Project Immortality, The Condemned of Altona, Serjeant Musgrave's Dance, Oh, What a Lovely War!, Macbeth, The Magistrate*—1966; *The Inspector General, Galileo, Phaedra, The Andersonville Trial, Major Barbara, Poor Bitos, The Trial of Lee Harvey Oswald, A Certain Young Man*—1967; *Hair, In Three Zones, The Cuban Thing, The Great White Hope, Love Match, Lovers and Other Strangers, Promises, Promises*—1968; *The Watering Place, My Daughter, Your Son, Edith Stein, Promises, Promises, Hair*—1969; *Gantry, Mahagonny, The Engagement Baby*—1970; *Lenny, Jesus Christ Superstar, Inner City*—1971; *Sugar, Julius Caesar, Antony and Cleopatra, Jesus Christ Superstar, Lulu, Lysistrata, Mary C. Brown and the Hollywood Sign, The Old Man's Place* (film)—1972; *Seesaw, Full Circle, Rachael Lily Rosenbloom and Don't You Forget It, Bette Midler Concert*—1973; *Mack and Mabel, Sgt. Pepper's Lonely Hearts Club Band on the Road*—1974; *A Chorus Line, The Red Devil Battery Sign, The Rolling Stones Tour of the Americas*—1975; *Hamlet Connotations, The Trojans*—1976; *A Chorus Line, Hair, West Side Story*—1977; *On the Twentieth*

Century, *Last Rite for Snow White*, *Ballroom*—1978; *George and Rosemary*, *Comin' Uptown*—1979; *Swing*, *42nd Street*, *One-Night Stand*—1980; *Semmelweiss*, *Dreamgirls*—1981; *The Barber of Seville*, *Mahalia*, *Rolling Stone Concert*—1982; *Merlin*, *Three Dances*, *Jewels*—1983; *Song and Dance* (Royale), *Measure for Measure* (New York Shakespeare Festival)—1985; *Chess*—1988; *Jerome Robbins' Broadway*—1989; *City of Angels*—1990.

Wagner, one of today's most successful stage designers, is known for scenographic spectacle and has designed some of the biggest musical hits since the late 1960s. His sets sometimes seem to overpower their shows, but such conceptual directors as Ed Sherrin, Michael Bennett, and Tom O'Horgan praise him as a true collaborative artist.

Although Wagner had no formal training in theatre, he got his start designing for several theatres in San Francisco. After moving to New York, his first production was *And the Wind Blows* at St. Mark's Playhouse in 1959. He continued to design for off-Broadway and regional theatres while assisting Ben Edwards* and Oliver Smith* on shows like *The Aspern Papers* and *Hello, Dolly!* From 1964 to 1967, Wagner was the principal designer at Arena Stage in Washington, D.C., for director Ed Sherrin.

Although his first Broadway show was *The Trial of Lee Harvey Oswald* in 1967, his design for *Hair* in 1968 established Wagner as a major designer. Beginning with *Promises, Promises* (1968), Wagner designed several shows for Michael Bennett, including *Seesaw* (1973), *A Chorus Line* (1975), *Ballroom* (1978), and *Dreamgirls* (1981). Developed over two years, *A Chorus Line* had a set comprised of simple *periaktoi* that helped change the scene from a bare stage to a wall of mirrors and to a glittery finale. Wagner's highly automated and sophisticated set changes in *Dreamgirls* were accomplished with five twenty-one-foot-high towers that became part of the choreography and ended up in new configurations.

Working with Tom O'Horgan on *Lenny* (1971), *The Trojans* (1976) at the Vienna State Opera, and especially *Jesus Christ Superstar* (1971), Wagner used more elaborate machinery. The latter show, for example, had special catwalks and pistons to create elaborate stage effects, including tilting the entire stage floor up to seal off the proscenium. Other productions that exemplify Wagner's technological style include *The Barber of Seville* (1982) at the Metropolitan Opera, *On the Twentieth Century* (1978) with Hal Prince, *42nd Street* (1980) with Gower Champion, and *Chess* (1988).

Awards: Wagner won Tony Awards for *On the Twentieth Century* (1978) and *City of Angels* (1990); the Joseph Maharam Award for *Seesaw* (1973); the Drama Desk Award for *Lenny* (1971), *Twentieth Century*, and *Dreamgirls* (1981); and the Outer Critics' Circle Award for *City of Angels*.

Further Reading: Aronson (see Bibliography); "Designers at Work." *Theatre Crafts Magazine* May 1987: 52; Fielding, Eric. "Contemporary American Designers: Robin Wagner." *Theatre Design & Technology* Winter 1983: 4–10; Gottfried, Martin. *Broadway Musicals*. New York: Harry Abrams, 1979; Pecktal (see Bibliography); Raymond, Gerard. "Robin Wagner Sets the Stage." *Theatre Week* May 16, 1988.

Ken Kloth

Wagner, Wieland. Director and designer (b. 1917, West Germany; d. 1966). Wagner, grandson of opera composer Richard Wagner, began studying design and direction under the tutelage of Heinz Tietjen and Emil Praetorius of the Berlin State Opera company. In addition, he had access to the ideas of Appia,* Craig,* and Meyerhold, and his own directing and design style reflected their influence. In 1951, when the Bayreuth festivals began again, Wieland and his brother Wolfgang took charge of directing and designing the operas for each festival season. The nonnaturalistic stage pictures that Wieland created were composed of platforms and abstract ''plastic'' forms, with a cyclorama in the background upon which abstract patterns were projected. Light, shadow, and color, inspired by their grandfather's music, were crucial design elements. As the director and designer of these operas, Wieland preplanned his stage designs before rehearsal with the performers. Once these rehearsals began, final lighting was adjusted and the singers were placed into these settings. What resulted were operas that were dark and dimly lit but that seemed to have translated Richard Wagner's ideas of *gesamptekunstwerk* into a modern technological idiom. Besides returning the Bayreuth festivals to their former greatness with his designs for *Tannhauser* (1954, 1964), *Parsifal* (1951), *Die Meistersinger*, *Tristan und Isolde*, and *The Ring Cycle* (1965), Wieland designed *Aida* (1962) for the Deutches Opera in West Berlin and *Lohengrin* for the Metropolitan Opera in New York. Since his death in 1966, his brother has continued to design and direct operas at Bayreuth.

Further Reading: Corathiel, Elizabethe H. C. ''Creative Artists in the Theatre: Wieland Wagner.'' *Theatre World* February 1955: 14–16; Loney, Glenn. ''And Wagner Said/Let There Be Light—But Not Too Much.'' *Theatre Crafts* September 1968: 28 +; Rood, Arnold, and Glenn Loney. ''Gordon Craig's Ghost Walks at Bayreauth: Wagner's Grandsons Fulfill Some Prophecies.'' *Theatre Crafts* May 1972: 5–18; Skelton, Geoffrey. *Wagner at Bayreauth*. New York: George Braziller, 1965; Skelton, Geoffrey. *Wieland Wagner: The Positive Sceptic*. New York: St. Martin's Press, 1971.

Andrea J. Nouryeh

Wahkevitch, Georges. Designer (b. 1907, Odessa, Russia). Wahkevitch spent most of his working career outside of Russia, especially in France. He was educated at the Ecole Superieure des Arts Decoratifs in Paris and was greatly influenced by artists Edwin Scott, Lazare Meerson, and Jean Perrir. He has designed more than eighty productions, two-thirds of these in France. His most noted designs include *The Little Hut* (1947), *Boris Godunov* (1948), *Jeanne la Folle* (1949), *Sud* (1953), *Faust* (1955), *Hymn a la Beaute* (1955), *Le Dialogue des Carmelites* (1957), *Don Juan ou le Festin de Pierre* (1959), and *Don Carlos* (1960).

James Fisher

Walton, Tony. Designer, director, and producer (b. October 24, 1934, Walton-on-Thames, England). Theatrical productions include *Worm's Eye*, *The Moon Is Blue*—1955; *Conversation Piece*—1957; *Valmouth*—1958; *The Ginger Man*,

Fool's Paradise, The Pleasure of His Company, Pieces of Eight—1959; *New Cranks, Valmouth, The Most Happy Fella*—1960; *Fairy Tales, Once There Was a Russian, One Over the Eight, A Wreath for Udomo*—1961; *A Funny Thing Happened on the Way to the Forum, Cindy-Ella*—1962; *The Rehearsal, A Funny Thing Happened on the Way to the Forum, The Love for Three Oranges, The Rape of Lucretia*—1963; *She Loves Me, Golden Boy, Caligula*—1964; *The Apple Tree*—1967; *Pippin*—1973; *Chicago*—1976; *A Day in Hollywood/A Night in the Ukraine*—1980; *Woman of the Year, Sophisticated Ladies*—1981; *The Real Thing, Hurlyburly, Whoopi Goldberg*—1984; *I'm Not Rappaport, My One and Only, Leader of the Pack*—1985; *Social Security, The House of Blue Leaves*—1986; *The Front Page, Anything Goes* (sets and costumes; Vivian Beaumont Theatre)—1987; *Songs of My Father* (Minskoff Theatre), *Waiting for Godot* (Mitzie E. Newhouse Theatre)—1988; *Grand Hotel, Lend Me a Tenor* (Royale), *Jerome Robbins's Broadway* (Walton's sets were re-created by Robin Wagner*; Imperial Theatre)—1989; *Square One*—1990.

After working as an illustrator of books and as a commercial artist in advertising, Walton took on his first New York design assignment in 1957 for a revival of Noël Coward's *Conversation Piece*. Since then, Walton has designed scenery, lights, and costumes for a wide variety of theatre productions. He has had particular success in designing contemporary musicals and comedies, for which he creates highly detailed and fanciful designs, such as for *A Funny Thing Happened on the Way to the Forum* (1962) and *Pippin* (1973). Walton has also directed and produced on occasion. Since 1959, he has been head of Theatre Projects, Ltd., a London company that services all technical areas of theatre. Along with his work in theatre, Walton has designed for television (including several Julie Andrews specials), opera, ballet, and especially film. His film credits include *Mary Poppins* (1965), *A Funny Thing Happened on the Way to the Forum* (1966), *Fahrenheit 451* (1967), *The Sea Gull* (1968), *Petulia* (1968), *The Boy Friend* (1971), *Murder on the Orient Express* (1974), *The Wiz* (1978), *All That Jazz* (1979), and *Star 80* (1983).

Awards: Walton has earned Tony Awards for *Pippin* (1973) and *The House of Blue Leaves* (1986); and an Academy Award for Art Direction for *All That Jazz* (1979).

James Fisher

Webb, John. Designer and artist (b. 1611, England; d. 1672). Webb began his prolific career in scenic design in England as a pupil and assistant of Inigo Jones.* His most important design, among many, was for *The Siege of Rhodes* (1656), produced by William Davenant at Rutland House. It was the first significant production heralding the start of the vigorous Restoration stage. His designs, which were undoubtedly taken from period engravings, depicted a landscape of a town and a harbor. Webb also designed *Mustapha* (1665).

James Fisher

White, Miles. Costume designer (b. July 27, 1914, Oakland, CA). Theatrical productions (all were in New York City, unless otherwise specified) include *Right This Way* (46th Street Theatre)—1938; *George White's Scandals* (Winter

Garden Theatre)—1939; *Best Foot Forward* (Ethel Barrymore Theatre)—1941; *The Pirate* (Martin Beck Theatre)—1942; *Ziegfeld Follies* (Ziegfeld Theatre), *Oklahoma!* (St. James Theatre), *Early to Bed* (Broadhurst Theatre), *Get Away, Old Man* (Cort Theatre)—1943; *Bloomer Girl* (Shubert Theatre), *Allah Be Praised!* (Adelphi Theatre), *Dream with Music* (Majestic Theatre), *Up in Arms* (film)—1944; *Carousel* (Majestic Theatre), *The Day Before Spring* (National Theatre), *Gypsy Lady* (Century Theatre), *The Duchess of Malfi* (Barrymore Theatre), *The Kid from Brooklyn* (film)—1946; *High Button Shoes* (Century Theatre)—1947; *That's the Ticket* (Shubert Theatre, Philadelphia, Pennsylvania), *Fall River Legend* (American Ballet Theatre)—1948; *Gentlemen Prefer Blondes* (Ziegfeld Theatre)—1949; *Bless You All* (Mark Hellinger Theatre)—1950; *Pal Joey* (Broadhurst Theatre), *Three Wishes for Jamie* (Mark Hellinger Theatre), *Two's Company* (Alvin Theatre), *The Greatest Show on Earth* (film)—1952; *Hazel Flagg* (Mark Hellinger Theatre)—1953; *The Girl in Pink Tights* (Mark Hellinger Theatre), *There's No Business Like Show Business* (film)—1954; *Ankles Aweigh* (Mark Hellinger Theatre)—1955; *Strip for Action* (Shubert Theatre, New Haven, Connecticut), *Around the World in 80 Days* (film)—1956; *Eugenia* (Ambassador Theatre), *Jamaica* (Imperial Theatre), *Time Remembered* (Morosco Theatre), *The Carefree Heart* (Cass Theatre, Detroit, Michigan)—1957; *Oh, Captain* (Alvin Theatre)—1958; *Cheri* (Morosco Theatre), *Show Business* (Curran Theatre, San Francisco)—1959; *Bye, Bye Birdie* (Martin Beck Theatre), *The Unsinkable Molly Brown* (Winter Garden Theatre)—1960; *Show Girl* (Eugene O'Neill Theatre), *Milk and Honey* (Martin Beck Theatre)—1961; *Song of Norway* (California tour)—1962; *Zenda* (California tour)—1963; *Oklahoma!* (New York State Theatre)—1969; *Candida* (Sarasota, Florida)—1970; *A Day in the Life of Just About Everyone* (Bijou Theatre)—1971; *A Quarter for the Ladies' Room* (Village Gate Theatre)—1972; *Tricks* (Alvin Theatre)—1973; *Sleeping Beauty* (American Ballet Theatre)—1974; *Best Friend* (Lyceum Theatre)—1976; *Toller Cranston's Ice Show* (Palace Theatre)—1977.

Throughout the 1940s and 1950s, White created costumes for some of the most popular musical comedies ever presented on the American stage. In addition, he has designed ten productions for the Ringling Brothers and Barnum and Bailey Circus, as well as three editions of the Ice Capades and a number of feature films. White studied art at the University of California at Berkeley and the California School of Fine Arts before moving to New York to finish his education at the Art Students League.

Noted for the elegance and detail of his costumes, White received his first credit on Broadway in 1938 with the production *Right This Way*. In the 1940s he designed the costumes for many successful productions, including *Oklahoma!* (1943) and *Bloomer Girl* (1944), and worked with noted designer Oliver Smith* on such productions as *Gentlemen Prefer Blondes* (1949) and *Pal Joey* (1952). In addition, White began to design film costumes in the mid-1940s, beginning with the musical *Up in Arms* (1944) and continuing throughout the 1950s with such Academy Award–winning films as *The Greatest Show on Earth* (1952) and

Around the World in 80 Days (1956). In the late 1950s and 1960s, White designed the costumes for revivals of many of his earlier hits, as well as new productions such as *Bye Bye Birdie* (1960) and *The Unsinkable Molly Brown* (1960).

White's technique may be best known for its liberal use of sequins and chiffon and for its vast scale. His approach, however, also takes into consideration the needs of the director and, in a musical, the choreographer of the show. For *Oklahoma!*, White created colorful costumes that were elegant but still flexible, enabling the performers to move easily while executing the complex choreography of Agnes de Mille. He got many of his ideas for the show from a 1900 Sears Roebuck catalog. Complementing what de Mille was attempting to do with her treatment of American folk dancing in the production, White stylized and slightly satirized the designs.

The costumes that White created for the Ringling Brothers and Barnum and Bailey Circus, however, probably offer the best example of this technique. Hired in 1944 to give the circus a "new look," White did away with the heavy brocades and dark colors the performers had been wearing and created a lighter atmosphere that continues to this day. "Dress the acrobats in blood-red velvet and they look as if they'd crash from heaviness," White was quoted as saying in the early 1950s. "Dress them in sequins and they seem to fly. With aniline dyes you get color that vibrates. Then you put sequins on top and you have the giddiest vibrations in the world."

Awards: White received two Tony Awards for "Best Costume Design" for *Bless You All* (1950) and *Hazel Flagg* (1953). In addition, he has won four Donaldson Awards for costume design for *Bloomer Girl* (1944), *High Button Shoes* (1947), *Gentlemen Prefer Blondes* (1949), and *Pal Joey* (1952); and three Academy Award nominations for Best Costume Design for *The Greatest Show on Earth* (1952), *There's No Business Like Show Business* (1954), and *Around the World in 80 Days* (1956).

Further Reading: "Sprangles in the Air." *Time* May 18, 1953.

Howard Gutner

Wilkinson, Norman. Designer (b. 1882, England; d. February 14, 1934). English artist and scene designer Wilkinson began his theatrical career designing a repertory of plays for Charles Frohman at the Duke of York's Theatre in 1910. His greatest fame rests on his designs for Harley Granville-Barker's productions of Shakespeare's plays at the Savoy Theatre between 1912 and 1914. Wilkinson's permanent setting for *Twelfth Night* and his gilded fairies and iridescent forest for *A Midsummer Night's Dream* were especially memorable. In later years, Wilkinson also designed for producers Nigel Playfair and C. B. Cochran. His significant productions include *Anatol*, *The Master Builder*, *Bonita* (all in 1911); *Iphigenia in Tauris*, *The Winter's Tale* (both in 1912); *The Dynasts* (1914); *Iphigenia in Tauris*, *The Trojan Women* (both in 1915); *The Rivals*, *The Would-Be Gentleman*, and *Lionel and Clarissa* (1925).

James Fisher

Williams, Piotr. Designer (b. April 17, 1902, Moscow, Russia; d. December 4, 1947, Moscow, Russia). Williams began his career in 1924 with a variety of painting assignments in Italy, France, and Germany, following his studies in

V. N. Meshkov's workshop and graduation from the Higher Technical Art Workshops. He joined the Lathe Artists Society in 1925 but did not truly begin his most significant work as a scene designer until 1929. From then, until his death in 1947, Williams designed sets and costumes for a wide variety of productions, mostly for the Moscow Academy Arts Theater, the Nemirovich-Danchenko Musical Theater, and the Bolshoi Theater, and won the Stalin Prize in 1943, 1946, and 1947. He was chief artist at the Bolshoi from 1941 to 1947, and, shortly before his death, he accepted a professorship at the Moscow Institute of Applied and Decorative Arts. Some of his well-known productions include *La Traviata* (1934), *Virgin Soil Upturned* (1937), *Prisoner of Caucasus* (1938), *Tartuffe* (1939), *William Tell* (1942), *The Last Days* (1943), *Ivan the Terrible* (1946), and *How the Steel was Tempered* (1947).

James Fisher

Wilson, Robert. Performer, playwright, director, designer, and artist (b. October 4, 1941, Waco, TX). Theatrical productions include *The Life and Times of Sigmund Freud, The King of Spain*—1969; *Deafman Glance*—1970; *Overture for Ka Mountain, GUARDenia Terrace* (all in Shiraz, Iran)—1972; *The Life and Times of Joseph Stalin*—1973; *Dia Log, A Mad Man A Mad Giant A Mad Dog A Mad Urge A Mad Face, A Letter for Queen Victoria*—1974; *The $-Value of a Man*—1975; *Spaceman, Einstein on the Beach*—1976; *I Was Sitting on My Patio This Guy Appeared I Thought I Was Hallucinating*—1977; *Prologue to Deafman Glance*—1978; *Death Destruction and Detroit, Edison*—1979; *The Man in the Raincoat*—1981, *Great Day in the Morning, The Golden Windows*— 1982; *the CIVIL warS*—1983; *Alcestis*—1986; *Parzival*—1987; *When We Dead Awaken*—1991.

Receiving his theatre experience at the Waco Children's Theatre at Baylor University and the University of Texas and his training in painting in Paris and as an architecture student at the Pratt Institute in Brooklyn, New York, Wilson became a total performance artist, writing, directing, and designing his own experimental works from the late 1960s to the present. As a youth, Wilson was cured of a speech impediment by Mrs. Byrd Hoffman, a name he later employed for his producing company—the Byrd Hoffman School of Byrds, founded in 1968—and one he used as a pseudonym in the 1960s and early 1970s.

In his earlier productions, Wilson explored the limits of language and collaborated with the autistic child Christopher Knowles, as well as with other deaf and brain-damaged children. In *A Letter for Queen Victoria*, produced at the Brooklyn Academy of Music in 1974, Wilson and Knowles performed against large backdrops of Knowles's geometric, but nonlinear writing. In *Dia Log* (1974) and *The $-Value of a Man* (1975), Knowles and Wilson collaborated on the writing and performing of these experimental works.

Although starting out in his Soho loft in New York City with minimal productions, Wilson eventually produced mammoth spectacles in some of the most prestigious venues in the world, including the Brooklyn Academy of Music, the

Metropolitan Opera House, the Deutsches Schauspielhaus in Hamburg, and the Opéra Comique in Paris. He has written, directed, and designed most of his works in collaboration with others and supervised such artists as choreographer Lucinda Childs, composer Philip Glass, lighting designer Beverly Emmons, set designer Lester Polakov, and others. His plays and operas include *Deafman Glance* (1970), *Overture for Ka Mountain* (1972), *A Letter for Queen Victoria* (1974), and *Einstein on the Beach* (1976). In the latter, Wilson designed mammoth settings and used backdrops, scrims, unit constructions, and dynamic lighting, as well as projections, to create what author Stefan Brecht describes as a "theatre of visions."

Wilson's plays, especially his design images, are usually nonrepresentational. They are the subjective images of the playwright and are visually striking and powerfully presented. In some of his productions, Wilson's characters move slowly, distorting the audience's sense of time and space through repetition of movement. In fact, many of his productions run for hours or, in the case of *Ka Mountain* (1972), for days. Wilson's sets, like the performers, undergo transformations throughout the course of the action.

During the 1980s, Wilson produced *The Man in the Raincoat* (1981), *Great Day in the Morning* (1982), *The Golden Windows* (1982), and *the CIVIL warS* (1983). These striking designs seem like surrealistic paintings that have come to life. In *the CIVIL warS*, a dioramalike set is moved past the characters as they walk in the opposite direction onstage and creates a treadmill effect.

Wilson's career has undergone a slight change with his decision to apply his unique approach to classic plays such as Euripides's *Alcestis* (1986) and Henrik Ibsen's *When We Dead Awaken* (1991), both produced at American Repertory Theatre in Cambridge, Massachusetts. He also staged Gluck's opera *Alcestis* in Stuttgart, Germany, at the Staatstheater in April 1987. For the play Wilson used an eclectic approach to the design of the props and scenery and did not adhere to the ostensible demands of the time and place required by the original script. The piece took place on three stages: on the main stage, on a down left platform that projected out, and within a "shadow box" down right. The heavily symbolic main stage set contained three dominant images that transformed through the action: a mountain range that had an eye appear on it with the use of a laser, a river in the floor that was mostly heard and not seen, and a stand of three cypress trees that were variously trees, smokestacks, and columns.

Further Reading: Brecht, Stefan. *The Theatre of Visions: Robert Wilson*. Frankfurt, Germany: Suhrkamp, 1978; Shyer, Lawrence. *Robert Wilson and His Collaborators*. New York: Theatre Communications Group, 1989. Shyer, Lawrence. "Secret Sharers." *American Theatre* September 1989: 12–19.

Thomas J. Mikotowicz

Wittop, Freddy (Fred Wittop Koning). Costume designer and dancer (b. July 26, 1921, Bossum, Holland). Theatrical productions (all were in New York City, unless otherwise specified) include *Follies* (Paris)—1937; *New Folies Bergère* (Paris), *Plaisirs de Paris* (London)—1938; *Folies Bergère* (San Francisco)—

1939; *Ice Capades*—1940; *Beat the Band*—1942; *El Amor Brujo, Pictures of Goya, Bolero* (American Ballet Theatre)—1944; *Madeleine Bastille* (Alhambra Theatre, Paris)—1946; *Heartbreak House* (Billy Rose Theatre)—1959; *Carnival!* (Imperial Theatre)—1961; *Judith* (London)—1962; *Hello, Dolly!* (St. James Theatre), *To Broadway with Love* (Texas Pavilion, New York World's Fair), *Bajour* (Shubert Theatre)—1964; *Hello, Dolly!* (London), *Kelly* (Paris), *Pleasures and Palaces* (Detroit, Fisher Theatre), *On a Clear Day You Can See Forever* (Mark Hellinger Theatre)—1965; *Three Bags Full* (Henry Miller's Theatre), *Breakfast at Tiffany's* (Majestic Theatre), *I Do! I Do!* (46th Street Theatre)—1966; *The Happy Time* (Broadway Theatre), *George M!* (Palace Theatre), *I Do! I Do!* (London)—1968; *Dear World* (Mark Hellinger Theatre), *A Patriot for Me* (Imperial Theatre)—1969; *Lovely Ladies, Kind Gentlemen* (Majestic Theatre)—1970; *Knickerbocker Holiday* (Curran Theatre, San Francisco, California), *Candide, Great Waltz, Dumas and Son* (Los Angeles Light Opera Company, Los Angeles, California)—1971; *Hello, Dolly!* (revival; Lunt-Fontanne Theatre)—1978; *The Three Musketeers* (Broadway Theatre)—1984; *Wind in the Willows* (Nederlander Theatre)—1985.

Wittop began his career in the theatre as an apprentice designer at the Opera House in Brussels in 1932. After leaving the Brussels Opera, he designed for the *Folies Bergère* (1937) and came to New York in 1940 to design costumes for the French casino revue in Manhattan. Using the stage name Frederico Rey, Wittop toured the United States between the years 1941 and 1943 as a partner to the Spanish performer Argentinita. He continued to design intermittently for Broadway with such productions as *Beat the Band* (1942), as well as the Metropolitan Opera's *Bolero* (1944) and the Ballet Theater's *Pictures of Goya* (1944). Throughout the 1940s and 1950s, Wittop toured Europe and the United States with his own dance company. During this period he was also the resident designer at the Latin Quarter in New York. In 1958, Harold Clurman and Maurice Evans saw Wittop's Latin Quarter costumes and asked him to design the wardrobe for their Broadway production of George Bernard Shaw's *Heartbreak House*. Wittop gave up his career as a dancer at this time and began to work exclusively as a costume designer. Throughout the 1960s and early 1970s, Wittop became one of Broadway's most prolific designers, creating costumes for such productions as *Carnival!* (1961), *On a Clear Day You Can See Forever* (1965), *I Do! I Do!* (1966), and *George M!* (1968) and working with noted designer Oliver Smith* on such productions as *Hello, Dolly!* (1965) and *A Patriot for Me* (1969). Wittop's approach is that the finished costume should not look like a costume; it should simply look appropriate to the character and the situation. Putting camouflaged ostrich feathers on Carol Channing in *Hello, Dolly!* helped to define her bold character for the audience. When Wittop wanted plumes for a hat he was designing for Mary Martin in *I Do! I Do!*, he advertised in the New York press for only the best, authentic bird of paradise feathers to suit Martin's high-class character. Wittop retired to Spain in the early 1970s and returned to Broadway in 1984 to design costumes for the musicals *The Three Musketeers* (1984) and *Wind in the Willows* (1985).

Awards: Wittop won a Tony Award in 1964 for "Best Achievement in Costume Design" for *Hello, Dolly!*

Howard Gutner

Wurtzel, Stuart. Set designer and art director (b. 1940, Newark, NJ). Wurtzel received his M.F.A. from Carnegie-Mellon University in 1965 and became the assistant scenic designer with the fledgling American Conservatory Theatre Company (ACT), which was then based in Pittsburgh. When the company went on tour later that year with sixteen productions, he became the resident designer, moving to San Francisco with the company in 1966. His work with ACT includes such productions as *Tartuffe, Man and Superman, A Flea in Her Ear, Rozencrantz and Guildenstern Are Dead, Charley's Aunt, Thieves' Carnival,* and *Hamlet.* In 1970, Wurtzel moved to New York City and established his career in design with such productions as *Sizwe Bansi Is Dead* (1974) at the Edison Theatre, *Summer Brave* (1975) at the ANTA Theatre, *Unexpected Guests* (1977) at the Little Theatre, *The Sorrows of Stephen* (1979), and *Wally's Cafe* (1981) at the Brooks Atkinson Theatre. During this time, he maintained a career in the regional theatres, including the Cincinnati Playhouse in the Park, the Milwaukee Repertory Theatre, and the Empire State Institute for the Performing Arts. In the 1980s, Wurtzel expanded his activities to include film and television and only occasionally designed for theatre. As art director, he designed *Hester Street* (1973), *Hair* (1978), *Ballad of Gregorio Cortez* and *Little Gloria . . . Happy At Last* (both 1982); Woody Allen's films, *Purple Rose of Cairo* (1984) and *Hannah and Her Sisters* (1986); and Neil Simon's *Brighton Beach Memoirs* (1986), among many others.

Awards: Wurtzel's design for *The Sorrow of Stephen* earned him the Maharam Award in 1979. In addition, he was nominated for an Academy Award for his art direction on *Hannah and Her Sisters* and an Emmy Award for the made-for-television film *Little Gloria . . . Happy At Last.*

Further Reading: "Designers at Work." *Theatre Crafts* May 1987: 36.

Penny L. Remsen

Y

Yakulov, Georgii Bogdanovich. Set designer (b. January 2, 1882, Tiflis, Russia; d. December 28, 1928, Moscow, Russia). First schooled as an artist, Yakulov attended the Moscow Institute of Painting, Sculpture, and Architecture from 1901 through 1903. In 1913 he went to Paris, where he became influenced by cubism, rayonism, and futurism. Upon his return to Russia. Yakulov began to design cubist settings, notably Claudel's *The Exchange* (1918). In 1919, he designed such classical plays as *Oedipus*, *Rienzi*, and *Measure for Measure* for the State Exemplary Theater. Ultimately attracted to the constructivist movement, Yakulov subsequently created decors for director Vsevelod Meyerhold, such as *Princess Brambilla* (1920), and for director Aleksandr Tairov, such as *Girofle-Girofla* (1922), at the Chamber Theater. These designs were characterized by a circuslike or carnival quality. Geometric shapes on painted flats were enhanced by movable platforms, rope ladders, traps, and passageways. In 1925, he traveled to Paris, where his work was exhibited at the Exposition Internationale des Arts Decoratifs. During this time, he collaborated with the composer Prokofiev on the scenario for a Diaghilev ballet, *Pas d'Acier* (1927). For this constructivist ballet, Yakulov provided the story line, the scenery, and the costumes. Unfortunately, this was to be Yakulov's final work for the stage. In 1928 he died of pneumonia in the USSR.

Andrea J. Nouryeh

Z

Zefferelli, Franco. Director, designer, and producer of film and theatre (b. 1923, Italy). Theatrical productions include *L'Italiana in Algeri* (La Scala)—1952 and 1953; *La Cenerentola* (La Scala)—1954; *Mignon, La Traviata*—1958; *Barber of Seville, Lucia di Lammermoor, Cavalleria Rusticana, Pagliacci* (latter three at Covent Garden)—1959; *Alcina, Don Giovanni, The Daughter of the Regiment, Romeo and Juliet* (Old Vic)—1960; *L'Elixir d'Amore* (Glyndebourne), *Othello* (Stratford on Avon), *Falstaff*—1961; *Don Giovanni, Alcina, The Lady of the Camellias* (New York)—1962; *Aida*—1963; *Tosca, Rigoletto, Falstaff* (the Metropolitan Opera), *After the Fall* (Rome), *Who's Afraid of Virginia Woolf?* (Paris), *Amleto* (National Theater)—1964; *La Lupa* (Rome), *Who's Afraid of Virginia Woolf?* (Milan), *The Taming of the Shrew* (film)—1965; *Tosca, Rigoletto* (Florence), *Days of Destruction* (film), *Much Ado About Nothing* (National Theatre)—1966; *Romeo and Juliet* (film), *Black Comedy, A Delicate Balance* (New York)—1967; *Pagliacci, Cavalleria Rusticana*—1970; *Missa Solemnis* (produced in Rome)—1971; *Otello* (Glyndebourne), *Don Giovanni* (Staatsoper-Wiengarden)—1972; *Brother Sun, Sister Moon* (film), *Saturday, Sunday, Monday* (National Theatre), *Tosca, Rigoletto, Antony and Cleopatra*—1973; *Otello*—1976; *Filumena* (Lyric), *Jesus of Nazareth* (film)—1977; *The Champ* (film)—1979; *La Boheme, Endless Love* (film)—1981; *Turandot, Traviata* (film), *Cavalleria Rusticana* (film)—1983; *Turandot, Tosca, Rigoletto*—1985; *Otello*—1986; *Hamlet* (film)—1990.

Zefferelli, best known as a theatre and film director, began his education at the Liceo Artistico, an art school in Florence, from which he graduated in 1941. Following his father's plans for a career in architecture, Zefferelli went on to study at the School of Architecture at the University of Florence, where he became director of the university's theatre company and gained his first operatic experience as director and designer. In 1943, Italy was under German occupation, and Zefferelli fought against the Nazis for a year as a partisan, for which he later received a silver medal. When the war ended in 1945, he abandoned his architectural studies and went to Rome. There, he began his theatrical career as a radio actor and soon joined Luchino Visconti's Morelli-Stoppa Company as an actor and stage manager.

After acting two years with the company, Zefferelli became a designer and assistant director for Visconti, perhaps the greatest influence on his work. In 1948, when Visconti took a sabbatical from the company to work on his film *La Terra Trema*, Zefferelli went with him to Sicily, where he subsequently worked on films with de Sica and Rossellini. His first stage design was in 1948, when he assisted Salvador Dalí with extra sets for the Morelli-Stoppa production of *As You Like It*. During 1948 and 1949, Zefferelli designed for a number of Visconti's productions and came into prominence with lavish sets for *Troilus and Cressida* in Florence and *The Three Sisters* in Rome in 1951. These productions brought him to the attention of the director of La Scala in Milan, where Zefferelli's first major assignment was Rossini's *L'Italiana in Algeri* (1952). A year later he directed and designed *La Cenerentola* at the same theatre.

Zefferelli started working abroad in 1956, with *Falstaff* for the Holland Festival. In 1957, he began a series of annual visits to the Dallas Civic Opera. He gained international attention in 1958 with his unorthodox design and staging of Verdi's *La Traviata*. That same year his *Mignon* was produced at La Scala. In 1959, Zefferelli received his English debut at the Royal Opera House, Covent Garden with *Lucia di Lammermoor*, which established him as an operatic director of the first rank. He directed *Romeo and Juliet* and the Old Vic the following year, and that production established him as a theatre director, as well.

Known for his spectacular and often expensive presentations, Zefferelli produces designs that typically are complete with such a vast array of visual details that some critics complain that the action of the story becomes lost. Others, however, praise his authentic re-creations of place and time that bring to life works that might otherwise remain detached from the audience.

Jonet Buchanan

Zipprodt, Patricia. Costume designer and teacher (b. February 24, 1925, Evanston, IL). Theatrical productions (all were in New York City, unless otherwise specified) include *The Potting Shed* (Bijou Theatre), *A Visit to a Small Planet* (Booth Theatre), *The Rope Dancers* (Cort Theatre), *The Virtuous Island, The Apollo of Bellac* (both at the Carnegie Hall Playhouse), *Miss Lonelyhearts* (Music Box Theatre)—1957; *Back to Methuselah* (Ambassador Theatre), *The Crucible* (Martinique Theatre), *The Night Circus* (John Golden Theatre)—1958; *The Gang's All Here* (Ambassador Theatre), *Our Town, The Quare Fellow* (both at the Circle in the Square)—1959; *The Balcony* (Circle in the Square), *Camino Real* (St. Mark's Playhouse), *Period of Adjustment* (Helen Hayes Theatre)—1960; *Laurette* (Shubert Theatre, New Haven, Connecticut), *The Garden of Sweets* (ANTA Theatre), *Madame Aphrodite* (Orpheum Theatre), *The Blacks* (St. Mark's Playhouse), *Sunday in New York* (Cort Theatre)—1961; *Oh, Dad,*

Poor Dad, Mama's Hung You in the Closet and I'm Feelin' So Sad, *Next Time I'll Sing for You*, *The Matchmaker* (all at the Phoenix Repertory Theatre), *Step on a Crack* (Ethel Barrymore Theatre), *A Man's a Man* (Masque Theatre), *Don Perlimplin* (Playhouse in the Park, Cincinnati, Ohio), *La Boheme*, *Madame Butterfly* (both at the Boston Opera Company, Massachusetts)—1962; *She Loves Me* (Eugene O'Neill Theatre), *The Dragon* (Phoenix Repertory Theatre), *Morning Sun* (Phoenix Repertory Theatre), *Calvary* (Princeton Experimental Theatre, New Jersey)—1963; *Fiddler on the Roof* (Imperial Theatre), *Too Much Johnson*, *The Tragical Historie of Doctor Faustus* (both at the Phoenix Repertory Theatre)—1964; *Anya* (Ziegfeld Theatre), *La Sonnambula* (National Ballet of Washington, D.C.)—1965; *Cabaret* (Broadhurst Theatre), *Pousse-Cafe* (46th Street Theatre), *Hippolyte Aricie* (Boston Opera Company, Massachusetts)—1966; *The Little Foxes* (Vivian Beaumont Theatre), *Katerina Ismailova* (New York City Opera Company, State Theatre), *L'Histoire Du Soldat* (ballet; Israel Cultural Foundation), *The Graduate* (film, Avco-Embassy)—1967; *Plaza Suite* (Plymouth Theatre), *Zorba* (Imperial Theatre), *The Flaming Angel* (New York City Opera Company, State Theatre)—1968; *Tales of Kasane* (National Theatre for the Deaf), *1776* (46th Street Theatre), *Les Noces* (American Ballet Theatre), *The Last of the Mobile Hot-Shots* (film, Warner Brothers)—1969; *Georgy* (Winter Garden Theatre), *The Poppet* (Joffrey Ballet)—1970; *Scratch* (St. James Theatre)—1971; *Pippin* (Imperial Theatre), *The Rise and Fall of the City of Mahagonny* (Boston Opera Company, Massachusetts), *The Mother of Us All* (opera; Guggenheim Museum), *Watermill* (New York City Ballet, State Theatre)—1972; *Waiting for Godot* (Tyrone Guthrie Theatre, Minneapolis, Minnesota), *Lord Byron* (Juilliard Opera), *Dumbarton Oaks* (New York City Ballet, State Theatre)—1973; *Mack and Mabel* (Majestic Theatre), *Dear Nobody* (Cherry Lane Theatre), *Dybbuk Variations* (New York City Ballet, State Theatre)—1974; *All God's Chillun Got Wings* (Circle in the Square), *Chicago* (46th Street Theatre), *The Leaves are Fading* (American Ballet Theatre)—1975; *Poor Murderer* (Ethel Barrymore Theatre), *Four Saints in Three Acts* (National Theatre for the Deaf), *Tres Cantos*, *Caprichos* (both at the Ballet Hispanico)—1976; *Tannhauser* (Metropolitan Opera)—1977; *Stages* (Belasco Theatre), *King of Hearts* (Minskoff Theatre), *Naughty Marietta* (New York City Opera, State Theatre)—1978; *Charlotte* (Belasco Theatre), *Swing* (Playhouse Theatre, Wilmington, Delaware)—1979; *One-Night Stand* (Nederlander Theatre)—1980; *Kingdoms* (Cort Theatre), *Fools* (Eugene O'Neill Theatre), *Fiddler on the Roof* (State Theatre)—1981; *Whodunnit* (Biltmore Theatre), *Alice in Wonderland* (Virginia Theatre), *Don Juan* (Tyrone Guthrie Theatre, Minnesota), *The Barber of Seville* (Metropolitan Opera), *Brighton Beach Memoirs* (Ahmanson Theatre, Los Angeles, California)—1982; *Brighton Beach Memoirs* (Alvin Theatre), *The Glass Menagerie* (Eugene O'Neill Theatre), *Sunset* (Village Gate Downstairs), *Estuary* (American Ballet Theatre), *Llamado* (Ballet Hispanico)—1983; *Accidental Death of an Anarchist* (Belasco Theatre), *Sunday in the Park with George* (with Ann Hould-Ward*; Booth Theatre), *Anna Christie* (Central Theatre Institute, Beijing,

China), *The Loves of Don Perlimplin* (San Francisco Opera), *Tito on Tambales* (Ballet Hispanico)—1984; *Helgi Tommasen* (Houston Ballet Company, Texas)—1985; *Sweet Charity* (Minskoff Theatre), *Big Deal* (Broadway Theatre)—1986; *Into the Woods* (with Ann Hould-Ward*; Martin Beck Theatre), *Cabaret* (Imperial Theatre)—1987; *Macbeth* (Mark Hellinger Theatre), *Fall of the House of Usher*, *Tango Opassioniada*, *Sleeping Beauty* (all at the New York City Ballet, State Theatre)—1988; *Shogun* (Marquis Theatre)—1990.

Zipprodt has been a leading costume designer in the theatre for more than thirty years and has designed more than one hundred productions, including theatre, opera, ballet, television, and motion pictures. In addition, Zipprodt has lectured and taught master classes at the Yale School of Drama, as well as at Wellesley, Smith, New York University's Tisch School of the Arts, and the Pratt Institute. From 1985 to 1986, she was Joseph Siskind professor of theater arts at Brandeis University.

After receiving a bachelor of arts degree in sociology from Wellesley College in 1947, Zipprodt pursued an education in theatre arts by attending classes at the Art Institute of Chicago and, later, the New School, the Art Students' League, and the Fashion Institute of Technology in New York. Beginning her career as an assistant to such noted designers as William and Jean Eckart,* Boris Aronson,* and Irene Sharaff,* Zipprodt received her first solo credit as a designer in 1957 with *The Potting Shed*. In the 1960s and early 1970s, her career on Broadway was formally established when she designed the costumes for a series of immensely successful musicals, including *Fiddler on the Roof*, *Cabaret*, and *1776*. Zipprodt began to design costumes for both opera and ballet at this same time. She began her opera career with Sarah Caldwell's Boston Opera Company and later designed several successful productions for both the New York City Opera and the Metropolitan Opera. In the late 1960s, she designed costumes for the Alvin Ailey Dance Company, the New York City Ballet, and the American Ballet Theater.

Throughout the 1970s and 1980s, Zipprodt provided the designs for a number of plays both on and off-Broadway, including *Waiting for Godot*, *Don Juan*, *Brighton Beach Memoirs*, *Mack and Mabel*, *Alice in Wonderland*, and *Sunday in the Park with George*. In addition, she maintained a successful collaboration with director-choreographer Bob Fosse that began with *Cabaret* in 1966 and continued for two decades, with such productions as *Pippin*, the 1986 revival of *Sweet Charity*, and Fosse's last musical, *Big Deal*, also in 1986.

Zipprodt sees herself as more than just a costume designer: "In this business, you have to be able to do a lot of things in addition to being able to draw. You must coordinate closely with the scenic designer. You have to know all about textiles, and how the color dyes will look under the lights." Creating depth and life onstage through variations of color and fabric textures is the hallmark of Zipprodt's technique, one that she shares with one of her mentors, Irene Sharaff. For example, in *Pippin*, a "vaudeville"-styled show that is set in the ninth century, the characters perform an opening number in black, then emerge dressed in off-white and tan. As the action progresses, the color slowly evolves, featuring tones with a secondary palette—orange and green—until the hero finally makes his appearance in bright crimson. "Everyone thinks that the theater is bright—and red," says Zipprodt. "But theater is really about holding back red so that you can use it with a wallop."

Zipprodt invented her own technique to achieve the effect she wanted for *Fiddler on the Roof* in 1964—one that involved painting, dyeing, texturing, and "underglazing" fabrics to create realism that was still vivid onstage. To make a pair of brown nineteenth-century peasant pants for the musical, she used rust fabric that was dyed brown. When the costume was "aged" and the brown color was rubbed away, bits of rust became visible. The juxtaposition of color was barely noticeable to the audience but nevertheless created a vibrancy under the lights that plain "brown" pants would never have achieved.

For *Sunday in the Park with George*, Zipprodt and her co-designer, Ann Hould-Ward, found that the same method was an ideal way to re-create the effect of pointillism, an artistic technique that created color out of the juxtaposition of light with other colors on a canvas. In addition, by using it for a limited number of costumes in the show, Zipprodt and Hould-Ward were able to achieve a contrast between the character of George Seurat—who is "real"—and the characters in the musical who have literally stepped off his canvas.

Awards: Zipprodt has won three Tony Awards for Best Costume Design for *Fiddler on the Roof* (1964), *Cabaret* (1966), and *Sunday in the Park with George* (1984; shared with Ann Hould-Ward). In addition, she has won Drama Desk Awards for *Zorba* (1968), *1776* (1969), *Pippin* (1972), and *King of Hearts* (1978); an Emmy Award in 1969 for the Anne Bancroft Special; and three Joseph P. Maharam Awards for *1776*, *Alice in Wonderland*, and *Don Juan* (1982), and *Sunday in the Park with George* (shared with Ann Hould-Ward).

Further Reading: "Designing Costumes for Broadway and Hollywood." *Theater Crafts* January/February 1973; "Mack and Mabel—Silent Era Re-created." *Theater Crafts* November/December 1974; Owen (see Bibliography); "Recreating Seurat—Sunday in the Park with George." *Theatre Design and Technology* Winter 1985.

Howard Gutner

Appendix A
Chronological List of Designers

Designer	Country of Birth	Born	Died
Vitruvius, (Marcus Vitruvius Pollio)	Italy	84 B.C.	14 B.C.
Alberti, Leon Battista	Italy	1404	1472
Serlio, Sebastiano	Italy	1475	1554
Peruzzi, Baldassare	Italy	1481	1537
Palladio, Andrea	Italy	1518	1580
Sommi, Leone Di Ebreo	Italy	1525	1592
Buontalenti, Bernardo	Italy	1536	1608
Aleotti, Giovanni Battista	Italy	1546	1636
Ingegneri, Angelo	Italy	c.1550	c.1613
Scamozzi, Vincenzo	Italy	1552	1616
Jones, Inigo	England	1573	1652
Sabbatini, Nicola	Italy	1574	1654
Francini, Tomaso	Italy	1576	1648
Parigi, Giulio	Italy	1580	1635
Vigarani, Gaspare	Italy	1586	1663
Furttenbach, Josef	Germany	1591	1667
Campen, Jacob Van	Holland	c.1595	1657
Bernini, Giovanni Lorenzo	Italy	1598	1680
Parigi, Alfonso	Italy	1600	1656
Mahelot, Laurent	France	?	?
Fuller, Isaac	England	1606	1672
Torelli, Giacomo	Italy	1608	1678
Webb, John	England	1611	1672

Bibiena Family	Italy	*1625 through 1787*	
Motta, Fabrizio Carini	Italy	1627	1699
Burnacini, Ludovico	Italy	1636	1707
Bérain, Jean	France	1637	1711
Mauro Family	Italy	*c.1650 through 1820*	
Quaglio Family	Italy	*1668 through 1942*	
Martin, Jean-Baptiste	France	1659	1735
Vanbrugh, Sir John	England	1664	1726
Juvara, Filippo	Italy	1676	1736
Fabris, Jacopo	Italy	1689	1761
Servandoni, Giovanni Nicolo	Italy	1695	1766
Boucher, François	France	1703	1770
Galliari Family	Italy	*1707 through 1823*	
DeLoutherbourg, Philip	Germany	1740	1812
Fossati, Domenico	Italy	1743	1784
Chiaruttini, Francesco	Italy	1748	1796
Gonzaga, Pietro Gottardo	Italy	1751	1831
Capon, William	England	1757	1827
Sacchetti, Lorenzo	Italy	1759	1829
Grieve Family	England	*1770 through 1882*	
Beuther, Friedrich Christian	Germany	1777	1856
Sanquirico, Alessandro	Italy	1777	1849
Ciceri, Pierre-Luc-Charles	France	1782	1868
Beazley, Samuel	England	1786	1851
Stanfield, William Clarkson	England	1793	1867
Planché, James Robinson	England	1795	1880
Roller, Andreas Leonhard	Germany	1805	1891
Telbin, William	England	1813	1873
Beverley, William Roxby	England	1814	1889
Godwin, Edward William	England	1833	1886
Craven, Henry Hawes	England	1837	1910
Armbruster, Mathias	Germany	1839	1920
Poelzig, Hans	Germany	1839	1936
Lautenschläger, Karl	Germany	1843	1906
Clare, Joseph	England	1846	1917
Belasco, David	United States	1853	1931
Moses, Thomas	England	1856	1931
Korovine, Konstantin	Russia	1861	1939

Appia, Adolphe	Switzerland	1862	1928
Golovine, Aleksandr	Russia	1863	1930
Bakst, Léon	Russia	1866	1924
Bragdon, Claude	United States	1866	1946
Ricketts, Charles	Switzerland	1866	1931
Matisse, Henri	France	1869	1954
Benois, Alexandre	Russia	1870	1960
Stettheimer, Florine	United States	1871	1944
Craig, Edward Gordon	England	1872	1966
Urban, Joseph	Austria	1872	1933
Bauchant, André	France	1873	1958
Dobuzhinsky, Mstislav	Russia	1875	1957
Linnebach, Adolf	Germany	1876	1963
Stern, Ernst	Romania	1876	1954
Anisfeld, Boris	United States	1879	1973
Strnad, Oskar	Austria	1879	1935
Derain, André	France	1880	1954
Larionov, Michel	Bessarabia	1881	1964
Bernstein, Aline	United States	1881	1955
Picasso, Pablo	Spain	1881	1973
Exter, Aleksandra	Russia	1882	1949
Komisarjevsky, Theodore	Italy	1882	1954
Yakulov, Georgii Bogdanovich	Russia	1882	1928
Wilkinson, Norman	England	1882	1934
Soudekine, Serge	Russia	1882	1946
Gropius, Walter	Germany	1883	1969
Vesnin, Aleksandr	Russia	1883	1959
Hume, Sam	United States	1885	1962
Sheringham, George	England	1885	1937
Laurencin, Marie	France	1886	1956
Jones, Robert Edmond	United States	1887	1954
Chagall, Marc	Russia	1887	1985
Schiller, Leon	Poland	1887	1954
Rosse, Herman	Denmark	1887	1965
Pronaszko, Andrzej	Poland	1888	1961
Schlemmer, Oskar	Germany	1888	1943
Simonson, Lee	United States	1888	1967
Thompson, Woodman	United States	c.1889	1955

Shelving, Paul	England	1889	1968
Popova, Liubov Sergeevna	Russia	1889	1924
Fraser, Claude Lovat	England	1890	1921
Erté, (Romain de Tirtoff)	Russia	1892	1990
Peters, Charles Rollo, III	France	1892	1967
Bel Geddes, Norman	United States	1893	1958
Hammond, Aubrey	England	1893	1940
Fedorovich, Sophie	Russia	1893	1953
Rabinovitch, Isaac	Russia	1894	?
Davenport, Millia	United States	1895	1990
Müller, Traugott	Germany	1895	1944
Gray, Terence	England	1895	?
Kiesler, Frederick	Austria	1896	1965
Neher, Caspar	Germany	1897	1962
Irving, Laurence Henry Forester	England	1897	1983
Throckmorton, Cleon	United States	1897	1965
Tchelitchew, Pavel	Russia	1898	1957
Gorelik, Mordecai	Russia	1899	1990
Berman, Eugene	Russia	1899	1972
Dmitriev, Vladimir Vladimerovich	Russia	1900	1948
Aronson, Boris	Russia	1900	1980
Appen, Karl von	East Germany	1900	—
Cook, Ansel	United States	?	?
Lissim, Simon	Russia	1900	1981
Pons, Helene	Russia	?	1990
Motley	England		
Audrey Sophia Harris		1901	1966
Margaret F. Harris		1904	—
Elizabeth Montgomery		1904	—
Mielziner, Jo	France	1901	1976
Oenslager, Donald	United States	1902	1975
Bérard, Christian-Jacques	France	1902	1949
Williams, Piotr	Russia	1902	1947
Gischia, Léon	France	1903	—
Adrian, Gilbert	United States	1903	1959
Kook, Edward	United States	1903	1990
Czettel, Ladislas	Hungary	1904	1949
Coutaud, Lucien	France	1904	—

Dalí, Salvador	Spain	1904	1989
Burian, E. F.	Czechoslovakia	1904	1955
Otto, Teo	Germany	1904	1968
Beaton, Sir Cecil Walter Hardy	England	1904	1980
Noguchi, Isamu	United States	1904	—
Messel, Oliver	England	1904	1978
Troester, Frantisek	Czechoslovakia	1904	1968
Burra, Edward	England	1905	1976
Visconti, Luchino	Italy	1906	1976
Carzou, Jean	France	1907	—
Wahkevitch, Georges	Russia	1907	—
Ballard, Lucinda	United States	1908	—
Jenkins, George	United States	1909	—
Hurry, Leslie	England	1909	1978
Feder, Abraham	United States	1909	—
Elson, Charles	United States	1909	—
Gérard, Rolf	Germany	1910	—
Ffolkes, David	England	1912	—
Bay, Howard	United States	1912	1986
Bonnat, Yves	France	1912	—
Izenour, George	United States	1912	—
Kerz, Leo	Germany	1912	1976
Nikolais, Alwin	United States	1912	—
Rosenthal, Jean	United States	1912	1969
Sharaff, Irene	United States	1912	—
Pène du Bois, Raoul	United States	1913	1985
Clavé, Antoni	Spain	1913	—
Delfau, André	France	1914	—
Moiseiwitsch, Tanya	England	1914	—
White, Miles	United States	1914	—
Clark, Peggy	United States	1915	—
Kantor, Tadeusz	Poland	1915	—
Colt, Alvin	United States	1916	—
Edwards, Ben	United States	1916	—
Herbert, Jocelyn	England	1917	—
Wagner, Wieland	West Germany	1917	1966
Duquette, Tony	United States	1918	—
Smith, Oliver	United States	1918	—

Sainthill, Loudon	Australia	1919	1969
Eckart, William and Jean	United States	1920, 1921	—
Nivinski, Ignati	Russia	?	?
Ter-Arutunian, Rouben	Russia	1920	—
Svoboda, Josef	Czechoslovakia	1920	—
Ayrton, Michael	England	1921	1975
O'Hearn, Robert	United States	1921	—
Daydé, Bernard	France	1921	1986
Luzzati, Emanuele	Italy	1921	—
Wittop, Freddy (Fred Wittop Koning)	Holland	1921	—
Acquart, André	France	1922	—
Szajna, Josef	Poland	1922	—
Ciulei, Liviu	Romania	1923	—
Damiani, Luciano	Italy	1923	—
Polidori, Gianni	Italy	1923	—
Zefferelli, Franco	Italy	1923	—
Elder, Eldon	United States	1924	—
Creuz, Serge	Belgium	1924	—
Koltai, Ralph	Germany	1924	—
Allio, René	France	1924	—
Heinrich, Rudolf	Germany	1925	1975
Bury, John	England	1925	—
Musser, Tharon	United States	1925	—
Georgiadis, Nicholas	Greece	1925	—
Zipprodt, Patricia	United States	1925	—
Pitkin, William	United States	1925	—
Larkin, Peter	United States	1926	—
Montresor, Beni	Italy	1926	—
Farrah, Abdelkader	Algeria	1926	—
Randolph, Robert	United States	1926	—
Schneider-Siemssen, Gunther	West Germany	1926	—
Toms, Carl	England	1927	—
Klotz, Florence	United States	1928	—
Hay, Richard	United States	1929	—
Armstrong, Will Steven	United States	1930	1969
Lee, Ming Cho	China	1930	—
Minks, Wilfried	Czechoslovakia	1930	—
Heeley, Desmond	England	1931	—

Mitchell, David	United States	1932	—
Jacobs, Sally	England	1932	—
Aldredge, Theoni	Greece	1932	—
Roth, Ann	United States	1932	—
Ponnelle, Jean-Pierre	France	1932	—
Pilbrow, Richard	England	1933	—
Jensen, John	United States	1933	—
Ronconi, Luca	Italy	1933	—
Wagner, Robin	United States	1933	—
Greenwood, Jane	England	1934	—
Arrocha, Eduardo	Cuba	1934	—
Borovsky, David	Russia	1934	—
Freyer, Achim	West Germany	1934	—
Walton, Tony	England	1934	—
Sagert, Horst	West Germany	1934	—
Firth, Tazeena	England	1935	—
Sequi, Sandro	Italy	1935	—
Rojo, Jerry	United States	1935	—
Kim, Willa	United States	1937	—
Fisher, Jules	United States	1937	—
Foreman, Richard	United States	1937	—
Kochergin, Edward	Russia	1937	—
Hockney, David	England	1937	—
Conklin, John	United States	1937	—
Tipton, Jennifer	United States	1937	—
Tilton, James	United States	1937	—
Rose, Jürgen	West Germany	1937	—
Dahlstrom, Robert	United States	1938	—
Nelson, Richard	United States	1938	—
Davidson, Jeannie	United States	1938	—
Eigsti, Karl	United States	1938	—
Howard, Pamela	England	1939	—
Lee, Eugene	United States	1939	—
Hersey, David	United States	1939	—
Baylis, Nadine	England	1940	—
Wurtzel, Stuart	United States	1940	—
Wilson, Robert	United States	1941	—
Pyle, Russel	United States	1941	—

Straiges, Tony	United States	1942	—
Rennagel, Marilyn	United States	1943	—
Robbins, Carrie	United States	1943	—
Kokkos, Yannis	Greece	1944	—
Loquasto, Santo	United States	1944	—
Napier, John	England	1944	—
Crow, Laura	United States	1945	—
Fingerhut, Arden	United States	1945	—
Kellogg, Marjorie	United States	1946	—
Funicello, Ralph	United States	1947	—
Beatty, John Lee	United States	1948	—
Mayrhauser, Jennifer von	United States	1948	—
Björnson, Maria	England	1949	—
Miller, Craig	United States	1950	—
Hould-Ward, Ann	United States	1951	—
Landesman, Heidi	United States	1951	—
Bloodgood, William	United States	1951	—
Dorsey, Kent	United States	1952	—
Militello, Anne E.	United States	1957	—
Asakura, Setsue	Japan	?*	—
Herrman, Karl-Ernst	Germany	?*	—

*Although their dates of birth are unknown, Asakura's work began in the 1960s and Herrman's work began in the 1970s.

Appendix B
Designers Listed by Country of Birth

Designer	Born	Died
Algeria:		
Farrah, Abdelkader	1926	—
Australia:		
Sainthill, Loudon	1919	1969
Austria:		
Urban, Joseph	1872	1933
Strnad, Oskar	1879	1935
Kiesler, Frederick	1896	1965
Belgium:		
Creuz, Serge	1924	—
Bessarabia:		
Larionov, Michel	1881	1964
China:		
Lee, Ming Cho	1930	—
Cuba:		
Arrocha, Eduardo	1934	—
Czechoslovakia:		
Burian, E. F.	1904	1955
Troester, Frantisek	1904	1968
Svoboda, Josef	1920	—
Minks, Wilfried	1930	—

Denmark:

Rosse, Herman	1887	1965

England:

Jones, Inigo	1573	1652
Fuller, Isaac	1606	1672
Webb, John	1611	1672
Vanbrugh, Sir John	1664	1726
Capon, William	1757	1827
Grieve Family	*1770 through 1882*	
Beazley, Samuel	1786	1851
Stanfield, William Clarkson	1793	1867
Planché, James Robinson	1795	1880
Telbin, William	1813	1873
Beverley, William Roxby	1814	1889
Godwin, Edward William	1833	1886
Craven, Henry Hawes	1837	1910
Clare, Joseph	1846	1917
Moses, Thomas	1856	1931
Craig, Edward Gordon	1872	1966
Wilkinson, Norman	1882	1934
Sheringham, George	1885	1937
Shelving, Paul	1889	1968
Fraser, Claude Lovat	1890	1921
Hammond, Aubrey	1893	1940
Gray, Terence	1895	?
Irving, Laurence Henry Forester	1897	1983
Motley	1901	1966
Beaton, Sir Cecil Walter Hardy	1904	1980
Messel, Oliver	1904	1978
Burra, Edward	1905	1976
Hurry, Leslie	1909	1978
Ffolkes, David	1912	—
Moiseiwitsch, Tanya	1914	—
Herbert, Jocelyn	1917	—
Ayrton, Michael	1921	1975
Bury, John	1925	—
Toms, Carl	1927	—

Heeley, Desmond	1931	—
Jacobs, Sally	1932	—
Pilbrow, Richard	1933	—
Walton, Tony	1934	—
Greenwood, Jane	1934	—
Firth, Tazeena	1935	—
Hockney, David	1937	—
Howard, Pamela	1939	—
Baylis, Nadine	1940	—
Napier, John	1944	—
Björnson, Maria	1949	—

France:

Mahelot, Laurent	?	?
Bérain, Jean	1637	1711
Martin, Jean-Baptiste	1659	1735
Boucher, François	1703	1770
Ciceri, Pierre-Luc-Charles	1782	1868
Matisse, Henri	1869	1954
Bauchant, André	1873	1958
Derain, André	1880	1954
Laurencin, Marie	1886	1956
Peters, Charles Rollo, III	1892	1967
Mielziner, Jo	1901	1976
Bérard, Christian	1902	1949
Gischia, Léon	1903	—
Coutaud, Lucien	1904	—
Carzou, Jean	1907	—
Bonnat, Yves	1912	—
Delfau, André	1914	—
Daydé, Bernard	1921	1986
Acquart, André	1922	—
Allio, René	1924	—
Ponnelle, Jean-Pierre	1932	—

Germany:

Furttenbach, Josef	1591	1667
DeLoutherbourg, Philip	1740	1812
Beuther, Friedrich Christian	1777	1856

Roller, Andreas Leonhard	1805	1891
Poelzig, Hans	1839	1936
Armbruster, Mathias	1839	1920
Lautenschläger, Karl	1843	1906
Linnebach, Adolf	1876	1963
Gropius, Walter	1883	1969
Schlemmer, Oskar	1888	1943
Müller, Traugott	1895	1944
Neher, Caspar	1897	1962
Appen, Karl von	1900	—
Otto, Teo	1904	1968
Gérard, Rolf	1910	—
Kerz, Leo	1912	1976
Wagner, Wieland	1917	1966
Koltai, Ralph	1924	—
Heinrich, Rudolf	1925	1975
Schneider-Siemssen, Gunther	1926	—
Aldredge, Theoni	1932	—
Freyer, Achim	1934	—
Sagert, Horst	1934	—
Rose, Jürgen	1937	—
Herrman, Karl-Ernst	?	—
Greece:		
Georgiadis, Nicholas	1925	—
Kokkos, Yannis	1944	—
Holland:		
Campen, Jacob Van	c.1595	1657
Wittop, Freddy (Fred Wittop Koning)	1921	—
Hungary:		
Czettel, Ladislas	1904	1949
Italy:		
Vitruvius, (Marcus Vitruvius Pollio)	84 B.C.	14 B.C.
Alberti, Leon Battista	1404	1472
Serlio, Sebastiano	1475	1554
Peruzzi, Baldassare	1481	1537
Palladio, Andrea	1518	1580
Sommi, Leone Di Ebreo	1525	1592

Buontalenti, Bernardo	1536	1608
Aleotti, Gian Battista	1546	1636
Ingegneri, Angelo	c.1550	c.1613
Scamozzi, Vincenzo	1552	1616
Sabbatini, Nicola	1574	1654
Francini, Tomaso	1576	1648
Parigi, Giulio	1580	1635
Vigarani, Gaspare	1586	1663
Bernini, Giovanni Lorenzo	1598	1680
Parigi, Alfonso	?	1656
Torelli, Giacomo	1608	1678
Bibiena Family	*1625 through 1787*	
Motta, Fabrizio Carini	1627	1699
Burnacini, Ludovico	1636	1707
Mauro Family	*c.1650 through 1820*	
Quaglio Family	*1668 through 1942*	
Juvara, Filippo	1676	1736
Fabris, Jacopo	1689	1761
Servandoni, Giovanni Nicolo	1695	1766
Galliari Family	*1707 through 1823*	
Fossati, Domenico	1743	1784
Chiaruttini, Francesco	1748	1796
Gonzaga, Pietro Gottardo	1751	1831
Sacchetti, Lorenzo	1759	1829
Sanquirico, Alessandro	1777	1849
Komisarjevsky, Theodore	1882	1954
Visconti, Luchino	1906	1976
Luzzati, Emanuele	1921	—
Damiani, Luciano	1923	—
Zefferelli, Franco	1923	—
Polidori, Gianni	1923	—
Montresor, Beni	1926	—
Ronconi, Luca	1933	—
Sequi, Sandro	1935	—

Japan:

Asakura, Setsu	?	—

Poland:

Schiller, Leon	1887	1954
Pronaszko, Andrzej	1888	1961
Kantor, Tadeusz	1915	—
Szajna, Josef	1922	—

Romania:

Stern, Ernst	1876	1954
Ciulei, Liviu	1923	—

Russia:

Korovine, Konstantin	1861	1939
Golovine, Aleksandr	1863	1930
Bakst, Léon	1866	1924
Benois, Alexandre	1870	1960
Dobuzhinsky, Mstislav	1875	1957
Exter, Aleksandra	1882	1949
Yakulov, Georgii Bogdanovich	1882	1928
Soudekine, Serge	1882	1946
Vesnin, Aleksandr	1883	1959
Chagall, Marc	1887	1985
Popova, Liubov Sergeevna	1889	1924
Erté, (Romain de Tirtoff)	1892	1990
Fedorovich, Sophie	1893	1953
Rabinovitch, Isaac	1894	?
Tchelitchew, Pavel	1898	1957
Berman, Eugene	1899	1972
Gorelik, Mordecai	1899	1990
Dmitriev, Vladimir Vladimerovich	1900	1948
Aronson, Boris	1900	1980
Lissim, Simon	1900	1981
Pons, Helene	?	1990
Williams, Piotr	1902	1947
Wahkevitch, Georges	1907	?
Nivinski, Ignati	?	?
Ter-Arutunian, Rouben	1920	—
Borovsky, David	1934	—
Kochergin, Edward	1937	—

Spain:

Picasso, Pablo	1881	1973

Dalí, Salvador	1904	1989
Clavé, Antoni	1913	—

Switzerland:

Appia, Adolphe	1862	1928
Ricketts, Charles	1866	1931

United States:

Belasco, David	1853	1931
Bragdon, Claude	1866	1946
Stettheimer, Florine	1871	1944
Anisfeld, Boris	1879	1973
Bernstein, Aline	1881	1955
Hume, Sam	1885	1962
Jones, Robert Edmond	1887	1954
Simonson, Lee	1888	1967
Thompson, Woodman	c.1889	1955
Bel Geddes, Norman	1893	1958
Davenport, Millia	1895	1990
Throckmorton, Cleon	1897	1965
Cook, Ansel	?	?
Oenslager, Donald	1902	1975
Adrian, Gilbert	1903	1959
Kook, Edward	1903	1990
Noguchi, Isamu	1904	—
Ballard, Lucinda	1908	—
Elson, Charles	1909	—
Jenkins, George	1909	—
Feder, Abraham	1909	—
Bay, Howard	1912	1986
Izenour, George	1912	—
Nikolais, Alwin	1912	—
Sharaff, Irene	1912	—
Rosenthal, Jean	1912	1969
Pène du Bois, Raoul	1913	1985
White, Miles	1914	—
Clark, Peggy	1915	—
Colt, Alvin	1916	—
Edwards, Ben	1916	—

Duquette, Tony	1918	—
Smith, Oliver	1918	—
Eckart, William and Jean	1920, 1921	—
O'Hearn, Robert	1921	—
Elder, Eldon	1924	—
Musser, Tharon	1925	—
Zipprodt, Patricia	1925	—
Pitkin, William	1925	—
Larkin, Peter	1926	—
Randolph, Robert	1926	—
Klotz, Florence	1928	—
Hay, Richard	1929	—
Armstrong, Will Steven	1930	1969
Mitchell, David	1932	—
Roth, Ann	1932	—
Jensen, John	1933	—
Wagner, Robin	1933	—
Rojo, Jerry	1935	—
Kim, Willa	1937	—
Foreman, Richard	1937	—
Fisher, Jules	1937	—
Conklin, John	1937	—
Tilton, James	1937	—
Tipton, Jennifer	1937	—
Eigsti, Karl	1938	—
Dahlstrom, Robert	1938	—
Davidson, Jeannie	1938	—
Nelson, Richard	1938	—
Lee, Eugene	1939	—
Hersey, David	1939	—
Wurtzel, Stuart	1940	—
Pyle, Russel	1941	—
Wilson, Robert	1941	—
Straiges, Tony	1942	—
Robbins, Carrie	1943	—
Rennagel, Marilyn	1943	—
Loquasto, Santo	1944	—
Fingerhut, Arden	1945	—

Crow, Laura	1945	—
Kellogg, Marjorie	1946	—
Funicello, Ralph	1947	—
Mayrhauser, Jennifer von	1948	—
Beatty, John Lee	1948	—
Miller, Craig	1950	—
Bloodgood, William	1951	—
Landesman, Heidi	1951	—
Hould-Ward, Ann	1951	—
Dorsey, Kent	1952	—
Militello, Anne E.	1957	—

Appendix C
Periodicals and Theatre Collections

American Theatre Magazine. New York: Theatre Communications Group.

This magazine contains information on contemporary theatrical artists, productions, and theatres. It usually has excellent documentation and photographs of recent American productions that have occurred at major theatrical institutions. There are also occasional articles on scenic and costume designers and design theory.

The Billy Rose Theatre Collection of the Performing Arts Research Center, the New York Public Library, Lincoln Center, New York City.

There are files of photographs, newspaper clippings, writings and correspondence, and actual production materials such as promptbooks and scenic and costume renderings at this collection. Most materials focus on American theatrical figures from the nineteenth and twentieth centuries, including many designers who were popular in the commercial or Broadway theatre.

Harvard Theatre Collection at Harvard University, Cambridge, Massachusetts.

This collection includes clippings and photographic files of theatrical figures and theatres. The researcher can find information on designers who have national and international stature. In fact, there are more than 15,000 costume and scenic designs. Original renderings, plan drawings, and actual three-dimensional scenic models can be found in this slightly restricted archive.

The Shubert Archive, the Lyceum Theatre, 149 West 45th Street, New York City.

There is a significant amount of early Broadway and commercial production data in this collection, comprised mostly of materials from shows produced by the Shubert Organization. Scenic and costume renderings, scenic drawings, architectural plans, contracts, and correspondence are only some of the original materials in this archive.

Theatre and Music Collection, the Museum of the City of New York, 103 Street and Fifth Avenue, New York City.

This museum contains many scenic and costume renderings, models, and drawings of New York City productions.

Theatre Crafts Magazine. New York: Theatre Crafts Associates, 1969–

Although the name implies a focus on the crafts of production, there are many interviews with designers, descriptions of design and technology, and theoretical writings included in this fine subscription magazine. All forms of theatre such as plays, operas, and dance, as well as film are covered.

Theatre Design & Technology. New York: The United States Institute for Theatre Technology, 1964–   .

Commonly referred to as *TD & T*, this journal of the USITT focuses on both historical and current design and technology. There is much information on scenography as well as theatre buildings. Articles range from "how-to" to scholarly papers. There is information on international design, design books, and on the group itself in this journal, which is distributed to its members and libraries.

Yale School of Drama Library and the Sterling Memorial Library, Yale University, New Haven, Connecticut.

This library contains data on major theatrical productions and designers. There are plenty of production photographs, newspaper clippings, costume and set designs, and periodicals in this collection.

Selected
Bibliography

Altman, George, Ralph Freud, Kenneth Macgowan, and William Melnitz. *Theatre Pictorial: A History of World Theatre as Recorded in Drawings, Paintings, Engravings, and Photographs*. Berkeley: University of California Press, 1953.
   This visually focused work is a good source for original graphics and photographs of set, costume, and lighting designs.

Appia, Adolphe. *The Work of Living Art & Man Is the Measure of All Things*. Trans. H. D. Albright and Barnard Hewitt. Miami: University of Miami Press, 1960.

———. *Music and the Art of the Theatre*. Trans. Robert W. Corrigan and Mary Dirks. Miami: University of Miami Press, 1962.
   Both of the above works contain Appia's theoretical writings and visionary staging suggestions for theatrical productions. These works focused on staging Wagner's operas but were influential in the development of modern scenic design practice.

Aronson, Arnold. *American Set Design*. (Foreword by Harold Prince.) New York: Theatre Communications Group, 1985.
   Contains historical analyses, photographs, and drawings of recent designers: John Lee Beatty, John Conklin, Karl Eigsti, Ralph Funicello, Marjorie Bradley Kellogg, Eugene Lee, Ming Cho Lee, Santo Loquasto, David Mitchell, and Robin Wagner.

Bablet, Denis. *The Revolutions of Stage Design in the Twentieth Century*. Paris: Leon Amiel, 1977.
   Translating from the French edition, Bablet traces the major trends in current world design. The work of many international designers is represented with a large selection of plates. Bablet's text illuminates the major and minor trends in design and production during this century.

Beaumont, Cyril. *Design for the Ballet: Past and Present*. London: Studio Ltd., 1957.
   This is one of the first complete documentations of ballet designers in history. Combining his previous works, *Five Centuries of Ballet and Design* and *Design for Ballet*,

Beaumont covers the Renaissance through the early part of the twentieth century. There are many plates showing the work of significant designers.

Brockett, Oscar, and Robert R. Findlay. *A Century of Innovation: A History of European and American Theatre and Drama Since 1870.* Englewood Cliffs, NJ: Prentice-Hall, 1973.

Brockett and Findlay describe the major trends in theatre of the period and document the significant productions of the past one hundred years. There are plenty of descriptions and photographs and drawings of the development of the scenography and technology of the period.

Buckle, Richard. *Modern Ballet Design.* New York: Macmillan, 1955.

This older work attempts to describe the theories of modern ballet scenography through many photographs of designs and copious descriptions of works. It is primarily focused on the first half of the century.

Burdick, Elizabeth B., Peggy C. Hansen, and Brenda Zanger, eds. *Contemporary Stage Design, U.S.A.* Middletown, CT: Wesleyan University Press, 1974.

Contains essays on design by famous artists Donald Oenslager, Howard Bay, Jerry Rojo, Richard Jenkins, Patricia Zipprodt, Boris Aronson, Ming Cho Lee, Rouben Ter-Arutunian, Charles Elson, and Eldon Elder. It contains many plates of designs by these luminaries, as well as information on some other, lesser-known artists.

Burian, Jarka. *The Scenography of Josef Svoboda.* Middletown, CT: Wesleyan University Press, 1974.

Regarded by many as one of the most innovative designers of our time, Svoboda redefines the meaning of scenic design. His term *scenography* encompasses a broader range of responsibilities and incorporates the newer technologies of the twentieth century. This book has plenty of visual material documenting Svoboda's use of technology in designing the classics.

Cheney, Sheldon. *Stage Decoration.* New York: Benjamin Blom, 1966.

Cheney traces the evolution, the general patterns, and the developments of theatre building and scenic design from antiquity.

Clarke, Mary, and Clement Crisp. *Design for Ballet.* New York: Hawthorn Books, 1978.

A more updated work on ballet design that includes plenty of photographs and descriptions of American and Continental design.

Craig, Edward Gordon. *The Art of the Theatre.* Edinburgh: T. N. Foulis, 1905.

This and the following works include this iconoclast's early theatrical theories and verbal assaults on the prevailing scenic practices of the day. Craig's works were influential and, like Appia's writings, laid the foundation for modern scenic practice. Some libraries have copies of *The Mask*, a journal that he wrote and edited intermittently.

———. *On the Art of the Theatre.* London: Heinemann, 1911. Reprint of *The Art of the Theatre.*

———. *Towards a New Theatre.* London: J. M. Dent and Sons, 1913.

Craig's theories and forty designs for the stage. Although some of his designs would be impossible, given the proportions of them, Craig's skill as an artist contributed to the very dynamic, atmospheric, yet simply composed renderings included in this volume.

Croyden, Margaret. *Lunatics, Lovers and Poets: The Contemporary Experimental Theatre.* New York: Dell, 1974.

Rare descriptions of productions and designs of the 1960s and 1970s experimental theatre.

Fuerst, Walter Rene and Samuel J. Hume. *Twentieth-Century Stage Decoration*, Vols. 1 and 2. (Introduction by Adolphe Appia). New York: Benjamin Blom, 1967.

A very complete history and documentation of design in the first half of the twentieth century throughout the world. There are plenty of plates of design, which make this double-volume work unequaled in its area.

Goodwin, John, ed. *British Theatre Design: The Modern Age*. New York: St. Martin's Press, 1990.

This recent book, with a foreword by Peter Hall, documents some of the most recent and exciting work in England. There are ample descriptions and plenty of color plates in this larger-sized work.

Gropius, Walter, ed. and intro. *The Theatre of the Bauhaus*. Trans. Arthur S. Wensinger. Middletown, CT: Wesleyan University Press, 1961.

This is considered by many the most important work on Bauhaus theories of design. Included are visionary essays, drawings, and photographs by Oskar Schlemmer, Laszlo Moholy-Nagy, and Farkas Molnar concerning art, performance, design, and theatre buildings.

Hainaux, Rene. *Stage Design Throughout the World Since 1935*. New York: Theatre Arts Books, 1956.

This book is the first of a series that details the art of design throughout the world. Set up very much like a yearbook, this set of books includes examples of dynamic design in hundreds of black and white photographs.

Hainaux, Rene, and Yves-Bonnat, eds. *Stage Design Throughout the World Since 1935*. New York: Theatre Arts Books, 1965.

———. *Stage Design Throughout the World Since 1960*. New York: Theatre Arts Books, 1965.

Hewitt, Barnard, ed. *The Renaissance Stage: Documents of Serlio, Sabbatini, and Furttenbach*. Trans. Allardyce Nicoll, John H. McDowell, and George R. Kernodle. Coral Cables, FL: University of Miami Press, 1958.

Excellent descriptions and line drawings of scenic machines and techniques used in the Renaissance. There is much insight to the philosophies toward production of these theatre practitioners.

Jones, Robert Edmond. *The Dramatic Imagination*. New York: Duell, Sloan, and Pearce, 1941.

The seminal work of one of America's most innovative designers. In this collection of lectures and essays, Jones examines scene design not just as technique, but as an intrinsic and fundamental element to drama.

Komisarjevsky, Theodore, and Lee Simonson. *Settings and Costumes of the Modern Stage*. London: The Studio, Limited, 1933.

With some color plates and plenty of black and white photographs, the two designer-authors show examples of modern scenic practice in production and in rendering.

Lacy, Robin Thurlow. *A Biographical Dictionary of Scenographers: 500 B.C. to 1900 A.D.* Westport, CT: Greenwood Press, 1990.

Covering the period from 500 B.C. to 1900 A.D., this dictionary provides information on historical figures involved with scene design and scene painting. There is an ample bibliography of 435 sources that detail the works of the scenic artists as well as a geographical/chronological appendix.

Larson, Orville K., ed. and intro. *Scene Design for Stage and Screen: Readings on the Aesthetics and Methodology of Scene Design for Drama, Opera, Musical Comedy, Ballet, Motion Pictures, Television, and Arena Theatre.* Westport, CT: Greenwood Press, 1976.
Reprinted from the 1961 edition of Michigan University Press. Included in this work are essays on various types of stage design by such famous artists as Oliver Smith and Howard Bay.

———. *Scene Design in the American Theatre from 1915 to 1960.* Fayetteville: University of Arkansas Press, 1989.
Larson traces, in a most complete manner, the development of American design through all of its significant designers. There are approximately fifty designers' chronologies included in this book. This recent work also includes plenty of color photographs of renderings and black and white production photographs.

Larson, Orville K., and C. Thomas Ault, trans. *The Theatrical Writings of Fabrizio Carini Motta: Translations of "Trattato sopra la struttura de'Theatri e scene," 1676 and "Costruzione de teatri e machine teatrali," 1688.* (Introduction by Larson.), by Fabrizio Motta. Carbondale: Southern Illinois University Press, 1987.
Through the writings of Motta, his drawings, and his etchings of the period, this work provides insight into actual seventeenth-century scenic design, technology, and theatre construction.

Lawrenson, T. E. *The French Stage in the XVIIth Century: A Study in the Italian Order.* Manchester, England: Manchester University Press, 1957.
A thorough book tracing the Italianate influences on French scene design during the seventeenth century.

Leeper, Janet. *Edward Gordon Craig: Designs for the Theatre.* Harmondsworth: Penguin Books, 1948.
The author captures the scope of this visionary's design and writing career.

Macgowan, Kenneth. *Continental Stagecraft.* (Foreword by Robert Edmond Jones.) New York: Harcourt Brace, 1922.
A very lucid work concerning the European theories of stage design that influenced an Art Theatre movement in the United States.

McNamara, Brooks, Jerry Rojo, and Richard Schechner. *Theatres, Spaces, Environments: 18 Projects.* New York: Drama Book Specialists, 1975.
This is an excellent work on both traditional and non-traditional performance spaces with descriptions of environmental theatre.

Marshall, Herbert. *The Pictorial History of the Russian Theatre.* (Intro. by Harold Clurman.) New York: Crown, 1977.
Using many rare illustrations, Marshall provides an account of the productions of the major theatres in Russia from the Middle Ages to the present. There are many photographs of great design for famous productions at the Moscow Art, the Kamerny, and Meyerhold's theatres.

Nagler, A. M., ed. *A Sourcebook in Theatrical History: Twenty-Five Centuries of Stage History in More Than 300 Basic Documents and Other Primary Material.* New York: Dover, 1952.

Including illustrations of many original documents, Nagler includes essays and firsthand descriptions of significant works by theatricians throughout the ages. Such essays as "Scenes, Machines, and Masks" by Greek writer Pollux and "The Wonders of Perspective Scenery" by Baldassare Castiglione make up a very interesting book of primary information.

Nicoll, Allardyce. *The Development of the Theatre.* New York: Harcourt, Brace, 1927.

There are plenty of photographs, engravings, renderings, and technical drawings included in this very complete work. Nicoll's descriptions of productions and scenic devices were culled from primary documents and heavily researched. While other books leave out many of the dimensions of theatres and settings, the author of this book attempts to be most complete in this area.

Oenslager, Donald. *Scenery Then and Now.* New York: W. W. Norton, 1936.

This work represents Oenslager's view of the historical development of scenic and theatre building methods. It is very informative, with many illustrations.

———. *Stage Design: Four Centuries of Scenic Invention.* New York: Viking Press, 1975.

After a brief introduction and background notes, Oenslager moves through the Renaissance, the baroque and rococo, the neoclassic and romantic, and the modern periods. With illustrations of renderings, some from his collection, the author includes basic biographies of almost one hundred designers from these periods.

Owen, Bobbi. *Costume Design on Broadway: Designers and Their Credits.* Westport, CT: Greenwood Press, 1987.

This book profiles more than 1,000 costume designers and illustrations of their work. The biographies include backgrounds and credits of each designer. There is an introduction to the history of costume design as well as appendixes of a chronological listing of plays and theatrical awards. Owen's forthcoming works, *Lighting Design on Broadway: Designers and Their Credits, 1915–1990,* and *Scenic Design on Broadway: Designers and Their Credits, 1915–1990,* will be published in October 1991 and will retain the same format.

Payne, Darwin Reid. *The Scenographic Imagination.* Carbondale: Southern Illinois University Press, 1981.

Payne's book is primarily a text for the design student. As such, it basically describes the process of design. The broader approach that this American text takes seems influenced by Svoboda's theories, as well as by a number of others.

Pecktal, Lynn. *Designing and Painting for the Theatre.* New York: Holt, Rinehart, and Winston, 1975.

Although Pecktal's book is primarily a "how-to" manual, it includes interviews with Jo Mielziner, Rouben Ter-Arutunian, Oliver Smith, Ben Edwards, Robert Randolph, Ming Cho Lee, Raoul Pène du Bois, Howard Bay, Donald Oenslager, and Robin Wagner.

Pendleton, Ralph, ed. *The Theatre of Robert Edmond Jones.* Middletown, CT: Wesleyan University Press, 1958.

This work chronicles the contributions of one of America's most significant designers through black and white illustrations of his renderings, as well as through essays by such luminaries as Donald Oenslager, Lee Simonson, Jo Mielziner, and Kenneth Macgowan. Pendleton's chronology of Jones's career is very complete, listing much historical information on the shows.

Rich, Frank, with Lisa Aronson. *The Theatre Art of Boris Aronson*. New York: Alfred Knopf, 1987.

This oversized book contains all of the information regarding the career of one of America's most prolific designers. Written and compiled by *New York Times* theatre critic Frank Rich and by Aronson's widow, who worked on the shows with her husband, this beautifully constructed book includes many color plates of Aronson's designs, which were ubiquitous on the American stage from the twenties through the eighties. Thus, it is a good document of the New York stage during this period.

Rosenfeld, Sybil. *A Short History of Scenic Design in Great Britain*. Totowa, NJ: Rowman and Littlefield, 1973.

Although it is short, it contains much information on the major designers throughout British history. Rosenfeld covers not only the London stage, but the provinces as well.

Russell, Douglas A. *Period Style for the Theatre*. Boston: Allyn and Bacon, 1987.

Russell's book is a standard text for design students and covers the major periods of theatrical design history. Through its descriptions of the philosophies and intellectual influences of the day, it focuses less on technology and more on the development of scenographic style through the ages.

Sellman, Merrill, and Hunton D. Lessley. *The Essentials of Stage Lighting*. Englewood Cliffs, NJ: Prentice-Hall, 1982.

This is a basic text on stage lighting.

Sheringham, George. *Design in the Theatre: Commentary by George Sheringham and James Laver, Together with Literary Contributions by E. Gordon Craig, Charles B. Cochran, and Nigel Playfair*. Ed. Geoffrey Holme. London: The Studio, Limited, 1927.

Focused primarily on the aesthetics of the early part of this century developed mostly by Appia and Craig, this treatise serves to document many productions. Most of them are British.

Simonson, Lee. *The Stage is Set*. New York: Theatre Arts Books, 1963; New York: Harcourt, Brace & Company, 1932.

A critical and philosophical perspective on the history of stage design. Simonson draws parallels between ancient practice and modern techniques, criticizes his contemporaries, and proposes new directions for the theatre.

Smith, Ronn. *American Set Design 2*. (Intro. by Ming Cho Lee.) New York: Theatre Communications Group, 1991.

Contains data on relatively recent designers Loy Arcenas, John Arnone, David Gropman, Robert Israel, Heidi Landesman, Hugh Landwehr, Adrianne Lobel, Charles McClennahan, Michael Merritt, Tony Straiges, George Tsypin, and Michael Yeargan.

Southern, Richard. *The Seven Ages of the Theatre*. Boston: Faber and Faber, 1979.

This is a history of the theatre with a broader scope in that it describes the design for more than theatrical plays. It also includes descriptions of the scenography and performance space for multicultural folk entertainments such as parades, festivals, and religious rituals.

University Art Museum. *The Twin City Scenic Collection: Popular Entertainment 1895–1929*. Minneapolis: University of Minnesota Press, 1987.

Excellent examples of European-inspired, American scenic backdrops and discussions of turn-of-the-century scenic studios are included in this work.

Volbach, Walther. *Adolphe Appia: Prophet of the Modern Theatre: A Profile*. Middletown, CT: Wesleyan University Press, 1968.

Volbach's book, with illustrations, is a thorough historical analysis of Appia's contributions to modern scene design.

Wickham, Glynne. *The Medieval Theatre*. New York: St. Martin's Press, 1974.

Thorough descriptions of medieval staging practices, as well as an in-depth understanding of the era, are included in Wickham's account of this period in theatre history.

Index

Page numbers set in boldface indicate the location of the main entry.

Abduction from the Seraglio, The, 20, 81, 133, 183, 231
Abduction of Figaro, The, 24
Abe Lincoln in Illinois, 50, 161
Abraham and Cochrane, 182
Absorbing Perdita, 106
Académie des Beaux-Arts, 60
Accent on Youth, 160
Accidental Death of an Anarchist, 77, 265
Achilles, 194
Achilles Has a Heel, 39
Acis and Galatea, 56–57
Acquart, André, **3**
Acrobats of God, 181
Act, The, 201
Adam and Creator, 106
Adam Had Two Sons, 183
Adam Solitaire, 239
Adaptation/Next, 224
Adding Machine, The, 106, 221
Adelmorn, the Outlaw, 43
Admirable Bashville, The, 107
Admirable Crichton, The, 202
Adrian, Gilbert, **3–4**, 71

Adriana Lecouvreur, 182
Adrienne Ambrossat, 231
Adventures of Huckleberry Finn, The, 63
Advise and Consent, 173, 238
Aelita, 85, 199
Affabulazione, 192
Affair, The, 79–80
Africanis Instructus, 95
After All, 153
After Magritte, 178
After the Fall, 24, 76, 162–163, 263
After the Rain, 174
After the Season, 23, 131, 242
Afternoon, 87
Afternoon Tea, 130
Agamemnon, 53, 153–154, 242
Agatha Sue, I Love You, 73
Age of Anxiety, 218, 223
Age of Innocence, The, 188
Agents, The, 43
Ages of Man, 74
Agnes of God, 146, 203
Agon, 101
Agrippo, 157
Ah, Wilderness!, 127, 152, 178, 242

Aida, 62, 101, 132, 167, 182, 193, 232, 245, 254, 263
Aimee, 145
Ain't Misbehavin', 23–25
Airs, 242
Akhnaten, 97
Akropolis, 235
Al Gran sole carico d'Amore, 115
Aladdin, 106
Albee Directs Albee, 76
Albert Herring, 81, 115
Alberti, Leon Battista, **4–5**
Albion's Triumph, 125
Alceste, 149
Alcestis, 55, 106, 181, 202, 258–259
Alchemist, The, 124, 168–169
Alcina, 263
Alcine, 30
Aldredge, Theoni V., **5–7**, 175
Aleko, 43
Aleotti, Giovanni Battista, xxii, xxiii, **7–8**, 244
Alexander the Great, 89
Alfie, 174
Alfred, 67–68
Alhambra and Tabarin Theater Revues, 83
Alice in Wonderland, 24–25, 48, 145–146, 217, 219, 224, 242, 265–267
Alice-Sit-By-the-Fire, 18
Alien Corn, 168, 240
Alison's House, 32, 107
All About Elsie, 72
All American, 162
All for Love, 106
All God's Chillun' Got Wings, 126, 130, 149, 195, 239–240, 265
All Good Americans, 105
All in Fun, 217
All in Good Time, 174
All in Love, 92
All in One, 79
All My Sons, 105, 125, 192
All Over, 41, 130, 178, 238
All Over Town, 225
All Summer Long, 162
All That Jazz, 255
All the King's Men, 92–93

All the Way Home, 54
All You Need Is One Good Break, 47, 132
All's Well That Ends Well, 5, 11, 91, 108, 148, 169, 207, 242
Allah Be Praised!, 123, 256
Allegro, 18, 161
Alligators, The, 5
Allio, René, **8**
Almoran and Hamlet, 67
Almost an Eagle, 77
Almost Perfect Person, An, 75, 108
Alone Together, 77, 109
Along Fifth Avenue, 47, 89, 223
Alphabetical Order, 130
Amadeus, 41
Amahl and the Night Visitors, 31, 147, 252
Amazing Adele, The, 47, 223
Amazing Grace, 79–80
Amelia Goes to the Ball, 183–184
Amen Corner, 77–78
America Kicks Up Its Heels, 153
America's Sweetheart, 183
American Buffalo, 93, 131–132, 153–154
American Clock, The, 77, 98
American Dream, 221
American in Paris, An, 218–219
American Jubilee, 17
American Landscape, 32
American Millionaire, An, 6
American Passion, 141
American Theatre, 243
American Tragedy, An, 230
American Way, The, 183, 217
Americana, 209
Amériques, 66
Amleto, 263
Amnon V'Tamar, 225, 242
Amor de Don Perlimplin con Belisa en su Jardin, 49
Amore e Psiché, 104
Amore Vince l'inganno, 158
Amorous Antic, The, 160
Amourous Flea, The, 22, 25
Amphytrion '38, 212, 221
Amphytrion, 30, 37, 228
Anastasia, 74

Anathema, The, 195
Anatol, 84, 160, 173, 257
Ancient Mariner, The, 126
Ancient Voices of Children, 21
And a Nightingale Sang, 77
And in the Tomb Were Found . . . , 106
And Perhaps Happiness, 184
And Stars Remain, 32
And the Wind Blows, 252–253
And Things That Go Bump in the Night, 92
Andersonville Trial, The, 11–12, 252
Andorra, 14, 132, 173
Andre and the Dragon, 232
Andrea Chenier, 175, 182
Androcles and the Lion, 87, 106, 168, 173–174
Androméda, xxviii, 245
Angel, 149
Angel City, 54, 60
Angel in the Pawnshop, 78
Angel in the Wings, 184
Angel Street, 87–88
Angela, 108, 200
Angelface, 94
Angelique, 133
Angelo's Wedding, 24
Angels Fall, 24, 159
Angels on Earth, 12
Animal Kingdom, The, 32
Animus, 148
Anisfeld, Boris, 8–9
Ankles Aweigh, 124, 256
Anna, 183
Anna Bolena, 148
Anna Christie, 75, 108, 126–127, 143, 265
Anna K., 178
Anna Karenina, 51
Annabel Lee, 67
Annajanska, 202
Anne of the Thousand Days, 162, 171
Annie, 6–7, 167–168, 189
Annie Get Your Gun, 18, 47, 52, 76, 161, 178, 200
Annula, An Autobiography, 131
Another Antigone, 70
Another Country, 131

Another Language, 240
Another Part of the Forest, 18–19, 63, 98, 161, 163–164, 179
Another Sun, 74
Antigone, 53, 106, 157, 166, 171, 174, 177, 179, 184, 189, 195, 202, 250
Antony and Cleopatra, 5, 34, 54, 108, 132–133, 139, 147, 161, 169, 171, 173, 188, 231, 252, 263
Any Other Business, 189
Any Resemblance to Persons Living or Dead, 178
Any Wednesday, 5, 173, 200
Anya, 200, 265
Anyone Can Whistle, 5, 72, 92–93
Anything Goes, 152, 183–184, 255
Aphrodite, 82, 84
Aphrodite Against Artemis, 201
Apocalypses, 43
Apollo of Bellac, The, 264
Apollon Apparaissant aux Bergers, 19
Apollon Musageté, 19, 67
Apothecary, The, 32
Appalachian Spring, 181
Appen, Karl von, 9
Appia, Adolphe, xxxv, xxxvi, xxxviii, xxxix, 9–10, 85, 107, 118, 127, 220, 222, 229, 234
Applause, 174, 200
Apple Cart, The, 182, 221
Apple Pie, 167
Apple Tree, The, 255
Approaching Zanzibar, 141
Arabella, 55, 102
Arabesque, 26
Arabian Nights, 48
Arcane, 66
Architettura, xx, 99, 216
Arcifanfano Re Dei Matti, 158
Ardèle, 54, 124
Are False, 20
Are You with It, 123
Argenide, 157
Ari, 200
Ariadne, 148
Ariadne auf Naxos, 133–134, 230–231, 233
Ariodante, 148, 215

Aristocrats, The, 25, 109
Arlecchino, 189
Armbruster, Mathias, **10–11**
Arminio, 157
Arms and the Man, 22, 70, 130, 179,
    201, 203, 221
Armstrong, Will Steven, **11–12**
Aronson, Boris, xxxix, **12–16**, 85, 112,
    149, 154, 190, 37,A A266
Around the World in 80 Days, 48, 50,
    124, 210, 256–257
Arrocha, Fernandez Eduardo, **16**
Arsenic and Old Lace, 131
Art of Comedy, The, 115
Art of Poetry, xx
Art of Scene Design, The, 222
Art of the Theatre, The, xxxvi, 57–58
Art Photographer, The, 240
Artaxerse, 156
Arthur, 109
Arturo Ui, 238
Artzte im Kampf, 132
As The Girls Go, 20
As Thousands Cheer, 217, 219
As You Desire Me, 52
As You Like It, 5–6, 17, 45, 54, 56, 59,
    64, 81–82, 87, 96, 103, 106, 115,
    147, 152–153, 169, 171, 173–174,
    182–183, 221, 228, 250, 264
Asakura, Setsu, **16**
Ascending Dragon, The, 183
Ascent of Mt. Fuji, The, 149
Ashes, 23, 25
Aspern Papers, The, 50, 74, 171, 244,
    253
Assassin, The, 13
Astarte, 201
At Home With Ethel Waters, 223
At the Gates of the Kingdom, 138
At the Gateway, 126
At the Grand, 87
At the Hawk's Well, 181
At War with the Army, 184
Athalie, 43
Atomtod, 232
Atonement of Tantalus, The, 245
Attila, 149, 201
Atys, 38

Au Pair Man, The, 6, 53
Au Soleil du Mexique, 83
Au Temps des Merveilleuses, 83
Aucassin und Nicolette, 171, 215
Auntie Mame, 47, 223
Autumn Crocus, 188
Autumn Garden, The, 20
Autumn Hill, 87
Avanti! Don Carlos, 184
Aventures et Nouvelles Aventures, 76
Awake and Sing!, 13, 15, 55, 60, 130,
    153, 179
Ayrton, Michael, **16**

Baal, 138, 176–177, 189, 196
Baba Goya, 76
Babbitt: A Marriage, 131
Babes in Toyland, 48
Baby, 24–25
Baby with the Bathwater, 242
Bacchae, The, 45, 54, 152, 195
Bacchus et Ariadne, 66
Bach Partita, 242
Bach Suite, 101
Bachanale, 64
Back Fire, 240
Back to Methuselah, 107, 138, 220–222,
    239, 264
Bad Seed, The, 123
Bagatelles, 53
Baintighearna An Ghorta, 168
Bajour, 48, 224, 260
Baker Street, 172, 224, 226
Baker's Dozen, 153
Baker's Wife, The, 6, 77
Bakst, Léon, xxxix, **17**, 29, 43, 61, 84,
    151–152, 202
Bal Tabarin Revue, 83
Balcony, The, 52, 87, 204–205, 264
Bald Soprano, The, 178
Ball at the Savoy, 171
Ballabile, 49
Ballad for a Firing Squad, 5, 240
Ballad of Baby Doe, The, 63, 79–80,
    184
Ballad of Gregorio Cortez, 261
Ballad of Johnny Pot, The, 51
Ballad of Soapy Smith, The, 146, 242

Ballad of the Sad Cafe, The, 74, 107, 109, 208
Ballade, 13
Balladyna, 129, 195
Ballard, Lucinda, **17–19**, 136
Ballet Ballads, 134
Ballet d'Alcina, 96
Ballet de la delivrance de Renaud, 96
Ballet des Elements, 155
Ballet du triomphe de Minerve, 96
Ballet Imperial, 243
Ballet Russes, 84
Ballets, 106
Ballets Africain, 66
Ballets de Moscou, 37
Ballets Haitians, 66
Ballets: U.S.A., 207–208
Ballroom, 6, 175, 253
Balustrade, 237
Banana Ridge, 120
Bananas, 76
Band Wagon, The, 48, 223, 226
Banjo Eyes, 217
Banjo On My Knee, 209
Banker's Daughter, The, 92
Barabau, 41
Barbary Shore, 167
Barber of Seville, The, 31, 53, 83, 127, 133, 148, 152, 169, 182, 202, 206, 243, 253, 263, 265
Barbiere di Siviglia, 193
Barchester Towers, 161
Barefoot Boy with Cheek, 50, 161
Barefoot in Athens, 13
Barefoot in the Park, 208, 224
Barnum, 6–7, 165–168
Baroque Ballet, 209
Barretts of Wimpole Street, The, 160, 239
Bartered Bride, The, 232–233, 238
Bartholomew Fair, 171, 115
Bartolucci, 233
Baruffe Chiozzotte, 65
Basic Training of Pavlo Hummel, The, 5, 7, 167
Bassarids, The, 91
Bastard Son, 145
Bastos the Bold, 106

Bathers, The, 131
Battle Hymn, 19–20
Battle of Angels, The, 22, 25
Battle of Legnano, 55
Battle of the Shrivings, 41
Battleship Gertie, 13, 15
Battleship Potemkin, The, 194–195
Bauchant, André, **19**
Bay, Howard, xxxix, **19–21**, 78, 135
Baylis, Nadine, **21–22**
Be Calm Camilla, 126
Beach Music Awards, 196
Beast in Me, The, 208
Beastly Beatitudes of Balthazar, The, 24
Beat the Band, 260
Beatlemania, 93–94
Beaton, Sir Cecil Walter Hardy, xxxix, **22**, 194
Beatrix Cenci, 53, 195
Beatty, John Lee, xxxix, **22–26**, 158
Beautiful Bodies, 179
Beautiful Galatea, The, 184
Beautiful Lady, The, 77
Beauty and the Beast, 31, 71
Beauty Part, The, 50, 178
Beaux' Stratagem, The, 8, 11, 79, 168, 173
Beazley, Samuel, **26**
Becket, 52, 59, 119–121, 171–172, 208, 223, 226
Becky Sharp, 127
Beclch, 53, 144, 178–179
Bed Before Yesterday, The, 23
Bedroom Farce, 91
Beekman Place, 224
Bees on the Boat, 120
Before You Go, 5, 93
Beg Bajazid, 245
Beggar on Horseback, 17, 106, 239
Beggar's Holiday, 46, 49, 223
Beggar's Opera, The, 20, 52, 78, 97, 130, 134, 158, 168, 171, 203–204, 207, 230
Beggars are Coming to Town, 161
Behold My Wife, 247
Bel Geddes, Norman, **26–28**, 33, 184, 240
Belamour, 83

Belasco, David, xxxv, **28–29**
Belissima, 192
Bell, Book, and Candle, 123–124
Bell for Adano, A, 171
Bell Witch Variations, The, 204
Belle of Amherst, The, 6
Bellerofonte, 244
Bells, The, 59, 181
Bells Are Ringing, 47, 188, 202–203
Beloved Friend, 225
Ben Bagley's New Cole Porter Revue, 92
Ben Franklin in Paris, 172, 224
Ben-Hur, 83
Benito Cereno, 11
Benois, Alexandre Nikolayevich, xxxix, 17, **29–30**
Bent, 90, 153
Bequest to the Nation, 224
Bérain, Jean, xxviii, **30**, 155
Bérard, Christian-Jacques, **30–31**, 60, 190, 237
Berenice, 157
Berman, Eugene, xxxix, **31**, 237
Bernini, Giovanni Lorenzo, **31–32**
Bernstein, Aline, **32–33**, 218
Beside the Seaside, 179
Best Foot Forward, 92, 161, 256
Best Friend, 256
Best Laid Plans, The, 48, 136, 224
Best Little Whorehouse in Texas, The, 130
Best Man, The, 5, 162
Best Years of Our Lives, The, 217, 219
Besuch der alten Dame, 215
Bethlehem, 56–57
Betrayal, 41, 243
Betrothal, The, 202
Bette Midler Concert, 252
Between Two Thieves, 252
Between Two Worlds, 32
Beuther, Friedrich Christian, **33–34**
Beverley, William Roxby, **34**
Beverly Hills, 183
Bewitched, 221
Beyond, 127
Beyond Desire, 87
Beyond Evil, 239
Beyond the Hills, 74–75

Beyond the Horizon, 108, 239
Beyond Therapy, 159, 179
Bibiena Family, The, xxix, **34–36**, 104, 197, 217
Bicycle Ride to Nevada, 20
Big and Little, 241
Big Blow, 87
Big Deal, 93–94, 266
Big Fish, Little Fish, 74
Big Knife, The, 20
Big Night, 105
Big People, The, 13
Big River, 141
Big Two, The, 161
Biggest Thief in Town, The, 132, 178
Bilby's Doll, 149
Billion Dollar Baby, 46, 223
Billy, 5, 93, 148, 150
Billy Barnes Revue, 47
Billy Bishop Goes to War, 146, 242
Billy Budd, 75, 77, 79, 145, 196
Biloxi Blues, 167, 175
Biography, 24, 160
Bird Cage, The, 13, 74
Bird of Our Fathers, 160
Bird Seller, The, 228
Birds, The, xv, 52, 56, 79, 106, 107
Bird's Nest, 168
Birds of Paradise, 93
Birds of Sorrow, 135
Birds Stop Singing, The, 183
Birth of the Poet, The, 95
Birthday of Infanta, The, 126
Birthday Party, The, 52, 152, 174
Birthright, 240
Bishop's Wife, The, 217
Bit O'Love, A, 183–184
Bits and Pieces, 130
Bitter Stream, 240
Bitter Sweet, 79, 228
Björnson, Maria, **36**
Black Chiffon, 74
Black Comedy/White Lies, 93, 152, 263
Black Masks, 138
Black Terror, The, 130
Black Velvet, 83
Black/White, 145
Blackpool Opera House Revue, 83

Blackpool Theatre Revue, 83
Blacks, The, 3, 264
Blasts and Bravos; An Evening With
  H. L. Mencken, 79
Bless the Bride, 168
Bless You All, 47, 223, 256–257
Blind Man's Bluff, 168
Blithe Spirit, 6, 179
Blood, 5, 184
Blood Knot, The, 41, 60
Blood Red Roses, 174
Bloodgood, William, **36–37**
Bloodstream, 160
Bloody Poetry, 25
Bloomer Girl, 78, 256–257
Blossom Time, 79
Blue Angel, 234
Blue Beard's Castle, 207
Blue Bird, The, 8
Blue Boy in Black, The, 5
Blue Denim, 50, 81, 142
Blue Peter, The, 239
Blues For Mr. Charlie, 87
Blues Whites and Reds, 117
Blvd. de Paris (I've Got the Shakes), 95
Boccaccio, 247
Bodies, 77
Body Beautiful, The, 13, 72
Body of Bricks, A, 204
Boesman and Lena, 76, 78
Bolero, 29, 260
Bolivar, 134
Bomarzo, 148
Bonanza Bound!, 46, 218, 223
Bondman, The, 59
Bonds of Interest, The, 188–189
Bone Songs, 146
Bonita, 257
Bonjour, La Bonjour, 130–131
Bonnat, Yves, **37**
Book of Beauty, Persona Non Grata,
  The, 22
Book of Costume, The, 65
Book of Job, The, 92
Book of Splendors (Part II): Book of
  Levers: Action at a Distance, 95
Booth is Back in Town, 52, 153
Borak, 252

Borderlines, 25, 159
Boris Godunov, 11–12, 37, 132, 137–
  138, 148–150, 167, 182, 232, 245,
  254
Born Yesterday, 60, 82, 183–184, 190
Borovsky, David, **37–38**
Borscht Capades, 81
Bosoms and Neglect, 135, 242
Boss, The, 203
Boucher, François, 38
Boudoir, 26
Boulevarde Solitude, 193
Bourgeois Gentleman, The, 138, 192
Bournonville Dances, The, 167
Bournonville Pas de Trois, The 153
Bow Bells, 209
Bowery After Art, 240
Box and Cox, 106
Boy David, The, 139
Boy Friend, The, 87, 174, 255
Boyd's Shop, 168
Boys and Girls Together, 217
Boy's in Autumn, The, 179
Boys from Syracuse, The, 161, 217–218
Boys of Winter, The, 167, 203
Bragdon, Claude, **38–39**, 56
Brand, 113, 138, 183, 231
Brass Ankle, 239
Brass Paperweight, The, 139
Bravo, 132
Bravo Giovanni, 200
Break a Leg, 6, 143
Breakfast At Tiffany's, 224, 260
Brecht: Sacred and Profane, 123
Bregenzer Festspiele, 182
Bridal Veil, The, 209
Bridal Wise, 160
Bride, The, 232
Bride of Chod, The, 232
Bride of the Lamb, 127, 239
Bride the Sun Shines On, The, 188, 240
Brief Moment, 160
Brigadoon, 46–49, 79, 89–90, 210, 218,
  223, 226
Bright Island, The, 138
Bright One, The, 169
Brighton Beach Memoirs, 167, 175, 261,
  265–266

Brilliant Traces, 25, 60
Bring Back Birdie, 167
Bring on the Girls, 188
Britannia Triumphans, 125, 134
Broadway, 23
Broadway, Broadway, 136
Broadway Bound, 167, 175
Broadway Follies, 51
Broadway to Paris, 17
Broken Jug, The, 120, 169
Brontosaurus, 60
Bronx Express, 12
Brooklyn, U.S.A., 20
Brother Sun, Sister Moon, 263
Brother to Dragons, 145
Brothers, 165
Brothers Karamazov, The, 52
Browning Version, The, 89
Brownstone, 179
Buccaneer, The, 127
Buddy System, The, 76
Build With One Hand, 20
Bullfight, 47
Bulls, Bears, and Asses, 240
Bully!, 54
Buontalenti, Bernardo, xxiv, **39**, 187
Burian, Emil Frantisek, **39–40**
Buried Child, 146, 230
Buried Inside Extra, 6
Burlesque, 239
Burn Me to Ashes, 132
Burn This, 25, 60–61
Burnacini, Ludovico Ottavio, xxviii, 35, **40–41**
Burning, The, 252
Burning Bright, 32, 162
Burning Glass, The, 223
Burra, Edward John, 16, **41**
Burrow, The, 100
Bury, John, **41**, 92
Bus Stop, 13
But For Whom Charlie?, 5, 162
But, Seriously . . . , 93, 224
Butterflies Are Free, 93
Buying Out, 76
By Jupiter, 161, 217
By the Beautiful Sea, 162, 218
By Your Leave, 160

Bye Bye Birdie, 47, 178, 200, 202–203, 256–257

C'est la guerre, 106
Cabal of Hypocrites, The, 167
Cabaret, 14–15, 190, 265–267
Cabin in the Sky, 13
Caccia al Tesoro, 83
Cactus Flower, The, 5–6, 224
Caesar and Cleopatra, 32, 101–102, 106–108, 149, 159, 195, 207
Café, 188
Cafe Amerique, 95
Café Crown, 13, 153–154, 179
Cages, 252
Caine Mutiny Court Martial, The, 179
Caius Marius, 212
Calculated Risk, 173, 200
Caliban of the Yellow Sands, 126, 247
California Dog Fight, 153
California Suite, 108
Caligula, 11, 208, 255
Call It a Day, 221
Call Me Madam, 79, 218
Call of Life, The, 160
Call on Kuprin, A, 136–137, 184
Calling All Stars, 87
Caludia, 183
Calvary, 265
Camel Through a Needle's Eye, 221
Camelot, 3–4, 71, 87–88, 115, 193–194, 223, 226
Cami, 115
Camille, 3, 32, 127, 149–150
Camino Real, 52–54, 152, 162, 264
Camp, The, 67–68
Campbell of Kilmhor, 106
Campen, Jacob Van, **42**
Can-Can, 71, 87, 162, 164, 167, 171, 218, 228
Can't Stop the Music, 93, 109
Candida, 78, 130, 168, 171, 183–184, 256
Candide, 48, 145, 147, 175, 218, 223, 226, 260
Candle in the Wind, 161
Canterbury Tales, The, 209, 213
Canticle for Innocent Comedians, 134

Cantique de la Vie, 196
Canto Campesino, 16
Cantorial, 131
Capon, William, xxxi, **42–43**
Caponsacchi, 39
Capriccio, 20, 83, 134
Caprice, 32, 71, 171
Caprichos, 265
Captain Blood, 121
Captain Brassbound's Conversion, 74
Captain Carvallo, 101, 169
Captain Jinks of the Horse Marines, 87
Captives, The, 195
Caravaggio, 163
Cards of Identity, 171
Carefree Heart, The, 47, 223, 256
Carefree Tree, The, 50
Caretaker, The, 76
Carib Song, 161, 171
Carmelina, 87, 225
Carmen Jones, 20–21
Carmen, 9, 20, 41, 49, 66, 79, 101–102,
    104, 115, 177, 182, 184, 193, 209,
    224, 232, 245, 247
Carmencita and the Soldier, 199
Carmina Burana, 174, 177
Carnival!, 11–12, 87, 221, 260
Carnival in Flanders, 18, 47, 223
Carnival of Venice, The, 67
Carnival Scenes, 45
Carousel, 47–48, 87, 136, 161, 209,
    223, 256
Carpenter of Rouen, The, 106
Carthaginian, The, 106
Cartney and Kevney, 168
Carzou, Jean, **43**
Casadh ant Sugain, 168
Casanova, 209
Case of Libel, A, 184
Casey Jones, 105
Casino du Liban Revue, 83
Cassaria, xx
Castor et Pollux, 38, 83
Cat and the Fiddle, The, 241
Cat Bird, The, 221
Cat on a Hot Tin Roof, 18, 24, 53–54,
    108, 119, 152, 162–163
Catch Me If You Can, 124

Catch My Soul, 174
Cathedral of Ice, 145
Catherine Was Great, 20
Catherine Wheel, The, 153, 224
Cats, xxxix, 115–116, 176
Catsplay, 23, 63, 76, 159
Caucasia, 85
Caucasian Chalk Circle, The, xxxviii, 9,
    22, 60, 79, 99, 153, 169, 178–179
Caught, 160
Cavalcade of Musical Theatre, 48, 132
Cavalleria Rusticana, 102, 263
Cave of the Heart, 181
Cécile Sorel, 83
Celebration, 153
Celeste, 183
Cenci, The, 103
Censored Scenes from King Kong, 179
Central City Lights, 127
Ceremony of Innocence, The, 135
Certain Joy, A, 20
Certain Young Man, A, 252
Cervantes, 235
Chagall, Marc, xxxix, **43–44**
Chairs, The, 114, 173
Chalk Circle, 176
Chalk Dust, 19
Champ, The, 6, 263
Champagne-Cocktail, 83
Champagne Complex, The, 81
Champagne Sec, 160
Chances, The, 67
Change Your Luck, 239
Changeling, The, 13, 206
Changes, 179
Channel Road, The, 127
Chantecler, 107
Chaparral, 11–12
Chapters and Verses, 153
Charade, 50–51
Charlatan, The, 175
Charles the King, 171
Charley's Aunt, 52, 171, 261
Charlotte, 265
Charmed Life, A, 245
Chauve Souris, 209
Cheap Detective, The, 6
Cheaters, 109

Cheezo, 106
Chekhov in Yalta, 54
Chemmy Circle, 132
Cheri, 47, 223, 256
Cherry, 79
Cherry Orchard, The, xxxv, 32–33, 45,
    52, 106, 116, 125, 139, 152–154,
    167–169, 171, 178, 242
Chess, 6, 253
Chez Nous, 54
Chiaruttini, Francesco, **44**, 96
Chic, 5
Chicago, 26, 93, 255
Chicken Every Sunday, 20
Chicken Soup With Barley, 114
Child, The, 77
Child and the Apparitions, The, 134
Child Buyer, The, 79–80
Child of Fortune, 182
Children, 6, 130
Children From Their Games, 224
Children of A Lesser God, 175
Children of Darkness, 127
Children of the Sun, 45, 233, 241
Children of the Wind, 132
Children! Children!, 163
Children's Christmas Story, The, 127
Children's Crusade, 131
Children's Hour, The, 20, 32–33
Child's Play, 163–164
China, 194
Chinese Lantern, The, 118
Chinese Prime Minister, The, 208, 224
Chloridia, 125
Chocolate Soldier, The, 18–19, 161, 209
Chorus Line, A, 6–7, 175, 201, 252–253
Chosen, The, 75
Chout, 142
Christ's Comet, 120
Christine, 50, 162
Christmas Carol, A, 204, 241
Christmas Eve, 161
Christmas in Las Vegas, 200
Christmas Oratorio, 183
Christmas Party, The, 196
Christmas Tale, A, 67
Chrysalis, 240
Chu-Chem, 20, 135

Church Street, 168
Ciceri, Pierre-Luc-Charles, xxxii, **44–45**
Cicero, 92
Cinderella, 59, 153, 206, 213
Cinders, 109
Cindy-Ella, 255
Circe, 181
Circle of Chalk, The, 107
Circle, The, 120, 183, 241
Circumstantial Evidence, 243
Cities in Bezique, 5, 148
City of Angels, 55, 136, 253
City Sugar, 241
Ciulei, Liviu, **45–46**
Civil Architecture, 99
Clandestine Marriage, The, 169
Clap Your Hands, 70
Clare, Joseph, **46**
Clarence, 241
Clark, Peggy, **46–49**
Clash by Night, 13
Class of '44, 75
Classe de farro, 212
Classical Therapy; or, A Week Under the
    Influence, 95
Claudian, 103
Clavé, Antoni, **49–50**
Clavigo, 97
Claw, The, 126
Clear All Wires, 32
Clearing in the Woods, A, 18, 87, 223
Cleopatra, 8, 46, 195, 218–219
Cléopâtre, 17
Cleopatra and Caesar, 86
Clerambard, 132
Clerical Error, A, 182
Climate of Eden, The, 207
Clive of India, 120
Clock Symphony, 30
Close of a Play, 24
Closed Circuit, 233
Clothes for a Summer Hotel, 201, 225
Clover Ring, 32
Clown, The, 232
Clowns in Clover, 209
Clutterbuck, 50
Clytemnestra, 181
Co-Respondent Unknown, 161

Coat, A, 32
Cock Robin, 160
Cock-A-Doodle Dandy, 240
Cocktail Hour, The, 70, 241
Cocktail Party, The, 177, 240
Coeur revelateur, 66
Coggerers, 168
Cold Storage, 76–78
Cold Wind and the Warm, The, 13, 87, 171
Colette, 5, 7, 55, 167
Collection, The, 75
Collector's Item, 81
Collision, 221
Collision Course, 224
Colored Girls, 150
Colt, Alvin, **50–52**, 108
Come Back, Little Sheba, 20, 22, 202
Come Blow Your Horn, 252
Come On Strong, 224
Come Play With Me, 87
Come Summer, 224
Comedian, The, 106
Comedians, 230
Comedy of a Marriage, The, 227
Comedy of Errors, The, 5, 11, 51, 108, 139, 148, 153, 173–174, 228
Comedy on the Bridge, 184
Comin' Uptown, 253
Coming of Christ, The, 121, 202
Coming Through the Rye, 222
Comings and Goings, 195
Command Decision, 161
Common Ground, 123
Commune, 204–205
Companes de Viena, 83
Company, 14–15, 165–166
Compulsion, 81, 142
Comrade Believe, 37
Comus, 34
Concert, The, 218
Concerto, 66, 153
Concerto Barocco, 31
Condemnation of Lucullus, The, 177
Condemned of Altona, The, 252
Confirmation, The, 130
Conflict of Interest, 241
Congai, 239

Conjur' Man Dies, 87
Conjuror, The, 163
Conklin, John, xxxix, **52–55**, 185
Connecticut, 74
Connecticut Yankee, A, 46
Conquering Hero, The, 208
Conquest of Everest, The, 178
Constant Wife, The, 184
Consul, The, 207, 215
Contemporary Dancers Company, 252
Contes Russes, 142
Continental Stagecraft, 128
Contrast, The, 23
Contredances, 225
Conversation Piece, 254–255
Conversations in the Dark, 147
Cook, Ansel, **55–56**
Cook for Mr. General, A, 11
Cool World, The, 20
Copacabana, 17
Coppelia, 182, 191, 238
Copper and Brass, 50, 72
Cordelia, 81
Coriolanus, 5, 11, 13, 50, 59, 65–66, 70, 87, 147, 157, 168–169, 174, 176–177, 184, 190, 212, 233
Corn Is Green, The, 6, 20, 179
Corner, The, 6
Corpse!, 131
Corsican Brothers, The, xxxiii
Cortege of Eagles, 181
Cosi fan tutte, xli, 53, 55, 63, 83, 101–102, 133–134, 167, 184, 196, 206, 247
Costake et la Vie Interieure, 45
Costanza, 106
Costumes of Shakespeare's King Henry IV, Parts 1 and 2, 191
Cotillon, 30
Count Me In, 20, 217
Counterattack, 46
Country Dances, 153
Country Doctor, A, 131
Country Girl, The, 13, 15, 87, 130, 247
Country Wife, The, 108, 171
Coup de Roulis Revue, 83
Court Singer, The, 120
Coutaud, Lucien, **56**

Cracks, 143
Cradle Will Rock, The, 87–88, 207–208
Craig, Edward Gordon, xxxv, 9, **56–59**,
    85, 96, 103, 107, 118, 127, 202, 214,
    220, 222, 229, 234–235
Cranmer of Canterbury, 120
Craven, Henry Hawes, xxxii, **59–60**
Crazy Quilt, 160
Cream in the Well, The, 161
Creation of the World and Other
    Business, The, 14
Creation of the World and Other Matters,
    The, 174
Creation of the World, 167
Creditors, 92
Creditors, The, 92, 203
Creeping Fire, 240
Creoles, 26
Cresco, 157
Crets, 67
Creuz, Serge, **60**
Crime and Punishment, 139, 217
Crime in the Whistler Room, The, 126
Crimes of Passion, 108, 178
Crimes of the Heart, 24–25
Criminal At Large, 240
Criminals, The, 240
Criss-Crossing, 178
Cristiano zwischen Himmel und Holle,
    231
Critic, The, 32, 67–68, 75, 168–169
Critic's Choice, 124
Cross Roads, 127
Crossing Niagara, 153
Crow, Laura, **60–61**
Crown Jewels, 83
Crucible, The, 13, 51–52, 125, 143,
    147–148, 163, 171, 173, 180, 203,
    264
Crucifer of Blood, The, 115–116
Crucifixion of Christ, The, 127
Cry, 196
Cry Aloud, 194
Cry for Us All, 20
Cry of Players, A, 79, 167
Cry of the Peacock, 47
Cuadro Flamenco, 189
Cuba and His Teddy Bear, 165

Cuban Swimmer, The, 149
Cuban Thing, The, 93, 252
Cunning Little Vixen, The, 91, 113, 245
Cup, The, 59, 103
Cup of Trembling, The, 81
Cure, The, 95
Curious Savage, The, 123
Curse of An Aching Heart, The, 23–24
Curse of Kulyenchikov, The, 24
Curse of the Starving Class, 76, 125, 153
Curtain Call, 240
Curtain Going Up, 47
Curtains Up!, 178
Cut of the Axe, 20
Cuttlefish, 129
Cyclopedia of Costume or Dictionary of
    Dress, A, 191
Cymbeline, 8, 54, 119, 139, 169, 228
Cynic, The, 103
Cyrano de Bergerac, 24, 30, 39, 52–54,
    79, 168–169, 233, 243
Cythere Assiegee, 38
Czech Manager, The, 232
Czettel, Ladislav, **61–62**
Czibi, 62

Da, 90, 130
Daddy, 76
Daddy Goodness, 153
Daddy's Gone A-Hunting, 126
Dahlstrom, Robert Andrew, **63**
Dalí, Salvador, xxxix, 41, **64**, 264
Dalibor, 232, 234, 245
Dame Julian's Window, 220
Dame Kobold, 215
Damer's Gold, 168
Damiani, Luciano, **64–65**
Damn the Tears, 26
Damn Yankees, 72–73, 125
Damn Your Humour, 221
Dance a Little Closer, 167
Dance Cameos, 106
Dance Me a Song, 162, 218
Dance of Death, The, 6, 60, 132, 152,
    179, 221
Dance with Your Gods, 183
Dances of Albion, 153
Dancin', 93–94, 135, 143

Dancing, 106
Dancing for the Kaiser, 159
Dancing in the Chequered Shade, 13
Dancing Pirate, The, 127
Dandelion Wine, 76
Dandy Dick, 106
Danger, 105
Danger Memory!, 63
Dangerous Woman, A, 81
Danny and the Deep Blue Sea, 179
Dans Notre Miroir, 83
Danse Brilliant, 71
Danses Concertantes, 71, 100–101
Danses sur des poésie, 66
Dante, 235
Danton, 229
Danton's Death, 45, 52, 102, 162, 177,
    189, 231
Daphne, 55, 215
Daphne in Cottage D, 5, 162
Daphnis and Chloe, 101, 206
Daphnis et Chloe, 44
Dark and Mr. Stone, The, 146
Dark at the Top of the Stairs, The, 18,
    74, 207
Dark Hours, The, 240
Dark is Light Enough, The, 177
Dark Lady of the Sonnets, The, 201
Dark Meadow, 181
Dark of the Moon, 46, 123–124, 252
Dark Pony, 23, 25
Dark Tower, The, 160
Dark Victory, 127
Dark Years, The, 45
Darling of the Day, 48, 224
Darling of the Gods, The, 28
Das Apostelspiel, 231
Das d'Acier, 262
Das gerhume Konig reich, 231
Das Kathchen von Heilbronn, 97
Das Leben des Orest, 231
Das Lockende Phantom, 231
Das Orchester, 206
Das Reich Gottes in Bohmen, 231
Das Rheingold, 9–10, 55, 198, 233
Das Salzburger grosse Welttheater, 231
Date With April, A, 182
Datterich, 177

Daughter of Silence, 223
Daughter of the Regiment, The, 62, 170,
    245, 263
Daughters of Atreus, 161
Davenport, Millia, **65**
Davidson, Jeannie, **65–66**
Davy Jones's Locker, 48
Dawn, The, 69
Dawns Are Quiet, The, 37–38
Day After Tomorrow, The, 89
Day and Night, 12, 14
Day Before Spring, The, 256
Day in Hollywood/A Night in the
    Ukraine, A, 255
Day in the Death of Joe Egg, A, 131,
    152
Day in the Life of Just About Everyone,
    A, 256
Day of the Locust, The, 210
Day of the Triffids, 213
Day the Money Stopped, The, 162
Day the Whores Came Out to Play
    Tennis, The, 135
Daydé, Bernard, **66**
Days and Nights of Beebee
    Fenstermaker, The, 252
Days of Destruction, 263
Days of Glory, 105
Days of the Commune, The, 190
Days to Come, 32
Days Without End, 221
De Architectura, xx, 216, 251
De Due Teatri, 32
De Montfort, 42
Dead Class, 129
Dead End, 26–27
Dead Pigeon, 72
Dead Souls, 8
Deafman Glance, 178, 258–259
Dear Barbarians, 87
Dear Charles, 184
Dear, Dead Delilah, 241
Dear Jane, 32
Dear Janet Rosenberg, 93
Dear Liar, 184, 208
Dear Me, the Sky Is Falling, 11
Dear Mr. Kooning, 93
Dear Nobody, 265

Dear Octopus, 171
Dear Queen, The, 168
Dear World, 224, 260
Death Destruction and Detroit, 258
Death in Venice, A, 54
Death of a Salesman, 75–76, 130, 149,
    162–164, 178, 192, 250
Death of Tarelkin, The, 85, 199
Death of Tintagiles, The, 201–202
Death of Von Richthofen as Witnessed
    from Earth, The, 179–180
Death on a Pear Tree, 236
Decameron, The, 52
Decline and Fall of the Entire World As
    Seen Through the Eyes of Cole Porter
    Revisited, 92
Deep Are the Roots, 20
Deep Blue Sea, The, 81, 169
Deer Park, The, 11
Deidre, 168
Deirdre of the Sorrows, 106
Delfau, André, 67
Delicate Balance, A, 5, 41, 77, 145,
    152, 174–175, 263
Deliverance of Renaud, The, xxvii
DeLoutherbourg, Philip, xxx, 67–69
Deluge, The, 126
Deluxe, 161
Densité 21.5, 66
Depths, The, 188
Deputy, The, 132–133
Der Boxen Oktaton Konig Reich, 231
Der Diamant des Geisterkonigs, 231
Der Einbrecher, 62
Der Fledermaus, 101
Der Freischutz, 133, 232, 243
Der Greischutz, 97
Der Gunstling, 177
Der Kliene Niemans, 231
Der Rosenkavalier, 62, 79, 84, 102, 132,
    182–184
Der Schweirige, 231
Der Untergang Karthagos, 177
Der Weisse Heiland, 231
Derain, André, 69
Dervorgilla, 168
Desert Incident, 20
Desert Rats, 120

Desert Song, The, 13, 48, 239
Design in the Theatre, 221
Design With Strings, 218
Desire Caught by the Tale, 189
Desire Under the Elms, 65, 74, 105,
    127, 149, 162, 173
Desk Set, The, 124
Desperate Hours, The, 20, 200
Desperately Seeking Susan, 153
Destry Rides Again, 50, 207, 223, 226
Detective Story, 13
Deuce o' Jacks, A, 168
Deuil en 24 Heures, 49
Deuil, 66
Development of the Theater, 227
Devil and Daniel Webster, The, 127
Devil in the Cheese, 26
Devil to Pay, The, 239
Devil's Advocate, The, 5, 162
Devil's Disciple, The, 106, 108, 221,
    243
Devil's Garden, The, 126
Devil's General, The, 177
Devil's Holiday, 31
Devil's Wall, The, 233
Devils Galore, 20, 46
Devils, The, 92, 238
Dia Log, 258
Dial M for Murder, 142–143
Dialogues of the Carmelites, 52, 82
Dialogues on Stage Affairs, 227
Diamond Cut Diamond, 121
Diamond, 230
Diamond Lil, 74
Diary of a Scoundrel, The, 22, 25, 50,
    70
Diary of Anne Frank, The, 13, 76, 193
Diary of One Who Vanished, 76
Diavolessa, 154
Dice of Death, The, 107
Did I Say No?, 239
Dido and Aeneas, 56–57, 133, 148, 184,
    224
Die Aegyptische Helena, 247
Die Burger von Calais, 177
Die Burgschaft, 177
Die Dreigroschenoper, 232

Die Fledermaus, 67, 95, 102, 132, 177, 182, 196, 207
Die Frau Ohne Schatten, 182, 233, 243
Die geschiedene Frau, 83
Die Gluckliche Hand, 127
Die Kluge, 234
Die Kraetur, 231
Die Kunst eine Widerbellerum zu zahmen, 166
Die Meistersinger, 182, 198, 233, 243, 245, 247, 254
Die Mitschuldigen, 206
Die Namenlosen, 231
Die Petroleuminseln, 177
Die Rauber, 166, 173, 195, 231
Die Reise einer Frau, 231
Die Soldaten, 233
Die Strasse der Verheissung, 231
Die Termporum fine commoedia, 215
Die Unberaten, 166
Die Verbrecher, 231
Die Verschworien des Fiesko zu Genua, 231
Die Vershworung des Fresco zu Genua, 166
Die Walküre, 9–10, 55, 132, 198, 233
Die Widerspenstigen Zahmung, 206
Die Wupper, 176
Diff'rent, 87, 127
Dime Museum Revue, The, 209
Dining Room, The, 73
Dinner at Eight, 3
Dionysus in '69, xl, 204–205
Diplomacy, 188
Disability: A Comedy, 77
Disappointment, The, 241
Discourse on Representational Poetry and the Manner of Presenting Stage Plays, 120
Disenchanted, The, 74, 207
Distaff Side, The, 5–6
Distant Bell, A, 5, 47, 105
Distant Drums, 160
Distant Fires, 131
Diversion of Angels, 181
Divertissment, 97
Divided by Three, 183
Divine Comedy, The, xxxviii, 26–27

Divine Drudge, A, 160
Divine Words, 105
Diviners, The, 24, 91, 159
Division Street, 98–99
Djamileh, 247
Dmitriev, Vladimir Vladimerovich, 69
Dmitry Donskoi, 138
Do Black Patent Leather Shoes Really Reflect Up?, 201
Do I Hear a Waltz?, 92
Do Re Mi, 13, 15, 218
Do You Turn Somersaults?, 225
Dobuzhinsky, Mstislav, 69–70
Doctor Faustus, 86, 138
Doctor Jazz, 87
Doctor Selavy's Magic Theatre, 225
Doctor's Dilemma, The, 50, 160, 168, 171, 183–184, 228
Dodsworth, 160
Dog Lady, 149
Doge of Venice, The, 34
Doll's House, A, 6, 41, 79, 106, 152, 178, 183, 196
Doll's Life, A, 91, 136
Don Carlos, 101–102, 114, 166, 199, 228–229, 231, 233, 247, 250, 254
Don Cézar de Bazan, 83
Don Giovanni, xli, 31, 81–82, 147, 169, 177, 182, 192, 215–216, 224, 231, 247, 263
Don Juan, 30, 41, 66, 95, 102, 106, 116, 148–149, 174, 221, 230–232, 245, 265–267
Don Juan in Hell, 201
Don Juan ou le Festin de Pierre, 254
Don Pasquale, 54, 66, 83, 133, 182, 184, 252
Don Perlimplin, 265
Don Quichotte, 55
Don Quixote, 41, 101, 153, 182, 242
Don Rodrigo, 5, 148
Don Sancho, 44
Don't Call Back, 225
Don't Drink the Water, 162
Donna Serpente, 142
Donnerstage Aus Licht, 36
Donogoo, 92
Door Must Be Open or Shut, A, 202

Dorsey, Kent, **70–71**
Dostigayev and Others, 69
Double Cross, The, 153
Double Dealer, 169
Double Suicide, 16
Doubles, 165
Dover Road, The, 106
Down By the River Where Waterlilies
   Are Disfigured Every Day, 22, 145,
   159
Down River, 77
Downstairs Boys, The, 77
Doxtor X, 239
Dr. Charcot's Hysteria Shows, 204
Dr. Faustus, 87, 99, 168, 204
Dr. Knock, 105–106
Dr. Selavy's Magic Theatre, 95
Dragon, The, 92, 265
Dragon's Tail, The, 244
Drakon, 212
Drama of the Nativity and the Murder of
   the Innocents, The, 209
Dramatic Imagination, The, 128
Drap d'Or, 83
Drat!, 178
Draw the Fires, 177
Dread, 160
Dream, The, 6
Dream Girl, 78, 164
Dream Girls, 175
Dream of Love, A, 144
Dream of Reason, A, 233
Dream on Monkey Mountain, 145, 174
Dream Play, The, 233
Dream Tantras for Western
   Massachusetts, 94
Dream With Music, 256
Dreamgirls, xxxix, 6–7, 175, 253
Dreams . . . , 178
Dreamy Kid, The, 106–107, 239
Drexler Plays, The, 79
Dreyfus in Rehearsal, 14, 136, 242
Drinker, The, 43
Drinks Before Dinner, 242
Driving Miss Daisy, 90
Drums Under the Window, 79
Drunkard, The, 178
Du Barry, 28

Duca d'Alba, 250
Duchess of Malfi, The, 53–54, 119, 207,
   256
Duchess of Wallenstein's Armies, The,
   234
Duck Hunting, 76
Duck Variations, 23
Dude, 145
Duenna, The, 220
Duet for One, 24, 109
Duet for Two Hands, 81
Duke Bluebeard's Castle, 234
Dumas and Son, 48, 224, 260
Dumb Man of Manchester, The, 106
Dumbarton Oaks, 265
Dumbwaiter, The, 75
Duquette, Tony, 3–4, **71**
Dusty Ermine, 171
Dutch Landscape, 141
Dybbuk Variations, 265
Dybbuk, The, 32–33, 76, 79, 105, 242
Dylan, 224
Dynamite Tonight, 135
Dynamo, 221–222
Dynasts, The, 201, 257

Each in His Own Way, 106
Eagle has Two Heads, The, 32, 81, 184
Early Girl, The, 159
Early to Bed, 123–124, 256
Earth, 239
Earth on End, 194
East Lynne, 65, 239
East Wind, 183
Eastward in Eden, 184
Easy Money, 146
Eater of Dreams, The, 107
Eccentric, The, 245
Eccentricities of a Nightingale, The, 6
Eccentricities of Davy Crockett, The, 92
Eccentrique, 224
Echo and Narcissus, 9
Eckart, Jean and William, **72–74**, 266
Eddie Fisher at the Winter Garden, 47,
   224
Edison, 258
Edith Stein, 61, 252
Edition Speciale, 83

Edna His Wife, 183
Educating Rita, 63
Education of Hyman Kaplan, The, 73
Edward II, 243
Edwards, Ben, **74–75**, 124, 253
Edwina Black, 132
Effect of Gamma Rays on Man-in-the-Moon Marigolds, The, 232
Egmont, 177
Egor Balycev, 245
Egyptian Night, 8
Egyptology: My Head Was a Sledgehammer, 95
Eight Bells, 240
800 Mètres, 56
84, Charing Cross Road, 225
Eigsti, Karl, **75–78**
Ein besserer Herr, 231
Ein Engel kommt nach Babylon, 233
Einstein On the Beach, xli, 258–259
El Amor Brujo, 232, 260
El Bravo!, 203
El Penetente, 181
El Salvador, 159
Elder, Eldon, 55, **78–81**, 110, 185, 230
Electra, 5, 60–61, 138, 147–148, 150, 201, 247
Electre, 206
Electric Grandmother, The, 159
Eleemosynary, 25
Elegy, 148
Elephant in the House, The, 22
Elephant-Steps, 94
11th Commandment, The, 232
Eli: A Mystery Play, 45
Elisa Regina de Tiro, 157
Elisabeth, 209
Elixer of Love, 196
Elizabeth d'Angleterre, 56
Elizabeth I, 45
Elizabeth of England, 202
Elizabeth the Queen, 87, 173, 221
Elmer Gantry, 131
Elson, Charles, **81–82**
Embattled Garden, 181
Embrace Tiger and Return to Mountain, 21
Emergence, The, 196
Emigres, 153
Emmanuel, 178
Empedokles, 232
Emperor Jones, The, 106–107, 113, 126–127, 133–134, 160, 183–184 209, 239–240
Empire Builders, The, 195
Enchanted, The, 127, 182
Enchantment, 127
Enclave, The, 200
Encyclopedia, 245
End of Summer, 221
End of the Beginning, The, 79, 168, 222
End of the War, 167, 178
Endgame, 60, 144, 195, 204–205, 225, 242
Endless Love, 263
Enemies, 91
Enemy, The, 160
Enemy of the People, An, 32, 39, 41, 60–61, 81, 145, 192, 203
Energetic People, 137
Engagement Baby, The, 93, 252
Enrico IV, 53, 102, 131, 134, 144
Enspigl, 245
Enter a Free Man, 167
Entertain a Ghost, 252
Entertainer, The, 79, 173, 232
Entertaining Mr. Sloane, 24
Entremeses, 84
Episode in the Life of an Author, 108
Equus, 176, 196
Era de Venerdi 17, 212
Erdgeist, 78
Ergo, 148
Eric XIV, 181
Ermine, 26–27
Ernani, 247
Eroe, 158
Eroffnung des indischen Zeitalters, 177
Errand into the Maze, 181
Erté (Romain de Tirtoff), **82–84**
Erwartung, 215
Escapade, 184
Escape Me Never, 139
Escape, 231
Esclaramonde, 170
Estate, The, 130

Esther, 79
Estuary, 225, 265
Eternal Road, The, 26–27
Ethan Frome, 131, 145, 161
Études, 66
Études de Bach, 84
Eubie!, 76
Eugene O'Neill: Journey Towards
    Genius, 159
Eugene Onegin, 40, 54, 102, 171, 199,
    206, 232
Eugene the Unlucky, 69
Eugenia, 47, 223, 256
Eunuch, The, 83, 106
Eurydice, 250
Eustace Chisholm and the Works, 145
Eve of Retirement, 45
Eve of St. Mark, The, 20
Evening With Agee, An, 79
Evening with Beatrice Lillie, An, 101–
    102
Evening with Cole Porter, An, 22
Evening With Fannie Kemble, An, 79
Evening's Frost, An, 252
Evensong, 120
Evergreen, 228
Everthing in the Garden, 174
Every Girl Should Be Married, 218
Every Good Boy Deserves Favour, 79
Every Night When the Sun Goes Down,
    178
Everybody Loves Opal, 162
Everybody Out, the Castle Is Sinking,
    124, 136
Everywhere I Roam, 127
Evgeny Onegin, 199
Evidence, 95
Evita, 91–92, 115–116
Evol Spelled Backward is Love, 241
Exchange, The, 262
Execution of Justice, 149
Exercise, The, 224
Exile, The, 20
Exiles, 145, 159
Exit the King, 79, 230
Expresso Bongo, 213
Exter, Aleksandra, xxxvii, 12, 14, **84–
    85**, 199, 237

Extra concubale, 212
Extravagances, 83
Extremities, 90, 131
Eyes of Laura Mars, 6
Ezio, 178

Fabris, Jacopo, **86**
Fabulous Invalid, The, 183
Facade, 134
Face of a Hero, 74
Facsimile, 217, 223
Fade Out—Fade In, 72
Fahrenheit 451, 255
Failures, The, 221
Fair, The, 32
Fair Circassian, The, 67
Fair Rosamund, 103
Fairy Queen, The, 16
Fairy Tale, A, 32
Fairy Tales, 255
Fait Accompli, 153
Faith Healer, The, 23, 109, 201
Faithful, The, 168, 188, 221–222
Faithful Shepherdess, The, 103
Fall of the City, The, 147
Fall of the House of Usher, The, 183,
    266
Fall River Legend, 49, 223, 225–226,
    256
Fallen Angels, 79, 160
Falling in Love, 153
Falstaff, 62, 65, 91, 133–134, 167, 174,
    182, 207, 224, 247, 263–264
Family, The, 13, 74
Family and a Fortune, A, 79, 178
Family Devotions, 135
Family Reunion, The, 11
Famira Kifared, 84
Fan, The, 153
Fancy Free, 83, 222, 226
Fanfare, 218
Fanfare for Europe, 24
Fanny, 50, 162
Fanny's First Play, 126, 201
Fantasio, 66
Fantasticks, The, 53, 178
Fantazy, 195
Far Country, A, 184

Farce of Scapin, The, 152
Fare-well Performance, 171
Farm, The, 23, 60
Farmer Takes a Wife, The, 183
Farrah, Abdelkader, **86–87**
Fashion, 126
Fashions of 1924, 3
Fashions of the Times, 133
Fata Morgana, 221
Fatal Weakness, The, 81, 183
Father, The, 78, 87, 131, 184
Father Malachy's Miracle, 161
Father Marek, 195
Father of the Bride, 64
Fathers and Sons, 130
Father's Day, 109, 163–164, 183
Faust, 9–10, 59, 82–83, 102, 127, 138,
    146, 148, 177, 193, 205–206, 221,
    228, 231–235, 244, 247, 254
Fear and Misery of the Third Reich, 177
Fearless Frank, 203
Feasting with Panthers, 145
Feathers in a Gale, 32
Feder, Abraham, **87–88**
Fedora, 54, 82, 174, 247
Fedorovich, Sophie, **88**
Feed Lot, 60
Fémina, 82
Femmes de bonne humeur, 69
Festival, 182
Festival Revue, The, 106
Feuerwerk, 49
Ffolkes, David, **88–90**
Fiddler on the Roof, 14–15, 190, 208,
    265–267
Fidelio, 14–15, 79–82, 97, 123, 134,
    148, 174, 177, 184, 215, 233, 247
Field Figures, 21
Fiery Angel, The, 232
Fiesco, 228
Fiesta, 239
Fifth Column, 20
Fifth of July, The, 23–26, 60–61
Fifty Million Frenchmen, 26
Fig Leaves Are Falling, The, 73, 174
Figaro, 101–102
Fighting Chance, 131
Fighting Cock, The, 20, 102

Figli d'Arte, 250
Figural Cabinet, The, 214
Figure of Fun, 169
Figures in the Sand, 75, 108
Figures of Chartres, The, 98
File on Jill Hatch, The, 77
Filling Station, 252
Filumena, 263
Final Balance, The, 12, 105
Find Your Way Home, 6
Fingerhut, Arden, **90–91**
Fings Ain't Wot They Used T'Be, 41
Finian's Rainbow, 20, 48, 50, 161, 178
Finishing Touches, 75, 108
Finn MacKool, the Grand Distraction,
    108, 178
Finta giardiniera, 66
Fiorello!, 72–73, 117
Fire in the Mindhouse, 167
Fire!, 20
Firebird, The, 32, 43, 206
Firebrand of Florance, The, 161
Firebug, The, 206
Firebugs, The, 53, 105, 178
First, The, 203
First Flight, 160
First Gentleman, The, 120, 171–172
First Impressions, 50, 81, 143
First Lady, 142, 183
First Little Show, The, 160
First Love, 5, 184
First Monday In October, 210, 225
First Mortgage, 160
First Mrs. Fraser, The, 81
First One Asleep, 5
First Stone, The, 32
Firstborn, The, 13, 173
Firth, Tazeena, **91–92**
Fisher, 75
Fisher, Jules, **92–94**, 165
Fisherman and His Wife, The, 178
Fitz and Biscuit, 144
Five Finger Exercise, The, 52, 173, 223
Five O'Clock Girl, The, 23–24, 26, 120,
    165
Five Plus One, 123
Five Posts in the Market Place, 178
Five, Six, Seven, Eight . . . Dance!, 179

Flahooley, 20, 89
Flaming Angel, The, 11, 265
Flaming Border, The, 232
Flawless Life, A, 233
Flea in Her Ear, A, 130, 261
Fledermaus, 209
Fleet of Clay, 26
Fleet's Lit Up, 83
Flieg roter Adler von Tirol, 177
Flies, The, 178–179, 202
Flight into Egypt, 162, 164
Flight to the West, 161
Floating Light Bulb, The, 153
Flora, the Red Menace, 72–73, 174
Florentine Irony, A, 106
Florentine Tragedy, A, 201
Florida Crackers, 25
Florimène, 125–126
Flower Drum Song, 47, 218–219, 223
Flower Festival Pas de Deux, 153
Flowering Cherry, The, 5, 13
Flowering Peach, The, 87, 105
Flowers of the Forest, 161
Flowers of Virtue, 183
Fly Blackbird, 92
Flying Blind, 241
Flying Colors, 26, 83
Flying Dutchman, The, 81, 114, 127,
    177, 232
Flying Ginzburgs, The, 183
Flying High, 247
Folies Bergère, 82–83, 259–260
Folies-Pigalle, 83
Follies, 14–15, 36, 136–137, 174–175,
    259
Follies of 1925, The, 26
Follow the Feet, 153
Follow the Girls, 20
Follow the Sun, 228
Follow Thru, 183
Fool for Love, 70, 146
Fool's Paradise, 255
Fool's Revenge, The, 103
Foolin' Around with Infinity, 196
Foolish Notion, 161
Fools, 24, 265
For Colored Girls Who Consider Suicide
    When the Rainbow is Enuf, 149, 242

For Services Rendered, 240, 243
For Sword and Song, 56
Force of Habit, 91
Forefather's Eve, 194–195, 214
Foreman, Richard, xl, xli, **94–95**
Forensic and the Navigators, 152
Forest of the Hanged, 45
Forget-Me-Not Lane, 175
Forsaking All Others, 183
Fortnight, 183
Fortuna, 135
Fortune Teller, The, 13
Fortune's Isles, The, 125
Forty Carats, 11–12
42nd Street, 6, 175, 253
Fossati, Domenico di Morcate, 44, **95–
    96**, 211
Found a Peanut, 109
Fountain, The, 127–128
Four Horsemen of the Apocalypse, The,
    71
Four Little Girls, The, 189
Four Marys, The, 224
Four On A Garden, 224
Four Plunderers, 199
Four Saints in Three Acts, 87, 148, 230,
    265
Four Seasons, The, 109, 153
Four Winds, 184
Fourposter, The, 18
1491, 48, 224
Fourteenth of July, The, 139
Fox Trap, The, 232
Foxfire, 24, 167
Foxhole in the Parlor, 221
Foxy, 200
Francesca da Rimini, 132, 159
Francesca, 133
Francini, Tomaso, **96**
Frankenstein, 94, 203, 209
Franklin Street, 20
Fraser, Claude Lovat, 81, **96–97**, 220
Fraulein Elsa, 139
Freaking Out of Stephanie Blake, The,
    74
Fred Waring Show, 20
Free and Clear, 77
Free for All, 183

Freischutz, 177
French Casino, 83
French Pastoral, A, 125
French Touch, The, 123
Freyer, Achim, **97–98**
Frimbo, 77
Frogs, The, xv
Frogs of Spring, The, 13, 50
From Morn to Midnight, 106, 221
From the House of the Dead, 177, 232–234
From Vienna, 183
Front, The, 130
Front Page, The, 11, 70, 76, 99, 135, 177, 192, 255
Front Street, 204
Frontier, 181
Frozen Deep, The, 228
Fruhlings Erunchen, 166
Fruits of Education, The, 199
Fuente Ovejuna, 195, 245
Full Circle, 93, 252
Full Hookup, 60
Fuller, Isaac, **98**
Fumed Oak, 11
Fun City, 93
Fun Couple, The, 79
Funicello, Ralph, **98–99**, 129
Funny Face, 167, 242
Funny Girl, 200, 218–219
Funny Thing Happened On the Way to the Forum, A, 190, 208, 255
Funnyhouse of a Negro, 135
Further Outlook, 139
Furttenbach, Josef, **99**, 172

G. R. Point, 143
Gabrielle, 46, 145
Galileo, 45, 53–54, 114, 146, 152, 163, 177–178, 185, 241, 252
Galliari Family, The, xxix, **100**, 104, 213
Gambler, The, 162
Game of Chess, A, 206
Game of Love and Death, The, 32
Gamelan, 135
Gandhi, 108, 148
Gang's All Here, The, 162, 264

Gangway, 62
Gantry, 93, 252
Garden of Earthly Delights, The, 109
Garden of Paradise, The, 126, 247–248
Garden of Sweets, The, 13, 173, 264
Gardenia, 153, 165–166
Garrick, 133
Garrick Gaieties, The, 187
Gas, 132, 220
Gas II, 133
Gaspard de la Nuit, 66
Gather Ye Rosebuds, 161
Gay Divorcee, 160
Gay Life, The, 18–19, 136, 208, 223
Gay New Orleans, 217
Gazebo, The, 162
Gazza ladra, 154
Gemini, 21
Generation, 124
Gentile Wife, The, 126
Gentle People, The, 13, 168
Gentlemen Dancing Master, The, 106
Gentlemen Prefer Blondes, 47, 49, 79, 223, 226, 256–257
Gentlewoman, 87, 105
Gently Does It, 123
George and Margaret, 168
George and Rosemary, 253
George Bataille's Bathrobe, 95
George Dandin, 8, 126, 228, 229, 239
George M!, 178, 260
George Washington: The Man Who Made Us, 126
George White's Revue, 83
George White's Scandals, 82–83, 255
Georgiadis, Nicholas, **100–101**
Georgy, 163, 265
Geranium Hat, The, 5, 178
Gérard, Rolf, **101–102**
Gershwin Concerto, 153
Gertie, 72
Gertrude Stein, 167
Get Away, Old Man, 256
Getting Even, 239
Getting Married, 32, 108, 130
Getting Out, 241
Ghost Dance, 145
Ghost for Sale, 240

Ghost Town, 187
Ghosts, 5–6, 87, 204, 206
Gianni Schicchi, 20, 133–134, 147, 182, 233
Giants, 143
Giants in the Earth, 78
Giants, Sons of Giants, 173
Gift of Time, A, 14, 208
Giftgas uber Berlin, 177
Gigi, 22, 159, 225
Gilda Radner Live From New York, 146
Gilded Age, The, 131
Gilles de Rais, 117
Gilles und Jeanne, 192
Gin Game, The, 167–168
Ginger Man, The, 92, 254
Gingham Dog, The, 5, 174
Girl Could Get Lucky, A, 11, 92
Girl Crazy, 60–61, 183, 184
Girl from Utah, The, 59
Girl from Wyoming, The, 46, 48
Girl in Pink Tights, The, 79, 256
Girl of the Golden West, The, 182
Girl of the Night, A, 5
Girl Who Came to Supper, The, 48, 218, 224
Girls in 509, The, 18, 178, 184
Girls of Summer, 13
Girofle-Girofla, 262
Gischia, Léon, **102–103**
Giselle, 16–17, 29, 31, 43, 87, 224
Give and Take, 153
Give My Regards to Broadway, 79
Give Us This Day, 240
Glad Tidings, 72
Glad to See You, 20
Glass Menagerie, The, 18, 45, 149–150, 153, 161, 163, 173, 178, 202, 250, 265
Glass Slipper, The, 221
Glencairn Cycle, The, 240
Glengarry Glen Ross, 70
Glittering Gate, The, 106, 126
Glorious Morning, 60
Glove, A, 32
Go Man Go!, 20
Go Show Me a Dragon, 92
Goat Song, The, 221

God and Kate Murphy, 74
God, Man, and Devil, 105
Goddess, The, 132
Gods We Make, The, 240
Godwin, Edward William, xxxvi, 56, **103**
Gogo Loves You, 92
Gold Eagle Guy, 183
Golda, 93, 153
Golden Age, The, 109, 225
Golden Apple, The, 50–51, 72–74, 92
Golden Boy, 22, 105, 132, 136, 174, 190, 255
Golden Cockerel, The, 138
Golden Cuckoo, 168
Golden Door, The, 13
Golden Rainbow, 200
Golden Six, The, 5
Golden Trumpet Ball, The, 79
Golden Windows, The, 258–259
Goldilocks, 87, 142–143
Golem, The, 12
Golovine, Aleksandr, 29, **103–104**, 227
Gondoliers, The, 202
Gonzaga, Pietro Gottardo, 44, **104–105**
Gonzague, 83
Good, The, 183
Good and Bad Times of Cady Francis McCullum and Friends, The, 145
Good as Gold, 142
Good Companions, The, 120
Good Doctor, The, 175
Good Earth, The, 221
Good Evening, 200
Good Gracious Annabelle, 126
Good Hope, The, 239
Good News, 183–184
Good Soldier Schweik, The, xxxviii, 233
Good Sports, 179
Good Woman, A, 32
Good Woman of Setzuan, The, 53, 65, 97, 105, 177, 185, 203
Goodbye Charlie, 47, 223
Goodbye, Fidel, 136
Goodbye My Fancy, 184
Goodbye People, The, 51, 153, 242
Goodness How Sad, 168
Goodtime Charley, 87, 135, 238

Gore ot ouma, 245
Gorelik, Mordecai, 33, 75, **105–106**
Götterdämmerung, 233
Government Inspector, The, 69, 107,
  138, 169
Governor's Lady, The, xxxv
Gracious Living, 225
Graduate, The, 265
Grand Ballet de la Reine représentant le
  Soleil, 96
Grand Distraction, The, 178
Grand Duchess, 48
Grand Hotel, 3, 32–33, 93–94, 153–154,
  255
Grand House in the City, 168
Grand Music Hall of Israel, 93
Grand Street Follies, 32–33
Grand Tour, The, 6, 20, 52, 149, 171
Grass Harp, The, 240
Grave Undertaking, A, 178
Gray, Terence, **106–107**
Gray Shadow, 239
Graziana, 50
Grease, 76, 203–204
Great Adventure, The, 168
Great American Goof, The, 13, 15, 87
Great Big Doorstep, The, 20, 46
Great Cyril, The, 199
Great Day in the Morning, 258–259
Great Expectations, 171
Great Gatsby, The, 6–7
Great God Brown, The, 11, 14, 127,
  128, 173–174
Great Grandson of Jedediah Kohler, The,
  60, 77
Great Hoss Pistol, A, 204
Great Indoors, The, 143, 174
Great Lady, 17
Great Magoo, The, 209, 230
Great Romance, 171
Great Sebastians, The, 207
Great Waltz, The, 48, 217, 224, 260
Great White Hope, The, 218, 252
Great Ziegfeld, The, 3
Greatest of These, The, 81, 183–184
Greatest Show on Earth, The, 256–257
Greeks, The, 55
Green Bay Tree, The, 127

Green Cockatoo, The, 32
Green Pastures, The, 127
Green Pond, 130
Green Ring, The, 32
Greenwich Village Follies, 240
Greenwich Village U.S.A, 92
Greenwillow, 50, 87, 143
Greenwood, Jane, **107–110**
Gregor und Heinrich, 177
Grey Fox, The, 160
Grey-Eyed People, The, 78
Grief Over the Message From Ur, 233
Grieve Family, The, xxxii, **110–111**, 228
Grin and Bare It, 167
Grind, 136–137
Gropius, Walter, xxxvii, **111**
GUARDenia Terrace, 258
Guardsman, The, 5, 160, 163, 243, 252
Guerramore, 76
Guests of the Nation, The, 77
Guibour, 126
Guilio Flavio Crispo, 157
Guillaume Tell, 45
Guilty Bystander, 132
Guitar, 178
Gun Play, A, 129, 152
Gustav Vasa, 106
Guys and Dolls, xxxix, 47–48, 50–51,
  115, 147, 162, 164, 209, 218, 223,
  226
Gyges und sein Ring, 151
Gypsies Wore High Hats, The, 132
Gypsy, 6, 162, 188, 200
Gypsy Baron, The, 102
Gypsy Lady, The, 13, 256
Gypsy, No Hard Feelings, 200

H.M.S. Pinafore, 79, 144, 173
Habeas Corpus, 242
Hail Scrawdyke!, 93, 135, 143
Hair, 5, 93–94, 148, 210, 252–253, 261
Hairy Ape, The, 106, 126–127, 132,
  239–240
Hakamadare wa dokoda, 16
Half a Sixpence, 92, 108
Half-Past Wednesday, 92
Halka, 214
Hallelujah, Baby!, 73, 174, 218

Halloween, 20

Hamlet, xxxvi, 5–6, 11, 24, 26, 32, 37–
38, 41, 45, 50, 53–54, 56, 58–60, 74,
76, 79, 89–90, 93, 105, 107–109,
119–120, 126, 128, 137–138, 147–
149, 151, 153, 161, 166–167, 169,
171, 174, 176, 178, 199, 207, 209,
217, 228, 231–232, 234, 238, 240–
243, 261, 263

Hamlet Connotations, 252

Hamlet of Stepney Green, The, 107,
178–179

Hammett, 146

Hammond, Aubrey, **112**, 220

Hand is on the Gate, Eh?, A, 93

Handful of Fire, 18, 162

Hands of Its Enemy, The, 24

Hanging Judge, 79

Hannah and Her Sisters, 261

Hansel and Gretel, 113–114, 247

Hapgood, 244

Happening-Cricotage, 129

Happiest Days of Your Life, The, 244

Happiest Girl in the World, The, 72

Happiest Millionaire, The, 124

Happily Ever After, 153

Happily Never After, 5, 143

Happiness Cage, The, 5, 129

Happy and Glorious, 107

Happy as a Lark, 171

Happy Birthday, 18–19, 161

Happy Days, 109

Happy End, 177, 203, 242

Happy Ending, The, 126

Happy Hunting, 162, 218

Happy Hypocrite, The, 93, 171

Happy Marriage, The, 120

Happy Time, 161

Happy Time, The, 24, 32, 171, 260

Happy to Die, 43

Happy-Go-Lucky, 83

Harbinger, 224

Harlequin and Cinderella, 111

Harlequinade, A, 89, 153

Harold and Maude, 136

Harold, 74

Harper's Bazaar, 84, 204

Harriet, 32

Harrigan 'n' Hart, 117, 167, 179

Harry and Walter Go to New York, 6

Harry Noon and Night, 145

Harry Outside, 22, 79

Harvest, The, 223

Harvey, 240

Hashish Club, The, 195–196

Hassan, 106, 168, 171

Hat, A, 32

Hatful of Rain, 105

Hatter's Castle, 139

Haunted Ballroom, The, 171

Have I Got a Girl for You!, 135

Hay, Richard L., **112–113**

Hay Fever, 108, 110, 159, 243

Hazel Flagg, 256–257

HcOhTiEnLa; or Hotel China, 94

He Was Born Gay, 171

He Who Gets Slapped, 134, 221, 252

He, 32

Head Hunters, The, 108

Heads Up!, 183

Heart Line, The, 139

Heartbreak House, 23, 65, 74–75, 77,
106, 109–110, 131, 153, 178, 221,
260

Hearts and Diamonds, 139

Hearts and Flowers, 209

Heat Wave, 120

Heavenly Express, 13

Heavenly Twins, 79

Heavens Above!, 89

Hedda Gabler, 5, 32–33, 41, 87, 109,
126, 130–131, 152, 159, 174

Heeley, Desmond, **113**, 125

Heinrich, Rudolf, **113–114**

Heiress, The, 171, 225

Helen, 135, 228

Helen Goes to Troy, 62, 127

Helen Hayes: Portrait of an Actress, 79

Helen of Troy, 65

Helen Retires, 133

Helena, 161

Helena in Troas, 103

Helena's Husband, 118

Helgi Tommasen, 266

Hell Freezes Over, 161

Hello, Dolly!, 208, 218, 224, 226, 253, 260–261
Hello Out There, 87, 222
Hellzapoppin, 200
Heloise, 5
Help! Help! The Globolinks, 148
Hempfield, 126
Henry IV: Part 1, 6, 8, 34, 70, 79, 82, 89, 102, 106–107, 148, 169, 171, 179, 182, 191; Part 2, 169; Parts 1 and 2, 5, 11–12, 148, 208, 228
Henry V, xxxii, 76, 79, 87, 103, 148, 152, 166–167, 169, 171, 173, 220, 228
Henry VI: Part 1, 115; Parts I, II and III, 150
Henry VIII, 59, 89–90, 106, 168–169, 202
Henry, Sweet Henry, 51, 200
Heptagon, 153
Heraclius, 106
Herbert, Jocelyn, 58–59, **114–115**
Hercules in Love, xxviii, 250
Here Come the Clowns, 87, 92
Here Comes Tootsie, 247
Here's Love, 50–51, 72, 173
Here's Where I Belong, 93, 148
Hernani, 45, 138
Hero, The, 233
Herodiade, 181
Herrman, Karl-Ernst, **115**
Hersey, David, **115–116**
Hester Street, 261
Hidden Horizon, 81
Hide and Seek, 24, 183
High Button Shoes, 46, 49, 209, 223, 226, 256–257
High Ground, The, 47
High Spirits, 92–93
High Summer Sky, A, 232
High Temperature, 168
High Tor, 161
Higher and Higher, 17, 161
Highest Tree, The, 184
Highland Fling, A, 89, 171
Hilda Crane, 20
Hippolyte Aricie, 265
His and Hers, 81

Histoires d'Eve, 83
Histoires Naturelles, 141
History of British Costume, The, 191
History of the American Film, A, 54, 230
Hit the Deck, 23, 124
Hobo, 178, 239
Hockney, David, **116**
Hoffman's erazhlungen, 231
Hold on to You, 87
Holdup, The, 24
Hole in the Head, A, 13, 207
Holeville, 141, 178
Holiday, 24, 36–37, 127
Holly and the Ivy, 169
Hollywood Holiday, 183
Hollywood Pinafore, 161
Homage to the Queen, 159
Homage to Varese, 66
Home, 93
Home and Beauty, 225
Home at Seven, 169
Home Chat, 188
Home Sweet Homer, 20
Homecoming, The, 41, 145, 152
Honeys, The, 74, 171
Honor, 95
Hooded Falcon, The, 4
Hook 'n Ladder, 78
Hook-Up, The, 87
Hooray! It's a Glorious Day . . . And All That, 93
Hope for the Best, 171
Hoppla!, 106
Horace, 37
Horatio, 76
Horizons, 26
Horse Eats Hat, 87, 207
Horseman Pass By, 242
Horses in Midstream, 184
Hostage, The, 36, 53, 152, 166, 202–203
Hot Buttered Rolls, 79–80
Hot l Baltimore, The, 60–61, 130
Hot Lunch Apostles, 131
Hot Money, 240
Hot Pan, 239
Hot September, 224
Hotel for Criminals, 95

Hotel New Hampshire, The, 114
Hotel Universe, 107, 221
Hothouse, The, 146, 243
Hould-Ward, Ann, **116–117**, 265–267
Hour Glass, The, 58
House, The, 138
House Beautiful, The, 160
House of Atreus, The, 169–170
House of Bernarda Alba, The, 23, 49,
    101, 105
House of Birds, 100
House of Blue Leaves, The, 76, 79, 98,
    108–109, 152, 255
House of Breathe, 145
House of Connelly, The, 81–82, 240
House of Flowers, 174, 207
House of Mirth, The, 130, 146
House of Women, The, 127
How I Wonder, 184
How it All Began, 141
How Music Came to Earth, 230
How Now, Dow Jones, 224
How the Other Half Loves, 48, 167
How the Steel Was Tempered, 258
How to Be a Jewish Mother, 200
How to Succeed in Business Without
    Really Trying, 48, 152, 200
How's the World Treating You?, 74, 108
Howard, Pamela, **117–118**
Howell of Gurent, 88–89
Huckleberry Finn, 218
Hue and Cry After Cupid, 125
Hume, Samuel, xxxviii, **118–119**
Hundred Percent Alive, A, 76
Hunter, The, 6
Hunting Cockroaches, 141, 179
Hurlyburly, 210, 242, 255
Hurry, Leslie, **119**, 168
Huui, Huui, 5
Hymenaei, 125
Hymn a la Beaute, 254
Hyperprism, 66

I Am a Camera, 13
I Am My Youth, 183
I Brandembergahesi in Bohemi, 245
I Can Get It For You Wholesale, 5, 11–
    12

I Capture the Castle, 171
I Capuleti e I Montecchi, 149
I Do! I Do!, 224, 260
I Don't Have to Show You No Stinking
    Badges, 196
I doni, 227
I Had a Ball, 11
I Have Been Here Before, 120
I Knock at the Door, 79
I Know What I Like, 183
I Love an Actress, 160
I Love My Wife, 167–168
I Married an Angel, 161
I Never Sang For My Father, 5, 163
I Pagliacci, 82
I Puritani, 149–150, 243
I Remember Mama, 18, 123–124, 167
I tre corsari, 212
I vespri siciliani, 233
I vinti, 192
I Want a Policeman!, 240
I Was Dancing, 224
I Was Sitting on my Patio This Guy
    Appeared I Thought I Was
    Hallucinating, 258
I Was Waiting for You, 160
I Won't Dance, 165
I'd Rather Be Right, 87, 183–184, 217
I'm Not Rappaport, 190, 255
I'm Old Fashioned, 136
I'm Solomon, 108
I've Got Sixpence, 13
Icare, 31, 189
Ice Capades, 260
Ice House, The, 104
Iceman Cometh, The, 75, 93, 109, 127–
    128, 148, 192, 203–204
Ida-Eyed, 94
Ideal Husband, An, 45, 126
Idiot, The, 9, 138, 178, 199
Idiot's Delight, 78, 217, 221
Idle Inn, The, 126
Idomeneo, 134, 149, 197, 232, 234
If, 32, 97
Il Ballo Delle Ingrate, 184
Il Campiello, 233
Il Candelaio, 206
Il Cappello a tre punte, 192

Il Cappotto, 192
Il diavolo in giardino, 250
Il était trois navires, 37
Il était une gare, 37
Il Favore degli Dei, 157
Il Fuoco Eterno, 40
Il Giardino d'Agrigento, 104
Il Giuramento, 148
Il Matrimonio Segreto, 83
Il mio nome e' nessuno, 193
Il Mondo della Luna, 158
Il Mondo di notte 2, 192
Il Nozze di Figaro, 62
Il Pomo D'Oro, 40
Il Racommandato di terro, 212
Il Signor Bruschind, 247
Il Tabarro, 147, 174
Il Tamerlano, 158
Il Trionfo d'Arianna, 158
Il Trovatore, 167, 171, 233
Il Vizio Assurdo, 192
Illya Darling, 5, 93, 224
Imaginary Invalid, The, 11, 51, 76, 144, 169, 174
Immoralist, The, 5, 87, 123, 171, 252
Immortal Hour, The, 106, 220
Immortal Thief, The, 39
Importance of Being Earnest, The, 5, 26, 52, 70, 98, 107, 144, 171, 178
Impossible Years, The, 190
Impresario from Smyrna, The, 250
Impromptu de Versailles, 240
Improvisation in June, 32
In a Garden, 127
In a Glass Darkly, 107
In a Jewish Grocery, 20
In Pasha's Garden, 134
In a Small Country House, 129
In Abraham's Bosom, 239
In Bed We Cry, 3
In Celebration, 24
In Praise of Love, 6
In Quest of the Sun, 149
In the Boom Boom Room, 6, 152, 167
In the Jungle of Cities, 176–177
In the Pasha's Garden, 133
In the Recovery Lounge, 60
In the Summer House, 47, 223

In the Train, 168
In the Well of the House, 204
In Three Zones, 252
In Trousers, 153
In White America, 252
Inaugural Program of the Radio City Music Hall, 127
Incident at Vichy, 14
Incomparable Max, The, 5, 167
Inconsequentials, 153
Increased Difficulty of Concentration, The, 167
Indians, 53, 224, 226
Infernal Machine, The, 31, 50, 147, 149, 159, 173
Infidelities, 55
Infinite, The, 152
Ingegneri, Angelo, **120**
Inherit the Wind, 87, 142–143, 146, 148, 150
Inheritors, 106
Injunction Granted, 87
Inner City, 252
Inner Journey, 202
Inner-City MacBeth, 75
Innocent Voyage, The, 32, 46
Innocents, The, 23, 162, 164, 171
Inns of Court Masque, 125
Inquest, 76, 93
Insect Comedy, The, 221, 232, 234
Insect Play, The, 106, 221
Inspector General, The, 45, 52, 199, 240, 249, 252
Inspector Kennedy, 239
Inspector's Recounting, The, 138
Intergrales, 66
Interior, 126
Interlock, 20
Interplay, 218, 223
Interpreter, The, 178
Intervention, The, 199
Interview, The, 178
Intimate Letters, 101
Into Light We Shall Return, 196
Into the Woods, xxxix, 117, 141, 179–180, 230, 266
Intoleranza, 232
Intoxication, 106

Intrados, 180
Investigation, The, 79–80
Invincibles, 168
Invisible Duke, The, 106
Invisible Lady, The, 181
Invitation, The, 101
Invitation to a Beheading, 5, 148
Invitation to a March, 18
Io, mammeta e tu, 212
Iolanthe, 239
Ionisation, 66
Iphégénie en Tauride, 30
Iphigenia in Aulis, 53, 93
Iphigenia in Concert, 5
Iphigenia in Tauris, 106, 133, 202, 257
Iphigenie en Tauride, 97, 243
Irene, 218
Irma La Douce, 23, 102
Iron Chest, The, 43
Iron Men, 26, 27
Irregular Verb to Love, The, 184
Irving, Laurence Henry Forester, **120–121**
Irving: The Actor and His World, 121
Is Life Worth Living?, 240
Is There Life After High School?, 24
Isadora, 114
Island Fling, 78
Island in the Sun, 89
Island of Goats, 171
Island of Jewels, The, 34
Island of the Mighty, The, 91
Islands of Goats, 162
Isle of Children, 20
Isn't It Romantic?, 131
Issé, 38
It Had To Be You, 203
It Happens on Ice, 26
It's a Bird . . . It's a Plane . . . It's Superman, 136, 200
It's a Long Way to Boston, 23
It's Getting Dark on Old Broadway, 209
It's In the Bag, 83
It's Me, 146
It's Up to You, 46
Italian Girl in Algiers, The, 244
Italian Lady from Algiers, The, 184
Italian Straw Hat, The, 16, 153, 167

Italian Voyage, 32
It's Only a Play, 24
It's Up To You, 20
Ivan the Terrible, 258
Ivanov, 11–12, 138, 238
Ivory Door, The, 239
Izenour, George C., **121–122**, 134

J. B., 13, 15, 18, 173, 175, 184
Jack and Jill, 171
Jack and the Beanstalk, 133
Jack MacGowran in the Works of Samuel Beckett, 148
Jack-in-the-Box, 69
Jacknife, 109
Jackpot, 127
Jacob Slovak, 239
Jacobs, Sally, **123**
Jacques and His Master, 109
Jacques Brel Is Alive and Living in Paris, 178
Jail Diary of Albie Sachs, 23
Jailbird, 168
Jakey Fat Boy, 93
Jamaica, 193, 223, 256
James Joyce Memorial Liquid Theatre, 195
Jane Clegg, 221
Jane Eyre, 74, 171
Janosik, 232
Janus, 184
Jardin Animé, 153
Jazz-out, 37
Jealous Moon, The, 160
Jeanne d'Arc au bucher, 37
Jeanne D'Arc, 27, 56
Jeanne la Folle, 254
Jeb, 161
Jedermann, 71, 177
Jeeves Takes Charge, 165, 243
Jenkins, George, **123–124**, 149
Jennie, 124, 208
Jenny, 160, 218
Jensen, John, **124–125**
Jenufa, 215, 233
Jeptha, 177
Jeremias, 231

Jerome Robbins's Broadway, 51, 225, 242–243, 253, 255
Jerry's Girls, 136, 175
Jest of Cards, 71
Jest, The, 126–127
Jesus Christ Superstar, 93–94, 252–253
Jesus of Nazareth, 263
Jeu de Cartes, 217
Jeux de Printemps, 56
Jeux, 37, 66, 187
Jew Süss, 12
Jewels of the Madonna, 247
Jewels, 253
Jezebel, 183
Jigsaw, 221
Jim Cooperkop, 12
Jimmy, 48, 224
Jitters, 24
Joan of Arc, 16
Joan of Lorraine, 203, 221
JoAnne!, 76
Johanna Balk, 177
John, 26
John Brown's Body, 51, 174
John Falstaff, 206
John Ferguson, 188–189
John Gabriel Borkman, 91, 168
John Loves Mary, 18–19
Johnny 2X4, 20
Johnny Belinda, 87
Johnny Johnson, 183, 195
Johnny On A Spot, 24
Joker, The, 239
Joker's Wild, 83
Jokers, The, 117
Jolanda, the Daughter of the Coraro Nero, 212
Jollyanna, 20, 47
Jones, Inigo, xxv, 32, 99, **125–126**, 186–187, 255
Jones, Robert Edmond, xxxviii, 26, 33, 39, 58, 105, 118, **126–128**, 143, 163, 184, 222, 229, 239–240, 247
Jonestown Express, 146
Jonny Spielt auf, 231
Josefs Legende, 234
Joseph and his Brethren, 133

Joseph and the Amazing Technicolor Dreamcoat, 77–78, 93
Jour de Fete au Village, 142
Journey to Jerusalem, 65, 161
Journey to the Center of the Earth, 89
Journey, The, 100
Journeys, 167
Journey's End, 54, 196
Joy to the World, 207
Joyous Season, The, 127
Juan Darien, 179
Juana, 103
Juarez and Maximillian, 221, 231
Jubilee, 161, 217
Judas, 106, 160
Judgement, 109
Judgment Day, 32
Judith, 14, 181, 202, 260
Judith Plays, The, 202
Judy Garland, 207
Julie, 183
Julietta, 177, 232
Juliette ou la Cle des Songes, 60
Julius Caesar, 11, 26, 29, 37, 45, 54, 74–77, 79–80, 90, 100, 106, 108, 112, 148–149, 169, 171, 174, 177–179, 202, 207, 208–209, 228, 231, 245, 252
Jumbo, 187
Jumpers, The, 22, 77, 135, 233, 244
Juniper and the Pagans, 208, 223
Juniper Tree, The, 242
Junius, 103
Juno, 47, 218, 223
Juno and the Paycock, 54, 127, 130
Just to Remind You, 239
Justine, 218
Juvara, Filippo, **128**

K2, 149–150
Ka Mountain, 258–259
Kabale und Liege, 233
Kaiser Franz Joseph van Oesterreich, 231
Kaiser in Messalina, 231
Kaleidoscope, 50
Kalkutta 4 Mai, 176
Kalldeway Farce, 115
Kameliendame, 206

Kantan, 105
Kantor, Tadeusz, **129**
Karaguez, 142
Karl and Anna, 160
Karl Marx Play, The, 76
Kaspar, 146
Kata Kabanova, 147, 232
Katalaunische Schlacht, 176
Katchen von Heilbronn, 176
Katerina Ismailova, 11, 265
Katerina, 32, 138
Kathleen, 81
Katie Roche, 168
Katya Kabanova, 36
Kaufman At Large, 24, 131
Kean, 54, 131
Keeper of the Keys, 183
Keeping an Eye on Louie, 159
Kellogg, Marjorie Bradley, xxxix, **129–132**, 148
Kelly, 174, 224, 260
Kenilworth, 111
Kennedy's Children, 153, 159
Kerz, Leo, **132–133**
Key Largo, 161
Kid Champion, 6
Kid from Brooklyn, The, 256
Kidnapped in London, 169
Kiesler, Frederick, **133–135**
Kikimora, 141, 142
Killdeer, The, 6, 130, 242
Killers, 239
Killing of Sister George, The, 108
Killycreggs in Twilight, 168
Kim, Willa, **135–136**
Kin Hubbard, 78
Kind Gentlemen, 224
Kind Lady, 161
Kind Sir, 162
Kindred, 127
King and I, The, 48, 87, 115, 136, 162, 164, 200, 210, 218–219
King Arthur, 59
King Bamba, 212
King Can Do No Wrong, The, 239
King Henry IV, 97; Part I, 93
King Henry V, 39
King Hunger, 105

King John, xxxii, 5, 11, 34, 59, 169, 171, 177, 191, 207, 237–238
King Lear, xli, 5–6, 10–11, 16, 59, 66, 70, 108, 119, 139, 144–145, 147–150, 152, 169, 171–174, 177–179, 181, 192, 201, 228, 231
King Lear's Wife, 106
King of Hearts, 153, 265, 267
King of Jazz, The, 209
King of Schnorrers, 178
King of Spain, The, 178, 258
King Richard II, 74, 89, 93
King Svatopluk, 245
King's Coat, The, 183
King's Threshold, The, 201
Kingdom Chums, 159
Kingdom of God, The, 106
Kingdoms, 265
Kingfisher, The, 109
Kismet, 47, 54, 71, 182, 225
Kiss Me, Kate, 47–48, 50, 79, 81, 178, 182, 193, 209
Kitchen, The, 93, 114
Kitty, 188
Klotz, Florence, **136–137**
Klute, 210
Knack, The, 5
Knickerbocker Follies, 179
Knickerbocker Holiday, 20, 161, 260
Knife, The, 109, 175
Knight of the Burning Pestle, The, 106–107
Knock, Knock, 23, 25, 63, 159
Knockout, 76, 78, 109
Knot Garden, The, 91
Knuckle, 241
Kochergin, Edward Stepanovich, **137–138**
Kokkos, Yannis, **138**
Koltai, Ralph, 92, **138**, 176
Komisarjevsky, Theodore, **138–139**, 221
Kongi's Harvest, 93
König Otakar, 233
Kook, Edward Frankel, **139–140**, 164
Kordian, 195
Korovine, Konstantin Alexeevich, 29, **140**

Krapp's Last Tape, 114
Kwamina, 11, 172

l diavoletto di Zvikov, 245
L'Affair Makropulos, 245
L'Aigle à Deux Têtes, 30
L'Aiglon, 32
L'Ambigu de la Folie ou Le Ballet des Dindons, 38
L'Ambizione depressa, 157
L'Amfione, 157
L'Amor in Ballo, 158
L'Amore de Tre Re, 170
L'Amore dei Tre Re, 83
L'Annonce Faite A Marie, 152, 249
L'Après Midi d'un Faun, 17
L'Arbore di Diana, 158
L'Architettura Civile Preparata Nello Geometria, 35
L'Arlesienne, 37
L'Autre Messie, 151
L'Avare, 102, 166
L'avventura della volpe furba, 245
L'Ecole des Femmes, 30, 66
L'Elixir d'Amore, 182, 263
L'Enfant et les sortileges, 134
L'Ennemi Publique No. 1, 105
L'Ennemie, 231
L'Etourdi, 102
L'Etrange Farandole, 156
L'eventail de Jeanne, 144
L'Heure Espagnole, 133
L'Hirifile, 227
L'Histoire du Soldat, 14, 183–184, 265
L'Homme et les Tantimes, 231
L'il Abner, 50–51, 72
L'Illusion Comique, 30
L'Inondazione del Tevere, 32
L'Invitation au Voyage, 32
L'Isola del tesoro, 37
L'Italiana in Algeri, 182, 263–264
L'Oiseau Bleu, 66
L'Oiseau de Feu, 104, 232
L'Ormindo, 148
L'Uomo e il fucile, 192
La Baiser de la Fee, 29
La Barbe Bleue, 152
La Bella Lauretta, 158

La Belle au bois dormant, 66, 140
La Belle et la Bête, 30
La Belle Hélène, 228
La Bohème, 60, 82–83, 101, 109–110, 147–148, 167, 182, 184, 193, 196, 230, 263, 265
La Bottega del Caffe, 166
La Boutique Fantasque, 69
La Cage Aux Folles, 6–7, 93–94, 167–168
La Calandria, xxvii, 102, 188
La Cambiale di Matrimonio, 130
La Celestina, 214
La Cena del Rey Baltazar, 166
La Cenerentola, 91, 170, 193, 207, 243, 263–264
La Chasse aux Folles, 83
La Clemenza di Tito, 81
La Cucaracha, 127
La Dafne, 152
La Dama Duenda, 85
La Dama Luende, 231
La Dama Spagnola e il Cavaliere Romano, 64
La Damnée, 37
La Difesa della, 7
La Donna del Lago, 149
La Donna Sullo Scudo, 85
La Dryade, 66
La Fanciulla del West, 145
La Farce des Encore, 151
La Favorita, 148
La Femme a Barb, 37
La Fille Mal Gardée, 153, 228
La Finta Pazzi, xxviii, 244–245
La Flora, 187
La Fontaine de Jouvence, 38
La Fontana di Trevi, 32
La Forza del Destino, 177
La Garde malade, 102
La Gazza Ladra, 213
La Gioconda, 170
La Gloria d'Amore, 156
La Grande-Duchesse de Gérolstein, 55
La Guerre de Troie n'aura pas lieu, 66
La Guerre involontaire, 37
La Java, 83
La Leç d'Amour dans un Parc, 83

La Légende de Joseph, 17
La Lupa, 263
La Machine Infernale, 30
La Malade imaginaire, 245
La Marche à L'étoile, 82
La Martyre de St. Sebastien, 66
La Mise en scene du drame wagnerien, 10
La Morte di Semiramide, 158
La Nama Sabella, 212
La Nave, 26
La Nipote Sabella, 212
La Nourvelle Eve Cabaret Revue, 83
La Nuit est une Sorciére, 66
La Nuit, 30
La Partenope, 157
La Pelligrina, 39
La Perichole, 23, 43
La Planète Fémina, 82
La Plume de Ma Tante, 81, 83
La Poule Noire, 83
La Princesse Lointaine, 83
La Profanateur, 102
La proprieta'non e' piu' un furto, 192
La Puta Vida, 165
La Quincaillère de Chicago, 83
La Reine Margot, 30
La Reine Morte, 101
La Rénè Fiomet, 8
La Revue de Saint Cyr, 82
La Ronde, 91
La Rondine, 99, 247
La Serva Padrona, 97, 209
La Signora senza Camelie, 192
La Sonnambula, 67, 232
La Sonnamnbula, 265
La Sorpresa, 158
La Strada, 148
La Sylphide, 66, 182
La Terra Trema, 264
La Tragedie de Salome, 227
La Traviata, 54, 82–83, 88, 102, 115,
    169–170, 177, 182–183, 196, 223,
    233, 243, 250, 258, 263–264
La Traviate, 113
La Troisieme femme, 37
La Valse, 29, 69
La vestale, 250

La Victoire de L'Amour, 66
La Vide Breve, 247
La Vie en Rose, 56
La Vie Parisienne, 62
La Ville, 102
La Voix Humaine, 30, 178
Labyrinth, 64
Lacheln am Fusse der Leiter, 66
Ladies and Gentlemen, 13
Ladies at the Alamo, 143
Ladies Leave, 127
Ladies' Money, 13
Lady and the Clarinet, The, 24, 141
Lady Audley's Secret, 106
Lady Beyond the Moon, 239
Lady from Albuquerque, The, 32
Lady from Colorado, The, 184
Lady from Dubuque, The, 179, 238
Lady from the Sea, 183
Lady in the Dark, 217
Lady Lies, The, 160
Lady of Rohesia, 168
Lady of Shalot, 71
Lady of the Camellias, The, 220, 263
Lady of the House of Sleep, The, 148
Lady Precious Stream, 245
Lady Who Came to Stay, The, 183
Lady Windmere's Fan, 22
Lady With a Lamp, The, 127
Lady's Not for Burning, The, 52, 81,
    130, 159, 177–178
Ladyhouse Blues, 241
Laffing Room Only, 46
Lag Boimer, 12
Lake, The, 160
Lamano, 157
Lancelot of Denmark, 106
Land in der Dammerung, 177
Land is Bright, The, 161, 217
Land of the Living, 183
Land's End, 81, 183
Landara, 132
Landesman, Heidi, **141**
Landscape, 41
Landscape of the Body, The, 153, 242
Lanval, 201
Largo Desolato, 95
Larionov, Michel, **141–142**

Lark, The, 50, 52, 162
Larkin, Peter, **142–143**, 185
Las Hermanas, 101
Last Days, The, 258
Last Days of Pompeii, The, 32, 213
Last Embrace, 109
Last Hour, The, 106
Last Love, The, 105
Last Meeting of the Knights of the White Magnolia, The, 76
Last Mile, The, 240
Last Night of Don Juan, The, 127
Last of the Mobile Hot-Shots, The, 265
Last of the Red Hot Lovers, 48–49, 75, 224
Last Ones, The, 232, 234
Last Rite for Snow White, 253
Last Sacrifice, The, 69
Last Savage, The, 170
Last Summer, 5
Last Summer in Shulimsk, 137
Last Tape and Testament of Richard Nixon, The, 196
Last Vacation, The, 233
Late Christopher Bean, The, 32
Latent Heterosexual, The, 92
Later, 241
Laterna Magika, 40, 232, 234
Latin Quarter Revue, 83
Laughing Lady, The, 126
Laughing Woman, The, 120
Launzi, 126
Laurencin, Marie, **143–144**
Laurette, 143, 264
Lautenschläger, Karl, xxxvi, **144**
Le Amiche, 192
Le Baiser de la Fee, 88, 206
Le Ballet de Galla, 64
Le Bargier de Seville, 97
Le Bourgeois Gentilhomme, 183, 199, 228–229
Le Bureau des Ideed, 142
Le Café de Chinitas, 64
Le Chant du Rossignol, 156
Le Chant du Tzigane, 83
Le Cid, 37, 102
Le Cinesi, 197
Le Cirque, 85

Le Cocu Magnifique, 139
Le Coiffeur-Miracle, 83
Le Coq d'Or, 8–9, 16, 148–149, 237
Le Corsaire, 30, 153
Le Dejeuner sur l'Herbe, 144
Le Dialogue des Carmelites, 254
Le Dieu Bleu, 17
Le Donne Curiose, 133
Le Faiseur, 102
Le Fortune di Rodope e di Damira, 156
Le Grand Macabre, 91
Le Loup, 43
Le Malade Imaginaire, 29, 106
Le Médecine Malgré Lui, 29, 102
Le Memoire de Mahelot, Laurent, et des Autre Décorateurs, xxvii
Le Minaret, 82, 84
Le Nozze di Figaro, xli, 49, 52, 79, 102, 250, 193
Le Nozze di Paride, 157
Le Pas d'Acier, 222
Le Pauvre Matelot, 183
Le Pavillon d'Armide, 29
Le Perichole, 102
Le poème électronique, 66
Le Poete, 56
Le Prezione Ridicole, 127
Le Provencale, 155
Le Roi de Labore, 8
Le Rossignol, 29, 227
Le Sacre du Printemps, 116, 232
Le Secret du Sphinx, 82
Le Seigneur de San Gor, 56
Le Soulier de Satin, 56
Le Tango, 82
Le Tricorne, 189
Le Triomphe de l'Amour, 30, 102
Le Vestale, 247
Le Vie en Rose, 56
Le Ville de la Mare, 37
Leader of the Pack, 255
Leading Lady, The, 184
Leaf People, The, 54
Lean Harvest, 120, 221
Lean On Me, 159
Lear, xli, 97, 148, 176, 193
Learned Ladies, 99
Leaves Are Fading, The, 149, 242, 265

Leda Had a Little Swan, 202–203
Lee, Eugene, **144–147**
Lee, Ming Cho, xxxix, 25, 77, 98, 112, 129, 131, 140, **147–151**, 154, 167, 230
Legend of Lovers, 78–79
Legend of Sarah, 74
Legend of Sleepy Hollow, The, 162
Legend of Tsar Saltan, The, 152
Legend, 136, 153
Legs Diamond, 93, 135
Leinen aus Ireland, 231
Lend Me a Tenor, 255
Lenin's Dowry, 32
Lenny, 93–94, 252–253
Leonard Bernstein's Theater Songs, 92
Leonce and Lena (and Lenz), 45, 242, 243
Leonce und Lena, 177
Les Ballets de Pakistan, 66
Les Biches, 144
Les Blancs, 77, 108, 110, 143
Les Cent Vierges, 83
Les Contes d'Hoffmann, 102
Les Deux Tisserands, 29
Les Éléments, 56
Les Elves, 30
Les Enfants et les sortilèges, 66
Les Fâcheux, 245
Les Femmes de bonne humeur, 17
Les Femmes Savantes, 102
Les Fêtes Chinoises, 38
Les Filles d'Eve, 83
Les Folle de Chaillot, 30
Les Forains, 31
Les Fourains, 30
Les Fourberies de Scapin, 30
Les Heures sont Belles, 83
Les Indes Galantes, 43
Les Joies du Capitol, 83
Les Liens, 66
Les Mamelles de Tirésias, 83
Les Miserables, xxxix, 115–116, 176
Les Monstres Sacrés, 30
Les Mouches, 66
Les Muets, 37
Les Muses, 30
Les Noces, 20, 224, 265

Les Noces de Psyche, 29
Les Orientales, 140
Les Paravents, 206
Les petits riens, 106
Les Rates, 221
Les Serments Indis, 67
Les Sirenes, 22
Les Soldat, 138
Les Songes, 69
Les Sylphide, 17
Les Sylphides, 66, 102
Les Travaux de Hercule, 83
Les Troyennes, 101
Les Troyens, 233
Les Vendanges de Tempé, 38
Lesson, The, 75, 173, 202, 243
Lesson from Aloes, A, 131
Let Freedom Ring, 105
Let it Ride, 72
Let Me Hear You Smile, 143, 203
Let the Artists Die, 129
Let's Make an Opera, 32
Letter for Queen Victoria, A, 258–259
Letter from Prison: In the Belly of the Beast, 146
Leucippe e Teonoe, 157
Levitation, 60
Liar, The, 171, 184
Lido and Tabarin Theatre Revues, 83
Lido Theatre Revue, 83
Lie, The, 43
Lie of The Mind, A, 165
Life, The, 204
Life Among the Lowly, 145
Life and Adventures of Nicholas Nickleby, The, 115
Life and Death of an American, 19
Life and Times of Joseph Stalin, The, 258
Life and Times of Sigmund Freud, The, 178, 258
Life Begins at 8:40, 217
Life Class, 130
Life in the Sun, A, 169
Life in the Theatre, A, 23, 25
Life is a Dream, 195
Life of Edward II, 176–177
Life of the Party, The, 78

Life With Mother, 184
Light Fantastic, A, 148
Light of Asia, 39
Lighthouse, The, 59
Lighting Dimensions, 88
Likely Tale, A, 171
Lilac Domino, The, 228
Lilian, 75
Liliom, 32, 139, 143, 174, 221–222
Lillian, 109
Lily, 178
Limited Mail, The, 11
Lindberg, 83
Line of Least Existence, A, 145
Lines of Vision, 95
Linnebach, Adolf, xxxvi, **151**
Liola, 192
Lion in Winter, The, 125, 174, 202
Lion Tamer, The, 32
Lionel and Clarissa, 257
Lisbo Traviata, The, 109
Lissim, Simon, **151–152**
Listen, Professor!, 17, 20
Listen to the Mockingbird, 132
Lithuania, 202
Little Bit of Broadway, A, 82
Little Black Book, The, 225
Little Black Sheep, 6, 167
Little Clay Cart, The, 32–33, 72
Little Dog Laughed, The, 161
Little Eyolf, 127, 160, 242
Little Family Business, A, 6, 179
Little Foxes, The, 19–20, 32–33, 136,
    152, 232, 265
Little Gloria . . . Happy At Last, 261
Little Hump-backed Horse, The, 140
Little Hut, The, 81, 254
Little Johnny Jones, 24, 200
Little Mahagonny, The, 176
Little Malcolm and His Struggle Against
    the Eunuchs, 152
Little Me, 200
Little Moon of Alban, 162
Little Murders, 5, 93, 148
Little Night Music, A, 14–15, 136–137,
    175, 190
Little Ol' Boy, 105
Little Prince and the Aviator, 146

Little Rascals, The, 146, 165
Little Sheba, 202
Little Shepherd, The, 126
Little Shop of Horrors, The, 115
Littlest Revue, The, 50
Live Wire, The, 184
Livin' Dolls, 24
Livin' the Life, 50, 72
Living Corpse, The, 32
Living Mask, The, 126
Living Newspaper, The, 20, 87
Livre de Splendeurs (Part 1), 95
Liza, 93
Liza with a Z, 200–201
Llamado, 265
Loco, 81, 183
Lohengrin, 10, 66, 81–82, 114, 132,
    138, 149–150, 198, 216, 254
Lolita, My Love, 148
London Docks, 107
London Symphony, 83
Lone Canoe, 23
Lonely Night, 5
Lonesome Train and Hard Travelin', 252
Long Day's Journey Into Night, 23, 75–
    77, 108–109, 135, 152, 171, 173, 175,
    178–179, 230, 242–243
Long Days, The, 78
Long Dream, The, 173
Long Ships, The, 89
Long Way from Home, A, 132
Look at Lightning, A, 147
Look Away, 75, 108
Look Back In Anger, 20, 171, 192, 213
Look Homeward, Angel, 25, 162, 171
Look Ma, I'm Dancin', 46, 223
Look to the Lillies, 163, 203
Loot, 24–25, 53, 179
Loquasto, Santo, 45, **152–154**, 185
Lord Blesses the Bishop, The, 240
Lord Byron, 167, 265
Lord Pengo, 18, 208, 224
Lords' Masque, 125
Lorelei, 51, 53, 221
Lorenzaccio, 102
Los Caprichos, 49
Losing Time, 76
Loss of Roses, A, 13, 18, 87

Lost Fairy Tale, The, 233
Lost in the Stars, 123, 224–225
Lost Leader, The, 168
Lost Silk Hat, The, 106, 107
Loud Speaker, 105
Louder, Please, 240
Louise, 82, 247
Louisiana Purchase, 188
Love Among the Ruins, 13
Love and Intrigue, 45
Love for Love, 65, 106, 127, 145, 189
Love for Three Oranges, The, 8, 95, 152, 199, 255
Love in a Village, 220
Love in Carnival Colors, 233
Love in E Flat, 184
Love in My Fashion, 240
Love Letters on Blue Paper, 79
Love Life, 13, 18, 47
Love Match, 93, 252
Love Me Little, 171
Love Me, Love My Children, 140, 163
Love Nest, The, 32, 92
Love of Four Colonels, The, 102
Love of Our Neighbor, 221
Love of Three Kings, 247
Love Revisited, 78
Love the Best Enchantment, xxvii
Love Thief, The, 138
Love's Labour's Lost, 11, 60, 91–92, 147, 169, 182, 243
Love's Triumph Through Callipolis, 125
Lovecraft's Follies, 145
Loved One, The, 238
Lovelies and Dowdies, 129
Lovely Ladies, Kind Gentlemen, 224, 260
Lovely Lady, 239
Lovely Me, 81
Lovely Sunday for Creve Coeur, A, 54
Lovely to Look At, 71
Lovers, The, 81, 174
Lovers and Friends, 171
Lovers and Other Strangers, 75, 252
Loves of Anatol, The, 241
Loves of Don Perlimplin, The, 266
Lower Depths, The, xxxv, 45, 78, 91, 153, 214, 230, 240–241

Lucia di Lammermoor, 148, 174, 182, 263, 264
Lucky One, The, 221
Lucky Sam McCarver, 160
Lucky Spot, The, 25, 159
Lucrece, 127
Lucretia Borgia, 213
Lucrezia, 216
Lullaby, 74
Lulu, 23, 54, 66, 79, 91, 114, 165, 176–177, 252
Luminalia, 125
Lunch Hour, 225, 242
Lunching, 131
Lunchtime Follies, 46
Luogo   Bersaglio (Place   Target), 95
Lute Song, 127
Luther, 166
Luv, 5, 152, 208, 224
Luzzati, Emanuele, **154**, 193
Lydie Breeze, 135
Lysistrata, 5, 11, 26, 81, 93, 101, 106, 135, 176, 178, 199, 228–229, 252

M. le Trouhadec, 106
Ma Mère l'Oye, 83
MacBeth, 5, 10, 16, 34, 39, 41–42, 45, 53, 55–56, 58–59, 65, 77, 87, 108, 114, 126, 132, 139, 145, 147, 152, 166–167, 171, 173, 177–178, 182, 202–203, 207–209, 228, 233, 235, 242–243, 245, 247, 250, 252, 266
Machiavelli, 183
Machinal, 127
Machine Wreckers, The, 106
Mack and Mabel, 252, 265–266
Mackeral Skies, 32
Macook's Corner, 169
Macrunes Guevarra, 241
Mad Man A Mad Giant A Mad Dog A Mad Urge A Mad Face, A, 258
Mad Tristan, 64
Mad World, A, 131, 179
Madam, 184
Madam Will You Walk, 127
Madama Butterfly, 167, 184
Madame Adare, 95
Madame Aphrodite, 264

Madame Bovary, 221
Madame Butterfly, 66, 81, 88, 147, 148, 149, 150, 174, 191, 196, 216, 265
Madame Chrysantheme, 209
Madame Curie, 217
Madame Mouse, 79
Madame Pepita, 106
Madame Pompadour, 228
Madame Sans-Gens, 37
Madeleine Bastille, 260
Mademoiselle Bourrat, 32
Mademoiselle Colombe, 13, 171
Madman and the Nun, The, 129
Madras House, The, 32
Madwoman of Central Park West, The, 6
Madwoman of Chaillot, The, 11, 31, 79, 174, 195, 241
Magdalena, 20, 218
Maggie, 47
Maggie Flynn, 73, 174
Magic, 87
Magic Circus, The, 233
Magic Flute, The, 34, 41, 44, 54, 71, 114, 116, 132–134, 148, 167, 170–171, 177, 198, 206, 231, 238
Magic of Light, The, 208
Magic Show, The, 178, 180
Magical City, The, 126, 221
Magistrate, The, 171, 252
Magnificent Cuckold, The, 194
Magnificent Yankee, The, 239
Magnolia Street, 139
Mahagonny, 233, 252
Mahalia, 253
Mahelot, Laurent, xxvii, **155**
Maid of Milan, The, 241
Maid of Orleans, The, 166
Maid of the Oaks, The, 67
Maiden of Pskov, The, 104
Maiden Voyage, 50, 162
Mail, 11, 179
Mais Oui, 174
Maitlands, The, 139
Major Barbara, 108, 130, 174, 184, 252
Major Molineux, 11
Majority of One, A, 171, 184
Makbeth, 204–205
Make Like a Dog, 93

Make Way for Lucia, 18
Makropoulos Affair, The, 232–233
Makropoulos Secret, The, 107, 173, 239
Makropoulos Case, The, 36
Malacon, 240
Malcolm, 135, 174
Male Animal, The, 32
Malheurs d'Orphée, 66
Mame, 73, 174–175, 178
Mam'zelle Angot, 69
Man, The, 37, 162
Man and Superman, 63, 89–90, 120, 178, 243, 261
Man and the Masses, 221
Man and the Universe, 174
Man Around the House, A, 178
Man Equals Man, 176–177
Man for All Seasons, A, 145, 169, 171–172
Man from Elsewhere, The, 233
Man in a Cloak, The, 168
Man in the Dog Suit, The, 184
Man in the Glass Booth, The, 93
Man in the Iron Mask, The, 121
Man in the Raincoat, The, 258–259
Man of Destiny, The, 201
Man of La Mancha, 20–21
Man of Mode, The, 91
Man on the Moon, 93
Man Who Ate the Popomack, The, 106–107
Man Who Came To Dinner, The, 183
Man Who Married a Dumb Wife, The, 126–127, 163, 201
Man Who Never Died, The, 239
Man Who Pays the Piper, The, 120
Man Who Was Thursday, The, 195, 249
Man with a Load of Mischief, The, 112
Man with Blonde Hair, The, 20
Man with Portfolio, 139
Man with Red Hair, The, 139
Man with the Flower in His Mouth, The, 106
Man with the Gun, The, 45
Man's a Man, A, 265
Man's Estate, 239
Man's Man, A, 239
Mandragola, 209

Mandrake, The, 63
Manfred, 9, 111
Manhattan Mary, 83
Manon, 62–63, 82–83, 101
Manon Lescaut, 167, 232, 250
Map of the World, A, 109
Marat/Sade, 52–53, 75, 123
Marathon '33, 143, 173
Maratondi danza, 250
Marching Song, 19–20, 178
Marco Millions, 106–107, 221–222
Marco Polo, 203
Marco Polo Sings a Solo, 6
Marcus in the High Grass, 92
Mardi Gras!, 48, 124, 178
Margin for Error, 183
Marguerite et Armand, 22
Maria, 66
Maria Baskirtscheff, 62
Maria Golovin, 81, 238
Maria Malibran, 133
Maria Stuarda, 148, 154
Maria Stuart, 61, 228, 231
Mariana Pineda, 64, 66
Marie Antoinette, 3–4
Marie Tudor, 102
Mariners, 160
Marines, 66
Marinka, 20
Mario e il mago, 250
Marionnette, The, 58
Marouf, 22, 25
Marquise, The, 160
Marriage á la Mode, 106, 120
Marriage Dance, The, 141
Marriage Go Round, The, 184
Marriage, The, 106, 199
Marriage of Figaro, The, 53, 55, 104, 133, 148, 170, 177, 182, 227, 243, 245
Marrying of Ann Leete, The, 91
Marta L'Amour dei Trere, 82
Martha, 49, 81–82, 184, 223
Martin, Jean-Baptiste, **155**
Martine, 127
Martinique, 221
Martyrdom of Peter Ohey, The, 195

Marvellous History of St. Bernard, The, 220
Mary Barnes, 131
Mary C. Brown and the Hollywood Sign, 252
Mary Goes To See, 120
Mary, Mary, 5, 47, 49, 223
Mary of Scotland, 127
Mary Poppins, 255
Mary Rose, 32, 87
Mary Stuart, 11, 50, 53, 60–61, 97, 149, 169, 173, 184, 195
Marysa, 232
Mask, The, xxxvi, 58
Mask and the Face, The, 106, 221
Maske in Blau, 83
Masked Ball, The, 62, 184
Masque of Blackness, The, xxv, 125
Masque of Kings, The, 221
Masque of Love, The, 56–57
Masque of Queens, The, 125
Masque of Venice, The, 160
Masquerade, The, 104
Mass, 225
Masses and Men, 106, 112
Master Builder, The, 13, 50, 53, 79, 138, 192, 257
Master Harold and the Boys, 63
Mata Hari, 162
Matchmaker, The, 169, 265
Mating Dance, The, 79, 136
Matisse, Henri-Émile-Benoît, **155–156**
Matrimony Pfd., 183
Matter of Gravity, A, 75, 108
Maulwerke, 97
Mauna Vanna, 82
Mauro Family, The, xxix, **156–158**
May I Have This Dance?, 77
May Time, 209
Maya, 32, 72, 107
Maybe I'm Doing It All Wrong, 141
Maybe Tuesday, 210
Mayerling, 101, 115
Mayor of Stilmond, The, 232
Mayrhauser, Jennifer von, **158–159**
Mazeltov, 43
Me and Juliet, 162, 218
Me and Molly, 132, 223

Measure for Measure, 5, 41, 78–79, 92, 98, 106, 108, 148, 153, 166, 169, 179, 192, 206–207, 238, 253, 262
Mecure, 189
Medal of Honor Rag, The, 76, 131
Medea, 46, 54, 56, 74, 75, 119, 167, 202, 212
Medium, The, 53, 106, 207, 223
Medusa, 24
Meet Me in St. Louis, 217, 219
Meet the Prince, 160
Mefistofele, 167
Megilla of Itzik Manger, The, 79
Meine Szene, 185
Member of the Wedding, The, 153
Memo, 5, 11
Memoire, 155
Memoirs of the Forties, 22
Memorandum, The, 5
Memory of Two Mondays, A, 13, 241
Memphis Bound, 18, 123
Men Working, 105
Men About the House, 171
Men in White, 105
Men of Distinction, 89
Men Should Weep, 25
Men to the Sea, 20
Men We Marry, The, 184
Menace, 239
Menschen Stoib, 12
Mephisto-Valse, 37
Mephistopheles, 8
Merchant, The, 183
Merchant of Venice, The, 5, 39, 59, 91, 103, 107, 139, 147, 161, 168–169, 171, 174, 202, 207, 209, 228–229, 231, 238, 240
Merchant of Yonkers, The, 13
Merlin, 6, 175, 253
Merrily We Roll Along, 115, 117, 146, 160
Merry Death, The, 126
Merry Widow, The, 20, 47–48, 54, 79, 124, 127, 174, 184, 202, 209, 228–229, 243
Merry Wives of Windsor, The, 11, 19, 60, 79, 91, 106, 108, 130, 139, 152, 169, 171, 173, 245, 247

Merrymount, 160
Mert and Phil, 6, 152
Merton of the Movies, 23, 54
Mes Amours, 83
Mesmer, 139
Message for Margaret, 184
Messel, Oliver, xxxix, **159–160**
Metamorphosis, 201
Methusalem, 133
Metropolis, 115, 138
Mexican Hayride, 123
Miami, 179
Michel Auclair, 127
Mid-Summer, 20
Middle Age Crazy, 6
Middle Ages, The, 23, 24
Middle of the Night, 132, 162, 171
Midgie Purvis, 74
Midnight Cowboy, 210
Midsummer Madness, 220
Midsummer Night's Dream, A, 5, 11, 20, 36, 45, 54, 59–60, 73, 79, 91, 113, 123, 131, 135, 141, 147, 152, 169, 171, 173–174, 176–178, 182, 191, 202, 206, 228, 231, 242–243, 245, 257
Midsummer Night's Sex Comedy, A, 153
Mielziner, Jo, xxxix, 12, 65, 75, 124, 140, 149–151, **160–164**, 184, 240
Mighty Gents, The, 153
Mignon, 263–264
Mikado, The, 59, 79, 184, 202
Mike Todd's Peepshow, 20, 218
Militello, Anne E., **164–165**
Milk and Honey, 20, 256
Milk Train Doesn't Stop Here Anymore, The, 162–163, 238
Miller, Craig, **165–166**
Millionairess, The, 202
Mind with the Dirty Man, The, 182
Minks, Wilfried, **166–167**
Minna von Barnhelm, 206
Minnie's Boys, 93
Minor Adjustment, A, 93
Minor Miracle, 5, 174, 200
Miracle, A, 201
Miracle, The, 26–27, 33, 228–229, 231
Miracle at Verdun, 221

Miracle in the Gorbals, 41
Miracle of St. Anthony, The, 106, 221
Miracle on 34th Street, 51
Miracle Play, 240
Miracle Worker, The, 76, 124, 173
Miraculous Mandarin, The, 50, 66, 233
Mirandolina, 245
Mireille, 37
Mirror to Mirror, 195
Misalliance, 60, 61, 70, 99, 109, 146, 152
Misanthrope, The, 53, 55, 131, 169, 179, 204, 240
Miser, The, 169, 252
Miss Firecracker Contest, The, 24, 159
Miss Havisham's Fire, 54
Miss Isobel, 142
Miss Julie, 50, 106, 189
Miss Liberty, 47, 49, 171, 223
Miss Lonelyhearts, 162, 264
Miss Margarida's Way, 153
Miss Quis, 183
Miss Saigon, 115, 176
Miss Underground, 13
Miss Universal Happiness, 95
Missa Brevis, 147
Missa Solemnis, 263
Mister Johnson, 72
Mister Pitt, 209
Mister Roberts, 161–162
Mister Universe, 132
Misunderstanding, The, 179
Mitchell, David, 131, **167–168**
Mixed Couples, 225
Mixed Marriage, 188
Mlle. Modiste, 48
Modern Khlestakov, The, 85
Moiseiwitsch, Tanya, **168–170**
Moliere, 137, 221
Molly, 93, 130, 203–204
Mon Mari et toi, 37
Mona Vanna, 247
Monday After a Miracle, 24–25
Mondongo, 167
Mongrel, The, 221
Monique, 173
Monkey, 240
Monologue About Marriage, 137

Monsieur Baucaire, 37
Montezuma, 149
Month in the Country, A, 23, 50, 54, 69, 106, 109, 169, 242
Month of Sundays, A, 131, 162, 175
Montresor, Beni, **170**
Montserrat, 20, 89, 178, 218
Monty Python, Live!, 76
Moon, The, 132
Moon Beseiged, The, 147
Moon for the Misbegotten, A, 54, 75, 93, 108–109, 127–128
Moon in the Yellow River, The, 240
Moon Is Blue, The, 254
Moon Is Down, The, 20
Moon Is a Gong, The, 105
Moon on a Rainbow Shawl, 92
Moon Vine, 17
Moose Murders, 131
Morals, 183
More Stately Mansions, 74, 108–110
Moritat, 177
Morning Star, 20
Morning Sun, 79, 80, 265
Mornings at Seven, 17, 161, 179–180
Moschopoulos, 177
Moses, Thomas, **170–171**
Moses and Aron, 41, 224
Moses' Rock, 168
Most Happy Fella, The, 48, 162, 164, 171–172, 255
Most Immoral Lady, A, 160
Most Important Man, The, 224
Mother, 37
Mother, The, 105, 133, 177
Mother Courage and Her Children, xxxviii, 53, 114–115, 145, 147, 149–150, 152, 172–173, 177, 185, 203–205, 232, 234
Mother Goose, 83
Mother Lover, The, 74
Mother of Us All, The, 178, 225, 265
Mother Was a Bachelor, 209
Mother's Kisses, A, 73
Motley, 112, **171–172**
Motta, Fabrizio Carini, **172**
Mouchoir des Nuages, 133
Moulin Rouge Revue, 83

Mound Builders, The, 22, 159
Mountain Man, The, 126
Mourning Becomes Electra, 14–15, 76,
    93, 108, 125, 127
Mozart and Salieri, 79
Mozartiana, 30
Mr. and Mrs. North, 161
Mr. Big, 183
Mr. Booth, 52
Mr. Broadway, 20
Mr. Gilhooley, 160
Mr. Moneypenny, 127
Mr. Pim Passes By, 221, 231
Mr. President, 5, 162
Mr. Prohack, 139
Mr. Roberts, 252
Mr. Welk and Jersey Jim, 75
Mr. Wonderful, 47, 223
Mrs. Cook's Tour, 160
Mrs. McThing, 18
Mrs. Moonlight, 74–75
Mrs. Murray's Farm, 23
Mrs. O'Brien Entertains, 161
Mrs. Partridge Presents, 160
Mrs. Warren's Profession, 6, 45, 167
Much Ado About Nothing, 5–6, 11–12,
    56–57, 79, 108, 148, 150, 169, 171,
    173, 178, 207, 228–229, 231, 238,
    263
Mud Cacklin' Hen, 153
Mulberry Bush, The, 120, 171
Müller, Traugott, **172–173**
Mummers and Men, 178
Murder Among Friends, 153, 242
Murder at the Howard Johnson's, 76, 178
Murder in the Cathedral, 102, 108, 120–
    121, 173–174
Murder in the Rue Morgue, 209
Murder on the Orient Express, 255
Museum, 242
Music and the Stage Setting, xxxv
Music Box Revue of 1921, 3–4
Music Box Theatre Revue, 82
Music in My Heart, 50
Music in the Air, 81
Music Is, 79
Music Man, The, 20–21, 166, 188
Music! Music!, 6

Musical Chairs, 48, 139
Musical Comedy Murders of 1940, The,
    159
Musser, Tharon, **173–175**, 201
Mustapha, 255
My Daughter, 252
My Dear Children, 183
My Dear Public, 17
My Dinner With Andre, 167
My Fair Lady, 22, 48, 70, 87–88, 182,
    193–194, 223, 226, 241
My Fiddle's Got Three Strings, 78
My Heart's in the Highlands, 79
My Kinsman, 11
My Life My Death, 95
My Lord, 20
My Masters, 131, 179
My Mother, My Father and Me, 20
My Name is Nobody, 193
My One and Only, 255
My Sister Eileen, 183
My Sweet Charlie, 162
My Three Angels, 13, 18, 209
Mystery Square, 239
Mystic, 74
Mystic, The, 82
Mystic Connecticut, 108
Mystic Pizza, 159
Myth of a Voyage, 148, 151

Nabucco, 70, 185, 232–233
Nail, 202
Naked, 106, 139
Naked Hamlet, 167
Napier, John, xl, **176**
Napoleon, 190, 239
Narbale, 158
Narcisse, 17
Narrow Road to the Deep North, 152,
    203
Nascosta sulle scale, 245
Nash at Noon, 6
Nat Turner, 178
Natalya Petrovna, 20
Nathan the Wise, 92, 240
Nathan Weinstein, 74, 108
National Health, The, 76, 79
Native Ground, 19, 87

Native Son, 207–208
Natural Affection, 224
Natural Look, The, 93
Nature's Way, 184
Naughty Marietta, 225, 265
Neal Maquade, 168
Ned McCobb's Daughter, 32
Neher, Caspar, xxxvii, xxxviii, **176–178**
Nella citta l'inferno, 212
Nelson, Richard, 120, **178–180**
Nelson Touch, The, 120
Neptune's Triumph, 125
Nerd, The, 24
Nerves, 160
Nervous Set, The, 5
Network, 6
Never Come Back, 120
Never Live Over a Pretzel Factory, 20
Never Love a Stranger, 132
Never No More, 160
Never Too Late, 72, 136
New Cranks, 255
New Faces of 1936, 87
New Faces of 1956, 47, 142
New Folies Bergère, 259
New Girl in Town, 238
New Life, A, 20
New Moon, The, 79, 183, 222
New Show, The, 146
New Theatres For Old, 105
New York Confidential, 132
Newsweek 50th Anniversary, 146
Next of Kin, 91
Next Time I'll Sing For You, 265
Nichevo, 106
Nicholas Nickleby, 116, 176
Nie wieder, 185
Nifties of 1923, 3
Niggerlovers, The, 224
Night and Day, 243
Night and the Laughter, The, 83
Night Before Christmas, The, 13
Night Chanter, The, 52
Night Circus, The, 264
Night in the House, 32
Night In Venice, A, 48, 79
Night Journey, 181
'Night Mother, 141

Night Music, 105
Night of 100 Stars, 51, 200–201
Night of 100 Stars II, 51
Night of 100 Stars III, 51
Night of the Auk, 20, 21
Night of the Iguana, 70, 87, 159, 179, 208, 223, 225–226
Night of the Tribades, The, 108
Night of Venice 1928, 85
Night Over Taos, 127
Night Rehearsal, 234
Night Shadow, 67
Night They Raided Minsky's, The, 73
Night Thoreau Spent in Jail, The, 148
Night Watch, 174
Night Wings, 148
Nightingale, The, 225
Nigorie, 16
Nikolais, Alwin, **180–181**
Nimbus, 223
Nina, 81
Nine Pine Street, 127
1959 Pink Thunderbird, 125
Ninety Sail, 120
Nirvana, 105
Nit-Gedajget, 199
Nivinski, Ignati, xxxvii, **181**
Nju, 26, 247
No Exit, 133, 223
No Hard Feelings, 6
No Time for Comedy, 23, 161
No Time for Sergeants, 47, 142–143
No Trifling With Love, 56–57
No Way to Treat a Lady, 5
No, No, Nanette, 79, 93, 188
Noah, 168, 171, 240
Nobilissima Visione, 237
Noble Mirror of Art, The, 99
Nobody Loves an Albatross, 11, 136
Nobody's Earnest, 53
Noctambules, 100
Nocturne, 37
Noguchi, Isamu, xxxix, **181**
None But the Lonely Hearts, 105
Norma, 81, 113, 213, 243
Normal Heart, The, 146
Norman Conquests, The, 200
Norman, Is That You?, 73, 136, 204

Not to Worry, 22
Not While I'm Eating, 178
Nota Kopek and Suddenly a Rouble, 138
Notes of a Madman, 137
Nourish the Beast, 76
Now, 199
Now and Then, 112
Nowhere to Go But Up, 143, 173
Nude with Violin, 47, 223
Nursery Rhymes, 97
Nutcracker Ballet, 182
Nutcracker, The, 14–15, 29, 53, 191,
    206, 225, 238, 242

O'Hearn, Robert, **182–183**
O Say Can You See!, 92
O.W., 53
Oberon, 111, 231
Oberon, the Fairy Prince, 125
Object of Virtue, An, 120
Obsession, 3
Occupations, 91
Ocean's Motion, 153
Octandre, 66
Octette Bridge Club, The, 24, 203
Odd Couple, The, 167, 175, 210, 224,
    226
Odds Against Tomorrow, 132
Ode to Liberty, 240
Odyssey, 20
Oedipe-Roi, 37
Oedipus, 20, 79, 102, 149, 262
Oedipus at Colonnus, 169
Oedipus in Athens, 104
Oedipus Rex, 16, 116, 127, 133, 169,
    186, 189, 201, 228–229
Oedipus Tyrannus, 106, 212
Oenslager, Donald, xxxix, 12, 58, 82,
    143, **183–185**, 240
Oesterreichische Komodie, 231
Of Love Remembered, 79
Of Mice and Men, 60, 70, 73, 124, 145–
    146, 183–184, 235
Of Thee I Sing, 47, 160, 218
Ofeus and Eurydice, 206
Off to Buffalo, 183
Offandes, 66
Office, The, 135

Oh Captain!, 162
Oh Dad, Poor Dad, Mama's Hung You
    in the Closet and I'm Feelin So Sad,
    72, 230, 264
Oh, Brother!, 179
Oh! Calcutta!, 240–241
Oh, Captain, 256
Oh, Kay!, 178
Oh, Men! Oh Women!, 72
Oh, What a Lovely War!, 41
Ohio, 223
Oil Islands, The, 106
Oklahoma!, 47–49, 79, 136, 210, 223,
    226, 256–257
Old Flag, The, 167
Old Foolishness, The, 183
Old Glory, The, 11, 135–136, 145
Old Ladies, The, 171
Old Love, 161
Old Maid, The, 53
Old Maid and the Thief, The, 133, 147
Old Man and His Family, The, 203
Old Man's Place, The, 252
Old Rascal, The, 239
Old Times, 23, 41, 91–92, 115–116,
    130–131, 145, 152, 174, 250–251
Old World, 153
Older People, 6, 148
Oldsmobile Show, The, 162
Olé, 83
Oliver Cromwell, 249
Oliver Cromwell's Sendung, 177
Oliver, Oliver, 179
Olympia, 231
Olympics, 148
Omai, 67
On a Clear Day You Can See Forever,
    22, 87, 224, 260
On an Open Roof, 136, 208
On Baile's Strand, 106
On Borrowed Time, 161
On Call, 239
On Cherche un Roi, 83
On Golden Pond, 165
On Stage!, 51, 223
On the Art of the Theatre, xxxvi, 57
On the High Road, 32
On the Lock In, 76

On the Razzle, 243–244
On the Rocks, 117
On The Swing Shift, 230
On the Town, xxxix, 46, 49–51, 174, 222, 226
On the Twentieth Century, 136, 252–253
On the Verge, 70
On Whitman Avenue, 183
On Your Toes, 47, 161, 217–218, 223
Once for the Asking, 87
Once in a Lifetime, 52–53, 76
Once More Frank, 153
Once There Was a Russian, 255
Once Upon a Mattress, 72, 173
Once Upon a Tailor, 13
Once Upon a Time, 153
Ondine, 52, 142, 169, 207, 237
One Act Plays, 201
One by One, 136, 184
One Eye Closed, 79
One-Ended Rope, 232
One Flew Over the Cuckoo's Nest, 11
One For the Money, 188
110 in the Shade, 172, 224
One Mo' Time, 76
One More River, 107, 124
One Night Stand, 253, 265
One Over the Eight, 255
One Shoe Off, 18
One Stage!, 50
One Third of a Nation, 19–20
1066 and All That, 106
One Touch of Venus, 20–21, 79, 165
One Trick Pony, 167
O'Neill Plays, The, 109
Only Game in Town, The, 5, 93, 124
Only In America, 143, 173
Only Way, The, 59
Only You, 25
Onward, Victoria, 6, 179
Open Admissions, 131, 175
Open Door, The, 32
Open Window, 131
Opera Comique, 75
Opera d'aran, 66
Operation Sidewinder, 135–136
Operetta, 232
Optimistic Tragedy, An, 233

Oratorio, 42
Orchards, 60
Orchestra, The, 108
Oresteia, The, 79, 106–107, 114–115, 206, 228, 234
Orfeo, 53, 177, 184, 197, 216
Orgasmo Adulto Escapes from the Zoo, 153, 242
Orghast, 145–146
Orlando Furioso, 206
Orphan, The, 6, 152, 175
Orphans, 77
Orphée aux enfers, 66, 228
Orpheus, 88, 127, 133, 177, 181
Orpheus and Eurydice, 9, 66, 67, 102, 184, 206
Orpheus Descending, 13, 18, 70, 87, 213
Orpheus in the Underworld, 66, 132
Osmane, 158
Otello, 113, 182–183, 215–216, 233–234, 263
Othello, 5, 11, 52, 70, 76, 79–80, 103, 108, 127, 147–148, 169, 171–172, 177, 182, 191, 207, 209, 228–229, 238, 263
Other Dances, 153
Other One, The, 240
Other Places, 24
Other Side of Midnight, The, 218
Other Voices, Other Rooms, 53
Otherwise Engaged, 108
Otto, Teo, xxxvii-xxxviii, **185**
Ou sont les neiges d'antan, 129
Our Daily Bread, 69
Our Man in Havana, 243
Our Militants, 233
Our Street, 105
Our Town, 54, 77, 109, 148, 150, 192–193, 242, 264
Out of Dust, 127
Out of Our Father's House, 23, 25
Out of the Sea, 188
Out of the Whirlwind, 120
Out of This World, 81, 87
Out West It's Different, 183
Outcry, 163
Outside Looking In, 127, 239
Over Here!, 203–204

Overtones, 221
Overture, 183, 258
Overture for Ka Mountain, 259
Overture, The Grand Tour, 53
Owl and the Pussycat, The, 136, 162, 210

P.S. I Love You, 5, 92
Pacific Overtures, xxxix, 14–15, 136–137, 175, 201
Page, The, 57
Page Pygmalion, 240
Pagliacci, 20, 102, 263
Pain(t), 95
Paint Your Wagon, 47, 171, 209, 223
Painted Veil, The, 120
Painting Churches, 141
Pair of Spectacles, A, 106
Paisley Convertible, The, 51, 162
Pajama Game, The, 47, 182
Pal Joey, 20, 47–48, 161, 164, 223, 226, 256–257
Palestrina, 176
Pallace of Augures, 125
Palladio, Andrea, xxii, xxv, 42, 126, **186**, 213, 251
Palladium Theater Revue, 82–83
PAMTGG, 163, 218
Panama Hattie, 79
Pandering to the Masses: A Misrepresentation, 95
Panic, 161
Pantagleize, 79, 152, 202, 240, 241
Pantaloon, 134
Pantomime, 77
Papa, 26
Papp, 135
Parade of Stars Playing the Palace, 51
Parade, 116, 189, 217, 221
Paradise, 239
Paradise Island, 47, 124
Paradise Lost, 13, 15, 242
Parenti terribles, 250
Parfums, 83
Parigi, Alfonso, xxiv-xxv, 39, 99, 126, **186–187**
Parigi, Giulio, **187**
Paris, 178

Paris '90, 184
Paris and Oenone, 201
Paris Bound, 127
Paris Is Out, 136
Parisian Nights, 209
Parisiana, 233
Park Avenue, 81, 183
Park Your Car in Harvard Yard, 24, 195–196
Parnell of Avondale, 168
Parsifal, 132, 177, 182, 247, 254
Part of a Lifetime, 222
Partage de Midi, 234
Particle Theory, 95
Partridge in a Pear Tree, A, 200
Parzival, 258
Pas d'Acier, 221
Pas de Deux, 153
Pasiphae, 102
Passacaglia, 45
Passage du Malin, 37
Passenger to Bali, A, 87
Passing Day, The, 168–169
Passing Present, The, 127
Passion, 24, 233
Passion Flower, The, 106
Passion of Antigona Perez, The, 76
Passion of Jonathan Wade, The, 11–12
Passion of Josef D., The, 11
Passion Play, The, 28
Passion, Poison, and Putrefaction, 178
Passionate Lovers, The, 125
Pastorale, 50–51, 141
Patience, 127
Patriarch, The, 183
Patriot, The, 26, 168
Patriot For Me, A, 224, 244, 260
Patriots, The, 20
Paul Bunyan, 130
Paul et Virginie, 144
Paul I, 139
Pavillon d'Armide, 8
Peace On Earth, 240
Pearl Fishers, The, 147, 175, 182
Peccadillo, 179
Peer Gynt, 5, 11–12, 20, 45, 52–53, 98, 107, 115, 145, 148, 150, 153, 166, 173, 178, 184, 189, 195, 221, 231

Peg, 136
Pelleas and Melisande, 83, 97, 167, 188, 193, 215, 232, 247
Pène du Bois, Raoul, **187–188**
Penguin Touquet, 95, 141
Penn & Teller, 25
Penny Arcade, 239
Penny for a Song, A, 63
Penny Wars, The, 108
People At Sea, 120
People Is the Thing That the World Is Fullest Of, 11, 48
Per un Don Chisciotte, 154
Perfect Marriage, The, 222
Perfect Party, The, 109
Perfect Pitch, 225
Perfect Setup, The, 82
Pericles, 53, 65, 91, 107, 152
Periferie, 231, 245
Period of Adjustment, 162, 264
Periphery, 106
Persée, 38
Persians, The, 159, 169, 201
Personals, 179
Peruzzi, Baldassare, **188**, 216
Pervaja Konnaja, 199
Pete Roleum and His Cousins, 20
Peter Allen—Up In One, 201
Peter and the Wolf, 17, 87
Peter Grimes, 91, 168–169, 177, 243
Peter Ibbetson, 147, 188
Peter Pan, 32, 47, 115, 142–143, 171
Peters, Charles Rollo, III, **188–189**
Petrouchka, 8–9, 29, 69, 84, 224, 227
Petticoat, 120
Petulia, 255
Pfarr Pedr, 177
Phaedra, 145, 181, 252
Phaedra Brittanica, 169
Phantasmagoria, 21
Phantom of the Opera, 36
Phèdre, 83, 233, 249
Phi-phi, 83
Philadelphia, Here I Come!, 22
Philadelphia Story, The, 3, 54, 127
Philanderer, The, 117
Philemon et Baucis, 29
Philip the King, 201

Phillip II, 199
Philodoxes, 5
Phoenix '55, 50, 52, 79
Photo Finish, 82
Photograph, A, 167
Photographer, The, 153
Physicists, The, 41
Picasso, Pablo, xxxix, 85, **189**
Piccadilly Hayride, 83
Pickwick, 92
Picnic, 24, 162, 164
Pictures at an Exhibition, 13
Pictures in the Hallway, 79
Pictures of Goya, 260
Pie in the Sky, 183
Pieces of Eight, 255
Piege pour un Homme Seul, 83
Pierre Patelin, 221
Pierrot Lunaire, 127
Pilbrow, Richard, **189–190**
Pilgrim of Love, The, 112
Pilgrimage, The, 127
Pilgrims, 168
Pillar of Fire, 161
Pillars of Society, The, 188
Pillars of the Community, 98
Pin to See the Peepshow, A, 87
Pink Jungle, The, 184
Pinocchio, 48
Pinwheel, 183–184
Pioniere in Ingolstadt, 177
Pipe Dream, 50, 52, 162
Pippin, 93–94, 255, 265–267
Pique Dame, 182
Pirate, The, 256
Pirates of Penzance, The, 239, 242
Pitkin, William, **190–191**
Place of Our Own, A, 18
Place Without Doors, A, 53
Places in the Heart, 210
Plague, The, 195
Plain and Fancy, 47, 188
Plaisir de France, 83
Plaisirs de Paris, 259
Planché, James Robinson, xxxi, xxxii, 34, **191**
Plaster Bambino, The, 252
Platonov, 45

Play, 59
Play by Aleksandr Solzhenitsyn, A, 124
Play of Daniel, The, 52
Play of Herod, The, 52
Play of Robin and Marian, The, 134
Playbill, 243
Play's the Thing, The, 153
Playboy of the Western World, The, 53,
    106, 168, 252
Player Queen, The, 106
Playroom, The, 5, 162
Plaza Suite, 152, 224, 265
Pleasure Garden, The, 106
Pleasure of His Company, The, 178,
    184, 255
Pleasure Reconciled to Virtue, 125
Pleasures and Palaces, 200, 260
Pleasures of the Enchanted Island, The,
    xxviii, 250
Plenty, 90, 109, 131, 149
Plots and Playwrights, 183
Plough and the Stars, The, 105, 168, 203
Plutus, 56
Poelzig, Hans, **191–192**
Poem of Fire, 232
Poema Extaza, 206
Poet and the Rent, 23
Poetics, xx
Point of No Return, 162
Point Valaine, 168
Pointe au Porc-épic, 107
Points on Jazz, 223
Poison Tree, The, 130
Poisoned Kiss, 133
Polidori, Gianni, **192–193**
Pollichino, 55
Polly, 203
Polonaise, 20
Polyekran, 232, 234
Pommes à l'Anglaise, 83
Pompey the Great, 106
Ponder Heart, The, 74
Ponnelle, Jean-Pierre, **193**
Pons, Helene, **193–194**
Poor Bitos, 144, 208, 252
Poor Murderer, 20, 265
Poor Richard, 48, 224
Poor Sailor, The, 133

Poor Thing, 32
Popova, Liubov Sergeevna, **194**
Poppet, The, 148, 265
Poppy, 87
Porcelain Palace, The, 32
Porcelain Year, The, 5, 143
Porgy, 239
Porgy and Bess, 115, 182, 200, 218,
    223, 227, 239–240
Port Said, 142
Portage to San Cristobal of A.H., The,
    55
Portrait in Black, 81, 184
Portrait of a Lady, 72, 183
Portrait of a Queen, 5
Portrait of Jenny, 18
Possibilities, 163
Postcards, 167
Postman Always Rings Twice, The, 161
Potting Shed, The, 266
Pousse-Cafe, 11, 265
Power, 19
Power and the Glory, The, 11–12, 177
Power of Darkness, The, 221
Power Without Glory, 81
Practice of Making Scenes and Machines,
    The, xxiii, 211
Prague Carnival, 233
Prazdnik and Kasrilovka, 199
Precious Sons, 179
Prelude to Exile, 221
Prescott Proposals, The, 184
Present Laughter, 47, 81, 131, 179, 183,
    223, 225
Pretenders, The, 56, 58, 106, 139
Prettybelle, 224
Price, The, 14, 152, 167, 178, 180
Price of Genius, The, 179
Pride and Prejudice, 55, 161
Pride of the Regiment, The, 107
Prima Donna, 79
Prime of Miss Jean Brodie, The, 108,
    163, 189
Prince Charming, 247
Prince Henry's Barriers, 125
Prince Igor, 138, 140
Prince of Grand Street, The, 109, 167
Prince of Homburg, The, 102

Princess Brambilla, 262
Princess Cygne, 29
Princess Rebecca Birnbaum, 93
Princess Turandot, 181, 235
Principia Scriptoriae, 24, 242
Printemps, 218
Prisoner, The, 134, 184
Prisoner of Caucasus, 258
Prisoner of Second Avenue, The, 174–175
Prisoners of War, 240
Private Affairs of the Grand Duchess, The, 79
Private Ear, The, 76
Private Life of the Master Race, The, 132
Private Lives, 6, 63, 81–82, 130, 167, 175, 240
Private View, A, 131–132
Processional, 105
Prodigal, The, 159, 252
Prodigal Daughter, The, 75, 108
Producing The Play, 88
Program for Two Players, 82
Progress, 106
Project Immortality, 252
Prologue to Deafman Glance, 258
Prologue to Glory, 87
Promenade, 93, 135–136
Prometheus, 9, 66, 106
Prometheus Bound, 10, 183–184, 202
Prometheus Project, 204–205
Promise, The, 174
Promise at Dawn, 5
Promises, Promises, 252–253
Prommesse di marinaio, 212
Pronaszko, Andrzej, **194–195**
Prosperpine, 217
Protective Custody, 142–143
Protée, 56
Protocolo, 66
Provok'd Wife, The, 106, 243–244
Psyche, 155
Public Enemy, 245
Public Opinion, 212
Public Prosecutor Is Sick of It All, A, 152
Pueblo, 183

Pueblo Incident, The, 20
Pulcinella, 66, 154, 189
Pump Boys and Dinettes, 179
Punch and Julia, 183
Punchinello, 120
Puntila, 177
Pure in Heart, The, 160
Purge, The, 232
Purlie Victorious, 74, 241
Purple Rose of Cairo, 261
Pursuit of Happiness, 74
Push Comes to Shove, 153
Puss in Boots, 83
Pygmalion, 62, 67, 79, 82, 87, 120–121, 130, 160, 171, 183
Pyle, Russel, **195–196**
Pyramis and Thisbe, 217

Quadrille, 81, 207
Quaglio Family, The, xxix, **197**
Quanto Sia Facile l'Inventore Decorazioni Teatrali, 212
Quare Fellow, The, 41, 166, 264
Quarter for the Ladie's Room, A, 256
Quartered Man, 196
Quattro libri dell'architettura, 186
Queen and the Cardinal, The, 103
Queen and the Rebels, The, 13
Queen Mab, 67, 68
Queen of Arragon, The, 125
Queen of Spades, The, 29, 139, 233–234
Queen's Enemies, The, 32–33
Queen's Silver Jubilee Gala, 243
Quiet City, The, 105
Quiet Place, A, 184
Quin's Secret, 168
Quintet, 17

Rabinovitch, Isaac, xxxvii, **199–200**, 237
Race of Hairy Men, A, 108
Race With a Shadow, The, 138
Rachael Lily Rosenbloom and Don't You Ever Forget It, 93, 252
Radio Days, 153
RA-D-IO (Wisdom); or Sophia = (Wisdom) Part 1, 95
Rag Dances, 21
Raggedy Ann, 179, 203

Rags, 93, 136
Ragtime Ballet, 84
Rain from Heaven, 221
Rain or Shine, 209
Rain, 54
Rainbow Terrace, 105
Rainbow, 240
Rainmaker, The, 45, 70
Rainy Day Friends, 196
Raisin in the Sun, A, 178
Rake's Progress, The, 91, 116, 148, 152, 203, 232
Ramshackle Inn, 46
Randolph, Robert, 112, **200–201**
Randy Newman Live at the Odeon, 146
Rape of Lucretia, The, 47, 148, 255
Rapid Transit, 239
Rapmaster Ronnie, 165
Rashomon, 70, 162
Rasputin, 173
Rat Race, The, 18, 184
Rausch, 231
Ravel Festival, The, 167
Raymonda, 101, 153
R.B.M.E., 206
Readings from the Bible by Judith Anderson, 184
Ready When You Are, C.B.!, 11
Real Inspector Hound, The, 178–179
Real McCoy, The, 162
Real Thing, The, 60, 175, 243, 255
Really Rosie, 203
Rear Column, The, 23
Rebel Armies Deep Into Chad, 25
Rebel Women, 23
Rebound, 127
Recreational Architecture, 99
Recruiting Officer, The, 8, 54, 145
Red-Bluegrass Western Flyer Show, 23
Red Cloak, The, 221
Red Devil Battery Sign, The, 252
Red Dust, 239
Red Eye of Love, 135
Red General, The, 160
Red, Hot and Blue!, 183
Red Letter Day, 178
Red Magic in New York, 94
Red Mill, The, 79

Red Nights of the Tcheka, 106
Red Planet, 221
Red Poppy, The, 13
Red Roses for Me, 20, 92, 169, 212
Red Rover, The, 106
Red Snake, The, 77
Red Sunday, 139
Red, Yellow, and Black, 12
Redemption, 126
Redemptor, The, 178
Rendezvous, 240
Redhead, 207, 238
Regina, 20, 32–33, 81
Regular Guy, A, 239
Rehearsal, The, 11, 255
Rehearsal Call, 79
Relapse, The, 182, 249
Remarkable Mr. Pennypacker, The, 74
Reminicience, 228
Remote Asylum, 148
Renard, 142
Renaud et Armide, 30
Rennagel, Marilyn, **201**
Requiem for a Heavyweight, 131
Requiem for a Nun, 171
Rescuing Angel, The, 126
Resistible Rise of Arturo Ui, The, 3, 53–54, 76, 152, 190
Resounding Tinkle, A, 91
Restless Sex, 82
Retreat to Pleasure, 183
Return of Odysseus, The, 129, 194
Return of Peter Grimm, The, 28
Return of Pinocchio, The, 242
Reuben, Reuben, 72
Reunion, 23, 25
Reunion in Vienna, 32
Revanche, 49
Revenger's Tragedy, The, 152, 166
Reverberation Fire Curtain, 24
Revisor, The, 195
Revizor, 245
Revues, 159
Rex, 54, 242
Rhapsody, 222
Rhinoceros, 132, 133
Rhoda in Potatoland, 95
Rhonda Roundabout, 171

Rib of Eve, 218, 223
Ricercare, 238
Rich and Famous, 6
Rich Full Life, A, 196
Rich Kids, 167
Rich Little Rich Girl, 143
Richard II, 45, 60, 77, 79, 82, 91, 102,
    169, 171, 173, 177, 241
Richard III, 5–6, 11–12, 43, 54, 87, 106,
    128, 148, 153, 169, 171, 173, 189,
    206
Richard of Bordeaux, 171
Richelieu, 11, 39
Ricketts, Charles, **201–202**
Riders to the Sea, 133
Riding Hood Revisited, 92
Riding to Lithend, The, 106
Rienzi, 262
Right of Way, 131
Right This Way, 255–256
Right You Are If You Think You Are,
    160
Righteous Are Bold, The, 47
Rigoletto, 31, 169–170, 177, 263
Rinaldo, 158
Ring, The, 138, 221, 222
Ring 'Round the Moon, 51, 143, 152,
    159, 230, 173
Ring Cycle, The, 36, 114, 215, 231, 254
Ring of the Nibelung, The, 119
Rink, The, 94
Rio Rita, 79, 247
Rip Van Winkle, 79
Rise and Fall of the City of Mahagonny,
    The, 66, 114, 177, 212, 230, 265
Rise of Silas Lapham, The, 221
Rivalry, The, 171
Rivals, The, 11, 26, 52–53, 79, 106,
    174, 188, 209, 257
River Line, The, 171
Riverside Drive, 132
Riverwind, 92
Riviera Girl, The, 247
Road, The, 234
Road Show, 60
Road to Mecca, The, 25
Road to Rome, The, 221
Roadside, 127

Roaming Stars, 12
Roar China, 221–222
Roast, The, 51
Rob Roy, 111
Robber, The, 232
Robbins, Carrie, **202–204**
Roberta, 79
Roberto Devereux, 148
Robin Hood, 139
Robin Landing, 183
Robinson Crusoe, 67
Rock Me, 183
Rock 'N' Roll! The First 5,000 Years,
    93–94
Rockabye Hamlet, 93
Rocket to the Moon, 105
Rodeo, 222, 225, 237
Rogue's Ballad, The, 232
Rojo, Jerry, xl, **204–205**
Roller, Andreas Leonhard, 68, **205–206**
Rolling Stones Tour of the Americas,
    The, 93, 252–253
Romance, Romance, 165
Romanoff and Juliet, 79
Romantic Comedy, 109
Romantic Young Lady, The, 32
Romeo and Juliet, xxiv, 4–5, 11–12, 16,
    31–32, 53–54, 59, 63, 66–67, 70, 79,
    84, 92, 101, 102, 103, 106–108, 126–
    127, 141, 148–149, 160, 165–166,
    168–169, 171, 173–175, 179, 188–
    189, 191, 206, 209, 228, 230–232,
    239, 243, 245, 263–264
Romilda e Constanza, 158
Romulus, 18, 47, 223
Ronconi, Luca, xl, **206**
Room in Red and White, A, 161
Room Service, 22, 54, 76, 148
Roomful of Roses, A, 184
Rooming House, The, 178
Roots, 114
Rope, The, 107, 168, 239
Rope Dancers, The, 13, 264
Rosalind, 106
Rosalinda, 47–48, 62, 182, 222, 250
Rose, The, 6, 194
Rose, Jürgen, **206–207**
Rose and the Ring, The, 112

Rose Bernd, 126
Rose Burke, 183
Rose of China, 247
Rose Tattoo, The, 13, 15, 23, 48, 54, 81, 152, 177
Rose Without a Thorn, The, 107
Rosebloom, 174
Rosemary, 5, 23
Rosencrantz and Guildenstern Are Dead, 54, 113, 152, 190, 206, 261
Rosenthal, Jean, 185, **207–208**
Roshomon, 159
Rosilena e Oronta, 157
Rosmersholm, 5, 56, 58, 106, 145, 171, 217, 239
Ross, 171
Rosse, Herman, 141, **209–210**
Roth, Ann, 98, **210**
Rothchilds, The, 190
Rouge et Noir, 156
Rough Crossing, 115, 244
Rout, 106
Rover, The, 25
Royal Audience, A, 106
Royal Family, The, 63, 74, 225
Royal Fandango, A, 126
Royal Hunt of the Sun, The, 74, 124, 145
Roza, 136
Rubber, 209
Rugantino, 79
Rugged Path, The, 161
Ruint, 127, 239
Ruling Class, The, 125, 132, 176
Rumble, 124
Rumors, 175, 230
Rumour, The, 106
Rumple, 50
Run, Little Chillun!, 240
Runaway, The, 67–68
Runaways, 242
R.U.R., 13, 133–134, 221
Rusalka, 153, 232–233
Russet Mantle, 183
Russian Bank, 139
Russian People, The, 13
Ruy Blas, 37, 39, 102, 127

S.S. Glencairn, 127, 239
S.S. Tenacity, The, 126
Sabbatini, Nicola, xxiii, 172, **211**, 244
Sabrina Fair, 184
Sacchetti, Lorenzo, 158, **211–212**
Sacred Flame, The, 132
Sadie Thompson, 13
Sadko, 8, 140
Safe Sex, 165
Sagert, Horst, **212**
Sail Away, 47, 223
Sailors of Cattaro, 105
Saint, The, 126
Saint in a Hurry, 168
Saint Joan, 45, 53, 76–77, 79, 106, 130, 149, 161, 169, 175, 202, 252
Saint Joan of the Stockyards, 114, 177
Saint of Bleeker Street, The, 66, 200, 207
Sainthill, Loudon, **212–213**
Saintliness of Mergery Kempe, The, 5
Sally, 247
Salmacida Spolia, xxv, 125–126
Salome, 53, 64, 66, 84, 85, 106, 114, 183, 188, 201–202, 206– 207, 250
Salt, 195
Salt Lake City Skyline, 131
Salut au Monde, 32
Salute To the American Musical Theatre, 87
Salvation, 127
Sambo, 129, 148
Same Time, Next Year, 108, 201
Samson, 91
Samson and Delilah, 126, 182
Samuel Zborowski, 194
Sandalwood, 239
Sandbox, The, 178
Sandhog, 20
Sandpiper, The, 218
Sanquirico, Alessandro, **213**
Sap of Life, The, 52
Sarah in America, 179
Sarah Siddons, the Greatest of the Kembles, 202
Saratoga, 50, 208, 222, 225
Sarava, 153
Sargasso, 238

Saturday Night Kid, The, 223
Saturday Night Live, 147
Saturday, Sunday, Monday, 76, 263
Saturday's Children, 160
Satyagraha, 97
Savages, 54, 60, 179
Save Me a Waltz, 161
Saved, 145
Saving Grace, The, 76, 135
Savitri, 97
Say, Darling, 47, 50, 178, 223
Scala Theater Revue, 83
Scamozzi, Vincenzo, xxii, xxv, 186, **213–214**, 251
Scandals, 3
Scapin, 240
Scapino, 204
Scaramouche, 178
Scarecrow, The, 54, 72
Scarlattiana, 192
Scarlet Fox, The, 239
Scarlet Letter, The, 146
Scenery, Then and Now, 185
Scenic Artist Handbook, 21
Scheherazade, 8, 17, 84, 156
Schiller, Leon de Schildenfeld, **214**, 232–233
Schinderhannes, 177
Schlemmer, Oskar, xxxvii, 111, **214–215**
Schneider-Siemssen, Gunther, **215**
School, 59
School for Husbands, The, 221
School for Scandal, The, 11, 26, 32, 72, 132, 171, 232
School for Wives, The, 31, 240
Schwanda, 231
Schwyk in zwesten Weltkrieg, 166
Scipio Africano, 157
Scorpions of Ysitt, The, 88
Scotch Symphony, 89
Scratch, 53, 87, 265
Screenplay, 77
Screens, The, 3, 135–136, 242–243
Scuba Duba, 93, 135, 143
Sea, The, 130
Seagull, The, xxxv, 24, 32, 45, 79, 109, 127, 130, 139, 143, 149, 171, 173, 178, 202, 232, 234, 240, 242, 255

Sea Marks, 130
Sea Plays, The, 125
Sea Shadow, 147
Searcher, The, 183
Searching for the Sun, 240
Searching Wind, The, 20, 32
Seascape, 241
Season in the Sun, 13, 15
Season of Choice, 11
Seasons, The, 181
Sebastian, 222
Second Avenue Rag, 131
Second Little Show, 160
Second Man, The, 160
Second Mrs. Tanqueray, The, 243
Second Threshold, 184
Secret, The, 233
Secret Affairs of Mildred Wild, The, 152, 203
Secret Honor, 196
Secret Life of Walter Mitty, The, 217
Secret Marriage, The, 65
Secret Place, The, 76
Secret Places, 148
Secret Service, 241
Seduced, 145
See How They Run, 178
See Naples and Die, 107, 127
Seed of the Brute, 160
Seeds of Discovery, 133
Seesaw, 93, 252–253
Segel am Horizont, 173
Seige of Rhodes, The, 255
Self Defense, 131
Selim and Azor, 67
Semi-Detached, 11, 13
Semi-Tough, 6
Semiramide, 157
Semmelweiss, 253
Señor de Manera, 66
Sensations, 73
Sentimental Centaur, The, 106
Sentimental Colloquy, 64
Sentinels, 240
Separate Tables, 178
Septuor, 37
Sequi, Sandro, **215–216**
Seraphic Dialogue, 181

Serena Blandish, 127

Sérénade, 67

Serenading Louie, 23, 131, 159, 179–180

Sérénite, 66

Serjeant Musgrave's Dance, 5, 76, 78, 93, 114, 252

Serlio, Sebastiano, xx, xxi, xxii, xxiii, xxv, xxvii, xxviii, 5, 7, 99, 126, 172, 188, 211, 213, **216**

Servandoni, Giovanni Nicolò, xxx, 38, **216**

Servant of Two Masters, The, 53, 107

Service for Two, 239

Servio Tullio, 156

Sethona, 67–68

Seven Brides for Seven Brothers, 200

Seven Deadly Sins, The, 152, 177, 238

Seven Descents of Myrtle, The, 108, 163

Seven Keys to Baldpate, 130, 145–146

Seven Lively Arts, The, 26–27

Seven Year Love, 127

Seventeen, 89

1776, 163–164, 265–267

Seventh Heaven, 87

Seventh Symphony, 30

Seventh Trumpet, The, 161

Seventy, Girls, Seventy, 108, 200

Sganarelle, 177

Sgt. Pepper's Lonely Hearts Club Band on the Road, 252

Shadow and Substance, 168

Shadow Box, The, 149–150

Shadow of a Gunman, The, 143, 173

Shadow of Doubt, The, 120

Shadow of Heroes, 178

Shadow of My Enemy, A, 184

Shadow of the Wind, 161

Shadows, 134

Shadowy Waters, 168

Shady Hill Kidnapping, 77

Shakespeare Revisited, 82

Shangri-La, 142, 218

Shanwis, 26

Sharaff, Irene, 136, 210, **217–220**, 266

Shaughraun, The, 34

She, 32

She Follows Me About, 120

She Had to Do Something, 168

She Loves Me, 23, 72, 189, 255, 265

She Means Business, 239

She Stoops to Conquer, 51–52, 66, 79, 99, 108, 116, 143, 174, 192, 243

Sheep on the Runway, 93, 108, 143

Shelter, 190

Shelving, Paul, **220**

Shepherd's Paradise, The, 125

Sheringham, George, **220–221**

Sherlock Holmes, 23, 243–244

Sherry, 200

Shewing Up of Blanco Posnet, The, 107

Shinbone Alley, 79–80, 171, 173

Shining Hour, The, 188

Shoe Shine Parlor, 167

Shoemaker's Holiday, The, 65, 106–107, 169, 207

Shoemaker's Prodigious Wife, 78

Shoestring Revue, 240

Shogun, 266

Shooter's Bible, 196

Short Eyes, 167–168

Short Happy Life, A, 5, 162

Short Plays by Merimee, 181

Shot in the Dark, A, 74

Show, The, 106

Show Boat, 8, 20, 48, 178, 207, 224, 247

Show Booth, The, 126

Show Business, 256

Show Girl, 223, 256

Show-Off, The, 130

Showdown at the Adobe Motel, 131

Showgirl, 47

Shrewing Up of Blanco Posnet, 168

Shrike, The, 20

Siamese Connection, The, 152

Side by Side by Sondheim, 136–137

Sideshow, 147

Sidewalkin', 203

Siege, 26

Siegfried, 37, 55, 206, 233

Sign in Sidney Brustein's Window, The, 6, 92, 152, 178, 180

Sign of Affection, A, 72

Sign of Winter, The, 132

Signalman's Apprentice, The, 79

Silence, 41

Silent Night, 5
Silent Night, Lonely Night, 162
Silk Stockings, 18, 162
Silkwood, 210
Silver Cord, The, 74, 239
Silver Jubilee, 168
Silver Lake, 177
Simon, 153
Simon and Garfunkel Concert, 146
Simon Boccanegra, 171
Simone Boccanegra, 232–233
Simonson, Lee, xxxviii, 33, 39, 58, 184, **221–222**, 239–240, 247
Simpleton of the Unexpected Isle, The, 221
Sin of Pat Muldoon, The, 105
Sinfonia, 71
Sing and Whistle, 240
Sing for Your Supper, 87
Sing Me No Lullaby, 74
Sing Out the News, 161
Sing Out, Sweet Land!, 18
Sing to Me Through Open Windows, 135
Singin' in the Rain, 153–154, 189, 210
Singin' the Blues, 183
Singing in the Rain, 242
Sisters of Mercy, 203
Sitting, 76
Six, 178
Six Books of Perspective, xxiii
Six Characters in Search of an Author, 50, 53, 92, 106, 115, 138, 239
Six Rms Riv Vu, 210
Sizwe Bansi is Dead, 76, 167, 261
Skin of Our Teeth, The, 52–53, 63, 87–88, 145, 152, 169, 173, 178, 193, 252
Skinflint Out West, 53
Skipper Next to God, 13
Skydrift, 171
Skylark, 183
Skyrocket, The, 160
Skyscraper, 5, 200
Skyscrapers, 127
Slapstick Tragedy, 148, 150
Slaughter on Tenth Avenue, 163, 218
Slave Ship, 145–146
Slavonika, 50
Sleep, 135

Sleep of Prisoners, 87
Sleeping Beauty, The 101, 133, 159, 199, 206, 225, 233, 256, 266
Sleeping Clergyman, A, 221
Sleeping Prince, The, 50
Sleeping Princess, The, 17
Sleepy Hollow, 89
Sleight of Hand, 179
Sleuth, 130, 204, 243
Slight, 95
Slightly Scandalous, 3
Slow Dance on the Killing Ground, 76, 224
Small Hours, The, 184
Small Miracle, 13
Small War on Murray Hill, 13, 218
Smile of the World, 184
Smiling the Boy Fell Dead, 5
Smiling Through, 74
Smith, Oliver, xxxix, 49, 88–89, **222–227**, 237, 253, 256, 260
Snegurochka, 140
Snow Laughed as It Fell, The, 233
Snow Maiden, The, 8, 13
Snow Man, The, 138
Snow on the Limba, 233
Snow Queen, The, 233
So Fien, 153
So Long on Lonely Street, 109
So Long, 174th Street, 178
Social Security, 201, 255
Sodom et Gomorrhe, 30
Soeur Beatrice, 227
Sogno d'una notte di mezza estate, 37
Soldaten, 166
Soldiers, The, 232
Soldier's Tale, The, 133
Soleil de Minuit, 141–142
Solid South, 160
Solitaire, 17, 161, 239
Solomon and Balkis, 133
Solomon Northrup's Odyssey, 77
Solomon's Child, 131, 179
Some of My Best Friends, 145
Some People, Some Other People, and What They Finally Do, 22
Someone Waiting, 74
Someone's Comin' Hungry, 93

Somerset Maugham Theatre, 20
Something Different, 11
Something for Everyone, 136–137
Something for the Boys, 20
Something Gay, 183
Something More!, 51, 200
Something Wonderful, 23
Something's Rockin' in Denmark, 196
Sommi, Leone Di Ebreo, xxi, **227**
Son of Learning, The, 106
Son of Man and The Family, 145
Sonata Pathétique, 66
Sondheim: A Musical Tribute, 136–137
Song and Dance, 93, 135, 253
Song Is Born, A, 218
Song of Noah, 135
Song of Norway, 47, 79, 124, 209, 256
Song of the Drum, The, 228
Song of the Grasshopper, 224
Songs of My Father, 93, 255
Sonja Henie Ice Revue, The, 87
Sons and Soldiers, 26
Sons of Giants, 143
Soon, 93
Sooner and Later, 183
Sophia   (Wisdom) Part 3: The Cliffs, 95
Sophie, 200
Sophisticated Ladies, 135–136, 242, 255
Sorceress, The, 199
Sorrows of Satan, The, 26
Sorrows of Stephen, The, 261
Sorrows of Young Werther, The, 40
Soudekine, Serge, 151, **227**
Sound of Music, The, 18, 48–49, 115,
    136, 208, 223, 226
Sourball, 204
Sourvenir, 6
South of Broadway, 240
South Pacific, 13, 47–49, 93, 113, 162,
    164, 171
South Seas Island Fantasy, 209
Souvenirs, 238
Spaceman, 258
Speak of the Devil, 87
Speaking of Murder, 178
Speck, 231
Spellbound, 64
Spellbound Child, 32

Spider's Banquet, The, 16
Spiel im Schloss, 231
Spiro Who?, 79
Spofford, 174, 184
Spokesong, 36, 63, 70, 130
Spook Sonata, The, 106, 126
Spookhouse, 165
Spoon River Anthology, 92–93
Spot in the Sun, A, 168
Spotlight, 200
Spread Eagle, 26
Spring Again, 183
Spring In Brazil, 20
Spring 1600, 171
Spring Song, 160
Spring Thaw, 183
Spring's Awakening, 40, 45
Springboard to Nowhere, 184
Springtime for Henry, 89, 240
Square in the Eye, 92
Square One, 255
Square Root of Wonderful, The, 162
St. Elizabeth, 247
St. Joan, 105, 231
St. Lazare's Pharmacy, 161
St. Matthew's Passion, 148
Stage Design Throughout the World, 37
Stage Design, 21
Stage Design: Four Centuries of Scenic
    Invention, 185
Stage Designs and Costumes, 160
Stage Door, 46, 183
Stage Hand's Lament, 240
Stage Is Set, The, 58, 222
Stage King, The, 135
Stage Lighting, 190
Stage Struck, 243
Stages, 95, 265
Staging of Wagner's Musical Dramas,
    The, xxxv
Stairs, The, 239
Stanfield, William Clarkson, xxxii, 110,
    228
Star and Garter, 217
Star 80, 255
Star Is Born, A, 81–82, 93, 210, 218
Star-Spangled Girl, The, 210, 224
Star-Wagon, The, 161

Stardust Memories, 153
Starlight Express, xl, 115–116, 176
Stars in Your Eyes, 161
Statira, 157
Steadfast Tin Soldier, The, 167
Steambath, 93, 167
Steaming, 131
Stempenyu, the Fiddler, 12
Step on a Crack, 265
Stephen D., 224
Stepping Out, 183
Stepping Sisters, 239
Stern, Ernst, xxxvii, 84, **228–229**
Stettheimer, Florine, **229–230**
Steve Martin Special, 146
Sticks and Bones, 5, 152–154
Stiletto, 51
Still Life, 11
Stirrings in Sheffield on a Saturday
    Night, 169
Stitch in Time, The, 203
Stolen Fruit, 188
Stop the World I Want to Get Off, 153
Storeyville, 23
Storm, The, 178, 190, 199, 232
Storm Beaten, 103
Storm Operation, 20
Storm Over Patsy, 32
Story of a Horse, The, 137
Story of a Right Man, The, 232
Story of Tzar Saltan, The, 29
Stove Pipe Hat, 18
Straiges, Anthony J., **230–231**
Strange Fruit, 123
Strange Interlude, 5, 160
Strange Orchestra, 171
Stranger, The, 13
Streamers, 230
Street Scene, 18–19, 160–161, 163
Streetcar Named Desire, A, 18–19, 23,
    45, 55, 60, 99, 142–143, 152, 161,
    163–164, 189
Streetheat, 146
Streets Are Guarded, The, 221
Streets of New York, The, 188
Streets of Paris, 217
Strife, 41
String of Pearls, 12

Strings, The, 20
Strip for Action, 256
Strip Tease, 196
Strnad, Oskar, xxxvii, **231**
Strong are Lonely, The, 102
Stronger, The, 50, 78, 106, 203
Struensee, 177
Student Prince, The, 48, 124, 178
Studs Edsel, 130
Subject to Fits, 5
Subject Was Roses, The, 92, 152
Suburban Tragedy, 93
Subway, The, 106
Subways Are For Sleeping, 11–12
Success Story, 105
Successful Calamity, A, 126
Such Good Friends, 238
Sud, 254
Suddenly Last Summer, 159
Suds, the Sixties Rocking Soap Opera,
    70
Sue's Leg, 153
Sueños de Viena, 83
Sugar, 51, 163, 252
Sugar Babies, 70
Suicide, The, 153
Sultan, The, 67
Summer, 109, 230
Summer and Smoke, 162
Summerfolk, 91–92, 131, 137
Sumurun, 228
Sun Always Shines in the Cool, The, 203
Sun Never Sets, The, 120
Sunday, 87
Sunday Breakfast, 74
Sunday Dinner, 135
Sunday in New York, 264
Sunday in the Park with George, 117,
    179–180, 230–231, 265–267
Sunday Morning, A, 32
Sundown Beach, 13, 74, 207
Sunny River, 217
Sunset, 152, 203, 265
Sunshine Boys, The, 175
Sunshine Sisters, 89
Sunup to Sundown, 19
Suor Angelica, 20, 79, 233
Suppliants, The, 107

Supporting Cast, The, 109, 179
Sur le Borysthene, 142
Survivors, The, 13
Susan and God, 161
Susannah, 47, 132, 148
Susanna and the Barber, 49
Susanna Don't You Cry, 127
Svoboda, Josef, xxxviii, xli, 40, 190,
    232–235
Swallows and Amazons, 190
Swan Lake, 17, 22, 53, 66, 100–101,
    206, 221, 224, 243
Swansong, A, 130
Swap Meet, 196
Sweat and Stanley Poole, 184
Sweeney Todd, 145–147
Sweeney Todd the Barber, 106
Sweet and Low, 160
Sweet Bells Jangled, 183
Sweet Bird of Youth, 5–6, 60, 76, 162,
    203
Sweet Bye and Bye, 13
Sweet Charity, 200, 218, 266
Sweet Dreams, 210
Sweet Liberty, 109
Sweet Little Evil, 221
Sweet Mystery of Life, 183
Sweet Peril, 120
Sweet Prince, 179
Sweet River: An Adaptation of Harriet
    Beecher Stowe's Uncle Tom's Cabin,
    183
Sweet Sue, 153
Sweet Table at the Richelieu, 55
Sweet Talk, 130
Swift, 169
Swindburne Ballet, 220
Swing, 253, 265
Swords, 126
Syllabaire pour Phèdre, 66, 148
Sylvia, 66, 146, 153
Sylvie, 38
Symphonie Concertante, 66
Symphonie Fantastique, 30, 233
Symphonie Italienne, 31
Szajna, Josef, **235–236**

Tabarin Theater Revue, 83
Table Ronde, 245

Table Settings, 141
Take a Chance, 209, 240
Take a Giant Step, 79
Take Her, She's Mine, 72, 136
Take Me Along, 165, 208, 223
Take One Step, 167
Take Two From One, 139
Taking of Miss Janie, The, 178
Tale of Cymbeline, The, 5
Tale of Lear, A, 90
Tale of the Country Priest and His
    Dunderhead Servant, The, 194
Tale of the Invisible City of Kitezh and
    the Maid Fevronia, The, 140
Tale of the Tsar Saltan, The, 140
Tale Told, A, 24, 60
Talent For Murder, 225
Tales from the Vienna Woods, 91
Tales of Hoffman, The, 83, 113, 133,
    148, 184, 231–232, 234, 247–248
Tales of Kasane, 265
Tall Story, 124
Talley and Son, 24, 60
Talley Method, The, 161
Talley's Folly, 23–26, 70, 125, 159
Tallis Fantasia, 182
Tambourines to Glory, 52, 55
Tamburlaine the Great, 41, 119
Taming of the Shrew, The, 60–61, 74,
    79, 98, 117, 121, 130, 139, 145, 147,
    169, 174, 182, 188, 191, 207, 218,
    228, 242–243, 263
Tango Opassionada, 266
Tannhauser, xli, 62, 91, 102, 177, 198,
    231, 233, 254, 265
Tap Dance Kid, The, 179–180
Tapestry in Gray, 183
Tartuffe, 8, 70, 77, 99, 108–110, 152,
    169, 178, 202, 212, 245, 258, 261
Taste of Honey, A, 41, 208, 223
Tavern, The, 178
Taverner, 138
Tchelitchew, Pavel, 30, 85, **237**
Tchin-Tchin, 5, 11
Tea and Sympathy, 162, 252
Teahouse of the August Moon, The,
    142–143
Teaspoon Every Four Hours, A, 200

Teatr Ogromny, 214
Teddy and Alice, 6, 175
Telbin, William, xxxii, 59, **237–238**
Telemachus Clay, 92
Telephone, The, 207
Temistocle, 157
Tempe Restor'd, 125
Tempest, The, 5, 21, 45, 52, 70, 86, 108, 112, 124, 132, 134, 146–147, 149, 152, 166–167, 171, 173, 177, 207, 212, 214, 231, 233, 238, 242
Temple of Love, The, 125
Temporary Mrs. Smith, The, 81, 183
Temptation, 106
Ten Little Indians, 20
Ten Million Ghosts, 183
Tender Land, The, 223
Tender Mercies, 109
Tensile Involvement, 180
Tenth Commandment, The, 12–14
Tenth Man, The, 148
Tents of the Arabs, The, 118
Ter-Arutunian, Rouben, xxxix, 149, **238–239**
Teresa, 132
Terra Nova, 55, 77
Terrain Vague, 37
Teseo, 156
Tethys' Festival, 125
Teufel von Loudun, 66
Tevya and His Daughters, 20
Texas Fourth, 225
Texas Trilogy, A, 75, 108
Thais, 82, 243
Thank you, Mr. Pepys!, 120
That Awful Mrs. Eaton, 160
That Championship Season, 6, 152–154, 178
That Is the Snow, 21
That Lady, 101, 102
That Summer . . . That Fall, 5, 162
That's Entertainment, 108
That's Life, 200–201
That's the Ticket, 47, 223, 256
The CIVIL warS, 258–259
The Cuckoo's Nest, 11
The Easiest Way, 29

Theatralischen Architectur und Mechanique, 86
Theatre Alcazar Revue, 82
Theatre and a Changing Civilization, The, 139
Theatre and School, 118
Theatre Arts Magazine, 27, 118
Theatre Arts Monthly, 128
Theatre Ba-Ta-Clan Revue, 82
Theatre des Ambassadeurs Revue, 82
Theatre Technology, 122
Theme and Variations, 153
There Was a Little Girl, 162
There Was a Time, 21
There's a Moon Tonight, 19
There's Always Juliet, 120
There's No Business Like Show Business, 256–257
Thermidor, 37
These Days, 127
These Modern Women, 239
Thésee, 38
Theseus, 245
They, 75
They Shall Not Die, 105, 221
They're Playing Our Song, 175, 210
Thief, 53
Thieves' Carnival, 52, 143, 261
Thinking (One Kind), 95
Third Little Show, The, 160
13 Daughters, 50, 124
13 of a Nation, 87
Thirty Minutes in a Street, 106
This is Cinerama, 132
This is Goggle, 13
This Side of Paradise, 92
This Was Burlesque, 178
This Winter's Hobby, 136, 224
This World of Ours, 106
Thomas Muskerry, 168
Thompson, Woodman, **239**
Thought, The, 106
Thousand Clowns, A, 124
Thousand Summers, A, 183
Thracian Horses, The, 89
Three Acts of Recognition, 95
Three Bags Full, 11, 260
Three by Offenbach, 147

Three Dances, 253

Three Days of the Condor, 6

Three Guardsmen, The, 11

Three Little Maids, 59

Three Men on a Horse, 13, 130, 178

Three Muskateers, The, 8, 66, 79, 228, 245, 247, 260

Three One-Act Plays for a Negro Theatre: The Rider of Dreams, ranny Maumee, Simon the Cyrenian,A - A126

Three Short Dances, 147

Three Sisters, The, 5–6, 11, 17, 45, 55, 75, 79, 87, 107, 108, 138–139, 153, 169, 171, 190, 204, 232, 250, 264

Three to Make Ready, 183

Three Ways Home, 165

Three Wilder Plays, 178

Three Wishes for Jamie, 87, 123, 256

Three x Three, 218

Threepenny Opera, The, 6, 16, 45, 47, 49, 53–54, 60, 93, 95, 132–133, 144, 145, 177, 190, 214, 240

Throckmorton, Cleon, **239–240**

Through the Leaves, 196

Thumby, 75

Thunder on the Left, 32

Thunder Rock, 105, 190

Ti-Jean and His Brothers, 6

Ticket of Leave Man, The, 81–82

Ticklish Acrobat, The, 252

Tidings Brought to Mary, The, 9, 221

Tiger At the Gates, 79

Tiger Ray, The, 92

Tiger, Tiger, Burning Bright, 18, 87, 224

Til Eulenspiegel, 126

Till, 199

Tiller in the Fields, The, 149

Tilton, James, **240–241**

Timber House, 183

Timbuktu, 230

Time for Elizabeth, 123

Time for Singing, A, 5, 148

Time of the Barracudas, The, 5, 48, 224

Time of the Cuckoo, The, 11–12, 74–75

Time of Vengeance, 178

Time of Your Life, The, 13, 45, 168, 178, 203, 207, 224, 241

Time Out for Ginger, 78

Time Out of Mind, 234

Time Remembered, 52, 87, 223, 256

Time the Comedian, 82

Time Vindicated, 125

Times Pocket, 168

Timon of Athens, The, 5, 113, 148, 169, 231

Tinder Box, The, 178

Tintypes, 60

Tiny Alice, 152, 210

Tip Toes, 23

Tipton, Jennifer, **241–243**

'Tis a Pity She's a Whore, 66, 250

Tito on Tambales, 266

Titus, 34

Titus Andronicus, 5, 113, 148

To Be Continued, 171, 184

To Broadway With Love, 260

To Dorothy, a Son, 72

To Grandmother's House We Go, 75, 109

To Quito and Back, 32

Tobacco Road, 23, 92

Tobias and the Angel, 106

Toi-C'est moi, 83

Toller Cranston's Ice Show, 256

Tom Jones, 145–146

Tomorrow and Tomorrow, 32

Tomorrow's Monday, 24

Toms, Carl, **243–244**

Tone Pictures and the White Peacock, 32

Tonight at Eight-Thirty, 51, 123, 127, 174

Tonight in Samarkand, 74

Too Late the Phalarope, 124

Too Many Girls, 161

Too Many Heroes, 161

Too Much Johnson, 72, 265

Tooth of Crime, The, 55, 70, 145, 204–205

Top Banana, 50, 162

Top Girls, 63

Top Man, 20

Top o' the Hill, 239

Topaze, 46, 223

Torch Song, 239

Torelli, Giacomo, xxiv, xxviii, 8, 35,
    211, **244–245**, 250
Torquato Tasso, 166
Tortilla Flat, 105
Tosca, 82, 83, 88, 182, 184, 263
Tot Family, The, 23
Total Eclipse, 179
Total Recall: Sophia (Wisdom) Part 2, 94
Touch and Go, 47
Touch of the Poet, A, 11, 51, 74, 75,
    130, 174
Touchstone, 123
Toussaint, 36
Tovarich, 102, 172
Towards a New Theatre, 58
Tower Beyond Tragedy, 87
Town House, 184
Toys in the Attic, 20–21, 52
Traces, 206
Trade Winds, 183
Tragédie á Vérone, 67
Tragedy of Fashion, A, 88
Tragedy of Nothing, 12
Tragedy of Richard III, The, 126
Tragical Historie of Doctor Faustus, The,
    87, 92, 265
Trainer, Dean, Liepolt and Company,
    202
Tramway Road, 91
Translations, 77
Traveler in the Dark, 201
Traveling Lady, The, 74
Travesties, 98, 243
Traviata, 263
Treasure Hunt, 168
Treasure, The, 221
Tree Grows in Brooklyn, A, 162, 218
Treize à table, 37
Trelawny of the 'Wells,' 5–6, 127, 167,
    188
Tres Cantos, 265
Triad, 147
Triadic Ballet, The, 214
Trial, The, 177, 207
Trial in Camera, 89
Trial of A. Lincoln, The, 152
Trial of Lee Harvey Oswald, The, 5, 93,
    252–253

Trial of Love, The, 233
Trial of Lucullus, The, 148
Trial of the Catonsville Nine, 79, 174
Trial of the Moke, The, 130
Trial of Three Million, The, 199
Trials of Oz, The, 93
Tribute to Lily Lamont, A, 23
Trick for Trick, 87
Tricks, 225, 256
Tricks of Scapin, The, 243
Trilby, 126
Trilogue des Wiedersehens, 115
Trip Back Down, The, 178
Trip to Bountiful, The, 47
Trip to Scarborough, A, 249
Triple Crossed, 239
Triple Sec, 134
Triple-A Ploughed Under, 87
Tristan, 223
Tristan und Isolde, 9–10, 41, 116, 147,
    183–185, 193, 198, 215, 231–233,
    235, 247, 254
Triumph of Honor, or, the Rake's
    Reform, The, 133
Triumph of Peace, The, 125
Triumph of Saint Joan, The, 134
Triumph of the Egg, The, 127
Triumphant Bachelor, The, 239
Triumphs of the Prince d'Amour, The,
    125
Trixie True, Teen Detective, 165
Troester, Frantisek, **245–246**
Troilus and Cressida, 3, 5, 82, 91, 107,
    132, 138, 145, 147, 171, 182, 264
Trois Jeunes Villes Nues, 83
Trojan Women, The, 5, 11, 92, 174, 257
Trojans, The, 252–253
Trouble in Tahiti, 79
Truckline Cafe, 13, 65
Trumpets of the Lord, 93
Truth About Blayds, The, 26, 240
Truth is Good But Happiness is Better,
    199
Tumbler, The, 173
Tunnel of Love, The, 178
Turandot, 9, 85, 91–92, 119, 123, 149,
    170, 173, 228, 231, 233, 263
Turk in Italy, The, 54, 147

Turn of the Screw, The, 50, 66, 115, 173
Turpentine, 87
Tutor, The, 177
Twelfth Night, 5, 11, 31, 45, 52–54, 59, 76, 79, 106–108, 130, 147, 149, 168–169, 173–174, 176–178, 202–203, 221, 225, 228, 238, 247, 257
Twelve Dreams, 141
Twelve Thousand, 106
Twentieth Century, 253
Twentieth-Century Stage Decoration, 118
27 Wagons Full of Cotton, 79, 241
Twice Around the Park, 241
Twice Nightly, 107
Twigs, 79, 143
Twilight Bar, 46, 223
Twist Appeal, 83
Twists, Arts, 123
Two by Pinter, 132
2x25, 12, 14
Two Farces, 192
Two for the See-saw, 124
Two Gentlemen of Verona, 5–6, 70, 91, 145, 148, 150, 169, 179, 202
200 Were Chosen, 183
Two Offenbach Operettas, 22
Two On an Island, 161
Two on the Aisle, 20
Two Part Inventions, 242
Two Queens of Love and Beauty, 178
Two Roses, 59
Two Rules of Perspective Practice, xxiii
Two Seconds, 240
Two's Company, 256
Twyla Tharp and Dancers on Broadway, 153
Tyl Eulenspiegel, 209, 232
Tyrannic Love, 98
Tzaddik, The, 14

Ubu Roi, 53, 116, 138
Ulysses, 59
Ulysses in Nighttown, 93–94, 209
Ulysses in Traction, 23, 60
Umbrella, The, 5
Umbrellas of Cherbourg, The, 109

Un ballo in maschera, 54, 177, 206–207
Un Chien Andalou, 64
Un Vrai Paradis, 83
Uncle Harry, 20, 46
Uncle Moses, 105
Uncle Tom's Cabin, 183
Uncle Tom's Cabin: A History, 145
Uncle Vanya, 52, 60, 93, 98, 106, 125, 138, 152–153, 160, 168–169, 178, 206, 242, 250
Uncommon Women and Others, 241
Unconquered, The, 13
Under Milkwood, 5
Under Statements, 242
Under the Ilex, 131
Under the Yum-Yum Tree, 47, 223
Under This Sky, 130
Underground, 5
Undivine Comedy, The, 194, 214
Une Femme Par Jour, 83
Une Saison en Enfer, 66
Unemployed Saint, The, 162
Unexpected Guests, 261
Union Pacific, 217
Unknown Soldier and His Wife, The, 93
Unknown Warrior, The, 106
Unpleasant Evening with H. L. Mencken, An, 79
Unseen, 160
Unseen Hand & Forensic and the Navigator, The, 152–153
Unsinkable Molly Brown, The, 47, 49, 223, 256–257
Unsophisticates, The, 239
Up in Arms, 256
Up in Central Park, 20–21, 78, 209
Uptight, 5, 152
Urban, Joseph, 134, 163, 219, **247–248**
Urfaust, 177
Uriel Acosta, 199
U.S.A., 53, 178–179
UTBU, 5
Utopia, 206
Utopia Limited, 59
Utter Glory of Morrissey Hall, The, 20

V & V Only, 25
Vacanza di'inverno, 212

Valentin and Valentina, 37, 137
Valmouth, 254–255
Valse Nobles et Sentimentales, 206
Valuable Rival, A, 106
$-Value of a Man, The, 258
Value of Names, The, 131
Vampire, The, 191
Vanbrugh, Sir John, **249**
Vanessa, 170
Varii Capricci, 116
Varsity Coach, The, 106
Varying Shore, The, 188
Vassiliev, 154
Vaudeville Vanities, 120
Velvet Glove, The, 184
Venere Gelosa, 244
Venice Preserved, 56, 58, 183
Ventodel Sud, 212
Venus and Adonis, 134
Venus at Large, 184
Venus et Adonis, 56
Venus Is, 162
Venus Observed, 78
Verdi's Requiem, 225
Veronique, 59
Verticle Mobility: Sophia = (Wisdom)
    Part 4, 95
Very Private Life, A, 75
Very Rich Woman, A, 224
Very Special Baby, A, 20
Vesnin, Aleksandr, **249–250**
Victim, The, 132
Victims of Duty, 205
Victoria Palace Theater Revue, 83
Victoria Regina, 209
Vienna Waltzes, 238
Vietnam Diskurs, 16
Vieux Carre, 108, 241
View From the Bridge, A, 5, 13, 52–53,
    193, 250, 252
Vigarani, Gaspare, xxviii, 30, 245, **250**
Vikings, The, 56–57
Viktoria and Her Hussar, 120
Village Romeo and Juliet, A, 6
Village Wooing, 168
Vincent, 178
Violet, 20
Virgin Forest, 204

Virgin Soil Upturned, 258
Virginia, 153, 217, 221
Virginia Sampler, 81
Virginius, 11
Virtuous Island, The, 264
Visconti, Luchino, 64, 192, **250–251**,
    264
Vision of the Bard, A, 111
Visions of Simone Machard, The, 125
Visit, The, 98
Visit of the Old Lady, The, 60
Visit to a Small Planet, A, 87, 223, 264
Visitor, The, 20
Vitruvius, xiv, xvi, xx, xxi, xxiii, 186,
    188, 216, **251**
Viva Madison Avenue!, 72
Vivat! Vivat, Regina!, 241, 243
Vogue, 163, 204
Voice of Ariadne, The, 243
Voices, 6, 163
Voices of Spring, 221
Volpone, 20, 45, 52, 105–106, 148, 167,
    169, 221
Voltaire, 126
Von Teufel geholt, 177
Voulez-Vous Jouer Avec Moi?, 30
Voyage of Edgar Allan Poe, The, 169
Voyage, 181

Wager, The, 22, 167
Wagner, Robin, **252–253**
Wagner, Wieland, **254**
Wahkevitch, Georges, **254**
Wait Until Dark, 124, 152
Waiting for Godot, 52, 117, 149, 232,
    242–243, 252, 255, 265–266
Waiting in the Wings, 171
Wake of Jamey Foster, The, 153, 242
Walk a Little Faster, 12, 14
Walk in Darkness, 147
Walk in the Woods, A, 242
Walk Into My Parlor, 105
Walk Together Chillun, 87
Walking Gentleman, The, 87
Walking Happy, 200
Wall, The, 20
Wall Street, 239
Wallenstein, 228

Wally's Cafe, 261
Walton, Tony, xl, **254–255**
Waltz Academy, 50, 222
Waltz Invention, The, 152
Waltz of the Toreadors, The, 54, 63, 74, 178–179
Wandering Years, The, 22
War, 40
War and Peace, 233
War Music, 117
War of the Roses, The, 5, 41, 148, 150, 166
Warp, 60–61
Warren Hastings, 106
Washington Square, 81, 101, 153, 183
Wasps, The, xv
Wastrels, The, 199
Watch on the Rhine, 161, 171
Water Engine (and Mr. Happiness), The, 23, 25, 60
Water-hen, 129
Watercolor, 178
Watering Place, The, 93, 252
Watermill, 265
Waves of the Danube, The, 45
Way of Life, A, 73
Way of the World, The, 52, 169
Ways and Means, 11
Wayward Stork, The, 11
WC, 143
We Come to the River, 55
We Interrupt This Program, 200
We Take the Town, 143, 171
We the People, 32–33
Weak Sisters, 239
Web, The, 146
Webb, John, **255**
Wedding Band, The, 6, 148
Wedding Breakfast, 72
Wedding in Paris, 171
Wedding of Iphigenia, The, 5
Week-End, 127
Weekend, 5, 224
Weep for Spring, 171
Weep for the Virgins, 13
Welcome to the Club, 175
Welded, 126
Well Hung, 145

Well of the Saints, The, 168, 202
Werther, 54, 66, 147
West Side Story, xxxix, 182, 201, 207–208, 218–219, 223, 226, 252
West Side Waltz, The, 75, 109
Western Waters, 13
Westminster, 168
Wetherby, 109
What a Lovely War!, 252
What Did He See?, 95
What Did You Say   What   For?, 178
What Do You Really Know About Your Husband?, 74, 108
What Every Woman Knows, 87, 89
What I Did Last Summer, 24, 159
What Price Glory?, 53, 177, 239
What the Butler Saw, 25, 53, 70, 109
What The Wine Sellers Buy, 152
What's Up, 13
When We Dead Awaken, 204, 258–259
When You Comin' Back Red Ryder?, 76
Where are the Snows of Yesteryear, 129
Where's Charley?, 48, 73, 79, 89, 130
Where's Daddy?, 74, 108
Whiff of Melancholy, A, 178
Whirlpool, The, 232
Whispers of Darkness, 149
Whistle, 5
Whistling in the Dark, 183
Whistling Wizard and The Sultan of Tuffet, The, 48
White, Miles, **255–257**
White Alice, 162
White Devil, The, 92
White Disease, The, 233
White Eagle, The, 199
White-Haired Boy, The, 183
White Horse Inn, 217, 228
White House, The, 92
White Rose and the Red, The, 252
White Storks Above Brest, 233
Whitehouse Murder Case, The, 125
Whitman Portrait, A, 79–80
Who Cares?, 163
Who Was That Lady I Saw You With?, 238
Who Will Remember?, 168

Who's Afraid of Virginia Woolf?, 5–6, 53, 60, 76, 108, 218–219, 263
Whodunnit, 265
Whoop-Up!, 162
Whoopee!, 23
Whoopi Goldberg, 242, 255
Widow Clair, The, 146
Widow in Green, A, 240
Wielopole, Wielopole, 129
Wife of Martin Guerre, The, 134
Wild Boy, 225
Wild Duck, The, 24, 106, 120, 126, 142–143, 146, 160
Wild Goose, The, 168
Wild Life, 131
Wild Violets, 112
Wildcat, 50–51, 82
Wilhelm Tell, 231
Wilkinson, Norman, 221, **257**
Will It Make A Theatre?, 80
Will of Song, The, 126
Will Rogers' USA, 79
Will Shakespeare, 26
Will Success Spoil Rock Hunter?, 47, 223
Will You Play With Me?, 107
Will You Walk, 184
William Tell, 258
Williams, Piotr, **257–258**
Willie Stark, 146
Willie the Weeper, 92
Willow and I, The, 32
Wilson, Robert, xl, xli, 25, 242, **258–259**
Wilson in The Promise Land, 145
Wind From the West, 168
Wind in the Willows, 165, 225, 260
Wind of Heaven, The, 171
Wind Remains, The, 222
Windy City, 161, 189, 243
Wine of Choice, 221
Wine Untouched, 131
Winesburg, Ohio, 207, 223
Winged Victory, 87
Wingless Victory, The, 161
Wings, 36, 70, 76
Wings of the Dove, The, 184

Winnie the Pooh, 48
Winslow Boy, The, 243
Winston Churchill Speaks, 77
Winter Garden Theatre Revue, 82
Winter Signs, 60
Winter's Eve, 100
Winter's Tale, The, 5, 54, 67–68, 108, 147, 169, 207, 183, 194, 207, 238, 243, 245, 257
Winterset, 161, 163
Wipe-Out Games, 152
Wise Child, 108, 143, 189
Wisecrackers, The, 239
Wish You Were Here, 162
Wisteria Tree, The, 18, 87, 162
Witch, The, 106–107
Witch of Edmonton, The, 171
Witch of Endor, The, 148, 151
Within A Glass Bell, 78
Within the Gates, 188
Without Love, 127
Without Warning, 87
Wittop, Freddy, **259–261**
Wiz, The, 175, 255
Wizard of Oz, The, 3, 191
Woman and Song, 247
Woman Bites Dog, 20
Woman in Mind, 25
Woman of the Year, 6, 201, 255
Woman's a Fool—To Be Clever, A, 183
Woman's Honor, 106
Women, The, 3, 161, 225
Women and Song, 248
Women Beware Women, 123, 230
Women Have Their Way, The, 32
Wonder Hat, The, 118
Wonder World, 92
Wonderful Town, 47–48, 79, 188, 200
Wonderful Zoo, 106
Wonderfull Yeare, A, 98
Wonders of Derbyshire, The, 67–68
Wonderworld, 51, 83
Wooden Dish, The, 184
Woods, The, 23, 131
Wookey, The, 161
Woolgatherer, The, 77–78

Words and Music: Sammy Cahn's Songbook, 200
Words on the Window Pane, 168
Work of Living Art, The, xxxv
Workhouse Ward, The, 106
Working, 167
Works of Samuel Beckett, The, 5
World, The, 46
World According to Garp, The, 210
World of Christopher Blake, The, 132
World of Ray Bradbury, The, 79
World of Sholom Aleichem, The, 32, 77
World of Suzie Wong, The, 162
World War 2 1/2, 145
World We Live In, The, 221
Worm in Horseradish, A, 252
Worm's Eye, 254
Would-Be Gentleman, The, 20, 32–33, 217, 257
Woyzeck, 97, 127, 177, 192, 206–207, 231, 245
Wreath for Udomo, A, 255
Writing on the Wall, The, 88–89
Wrong Box, The, 196
Wrong Side of the Park, 169
Wrong Way to Light a Bulb, The, 108, 184
Wurtzel, Stuart, **261**
Wuthering Heights, 46

XX, 206

Yakulov, Georgii Bogdanovich, **262**
Yale Repertory Season of Story Theatre, 152
Yankee Doodle Comes to London, 178
Year Boston Won the Pennant, The, 202
Yearling, The, 93
Years Ago, 81, 183
Years of the Locust, 145
Yegor Bulychov and Others, 69
Yellow House, The, 204

Yellow Jack, 160
Yellow Mask, The, 209
Yentl—the Yeshiva Boy, 76, 203
Yeoman of the Guard, The, 51
Yes and No, 120
Yolanda and the Thief, 71
Yolanda of Cyprus, 127
York Mystery Cycle, 41
Yoshke Musikant, 12
You Bet Your Life, 83
You Can't Take It with You, 76, 145, 152, 183–184, 240–241
You Know I Can't Hear You When The Water's Running, 5, 93
You Never Can Tell, 176
You Said It, 183
You Touched Me!, 171
You're A Big Boy Now, 5
You're a Good Man Charlie Brown, 93
Young Alexander, 160
Young and the Beautiful, The, 79, 87, 171
Young Baron Neuhaus, The, 231
Young Couple Wanted, 183
Young Go First, The, 105
Young in Heart, 83
Young King, The, 120
Young Man's Fancy, A, 247
Young Marrieds Play Monopoly, 93
Young Mr. Disraeli, 89
Young Playwright's Festival, 24
Your Son, 252
Yr. Obedient Husband, 161

Zalmen, or the Madness of God, 178
Zanetto, 252
Zaubergeige, 177
Zaza, 82
Zeal of Thy House, 120
Zefferelli, Franco, 193, **263–264**
Zelda, 5, 11
Zelig, 153
Zenda, 256
Zenobia, 158

Ziegfeld Follies, The, 47, 71, 82, 175, 217, 247–248, 256
Zipprodt, Patricia, 117, **264–267**
Zizi Je T'Aime, 84
Zizi Jeanmaire Show, 83–84

Zorba, 14–15, 190, 265, 267
Zu ebener Ende und erster Stock, 231
Zulu and the Zayda, The, 72
Zykovs, The, 91

About the Editor
and Contributors

JONET BUCHANAN earned a B.F.A. with distinction from the University of Oklahoma in 1981 and a master of science in music, scene design and stagecraft technology from Indiana University in 1988. She worked as an associate instructor in the technical department at Indiana University Opera Theatre from 1984 to 1987 and is currently associate professor at Antelope Valley College in Lancaster, California, where she is the designer-technical director in the theatre arts department. She has won awards for her set and lighting designs.

ELBIN L. CLEVELAND is a professor and designer-technician at the University of South Carolina in Columbia, where he has served since 1975. He has provided scene or lighting design and technical direction for over two hundred productions for academic and professional theatres. He has been active with professional associations at state, regional, and national levels and has served as president of the South Carolina Theatre Association (SCTA) and the South Carolina Alliance for Arts Education. He received the SCTA Founders Award in 1988 for his extensive work on behalf of theatre arts and theatre education in South Carolina. He is the South Carolina representative to the board of the Southeastern Theatre Conference and is design and technology editor of *Southern Theatre*. He chairs the national Publications Committee for the USITT and is the associate editor for education for *Theatre Design Technology*.

JAMES FISHER, associate professor of theatre at Wabash College, was named McLain/McTurnan/Arnold Research Scholar at Wabash for 1988, an honor that permitted him to complete work on a book entitled *Theater of Yesterday and Tomorrow: Commedia dell'arte on the Twentieth Century Stage*. He has published articles, book reviews, and theatre reviews in many journals and periodicals, serves as book review editor of the *Journal of Dramatic Theory and Criticism*, and is the national business manager of Alpha Psi Omega, the national theatre fraternity, and editor of its annual publication. He recently served as curator for an exhibition on the history and influence of commedia dell'arte for the Actors Theatre of Louisville's "Classics in Context" Festival in October 1990.

HOWARD GUTNER holds a master's degree in film studies from Northwestern University, as well as a graduate degree in journalism from the University of Illinois. He is senior editor at Scholastic, Incorporated, in New York City, and is currently working on a book about Gilbert Adrian and his work at MGM in the 1930s.

BRIAN R. JONES is an assistant professor of theatre at Weber State University in Ogden, Utah, where he is the resident lighting and set designer and teaches design and general theatre courses. He is active in USITT and serves as a regional representative. He received his B.A. from Wabash College and his M.F.A. from the University of Florida in Gainesville.

KEN KLOTH is on the faculty at Marquette University, where he designs for the theatre department. He has designed scenery and lights for several theatres in the midwest, including Milwaukee Repertory Theatre. Active in the USITT, he has written for their publications, *TD&T* and *Sightlines*.

KURT LANCASTER received his master's degree in theatre in 1991 after serving as a graduate student and research assistant in the department of theatre/dance at the University of Maine. He has directed an original, experimental, multimedia production, as well as one of his own original science fiction scripts, and also wrote a performance studies' paper on live action role-playing games. In 1989, he served as a journalist for the *Piscataquis Observer* in Maine. He also received his B.A. in English in 1989 from Principia College in Elsah, Illinois.

TOM MIKOTOWICZ is an assistant professor of theatre in the department of theatre/dance at the University of Maine and supervises the directing program. After receiving his doctorate in performance studies from New York University in 1985, he became an associate editor, book reviews for *Theatre Design & Technology*, the journal for the USITT, and director of marketing at Kliegl Bros. Stage Lighting. His doctoral thesis on producer-designer Oliver Smith is currently under consideration for publication. In addition, he has published articles and delivered papers on such varied topics as street performers, puppetry, postmodern directing, and design in such publications as *TD & T*, *Puppetry Journal*, *Theatre Topics*, *Contemporary Designers* (MacMillan), and *Cambridge Guide to World Theatre*. In addition, he has directed and designed more than seventy-five major productions at community, educational, and professional theatres in Pennsylvania, Texas, Illinois, New York, and Maine.

ANNIE MILTON lives in Los Arboles, New Mexico, and is presently pursuing interests in computer-aided design applications in theatre technology. She was the former resident costume designer at the University of Maryland in College Park, where she served as an assistant professor from 1986 to 1990. In 1989, her article "The Automated Costume Designer" was published in *Sightlines*. She received a B.A. degree in 1980 from the University of Oregon and an M.F.A. from the University of Wisconsin in Madison.

ANDREA J. NOURYEH has served as the archivist for the Roundabout Theatre and as dramaturge for the department of theatre/dance at the University of Maine. She has taught at Baruch College, CUNY and is currently an assistant professor of theatre at St. Lawrence College. She received her Ph.D. in performance studies at New York University and was the recipient of the Monroe Lippman Memorial Award for Distinguished Doctoral Dissertation in 1988 for her thesis on the Mercury Theatre. Her lecture "You've Taken My Blues and Gone," dealing with the role of Afro-Americans in American theatre, has been included in the 1990–1993 Speakers in the Humanities Program for the New York Council for the Humanities. She has contributed to *Cambridge Guide to World Theatre*, has served as field bibliographer in Afro-American performance for the *International Bibliography of Theater*, and has acted as consultant on a documentary about Orson Welles. Her articles and book reviews have been published in *Theatre Design Technology, Broadside, Black American Literature Forum*, and *Shakespeare on Film Newsletter*.

PENNY L. REMSEN is a lighting designer for theatre, dance, "industrials," and architecture. Her credits include work with the Boston Conservatory, the New Erlich Theater, the Philadelphia Drama Guild, the Quaigh Theatre in Houston, and the Wayside Theatre in Middletown, Virginia. Recently, she created the lighting for a computer-video installation, LANDSCAPE, which premiered at Zone Art Center in Springfield, Massachusetts. She is an assistant professor and resident lighting designer at the department of theatre, University of Massachusetts at Amherst.